THE MYTH
OF THE GODDESS

EVOLUTION OF AN IMAGE

ANNE BARING
AND
JULES CASHFORD

VIKING ARKANA

VIKING

Published by the Penguin Group
Penguin Books Ltd, 27 Wrights Lane, London w8 5tz, England
Penguin Books USA Inc., 375 Hudson Street, New York, New York 10014, USA
Penguin Books Australia Ltd, Ringwood, Victoria, Australia
Penguin Books Canada Ltd, 10 Alcorn Avenue, Toronto, Ontario, Canada m4v 3b2
Penguin Books (NZ) Ltd, 182–190 Wairau Road, Auckland 10, New Zealand

Penguin Books Ltd, Registered Offices: Harmondsworth, Middlesex, England

First published 1991
1 3 5 7 9 10 8 6 4 2

Set in 10/12 pt Lasercomp Plantin Light
Printed in England by Clays Ltd, St Ives plc

A CIP catalogue record for this book is available from the British Library

ISBN 0–670–83564–1

CONTENTS

FOREWORD
BY
SIR LAURENS VAN DER POST

This is a long book but it is not a page too long. It is a very important
book and of great significance for the reappraisal – which is grossly
overdue – of our approach to history. History as a record of the past has
been told almost entirely in terms of its outer eventfulness and, in a sense,
this is the least of history. History progresses on two levels, a manifest
one and a profound one which is irresistible but not fully expressed,
demanding to make itself known through the way we shape our lives in
the world without, and through the failures and disasters brought about
because this hidden, inner eventfulness is not fully recognized and given
its due role in the human spirit and its societies.

There is no dimension of history of which this is more true than the
way the feminine half of the human spirit has been dealt with by masculine-
dominated societies, and inadequately acknowledged and evolved in our
cultures and civilizations. We see the result of this neglect, which is
with us still, in the decay of the feeling and the caring values of life and in
the pursuit of the masculine rationalism which seems to be the dominant
element in the establishments of today.

But here at last is a work of immense pioneering significance. It is
pioneering that has been done admirably in all sorts of sorties and forays
of imaginative men into this undiscovered dimension, but it has never
been done as it should have been done – by women, by the feminine itself
looking for the feminine, as we have looked for the masculine in the
remote origins of life on earth and our progression into this great and
tumultuous time of ours.

Jules Cashford and Anne Baring have done precisely this. They have
gone as far down into history as one can go and followed it through into
the present day. It is a great story that they have to tell and it is a timely
story, because it is the loss of this feminine eventfulness which has led to
the most urgent and dangerous problem of our time: the exploitation and
also the rejection of our Mother Earth, our mother not only deprived of
the great store of life it had prepared for us but increasingly being denied
the chance to do more.

Here, for the first time to my knowledge, the story is told in full. It is
the awful, yet at the same time strangely inspiring story of the feminine,
still unvanquished and undismayed, which we are all called to honour and

obey if we are not also to vanish, like so many other cultures in the labyrinth of the past through which the authors follow this golden thread. The horizon behind us is littered with the rubble of civilizations which have failed to renew themselves, have failed a challenge somehow to transcend their opposites in something that will combine in balance both the masculine and the feminine and, in their union, create something greater than the sum of their parts.

Laurens van der Post
October 1990

PREFACE

When we began this book we intended simply to gather together the stories and images of goddesses as they were expressed in different cultures, from the first sculpted figures of the Palaeolithic era in 20,000 BC down to contemporary pictures of the Virgin Mary. This seemed worth doing because one way in which humans apprehend their own being is by making it visible in the images of their goddesses and gods. But in the course of this research we discovered such surprising similarities and parallels in all the goddess myths of apparently unrelated cultures that we concluded that there had been a continuous transmission of images throughout history. This continuity is so striking that we feel entitled to talk of 'the myth of the goddess', since the underlying vision expressed in all the variety of goddess images is constant: the vision of life as a living unity.

The Mother Goddess, wherever she is found, is an image that inspires and focuses a perception of the universe as an organic, alive and sacred whole, in which humanity, the Earth and all life on Earth participate as 'her children'. Everything is woven together in one cosmic web, where all orders of manifest and unmanifest life are related, because all share in the sanctity of the original source.

However, it was evident that in our present age the goddess myth is nowhere to be found. Of course, in the Catholic version of Christianity Mary, 'the Virgin', 'Queen of Heaven', is clothed in all the old goddess images – except that, significantly, she is not 'Queen of Earth'. The Earth used to have, as it were, a goddess to call her own, because the Earth and all creation were of the same substance as the Goddess. Earth was her epiphany: the divine was immanent as creation. Our mythic image of Earth has lost this dimension.

So we set out to discover what had happened to the goddess image, how and when it disappeared, and what were the implications of this loss. Since mythic images implicitly govern a culture, what did this tell us about a particular culture – such as our own – that either did not have or did not acknowledge a mythic image of the feminine principle? It began to seem no coincidence that ours is the age above all others that has desacralized Nature: generally speaking, the Earth is no longer instinctively experienced as a living being as in earlier times, or so it would seem from the evidence of pollution (itself a term that originally meant the profaning of what was sacred). And now is also the time when the whole body of the Earth is threatened in a way unique to the history of the planet.

Consequently, the second aim of this book became to explore the way in which the goddess myth was lost; when, where and how the images of 'the god' arose, and how goddess and god related to each other in earlier cultures and times. It soon became clear that, from Babylonian mythology onwards (*c.* 2000 BC), the Goddess became almost exclusively associated with 'Nature' as the chaotic force to be mastered, and the God took the role of conquering or ordering nature from his counterpole of 'Spirit'. Yet this opposition had not previously existed, so it needed to be placed in the context of the evolution of consciousness. One way of understanding this process is to view it as the progressive withdrawal of participation from nature, which makes possible an increasing independence of natural phenomena and a gradual transference of 'nature's life' into humanity. This is how it seems to be that Humanity and Nature become polarized. But while this polarization can be seen to be a first stage in this process – perhaps even an inevitable one – it does not constitute an absolute description of the two terms that were once one. Yet so much are we still living with the thought structures initiated in the late Bronze and early Iron Ages that we were obliged continually to remind ourselves that this was not intrinsic to the way in which we had to reflect upon these terms.

It came, then, as a surprise to discover the extent to which our Judaeo-Christian religion or mythology (depending on the point of view) had inherited the paradigm images of Babylonian mythology, particularly the opposition between Creative Spirit and Chaotic Nature, and also the habit of thinking in oppositions generally. We find this, for instance, in the common assumption that the spiritual and the physical worlds are different in kind, an assumption that, unreflectively held, separates mind from matter, soul from body, thinking from feeling, intellect from intuition and reason from instinct. When, in addition, the 'spiritual' pole of these dualisms is valued as 'higher' than the 'physical' pole, then the two terms fall into an opposition that is almost impossible to reunite without dissolving both of the terms.

We concluded that, for the last 4,000 years, the feminine principle, which manifests in mythological history as 'the goddess' and in cultural history as the values placed upon spontaneity, feeling, instinct and intuition, had been lost as a valid expression of the sanctity and unity of life. In Judaeo-Christian mythology there is now, formally, no feminine dimension of the divine, since our particular culture is structured in the image of a masculine god who is beyond creation, ordering it from without; he is not within creation, as were the mother goddesses before him. This results, inevitably, in an imbalance of the masculine and feminine principles, which has fundamental implications for how we create our world and live in it.

We also found that even when the goddess myth was debased and devalued, it did not go away, but continued to exist in disguise – in images that were prevented from expressing themselves vitally and spontaneously, particularly in the Judaeo-Christian tradition. In Greek mythology, for example, Zeus 'married' the old mother goddesses, one after the other, and they continued to rule the provinces of childbirth, fertility or spiritual transformation in their own right, even though they were finally answerable to the Father God himself. But in Hebrew mythology the goddess went, so to speak, underground. She was hidden in the chaotic dragons of Leviathan and Behemoth, whose destruction was never complete, or in the ineluctable appeal of the forbidden Canaanite goddess Astarte, or, more abstractly, in the feminine personification of Yahweh's 'wisdom' – Sophia – and his 'presence' – the Shekhinah. Eve, though human and cursed, was given by Adam the displaced name of the mother goddesses of old – 'the Mother of All Living' – though with fatally new and limited meaning. The Virgin Mary, as the 'Second Eve' – who has been gathering importance over the centuries in answer, it must be, to some unfulfilled need of many people – was finally declared 'Assumed into Heaven, Body and Soul' as Queen only in the 1950s.

In all these instances, as we hope to show, the myth of the goddess continued to act on the prevailing world view of the time. However, since this myth was contrary to formal doctrine, its action had to be implicit and indirect in the manner of any less-than-fully conscious attitude, which meant that its unacknowledged but persistent presence often distorted even the finest expressions of the prevailing myth of the god. It seemed clear that the feminine principle was an aspect of human consciousness that could not and should not be eradicated. Consequently, it needed to be brought back into consciousness and restored to full complementarity with the masculine principle if we were to achieve a harmonious balance between these two essential ways of experiencing life.

So where was the goddess myth now? Turning then to the discoveries of the 'new' sciences, it appeared, astonishingly, as if the old goddess myth were re-emerging in a new form, not as a personalized image of a female deity, but as what that image represented: a vision of life as a sacred whole in which all life participated in mutual relationship, and where all participants were dynamically 'alive'. For, beginning with Heisenberg and Einstein, physicists were claiming that in subatomic physics the universe could be understood only as a unity, that this unity was expressed in patterns of relationship, and that the observer was necessarily included in the act of observation. Characteristically, these conclusions were themselves expressed in many of the images that belonged to the old goddess myth. The web of space and time that the mother goddess once spun from her eternal womb – from Neolithic goddess figures buried with spindle whorls, through the

Greek spinners of destiny, down to Mary – had become the 'cosmic web' in which all life was related. All the mother goddesses were born from the sea – from the Sumerian Nammu, the Egyptian Isis, the Greek Aphrodite, down to the Christian Mary (whose name in Latin means sea). Now this image had come back into the imagination as the 'ocean of energy' of the 'Implicate Order'.

From a mythological perspective, the goddess myth can also be seen in the attempts of many human beings to live in a new way, allowing their feeling of participation with the Earth as a whole to affect how they think about it and act towards it, aware of the urgent need to comprehend the world as a unity. Einstein is the spokesman for this need: 'With the splitting of the atom everything has changed save our mode of thinking, and thus we drift towards unparalleled disaster.'

But the predominant mythic image of the age – which could be characterized as 'the god without the goddess' – continues to support the very oppositional and mechanistic paradigm that the latest scientific discoveries are refuting. This means that two essential aspects of the human mind are out of accord with each other. It may seem a lot to claim that mythic images are so important to all areas of human experience, but the discoveries of Depth Psychology have shown how radically we are influenced and motivated by impulses below the threshold of consciousness, both in our personal and in our collective life as members of the human race. We cannot, then, afford to be indifferent to the prevailing climate of thought. It would seem necessary to make the attempt to move beyond our mythological inheritance in the same way that we try to gain some perspective on our individual inheritance – our specific family, tribe and country.

One way of bringing the myth of the goddess back into consciousness is to tell again the stories people have told down the millennia, and to follow the continuous chain of images through different cultures from 20,000 BC onwards, gathering them all together so that their underlying unity can appear. Then this neglected, devalued but apparently unquenchable tradition may speak for itself. This we have tried to do, in the hope that the vision of life as a sacred whole, which at its finest the goddess myth embodies, might be brought into relation with the god myth, and so contribute to the new mode of thinking for which Einstein calls.

We took a decision to focus on the Western tradition and so we have not attempted to tell the stories of India, Africa and the Far East. This is obviously a limitation, but the book is long enough already! Perhaps readers will see parallels and points of contrast that would contribute to a truly universal theme.

One word about myth. Myth, as the foremost exponent of mythology, Joseph Campbell, has written, is a dream everyone has, just as everyone also dreams her or his own personal myths: 'Dream is the personalized myth, myth the depersonalized dream':

Throughout the inhabited world, in all times and under every circumstance, the myths of man have flourished; and they have been the living inspiration of whatever else may have appeared out of the activities of the human body and mind. It would not be too much to say that myth is the secret opening through which the inexhaustible energies of the cosmos pour into human cultural manifestation. Religions, philosophies, arts, the social forms of primitive and historic man, prime discoveries in science and technology, the very dreams that blister sleep, boil up from the basic, magic ring of myth.[1]

Myths are the stories of the human race that we dream onwards. In fact, the most we can do, according to Jung, is 'to dream the dream onwards and give it a modern dress'.[2]

Back in the Bronze Age a union of the mythic images of the feminine and the masculine principles was symbolized in the 'sacred marriage' of the goddess and the god, a ritual ceremony that was believed to assist the regeneration of nature. With the greater self-consciousness of 4,000 years later, may it not be possible to re-create in the human imagination the same kind of insights that once were enacted in unconscious participation with the same purpose: the renewal of creative life? What would the modern dress of this ancient dream be? With the restoration of the feminine to a complementary relation with the masculine, might there then be the possibility of a new mythology of the universe as one harmonious living whole? Nature and Spirit, after the many millennia of their separation, newly embraced as one and the same?

PART I
THE MOTHER GODDESS
AND HER SON-LOVER

Figure 1. Goddess of Laussel; rock carving, *c.* 22,000–18,000 BC, height 17 in. (43 cm). Dordogne, France.

1
IN THE BEGINNING:
THE PALAEOLITHIC MOTHER
GODDESS

Every part of this earth is sacred to my people. Every shining pine needle, every sandy shore, every mist in the dark woods, every meadow, every humming insect. All are holy in the memory and experience of my people. We know the sap which courses through the trees as we know the blood that courses through our veins. We are part of the earth and it is part of us. The perfumed flowers are our sisters. The bear, the deer, the great eagle, these are our brothers. The rocky crests, the juices in the meadow, the body heat of the pony, and man, all belong to the same family. The shining water that moves in the streams and rivers is not just water, but the blood of our ancestors. Each ghostly reflection in the clear water of the lakes tells of events and memories in the life of my people. The water's murmur is the voice of my father's father. The rivers are our brothers. They quench our thirst. They carry our canoes and feed our children. So you must give to the rivers the kindness you would give any brother ... Remember that the air is precious to us, that the air shares its spirit with all the life it supports. The wind that gave our grandfather his first breath also receives his last sigh. The wind also gives our children the spirit of life ... Will you teach your children what we have taught our children? That the earth is our mother? What befalls the earth, befalls all the sons of the earth. This we know: the earth does not belong to man, man belongs to the earth. All things are connected like the blood which unites us all. Man did not weave the web of life, he is merely a strand in it. Whatever he does to the web, he does to himself.

Chief Seattle, 1855[1]

Long ago, some 20,000 years ago and more, the image of a goddess appeared across a vast expanse of land stretching from the Pyrenees to Lake Baikal in Siberia. Statues in stone, bone and ivory, tiny figures with long bodies and falling breasts, rounded motherly figures pregnant with birth, figures with signs scratched upon them – lines, triangles, zigzags, circles, nets, leaves, spirals, holes – graceful figures rising out of rock and painted with red ochre – all these have survived through the unrecorded generations of human beings who compose the history of the race.

At what point in human history did these sacred images appear? Fire was discovered about 600,000 years ago. What happened in the half a million years or so between this time and the beginning of the Upper

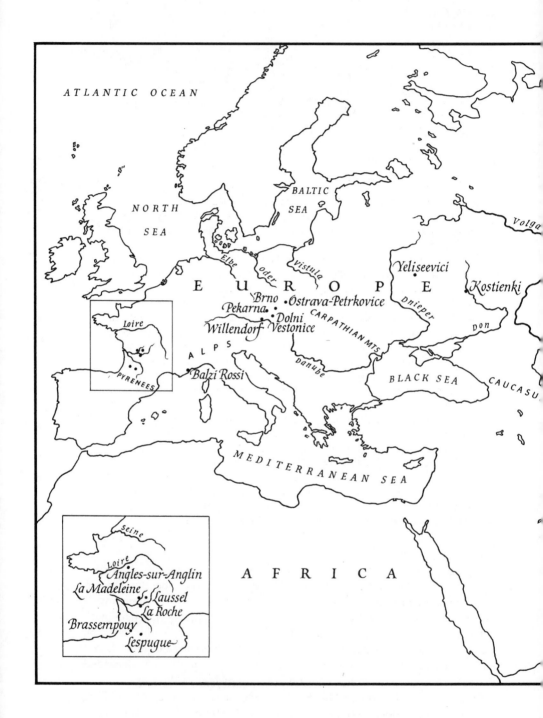

ATLANTIC OCEAN

NORTH SEA

BALTIC SEA

Volga

N O R T H

S E A

Elbe

Oder

Vistula

E   U   R   O   P   E

Yeliseevici

•Kostienki

Brno •Ostrava-Petrkovice
Pekarna•   •Dolni
Willendorf• Vestonice

CARPATHIAN MTS

Dnieper

DON

A L P S

Danube

•Balzi Rossi

BLACK SEA

CAUCASUS

Loire

PYRENEES

M E D I T E R R A N E A N   S E A

Seine

Loire
Angles-sur-Anglin
La Madeleine •Laussel
• La Roche
Brassempouy
Lespugue

A   F   R   I   C   A

Map 1. Distribution of Goddess figurines in the Palaeolithic era.

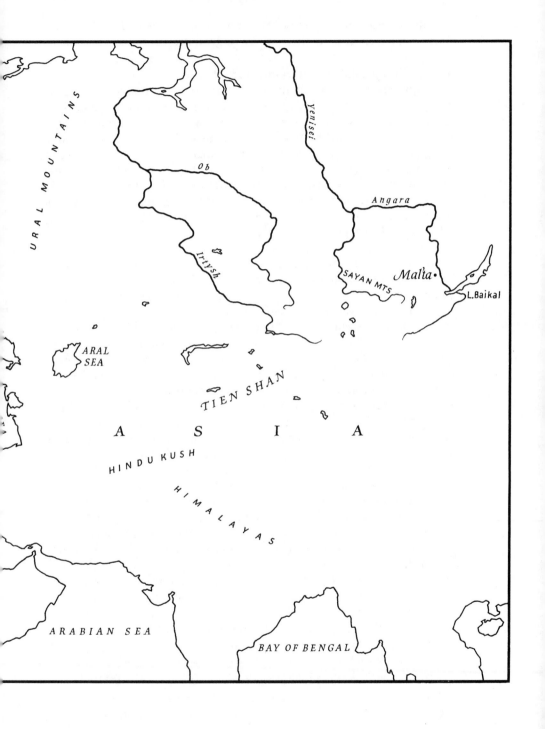

URAL MOUNTAINS

Yenisei

Ob

Angara

Irtysh

SAYAN MTS

Malta •

L.Baikal

ARAL
SEA

TIEN SHAN

A   S   I   A

HINDU KUSH

HIMALAYAS

ARABIAN SEA

BAY OF BENGAL

Palaeolithic era, about 50,000 BC? What dreams were dreamed, what
stories were told around the fire? Four great ice ages, each one taking
thousands of years, came and went. When the glaciers that had covered
much of Europe and Asia were melting – between 50,000 and 30,000 BC
(although they did not finally disappear until about 10,000 BC) – a type of
human being emerged with whom we can feel a sense of affinity: *Homo
sapiens.* Before this, few animals could live on the frozen ground except
the woolly mammoth, the woolly rhinoceros and the reindeer; but now
grassy steppeland began to grow, which supported great herds of bison,
horse and cattle. Later on – between 20,000 and 15,000 BC – the grasslands
gave way to thick forests and so the herds moved eastwards, with the
hunters following them. Some tribes stayed behind, like those in south-
western France, making their homes in the caves of the fertile river
valleys of the Dordogne, the Vézère and the Ariège. This was the time when
the walls of the caves were painted and statues of goddesses were carved.

More than 130 of these statues were discovered resting in rock and soil
among the bones and tools of the people of the Palaeolithic time, or
appeared, when more closely observed, sculpted on ledges and terraces of
rock above the caves where many of the people lived. The statues are
always naked, generally small and often pregnant. Some look like ordinary
women, but most of them have the look of mothers, as though all that
were female in them had been focused on the overwhelming mystery of
birth. Many figures have been sprinkled with red ochre, the colour of life-
giving blood, and frequently they taper to a point without feet, as if they
were once fixed upright in the ground for a ritual purpose. The tribes
who lived just inside the caves, painting the dark inner walls with the
vibrant reds, ochres and browns of wild animals, would place the statues
outside the cave, at the entrance to their home or their sanctuary.

Over a rock shelter in Laussel in the Dordogne, only a few miles from
the great cave at Lascaux where the most brilliant of these paintings still
cover the walls, the figure of a woman 17 inches (43 cm) tall once gazed
out over the valley (Fig. 1). Palaeolithic sculptors chiselled her out of
limestone with tools of flint, and gave her to hold in her right hand a
bison's horn, crescent-shaped like the moon, notched with the thirteen
days of the waxing moon and the thirteen months of the lunar year. With
her left hand she points to her swelling womb. Her head is tilted towards
the crescent moon, drawing a curve of relationship from her fingers on
the womb up through the incline of her head to the crescent horn in her
hand, so creating a connection between the waxing phase of the moon and
the fecundity of the human womb. In this way the pattern of relationship
between the earthly and the heavenly orders is acknowledged.

Joseph Campbell makes the connection between past and present:

> The phases of the moon were the same for Old Stone Age man as they are
> for us; so also were the processes of the womb. It may therefore be that the

initial observation that gave birth in the mind of man to a mythology of one
mystery informing earthly and celestial things was the recognition of an
accord between these two 'time-factored' orders: the celestial order of the
waxing moon and the earthly order of the womb.[2]

A hundred miles (161 km) to the south, in the foothills of the Pyrenees
at a place called Lespugue, the delicate statue shown in Figure 2 lay
resting for millennia in a muddy ditch. She was carved from the ivory of a
mammoth, only $5\frac{1}{2}$ inches (14 cm) high. She has no hands or feet and her
legs taper to a point, suggesting that she was pressed into the earth or
fixed into wood to enable her to stand where she could be seen. Her
upper chest is flattened into a curve, rising upwards to an almost serpentine head, which inclines forwards, so that all the emphasis of her
fragile body falls upon her capacity to give birth and nourishment.

Large, pendulous breasts, with her arms resting on them, merge into
her full and rounded womb; her buttocks and thighs are disproportionately
swollen, as though also contributing to the act of birth. Her breasts and
buttocks give the feeling of four great eggs carried in the nest of her
pregnant body. Ten vertical lines have been etched from beneath her
buttocks to the back of her knees, giving the impression of the waters of

Figure 2. Goddess of Lespugue, front and back view; mammoth-ivory
statue, *c.* 20,000–18,000 BC, height $5\frac{1}{2}$ in. (14 cm). Haute-Garonne, France.

birth falling profusely from the womb, like rain. The ten lines are suggestive of the ten lunar months of gestation in the womb.

What are the grounds for claiming that these sculptures of women are goddesses, not simply the beauties of the local tribe or the girls in the cave next door? Firstly, the sculptures are not naturalistic, unless we assume that the Palaeolithic artist had no sense of proportion for human females while having exquisite artistry for animals. To describe them in the cautious language of 'Statue of a Woman' often found on museum plaques is to overlook the symbolism of arranging all the features of the body in such a coherent and consistent manner. Because the whole of the body is concentrated on the drama of birth, the story that these and many other figures tell is the story of how life comes into being.

The female figure is the only evidence before us in each case. We can interpret this as a particular woman, or women in general, or a woman whose specific characteristics are given ritual significance and made translucent to convey something beyond what any particular woman is or does. No similar male figures have been found. Why, then, would the figure of a woman, or, more precisely, the figure of a woman giving birth, be ritualized? Here we leave the evidence and come to interpretation.

The mystery of the female body is the mystery of birth, which is also the mystery of the unmanifest becoming manifest in the whole of nature. This far transcends the female body and woman as carrier of this image, for the body of the female of any species leads through the mystery of birth to the mystery of life itself.

If we acknowledge the religious significance of these figures, we cannot then dismiss them in the term 'idols of fertility'. For the word 'idol' invariably trivializes the numinosity of the religious experience since it is used only of other people's forms of worship, and the word 'fertility' also, rather grandly, overlooks the fact that many people in our time pray to the Virgin Mary to grant them children. Similarly, to call them 'Venus figurines' – as in *Venus of Laussel* or *Venus of Lespugue*, which are their usual names – is to reduce the universality of a first principle – the Mother – to the name of the Roman goddess of love, who was by then only one goddess among many, all of them long superseded by the Father God as ruler if not creator of the world. So, to try to restore to the Palaeolithic figures their own original dignity, we prefer to ascribe the name of 'Mother Goddess', or simply 'Goddess', to these sacred images of the life-giving, nourishing and regenerating powers of the universe.

We shall not try to define 'the sacred' and 'the numinous', since they are terms that point to an ultimate reality that is unique for each person, yet whose shared meaning appears over the millennia to change imperceptibly from age to age. What is important is that an experience of a sacred dimension is found in all cultures whether their organization is simple or very complex. This suggests that the sacred is not a *stage* in the history of consciousness but an element in the *structure* of consciousness,

Figure 3. Head of Goddess; mammoth-ivory,
c. 22,000 BC, height 1⅜ in. (3.65 cm).
Brassempouy, Landes, France.

belonging to all people at all times. It is therefore part of the character of the human race, perhaps the essential part. So it is crucially necessary for an understanding of that other aspect of being human, which is to have been born at a particular time into a specific family within a certain tribal group. If we accept that the images of other cultures have an equally valid claim to the sacred, then we are less likely to overlook similarities between our own numinous images and those of others.

The oldest sculpture of a goddess, from about 22,000 BC, is the one that looks most modern, of which only a tiny head remains (Fig. 3). She was carved from mammoth-ivory, only 1⅜ inches (3.65 cm) tall, with fine, delicate features: a long neck framed by long straight hair, a most distinctive nose and eyebrows, and the design of a net precisely chiselled over the full length of her hair. She comes from Brassempouy in the Landes area of France.

THE MOTHER GODDESS AS THE CREATIVE SOURCE OF LIFE

Looking back so many thousands of years later at these earliest figures, it seems as if humanity's first image of life was the Mother. This must go back to a time when human beings experienced themselves as the children of Nature, in relationship with all things, part of the whole. It may seem astonishing that people who lived then were already speaking a language that is still intelligible to us today. Yet, exploring the art of that time from the perspective of the present, it seems that many of the images known to us later from the worship of the Mother Goddess in more complex traditions had here their earliest manifestation. Images of giving birth, offering nourishment from the breast and receiving the dead back into the womb for rebirth occur in the Palaeolithic as they do 10,000 years later in the Neolithic and 5,000 years after that in the Bronze and Iron Ages – and, indeed, are present to this day in Western culture in the rituals surrounding the Virgin Mary. It is not surprising that these images of the goddess appear throughout human history, for they all express a similar vision of life on Earth, one where the creative source of life is conceived in the image of a Mother and where humanity feels itself and the rest of creation to be the Mother's children.

Moving from west to east, the Goddess of Willendorf in Austria (Fig. 4) is only 4⅓ inches (11 cm) tall but seems massive. Made of limestone, this figure is weighed down with fertility, so rooted in the earth that she seems to be part of it. The centripetal heaviness of her body – where breasts, womb and thighs fall into a round and the arms rest on top of the hugely swollen breasts – forms a distinct contrast to the separateness of the head with its precisely carved notations. The curiously bulbous head is vertically layered in seven strata, with each layer notched horizontally all the way round, giving the appearance of seven circles around the head. The number seven, as one quarter of the moon's full circle and the number of the moving planets, may here be coincidental, but certainly was a sacred number of wholeness by the time of the Bronze Age (*c.* 3500 BC), 15,000 years later.

The flowing breast is the essential image of trust in the universe. Even the faintest pattern of stars was once seen as iridescent drops of milk streaming from the breast of the Mother Goddess: the galaxy that came to be called the Milky Way. In the ivory figurine from Pavlov, near Dolní Věstonice in Czechoslovakia, in Figure 6, the breasts are the entire focus of meaning, and everything else has been abstracted away to render the central theme of nourishment all-inclusive. The lines etched around the

Figure 4. (*Left*) Goddess of Willendorf, front view; limestone, 20,000–18,000 BC, height 4⅓ in. (11 cm). Austria.
Figure 5. (*Right*) Goddess of Willendorf, close-up of the top of the head, showing seven strata of notched circles.

Figure 6. (*Left*) Ivory rod with breasts; *c*. 25,000–20,000 BC. Dolní
Věstonice, Czechoslovakia.
Figure 7. (*Right*) Goddess; fired clay, *c*. 20,000 BC, torso height 4¼ in
(11.5 cm). Dolní Věstonice, Czechoslovakia.

outside of the breasts and the horizontal lines beneath them direct attention to the sacred source. It seems incredible that when this image was
found in 1937 it was described as 'a diluvial (i.e. Ice Age or pre-Flood)
plastic pornography'.[3]

The strange dark goddess in Figure 7, found near a hearth also in Dolní
Věstonice, was sculpted from clay and pulverized bone and fired rock-
hard. Her face has two upward slanting slits for eyes and a downward
stroke for the nose, and in the top of her head four holes were made in the
wet clay to hold flowers, leaves or feathers, forming her 'hair' or 'head-
dress' – an image, perhaps, that explores how plants grow. Again, it is the
feeling of fecundity that predominates: the shape of the full hanging
breasts followed in the swelling curve of the hips and belly, with a large
hole for the belly button, emphasizing the umbilical cord and possibly
taking the place of the vulva, which is absent. Since her legs end in a
point, she would also have been placed upright in soil or wood, or carried
by hand.

The goddess as the creative source of life was also frequently rendered
abstractly in the shape of a triangle (Fig. 8) or in a distinct division of the
legs opened at the entrance to the womb. There are more than 100 images
of the vulva in Palaeolithic France alone, suggesting that stories of the
goddess who gives birth were so familiar that they could be instantly
recognized. Sometimes the vulvas have seeds and sprouts drawn over or
beside them, or even the rippling movement of water, suggesting that the

Figure 8. Genital triangle, meanders and chevrons incised on bone figurines, 30,000–20,000 BC. Mezin, western Ukraine.

cosmic womb was recognized as the source of the vegetative world and also of the waters of life. In Figure 8 the meander of chevron patterns that are incised on the ivory may be the markings of bird wings or the wavy lines of water.

In the forked bone pendant in Figure 9, again from Dolní Věstonice, the body is abstracted to form a symbol, its meaning focused on the deeply marked groove where the 'legs' divide. Over 10,000 years later, the bone engraving from Teyjat in the Dordogne (Fig. 10) looks like an evolution of this image: the figure is also abstract, yet it may be more readily recognized as a goddess. She has a tiny head, angular shoulders, a serpentine design down the outer length of the body and curious rectangular shapes engraved upon it. The vulva or womb is drawn as a double oval with the two horizontal lines beneath it, further emphasized by the cleft between the tapering legs.

Moving further eastwards across to Siberia, an extraordinary burial site was discovered at Mal'ta near Lake Baikal, dating to c. 16,000–13,000 BC; in this site, along with fourteen animal burials, there were at least twenty

Figure 9. (*Left*) Ivory pendant; c. 20,000 BC. Dolní Věstonice, Czechoslovakia.
Figure 10. (*Right*) Drawing of goddess engraved on bone; c. 10,000 BC. Teyjat, France.

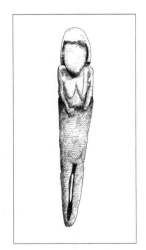

Figure 11. Goddess figure carved from
mammoth-ivory; *c.* 16,000–13,000 BC.
Mal'ta, Siberia.

mammoth-ivory figures of goddesses, all from $1\frac{1}{4}$ to $5\frac{1}{4}$ inches (3.2 to
13.3 cm) tall, one of them apparently clothed in a lion's skin. The small
thin goddess in Figure 11 has unusually defined arms, with the breasts
and head emphasized, and again she has tapering legs that allow us to
imagine her standing upright, fixed into the earth, just like the Goddess
of Lespugue. The resemblance of many of the goddess figures all the way
from France to Russia suggests that there was a continuity of religious
structure stretching from Europe to Siberia, unimaginable before the
excavations of the twentieth century.

THE GODDESS AS BIRD

The bird who appears out of a distant sky has always been a messenger of
wonder as the visible incarnation of the invisible world. In many Bronze
Age myths the cosmic egg of the universe was laid by the Cosmic Mother
Bird, and its cracking open was the beginning of time and space. The
ivory bead from Dolní Věstonice in Figure 12 is the centre-piece of a
necklace of beads, carved from the ivory of a mammoth tooth. It has a
long, faceless neck and two breasts, which could also be the wings of a
bird, because the sign of the double V chevron engraved on them resembles the striped markings of many birds, as do the grooves on the
lower tips. It anticipates similar figures in the Neolithic era (10,000–3500
BC), by which time the power and protection of the one Mother Goddess
has clearly differentiated into the three regions of Sky or the Upper
Waters, Earth, and the Lower Waters or the Waters Beneath the Earth.
From the evidence of art, the notion of 'the underworld', with its connotations of darkness, lifelessness and menace, was not present before the

traumas and anarchy of the late Bronze Age. The Goddess of the Upper Waters in the Neolithic is the Bird Goddess who brings the life-giving rain, just as, even in much later times, birds were believed to make the weather or be a sign of weather to come. The stork who in folk-lore brings the baby through the air was once the Stork who brought back the spring, the rebirth of the year. The Neolithic goddess in Figure 13 has the head of a bird, and sometimes she also has a bird body with wings; or her body becomes the pots and vases holding the waters of life, her bird face staring out from them and rain torrents streaking across them.

Nearly 15,000 years lie between these two images, yet they and many others travelled across many thousands of miles and many hundreds of centuries, carried either by the constantly dispersing tribes as they moved into new lands, or re-enacted, more obscurely, by successive generations moved by the same need to articulate a similar feeling in a similar way. The debate on whether some recurrent images radiate from a central source or are a spontaneous recurrence brought about by constant characteristics in the nature of the human psyche is virtually unsolvable once both alternatives are held to be possible. When we talk of archetypal images here we are assuming that even if an image were, so to say, physically transported from one place to another (as many undoubtedly were), it would not have caught the imagination of the inhabitants of any new place if there had not been some essential resonance in the hearts and minds of all the people.

Figure 12. (*Left*) Pendant bead (enlarged) of mammoth-ivory in the shape
of an elongated neck with pierced hole and two breasts engraved
as wings on the front; *c.* 20,000 BC, height 1 in. (2.5 cm).
Dolní Věstonice, Czechoslovakia.
Figure 13. (*Right*) Bird goddess with breasts and chevrons; terracotta,
c. 6000 BC. Sesklo, Thessaly, Greece.

Figure 14. (*Left*) Female figurine; coal, *c.* 14,000 BC, height 1¾ in. (4.4 cm).
Petersfels, Germany.
Figure 15. (*Right*) Engraving of female figure with cosmic egg; *c.* 18,000–
14,000 BC. Fontales, France.

Egg-shaped buttocks or buttocks round enough to hold an egg also render the goddess as the source of life through the metaphor of a bird. Many so-called 'buttocks' figures were engraved on cave walls in south-western France from 30,000 BC to 10,000 BC (from the Aurignacian to the Magdalenian periods). The tiny piece of coal from a cave in Petersfels, Germany, in Figure 14, beautifully carved and polished to a smooth ebony, is only 1¾ inches (4.4 cm) tall and has a hole at the top, so it might have been hung around the neck by a leather thong. The egg inside the buttocks of the engraving from Fontales in southern France in Figure 15 may suggest a fusion of the goddess with the bird who lays the cosmic egg, or it may be that the egg is placed inside the body of the goddess to make an analogy between the miraculous way a baby bird comes forth from the egg and the way the world is imagined as coming forth from the body of the goddess.

THE CAVE AS THE WOMB OF THE MOTHER GODDESS

Scarcely more than 100 years ago no one knew that there was human life at the time when the woolly mammoth ranged over the frozen wastes that covered most of Europe and Asia. Then came the astonishing discoveries of the Palaeolithic caves of northern Spain and south-western France: first, Altamira (1879); then La Pasiega (1911), Les Trois Frères (1912), Tuc d'Audoubert (1914), Niaux, Les Combarelles, Pech-Merle and Las-caux (1940), to mention only the best known. Layer after layer, painstak-ingly lifted from the floors of these caves, has revealed a continuity of life inside them over an immense span of time. The excavations at El Castillo in northern Spain, for instance, show that Neanderthal Man (*Homo sapiens neanderthalensis*), who preceded Modern Man (*Homo sapiens sapiens*), lived here before the Riss–Würm interglacial period, that is, before 186,000 BC.[4] In the past century more than 100 decorated caves have been un-covered, overturning earlier theories of barely human warrior-hunters lurking at the dawn of history and sleeping unquietly in the depths of the human heart.

The story of a great primeval goddess is told in the caves of south-western France through the art and the rituals that took place inside them. For at least 20,000 years (from 30,000 to 10,000 BC) the Palaeolithic cave seems to be the most sacred place, the sanctuary of the Goddess and the source of her regenerative power. Entering one of these caves is like making a journey into another world, one which is *inside* the body of the goddess. To those who would have lived in a sacred world, the actual hollowed shape would have symbolized her all-containing womb, which brought forth the living and took back the dead. The cave as the place of transformation was the binding link between the past and future of the men and women who lived in the forefront of it and held their religious rites deep in its interior sanctuary. Inside the cave were placed the stones that represented the souls of the dead who would be reborn from her womb. On the exterior walls her image was sculpted; on the interior walls were painted the male and female animals who may have embodied the different aspects of her being, and the artist-shamans who could hear her voice in the voice of the animal.

Just before 1914, in the Ariège region of south-western France, a vast complex of labyrinthine caves was discovered 60 feet (18 metres) below the surface of the ground. Campbell points out that this cave-labyrinth of Tuc d'Audoubert and Les Trois Frères together was used for at least 20,000 years and was one of the most important centres of religion, if not the greatest in the world.[5]

All the magnificently decorated caves of the Palaeolithic tribes were guarded by a formidably arduous approach. Going from daylight into complete darkness, it is impossible not to feel a tremor of fear and awe, treading the same path into the heart of the earth as people did 30,000 years ago. They had only lamps of hollowed stone with juniper twig wicks and oil made from animal fat to give them light. How did they find the courage to creep and slither and gasp their way through narrow laby-rinthine passages, through caverns vast enough to contain a cathedral, to a sanctuary at the end, often 1–2 miles (2–3 km) from the mouth of the cave? Following the tortuous pathway to the sanctuary or descending into an enormous light and spacious womb-cavern has all the characteristics of a tribal initiation of the kind still practised by some contemporary tribes. The vision at the end of this journey at Lascaux – the dazzling animals known only from field and forest – must have felt like a 'second birth' into a new dimension. Dr Herbert Kuhn describes his breakthrough into

Figure 16. Interior of the great cave at Lombrives, near Tarascon-sur-Ariège, France.

the ultimate cavern at Les Trois Frères in 1926:

> The hall in which we are now standing is gigantic. We let the light of the lamps run along the ceiling and walls; a majestic room – and there, finally, are the pictures. From top to bottom a whole wall is covered with engravings. The surface has been worked with tools of stone, and there we see marshaled the beasts that lived at the time in southern France: the mammoth, rhinoceros, bison, wild horse, bear, wild ass, reindeer, wolverine, musk ox; also, the smaller animals appear: snowy owls, hares, and fish . . . And one sees darts everywhere, flying at the game. Truly a picture of the hunt; the picture of the magic of the hunt.[6]

Inside the caves an inspiration for the art of sculpture may have been offered by the elongated stalactites that hung from the roof to the floor, as well as by the rounded stalagmites thrown upwards from the ground. Watching and listening to the constant dripping of water on to stone, the cave dwellers may also have seen the connection of what is above with what is below as symbolizing a universal relationship between heaven and earth. Some cave shapes at least were alive with meaning: at Pech-Merle in France, for instance, red and black dots were painted around stalactites, transforming them into breasts.

André Leroi-Gourhan, the pioneering French Palaeolithic scholar, who analysed thousands of paintings and sculptures from a great number of caves, proposed that the figures and signs could be distinguished into what he called 'feminine' and 'masculine' categories, and that there was a fundamental, though very complicated, emphasis on 'pairing' of polarized forces. Not every animal of all those known to have been alive then was portrayed, so that those especially selected were, he concluded, chosen for their dramatic role in a specific mythology, the main actors being the bison and the horse. What is fascinating is his observation that the figures, animals and signs he interpreted as feminine were situated in a central position, which was clearly 'the special heart and core of the caves'.[7] The masculine animals and signs, by contrast, supplemented the feminine signs: either they were arranged around the feminine signs or they featured only peripherally in the narrow entrances towards the sanctuary or in the narrow tunnels at the back.[8]

THE GODDESS AS THE MOON

When we try to construct a picture of how Palaeolithic people lived and thought, imagining ourselves at the mouths of their caves looking out, do we not see, as the most mysterious phenomenon, the moon – and the faces of the moon, which constantly change in a way that is constantly the same? The two terms, the fixed and the variant, give the first notion of sequence, measurement and time. This meaning of the moon is still hidden in our language: Greek *mene* means moon, Latin *mensis* means month, and *mensura*, with the same root, means measurement, from which the name of the menstrual cycle comes; for the changes of the moon made possible the earliest measurement of time longer than a day (which could be reckoned by the sun).

But this is secular language, not the sacred and symbolic language of myth. For these early people in the history of humanity we could imagine that the moon, as the whole of nature, was experienced as the Mother Goddess, so that the moon's phases became phases in the life of the Mother. The crescent moon was the young girl, the maiden; the full moon was the pregnant woman, the mother; the darkening moon was the wise old woman, whose light was within.

There was a trinity of goddesses found in a cave at the Abri du Roc aux Sorciers at Angles-sur-l'Anglin, coming from the time between 13,000 and 11,000 BC. Three huge goddesses were hewn out of the cave rock, with their capacity to give birth definitely emphasized and their heads and the upper parts of their body vanishing upwards out of sight. The three figures are standing on a bison, recalling the Goddess of Laussel holding the bison's horn as the crescent moon, carved nearly 10,000 years before. Are they the goddesses of the three visible phases of the moon, who assume separate names and roles in later ages? Laurens van der Post considers the African Bushman to be one of the oldest races on Earth alive today. He tells the story of how, when he was travelling with them and it was night and they had a long day ahead, he wondered why everyone was dancing and no one was going to sleep. When he asked them, they told him that they would be dancing all night because the moon was going to wane: 'We must show her how we love her or she won't come back.'[9]

Tales of the moon are found all over the world, and in many of them the cyclical rhythms of the moon enact a pattern that is felt to belong to human life also, a feeling portrayed in the sculpture of the Goddess of Laussel. In the rhythmical phases of light and darkness the Palaeolithic tribes must have seen a pattern of growing and decaying endlessly renewed, and this would have given them trust in life. In the waxing of the moon they would have felt life growing and felt the growth of their own lives. In the full moon they may have marvelled at the increase of life that overflowed into new life. In the waning moon they would have mourned the withdrawal of life, the departure of the goddess; and in the darkness of the lost moon they would have longed for her and her light to return. With the passage of time, they must have come to trust in the reappearance of the crescent moon, and so to recognize darkness as the time of waiting before the resurgence of new life. With death they would have felt that they were taken back into the dark womb of the Mother and believed that they would be reborn like the moon.

This experience gave birth in them to the power to see life imaginally. Darkness was not something antagonistic to light, nor death to life, but an aspect of the being of the Mother Goddess. Everything that existed, including themselves, was an expression of the Goddess. Everything, therefore, was an image that confirmed their relationship to her. Out of this ability to experience life imaginally arose the inexhaustible creativity of humanity. Myth was the expression of this primordial experience.

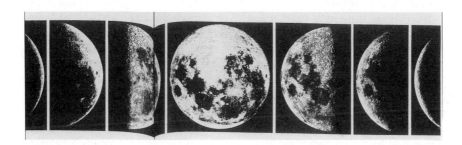

Figure 17. The phases of the moon.

Alexander Marshack's remarkable book *The Roots of Civilization* shows
that Palaeolithic people used a system of lunar notation as early as 40,000
BC. This brings them much closer to us, urging us to value their intelligence and skills more highly than we have. In 1963 Marshack was research-
ing a book about the technological achievements that enabled human
beings to travel to the moon in a spacecraft, but his researches left him
with the feeling that something was missing in the archaeological record.
Humanity, he felt, could not 'suddenly' have invented writing, mathematics, astronomy. What had happened before the Bronze Age that laid
the foundations for these 'sudden' discoveries? His search led him to a
piece of bone from Ishango near the headwaters of the Nile. Examining
this intently, he had the intuitive idea that the lines engraved on it might
be lunar notations. What followed is as exciting as the story of any great
discovery. The lunar notations he found on bone, stone, antler and goddess figure must, he thought, have laid the foundations for the discovery
of agriculture, the calendar, astronomy, mathematics and writing. In this
case all these achievements would have developed over immense periods
of time and not 'suddenly' as we had assumed:

> Apparently as far back as 30,000 BC, the ice-age hunter of western Europe
> was using a system of notation that was already evolved, complex and
> sophisticated, a tradition that would seem to have been thousands of years
> old by this point. Apparently it was also in use by other types of modern
> man, such as Combe Capelle man of the East Gravettian culture in Czech-
> oslovakia and Russia and by other peoples and sub-cultures in Italy and
> Spain . . . The tradition seems so widespread that the question arises as to
> whether its beginnings may not go back to the period of Neanderthal man
> . . . These facts are so new and important . . . they raise profound questions
> concerning the evolved intelligence and cognitive abilities of the human
> species.[10]

It is possible that an ability to think abstractly developed from an
understanding of the moon's phases as four instead of three. To the three
visible phases – the waxing, the full and the waning – was added the
fourth phase, the three days' darkness where the moon cannot be seen and
can only be imagined. The fourth, invisible phase may have been understood as the invisible dimension where new life is gestated and from
which the old moon is reborn as the new moon. When the dark phase of
the moon is included as an essential part of the continuing cycle of light,
it requires the capacity to hold as present in the mind an image of what is
not actually visible to the eye. Meanders and spirals (see p. 23) are
evidence of abstract thought, and later, on Neolithic pots, images of a
four-armed cross represent the four phases of the moon.

For Palaeolithic people, whatever they observed was defined by a
seasonal rhythm. If they looked to the sky, they saw the migrating and
returning birds, among them the crane, goose, heron and swan. They saw
the salmon leaping upstream in the great rivers at definite times of year.

They saw the sequence of budding, blossoming and fruiting of the many different kinds of tree, and the fall of the leaf. They saw the gestation and birth, growth and death of all kinds of animals in a predictable rhythm. Their own lives followed the same rhythmic pattern, as one season changed into another. In summer they followed the animals and their lives were focused on the hunt. In winter, when short days and arctic cold made hunting difficult, life was concentrated around the caves, where they mastered the art of tool-making. There was a season for making tools and a season for using them, one for transforming skins and furs into clothes and covering, and one for killing the animals that provided them. In the summer they must have delighted in the greater warmth and increase of life. In winter, around the fire, they probably told the stories that have come down to us as myth, legend and fairy-tale. Their rituals were timed to the seasons and promised the fertility of the animals, the success of the hunt and the lasting through winter's terrible cold. The skills they developed in observing the phases of the moon and the circular movement of the stars, the stories they told to accompany these rituals, all expressed the specifically human instinct to recognize analogies between different orders and dimensions of life. It must have been this power to think analogically that enabled them to perceive the relationship between a heavenly order, symbolized by the moon, and the earthly order they saw around them.

The moon was undoubtedly the central image of the sacred to these early people because, in its dual rhythm of constancy and change, it provided not only a point of orientation from which differences could be measured, patterns conceived and connections made, but also, in its perpetual return to its own beginnings, it unified what had apparently been broken asunder. As the great light shining in the darkness of the night, the moon, in all mythologies up to the Iron Age (*c.* 1250 BC), was regarded as one of the supreme images of the Goddess, the unifying power of the Mother of All. She was the measure of cycles of time, and of celestial and earthly connection and influence. She governed the fecundity of woman, the waters of the sea and all the phases of increase and decrease. The seasons followed each other in sequence as the phases of the moon followed each other. She was an enduring image both of renewal in time and of a timeless totality, because what was apparently lost with the waning moon was restored with the waxing moon. Duality, imaged as the waxing and waning moon, was contained and transcended in her totality. So, analogously, life and death did not have to be perceived as opposites, but could be seen as phases succeeding each other in a rhythm that was endless. It is not surprising, then, that lunar mythology preceded solar mythology in many, if not all, parts of the world.

The lunar notations sometimes follow a serpentine path on the fragments of bone that have come down to us, and this helps to understand the ancient connection between the moon and the serpent (Fig. 18). The

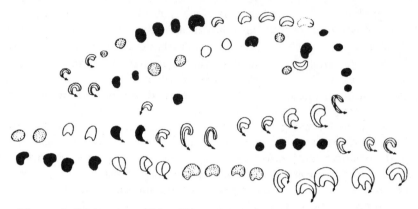

Figure 18. Schematic rendition (from microscopic analysis) of the engraved
marks, indicating the strokes structuring the serpentine form, on the plaque
from the rock shelter at Blanchard.

moon died and came to life again; the serpent sloughed its skin yet
remained alive. The serpent must have already become what it was always
afterwards to be – an image of rebirth and transformation.

THE GODDESS OF DEATH AND REBIRTH

Over 100,000 years ago, in the Riss–Würm interglacial period (186,000–
75,000 BC), the burials of Neanderthal Man, who preceded *Homo sapiens
sapiens* in the Stone Age, suggest that human consciousness had already
developed the capacity to recognize death and to give it the status of a
mystery that required honouring rituals. Bodies have been found, some
60,000 years old, arranged in the foetal position, facing east – the direction
of the rise of the full moon, the last crescent and of sunrise – covered in
flowers and sprinkled with the red ochre dye that mimed, perhaps, the
renewal of blood and the quickening of the life-force for the new life.[11]

When the sign of the vulva is incised on a lunar disc and found in a
grave (Fig. 19), there may be a coincidence of meanings in which the
birth-giving vulva becomes the womb of rebirth. Does this cleft also symbolize the three days' dark passage between the death of the old moon and
its rebirth as the crescent of the next round? Certainly, the lunar model
suggests that human beings, when they died, vanished like the moon from
the world of the living, perhaps to be reborn in another world, perhaps to
return to this one. Here, the womb of the goddess takes back the life she
has given so that the life may be born anew.

The burial site in Mal'ta in Siberia mentioned earlier (see p. 12) was
also interesting for showing the goddess figures set in the midst of many
of the images that consistently surround the Goddess in much later times:
the bird and fish, meander and spiral, and the wild animals that gave her

Figure 19. Lunar disc made from a mammoth tooth (enlarged); *c.* 20,000 BC. Brno, Czechoslovakia.

the title 'Goddess of the Animals' or 'Lady of the Beasts'. Beside the twenty tiny goddesses was an ivory plaque with a spiral design on one side and three serpents with cobra-like heads engraved on the other (Figs. 20, 21). A group of six ivory birds, either geese or swans, carved as if in flight (Fig. 22), were found alongside them, and also an ivory fish, engraved on one side with the stipple design of a labyrinth or meander. There were also a shaman's ivory baton, the skeletons of some fourteen ritually buried animals and a four-year-old child lying in the foetal position, facing east to rise with the sun. The ceremony of the child's burial is given in the plentiful red colouring in the grave and in the care taken with the decoration of the little body: a mammoth-ivory crown around the forehead with matching bracelet and a necklace of ivory beads, from which hung a pendant in the shape of a flying bird.

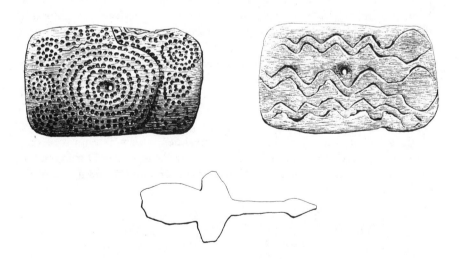

Figure 20. (*Above left*) Buckle or plaque showing spiral design; *c.* 16,000–13,000 BC, length 5½ in. (14 cm). Mal'ta, Siberia.
Figure 21. (*Above right*) Other side of plaque, showing three serpents.
Figure 22. (*Below*) Flying goose or swan carved in ivory; *c.* 16,000–13,000 BC. Mal'ta, Siberia.

The burial site at Mal'ta, occupied between 16,000 and 13,000 BC, is one of several similar sites discovered in Russia. But this one is highly significant because, as Campbell says, it was 'the crucial centre of an archaic cultural continuum running, on the one hand, back to the Aurignacian rock shelter of Laussel, on the other, forward to the Blackfoot Buffalo dance of the nineteenth century AD'.[12] In Palaeolithic times there was a land bridge between Siberia and Alaska, and it was across this bridge that the Stone Age people travelled to the Americas.

THE SPIRAL AND MEANDER

Like the labyrinthine passage through the cave, the spiral and meander symbolize the sacred way of approach to a dimension invisible to human senses. They are found incised on the goddess figurines as well as on or around the images of the animals carved on antler, stone and bone, and also on the walls of the caves. The earliest known spiral is the one on Figure 20, where a spiral of dots on mammoth-ivory winds round seven times towards or out of a central hole. The seven-fold spiral design appears highly deliberate, and the number seven, recalling the seven strata notched round the head of the Goddess of Willendorf, gains in possible significance. On the other side, serpents wind across the buckle like waves of water. The archaeologist Gertrude Levy, in her pioneering book *The Gate of Horn*, writes that spirals are the most frequent decorative motif on the Magdalenian ceremonial wands, or *bâtons de commandement*, as Leroi-Gourhan has called them.[13] The spiral form is found in the eddying of water, sea-shells, the intestines, the spider's web and the whirling galaxies of space.

Both water and the serpent are closely associated with the spiral, as they are with the meander and labyrinth. The labyrinth winds like a serpent or like the serpentine movement of water through the womb of earth, which is the cave. The oldest meander known is engraved on a bone that is 135,000 years old, from Pech de l'Aze in the Dordogne. All these form an enduring constellation of images related to the figure of the

Figure 23. Meander incised on bracelet of mammoth-ivory; *c.* 20,000 BC.
Mezin, western Ukraine.

Goddess, for they symbolize the intricate pathway that connects the visible world to the invisible, of the kind that the souls of the dead would have taken to re-enter the womb of the Mother.

Figures of goddesses, images of the moon, the crescent horns of bison and bull, the bird, serpent, fish and wild animals, the chevrons of water or birds' wings, the meander, labyrinth and spiral – all these reappear in the myths and images of later ages, often clearly reminiscent of their earliest beginnings. Together they point to a culture with a highly developed mythology that wove together all these elements in stories long since lost to us, but whose traces may still linger in the enchanting convolutions of fairy-tales. The miraculous survival of these images of the Mother Goddess throughout 20,000 years is a testament to a surprisingly unified culture – or, at the very least, a common nexus of belief – lasting for a much longer period of time than their successors, images of the Father God. Campbell summarizes:

> From the Pyrenees to Lake Baikal, the evidence now is before us of a Late Stone Age mythology in which the outstanding single figure was the Naked Goddess . . . She was almost certainly a patroness of childbirth and fecundity. In that Palaeolithic age she was specifically a goddess of the hunt, but also, apparently, of vegetation . . . The Mal'ta burial suggests that it was she who received the dead and delivered their souls to rebirth.[14]

Our assumptions about human nature, in particular our beliefs about the capacity of human beings to live in harmony with the rest of nature and to shape a peaceful world, are crucial to whether or not we can actually create a better way of being. If we hold that human beings are and always have been primarily hunters and warriors, then we are more likely to overlook evidence to the contrary and conclude that war-like aggression is innate. No evidence has been found that Palaeolithic people fought each other.[15] It is then moving to discover that our Palaeolithic ancestors have something to teach us, specifically about the way we have misinterpreted their art, and so their lives, by pressing them into a world view belonging to the twentieth century.

The two misconceptions are interestingly related. Firstly, the goddess figurines were originally classified as erotic or pornographic art, a conception that would be unthinkable if the feminine principle were recognized as sacred, or, to speak colloquially, if 'God' were a Mother as well as a Father – that is to say, if our image of the deity contained both feminine and masculine dimensions. Secondly, the many stick and line forms engraved on stone and bone and painted on the walls of the caves were assumed to be weapons for hunting or male signs, but, on closer microscopic examination, proved to be plants, leaves, branches and trees. Again, this discovery is due to Marshack, who brought the goddess figures and the lunar reckoning to the notice of the world, and who was not bound to the prevailing view of these drawings as 'masculine objects' and 'barbed signs'. Significantly, both the symbolic potentiality of the birth-giving female figure and the myriad forms of vegetative life have been excluded, for the last 3,000 years, from the categories of the sacred. As Riane Eisler observes in her important book *The Chalice and the Blade*, Palaeolithic art 'bespeaks psychic traditions we must understand if we are to know not only what humans were and are but also what they can become'.[16]

THE ANIMALS

Figure 24. Bison bellowing, with plants and cones (face of doe on reverse side); engraving on mammoth-ivory 'knife' or 'polisher', *c.* 10,000 BC. La Vache cave, Ariège, France.

The most startling difference between the Palaeolithic and our contemporary sensibility lies in the awe and reverence that these early people accorded to the animals. In the beginning of the Judaeo-Christian tradition human beings are told to 'replenish the earth and subdue it: and have dominion over the fish of the sea, and over the fowl of the air, and over every living thing that moveth upon the earth' (Gen. 1:28). Such isolation from the earth and the animal, bird and sea world would be sacrilege in the Palaeolithic. There, the animals were sacred beings, teachers of fundamental laws within which both human and animal were bound. In the art of the caves it is the animal who rules supreme, exquisitely and lovingly drawn, brilliantly coloured and vibrantly alive. The Abbé Breuil, whose devoted work in recording these images has saved many of them from extinction, here describes the scene:

> When we visit a painted cave, we enter a sanctuary, where, for thousands of years, sacred ceremonies have taken place, directed no doubt by the great initiates of the time, and introducing the novices called to receive in their turn the necessary fundamental instruction for the conduct of their lives.[17]

What was the nature of the bond between human and animal, which is so moving in this art? When the ice was at its thickest and the ground was frozen tundra, only meat could sustain life and so the Palaeolithic tribes had to hunt animals to survive. Animals also provided the furs and skins that gave the people warmth, shelter and clothing. Their bones, tusks, horns and antlers gave the people the material to shape into tools and carve and paint their sacred images; they gave them instruments for reckoning the passage of time, even needles with which to sew together their clothes. Animal bones, teeth and claws were transformed into necklaces, and their fat provided oil for lamps. The animals must have been seen as the embodiment of divine power, the gift of life to the tribe. Were the animals experienced as the generative powers of the Goddess, which guaranteed the continuation of life? It is likely that they were already regarded as diverse expressions of the all-encompassing reality of the Great Mother Goddess, who was carved outside the caves, which held inside, on their womb-like walls, images of the bewildering variety of forms to which she had given birth.

The identity between animals and human animals was broken at some point in the last 3 million years when a new kind of thinking set humanity apart from the rest of nature. But in the art of the caves this ancient bond was remembered and reforged. Perhaps in the rituals celebrated in the caves the people could once again experience the spontaneity of the animal life within them that was sacrificed with the birth of consciousness, reflecting upon itself.

The animals appeared to live in the moment, with no discernible awareness of an ending, yet they knew when to move according to the seasons. Because they seemed to answer to invisible rhythms, they could also embody the souls of the tribal ancestors, those who lived in the 'dream time' of eternity. There were no written records of the past, so human memory alone could give the tribe a feeling of continuity. But tribal memory is continually revised as the generations move forward, and the years and decades and centuries behind become compressed into stories of origins and merge into sacred time – what happened once upon a time – when the deeds were performed that gave birth to present time. The stories that were handed down from generation to generation must have created the beginnings of a tribal tradition. Telling and dancing the stories linked the 'dream time' of the immemorial past with a present made sacred by the re-enactment of a primordial myth.

In 1989 some Brazilian Indians, whose nations until the last decade had been living undisturbed for many centuries, if not millennia, in the Amazon jungle, described their own experience in very similar terms: the Great Chief of the nation, who had dreamed their destiny in the beginning, had said then that now was the time when the tribe should act to save the forest and their common home. Now, because their trees and their animals had been destroyed, the elders of the tribe could no longer dream, and without dreaming the tribe would lose direction. Cutting down the jungle and giving them cattle to rear on the stubbled grass would give them only 'cowboy dreams', not the dreams proper to their own tribe, which can guide them rightly. Only their own animals, who, like them, belong to the forest, can give them their 'dreams'; for, the Indian added, in language Chief Seattle would have understood, the animals are our brothers, and the rivers are our veins, they run with our blood; if you block them and dam them, you stop the flowing of blood in our veins and then the heart stops.[18]

The Palaeolithic sensibility does not seem far away. So it is likely that the animals painted on the walls of the caves may have been characters in stories that were told over and over again from the beginning. In this way, certain animals could have become totem animals essential to the dream of the tribe, even perhaps dreaming for the tribe as their ancestral spirits, speaking to the shamans in trance and giving the people their sense of unity and identity.

By the close of the Aurignacian period (30,000–25,000 BC), the woolly mammoth, rhinoceros, cave bear and cave lion had vanished, probably to become figures in Palaeolithic legend of a far-distant past. Even today certain animals 'stand for' certain tribes or peoples: the bear for Russia, the lion for England, the eagle for America and Germany. Teddy bears still have their picnic in the woods, and animals reassume their awesome nature nightly in dreams.

In the sanctuary at Les Trois Frères there are from 300 to 500 engravings of animals overlapping and superimposed on each other. At Lascaux there are 2,000 engravings and paintings, some of them as old as 30,000 BC, though most of them belong to the Magdalenian period (15,000–10,000 BC). It is hard to grasp the immensity of time during which these sanctuaries were used, later artists drawing their own images on top of those already thousands of years old. This raises the question why or how did the 'religion of the caves' endure for so long?

The oldest animal hunted for food in the northern hemisphere, and also the oldest animal whose remains have been given a ritual significance, is

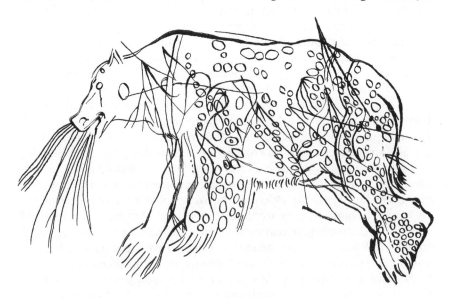

Figure 25. Wounded bear; *c.* 16,000–12,000 BC. Les Trois Frères cave, Ariège, France.

the bear. Bear skulls have been found high up in the Swiss Alps in caves over 7,000 feet (2,100 m) above sea-level, which means that they must have been put there before the beginning of the last ice age – that is, before 75,000 BC – when the mountains became inaccessible because of the glaciers that covered them. The bear skulls are piled in hollows made of stone slabs, relics of a ritual of sacrifice in which, perhaps, the bear's soul was sent as a messenger to the other world, as the source of life, to ask for the right to take these particular lives in the hunt. At Les Trois Frères the engraved image of a wounded bear is transfixing (Fig. 25). Its body is covered in tiny circles. Darts and spears pierce its flanks and blood pours from its mouth. The picture is often understood as part of a hunting ritual in which the bear is drawn with the wounds that are hoped for so as to ensure the success of the hunt – an early example of magical wish-fulfilment. A further idea is sometimes added, that the painting is in itself a rite of propitiation whereby the wrath of the animal was appeased and the tribe enabled to take the animal's life without fear of retribution. The wholly secular character of these kinds of interpretation should alert us to their inappropriateness. If, on the other hand, the taking of life were understood as the rupturing of a sacred order, then the engraving of the sacrificial image of the bear would perform a dual purpose: it would prepare the tribe for the enormity of slaying the animal and at the same time honourably ask the animal for his consent to be slain. In the latter interpretation the painting is an ethical act: it honours the bond between human and animal, and the bond of both with the whole. In the first kind of interpretation the painting is merely an expedient of survival. It is important not to confuse the two kinds of action, nor to read our own reductions back into history by assuming that the predominant feeling for the bear was self-interest.

Imagining ourselves back into a world where all life is interrelated, there is blood-guilt for taking the life of a 'brother', and this has to be atoned for by careful ritual when human being and animal are part of the same unity. When an animal is killed, the 'One' is wounded. Some fairy-tales tell the story of an animal whom the hero has to kill in obedience to the animal's own instruction. He kills him in sorrow and finds to his amazement that the animal is transformed into a long-lost brother or a royal prince held under enchantment in an animal form. It may be that this is an ancient Palaeolithic story, where the animal to whom due rites are given is reborn into human life and takes his place again beside his brother. The relation between the human hunter and the hunted animal is certainly not simple, since of the many human figures found with animals in Upper Palaeolithic art none is found carrying weapons, though many wear some kind of ceremonial dress or carry symbolic objects, either clothed in animal skins or naked.

There are only thirty engravings or paintings of a lion or lioness in the Pyrenean caves so far discovered – a tiny proportion in relation to the

Figure 26. Lioness; *c.* 25,000–12,000 BC. Les Trois Frères cave, Ariège, France.

bison or horse – and of these, six or seven are in Lascaux, four are in Les Trois Frères and one, engraved on a rib fragment, is from La Vâche cave in the Ariège. In Les Trois Frères the lioness (Fig. 26) is given the most prominent place directly facing the one who approaches the innermost sanctuary of the cave. As the most ferocious animal and the 'King and Queen of the Beasts', the lion as the guardian would have commanded most respect. Unlike the other animals, this lioness is not engraved in profile but confronts head on. With the startling impact of her eyes she appears to be challenging the one about to enter the sacred cave, as though guarding the mysteries against the uninitiated. In later times lions are the guardians of temples all over the world, and everywhere the Goddess is conceived as seated upon a throne of lions – from seventh-millennium-BC Anatolia to second-millennium-AD Europe in the figure of the Virgin Mary (see Chapter 14, Fig. 21).

A third of all the cave animals are horses – over 600 paintings in all. Bison, aurochs and wild ox make up nearly a third also. About a tenth of the total animals are stags or hinds. Strangely, reindeer, which were hunted with the woolly mammoth and whose bones were found in great profusion at Lascaux, hardly appear at all in the paintings. This raises the question why the horse, horned bison and bull (or aurochs) were depicted more than any other animal. Of course, they would have been close to human life and essential to survival, but they may have had a mythic status as well. They are all animals of power and great fertility, and the horns of bison and bull, shaped to the curve of the crescent moon, may already symbolize the regenerative forces of life that were later to take masculine form as the bull and the god. It may be that the Bronze Age myth, which connected the bull through the moon to the cyclical death and rebirth of the life-force, took its origin from this time 15,000 years earlier, imaged first of all in the goddess holding a bison's horn in her hands at Laussel. This central myth will be discussed in Chapter 4.

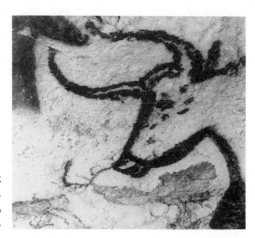

Figure 27. Head of great black aurochs; *c.* 15,000–12,000 BC. Lascaux cave, Dordogne, France.

A similar sacred meaning could be given to the horse (Fig. 28). Many fairy-tales tell the story of the horse as guiding voice, leading the hero or heroine through the trials and perils of the quest, as in the Irish story of Conneda or the story of Fallada and the Goose Girl. In certain parts of the world the horse is the guide to the souls of the dead and also carries the shaman on the ecstatic flight of the soul to forbidden regions.[19] The mare is often pregnant in the cave paintings, sometimes with a branch or

Figure 28. Mare with plants or branches; *c.* 15,000–12,000 BC. Lascaux cave, Dordogne, France.

plant close to her, suggesting a symbolic role in seasonal rituals of fertility and the renewal of the life-force.

The genius of the Palaeolithic artist was sometimes able to 'see' the form of an animal in a natural bulge of the cave wall and 'draw' it out by the carving of eyes or the placing of antlers or horns, completing the form given by nature. There are very few birds and fish in relation to the other animals, and no reptiles. But these all appear, exquisitely engraved, on the shamanic wands, staffs or *bâtons de commandement*, whose precise use is still unknown. These have a round hole at one end, sometimes in the place of the animal's or bird's eye.

THE SHAMAN

Mircea Eliade, the great historian of religions, wrote in his book *Shamanism*: 'It is impossible to imagine a period in which man did not have dreams and waking reveries and did not enter into "trance" – a loss of consciousness that was interpreted as the soul's travelling into the beyond.'[20] The shamans through their trance-flights visited a dimension inaccessible to ordinary tribal consciousness, believing that the living visible world rests on the invisible world. Their task was to give an infinitely profounder meaning to the human cycle of growth, flowering and decay. They could have transmitted the understanding that the animal still lived in the oldest and deepest human memories, so that it could continue to convey its wisdom in the sacred ritual. Palaeolithic people, living amongst the animals, would have known, as the Bushmen know, that the animals had superior powers.[21] They could see and find their way in the dark. They knew how to recognize danger. They had immense strength, fleetness of foot, a miraculously perceiving eye and ear. The gifts of the shamans were like those of the animal: they could also 'see in the dark'; that is, they could see farther and better, more intensely than the majority of the tribe.

Campbell, in *The Way of the Animal Powers*, quotes this passage transmitted by a Pawnee Indian:

> When man sought to know how he should live, he went into solitude and cried until in vision some animal brought wisdom to him. It was Tirawa, in truth, who sent his message through the animal. He never spoke to man himself, but gave his command to beast or bird, and this one came to some chosen man and taught him holy things. Thus were the sacred songs and ceremonial dances given the Pawnees through the animals.[22]

High above the jostling throng of animals in Les Trois Frères is the large and startling figure of what is usually called 'the Sorcerer' or 'Animal Master' (Fig. 29), recorded, as were all the animals in the sanctuary, by the Abbé Breuil. He is 30 inches (76 cm) high and 15 inches (38 cm) across, and the only picture in the entire chamber that has been painted –

Figure 29. 'Animal–shaman' dancing. Les Trois Frères cave, Ariège, France.

in black paint – so he stands out far beyond the rest. He could be the animal–shaman, who is there to teach the tribe about the animal world, the origin of the figure who became the 'Lord of the Beasts'. Only the dancing feet are definitely human. The whole feeling of the painting confuses the distinction between the human and the animal, so that we do not know whether he is an animal with human feet or a human dressed in animal form. He has the large round eyes of a lion or an owl, the antlers and ears of a stag, and the two raised front paws of a lion or a bear. He has the genitals of a feline, and the tail of a horse or a wolf. The flowing 'beard' in itself is like a lion's mane, and appears to be a human beard only because of the numinous look in the eyes that it frames, for the most arresting thing about this magnificent god-like being is his expression, which seems to gaze towards you and beyond, as if beckoning into an unfathomable dimension. Is he the animal ancestor or the soul of the tribe, or is he the incarnate figure of our own animal humanity? His feet are firmly on the ground, making possible the upright position, one of the defining characteristics that distinguish us from the other animals. Although he seems to be dancing, his face is still, as if asking us to enter the meaning of his mystery – perhaps the paradox of being human yet at the same time animal?

The sacred dance was another way of evoking the animal soul of humanity. The imprint of feet in a circle has been discovered in the caves at Tuc d'Audoubert and Montespan in south-western France. Men and women dressed in the skins of animals may have danced here the rituals of the hunt and fertility focused on certain animals, such as the bear, horse and bison (Fig. 30). The study of surviving Stone Age cultures has shown how vital is the maintenance of a living relationship between human customs and the unseen powers of life embodied in the animal. The Cretan labyrinth dance invoking the mystery of death and rebirth, the dance of the Greek Korybantes (ritual dancers) at the birth of the god, the bear dance of the Sioux Indians and the mantis dance of the Bushmen – all these and many others suggest the transmission from a very ancient past of the tradition of the sacred dance that brought about a renewal of life. The drumming of human feet in later periods was a fertility ritual, and the masked dance was a deliberate means of approach to the deepest layers of the psyche, where the ecstatic reunion of human and animal nature took place.

Figure 30. Dancing shamans; *c.* 14,000 BC. Les Trois Frères cave, Ariège, France.

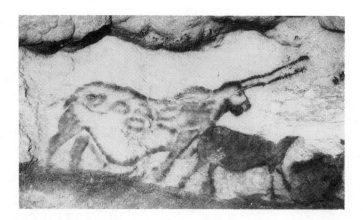

Figure 31. Animal with extended horns; *c.* 15,000–12,000 BC.
Lascaux cave, Dordogne, France.

Entering the great rotunda at Lascaux, the first sight is the figure of an animal with large ovals and arcs inscribed on its side and two straight horns extended as far beyond its body as half its length again (Fig. 31). It has been called a 'wizard beast' and the 'double unicorn', as though to express the disbelief of the twentieth century that such an animal could have existed anywhere except in the human imagination. Its pregnant belly hangs almost to the ground, and yet all the weight of the body is drawn upwards and outwards through the outstretched horns by the paralleling of the line of the belly and the horns. This creates an unequivocal relationship between the visible new life within the body and the invisible new 'life' beyond the last tip of the horns. Are these horns, then, images of extended vision, the animal here pointing the way for the shamanic flights that take place deeper inside the cave where a new vision is symbolically brought to birth?

In the most secret part of the same cave at Lascaux, at the bottom of a 16-foot (5-m) well, lies a man with a bird's head and bird-like hands, who may be a shaman in a trance, flying like a bird, as do the other shamans of later and better documented times. Many different interpretations have been offered for the strange configuration of man, bird, bison and rhinoceros at Lascaux (Fig. 32), where the detailed involvement of the figures with each other suggests that a precise story is being told. The man–bird lies stretched on the ground with erect phallus, one bird-hand pointing to the bison on his left and the other to the bird on his right below him, perched on top of a staff or stick. The enormous bison is mortally wounded, with his entrails cascading on the ground; beneath his upright tail a spear, the wounding weapon, lies across his body from the anus to the belly as though having passed through the body, hurled from some place or by some person not shown. The end of the spear points to the man–bird's ceremonial staff, which lies on the ground. On the far left a

Figure 32. Scene of shaman, bird, bison and rhinoceros; 15,000–12,000 BC.
Lascaux cave, Dordogne, France.

rhinoceros, facing away from the rest of the scene, has a raised tail, from
beneath which six black dots emerge, suggesting a fresh dropping of
dung.

If we become aware of what the lines of the painting are doing to the
eye of the one contemplating it, then we realize that at whichever point
we enter the picture, we are drawn around in a circular process that unites
the bison, the bird and the man–bird in one meaning. The bird on top of
a long stick or perch occupies the central part of the 6½-foot (2-m) long
picture. The bird leads directly to the bird-hand of the man above, in
turn leading to the bird-head of the man, suggesting that the man, on the
occasion of the death of the bison, has taken on the spirit of the bird who
flies far distances into unknown regions, the metaphorical clothing of
shamans of all times.

The Bushmen describe a shamanic ritual in similar terms, where the
animal of power is an eland:

> The body feels stretched, elongated. The spirit soars out of the head towards
> the supernatural world. Here the shaman's spirit gains its energy from
> powerful creatures. He feels himself transformed into an animal. The source
> of his power is the eland. As the dying eland releases his potency, the
> shaman absorbs it and goes deeper into trance. The dying eland is a meta-
> phor of the 'dying' shaman who is becoming like an eland. The eland is the
> source of the man's power and the shaman uses this power to go into
> trance.[23]

The parallels between the Bushman tale and the drama of the Palaeolithic painting are very striking, especially as the death of the bison and the 'flight' of the man are obviously related. The appearance of the bison as the animal of power who bequeaths vision recalls the bison horn of the Goddess of Laussel and the bison beneath the three goddesses at Angles-sur-l'Anglin, suggesting that the lunar mythology of transformation was a well-known myth, perhaps even a founding legend of cave life. In Niaux, in the Pyrenees, in about 12,000 BC a bull was painted on the cave floor with a large crescent moon above the generative organs and three round 'eggs' in increasing size – suggestive of the phases of increase to the full moon – moving towards his head, indicating a ritual of rebirth.[24]

Where, then, is this shaman travelling, and what vision are we to understand that he is experiencing as he lies there, rapt and erect? The position of the shaman's hand points between the horns of the bison, who apparently turns his head to gaze upon his wound, a wound of such finality as to be his death. Could it be that the shaman – notably the only human figure in the whole cave – has gone to contact the soul of the bison in his death-moment, to learn from the animal the mystery of death and of rebirth? The dung of the rhinoceros directly facing the bird is given such prominence as to suggest that, even in the act of apparently passing out of the life cycle, the dung still contains the seeds of fruit or grain that will begin a new cycle.

Eliade's books on shamanism and initiation rites throw much light on Palaeolithic shamanism, partly because so much shamanistic lore and ritual has been preserved in present day Siberia, where another 10,000 years seem to have made little difference to the beliefs of the 20,000 that preceded them. He points out that Siberian, Eskimo and North American shamans all 'fly'!

Two mythological motifs have contributed to giving the symbolism of magical flight its present structure: the idea of birds as guiding the soul through the realm of the dead and the image of the soul in the form of a bird. This may give a further meaning to the six flying birds from the burial scene at Mal'ta. Eliade adds that 'the bird perched on a stick is a frequent symbol in shamanic circles. It is found ... on the tombs of Yakut shamans.'[25]

The passage between dimensions or the worlds of life and death is dangerous, as the actual pathway leading to the cave sanctuaries demonstrates. In shamanic ritual the ecstatic flight is often symbolized by a bridge or ladder or by a spiral, and has to be prepared for by careful initiation. It is interesting that in Lascaux, in the same pit where the shaman lies in trance, the fossilized remains of a rope have been found:

> By crossing, in ecstasy, the 'dangerous' bridge (or the spiral staircase) that connects the two worlds and that only the dead can attempt, the shaman proves that he is spirit, is no longer a human being, and at the same time

Figure 33. Sculpture of bison; Magdalenian period, *c.* 12,000 BC, length 4 in. (10 cm). Cave of La Madeleine, south-west France.

attempts to restore the 'communicability' that existed *in illo tempore* between this world and heaven.[26]

Without art there would be no way of imagining the past. 'The backward half-look over the shoulder, towards the primitive terror',[27] which was once the generally assumed attitude towards our earliest known forebears, has had to be completely revised in the light of the magnificent paintings on the cave walls, which few people today could do themselves. Our view of history, and any assumption of a purely linear idea of the evolutionary course of human nature, is therefore infinitely complicated by the discovery that the Palaeolithic people were exceedingly fine artists as well as 'primitive' hunter–gatherers.

The artist and the shaman were probably one and the same, as artists ever since have consistently claimed. Through their magical power to re-create the animal on the walls of the temple caves, they – the artist-shamans – connected the tribe with the source of life that animated both human and animal, becoming themselves vehicles of that source, creators of the living form like the source itself. Leroi-Gourhan, who has devoted his life to understanding the symbolism of the art of the caves, says of Lascaux: 'Behind this decoration we can perceive the involvement of a whole community who maintained a few artists of high talent during the long weeks they spent preparing the scaffolding, the colouring matter and the lighting.'[28]

PALAEOLITHIC MYTHOLOGY

The first question that arises from a consideration of Palaeolithic art is why was the mother goddess only sculpted and not painted on the cave walls? And what was her relation to the animals that were painted but not sculpted? One inference from this evidence is that there were two fundamental kinds of vision explored in the culture of the Stone Age. One is expressed in stone, bone and mammoth-ivory, the enduring substances in which the sculptures of the mother goddess were carved, either chiselled out of the structure of the cave rock or modelled into small statues in burial sites. The other is expressed through painting, on the inside walls of the caves, where the animals come alive, where the ritual of the hunt is dramatized and reflected upon, and where human and animal shamans offer the rites of initiation.

Can we understand from this that there were originally not one but two basic myths: the myth of the goddess and the myth of the hunter? The pregnant figures of the statues suggest that the myth of the mother goddess was concerned with fertility and the sacredness of life in all its aspects, and so with transformation and rebirth. By contrast, the myth of the hunter was concerned above all with the drama of survival – the taking of life as a ritual act in order to live. The first story is centred on the goddess as the eternal image of the whole. The second story is centred on humanity, who, as hunter, has continually to rupture this unity in order to live the daily life of time. These two stories, both essential to human experience, tend to pull apart in response to two apparently different human instincts: the instinct for relationship and meaning, and the instinct to survive. They seem, then, to tell different and even mutually exclusive stories: one where life and death are recognized as phases of an eternal process; the other, where the death of animal and human being loses its connection to the whole and is no longer sacred. Here death becomes final, and our experience of life tragic.

In the mother goddess story the human hunter and the animals that are hunted are both contained in one vision. There is a continuum of relationship in which both hunter and hunted participate, so that the myth of the hunter is ultimately included in the myth of the goddess, along with all other aspects of life that are part of the whole. This is the symbolism of the paintings on the inside of the cave experienced as the womb of the goddess. But, from within the story of the hunter, which is concerned with mortal life in time, the foundation of the hunter myth in the goddess myth can be forgotten. In the myth of the hunter, animals and human beings compete for survival and the life of the one is often the death of the other. The two stories are then seen in opposition to each other. When this happens, the connection with the invisible dimension out of which both life and death come, and which confers sanctity on both, is lost. The goddess myth contains the hunter myth, but the hunter myth cannot contain the goddess myth.

The presence of the shaman in the cave suggests that Palaeolithic people knew how vital it was for the well-being of the tribe not to forget the essential relation between these two stories, and perhaps also to continue to explore the different ways in which their relation can be understood. Shamans mediated between two worlds of human experience, and their flight into darkness took place, necessarily, in the most secret part of the cave, where ordinary limits of perception could be more readily transcended. There they were able to *re-member* the fundamental relationship between these two myths, and to honour the essential need to relate the hunt to the deeper vision of the whole. Such an interpretation can help to explain the intense importance of the hunting rituals even to this day in certain tribes.

In this way the myth of the goddess expressed what we might call the moral vision of the age. It persisted for thousands and thousands of years, gathering substance in the Neolithic era from the regulation of plant and animal life to the seasonal cycles of moon and sun, month and year. But by the middle of the Bronze Age (*c.* 2000 BC), with the continuous invasion of nomadic warrior tribes from the old Palaeolithic hunting grounds of the steppes, the myth of the goddess lost its central place in the moral feeling of humanity, and the vital connection between the myth of the hunter and the myth of the goddess was weakened and often apparently lost. Life in time came to be separated from the vision of eternity as the part broke away from the whole.

In the course of the Bronze Age the old myth of the hunter grew into the myth of the warrior-hero and came to overshadow the myth of the goddess, which was gradually relegated to the unconscious psyche of humanity. Yet we can find the lost primordial myth scattered throughout the symbolic images, myths and fairy-tales of every civilization, frequently unrecognized, often unconnected with each other, but always present. The goddess, and the vision of the whole that the image of her embodies, has not been lost but obscured by the pressing claims of the other story, the myth of the hunt and the need to survive.

We can, therefore, still recover the lost myth of the goddess through her images. Wherever we find the cave, the moon, the stone, the serpent, bird and fish; the spiral, meander and labyrinth; the wild animals – the lion, bull, bison, stag, goat and horse; rituals concerned with the fertility of the earth and of animals and human beings, and the journey of the soul to another dimension, then we are in the presence of the images that once enacted the original myth. They exist as living testimony in the human psyche to its vision of the unity of life, originally imagined as the mother goddess who gives birth to the forms of life that are herself. For the psyche, as Jung writes, is 'not of today':

> Its ancestry goes back many millions of years. Individual consciousness is only the flower and fruit of a season, sprung from a perennial rhizome beneath the earth; and it would find itself in better accordance with the truth if it took the existence of the rhizome into its calculations. For the root matter is the mother of all things.[29]

The formal religious images of today are pre-eminently those of the father god who created heaven and earth through his word, so that he is beyond his creation not within it. We are used to a mythological tradition in which nature, the earth, the animals, seas, rivers, birds and mountains are not sacred. This myth will be explored in Chapters 7 and 10, so at this point we can only draw attention to the fact that this view of life is but the flower and fruit of a season. The vision of the unity and sacredness of life has lived in the roots of the human psyche for an inestimable number of years longer than this late addition to religious thought, which seems inevitable only because we have experienced – in the official mythic images of our time – nothing else. The doctrinal Christian position has long dismissed as animism the feeling of people for whom nature is truly alive – and so cannot learn from them – and also largely overlooks the contemporary discoveries of archetypal psychology, which show us that the knowledge of all the human race is stored within the psyche, as the rhizome, and so is potentially available to every one of us. The significance of this ancient symbolism is only now being recognized as Depth Psychology explores the roots of consciousness in the 'womb of the mother' – the human soul.

We should not assume that the Palaeolithic moral order died with the Palaeolithic Age. Although we are accustomed to thinking of the historical past as finished and, as it were, left behind as the race moves onwards into its future, this century's exploration into the unconscious mind may offer another way of looking at the phenomenon of 'memory' and at 'the past'. Jung proposed the idea that human beings have not just a personal unconscious exclusive to each individual, but also what he calls a 'collective unconscious', an unconscious mind that is inherited by every member of the human race, along with all the other physical, mental and spiritual characteristics by virtue of which we call ourselves human. According to this idea, an experience of the race is never lost but is transmitted down the race, as are the more obvious instinctive and learned processes. It follows from this that at any one time the experience of earlier generations and, indeed, the whole history of the race is in some way always alive in the psyche as part of being human. This is the same sort of assumption that Laurens van der Post is making when he asks us to look for the Bushman within us.[30]

We might imagine a geological analogy for the collective unconscious in which the oldest layer of the psyche consists of the millions of years of instinctive animal life. After this, the first and the oldest cultural layer is the Palaeolithic experience, followed by the Neolithic as the next layer, followed by the Bronze Age layer, and so on throughout the ages until the present – the surface layer of the twentieth century still accessible to what we call 'living' memory.[31] In a different metaphor, Jung suggests that the totality of this human consciousness could be described

as a collective human being combining the characteristics of both sexes, transcending youth and age, birth and death, and, from having at its command a human experience of one or two million years, practically immortal.

If such a being existed, it would be exalted above all temporal change; the present would mean neither more nor less to it than any year in the hundredth millennium before Christ; it would be a dreamer of age-old dreams and, owing to its limitless experience, an incomparable prognosticator. It would have lived countless times over again the life of the individual, the family, the tribe, and the nation, and it would possess a living sense of the rhythm of growth, flowering and decay.[32]

If this is true, or is valid as a metaphor, then it is not surprising that there are traces of the old goddess myth scattered throughout every religion of the world, remembered or re-created anew to explore this particular dream of life on earth. Wherever there appears an arrangement of stones in a circular, spiral or serpentine form, as at Stonehenge or Avebury, or wherever the cave or crypt has been marked as the place of birth or revelation, there is the tradition of the Mother Goddess, who for at least 25,000 years was conceived as both origin and goal: the giver of life and dwelling place of the dead; the transformer of the life she brought out of herself and took back into herself in a cycle of time as perpetual and enduring as that of the moon.

From the labyrinthine passages of the Palaeolithic caves to the labyrinth inscribed on the floor of Chartres Cathedral there is a distance of twenty-five millennia in linear time, but an identity of symbolic image that nullifies the passage of the centuries. The flying birds in the burial site at Mal'ta reach forward to the Bird Goddess of Neolithic times, as well as to the doves belonging to the Sumerian Goddess Inanna, the Egyptian Isis, the Greek Aphrodite, and the dove of the Holy Spirit. The bird on the top of the shaman's staff at Lascaux (Fig. 34) prefigures the dove of

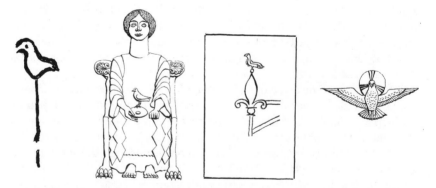

(From left to right) Figure 34. Detail of bird from shaman's staff; *c.* 15,000–
12,000 BC. Lascaux cave, Dordogne, France.
Figure 35. Persephone with dove; *c.* 450 BC. Locri, Italy.
Figure 36. Detail of a bird on sceptre of Mary; twelfth century AD.
Figure 37. Dove of the Annunciation; drawing of detail from *The Mystic
Lamb* in the Ghent Altarpiece, Hubert and Jan Van Eyck, AD 1432.

Noah's ark, the dove nestling in the lap of the Greek goddess Persephone
in the fifth century BC (Fig. 35), the bird standing on the sceptre of Mary
in the twelfth century AD (Fig. 36) and the fifteenth-century painting of
the dove of the Annunciation (Fig. 37).

The serpent on the Mal'ta plaque (Fig. 38) reappears with the Sumerian
Tree of Life, standing behind the goddess (Fig. 39), and later speaks to
Eve from the Tree of Knowledge (Fig. 40). Intertwining serpents form
the hieroglyph of the Sumerian god Ningizzida as well as the spiral of the
caduceus of the Greek god Hermes, guide of souls (Fig. 41), and a serpent
winds round the staff of Asclepius, Greek god of healing.

Figure 38. (*Left*) Serpents on plaque; 16,000–13,000 BC. Mal'ta, Siberia.
Figure 39. (*Right*) Goddess and horned god with tree and serpent; Sumerian
cylinder seal, *c.* 2500 BC.

Figure 40. (*Left*) Adam, Eve and the Serpent; Spanish woodcut, AD 976.
Figure 41. (*Right*) Caduceus; Swiss woodcut, AD 1615.

Figure 42. (a) Goddess of Laussel; 22,000–18,000 BC. (b) Astarte with the
crescent moon on her head; second century BC. Babylon.[33]

Figure 43. Virgin Mary with moon beneath her feet;
The Glorification of the Virgin, Geertgen tot St Jans, AD 1490.

From the dancing shamans of Les Trois Frères, through the labyrinth dance of Crete to the circular dance of Christ's disciples in the Gnostic Gospels, there is a constant thread of transmission that has much wider implications for our conception of the human psyche than has yet been fully recognized. The crescent moon in the hand of the Goddess of Laussel leads forward to the crescent on the head of the Babylonian Astarte of 200 BC (Figs. 42a–b) and again to the crescent moon resting beneath Mary's feet (Fig. 43). From the Palaeolithic cave sanctuary with the animals painted on the walls to the stable of Bethlehem with the ox and the ass, from the ancient Mother Goddess to the Virgin Mary, there runs an ancient and extraordinary pattern of relationship that can be traced only through a knowledge of the symbolic image. In the Neolithic era, as we shall see in Chapter 2, these images explore a new dimension of the myth of the goddess with the discovery of planting and the art of agriculture.

If we entertain the idea of Jung's 2-million-year-old human being – woman and man – who is present in each one of us, then the Palaeolithic vision is still accessible to us today. As Jung also wrote: 'Nothing to which the psyche belongs or which is part of the psyche is ever lost. To live fully, we have to reach down and bring back to life the deepest levels of the psyche from which our present consciousness has evolved.'[34]

2

THE NEOLITHIC GREAT GODDESS
OF SKY, EARTH AND WATERS

Thou knowest that I sit waiting for the moon to turn back for me, so that
I may return to my place; that I may listen to all the people's stories . . .
that I may sitting listen to the stories which yonder came, which are
stories that come from a distance, for a story is like the wind, it comes
from a far-off quarter and we feel it . . .

Xhabbo the Bushman [1]

The Neolithic was the great age of discovery and the result was no less
than a new relation to the universe. This was the time when humanity
was released from the need to live in complete accord with what nature
offered or withheld and now learned to participate in the mysterious
processes of growing. With the realization that certain seeds changed into
wheat and corn, which could be transformed into bread, and that certain
animals would live close to the home and provide milk, eggs and meat, a
new spirit of conscious co-operation between human beings and their
world was born.

The life of the cosmos became a story that included humanity as one of
the characters. The role was a minor one, but it was beginning to contribute to the direction of the drama, if only sometimes by listening to a

Figure 1. Vase decoration with patterns of snakes and a womb-shaped
design enclosing a female figure; late Classical Cucuteni vase, *c.* 4000 BC.
North-eastern Romania.

voice not heard before. We know this not just from the evidence of agriculture and the domestication of animals, but from art, the oldest human record. The art of this time has a new and exciting sense of narrative: images weave together to tell a story, separate and rephrase in a continual act of exploring the relation between the different orders of creation. These stories have come down to us in the great legacy of fairy-tales all over the world; for a story, as Xhabbo, a twentieth-century Bushman, tells us, 'is like the wind: it comes from a far-off quarter and we feel it'.

The Neolithic, or New Stone, Age begins about 10,000 BC and ends about 5500 BC. It is followed by the Chalcolithic, or Copper, Age about 5500–3500 BC, though the two ages are generally grouped together as the Neolithic.[2] What distinguishes this era from the inestimable number of years before it is the discovery of agriculture. For at least two million years human beings had hunted animals and gathered fruits, but now they learned to cultivate the soil, to domesticate and breed animals, to weave cloth and to make pots to hold the food they could store for the first time. They began to stay in one place, to build houses, temples and villages, and to share in a permanent community life. No longer did the tribes have to follow the wild animals in their long trails across the earth. Now their energies were engaged in a new way: contained and concentrated on the precise nurturing of the crops and the continual care of the domestic animal. The last glaciers had gone and the climate grew warmer; forests began to grow where before there had been only frozen tundra. The bison and reindeer withdrew to the colder regions in the north and east, and life settled in the fertile river valleys and the upland pastures where the smaller varieties of wild game grazed.

The evolution from one age to another was not sudden and spectacular, not 'revolutionary' as it was first believed to be, but slow and irregular. In Europe in the late Magdalenian period (12,000–10,000 BC) Palaeolithic people already lived in caves, leaving only for the seasonal hunt and coming back to them afterwards. When the climate changed and they no longer needed caves as protection against the cold, they began to build summer dwellings, which they may eventually have lived in all year round. In the Mesolithic, or Middle Stone, Age,[3] reckoned from 10,000 to 8000 BC, the tribes were still hunters and gatherers, yet were beginning to settle and sow seeds of grain. Somewhere between 10,000 and 8000 BC the Old and New Stone Ages meet and merge, and an archaic way of life extending over countless thousands of years is gradually transformed into a way of life that appears closer to our own.

The movement of consciousness in the Neolithic is one of differentiation and proliferation, but there is no loss of the original sense of unity, which is now explicitly explored through the myth of the goddess. The Mother Goddess in the Neolithic Age is an image that, more obviously than before, inspires a perception of the universe as an organic, alive and sacred whole, in which humanity, the earth and all life on earth participate as 'her children'. As the Great Mother, she presides over the whole of creation as goddess of life, death and regeneration, containing within herself the life of plants as well as the life of animals and human beings. There is the same recognition of an essential relationship between an invisible order, governing the revolving phases of the moon, and a visible earthly order, embodied earlier in the cycles of human and animal life, and now in the cycle of the seasons and the agricultural year.

The ascending and descending spiral on the pregnant womb of the goddess of 6,500 years ago shown in Figure 2, found in a tomb, suggests that she is goddess of life, death and rebirth. A lozenge is incised on her buttocks (not shown) and this rectangular figure is so frequently drawn on pregnant goddesses that it must be an image of growth; when there is a dot in the centre, it may symbolize the seed sown in the fertile field.[4] The serpentine spiral on her belly points to the stirring energy in the womb. She feels as heavy as the weight of the gravid earth, with the throne on which she is seated drawing her centre of gravity still further downwards. Her face is abstracted or masked, with six holes for her lower lip and long hair hanging down her back. The Goddess is here the goddess of vegetation and the fruitfulness of nature, whose womb is the depths of the earth: from her new life comes forth and back to her that life, grown old, returns.

Figure 2. *The Lady of Pazardzik*; East Balkan civilization, *c.* 4500 BC. Central Bulgaria.

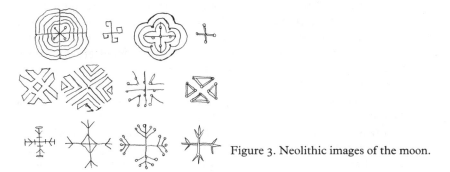

Figure 3. Neolithic images of the moon.

The moon is still the primal image of the mystery of birth, growth, decay, death and regeneration. The lunar cycle must have offered a way of comprehending how a seed grows into flower and fruit, which, falling back into the darkness of earth, returns as the regenerated seed. The 'four' seasons that mark the stages of the life of vegetation and chart one passage of the sun back to its original place reflect the four phases of the moon. Spring, summer, autumn and winter parallel the waxing, full, waning and dark moon – the stage of gestation when creative life is invisible. The four lunar phases are often drawn on pots and vases as the four arms of a cross and evolve into swastikas with four or eight arms, images that in Classical Greece 5,000 years later covered the cloaks of the goddesses Artemis and Athena like stars (see Chapter 8, Figs. 10, 11, 19).

The people of that time could not have failed to experience the analogy between the growth of their own lives and the seeds that, planted in the soil, gestated and re-emerged as the green and golden grain. The rituals that evoked the birth, mourned the death and celebrated the rebirth of the corn show how vital was this analogy to the human imagination, for it placed regeneration at the heart of life. The cyclical pattern, during which invisible life grew to become visible and visible life diminished until it was invisible again, could now be followed in the annual round of sowing and reaping, as before it was recognized in the monthly round of the moon. The secret source of life was still invisible: where the dark womb of the Palaeolithic Goddess had been the cave-temple, now it was hidden deep inside the earth. Human beings are still born from her, nourished by her and taken back by her. They sow the seed in her womb and harvest it as the substance of her body, transforming it themselves into bread. Plants, fruit, crops and animals that give milk, eggs, meat, wool and skins are all, like them, her children and are all, therefore, sacred.

Moon, woman, earth – and the cycle of gestation in all three – can be seen to be governed by rhythm, order and an exact sequence of development. Woman, with the formation of the child in her womb tied to the precise time of ten lunar months, continues to embody a sacrality that is possibly even more pronounced than it had been in the Palaeolithic.

Campbell writes that woman 'participated – perhaps even predominated – in the planting and reaping of the crops, and, as the mother of life and nourisher of life, was thought to assist the earth symbolically in its productivity'.[5] By the very fact that her body in the act of giving birth portrays the mysteries of creation, she becomes in some sense endowed with magical power to embody the relationship between the invisible and visible orders, helping the crops to grow, the trees to bear fruit and the animals to remain fertile.

The sowing and reaping of grain, the transformation of grain into bread, the making and baking of clay pots and ritual vessels and their decoration, the art of dyeing wool and weaving cloth and the gathering of herbs to transform into healing potions – all these may have been, to begin with, as Briffault concluded, the invention of women, whose skills were transmitted from mother to daughter.[6] These were all activities that reflected the powers of the goddess to nourish, form, weave and transform life. Eliade writes that in this era

> woman and feminine sacrality are raised to the first rank. Since women played a decisive part in the domestication of plants, they become the owners of the cultivated fields, which raises their social position and creates characteristic institutions, such as, for example, matrilocation, the husband being obliged to live in his wife's house.[7]

It is likely that women played a central role in the care of plants and fruit-bearing trees, and in the actual process of discovering agriculture. Remaining close to the home to care for the children, they would have noticed that the seeds of wild grasses came back the following year. They could have gathered the strongest and planted their seeds in a special place so that each season the seed gave better grain. There is also evidence that only women made pots at the beginning, baking the clay on the hearth, and even into Greek times these activities were the province of goddesses and not gods.

The myriad forms of Neolithic pottery reveal the imaginative reach of the people, who reflected upon the mystery of birth and related it to the larger mystery of the birth of all life through the 'body' of the goddess. Images of the goddess show her as the door or gate through which lives enter and leave this world. In Figure 4 the goddess has the labyrinth or meander design inscribed on her front and back. In Figure 5 she is drawn as the Bird Goddess (with her head restored) and appears as the vessel that is both labyrinth and door to the dimension beyond human life. During this era images of the labyrinth, spiral and meander become highly articulated, carved on stone and painted on the ritual vessels that were used in shrines and homes.

In the Palaeolithic era the decoration of the cave with the animals was considered to be so vital to the life of the tribe that certain individuals were supported by the rest in order that this work could be done. In the

Figure 4. (*Left*) The Szvegár enthroned goddess; Tisza culture, *c.* 5000 BC,
height 8⅔ in. (22 cm). South-eastern Hungary.
Figure 5. (*Right*) Clay model of a temple with a bird's head (restored),
decorated with meanders; *c.* 5000 BC. South-western Romania.

Neolithic, the gradual accumulation of a food surplus would have allowed
any artistically inclined members of the group more freedom to express
their vision of life and a new medium through which to do so – pottery.
In one sense nothing changed. Neolithic artists continued to explore their
feeling for the whole through the figure of the Mother Goddess, experiencing earth, animals and plants as an epiphany, or 'showing forth', of her
presence. As before, the bird and the serpent manifest her divinity, but
now this reflection is extended through intricate and elaborate designs
upon the many different figures. The crane, swan, goose, duck, owl, diver
bird and vulture are all sculpted and painted, as are the butterfly and bee.

In a more specific sense, though, a revolution had occurred. A new
image appeared, the Goddess of Vegetation, who was to be the guardian
of the sowing and reaping of grain for many millennia afterwards, and can
still be glimpsed beneath European agricultural folk rituals even today.
With the focus on agriculture, new animals of every kind come into view:
tiny ones, like the hedgehog, caterpillar, weasel and toad; larger ones, like
the ram, dog and pig. The Palaeolithic animals – bull, cow, lion, bear,
stag and serpent – continue their central role in life and art, but, curiously,
the horse disappears.

Serpents wind over pots and coil around the womb of goddess figures,
undulating across vessels, like rain water falling from above and waters
rising up from within the earth. A whole language of signs and symbols

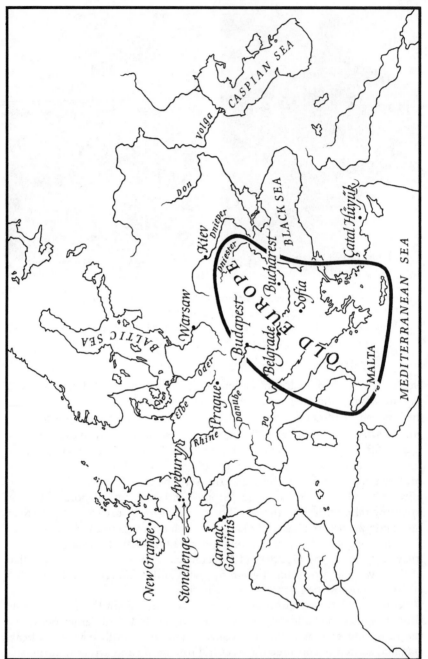

Map 2. Neolithic Old Europe, 7000–3500 B.C.

emerges – spirals, chevrons, zigzags, meanders and net-like patterns – embodying aspects of the goddess's powers. Altogether they compose, as Marija Gimbutas suggests, 'an alphabet of the metaphysical . . . by which an entire constellation of meanings is transmitted'.[8] It is easy to make the mistake of believing that Neolithic people were merely using these as decorative motifs with no particular significance, or that they were actually worshipping animals, if the amplifying and unifying symbolism of the Great Mother is not understood.

OLD EUROPE

For many centuries the Neolithic remained an obscure and unfocused time, but the work of many archaeologists in the last few decades has begun to bring it back to life and, as methods of dating become more accurate, it has been placed even farther back in time. Now it seems that isolated centres of Neolithic culture existed as early as 7000 BC in places as far apart as eastern Europe, southern Turkey, Egypt, Palestine, Mesopotamia and the Indus Valley. The picture that is emerging is of a single cultural matrix that underlies and relates all these different areas to each other. Almost identical figurines and sculptures of the goddess have been found in eastern Europe and in the Indus Valley (in a place called Mehrgarh). If people had travelled from one far-off place to another, they would have recognized the images and understood their meaning, even if they could not have understood the language of a different tribe, for at this stage in the evolution of consciousness there were no tribal gods, only a universally worshipped goddess.

The implications of uncovering these highly developed Neolithic cultures have not yet informed the general understanding of our time, which continues to believe that the 'cradle' of civilization was Bronze Age Sumeria and Egypt. In the art world, images of Neolithic goddesses, like those of the Palaeolithic, are still referred to as idols or seen as the earliest expression of abstract art, often without any knowledge of their meaning or their relation to images before and after them.

The work of a single individual has brought one of these cultures to life in the last decade, completely transforming our understanding of a vitally important phase of human evolution. What Heinrich Schliemann did for Troy and Arthur Evans did for Crete, Marija Gimbutas has done for the Neolithic era, unearthing the treasures of the amazingly rich and advanced civilization she has named 'Old Europe'. Her long study and interpretation of the images give a unique insight into the symbolic imagery of a Neolithic culture that flourished between 7000 and 3500 BC.

In her two books *The Goddesses and Gods of Old Europe* and *The Language of the Goddess* Gimbutas explores in detail the Neolithic and Chalcolithic art of Old Europe. This area includes Hungary, south and central Yugoslavia, Bulgaria, Romania and eastern Austria. It extends northwards into southern Czechoslovakia and southern Poland, and eastwards into the Ukraine as far as Kiev. To the south it includes southern Italy and Sicily, Malta, Greece, Crete and the Cycladic, Ionian and Aegean islands, as well as the western coastal region of Turkey. The legacy of this civilization to the later Cretan and Greek civilizations and, through them, to our own is incalculable, and the sculpture and painting of Neolithic Old Europe are evidence of a transmission of imagery from the Palaeolithic era to the Bronze Age. This makes a connection between two ages previously unrelated in history and offers an image of the continuity of the human tradition that was not possible before.

Approximately 30,000 miniature sculptures made of clay, marble, bone, copper and gold have been discovered in some 3,000 sites. Vast numbers of ritual vessels, shrines, altars and implements of sacrifice, painted vases, inscribed objects, as well as clay models of temples and actual temples are testament to a genuine civilization. The focus of this hitherto unknown culture, Gimbutas writes, was the figure of a Goddess 'incarnating the creative principle as Source and Giver of All'.[9]

These fascinating books reveal the cultural matrix that underlies European, Near Eastern and Mediterranean civilizations. What she has discovered and interpreted parallels the discoveries of other Neolithic cultures, such as Çatal Hüyük in Anatolia and the communities in the Indus Valley. Before radio-carbon dating (discovered in 1952) and tree-ring dating (dendochronology) had been synchronized (an achievement that revolutionized the chronology of prehistoric material), the cultural momentum was believed to have spread westwards from the Near East, in particular from Egypt and Sumeria, during the fourth and third millennia BC. But the study of Old Europe shows that this was an autonomous culture, which developed parallel with other cultures in the Near East and Anatolia from the seventh to the fourth millennium BC. Moreover, the astonishing variety, richness and sheer volume of material gathered from Old Europe far surpass anything found so far in other Neolithic cultures.

In the civilization of Old Europe settlements grew into villages and villages into small towns housing several thousand people. This happened many thousands of years before anything like it occurred in western and northern Europe – undoubtedly because of the increasing mastery of agriculture – and reached its peak in the fifth millennium BC. All kinds of skills, such as pottery and stone- and copper-working techniques – even the formulation of a rudimentary linear script in the sixth millennium BC – attained a remarkable level of achievement long before the rise of Bronze Age Sumeria. One in every hundred figurines in Old Europe carried the incisions of this script, as did vessels, dishes and spindle whorls (the disc of the spindle that steadies its motion).[10]

So advanced was this civilization that for a long time no one knew how very old it was. In other words, if a culture was considered 'advanced',

Figure 6. (a) Spindle whorl decorated with primitive script; East Balkan civilization, *c.* 4500 BC. (b) Shallow vessel inscribed with primitive script; Vinca culture, *c.* 5000 BC. Western Bulgaria. *a*  *b*

then it was assumed, on a precisely linear model of evolution, to be later rather than earlier; closer, by definition, to our own. The Vinca culture in Yugoslavia, for example, where nearly 2,000 figurines were found, was thought to be a colony of the Romans or the Greeks until radio-carbon dating gave the true dates as 5300–4000 BC.[11] Here, in the Vinca culture, towns as large as 20 acres (8 ha), rather than villages, have been discovered spreading beside rivers, their streets lined with spacious houses with two or three rooms in them, some 7,000 years old.

In the painted vessels and images of Old Europe there appears to be a direct continuity with the imagery of the Palaeolithic cave paintings in south-western France. Some of the groups of hunters who followed the herds as far eastwards as Lake Baikal in Siberia may have decided to settle in the now forested river valleys that lay along their route. Cave dwellers along the Danube and elsewhere were able to leave their caves as the climate grew warmer. They chose sites that were fertile, close to water and rich pastures, sheltered from the wind and lovely to look at. There they re-created the older cosmology through the new media of pottery, weaving and sculpture. A continuity with the Palaeolithic seems unmistakable, particularly in the sculptures of goddess figures and in the building of shrines or temples, which continue the tradition of the cave sanctuary.

The 2,000 to 3,000 years that elapsed between the 'end' of life focused on the caves and the 'beginning' of established communities in the river valleys of Old Europe is not long, given the immense time span of the Palaeolithic era. Moreover, the people seem to have enjoyed peace as well as prosperity for 2,000 years, for there is no sign of any disruption to their culture until the first Indo-European (Kurgan) invasions in 4500 BC. Before this, there is no emphasis on choosing hill sites, building massive walls or making weapons that would offer protection against enemies. Indeed, the hill or mountain was chosen as the site of a shrine, not as a citadel or fortified encampment.

There is another, possibly related, feature of this civilization. The deities of these people, as Eisler has noted, carry no spears, swords or thunderbolts, nor are there any lavish chieftain burials suggesting a hierarchical organization of society with powerful leaders and a submissive population. There are no pictures that celebrate or even depict war. Rather, the myriad images from nature attest to their feeling for the beauty and sanctity of life.[12] The primary purpose of life was evidently not to conquer, pillage and loot, nor was the relation with the divine one of fear and obedience.[13]

As to the relations between women and men in Old Europe, the archaeological evidence suggests that there was no apparent social superiority of males over females, and, generally, the distribution of goods in the cemeteries of Old Europe points to an egalitarian and clearly non-patriarchal society.[14] Gimbutas observes that this was a matrilineal society in which descent and inheritance passed through the mother[15] and where women played essential roles in religious rituals:

> In the models of house-shrines and temples females are shown supervising the preparation and performance of rituals dedicated to the various aspects and functions of the Goddess. Enormous energy was expended in the production of cult equipment and votive gifts. Temple models show the grinding of grain and the baking of sacred bread ... females made and decorated quantities of various pots appropriate to different rites. Next to the altar of the temple stood a vertical loom on which were probably woven the sacred garments and temple appurtenances. The most sophisticated creations of Old Europe – the most exquisite vases, sculptures, etc. now extant – were woman's work.[16]

The Great Mother: Goddess of Life, Death and Regeneration

Images of the Mother Goddess – where the body of a woman has been stylized to render her capacity to give birth transparent to the mystery of birth itself – have been found all over the river valleys and islands of Old Europe. In fact, so many images of the goddess have been found in Old Europe that they alone would fill many volumes. In this chapter we can give only a glimpse of the mythological heritage that Gimbutas has brought back to life. Some of the goddess figures were modelled as early as 6000 BC; some of them are tiny, and some are as much as $11\frac{4}{5}$ inches (30 cm) high. Often they have a pillar-like neck and head (Fig. 7a) or their arms are folded on top of the breasts (Fig. 7b) like the Palaeolithic goddesses of Lespugue and Willendorf. Sometimes they have an enormous incised genital triangle, like those outlined later on Cycladic goddesses from the islands of the Aegean. These figures are made of clay, white marble, bone or even gold. Over some 4,000 years, they show no more than a very gradual change of style, which culminates in the more familiar Cycladic figures of the third millennium BC.

The statues were placed in shrines and graves on their own, in pairs and even in dozens. Gimbutas interprets the folded arms of the goddesses as being typical of the way the dead were actually buried in the cemeteries of Old Europe. She comments that babies and children were laid in large egg-shaped urns with their arms pressed tightly against their bodies. This foetal position in the urn-womb echoed the position of the infant in its

Figure 7. (a) Pregnant goddess with pillar head; *c.* 5000 BC. Cernavoda Cemetery, Romania. (b) Goddess with folded arms; *c.* 6000 BC, marble. Aegean area.

mother's womb. Miniature vessels were filled with red colour and placed in the graves as the blood that would restore the child to life.[17]

There is as yet no distinction between the goddess who brings life and the goddess who brings death, as there was to be in the Bronze Age. For the Neolithic feeling, like the Palaeolithic, was to experience both as a unity through the image of the Great Mother as the totality of life-and-death. Figures of the goddess were often placed in graves, transforming the experience of death into one of rebirth into another dimension. Spindle whorls found with the statues suggest a mythology of the goddess as the spinner of the thread that is woven into the great web of life, which is later spun in Greece by the three lunar 'Fates', or goddesses of destiny.

Images of a goddess with one body and two heads are sometimes carved with the head or a mask of a bird, or incised with the chevrons and meanders already familiar from the Palaeolithic (Fig. 8). The meander, as a stylized rendering of the snake, signifies the waters of the dimension of the beyond, which is also symbolized by the labyrinth. Frequently placed on the womb of the goddess, the meander locates the central mystery of life as the mystery of birth. What is often called the dual goddess, because there are two heads, may be understood rather as the principle of unity beyond duality. This principle manifests as an image of the source and the manifestation of the source as one and the same. The image is often rendered as the mother and the daughter: she who has borne life and she who carries the life to come. This is one of the meanings of the full and

Figure 8. Double-headed goddess;
Early Vinca culture, *c.* 5000–4800 BC.
South-western Romania.

crescent moon, whose story is unfolded several thousand years later in the Greek myth of Demeter and Persephone. When the source is imagined as invisible, the 'mother' is the totality of the lunar cycle and the changing phases are the 'daughter'. (This will be explored in Chapter 4.) The image of the goddess of life-and-death, which comprehends the waxing and waning moon as a totality, is often rendered as two sisters: Inanna and Ereshkigal of Mesopotamia, for instance, or the Egyptian Isis and Nephthys, goddesses of light and darkness, who together compose the whole.

The Bird Goddess: the Mistress of the Upper Waters

To people of all times, the breaking of the waters of the womb heralds the birth of a child. In the Neolithic era the goddess was believed to be the source of the life-sustaining water that fell from the sky as rain and welled up from beneath the ground as spring, lake and river. Just as the luminous swathe of stars known as the Milky Way suggested the stream of nourishment emanating from her breasts, so it was as if the earth were encircled by waters that, falling as rain, impregnated her so she could give birth. Water was now needed for plants and animals as well as humans, so it must have seemed the very embodiment of the Great Mother's generative power: the life-force she offered or withheld.

The vessel holding water or milk was, therefore, a paramount image of the goddess herself, a tradition continued in Egypt, where the hieroglyph for the sky goddess, Nut, was a water jar, and in Mesopotamia, where a goddess is sculpted holding in her hands the vessel of life, which is herself (see Chapter 4, Fig. 5). Many vessels have raised breasts and are decorated with meanders and zigzags signifying the movements and patterns of water, and symbolizing the sky mother, whose rain falls as milk from her breasts (Fig. 9). Painted water jars with breasts appear everywhere in Bronze Age Crete.

The bird was the life of the waters, the epiphany of the goddess as the deep watery abyss of cosmic space and as the seas and rivers, underground

Figure 9. Pot with mask and breasts of goddess, marked with chevrons and triple lines suggesting water; end sixth millennium BC. North-eastern Hungary.

wells and streams. The bird that flies far above the earth and the bird that swims on waters resting upon the earth linked two dimensions that were not the native element of human beings yet surrounded them above and below. The image of the bird at home in both dimensions brought the upper and the lower waters together, offering an image of a unified world.

The Bird Goddess as the bringer of life appears as a composite image of woman and bird, with the emphasis falling on her long, slender neck and egg-shaped body, imagery familiar from the Palaeolithic period. The image of the Bird Goddess as primordial creatrix endures for some 25,000 years, from the thirtieth to the fifth millennium BC, descending to all the later civilizations, especially to Crete and Boeotia in Greece. The goddess takes

Figure 10. (*Left*) Head of Bird Goddess; *c.* 6000 BC, height 2⅔ in. (6.1 cm). Achilleion, Thessaly.
Figure 11. (*Right*) Bird Goddess; *c.* 6000 BC, terracotta. Sesklo, Thessaly.

the guise of many different birds: crane, swan, diver-bird, duck, goose, dove and owl. Figure 10 shows one of the most memorable of these images, discovered by Gimbutas in Thessaly in 1973. The goddess is also fashioned as a vase with the features of a bird or as a woman who wears the mask of a water-bird or duck.

The vase or vessel becomes also an image of the womb of the goddess from which the life-giving waters flow. Her rain, milk or water is painted as a pattern of parallel, serpentine or wavy lines (Fig. 12) and zigzags, spirals and M signs.[18] Chevrons symbolize the wings or beak of a bird, birds in flight or the rippling wake made by a bird moving through water. Gimbutas adds that the V of the chevron is also a hieroglyph for the genital triangle and for the life that emerged from the goddess's womb.[19] The vase or vessel as the Bird Goddess is explicitly shown in Figure 13, where her face is drawn on the neck of the vase and rain bands as wings form the decoration of her body.

The tradition of the very ancient relationship between goddess and bird can be traced through the Egyptian, Sumerian, Minoan and Greek civiliz- ations. The figures of the Egyptian Isis and her sister, Nephthys, guard the sarcophagus of the pharaoh like two great-winged birds (see Chapter 12, Fig. 4). The swallow and the dove are sacred to the Sumerian goddess Inanna and the Egyptian Isis, and the swan and the goose belong to Aphrodite (see Chapter 9, Figs. 4, 5, 7). In her aspect as the bringer of death and regeneration the Bird Goddess appears as the Sumero-Babylonian goddess Inanna–Ishtar flanked by owls and standing on a pair of lions (see Chapter 5, Fig. 30), and as the Egyptian Sphinx guarding the tomb of the pharaohs. Isis also takes the form of a kite to fan her dead husband back to life with the sweeping of her vast wings. The owl, bird of the goddess Athena, continues to be the messenger of death and also the comforter of the bereaved even to the present day. Its round eyes stare

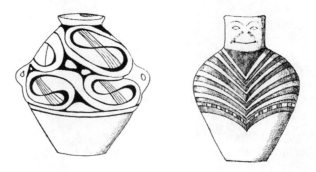

Figure 12. (*Left*) Vase with snake-like bands; end fifth millennium BC.
Western Ukraine.
Figure 13. (*Right*) Vase with face of Bird Goddess and chevron-like bands;
Vinca culture, *c.* 5300–5000 BC. Central Macedonia.

from Neolithic pots and vases, as once they did from the Palaeolithic cave of Les Trois Frères, and are often incised with the zigzag and net signs of the life-force. As with the chrysalis, models of the owl goddess were laid in the tholos tombs and shaft graves of Mycenaean Greece in the fifteenth century BC.

Although in the Judaeo-Christian tradition the dove is pre-eminently the bird of epiphany, discovering land and signalling the end of the flood in the story of Noah, and symbolizing the Holy Ghost in the baptism of Christ and at Pentecost, the original relationship between the dove and the goddess is long forgotten. Yet there are many stories of swan maidens and talking birds woven into the fairy-tales of Europe that may come from this ancient time: the swan princess (and her black counterpart) in the ballet *Swan Lake*, the goose with the golden egg, and pantomime's Mother Goose.

The egg

Figure 14. Egg design; *c.* 4500 BC. Western Ukraine.

The egg belongs to the mythology of the Bird Goddess as the source of life. The egg is also related to water as the primordial element in which life gestates, because the foetus-egg first comes alive in the waters of the womb. The egg and egg-shaped womb are both images of the beginning of life: the single egg divides, becomes two, and from the separation of the two halves – female and male, heaven and earth – creation comes. This motif, originating in the Palaeolithic era, is clearly painted on Neolithic vessels several thousand years before it appears in the great Bronze Age civilizations of Sumeria, Egypt and Crete. The memory of this myth lingers in the custom of Easter eggs, and also in the old wives' tale of the stork bringing the baby.

The egg as womb is a favourite image of the artists of Old Europe. Double eggs inside the buttocks of the goddess (Figs. 15a–b) swell them into a pregnantly rounded shape that tapers to an elongated head at one end and narrow legs at the other. Bird goddesses are sculpted with great emphasis given to the egg-shaped body. Stylized eggs adorn countless vases, intricately combined with water and snake symbolism (Fig. 15f). The Palaeolithic sculptures and abstract drawings on the walls of the cave are here developed into figurines and vessels whose form gradually evolves into the vases and huge jars, or *pithoi*, of Minoan Crete. Figure 15g shows

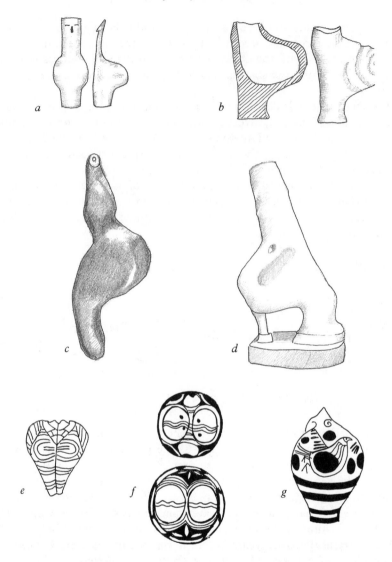

Figure 15. Images of the egg; 16,000–1500 BC. (a) Bird-woman with egg-shaped buttocks; east Balkan Neolithic, early sixth millennium BC. Near Sofia, Bulgaria. (b) Figurine with a hollow egg-shaped space in buttocks and a snake winding around them; central Balkan Neolithic, early sixth millennium BC. Northern Yugoslavia. (c) Sculptured figure with egg-shaped buttocks; c. 14,000 BC. Petersfels, Germany. (d) Seated goddess with cylindrical neck and egg-shaped buttocks; Vinca culture, early sixth millennium BC. (e) Double egg within the womb of figurine with double-egg motifs incised on front and back; end fifth millennium BC. Soviet Moldavia. (f) Snakes winding across double eggs; Late Cucuteni, mid-fourth millennium BC. Western Ukraine. (g) Design of bird with large egg inside its body, painted on a Minoan vase; c. 1450 BC. Crete.

a Cretan vase with a bird containing an egg. Goddess, egg, bird and serpent are four elements that are inseparable in the mythic images of Old Europe.

The tiny Palaeolithic amulet from Petersfels (Fig. 15c; see also Chapter 1, Fig. 14), carved from a piece of coal, is one of the earliest images of the Bird Goddess whose body contains an egg. The figure from Neolithic Vinca (Fig. 15d), with her egg-shaped body and tall, cylindrical neck, continues the highly schematized tradition of the Palaeolithic goddess. The androgyny of the goddess – the union of feminine and masculine forms – is exactly rendered in the elongated neck and egg-shaped body shared by the images from Petersfels and Vinca, although they are separated by some 8,000 years.

Figure 16. Egg-womb design; *c*. 4000 BC. North-eastern Romania.

In later myths the 'cosmic egg' was the beginning of all life. In one Bronze Age Egyptian myth the egg is laid by a large goose – 'The Great Cackler' – and in Greek Orphic myth the world-egg was laid by uncreated Night, imagined as a black-winged bird. Many African and Arctic myths tell of a mythical water-bird who laid the egg of the world, from which creation emerged.

The Fish Goddess

The theme of the egg appears in the great carved stones found at a site called Lepenski Vir, beautifully situated on the shores of the River Danube in northern Yugoslavia (Fig. 17). These monumental stones – part human and part fish – were placed at the head of triangular shrines with red-lime plastered floors.[20]

The natural element of the child before birth, like that of the fish, is water, and the sign of imminent birth is the breaking of the waters of the womb. These fish deities are shaped like an egg or womb. Is this because, like the child born of the waters of the womb, the fish is the new life that emerges from the egg in the watery womb of the sea or river? The human quality of these fish-faces creates an unusual identity of feeling between the human and sea dimensions. In the enchanted world of fairy-tales fish speak to humans and bring them great riches, as in Grimm's fairy-tale of the fisherman and his wife. The fish is still the central image of fertility and rebirth in the Chaldean myth of the fish-god Oannes, who emerges from the sea to teach humanity the arts of civilization. The phallus of the dismembered Egyptian god Osiris was swallowed by a fish, returning the

Figure 17. Fish Goddesses; stone, *c.* 5800 BC. Lepenski Vir, Yugoslavia.

impulse of regeneration to the depths of the waters. The fish – *Ichtheus* – was also the early Christian symbol of Christ, fisher of men. Christ is portrayed later seated in the fish-shaped oval that is both egg and womb, carved on the portals of Romanesque and Gothic cathedrals. The wounded Fisher King of the later Grail legends belongs to these rituals of regeneration, whose origins may lie in the Neolithic era.

The Serpent Goddess: the Goddess of the Lower Waters

The coiling path of the serpent, like the great rivers of the earth winding from mountain to sea, traces the spiralling of the life energy as it travels from one dimension to another. The serpent, with its quick and fluid shape and movement, came to symbolize the dynamic power of waters beyond, beneath and around the earth, and appears in many different mythologies as the creative source or generator of the universe. In Sumerian myth Nammu, the great serpent goddess of the abyss, gives birth to earth and heaven (see Chapter 5). The image of the serpent with its tail in its mouth forming a closed circle – sometimes called the *uroboros* – represents in many cultures the primordial waters encircling the earth.

The umbilical cord connecting the child to its mother has the form of intertwined double snakes, and this universal and evocative image of relationship may lie behind the image of the serpentine meander and labyrinth connecting this world to the one beyond. To this day the copulating serpents appear as an image of healing. Because of its coiling movement and its power to regenerate itself by sloughing its skin, the serpent became an image of the goddess's power of renewal, especially her power to restore life to the dead. Its cyclical pattern of hibernation may also have suggested the continual awakening of life from the temporary sleep of death. The meander, as the stylized snake, signifies the energy of transformation whose source lies beyond the reach of human consciousness – the watery dimension that is visited only by the dead. The underworld river Styx is the (greatly diminished) Latin version of this idea. The design of the net, portrayed in the Palaeolithic era, is now painted on figurines of the goddess and on water vessels, and may symbolize the watery womb of life, the cosmic 'net' in which all life is contained.

In Figure 18, which was found in Thessaly, snakes are coiling over the body of the enthroned goddess and the child she holds in her arms. This may be one of the earliest images of the snake goddess, who is found in other Neolithic cultures as far away from Old Europe as Ur in Mesopotamia and the Indus Valley (Mehrgarh). Sometime in the seventh millennium BC the attributes and powers of the goddess are distinguished into female and male on the analogy of fecundating womb and fertilizing phallus, and then the serpent comes to personify the autonomous male power of regeneration. In Bronze Age myths the serpent was imagined as the consort of the goddess, who unites with her to bring fertility to the earth.

Figure 18. Enthroned goddess holding her child, with spiralling snakes; fifth millennium BC. Sesklo, Thessaly.

Figure 19. (*Left*) *The Lady of Sitagroi*, with a double spiral or two snakes
engraved on belly; *c*. 4500 BC. Sitagroi, Macedonia.
Figure 20. (*Right*) Androgynous figure with phallic head and snake design
on womb; *c*. 4500 BC. Sitagroi, Macedonia.

In the Neolithic age, as later in Minoan Crete, snakes and spirals (the
snake in abstract form) are wound around vases and sculptures, coil over
pregnant bellies, buttocks and phalluses (Figs. 19, 20) or undulate between
moon, sun, stars and rain, as the dynamic principle of the life-energy that
never runs out. Spiral forms tracing the movement of water decorate
vases and pots. The images in Figure 21 suggest the serpent is the power
beneath the earth that makes the plants grow. The term 'serpent power',
meaning the 'coiled-up' energy of 'Kundalini' at the base of the spine in
the Indian system of Kundalini yoga, may derive from this idea.

A fascinating image from the Pyrenees (Fig. 22) shows the persistent
power of this symbolism, for here, much closer to our time, the goddess is
sculpted giving birth to life as a snake that she nourishes with her breasts.
In modern science the serpent image emerges once more in the spiralling
form of DNA.

The three striking Boeotian goddesses (Figs. 23–25), from 750–700 BC
(4,000 years later), have woven together images that, in the Neolithic,
appear separately.

Figure 21. Serpent spirals with plant forms and snakes; mid-fourth
millennium BC. Western Ukraine.

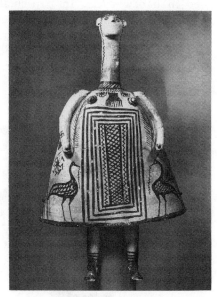

Figure 22. Sculpted figure showing the Goddess giving birth to a snake and suckling it; date unknown, possibly Gallo-Roman. The village of Oô in the Luchon region of the Pyrenees, south-western France.

Figure 23. (*Left*) Boeotian goddess with swastika and water-birds; eighth century BC.
Figure 24. (*Right*) Boeotian goddess with labyrinth and water-birds; eighth century BC.

Figure 25. Boeotian goddess with fish womb, animals and birds; eighth century BC.

The Goddess of Vegetation

A new image of the goddess appears in the Neolithic era: the goddess of wheat and corn, guardian of the rituals of sowing and harvesting, to whom the first fruits of the crops were dedicated. It is difficult to separate the Goddess of Vegetation and the Harvest from the Great Mother, since, like the moon, all plants, wild or cultivated, are born, die and are regenerated in a new cycle. In particular, the pregnant vegetation goddess (Fig. 27) draws a relationship between the fertility of woman and earth. The abdomen is characteristically emphasized and, as often on the body, there is a diamond- or lozenge-shaped design suggestive of a field, which

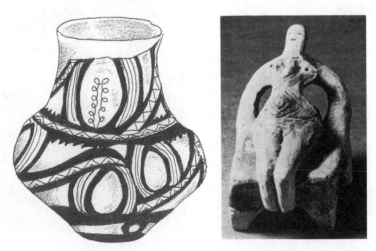

Figure 26. (*Left*) Plant form within an egg or vulva; painted vase, dark brown on orange-red, Late Cucuteni, *c.* 4000 BC. Western Ukraine.
Figure 27. (*Right*) Pregnant goddess figure with lozenge incised on womb; *c.* 4500 BC, height 4 in. (10 cm). Central Bulgaria.

is sometimes further divided into four sections or 'fields', with dots for seeds.[21] In this figure the dot is placed centrally as the umbilicus.

Because the pig grew very fast, had many children and seemed to 'plough' the soil as it rooted in the earth with its snout, its life cycle was an image of the earth's fertility. So it belonged inevitably to the lunar rites of agriculture, which were believed to assist the goddess of vegetation to give birth. In Figure 28 the goddess has the head of a sow, an image inherited by the Egyptian sow goddess in Figure 29, anticipating the goddess Isis, who is later depicted giving birth on the back of a pig (see Chapter 6, Fig. 15). Death was also imagined through the pig as part of the cycle of the withering crop, whose seed must fall back into the body of the earth for renewal. In many countries the boar brings death: in Babylonia, Tammuz, lover of the goddess Ishtar, in one version of his story, is killed by a boar, as is Attis in Anatolia. In Egypt, Seth, who had already killed his brother Osiris, was hunting the boar on the night of the full moon when he discovered Osiris's body in the marshes and dismembered it. A similar tradition in Greece has Adonis, the lover of Aphrodite, gored to death by a wild boar when out hunting. In the harvest festival of the Thesmophoria in Greece pigs were cast into pits, and the remains of last year's pig sacrifice dug up. In the Eleusinian Mysteries piglets were washed in the sea and sacrificed – perhaps as an image of the old life that had to die so that the initiate could be reborn.

Figure 28. (*Left*) The Goddess of Vegetation with the head of a sow; Vinca culture, *c.* 4500 BC, height $3\frac{1}{2}$ in. (9 cm). Western Romania.
Figure 29. (*Right*) Egyptian Pig Goddess, forerunner of Isis; *c.* 3000 BC.

The Goddess of the Animals

The sculpted animals of Old Europe may be seen, with Gimbutas, as epiphanies of the Mother Goddess, incarnating the various different aspects of her powers.[22] Buffie Johnson, in her book *Lady of the Beasts*, explores in depth the many animals in whom the image of the goddess was perceived, and so here we will only briefly touch on a few of them. Ritual masks of animals of all kinds, often covering the heads of female bodies, have been found in many places that were used as shrines or temples. Pictures of animals decorate pots and vessels, and the vessels themselves are often shaped as animals – frequently the doe or bear – and would seem to be an essential part of a ritual.

It was suggested in Chapter 1 that the Palaeolithic caves whose walls were covered with paintings of animals might be understood as symbolizing the womb of the goddess,[23] particularly because sculptures of goddess figures have been found on the outside of caves (Laussel) or in the ground close by (Lespugue), which makes some kind of relationship between the goddesses outside and the painted animals inside. In the Neolithic era the art of Old Europe and of Çatal Hüyük in Anatolia explores a precise relationship between goddess and animal, inviting the term 'Goddess of the Animals' or 'Lady of the Beasts' as a way of understanding how animals were experienced as immanent realities, full of divine presence.

The bear

The bear is probably the oldest sacred animal of all, known from the carefully arranged skulls in the mountain caves used by the Neanderthal race before the beginning of the last Ice Age about 75,000 BC. Figure 30

Figure 30. Goddess and baby as bear mother and cub; Vinca culture, *c.* 4500 BC, height $2\frac{1}{4}$ in. (5.7 cm). Kosovska Mitrovica, Yugoslavia.

may be the earliest image of a mother with her young, and expresses a feeling that has not been found in the Palaeolithic era. The sculptor has taken the notable tenderness of the mother bear for her cub as an image for human mothering, so creating a relationship between the animal and human worlds. Care of an animal for her young is experienced as common to both animal and human, and this may explain the arrestingly human emotion evoked by this image of a bear and her cub, which still echoes today in the devotion of a child for its teddy bear.

The mother animal with her child, whether bear, bird or serpent, illustrates the dual image of the Great Mother as source and what comes from the source – the child as the constantly renewed cycle of life. The later image of a 'human' goddess mother with her child celebrating the mystery of birth is common to all civilizations, from the Cretan goddess holding up her child, to the Egyptian Isis with the child at her breast, to the Christian Mary with the child upon her knee. The mother–child figure is also inspired by the experience of humanity cradled like a child in the lap of 'the Mother' in its ultimate dependence on 'Nature'.

The doe

The doe was one of the epiphanies of the goddess as Mother of Life and this archaic tradition has been handed down through legends and folk memories in many lands. The sacrality of the doe may have come from the vital importance of the deer and reindeer as a source of food in Palaeolithic times. Because of the rapid growth of its antlers, the deer (as the bull with its fast-growing horns) symbolized the waxing phase of the moon and so the generative principle of life. Deer's antlers have always been worn by male and female shamans and, up to this century, were worn by the people of Eastern Europe and England in the ritual cere-monies celebrating the coming of spring.[24] Hunters in the far north of Europe still hold an image of the Great Mother of the universe as an elk doe or a reindeer doe, and their myths speak of mothers, pregnant and looking like deer, with horns of reindeer on their heads and the hair of

 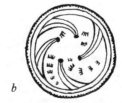 

a   b   c

Figure 31. (a, b) Painted bowls, perhaps showing does in the shape of lunar crescents; fourth millennium BC. Western Ukraine. (c) Bowl painted with a design of crescent shapes, perhaps antlers, with a central design of the lunar cross; Late Cucuteni, early fourth millennium BC. North-western Ukraine.

deer on their bodies. The beautifully painted dishes represented in Figure 31 show two or four does circling in a pattern of crescents, suggesting an association of the doe with the moon. One dish has the image of the goddess on one side, and two deer with stylized antlers circling round a four-armed cross on the other.

The dog

The dog is one of the most ancient animals belonging to the goddess as the guardian of her mysteries. In Greece dogs were sacred to Hecate, goddess of the dark phase of the moon and so of the crossroads and the underworld. The culture of Old Europe reveals the very ancient origin of the link between dog, dark moon, black night and goddess. The finest materials – marble, rock-crystal and gold – were used to fashion dog figurines or vessels shaped as dogs.[25] On vases from Cucuteni (eastern Romania and western Ukraine) dogs guard a tree, centrally placed to signify the Tree of Life (Fig. 32b).

The Neolithic images are the earliest to show the relationship between these guardian animals and the tree that once symbolized the goddess herself. But the dog also appears with the caterpillar on the vases of Old Europe and so it becomes an image of death and rebirth. In later civilizations the dog guards the threshold between the realms of the living and the dead: in Egypt, the jackal god, Anubis, becomes the guide of the souls of the dead into the underworld and assists at their transformation; in Greece, the three-headed dog, Cerberus, guards the entrance to the realm of the dead.

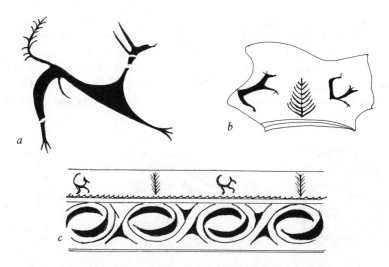

Figure 32. (a) Dog painted on a pear-shaped vase; *c.* 3500 BC. Soviet Moldavia. (b) Dogs guarding the Tree of Life; painting on a vase, mid-fourth millennium BC. Sipintsi, western Ukraine. (c) Dogs and Tree of Life; painting on a vase, fourth millennium BC. Sipintsi, western Ukraine.

The butterfly and bee

The butterfly is one of the oldest images of transformation. No one who, as a child, has waited for a caterpillar to turn into a butterfly can forget the moment when the earth-bound caterpillar becomes the beautiful winged creature that flies away. Some 8,000 years ago the caterpillar and the butterfly suggested that there were two aspects to a single life-form: one was 'born' out of the other. Thus it became one of the oldest images to suggest the regeneration of life from an outworn form and, analogously, the survival of the soul after the death of the body. The two images in Figure 36 are the earliest known images of a butterfly in Europe.

Figure 33. Engravings of butterflies on Neolithic vases; Linear Pottery culture, fifth millennium BC. Czechoslovakia.

Bees, like all insects that spin cocoons or weave webs, serve as images of the miraculous interconnectedness of life. The intricate cellular structure that secretes the golden essence of life is an image of the network of invisible nature that relates all things to each other in an ordered harmonious pattern. Perhaps this is the meaning of the tale in which the infant Zeus is fed on honey in Crete, and why honey was the nectar of the gods. Furthermore, the busy bee, following the impulsion of its nature to pollinate the flowers and gather their nectar to be transformed into honey, was an example of the continual activity required of human beings to gather the crops and transform them into food. The queen bee, whom all the others serve during their brief lives, was, in the Neolithic, an epiphany of the goddess herself. For a watchful eye, the relationship between the queen bee and the goddess must have seemed irresistible, and in Minoan Crete 4,000 years later the goddess and her priestesses, dressed as bees, are shown dancing together on a golden seal found buried with the dead. The hive was her womb – perhaps also an image of the underworld – and later reappears in the beehive tombs of Mycenae.[26]

Figure 34. Partly reconstructed frieze of Bee Goddess (?) painted on a vase; *c.* 6400–6200 BC. Otzaki, Thessaly.

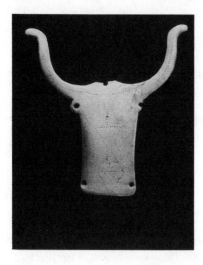

Figure 35. Bull-horned goddess in the shape of a bee picked out in dots on a stylized bull's head of bone; Late Cucuteni, fourth millennium BC. Western Ukraine (now Poland).

The earliest known image of the goddess in the shape of a bee has been scratched in dots on the stylized head of a bull from the western Ukraine (Fig. 35). It shows the earliest association between the bull and the bee – both images of renewal – which is later central to Minoan and Greek mythology. It was a common Greek and Roman belief that the bee was born from the carcass of a slain bull, and that both of these belonged to the regenerative power of the moon.[27]

The God

Since all things were contained in the Great Mother, for a long time she embodied male as well as female attributes. The female principle is clear in the egg-shaped 'body', or when the rounded, birth-giving aspect of the body is emphasized, as in Palaeolithic artefacts. The male principle is given in the tall, phallic neck and head. Many of the composite androgynous figures convey the sense of the source that continually generates itself – the original meaning of 'virgin'.

One of the ways in which consciousness evolves is through the differentiation of what was once experienced as a unity. It seems in accordance with this that in the course of the seventh and sixth millennia BC the androgynous goddess of Old Europe with phallic neck and egg-shaped body (see Fig. 7) separates into female and male elements, the male becoming the fertilizing power and the female the gestating womb. The image of the god appears in Old Europe about the same time as in Anatolia. The differentiated male principle is embodied as the phallus, as the bull or horned animal – ram and goat – and as the phallic-shaped serpent. It is also personified by a figure that is half-man, half-animal (bull or goat), and by the figure of a man portrayed as a god.

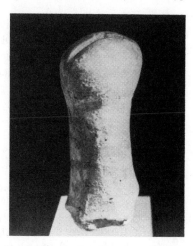

Figure 36. Clay phallus; *c*.6000 BC.
Tsangli, Thessaly.

The bull was the principal animal epiphany of the god. Either the whole body is that of a bull, or a bull's body bears a human head, or a male body carries the horns of a bull. All these compositions are images of the dynamic fertilizing power that calls out or awakens new forms dormant in the old. Later Sumerian, Egyptian, Minoan and Greek myths dramatize the bull-god as the 'son' of the mother goddess, and an actual bull was often sacrificed as the epiphany of the son returning to the mother for rebirth, renewing, in this way, the life-force that he incarnated.

The human forms of the god are of particular fascination in Old Europe, not just for their beauty of form but also for the human characteristics

Figure 37. (*Left*) Ithyphallic figure of a seated god; mid-fifth millennium BC. Dimini, near Volos, Thessaly.
Figure 38. (*Right*) Enthroned god; Sesklo culture, sixth millennium BC. Pyrasos, Thessaly.

that were chosen to portray divinity. The god emerges more clearly in human form in the culture of Old Europe than he does in Neolithic Çatal Hüyük (see pp. 91–2). A terracotta figure of a god from Thessaly (Fig. 37), with one hand on his erect penis, raises the other to his head in the manner of the young Minoan god; another figure of an enthroned god (Fig. 38), found also in Thessaly, anticipates the beautiful Cycladic figure of the man playing a harp.

In another sculpture from 5000 BC, found in Hungary, goddess (Fig. 39a) and god (Fig. 39b) need to be placed side by side or face to face since they belong together as a unity. The god appears seated on a throne, wearing a wide decorated belt and bracelets on each arm. He carries a large sickle over his right shoulder, which shows him as the reaper of the corn, or perhaps, in a more complex expression, he may be an image of the corn itself, which is cut down and reborn in the annual cycle of agriculture. He may then also personify the god of the yearly cycle, who is 'cut down' with the passing of the year, yet at the same time reborn as the new year (Time, the reaper). The sickle anticipates the ritual sickle that was part of the Mysteries of Eleusis, where its crescent shape symbolized the rebirth or renewal of the life-force.

The strangely modern figures of goddess and god (Figs. 40, 41) from the cemetery at Cernavoda at Hamangia on the edge of the Black Sea (now Romania), apparently sculpted by the same hand, may be one of the

a   b

Figure 39. (a) Goddess and (b) god; Tisza culture, *c.* 5500–5000 BC.
South-eastern Hungary.

Figure 40. Goddess; *c.* 5000 BC, height $4\frac{1}{2}$ in. (11.3 cm).
Cernavoda, eastern Romania.

Figure 41. God; *c.* 5000 BC, height 4½ in. (11.3 cm). Cernavoda, eastern
Romania.

earliest portrayals of the god as consort of the goddess. The god's reflective pose recalls that of Rodin's *Penseur*.

Figure 42 is the earliest image of the sacred marriage between goddess and god, which was to endure for 5,000 years until it formally died with Hebrew and Christian monotheism. The tenderness between the masked figures of a woman and a man – his embracing of her with his right arm – is intensely human, not remotely divine. The fertility of their sexual union is emphasized, but the quality of human feeling conveyed by the position of their heads and arms, as well as the closeness of their bodies, is primary.

The brilliant civilization of Old Europe flowered undisturbed for 2,000 years, from 6500 to 4500 BC, until, suddenly, it was disrupted by the arrival of nomadic tribesmen from the East – the first wave of peoples later known as Indo-European (or Aryan), who were in fact neither Indian nor European. Gimbutas names them as the Kurgan (Barrow) peoples and suggests that their homelands were the steppeland between the Dnieper and Volga rivers. These people, who led a predominantly nomadic life, worshipped sky gods who wielded the thunderbolt and the axe, and rode the horse, which they had domesticated as early as 5000 BC, enabling them to cover vast distances at a previously unimaginable speed. Suddenly the battle-axe and the dagger appear in the Old European sites. Then, simultaneously, Gimbutas writes:

> millennial traditions were truncated: towns and villages disintegrated, magnificent painted pottery vanished; as did shrines, frescoes, sculptures, symbols and script. The taste for beauty and the sophistication of style and

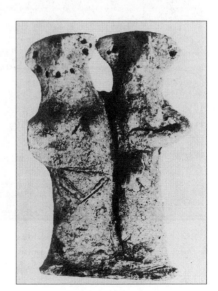

Figure 42. *The Gumelnitsa Lovers*; East Balkan civilization, *c.* 4500 BC, height 2⅔ in. (6.8 cm). Cascioarele, Romania.

execution withered. The use of vivid colors disappeared in nearly all Old European territories except Greece, the Cyclades, and Crete where Old European traditions continued for three more millennia, to 1500 BC.[28]

The resemblance of the goddess sculptures in Figures 43 and 44 to much earlier Old European goddesses, and to each other, shows that Old European culture did not entirely die out but continued in some form on the western coast of Anatolia and the Cycladic islands of the Aegean, passing to Minoan and Mycenaean culture and then to Greece. In both figures the outlining of the genital triangle draws the focus of the sculpture to the mystery of birth. The divided and curved arms of the Anatolian goddess recall the wings of the older Bird Goddess, as does the beaked nose upon her face.

But the ruthless imposition of an alien mythology, a war-like ethos and hierarchical customs on the agricultural peoples of Old Europe all but obliterated the older culture. The disruption and suffering caused by the nomadic tribes, the 'ceaseless flight' of displaced peoples throughout the fourth millennium BC,[29] can be imagined only by comparing them with the events in this century in central and eastern Europe – strangely enough, almost the same area as Old Europe – where so many terrified people, caught between highly mechanized armies, had nowhere to flee. It is Gimbutas's view that the Kurgan tribes that entered the area of Old Europe in three waves of infiltration (4300–4200 BC, 3400–3200 BC, 3000–2800 BC) changed the course of European prehistory by imposing a

Figure 43. (*Left*) Bird Goddess; marble sculpture, *c.* 2700–2400 BC.
Gallipoli Peninsula.
Figure 44. (*Right*) Cycladic goddess; marble sculpture, Keros-Syros culture, *c.* 2500 BC.

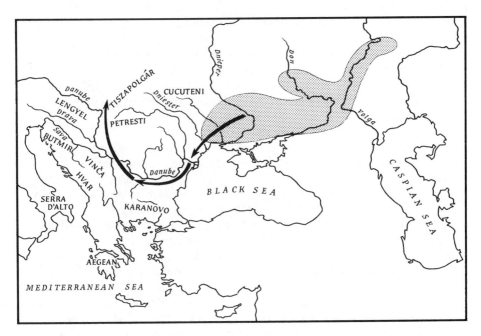

Map 3. Kurgan Wave One (*c.* 4300–4200 BC). Arrows show main invasion routes for earliest Kurgan incursion primarily into Old European cultures of Karanova, Vinca, Lengyel and Tiszapolgar.

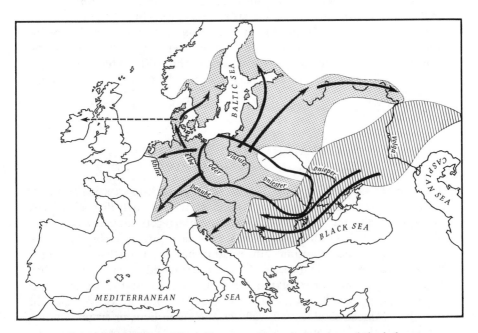

Map 4. Kurgan Wave Three (*c.* 3000–2800 BC). Arrows and shaded areas show later incursions by Kurgans from steppes (eastern area of dark bars) and from hybridized cultures (e.g. oblong area in centre of map). Dotted line shows possible route to Ireland.

culture that was 'stratified, pastoral, mobile and war-oriented' on a culture that was 'agricultural and sedentary, egalitarian and peaceful'.[30] Their social system was hierarchical and dominated by the most powerful males, with a male priesthood. They practised human and animal sacrifice (selecting particularly the horse), immolating the living wives and children of their dead chieftains along with them.

The peoples of the goddess culture had little defence against the taller, stronger, well-armed and mounted invaders, and gradually succumbed to them.[31] The Kurgan people spread southwards into the Macedonian plain and western Anatolia, building citadels and massive stone walls as they went, of which the walls of Mycenae and Tiryns are a late example. Once the route of invasion was established, there was a continuous migration of new generations, which reinforced the cultural disruption.[32] The Dorian invasions, which finally destroyed Minoan civilization, were perhaps the last phase of an historical process that had begun 3,000 years earlier. The cyclical lunar imagery of the goddess culture was either gradually replaced by the predominantly male deities and solar mythology of the Kurgan peoples, or fused with them in the often uneasy union that is transmitted to later Greek and Celtic culture. What developed after *c.* 2500 BC, Gimbutas concludes, was 'a melange of the two mythic systems, Old European and Indo-European'.[33]

We have been taught that our finest perceptions come from Greek civilization, yet the origins of the artistic achievements of the Greeks, in their search for a way of life that is lived in harmony with the life of the universe, are 6,000 years older. We are the inheritors, via the Bronze and Iron Ages, of two utterly different visions of the world, whose mythology must be differentiated before the legacy of their long conflict can be transformed.

ÇATAL HÜYÜK, ANATOLIA

The Mother Goddess of Çatal Hüyük sits on a rock-like throne and rests her hands, in the act of giving birth, upon the wild animals that accompany her in later cultures (Fig. 45). This sculpted terracotta figure, 8,000 years old, with massive head, hips and legs, is in fact only 4⅔ inches (11.8 cm) tall and was found in a grain bin, relating her act of birth-giving to the 'birth' of the crops from the earth. The Mother Goddess with her guardian felines is the forerunner of the Great Goddesses of the Bronze Age: Inanna–Ishtar in Mesopotamia, Isis and Sekhmet in Egypt and the unnamed Minoan Goddess all walk with or upon lions or sit upon a lion throne. In the Iron Age, Cybele, the Great Goddess of Anatolia and Rome, rides in a chariot drawn by lions, in a direct line of descent from the goddess of Çatal Hüyük. A hymn to Cybele, from the second century AD at Pergamum, invokes her as 'the mother of the immortal gods', seated

Figure 45. Mother Goddess giving birth between lions or leopards; terracotta sculpture, *c.* 6000–5800 BC. Shrine in Level 11, Çatal Hüyük.

in a chariot drawn by 'bull-killing lions. . .who occupies the central throne of the cosmos, and thus of the earth. . .who rules the rivers and the entire sea.'[34]

Çatal Hüyük on the Konya plain of southern Anatolia (now modern Turkey) is the largest Neolithic site in the Near East, covering some 32 acres (13 ha.), yet only one-twentieth of it has been excavated. It gives a very early picture of another advanced and distinctive culture that, like the civilization of Old Europe, was centred on the figure of the Mother Goddess. It thrived from 7000 to 5000 BC, when the site was deserted, though no one knows why. Çatal Hüyük was discovered in 1957 by the archaeologist James Mellaart, who described it as shining 'like a supernova among the rather dim galaxy of contemporary peasant cultures'.[35]

The great plain of Konya was once covered with trees and open parkland, roaming herds of red deer and wild cattle, abundant food for the Neolithic people of Çatal Hüyük. By the seventh millennium BC, some 3,000 years before the rise of Sumeria, there were many established groups whose work was already highly specialized: work such as stone carving, weaving, cloth dyeing, pottery, basket work, spinning, the cultivation of crops and the building of houses and shrines. When and where, Mellaart asks, did the people of Çatal Hüyük learn to smelt copper and lead? Certainly it was by 6400 BC, long before the Chalcolithic discovery of copper.

Bulls' horns (bucranium) as well as the giant heads, plaster reliefs and paintings of the bull appear in many of the shrines and houses that have been excavated in Çatal Hüyük. The bulls' horns of consecration are already familiar from the culture of Old Europe, but, as no shrines there have survived intact, we cannot know exactly how or where they were placed. Here they are vividly arranged on the walls of many of the shrines. The pillars in the shrine shown in Figure 46 stand for the goddess, while the horned bull incarnates her regenerative power or the power of the god, her son. This consistent imagery of the goddess and the ram and bulls' horns shows a remarkable affinity not only with the contemporary civilization of Old Europe but also with Minoan–Mycenaean culture.

The central image of the religion of Çatal Hüyük was the Mother Goddess, who appears in three aspects: as a young woman, a mother giving birth and an old woman. Only the goddess was sculpted in relief or painted on the walls of the shrines; the god was represented as the bull, and the images and statuettes of the goddess far outnumber those of the god. Mellaart comments on the absence of specific sexual imagery – of the phallus or vulva – at Çatal Hüyük and surmises that the religion may have been the creation of women who elaborated a mythology where the birth-giving and nourishing capacity of the goddess image was emphasized, and where the male principle was represented by the horned animal. The priestesses who may have conducted her rites gave greatest importance to the experience that was most numinous to them – the birth and regeneration of life. 'Sometime during the fifty-eighth century BC', Mellaart writes, 'agriculture finally triumphed over the age-old occupation of hunting and with it the power of woman increased: this much is clear from the almost total disappearance of male statues in the cult.'[36]

The goddess in Figure 48 has two heads and two pairs of breasts but only one set of arms, suggesting that she is both mother and maiden, and

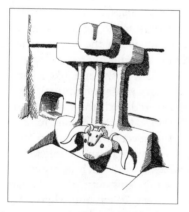 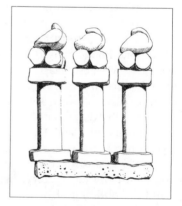

Figure 46. (*Left*) Restoration of relief of the twin goddess and her son imaged as the bull; *c.* 5800 BC. Shrine VI.14, Çatal Hüyük.
Figure 47. (*Right*) Minoan shrine with doves; *c.* 1500 BC.

Figure 48. White marble figure of the dual goddess; *c.* 5800 BC. Shrine VI.A.10, Çatal Hüyük.

so the predecessor of the ivory figure of the mother and daughter with the child from Mycenae (see Chapter 3, Fig. 38) and of Demeter and Persephone from Greece. She may represent the goddess in her dual aspect as the source of life and its manifestation.

Twin goddess figures exist in several shrines. In Figure 49 two figures sit side by side, again perhaps personifying the goddess as mother and daughter, like the 'Two Ladies' of the later Minoan texts from Knossos. While the figure on the right has no breasts, the V shape below the neck could be a necklace or the line of a robe, as it is in a stone statuette of the

Figure 49. The two goddesses and the bull; *c.* 5800 BC. Reconstruction of the north and east walls of Shrine VII.8, Çatal Hüyük.

daughter goddess (see Fig. 54) found in another shrine, but originally, Mellaart believes, belonging to this one. On the adjoining wall, a huge bull faces towards them, charging the whole shrine with its energy.

The Birth-giving Goddess

The physical gesture of birth is the paramount theme in many of the shrines at Çatal Hüyük. In Figure 50 the goddess, with legs outstretched in the stylized birth position repeated in many different shrines, seems to have given birth to the three bulls' heads placed beneath her. The shape emerging from her womb may be the muzzle of a fourth bull, giving the impression that she is perpetually giving birth. It is curious that in Old Europe images of the goddess in the act of giving birth are very rare, whereas here they are extremely prolific, as though this culture wanted to catch life at the moment of its greatest drama. Because of this a special shrine may have been set aside in which women came to give birth, named by Mellaart the 'Red Shrine' because the plastered walls and floor were coloured red – the colour of life – throughout.[37]

Sometimes the body of the goddess is marked with giant flower forms and on one occasion she emerges between doorposts as if she were coming through the door as an apparition to her worshippers. In the striking plaster relief represented in Figure 51 the goddess is shown as Mellaart describes her:

> with head and body in profile, her long hair floating behind her in the wind. Arms and legs are outstretched and foreshortened, thus strengthening the impression of swift motion. The goddess appears to be running, dancing or whirling . . .[38]

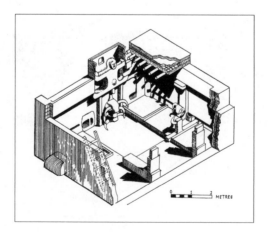

Figure 50. The Birth-giving Goddess; *c.* 5800 BC. Restoration of the north and west walls of Shrine VI.A.10, Çatal Hüyük.

Figure 51. Goddess with flowing hair; *c.* 6100 BC. East wall of
Shrine VII.31, Çatal Hüyük.

The shrine of the vultures is the most impressive image of the Goddess of Death and Regeneration in Neolithic art. In Figure 52 the seven huge vultures are overwhelming. Painted not black but blood-red on a pink background, they hover over headless human beings with their life-size wings outspread, covering two walls. The headless figures, with their raised arms forming the gesture of epiphany, appear to be greeting the goddess in her vulture form, even possibly flying with her, like birds themselves, in the world beyond death. This gesture of recognition creates the mood of the experience, so, despite the formidable presence of the vultures, the scene conveys a confidence that the goddess in her vulture form has the power of regeneration as well as death. For the vulture,

Figure 52. Earliest paintings of vultures; *c.* 6100 BC. North and east walls of
Shrine VII.8, Çatal Hüyük.

feeding on carrion, does not so much 'bring' death as transform what is already dead back into life, beginning a new cycle by assimilating the end of the old one. In this way the goddess of death and the goddess of birth are inseparable.[39]

The Goddess of the Animals

At Çatal Hüyük the leopard was the sacred animal of the goddess. Yet it appears on the walls of only one shrine, even though, in small statues, the goddess rests her hands on them as she gives birth (Fig. 45) or carries them on her shoulders or clothes herself with their skins. One of the most remarkable wall decorations in the shrines, remoulded and painted some forty times over, is of two leopards face to face – the female on the left, the male on the right – their spots drawn as a flower design and their tails raised in perfect symmetry (Fig. 53). It is as though the leopards, like the Palaeolithic lions, act as guardians to a mystery that must not be profaned.

In Figure 54 two goddesses stand behind leopards, as if stroking them, wearing leopard-skin dresses. The one on the right is an older, mother figure, sculpted in brown limestone, and the one on the left is a younger, daughter figure, sculpted in blue limestone. The third figure in the group, of brown limestone like the mother figure, is a young boy riding on the back of a leopard. The relationship between these three figures instantly evokes the trio of two goddesses and a young god from Mycenae sculpted in 1300 BC (see Chapter 3, Fig. 38). There is a similar resemblance between the figure of the Anatolian daughter goddess and the Mycenaean goddess in Figure 55, which is dated at 1500 BC. Certain sculptures of the Minoan goddess also have this distinctive dress and posture (see Chapter 3, Fig. 11). Some 4,000 years separate these two goddesses, so similar in form and grace of line, suggesting a relationship between Anatolia and Crete that fostered an undisrupted transmission of imagery over this immense span of time.

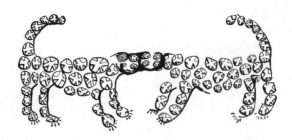

Figure 53. Painting of two leopards; *c.* 5900 BC. North wall of
the Leopard Shrine VI.B.44, Çatal Hüyük.

Figure 54. (*Above*) Mother and daughter goddesses and young god with leopards; *c.* 5800 BC. Çatal Hüyük.
Figure 55. (*Right*) A goddess; ivory, *c.* 1500 BC. Mycenae.

The Goddess of Vegetation

The association of the goddess with plant life and agriculture is clear from the flower and plant patterns painted on the figures of goddesses and on the walls of the shrines, and from the placing of the statues in grain bins.

The beautiful paintings at Çatal Hüyük range from frescoes of the deer and bull hunt, to paintings of flowers, plants, insects and even textiles. In one painting a rectangular honeycomb design painted in red had some of the cells left empty. As the eye moved to the right, other cells were filled with the forms of flowers and insects (Fig. 56); some insects – perhaps bees – had wings, others were wingless. Encasing the flower and insect forms and the honeycomb design was a line of hand imprints, the upper line painted in pink and black, the lower in pink and white.

Figure 56. Copy of a painting of insects and flowers on the walls of
Shrine VI.B.8; *c.* 6000 BC. Çatal Hüyük.

Figure 57. Butterfly, four-armed ritual images and two 'goddesses' with
lines of energy or water flowing between them; *c.* 5800 BC.
Shrine VI.A.66, Çatal Hüyük.

Amazingly, the weaving of kilims may go back 8,000 years, for the
painting on the walls of the shrines show that it was already a highly
developed art at Çatal Hüyük and that the wall paintings were copied
from the woven kilims, rather than the other way round. One of the latest
of these kilims, painted in bright colours on a beige ground, shows a
pattern that is quite as complicated as a modern woven one.[40] Perhaps the
shrines were actually hung with kilims and the walls were literally tapes-
tried in the colours and intricate designs that are still woven to this day
in Turkey. Some of the walls are almost completely covered with these
designs (Fig. 58), as if the artists who painted them were hanging a single
piece of woven cloth all the way round the room. It is possible that the
designs have changed little over the millennia, and that then, as now, each
knot told a story.

Certain shrines decorated with intricate geometric patterns and images
of flowers seem to have been reserved specifically for women, and may
have been decorated by them, for their palettes have been found buried
with them, still bearing traces of the colours used to paint the walls.[41]

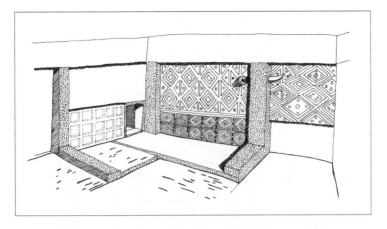

Figure 58. Reconstruction of the north and east walls of Shrine VII.1, with wall paintings of textiles similar to kilims; *c.* 6100 BC. Çatal Hüyük.

The God

Even though the myth of the goddess presides over all the activities of the community at Çatal Hüyük, the myth of the god was not absent, for although only eight statuettes of the god have been found there (compared with thirty-three of the goddess), his story is interwoven with hers, as can be seen from the relation of the bull-child to the goddess giving birth. The tiny statuettes tell a story of different aspects of the lives of the deities, which is also a story of changing episodes in the life-cycle of the seasons, the crops and the lives of human beings in relation to the greater life that contained them.[42]

Figure 59. (*Left*) White marble figure of a god; *c.* 5800 BC. Found in a vulture shrine (VI.A.25), Çatal Hüyük.
Figure 60. (*Right*) White marble figure of a god wearing a leopard-skin cap and bracelets on his upper arm; *c.* 5800 BC. Çatal Hüyük.

Figure 61. Unique green schist-plaque showing four figures in bold relief;
c. 5800 BC. Shrine VI.A.30, Çatal Hüyük.

As the male principle emerging from the goddess, the god appears as a
bull in the shrines. In the statuettes he is drawn in the form of a boy –
perhaps a figure in a story with a name and a role – as in Figure 54, where
he is sitting on a leopard. He is also depicted as a hunter wearing a
leopard-skin hat and seated on a bull. In Figure 59 he is the son of the
goddess; in Figure 60, her consort. So each deity, goddess and god, had
two aspects: mother and daughter, son and consort. The essential unity of
these four figures is shown in the magnificent carved relief where the
goddess and god are embracing each other and the goddess is holding her
child (Fig. 61). Mellaart comments that 'the goddess remains the same,
the male appears either as husband or as son',[43] a drama that is explored
later in the Bronze Age myth of the mother goddess and her son–lover.

There is no evidence that Çatal Hüyük was conquered by invaders, but
the civilization appeared to die out in the sixth millennium BC. The
fragments that have been excavated leave a tantalizing image of what
hidden treasures might still lie beneath the Konya plain and in other
places yet undiscovered. But even these fragments add to a more complete
picture of Neolithic culture in a setting where it was able to evolve
undisturbed. Moreover, the vitality and strength of this culture may have
laid the foundations for the endurance of the cult of the mother goddess
in Anatolia, which will be explored in Chapter 10.

THE MEGALITHS

The gigantic stones of the Megalithic[44] culture strewn across Europe stand as a visibly unanswered question in any attempt to reach back into the past with a modern mind. As Eliade observed, 'Desacralization pervades the entire experience of the nonreligious man of modern societies', and this makes it increasingly difficult for us to 'rediscover the existential dimensions of religious man in the archaic societies'.[45] What we have lost is their understanding that the life of the cosmos and the life of humanity are one life. So we can approach the intention of these people only by trying to see through their eyes: experiencing the ground they walked on and the air they breathed as belonging to a world that was wholly sacred. Even now, few people can look upon stones like those of Callenish (Fig. 62), for example, without being deeply moved by them.

Sometime during the fifth millennium BC, and later, people with considerable engineering, geometric and astronomical skills raised giant stones to form circles, alignments and burial chambers – all of which required an extraordinary amount of time, labour and knowledge to build. Malta seems to have been an especially sacred island and has the remains of as many as thirty temples. The startling alignments at Carnac, in Brittany, have some 3,000 upright stones laid out in lines that extend for nearly 2½ miles (4 km) and may have formed part of a lunar observatory or a processional way for an unknown seasonal ritual. The stones of Avebury

Figure 62. The Stones of Callenish; *c.* 2000 BC. Isle of Lewis.

in Wiltshire were once disposed in the shape of a gigantic serpent carrying two 'eggs' in its belly (Fig. 69). Silbury Hill (see pp. 99–100), which was part of this linear temple, is the tallest prehistoric structure in Europe, described by Michael Dames as an effigy of the goddess 'arranged with stupendous deliberation'.[46]

Stonehenge (see p. 100) belonged to the Avebury temple complex, and though we know that there were three phases of building – the first about 2800 BC and the last about 1500 BC – the full range of their astronomical significance can still only be surmised.[47] None the less, their building was surely a sacramental undertaking meaningful to the whole community, as was the building of Chartres, whose stones were hauled in wagons drawn by rich and poor together. It is highly unlikely that the lifting and placing of these enormous stones was a labour imposed on the people by a powerful and autocratic priesthood intent on maintaining its power by means of its astronomical knowledge. To interpret the building of the temples in this way is to see the Neolithic past through the veil of our own cultural assumptions.

The Great Mother was the spiritual focus of the Megalithic culture of Western Europe, as she was of the Neolithic cultures of Old Europe and Çatal Hüyük. Professor Glyn Daniel writes that the megalithic tomb builders of Western Europe

> were imbued by a religious faith, were devotees of a goddess whose face glares out from pot and phalange idol and the dark shadows of the tomb walls, whose image is twisted into the geometry of the Portuguese schist plaques and the rich carving of Gavrinis (Brittany) and New Grange (Ireland).[48]

Only thirty years ago the Megalithic culture used to be placed in the second millennium BC, but the discovery of radio-carbon and tree-ring dating has allowed its beginnings to recede into the fifth millennium BC. It is now known that Neolithic farming communities were established in France and the Iberian Peninsula as early as the sixth millennium BC, and in Britain and Ireland towards the end of the fifth millennium BC. Then, about 4500 BC, the practice of collective burial begins to appear along the south-eastern and western coasts of the Iberian Peninsula, in Brittany and, about 500 years later, in Ireland.

Tombs disclosing the ritual of collective burial have been found as far apart as Ireland, the Iberian Peninsula and Malta, and the great stone temples and temple tombs built between 3500 and 1500 BC can still be seen in Ireland, Britain, Brittany and Malta. The mystery of their origins is not entirely resolved. The graves and temples may have been built by seafaring travellers venturing beyond the Mediterranean up the western coastline of Europe, and bringing with them astronomical and geometric skills learned in other cultures. Or they may have been built by Neolithic farming communities already settled in Western Europe, or even from a

Figure 63. Engraved stone from the passageway at Gavrinis; *c.* 4000 BC. Gulf of Morbihan, Brittany.

fusion of the two. And it is just possible that the Megalithic people in Western Europe were the cultural descendants of their Palaeolithic ancestors. (The megalithic 'beehive' stone chamber in the passage grave can be understood as the first articulation of a temple, which can itself be seen as an externalized form in stone of the Palaeolithic cave. The flat stones laid across the raised stones to form a passage can be recognized as the 'cave roof' and, when covered with earth, as many of them were, the dark area enclosed re-enacts the womb experience of the cave. The temple is no longer 'given' as the cave. Human beings themselves now construct the stone chamber as the womb of the goddess in which they lay their dead as the seed from which new life will come.)

France has over 5,000 megalithic tombs extending in a line from Brittany to the Mediterranean. Of all these, the passage grave or temple-tomb of Gavrinis in the Gulf of Morbihan in Brittany is the most remarkable. It is aligned to the rising sun at the winter solstice, but the main orientation of the passage is towards an extreme position of the rising moon.[49] Twenty-three of the twenty-nine great upright stones lining the passageway are covered with strange designs that look like giant fingerprints, swirling water or patterns of energy – possibly the inexhaustible life-force of the goddess and her 'primordial waters' – though they may also represent the pathway spiralling between this world and the world of the ancestral dead (Fig. 63). Dowsers, who are perhaps closest to the Neolithic understanding of the earth, have remarked that the pattern of energy emerging from the ancient stones may take the form of a spiral.

Images of the goddess have been found inside some of these tombs, at the entrance of rock-cut tombs, and standing by themselves without any apparent relation to the burial sites (Fig. 64). Daniel writes that 'these figures are without doubt the goddess-figure which appeared on the Iberian cult objects and tombs and in a different guise on the statue-menhirs of southern France'.[50] A distinction is occasionally drawn between a 'funerary' goddess, such as those found incised on the stones lining a tomb, and

Figure 64. Goddess figures incised on chamber tombs; *c.* 4000–3000 BC. France and Spain.

a 'fertility' goddess, found elsewhere. But to separate these two aspects of the goddess is to miss the significance of placing her image in or close to a burial chamber; for, if read symbolically, this promises the fertility of the life to come.

Upright stones carved with the features of a goddess have been found in isolated places in France, maybe marking a burial site or sacred place (Fig. 65). The stone, which lasts so long it seems timeless, offers an image of a reality that survives the passing of time. We now call this 'eternity', but, in the Neolithic as in the Palaeolithic, it may once have been contained in the image of the goddess. The stone symbolized the essential being: the soul or spirit of animate life that was not subject to decay, but endured beyond and beneath all appearances. 'The megalithic cult of the dead', Eliade comments, 'appears to include not only a certainty of the soul's survival but, above all, confidence in the power of the ancestors and the hope that they will protect and help the living.'[51] The menhirs, or standing

a   *b*

Figure 65. *La Dame de St Sernin*, (a) front and (b) back views; *c.* 3000 BC. Rodez, France.

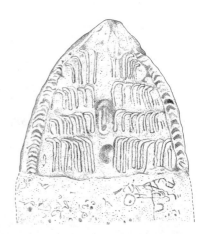

Figure 66. The great stone in the
burial chamber La Table des
Marchands; *c.* 4000–3000 BC.
Locmariarquer, Brittany.

stones, were believed to be the 'dwelling' or 'body' of the dead, whose
souls, when summoned, would 'inhabit' the stone erected to receive them.
The belief that stones could engender fertility originates in the idea that
the spirit of the ancestor 'animated' the stone, and continues into this
century in the custom of women touching or rubbing themselves against
the stone to help themselves become pregnant. Above all, the erection of
the stone is an act of remembering. The faint resonance of this original
belief lives on in our custom of marking the burial place of the dead with
a gravestone or, in the case of those killed in war, a war memorial, often
found in the centre of villages and towns.

The triangular stone standing at the end of the passage grave has
baffled many archaeologists. Its shape suggests a hill or mound, the image
of the goddess herself, the sacred place of life. It has a design of hooks or
sickles incised on it, similar to a design that appears on many goddess-
menhirs elsewhere in France and all over Old Europe. These designs
increase in number as the stone widens. The two groups are divided by a
central space marked by an oval design, which Gimbutas has identified as
a vulva. The hook or sickle is so similar in shape to a serpent and so
ubiquitous in Neolithic imagery that it may not be too far-fetched to read
it as an image of regeneration such as would appear naturally in a place of
burial. These hook-like images might then be understood both as emanations of energy emerging from the vulva of the goddess and also as the
dead brought back to life – serpents that have sloughed their skin, images
of ancestral spirits.

Ireland has some 500 megalithic tombs or temple-tombs, of which the
great passage grave of New Grange on the River Boyne is the most
fascinating (Fig. 67). Built over 5,000 years ago, about 3200 BC, no Neolithic temple illustrates more graphically the response of the people of
this time to the mysterious movements of the moon, stars and sun. It is
possible that all the events of their communal lives may have been aligned
in some way with the cyclic drama taking place in the sky.

Figure 67. The temple-tomb at New Grange, Ireland; *c.* 3200 BC.

Horizontally in front of the doorway lies a huge stone decorated with the triple spirals, lozenges and wave-like lines that are familiar from Old Europe (Fig. 68). The passage grave was constructed so that for a few days either side of the winter solstice – and for that time only – a ray of sunlight could penetrate through the narrow opening above the stone lintel of the doorway and flow along the inner passage until it illuminated the furthest recess at the far end of the corbelled chamber. There, it touched the rim of a carved white stone basin and the triple spirals carved on the face of a great stone slab behind with a soft radiance. For the rest of the year the interior of the temple was in darkness. The ritual enacted must have been one of the sun fertilizing the 'body' of the earth and so awakening her after her winter sleep to the renewed cycle of life. It may also have been a ritual for the regeneration of the dead, asleep like winter, for in all Neolithic imagery death is inseparable from regeneration.

Figure 68. The great stone in front of the entrance passage.

Some 900 stone circles, or henge sites, have survived, or at least are known to have existed in Britain, and many of these seem to have been built in a great surge of activity between 2600 and 1500 BC. Avebury was the greatest of all, although it was despoiled and destroyed in the Middle Ages and even in recent centuries by Christians intent on removing all traces of pagan rituals, or simply by village people using its stones to build their houses. The whole complex of Avebury is a testament to the Neolithic mythology of the Great Goddess: the adjacent long-barrow burial mound at West Kennet, whose entrance is marked by great horn-shaped stones, and the earthworks and stone alignments, with Silbury Hill nearby.

For us, as Professor Henri Frankfort observed, the phenomenal world is primarily an 'it', but for the people who built the megaliths, 'it' was a 'thou'.[52] Wandering among the remaining stones of Avebury, watching how the modern dowsers can still find the exact position of a missing stone with their rods, it seems undeniable that the power of this 'thou' drew devoted labour over many years from people apparently equipped only with flints, antler picks and shoulder-blade shovels. And it is not difficult to imagine the ritual dramas that took place during the year, the dances within the circles and along the processional ways, imitating perhaps the cosmic dance of the stars, rituals of birth in spring, the marriage ceremony in early summer and rituals of death and rebirth in autumn and mid-winter.

Silbury Hill in Wiltshire, with its flattened summit, soaring 130 feet (39.6 m) from the ground, was the earliest part of this temple complex after the West Kennet burial mound, and looks the same today as it did

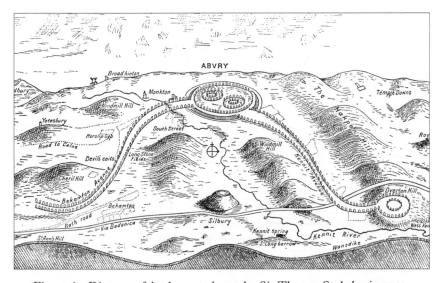

Figure 69. Diagram of Avebury as drawn by Sir Thomas Stukeley in 1740.

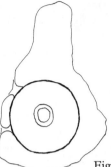

Figure 70. The image of Silbury Hill as the Goddess.

when it was constructed some 4,600 years ago. It probably took 500 men fifteen years to build it.[53] It is not a Bronze Age burial mound concealing a great king or chieftain, as was originally thought, but is fashioned from the earth in the image of the goddess seated in the position of giving birth, like so many Neolithic sculptures. In Michael Dames' vivid interpretation, the mound is the pregnant womb of the goddess, her 'body' being the water-filled ditch surrounding it (Fig. 70). The ditch was no hastily dug trench, but was, as he says, 'immaculately worked'.[54]

At the full moon in late July or early August – the moon that silvered the harvest soon to be reaped – the goddess came to life and began to play her part in a sacred drama created by the collaboration of the moon and the earth and the human imagination. The momentous annual birth of her child began when the moon was reflected in the still waters of the moat so that it appeared as the child's head emerging from her womb. As the moon moved upward in the sky, the lunar reflection touched her breast, as if setting in motion the suckling of her child. Then, as the moon rose still farther into the sky, the 'milk' was released and the moat became opaque with lunar light. Obviously, a clear night was needed for this drama to take place, but when it did, the moment must have been numinous to all who watched their hill give birth and knew that with the 'cutting' of the umbilical cord the signal was given to begin reaping the harvest – the child gestated in the mound of earth during the months of growth following the sowing of the seed.

Stonehenge is the most dramatic of the megalithic temples. It has inevitably attracted the most attention because it is the most complete of the temples that remain. But, in fact, there were several temples built at Stonehenge and what we see today are only the fragments of the last one, constructed about 1500 BC. The first temple was built about 2800 BC with what is thought to be a lunar orientation, but this was replaced by the second temple, about 2400 BC, which had a solar orientation.

The temples of New Grange, Avebury and Stonehenge and the great mound of Silbury reveal that the sky was a mystery of incalculable fascination to Neolithic, as to Palaeolithic, people. It inspired their myths, evoked their intelligence and regulated their festivals and rituals. Enough evidence exists to confirm that the society that built these temples lived within a universe imagined as a goddess and was passionately concerned with participating in her earthly and celestial rhythms. Professors Alexander Thom and Gerald Hawkins have suggested that the geometrical and astronomical knowledge of the Megalithic peoples may have been far greater than has so far been imagined. Living so close to earth and sky, they had every opportunity to observe the movements of the moon, sun and stars, and to erect stones in such a way as to help them to see and measure more precisely. There is no reason to suppose that the astronomical knowledge developed in the Palaeolithic era simply vanished in the Neolithic. It is much more likely that it was extended and deepened.

Malta

In the museum at Valetta in Malta there is a flat megalithic stone on which a sun, moon and stars have been carved with distinct lines drawn between them, suggesting that an interest in the heavens was shared by the temple builders of Malta.

Malta is the most southern part of the large area designated as Old Europe by Gimbutas, yet it must also be considered as a Megalithic culture because of its astounding stone temples. Malta has the earliest and most interesting complex of megalithic temples in the world (apart, perhaps, from Stonehenge and Avebury), but, strangely, few people are aware of their existence until they visit the island. Was Malta a mid-point between the eastern and western Mediterranean, and so a sacred centre of influence? The goddess figures of Malta (Fig. 71) have the same massive

Figure 71. (*Left*) Figure of the Goddess; *c.* 3000 BC. Malta.
Figure 72. (*Right*) Goddess; *c.* 6000 BC. Çatal Hüyük.

bodies as those of Çatal Hüyük (Fig. 72), as though one vision had informed both, yet no firm evidence has emerged to link Malta with Anatolia. It is known that people arrived in Malta from Sicily about 5000 BC, and the earliest figures of the goddess belong to this time. Fifteen hundred years after this, around 3500 BC, a further influx of people arrived from Sicily and it was these who are thought to have built the thirty temples, of which only a handful remain today. The great phase of temple building lasted only 1,000 years, from 3500 to 2500 BC, then abruptly ceased at the point when the temples of Avebury and Stonehenge appeared. The Maltese temples are formed of colossal blocks of stone and were once much higher than they now appear, for they were covered with beehive roofs made of corbelled blocks of stone, like those in Brittany and Ireland, and sometimes they had wooden or thatched roofs. Some of them were painted red inside, like the 'birthing room' of Çatal Hüyük.

The ground plans of the Maltese temples show how closely they followed the contours of the body of the goddess, as they did in other megalithic sites as far away as Ireland. Figure 73 shows there are two 'goddess' figures in the Ggantija temples on Gozo; could they be mother and daughter? Their giant stones enclose curved spaces, suggestive of the goddess's breasts and womb. A central passage opens out on either side into circular 'chapels' and ends in a circular chamber. These rounded chambers were once covered with a stone or wooden roof. Great stones carved in the shape of horns stood at their entrance, as they do at the entrance to West Kennet Barrow near Avebury. The strange-sounding names of the temples have come down to us from a past so remote that it has almost remained hidden: Hal Tarxien and the Hypogeum at Hal Saflien, which now stand in the midst of modern buildings; Hagar Qim and Mnajdra, which appear lost and dream-like on the south-west coast of the island; and the Ggantija temples on the adjacent island of Gozo – incredible for the sheer size of the stones that enclose them. These temples evolved from the rock-cut tomb and the tomb built above the ground.[55]

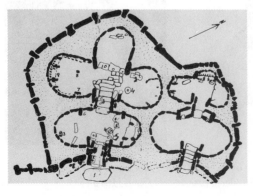

Figure 73. Ground plan of the Ggantija temples, Gozo.

Figure 74. Sleeping priestess or goddess; brown clay with red ochre traces,
c. 3800–3600 BC. The Hypogeum, Malta.

Statues with deformed limbs suggest that these temples were used for healing, among other rituals. A monumental figure of a goddess stands in her temple at Tarxien. A tiny female figure (Fig. 74) was found in a recess of perhaps the most mysterious temple of all, the Hypogeum. Is she the goddess dreaming the world into being, or a priestess undergoing a rite of incubation, or a pregnant woman receiving the spirit of her child into her care? The Hypogeum, laboriously hollowed out beneath the ground, gives the impression of a vertical labyrinth, for it has several levels. Here the bones of some 7,000 people were discovered, suggesting that it was a sacred burial site, but who was buried here over some 600 years – a priesthood or part of the general population? The Hypogeum has a strange atmosphere, which, like the cave, is unbearable to some people. Did the living come here to communicate with the ancestral dead in these womb-like burial chambers?

The temples of Hal Saflien and Hal Tarxien are decorated with the remains of paintings, with spiral designs, and with the animals that appear on the pottery of Old Europe. A design of spirals in red ochre was once traced on the stone ceiling of the Hypogeum together with a tendril pattern carved in stone. The magnificent spirals from the temple of Tarxien are related to those of Old Europe and long precede those of Crete and Mycenae. Fish, bulls and other animals adorn the walls of other temples. A sow suckling thirteen piglets is carefully drawn in stone. The pillar altar at Hagar Qim has a tree sculpted on each of its four sides, and is the earliest sculptural representation of what later came to be known as the 'Tree of Life' (Fig. 75).

Some 5,000–6,000 years before the age of Classical Greece, the people of the Neolithic developed the mythic imagery of the Palaeolithic era into a

Figure 75. (a) Pillar altar and (b) detail of the 'Tree of Life'.
Temple of Hagar Qim, Malta.

vital cultural matrix which became the foundation of the great cultures of
the Bronze Age. It is as if the goddess imagery first formulated in the
Palaeolithic era becomes a cultural unity in the Neolithic. What is amazing
is that the same ritual structures and images of the goddess are found as
far apart as Britain and Malta, Malta and Old Europe, Old Europe and
Anatolia, Anatolia and the immense territory between Syria and the Indus
Valley.[56] Gradually, our view of the prehistoric past is being extended to
include new evidence of civilizations established long before we thought it
possible for them to exist – civilizations that laid the foundations of
architecture, astronomy, mathematics, writing and cultural relations in
places believed to be too isolated and too primitive to be able to communicate with each other. The unity and coherence of the metaphysical ideas of
these ancient peoples become more accessible if we are aware of the
limitations of our own minds in approaching them. If earth and sky were
resacralized, it might be easier for us to rediscover the 'language' of the
goddess.

   The discovery of these centres of Neolithic civilization, some 6,000 to
8,000 years after they came into being,[57] must have implications for our
conception of the evolution of consciousness. We will at least have to give
up the idea of primitive tribes lurking in the darkness of prehistory
awaiting our civilized minds to enlighten them. We would also lose the
condescending terminology of 'idols', 'Venus figurines' and 'fertility

cults'. Eisler has commented that 'the Neolithic agrarian economy was the basis for the development of civilization leading over thousands of years into our time. And almost universally, those places where the first great breakthroughs in material and social technology were made had one feature in common: the worship of the Goddess.[58] Gimbutas brings this image to life at the conclusion of her book *The Language of the Goddess*:

> The Goddess in all her manifestations was the symbol of the unity of all life in Nature. Her power was in water and stone, in tomb and cave, in animals and birds, snakes and fish, hills, trees, and flowers. Hence the holistic and mythopoeic perception of the sacredness and mystery of all there is on Earth.[59]

Jung, striving to restore to the psyche this forgotten knowledge of the unity and sacrality of all life, knew that the Neolithic experience is not dead and gone, but still lives on in us as the archaic ground of the twentieth-century psyche. It is found, for instance, in the spontaneous world of the child, which is lost with the adaptation to a desacralized society. If the collective unconscious can be imagined, as Jung saw it, as 'the mighty deposit of ancestral experience accumulated over millions of years . . . to which each century adds an infinitesimally small amount of variation and differentiation',[60] then the millennia of the Neolithic must have registered, as a deep layer of the soul, a vision of life as a constant celebration of being. The next chapter will explore a culture on the threshold between the Neolithic and the Bronze Age, when this vision was still a living reality and had not yet become a memory and a dream.

3
CRETE: THE GODDESS OF LIFE, DEATH AND REGENERATION

There is a poem at the heart of things.

Wallace Stevens

'Out in the dark blue sea there lies a land called Crete, a rich and lovely land, washed by the waves on every side . . .'¹ Homer's words evoke a visionary island, shimmering emerald and gold in spring, violet and indigo in summer, surrounded by a furling strip of white sea-foam. Precipitous cliffs soar above deep gorges. Caves used as cult sites for over 4,000 years conceal the stalactites and stalagmites that once revealed the forms of goddesses and gods. The rare naturalism of Cretan art reflects a delight in the beauty and abundance of nature. It is a vision that recalls the vitality of the cave paintings of the Palaeolithic era, and, indeed, the cave and the

Figure 1. Goddess of the Double Axe; second millennium BC. Palace of Minos, Knossos, Crete.

palace-temple were the main focus of Cretan religious life, with the labyrinth as the image of an initiatory path leading to the central mystery of
Minoan ritual.

In Crete the great goddess was experienced as a flowing, dynamic
energy that could manifest in a swarm of bees, a dolphin's joyous leap, a
flight of birds, the coiling of serpents and sea creatures as well as in the
human gesture. Nikolaos Platon, the director of the museum in Herakleion
where most of the Minoan art can still be seen, captures the essence of the
culture when he says that 'a hymn to Nature as a Goddess seems to be
heard from everywhere, a hymn of joy and life.'[2] The goddess is sculpted
with serpents entwined around her body or rising from her arms, or she is
drawn holding the double axe in her hands. Sometimes she has doves or
poppies on her head. On seals she is engraved resting in the shape of a
bee, or standing upon her mountain with lions, or raising her arms as the
wings of the bird goddess, or sitting beneath the Tree of Life offering the
fruits to her priestesses. She was worshipped as the Great Mother of Life,
Death and Regeneration, the Goddess of the Animals, and the Mistress of
the Sea and of the Fruits of the Earth.

Once Crete was covered with great forests of oak, cypress and fir,
which today have left no trace. Unlike Sumeria and Egypt, Crete did not
have to import any wood to build its tiered and pillared palaces or the
cedar shafts of its ceremonial bronze axes. Water from the snows high in
the mountains flowed down continuously to the plains. There was never a
shortage of food or difficulty in growing it. Herds of oxen, sheep and
swine grazed the plains. Olive oil, honey, fish, fruit and every kind of
aromatic herb were exported in Cretan ships all over the Mediterranean.
Cretan palaces were spacious, often several storeys high, with many courtyards; they were exquisitely decorated with images of flowers, sea and
bird life, and imaginal animals, as well as the double-headed axe, the rose
and the lily. Bulls' horns formed a frieze to the temple-palaces, and
Cretan pottery was intricately painted with every aspect of natural life. A
gaiety pervades their art that is not found in any other contemporary
culture in the Near East. 'In Minoan art', the classical scholar Carl
Kerenyi writes, 'man is never without gesture.'[3]

H. A. Groenewegen-Frankfort, in her book *Arrest and Movement*,
captures the genius of Cretan art in the second millennium BC:

> Cretan art ignored the terrifying distance between the human and the trans-
> cendent which may tempt man to seek a refuge in abstraction and to create a
> form for the significant remote from space and time; it equally ignored the
> glory and futility of single human acts, time-bound, space-bound. In Crete
> artists did not give substance to the world of the dead through an abstract of
> the world of the living, nor did they immortalize proud deeds or state a
> humble claim for divine attention in the temples of the gods. Here and here
> alone (in contrast to Egypt and the Near East) the human bid for time-
> lessness was disregarded in the most complete acceptance of the grace of life

the world has ever known. For life means movement and the beauty of movement was woven into the intricate web of living forms which we call 'scenes of nature'; was revealed in human bodies acting their serious games, inspired by a transcendent presence, acting in freedom and restraint, unpurposeful as cyclic time itself.[4]

Crete used to be simply a land of legend in the Greek imagination of its past: the sacred place of origin, where many of its own goddesses and gods were born. Homer, who wrote in the eighth century BC, was once the only source for these fabulous beginnings, and no one could be certain that his poetic vision was also historically true.

How exciting, then, when, in the first quarter of this century, the archaeologist Sir Arthur Evans lifted the layers of over four millennia of history and laid bare a civilization apparently as magical as Homer had intimated. Starting with the palace at Knossos, the focus of this culture, the excavations revealed five great palace complexes whose life was broken off abruptly in 1450 BC by the second and the greater of two earthquakes; for exactly beneath these ruins were the ruins of other palaces, which had been constructed about 2000 BC and destroyed by an earthquake in 1700 BC. And mixed in with the rubble of stones and earth of both these levels fragments of painted pots appeared, brightly coloured mosaics, golden seals with dancing figures, necklaces of bees and butterflies, urns decorated with flying dolphins, serpents and spiralling flowers, tiny statues of bulls, large bulls' horns, and statues of goddesses, which, pieced together, composed a culture of joyousness, grace and elegance centred for hundreds of years around the worship of a great goddess.

Evans called the culture 'Minoan' after the King Minos of whom Homer speaks, and distinguished three main periods within the culture: Early Minoan, or 'Pre-palatial', up to about 2000 BC; Middle Minoan – 'Early Palatial' – from 2000 to 1600 BC; and Late Minoan – 'High Palatial' – from 1600 to 1150 BC. In the Middle Minoan period the Minoans used a hieroglyphic and later a linear script (called Linear A), which has not yet been deciphered. The civilization reached its peak in the first phase of the Late Minoan period, between 1600 and 1450 BC, when relations were established with the Mycenaeans – the Indo-European or Aryan people who built Mycenae in mainland Greece. They brought with them a script known as Linear B, an early form of Greek, which was decoded only in 1953, revealing the names of just those goddesses and gods that Classical Greek myth had always placed there: 'To the Dictaean Zeus, oil'; 'To the Lady of the Labyrinth, a jar of honey'; 'To the mistress of At(h)ana . . .'. The Mycenaeans seem to have gone back and forth between Crete and Mycenae, gradually absorbing and adopting Minoan culture as their own, before finally settling there after 1450 BC, when violent earthquakes and tidal waves coming from the volcanic eruption on the island of Thera to the north shook all the palaces to the ground. The arrival of another wave of invaders, the Dorians, in 1150 BC brought this civilization to an end.

Figure 2. (*Left*) Neolithic Snake Goddess; terracotta, *c.* 4500 BC, height
5$\frac{7}{10}$ in. (14.5 cm). Kato Ierapetra, Crete.
Figure 3. (*Right*) Minoan Goddess with snakes; gold and ivory,
c. 1600–1500 BC, height 6$\frac{1}{2}$in. (16.5 cm). Knossos, Crete.

Unlike many surrounding cultures the island of Crete was not invaded
in the 1,500 years from 3000 to 1500 BC, and so it offers a unique insight
into how a Neolithic society evolved without disruption into a Bronze
Age one while still retaining its belief in the unity of life. Although,
reckoning by dates, Minoan society is chronologically within the province
of the Bronze Age (3500–1250 BC) and was flourishing at the same time as
the Bronze Age cultures of Mesopotamia and Egypt, we place it here
directly after the Neolithic because its characteristic temper and tone
seem closer in feeling to the spontaneity and peacefulness of the Neolithic
vision. Also because, ultimately, Crete, like the Neolithic, has the mute-
ness of a culture whose writing has not been deciphered, so that its story
has to be told through the image alone.

As Gimbutas has shown, Crete was the direct inheritor of the Neolithic
culture of Old Europe.[5] Immigrants from south-western Anatolia also
arrived on the shores of Crete, possibly as early as the sixth millennium
BC;[6] and from an early time Minoans were trading with Egypt, which was
only a few hundred miles away to the south. Crete lay at the centre of the
sea routes that connected it with all the other great cultures: to the north,
with Old Europe; to the east, with Anatolia and Syria, and Sumeria
beyond; to the south, with Egypt; and further to the west, with the
islands of Malta and Sicily. Spirals of decoration in Maltese and Minoan
design, for instance, are virtually identical.[7]

But while Crete had many towns, it did not have the enormous cities of
Sumeria and Egypt, and Minoan religion was far more intimately involved
with natural life than that of these two cultures. The goddess flanked by

Figure 4. Griffins in the throne room of the Palace of Minos; *c.* 1450 BC. Knossos, Crete.

lions, the griffins painted on the walls of the throne room at Knossos (Fig. 4), the pillared shrines, bulls' horns and the serpents – all proclaim the signature of the older Neolithic Mother Goddess. The griffin, for instance, a composite image of bird, lion and snake, embodies the three dimensions of sky, earth and waters beneath the earth, which, in Neolithic Old Europe, were three aspects of the Great Goddess.

Crete was the meeting place for many cultures, and many mythic images from these earlier cultures reappear later in Crete, showing the persistence of symbolic forms throughout 3,000 years. For example, the bulls' horns of consecration from seventh-millennium-BC Çatal Hüyük in Anatolia, fifth-millennium-BC Vinca in Old Europe and second-millennium-BC Knossos in Crete in Figure 5 are almost indistinguishable.

In the six volumes of his great work *The Palace of Minos*, Evans concluded that the goddess images that he found everywhere represented 'the same Great Mother with her Child or Consort whose worship under various names and titles extended over a large part of Asia Minor and the Syrian regions beyond'.[8] Although originally disputed,[9] Evans' claim has been irrefutably confirmed by the ever-increasing evidence of the kind offered above, where similar complexes of images have been found in

Figure 5. Horns of Consecration. (a) Çatal Hüyük, Anatolia, seventh millennium BC. (b) Vinca, Old Europe, fifth millennium BC. (c) Knossos, second millennium BC.

Figure 6. (*Left*) Minoan Snake Goddess; faience, *c.* 1600 BC, height 13⅓ in.
(34 cm). Knossos, Crete.
Figure 7. (*Right*) Minoan Snake Goddess; faience, *c.* 1600 BC.
Knossos, Crete.

places as far apart as Mesopotamia, Egypt, north-western India, Old
Europe and Greece.

The Old European Serpent Goddess reappears in Crete with a new
distinctness that allows her story to continue to unfold. Only 13⅓ inches
(34 cm) tall and dating from 1600 BC, the image of the goddess in Figure
6 was found in a stone-lined pit in the underground treasury of the
central sanctuary at Knossos, together with the one in Figure 7. Is she a
priestess or a goddess? Although the goddess was often identified with the
priestess who represented her, both assuming the same posture,[10] here the
presence of so many snakes suggests that she is a goddess. She holds the
head of a snake in her right hand and its tail in her left hand, its body
wrapped around her shoulders and back. Two other snakes entwine themselves around her waist and coil up her arms, one of them winding
spirally around her head-dress and appearing above it, like the uraeus on
the head-dress of Egyptian goddesses and gods. The open bodice with the
bared breasts is eloquent of the gift of nurture, while the caduceus-like
image of intertwined snakes on the belly suggests that the goddess whose
womb gives forth and takes back life is experienced as a unity.

The goddess in Figure 7 is holding a snake high in each hand with all the
ritualized gesture of divine statement. The trance-like, almost mask-like,
expression of these two goddesses composes a meditation upon this theme
of regeneration. In contrast to the Neolithic snake goddesses the sharp
focus of this figure is designed to convey an explicit meaning. Are these the
snakes of life and death, which belong to her as manifestations of her power
to give and withdraw life? The lion cub that sits tamely on her head is also
guardian, as a full-grown lion, to the Goddess of the Animals in Anatolia,

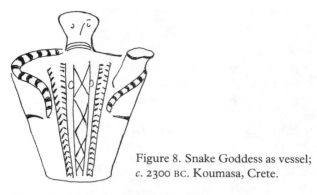

Figure 8. Snake Goddess as vessel;
c. 2300 BC. Koumasa, Crete.

Sumeria and Egypt. The net pattern on her skirt, which gathers significance from its Palaeolithic and Neolithic ancestry, suggests she is the weaver of the web of life, which is perpetually woven from her womb. Her skirt has seven layers, the number of the days of the moon's four quarters, which divide into two the waxing and waning halves of the cycle, like the Neolithic cross inside the circle. Although seven was also the number of the visible 'planets', this is probably a lunar notation of series and measure, so that sitting in the lap of the goddess, as the overlapping panel of her gown invites, would be to experience time supported by eternity, and eternity clothed in time. For the goddess, by virtue of holding the two snakes, is herself beyond their opposition; or rather, she is the one who contains the two poles of dualism and so prevents them falling apart into the kind of opposition that our modern consciousness assumes as inevitable. Now we talk of the goal of reconciling or transcending opposites – whether of life and death, time and eternity, or unity and multiplicity – but these images ask us to contemplate the possibility of a different kind of reality: one in which (to keep the language of the image) the two are, as it were, small in relation to the One, who holds them both in the palm of the hand.

The snake goddess sometimes takes the form of a vessel, like the one in Figure 8, found at Koumasa just outside the tombs, suggesting that she was designed to pour libations for the dead. Serpents were a constant motif in Minoan art, twining around pots, urns and vases, combining with the fluid forms of sea creatures, and even creating the circular form of the disc found at the palace of Phaestos.

THE GODDESS OF THE DOUBLE AXE

Double images poised in such precise balance as to render an experience not of duality but of unity are the hallmark of Minoan art, for the same motif is found not only in two snakes unified in the figure of the goddess, but also in the double-headed axe emerging from its great shaft and in the curving horns of the bull. The double axe is a very ancient symbol, and has been found in the Palaeolithic cave of Niaux in south-western France

Figure 9. Vase with double axes; *c.* 1400 BC.
Knossos, Crete.

and in the Neolithic Tell Halaf culture in Iraq.[11] In Crete the great bronze double-headed axes stood on shafts some 6½ feet (2 m) high on either side of the altars of the goddess, where priestesses, celebrating her rites, held them in their hands or upon their heads. They also marked the entrance to her sanctuaries just as in Sumeria the stylized twin reed pillars marked the entrance to the temple of the goddess Inanna. The vase with the double axes in Figure 9 is patterned with roses, and others are decorated with lilies, both flowers that call forth the goddess, in the way that in Christian art (to anticipate) they evoke the presence of the Virgin Mary.

The two double axes held in the goddess's hands (Figs. 1, 10a) may be understood, like the serpents, as symbolizing her rulership over the related domains of life and death. The sacred axe was the ritual instrument that sacrificed the bull, the cult animal who embodied the regenerative power of the goddess. As suggested in Chapter 2, the sacrifice of the male animal who became the focus of fertility was believed to renew the life-cycle, as was the cutting down of the tree, which was probably an annual ceremony.

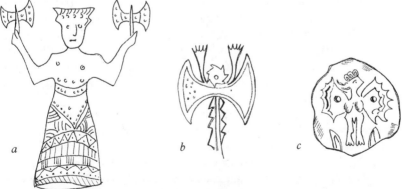

Figure 10. (a) Goddess of the Double Axe; *c.* 1500 BC. Knossos, Crete.
(b) Goddess with butterfly wings; seal impression, *c.* 1700 BC. Zakro.
(c) Goddess with butterfly wings in the shape of a double axe;
c. 1600 BC. Mochlas.

Figure 11. Goddess of the
Double Axe beside the Tree
of Life; Mycenaean seal,
c. 1500 BC.

In Crete (as in Egypt) the tree was worshipped as the image of the
goddess herself, and a special rite and a sacred axe were required when a
tree was cut down.[12] Since the axe never appears in Crete held by a man
or a male priest, it does not seem to carry the later Aryan association of
the axe with the god of thunder and the battle-cry.

Gimbutas suggests that the double blades of the axe evolved from the
Neolithic butterfly, and that the double double-axe in particular precisely
imitates the double wings of the butterfly (Fig. 10b, c). The butterfly is
still in many lands an image of the soul, and in Greek the word for
butterfly and the soul were the same – *psyche*. Both the axe and the
butterfly, Gimbutas adds, are images of the goddess.[13]

Although the seal in Figure 11 is Mycenaean in contrast to the Minoan
images in Figure 10, the similarity of image and feeling shows how difficult it is to separate the two cultures. It is clear, as J. V. Luce suggests,
that Mycenaean culture gradually absorbed the genius of Minoan culture,
probably by Minoan princesses marrying into the houses of Mycenaean
lords, Minoan architects designing the mainland palaces and Minoan
painters adorning them with frescoes. He adds that 'Greek first became a
written language in the hands of Minoan scribes.'[14] Artistically, it seems
as if, for the most part, Mycenaean art elaborated the Minoan vision by
giving it a more complex narrative form, as here, where the meaning
unfolds dramatically.

The focus of this seal ring is the double axe of life-and-death in the
centre, which both separates and unites the scenes on either side of the
blades. On the left is a scene representing the sacrificial, death-bringing
aspect of the goddess, showing six animal heads and above them a tiny
figure covered by a Mycenaean warrior's shield, holding a sceptre or staff
and pointing at the severed heads. On the right is a counterbalancing
scene embodying the life-giving aspect of the goddess, showing a plentiful
fruit tree, perhaps a mulberry, with the figure of a child or young girl
apparently rising from the earth, about to pick the fruit.

The goddess is seated beneath the Tree of Life, which, as in Mesopotamia and Egypt, signifies her nurturing power as food-giver, emphasized by her left hand offering her breast. She welcomes two priestesses with snake-like head-dresses similar to her own, holding out to them in her hand three poppy pods full of seeds, the fruit of transformation. Between them, below the outstretched arm of the priestess, a small female figure seems to have come up from the earth, holding in one hand a minute double-headed axe and in the other a flowering branch. Below her are new shoots of vegetation. She may be the daughter of the goddess, emerging from the earth as the new life born from death in the principle of continuous renewal. The handle of the large double-headed axe leads directly down to this tiny axe, perhaps relating the daily life to the all-embracing symbolic life, and this particular rebirth after the death of winter to the life-cycle of regeneration. Campbell comments that this small figure represents the mid-point of balance between the small descending figure with the shield and the small ascending one picking fruit.[15] The double-headed axe of life-and-death holds the central meaning of the scene, in which the priestesses come towards the goddess from the side of death while the goddess is seated on the side of life, healing this division through her presence. The joyful tone of the picture suggests that here is an image of rebirth after the sacrifice of death, as would also be intimated through the placing of the vibrant sun beside the waning moon.

Returning to the image of the 'daughter', or the young goddess, rising up from the earth, there is another seal that suggests that the myth of spring as the return of the goddess originated in Crete (Fig. 12). Here, the goddess is coming up from the earth between two sprouting shoots of vegetation, clasping those same poppy pods that, as seated goddess amid the full bloom of the tree, she also holds in her hands in Figure 11.

This central myth is familiar from Classical Greece as the tale of Persephone, daughter of Demeter, the Corn Goddess, who lives for the winter

Figure 12. (*Left*) Goddess rising from the earth; gold bead seal, *c.* 1500 BC. Thisbe, Boeotia.
Figure 13. (*Right*) *The Birth of Erichthonius*; Gaia, Goddess of Earth, rising from below with child, vase painting, *c.* fifth century BC.

months in the underworld and returns to be with her mother in spring
and summer. The same theme is found in pictures of Aphrodite rising
from the waves between two attendants, also entitled 'the return of the
maiden', and of Gaia, Goddess of Earth, rising from beneath the earth. In
Figure 13 the pictorial scene suggests that (whatever the later Classical
story around it) Gaia is offering to the upper world the child who symbolizes the new life of vegetation born below. The Mycenaean fresco of a
goddess or priestess displaying two sheaves of corn in her hands as a
celebration, seen in Figure 14, anticipates almost exactly the sculpture of
Demeter, Goddess of the Harvest, who in Roman times was named Ceres,
in Figure 15.

It is most likely that the myth of Demeter and Persephone itself originated
in Crete, for, as well as the stories that place Demeter in Crete, there are two
images in the museum at Herakleion from *c.* 1800 BC that suggest the motif
of going down and coming up – the *kathodos* and *anodos* – rites commemorated in the Mysteries at Eleusis. In the first image (Fig. 16) two female
figures appear, from the drooping gesture of their arms, to be mourning a
third figure between them apparently about to pick a narcissus (as did
Persephone), and the direction of the picture is downwards into the earth.
In a second image (Fig. 17) the same three figures are gesturing upwards

Figure 14. Seated goddess or priestess holding sheaves of wheat or red
barley; Mycenaean fresco, thirteenth century BC.

Figure 15. Demeter (Ceres), Goddess of the Harvest, holding wheat; Hellenic, terracotta relief, third century BC. Magna Graecia.

together as in a celebration, the central one holding up a flower in each hand, and the scene has the feeling of rising movement, such as a return from below the earth. The scene may also relate to a similar configuration of three female figures and spring flowers on two frescoes found at Akrotiri in Thera. In the upper fresco crocuses are being offered to a goddess; in the lower fresco a female figure sitting in a field of flowers directly before a flower in blossom – possibly a narcissus – is wounded in the foot and contemplates the blood dripping on to the earth, as though in a spring ritual of regeneration.

Figure 16. (*Left*) *Descent of the Goddess*; Minoan painting, *c.* 1800 BC.
Figure 17. (*Right*) *Return of the Goddess*; Minoan painting, *c.* 1800 BC.

THE BEE GODDESS

Bee and butterfly belong together as images of the Great Goddess of Regeneration. It was a very ancient belief that bees arose out of the dead carcass of a bull, and the association of bee and bull is made as early as the Neolithic in the image of the bee goddess incised on the head of a bull (see Chapter 2, Fig. 35). In the third century AD the Greek traveller Porphyry talks of these later goddesses of Greece in the same imagery:

> The ancients gave the name of *Melissae* ('bees') to the priestesses of Demeter who were initiates of the chthonian goddess; the name *Melitodes* to Kore herself: the moon (Artemis) too, whose province it was to bring to the birth, they called Melissa, because the moon being a bull and its ascension the bull, bees are begotten of bulls. And souls that pass to the earth are bull-begotten.[16]

Here, bee, bull and moon are united in the symbolism of renewal, and in Crete also the bee signified the life that comes from death, as did the scarab in Egypt. Probably for this reason, the gold ring seal in Figure 18 was placed in a tomb. Here the bee goddess, the figure in the centre descending to earth among snakes and lilies, is being worshipped by her priestesses, who, characteristically, take the same form as she does, all raising their 'hands' in the typical gesture of epiphany. Honey was used to embalm and preserve the bodies of the dead, and some of the great jars, or *pithoi*, found at Knossos were used to store honey. The importance of bee-keeping to the Minoans is documented in the Linear A hieroglyphs, where there are already drawings of actual beehives, testifying to a long history probably going back to the Neolithic era. The onyx gem from Knossos (Fig. 19) shows the bee goddess bearing upon her head the bull's

Figure 18. (*Left*) Epiphany scene showing Bee Goddess, priestesses and child in a field of lilies; gold seal ring, *c.* 1450 BC. From a tomb at Isopata, near Knossos.

Figure 19. (*Centre*) Bee Goddess with winged dogs; onyx gem, *c.* 1500 BC. Knossos, Crete.

Figure 20. (*Right*) Goddess in the shape of a bee; yellow steatite bead seal, *c.* 2400–2200 BC.

horns with the double axe inside their curve. The dogs – later the dogs of the underworld belonging to Hecate and Artemis – are winged and flying so close to the goddess that their wings, at first glance, appear as hers. The goddess in the shape of a bee in Figure 20 is engraved on a yellow steatite seal that has three sides, and the other sides show the head and foreparts of two dogs also. The position of the figure recalls the birth-giving goddess in Çatal Hüyük, who had apparently given birth to three bulls (see Chapter 2, Fig. 50).

Honey also played a central part in the New Year rituals of the Minoans. The Cretan New Year began at the summer solstice, when the heat was at its greatest, and 20 July was the day when the great star Sirius rose in conjunction with the sun, as it did also in Sumeria and Egypt. In these two other countries Sirius was explicitly the star of the goddess (Inanna in Sumeria, and Isis in Egypt), and Minoan temple-palaces in Crete were orientated to this star. The rising of Sirius ended a forty-day ritual during which honey was gathered from the hives of the bees in the darkness of the caves and the woods. The honey was then fermented into mead and drunk as an intoxicating liquor, accompanying the ecstatic rites that may have celebrated the return of the daughter of the goddess as the beginning of the new year – as, perhaps, in the seal of the double axe in Figure 11. All these rites are present in the Classical Greek myths of Dionysos, himself originating in Crete and called the Bull God. A bull was sacrificed with the rising of the star Sirius, and the bees were seen as the resurrected form of the dead bull and also as the souls of the dead. Kerenyi comments that this festival for the rising of Sirius that initiated the New Year was thereby 'raised to the level of a myth of *zoe* (indestructible life): the awakening of bees from a dead animal'.[17] (The important Greek term *zoe* will be discussed in Chapter 4.)

This intense drama of epiphany suggests that, as well as these connotations, the humming of the bee was actually heard as the 'voice' of the goddess, the 'sound' of creation. Virgil, for instance, describing the noise of howling and clashing made to attract swarming bees, says: 'They clash the cymbals of the Great-Mother.'[18] The tombs at Mycenae were shaped as beehives, as was the omphalos at Delphi in Classical Greece, where Apollo ruled with his chief oracular priestess, the Pythia, who was called the Delphic Bee. In the Greek Homeric 'Hymn to Hermes', written down in the eighth century BC, the god Apollo speaks of three female seers as three bees or bee-maidens, who, like himself, practised divination:

> There are some Fates,
> sisters born, maidens,
> three of them, adorned with swift wings.
> Their heads are sprinkled over
> with white barley meal,
> and they make their homes
> under the cliffs of Parnassus.

Figure 21. (*Left*) Lion genii with bee-skin coverings, holding jugs (with honey?) over a plant growing from bull's horns; Mycenaean lentoid gem, *c.* 1500 BC. Vapheio.

Figure 22. (*Right*) Bee Goddess; gold plaque, *c.* 800–700 BC. Kameiros, Rhodes.

> They taught divination far off from me,
> the art I used to practise
> around my cattle while still a boy.[19]

These holy bee-maidens, with their gift of prophecy, were to be Apollo's gift to Hermes, the god who alone could lead the souls of the dead out of life and sometimes back again. The etymology of the word 'fate' in Greek offers a fascinating example of how the genius of the Minoan vision entered the Greek language, often invisibly, as well as informing its stories of goddesses and gods. The Greek word for 'fate', 'death' and 'goddess of death' is *e ker* (feminine); the word for 'heart' and 'breast' is *to ker* (neuter); while the word for 'honeycomb' is *to kerion* (neuter). The common root *ker* links the ideas of the honeycomb, goddess, death, fate and the human heart, a nexus of meanings that is illumined if we know that the goddess was once imagined as a bee.

THE GODDESS OF THE SACRED KNOT

A knot of cloth, corn or hair hung at the entrance to shrines or pinned up on the ceremonial occasions of bull vaulting was a sign of the presence of the goddess, and came to stand for the goddess herself. Figure 23 shows a knot similar to the ones found on gems, which indicates that it had a ritual status. The resemblance to the curved reed bundle that was the image of the goddess Inanna in Sumeria (Fig. 24) is remarkable;[20] so also

Figure 23. (*Left*) Sacred knot; *c.* 1500 BC. Knossos, Crete.
Figure 24. (*Centre*) Reed bundle as 'Knot' of Inanna; *c.* 3000 BC. Sumerian.
Figure 25. (*Right*) Minoan priestess with sacred knot; fresco, *c.* 1500 BC.
Knossos, Crete.

is the resemblance to the knotted headband or necklace of the Egyptian goddesses Hathor and Isis, called the *menat*. In the Minoan fresco in Figure 25 the priestess carries the knot at the nape of her neck, probably indicating her role in the rites of the goddess, together with other women, while the priest's function may have been reserved for the sacrifice of the bull (see p. 140). If the Minoans followed the practice of contemporary Near Eastern cultures, the queens and princesses of Crete would have been high priestesses, and would themselves have worn the sacred knot of the goddess as a sign of their role. It is not inconceivable that what the Greeks called 'Ariadne's thread' referred to the priestess's knot, which was unravelled at various ceremonies with a particular ritual meaning.

The beauty and elegance of Minoan women is evident in the frescoes of Knossos, and is reiterated in the seals of the goddess, who, like her priestesses, is drawn wearing the bare-breasted and embroidered jackets, and the many-tiered, flowered and flounced skirts that display the joyousness and assurance of this unselfconscious culture. As Platon observes, women participated actively in every sphere of Minoan society,[21] and there is no evidence of dominance of either sex by the other. In fact, where men and women appear together in Minoan art, it is as partners in relationship, most strikingly in the bull-vaulting seals and frescoes, where they entrust their lives to each other. In religious ceremony, though, the priestess presided on behalf of the goddess.

Figure 26. (a, b) Minoan pots showing figure with double axe and the sacred knot. (c) Egyptian pot with figure in shape of an *ankh*. (d, e) Minoan seals showing sacred knot. (f) Minoan sacred knot similar to Egyptian *ankh*.

In the various Minoan signet rings and images in Figure 26 the ritual status of the sacred knot is unmistakable. When the knot is drawn on its own, it can often look very like the butterfly whose wings are stylized to represent the double axe. It may have then been understood as a composite symbol, holding as one idea the images of the knot, the double axe and the butterfly, and evoking as well the figure of the goddess herself, where the wing–axes become arms and the vertical knot the body. In Egypt the symbol of eternal life – called the *ankh* – which was held by the goddesses and gods as a sign of their divinity, bears a similar shape to the knot, and also sometimes appears as a human figure holding two staffs in the 'hands', as in the painted vase in Figure 26c.

THE GODDESS OF THE ANIMALS

The Goddess of the Animals, sometimes called the Lady of the Beasts, is a familiar figure from the art of Old Europe and Çatal Hüyük, and farther back, perhaps, she was Goddess of the Hunt in the Palaeolithic era. In Crete the animal world – both the wild and the tamed – was sacred to the goddess. In Figure 27, sceptre in her hand, the goddess stands upon her mountain, the mountain of the world, as though she had just emerged

Figure 27. (*Left*) Goddess on mountain with lions and worshipper; seal,
c. 1500 BC. Knossos, Crete.
Figure 28. (*Right*) Gate of Mycenae with lions flanking central pillar;
c. 1500 BC.

from it, while behind her is a large shrine of bulls' horns, stacked one on top of the other. Two lions rise upwards on either side of her as her guardians, whose posture closely resembles the lions flanking the pillared Gate of Mycenae (Fig. 28).

In this seal a male figure stands facing the goddess in the attitude of adoration while she holds out her staff towards him, acknowledging him. He appears to be saluting, or shading his eyes to shield him from the numinosity of her presence (perhaps the *ritual* origin of the salute?). He may be a devotee or, more likely, the young god, for numerous small statues of young male figures in this posture have been found in caves and tombs, suggesting some ritual relation to the goddess. The lion as an image of the goddess of death and regeneration is found on its own in the ring seal of the after-life (Fig. 35).

THE BIRD GODDESS

The Neolithic Bird Goddess re-emerges in Crete as the Minoan and Mycenaean bird goddesses, whose wings have become upraised arms and whose beaked head has become a human face. This imagery was in turn inherited by the goddesses of Classical Greece, in particular Athena, whose association with the owl, snake, olive tree and shield point to her descent from the bird, snake, tree and shield forms of the Minoan great goddess. Many times in the *Odyssey* Athena manifests as a bird and is recognized as the goddess in six different bird forms, just as it would have happened in Minoan Crete: 'Thus she spoke and Athene of the flashing

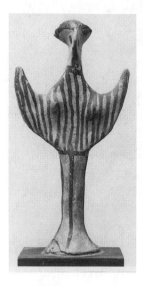

Figure 29. (*Left*) Bird Goddess; *c*. 1400–1200 BC. Tiryns, near Mycenae.
Figure 30. (*Centre*) Goddess with crown of doves and bull's horns; *c*. 1400–
1200 BC. Knossos.
Figure 31. (*Right*) Goddess with poppy crown; *c*. 1400 BC. Knossos, Crete.

eyes disappeared, flying up into the air, like a bird.'[22] Later on, 'she herself darted up and perched on the smoky roof-beam of the hall, in the actual form of a swallow.'[23]

The bird, since Palaeolithic times the messenger of the vast incomprehensible distance and so of the whole invisible world, was taken by the Minoans, as by many another culture, to constitute the supreme image of epiphany. ('Epiphany' in Greek means literally the 'showing forth' of the sacred, which is the presence of the divine recognized as *immanent* in creation.)

The raised wings of the Mycenaean bird goddess from Tiryns (Fig. 29) are still those of a bird, but they become the gesture of epiphany for any manifestation of the deity. The same basic gesture of greeting defines the upraised arms of the goddess who carries two doves on her horned crown (Fig. 30), the goddess with the crown of poppy pods (Fig. 31) and the goddess in the funerary shrine (Fig. 32e). The two doves resting on either side of the horns of consecration make a parallel with the upraised arms. The dove was a central image of the goddess throughout Minoan culture, and its clay form has been found in many caves as a votive offering. The seed pod of the poppy is often held in the hands of the goddess or her priestess, as in Figure 11. The poppy was grown in great quantities in Crete and was undoubtedly used in the shrines and temples of the goddess to elicit visionary experience, later re-emerging in the cult of Demeter, which was taken from Crete to Eleusis.[24]

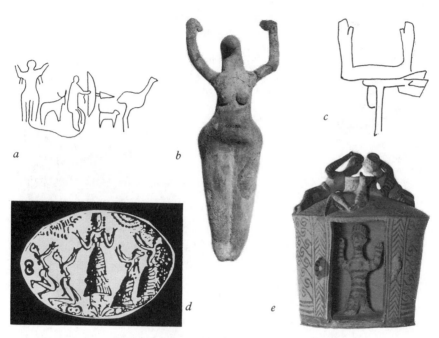

Figure 32. Gestures of epiphany from the Palaeolithic era to Bronze Age
Crete. (a) Palaeolithic scene. (b) Neolithic Egyptian figure with raised arms;
c. 4000–3500 BC. (c) Hieroglyph of the Egyptian *Ka*. (d) Mycenaean seal
with goddess and worshippers; *c*. 1500 BC. (e) Minoan funerary shrine with
figure inside making gesture of epiphany; 1100–1000 BC.

The tradition of the symbolic gesture of the raised arms originates in
the Palaeolithic, is continued in the Neolithic and extends to Bronze Age
Egypt (Fig. 32). In Egypt the gesture of the raised arms was the hieroglyph
for the *Ka*, the Egyptian image of a person's greater soul, who came to
meet the individual soul (the *Ba*) after death. The image of the *Ka* was
the bennu bird or the phoenix, and was sometimes called the mother:
'Behold I am behind thee, I am thy temple, thy mother, forever and
forever.'[25] A Neolithic Egyptian figure dating to 3500 BC (Fig. 32b) takes
the same attitude as the later hieroglyph (Fig. 32c). The figure inside the
Minoan shrine, perhaps the deceased man or woman, makes the same
gesture as those on the seal in Figure 32d.

There is no doubt that the Minoans 'saw' their goddess, just as in the
Christian tradition people have 'seen' the Virgin Mary. They saw her on
the mountain tops, deep in the labyrinthine caves, in a grove of trees,
sailing her crescent boat or riding a bull on the waves of the sea. They
may have worshipped her with the same gesture as the young male figure
in Figure 27, labouring with their offerings up the steep slopes to her
sanctuaries on the mountain peaks, seeking her in caves or groves of oak

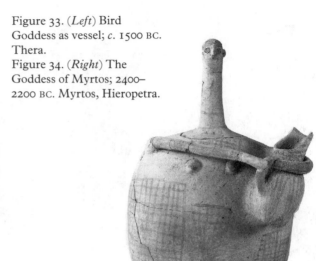

Figure 33. (*Left*) Bird
Goddess as vessel; *c.* 1500 BC.
Thera.
Figure 34. (*Right*) The
Goddess of Myrtos; 2400–
2200 BC. Myrtos, Hieropetra.

and olive. They may have glimpsed her form in the brilliantly clear light
of spring and autumn when strange reflections were thrown up from the
valleys on to the hills. Kerenyi comments that accounts of ancient religions
give too little emphasis to the visionary faculty in human nature, which
has become more and more rare with the passage of the centuries until
now it is regarded as an anomaly rather than the norm: 'Vision and myth,
epiphany and mythology, influenced and engendered one another and
gave rise to cult images. But in man's relation to the gods, epiphany has a
priority grounded in the immediacy of every true vision.'[26]

The ritual nature of what we might call everyday life can be seen in the
kind of sacred implements that served the ordinary purposes of living.
The vessel in Figure 33, for example, is shaped in the image of the
with human breasts and the beaked head of a bird. The beaked spout with
the eye, the necklace decoration at the 'neck' of the vase, and the raised
breasts outlined with dots transform the simple act of pouring water into
an offering of milk from the nourishing body of the mother goddess –
water transformed into the water of life. The sacredness of the vessel, or
the vessel as the containing body of the goddess, is shown in the Pre-
palatial sculpture in Figure 34 of the goddess and her 'child', the smaller
vessel, whose spout is the only opening into the body of the goddess. The
pattern of the net is drawn on the body, recalling the net on the dress of
the snake goddess (Fig. 6).

THE GODDESS OF REGENERATION

Art in Crete cannot be separated from ritual, nor ritual from the unseen dimension that informs all life. In the engraved scene on the beautiful 'Ring of Nestor' in Figure 35, found by a peasant in a beehive tomb at Pylos in the Peloponnese, many of the images of the great goddess so far found in separation combine to create a fascinating drama of transformation: the Tree of Life, the lion, the butterfly, the bird, the dog and the griffin. This gold ring is one of the most eloquent images of the after-life as the Minoans and early Mycenaeans must have imagined it.

The seal is structured by the gnarled and knotted Tree of Life, which grows out of a mound covered in fresh shoots in the centre, with its two lateral branches dividing the scene into the underworld below and the after-life above. Entering the scene from the lower left, a bird-headed priestess bars the way of entry to an intruder, her raised arms suggesting that here are mystery rites that may not be profaned by the uninitiated. A young couple holding hands are beckoned towards the other side of the tree trunk by another bird-headed priestess. Facing the other way, two more bird-headed figures pay homage with the raised arms of the gesture of epiphany to a griffin seated on a throne in front of the goddess who stands apart behind it. Her right arm points downwards to the griffin and her left arm upwards to the scene above, as though she is ultimately the one with the power of movement from the underworld to the after-life.

The scene beneath the main branches recalls the Egyptian Halls of Judgement, where a similar procession leads the dead person into the presence of the god Osiris. In the Egyptian ceremony the god Thoth – who has the head of a long-beaked bird, the ibis – records the result of the

Figure 35. The Tree of Eternal Life on the Mycenaean gold 'Ring of Nestor'; *c.* 1500 BC.

judgement in which the heart of the dead person is weighed against the feather of truth, the image of the goddess Maat. Here, interestingly, the attendants approaching the griffin seated on the throne of judgement also have bird heads. Behind the griffin stands the goddess, in the way the goddess Isis often stands behind the seated Osiris.

The dog at the root of the tree, looking remarkably like a dachshund, recalls firstly the Neolithic dog guarding the Tree of Life from Old Europe, then the jackal Anubis, who in Egypt guides the souls of the dead, and anticipates the dog Cerberus, who in Greek mythology belongs to Hecate, goddess of the underworld. Within the roots of the tree are tiny oblong forms that suggest the shoots of plants, images of the new life in preparation. If, following the gesture of the goddess, we assume that the dead couple have satisfied the court of judgement represented by the sphinx-like griffin, then the couple would pass to the upper right part of the seal, where they must encounter the awesome power of the goddess symbolized by the disproportionately huge lion. The lion rests on a kind of platform upheld by two female figures. Reposing and vigilant, it guards the mysteries of the goddess just as it did in the Palaeolithic cave of Les Trois Frères. From the upper part of the tree next to the lion emerge branches of ivy, whose spiral growth and evergreen leaves are a symbolic image of the immortality of life, anticipating Virgil's 'Golden Bough' (*Aeneid* VI).

The couple are absent in the upper right scene where the lion holds sway, but re-emerge joyously together on the other side of the tree trunk – as though the rite of passage were through the body of the lion – and there the woman's gesture of epiphany may indicate an expression of amazement and delight at their new transformed state, so similar to the old. There, seated on the branch, no longer apart from them, is the Minoan goddess and another figure with whom she appears to be having an 'animated conversation', as Evans phrases it, while above her head flutter two butterflies. Evans continues:

> The symbolic significance of these, moreover, is emphasized by the appearance above them of two small objects showing traces of heads at the tip and with hook-like projections at the side, in which we may reasonably recognize the two corresponding chrysalises . . . Placed as they are here in connection with their pupal forms, it is difficult to explain them otherwise than as an allusion to the resurgence of the human spirit after death.
>
> It can hardly be doubted, moreover, that they apply to the two youthful figures who appear beside them on the ring, and must be taken to be symbolic of their reanimation with new life . . . We see here, reunited by the life-giving power of the Goddess and symbolized by the chrysalises and butterflies, a young couple whom Death had parted.[27]

THE GODDESS AND THE BULL

A large stone sculpture of the double-horned bull still stands facing the west in the temple-palace at Knossos, and to watch the sun disappearing through the centre of the horns is even now a wondrous event. Bulls' horns once formed a frieze around the courtyard and along the walls of the palace of Knossos, as if framing the human world within. The horns were placed upon the roofs of household shrines, in the pillar crypts and on the altars that stood between the double-headed axes of the goddess. Splendid vessels (called rhytons) in the shape of a bull's head were used for pouring libations in Minoan rituals. Countless models of bulls were found in caves and tombs, as the sign and promise of regeneration in the life to come.

The importance of the bull and its horns as symbolic of the creative life-force of the goddess has already been seen in the Neolithic cultures of Old Europe and Çatal Hüyük, and its association with the goddess and her lunar crescent was suggested as far back as the Palaeolithic era. In Çatal Hüyük the goddess gave birth to the bull as her child, and in Crete also the bull could be called the 'son' of the goddess, as it was all over the Near East, the visible image of her regenerative power on earth. Sometimes the rosette of the goddess is pinned to the brow of the bull, or the lunar cross and the chevron are painted on the bull's clay face. Sacred horns of consecration, inherited from Old Europe and Anatolia,[28] were found in great numbers and generally have a central hole to receive some object that was made of perishable material. In Crete the horned altar is far more ancient than Minoan civilization, and the double axe is often found between the horns. Fresh vegetation often sprouts from between the horns, as well as from the double axes, just as it grows out of the backs of bulls. In the seal in Figure 37 shoots are emerging from the

Figure 36. (*Left*) Bull's head; *c.* 1500 BC, Minoan.
Figure 37. (*Above*) Bulls sprouting plants, with growing plant in centre; crystal signet ring, *c.* 1500 BC. Mycenae.

backs of two young bulls, with a central plant between them growing from a seed pod. Here the life-force is symbolized as the 'seed' of renewal contained within the bulls, which makes the shoots grow. In Egypt also we shall find corn growing from the body of the god Osiris, himself known as the bull god.

Other seals have the criss-crossed pattern of the net incised upon them, and this may refer to a goddess who was later called Dictynna, goddess of the net (*dictyon* means net), and also links to the snake goddess (see Fig. 7). The Greek story told of a maiden called Britomartis, who was pursued by the Minoan King Minos for nine months (time enough to gestate a child), until she threw herself into the sea and was saved by the nets of some fishermen.[29] Afterwards she was called Dictynna – a name whose resemblance to the Dicte Mountain in which Zeus was born cannot be coincidental. The net as the spinning womb of birth, destiny and time was patterned on Neolithic vases and scratched on the walls of Palaeolithic caves, and in this story is specifically linked to the transformation of maid into mother.

TWO GODDESSES AND THE CHILD

In an important ivory sculpture from Mycenae in the last phase of the Bronze Age, about 1300 BC, two goddesses sit together, one slightly smaller than the other, both clothed in flounced dresses and adorned with necklaces, a single cloak enfolding them (Fig. 38). The arm of one rests on

Figure 38. Two goddesses and the child; ivory sculpture, *c.* 1300 BC. Mycenae.

the shoulder of the other, who lifts a hand to clasp her hand. This may be the earliest known sculpture of the goddess with her daughter and the child, who personifies the new life of the year or the grain. They could be the goddess in her dual form as Queen of Life and Death. They may be the 'Two Queens and the King' or the 'Two Queens and the Young God' spoken of in the Linear B tablets found at Pylos, on the west coast of the Peloponnese. The child is climbing from the lap of the larger figure, probably the mother, to the lap of the other, necklaced goddess, perhaps the daughter, rather in the way that, in Classical Greece, the young man Triptolemos moves between Demeter and Persephone, bringing the knowledge of the mysteries of regeneration from the underworld to the light (see Chapter 9, Figs. 18, 19).

Campbell points out the parallel between this Mycenaean threesome and the triad of the Sumerian Inanna, goddess of the world above, and her sister, Ereshkigal, goddess of the world below – or the one goddess in dual form – and the dying and resurrected god Dumuzi, who belongs to both of them.[30] This 'divine family' has appeared already in the Neolithic culture of Çatal Hüyük; it reappears later in Classical Greece, and still later – it will be suggested in Chapter 14 – in Christian images of St Anne, the 'grandmother', and her daughter Mary with the child Jesus, who also is often pictured climbing across the lap of one to the other.

THE SON-LOVER OF THE GODDESS

Archaeological research has so far uncovered no image of a god in Neolithic Crete. The male aspect of the goddess, who was at that time still androgynous, uniting both male and female roles, was symbolized then by the crescent horns of the bull or by a male animal – the bull, ram or stag. In the Minoan age of Crete it is as though the male has separated from the female, but is not yet independent from her, so the relation of masculine to feminine principles is rendered in the image of a great goddess and a young god. A male figure, diminutive in size in relation to the goddess, gradually appears on seal stones, either descending from the sky towards her or standing bent backwards in adoration before her. There are many small statues of a young male, generally in the posture of salutation, which are likely to have been portrayals of a young god because they were found in tombs and caves together with small statues of bulls. Amazingly large numbers of both god figures and bulls were discovered, wedged between hanging stalactites, in the massive and eerie Dictaion cave where Zeus was born – as the story has it in Classical myth, written down at least 1,000 years later. Certainly the models and statues suggest that this was the cave-womb of the mountain mother, where the divine child was brought forth for the renewal of the people, and in the unique sculpture in Figure 39, found near Knossos, the goddess holds up a baby in her arms as a celebration. Yet this male child never reaches full

Figure 39. Mother goddess and child; painted terracotta statue, *c.* 1350 BC. Mavro Spelio, near Knossos, Crete.

adulthood, for, as archaeologists and historians agree, there is no proof of the existence of an adult male god,[31] except perhaps one nearly full-size portrayal of a naked figure standing between the horns of consecration.[32]

Since this late emergence of the adult male god in Crete is unique in the contemporary history of the third and second millennia BC, we might wonder if it had anything to do with the fact that the masculine principle was still tied to the rhythms of the agricultural year, and so involved with the annual death and rebirth of vegetation; it was not isolated and elevated in the need for self-defence, as it was in other countries in the Near East. On the *Vase of the Harvesters* (Fig. 40), harvesting is obviously a male activity, and all the harvesters carry their corn in a procession, as though celebrating a ritual of cutting the corn, one, perhaps, where the first fruits of the harvest were offered to the goddess. Cretan towns were not enclosed with defensive walls, and nowhere in their art is war or violence celebrated

Figure 40. The *Vase of the Harvesters; c.* 1500 BC. Haghia Triada, Crete.

or even depicted, with the exception of the occasional helmet and some swords now in the museum at Herakleion. None the less, they were not likely to have been entirely innocent of the warrior role, if we are to believe the dates given by the Greek historian Thucydides, writing in the fifth century BC, who speaks of King Minos as the first leader to acquire a strong navy and to keep a firm peace in the Aegean. But protected by the sea, the Minoans were not exposed, like the Sumerians and Egyptians, to the fate of being attacked on every side by war-like peoples, and though after the fifteenth century BC the Mycenaeans brought a more combative culture with them, it was only when the Dorians invaded in the twelfth century BC that the Cretan sense of sovereignty was finally lost. The only calamity the Minoans suffered was the earthquake, at least three per century, and this was presumably experienced as belonging to the province of the great goddess.

Certainly, when the young god and the goddess are depicted together, as they are in the seals, the relation is not one of equality, but of service – the god giving necessary homage to a greater power. It would seem that the god, like his animal forms the bull, goat and ram, was still the 'son' of the goddess, personifying the dynamic force of growth, which must, like the tree, die an annual death into the body of the goddess in order to be reborn from her the following spring. In this way he incarnates the form of life that has to change, while she remains as the principle of life that never dies and continually renews itself through its changing forms. Willetts, in his *Cretan Cults and Festivals*, comments that the god 'represents the element of discontinuity, of growth, decay and renewal in the vegetation cycle, as the goddess represents continuity. Because he shares in the mortality of the seed, he is an annually dying god.'[33] This is the 'year god', who dies and is reborn every year, and whose rebirth was celebrated in the mountain caves and probably also in the labyrinth of the temple-palace at Knossos.

On the Minoan gold ring in Figure 41 a tiny young god holding a staff is descending from the sky in front of a pillar, which marks a shrine with the Tree of Life growing from it. The goddess, with plants behind her, welcomes him, perhaps as the spirit of the new life that is returning from

Figure 41. (*Left*) Goddess and young god; Minoan ring, *c.* 1450 BC.
Figure 42. (*Right*) Seated goddess and young god; Mycenaean seal,
c. 1500 BC.

Figure 43. (*Left*) Goddess, young god and priestess beside the Tree of Life;
Mycenaean seal, c. 1500 BC.
Figure 44. (*Right*) Young god with tree and goat sprouting branches;
Mycenaean seal, *c.* 1500 BC.

the heavens, possibly in the form of rain. On the Mycenaean seal in Figure 42 the imposing goddess sits on her throne before the Tree of Life while a slender young man or god with a sceptre or staff stands before her, leaning slightly away from her. His hand points towards her as hers, crossing behind his, points towards him, seeming to bind them to each other as in a knot. Here, it would seem, is an exact depiction of the relation of the goddess and her son–lover, which is to be the theme of the Bronze Age myths in Sumeria and Egypt.

This drama may be depicted on the Mycenaean seal in Figure 43. There the goddess stands in the centre beating her thighs in the traditional attitude of mourning, her priestess is weeping prostrate on the right, while the young god is apparently uprooting a tree from the goddess's shrine. This may be an image of the son–lover of the goddess, who is himself to be uprooted, like the tree that personifies him, at the end of his

Figure 45. Heracles slaying the Cretan Bull; Greek vase painting,
c. 530–510 BC.

particular cycle of growth in order that the principle of growth may persist. His death as the annual death of the life of the tree and all vegetation may explain the mourning of the goddess and the priestess. The association of the son–lover with the tree, and the ritual of cutting down the tree as the death of the son–lover or 'year god' is found also in Sumerian and Egyptian myths.

In the Mycenaean seal in Figure 44 the young god stands alone touching the Tree of Life growing from a shrine on his left. Behind him is a horned male goat with a similar tree growing from his back, as it does from the backs of bulls in other seals, and anticipating also the later Greek vase painting of Heracles and the Cretan Bull (Fig. 45), where branches appear to grow out of the body of the bull, pointing to the continuity of this tradition. Here the regenerative principle, which in earlier times belonged entirely to the androgynous goddess, has now become fully embodied in the male animal and in the young god.

THE 'LADY OF THE LABYRINTH'

The shape of the labyrinth is already familiar from Palaeolithic and Neo-lithic drawings of the meander, symbolizing the waters beneath the earth, also imagined as a serpent, and referring to the dimension of the other world. The labyrinthine passages of approach to the inner sanctuary of the Palaeolithic cave also share in this symbolism. Here, in Crete, these ancient meanings become more specific. The word 'labyrinth' is not Greek in origin, though we know that the word *labrys* meant the double-headed axe. So the labyrinth was both the 'House of the Double Axe' – that is, the temple of the goddess, where her mysteries were celebrated – and the place of rebirth. The goddess was probably the 'Lady of the Labyrinth', to whom a jar of honey, the divine nectar, was humbly offered.

A labyrinth was drawn on the ground floor corridor of the Palace of Knossos and – in a striking persistence of imagery across 1,000 years – the later Greek myth of Theseus and the Minotaur is also centred round an impenetrable labyrinth. A similar labyrinth is found on an early seal from the Minoan palace of Haghia Triada, another on a clay tablet from Pylos in the Peloponnese, and still others on late coins from Knossos from the Classical Greek period, about 350 BC onwards, one with a crescent moon in its centre and one with a rose. A similar spiralling, labyrinthine motif appears on the strange circular stone known as the Phaestos Disc.

Homer makes a suggestive link between dancing and the labyrinth in his image of Ariadne's dancing floor at the Palace of Knossos, for, as the daughter of King Minos and Queen Pasiphae in the later Greek story, she would have been the high priestess who conducted the ceremonies. Cer-tainly in Egypt ritual dances and dramatized performances of living myth were given in the temples. Dance, in all early cultures, was a way of communicating with the goddess, drawing her through ritual and ecstatic gesture into the midst of the spiralling forms that became, as they were danced, her epiphany.[34] In the *Iliad* Homer draws a parallel between Daedalos, the master-architect of Crete, and Hephaestos, the later Greek god of craftsmen. In one of the scenes on the shield he made for Achilles, Hephaestos

> depicted a dancing-floor like the one that Daedalos designed in the spacious town of Knossos for Ariadne of the lovely locks. Youths and marriageable maidens were dancing on it with their hands on each other's wrists, the girls in fine linen with lovely garlands on their heads, and the men in closely woven tunics showing the faint gleam of oil, and with daggers of gold hanging from their silver belts. Here they ran lightly round, circling as smoothly on their accomplished feet as the wheel of a potter when he sits and works it with his hands to see if it will spin; and there they ran in lines to meet each other. A large crowd stood round enjoying the delightful dance, with a minstrel among them singing divinely to the lyre, while a couple of acrobats, keeping time with his music, threw cart-wheels in and out among the people.[35]

It is possible that this is a folk memory handed down through the generations of a ritual dance that did actually take place on the dancing floor of the labyrinth. Dances of later times suggest that lines may have been marked on the ground for the dancers to follow, and that their movements traced the movement of the sun and moon as they circled the ecliptic. Another interpretation has the labyrinthine turnings representing the soul's wandering before or after death, where the obstacles in the way of reaching the centre symbolize the sacrifices that progressively

Figure 46. Dance of the goddess and the young god beside the Tree of Life, with butterfly and sacred knot; Mycenaean ring, *c.*1450 BC. From the Tholos tomb, Vapheio.

make possible the way forward, until at the centre the union creates transformation, and the way out again allows rebirth.

Plutarch, in his *Life of Theseus*, tells a story of how, when Theseus left Crete with Ariadne, his ship put into the harbour at Delos. There he offered a sacrifice to the god Apollo, dedicating a statue of the goddess that had been given to him by Ariadne. With his companions, he performed a dance that imitated the circular pathways of the labyrinth, winding the thread of Ariadne into the centre and back again, the direction of involution and death followed by evolution and birth. It was called the Crane Dance, after the sinuous turnings of the cranes' necks in their mating rituals, and also perhaps after the fact that the returning cranes brought the spring, and Theseus danced it round the Horned Altar.[36] There was a Crane Dance in Troy, and Virgil in Roman times describes a dance called 'The Game of Troy' as winding like the turnings of the Cretan labyrinth.[37] This dance became the prototype of early Christian dances, where the Minotaur became the Satan of the underworld, and Theseus became Christ who overcomes him and returns to life, bringing eternal life to all. The labyrinths at Chartres and Auxerre point to the persistence of this ancient symbolism.

THE LEGEND OF THE MINOTAUR

The Classical Greek myth of Theseus and the Minotaur is the first story we have of Crete, even though it is told 1,000 years later from a perspective of a culture much changed from the original one, and so inevitably remembering and re-creating the earlier one from its own point of view. The story was painted on Greek vases from the eighth century BC onwards, and written down by Homer, Hesiod, Thucydides, Pindar, Plutarch and others, as well as by Ovid in his *Metamorphoses*.

One day, so the story goes, Zeus saw Europa picking flowers by the sea-shore, and he transformed himself into a bull. The princess, suspecting nothing, climbed on to his back, when suddenly the bull plunged into the sea and carried her across the waves to Crete. A son, Minos, was born from this union. Europa, who was the princess of Phoenicia, then married the King of Crete, Asterios, and in due course Minos became king.

Minos, in his turn, married Pasiphae, daughter of Helios, the sun god, and the nymph Perseis, and they lived in the Palace of Knossos with their children. It so happened that, in order to settle a dispute with his brothers, Minos prayed to Poseidon to send him a bull as a sign that the throne belonged only to him, and he promised to sacrifice the animal immediately. Poseidon sent him a magnificent white bull from the sea, but when Minos saw it, he could not bear to part with it, and so he sacrificed another in its place, imagining the god would not know the difference, which, of course, he did.

Figure 47. *Europa and the Bull*; archaic Greek sculpture, *c.* 600 BC.
Temple at Selinus, Sicily.

In fact, so angry was Poseidon that he aroused in the Queen a great passion for the bull. She begged her craftsman Daedalos to make a model of a cow and hid herself inside it, hoping the bull would not know the difference, which he did not. A son was born to Pasiphae with the body of a man but the head and tail of a bull. Daedalos then made a vast labyrinth deep under the ground, and so they hid the Minotaur away.

Now King Minos, who ruled the seas, had won a campaign against Athens, and demanded as annual (some say octennial) tribute from the Athenian king, seven boys and seven girls, who were to be given to the Minotaur in the labyrinth. Theseus, the king's son, came to Crete as one of the fourteen in order to slay the Minotaur and set his country free. Ariadne, daughter of King Minos and Queen Pasiphae, fell in love with Theseus and offered to help him. So she asked Daedalos to give her a skein of thread, which she then gave to Theseus, who, tying one end to the entrance and unravelling the ball as he went deeper and deeper inside, was at last able to reach the heart of the labyrinth. There he killed the Minotaur and, ravelling up the thread in and out of the winding pathways, he at last found his way back to the light. Theseus then escaped from Crete, taking Ariadne with him as he had promised, and on the way to Athens they stopped at the island of Naxos. But while Ariadne was sleeping on the beach, Theseus sailed away and left her. Then Dionysos, the bull god, saw her lying there asleep, and he fell in love with her, and so they were married and had three sons.[38]

If we had no knowledge of Crete, we would take this story simply as a tale of a hero vanquishing a monster and freeing his country from a cruel oppression. But, with some knowledge of Minoan ritual, it is clear that

Figure 48. Theseus slaying the Minotaur; cup by Apollodorus,
510 BC. Chiusi, Italy.
Figure 49. The ritual slaying of the bull; Minoan gold bead seal,
c. 1400–1100 BC.

there is another story here also, one much older and more complex: a story of the sacred marriage rituals at Knossos, which were celebrated by the priestess-queen and the priest-king wearing the horned masks of the cow and bull. 'Minotaur' means 'the bull of Minos', or 'Minos, the bull', a name that refers us to all the other 'bulls' in the tale: Zeus, who turned into a bull; Poseidon, brother to Zeus, called the bull god, who sent a bull from the sea, a form of himself; Theseus, whose divine father was said to be Poseidon; and Dionysos, the bull god. This proliferation of bulls is not taken up by the explicit meaning of the story, so we are introduced to two levels in the tale, the narrative and the image.

The myth then illustrates the way in which Aryan Greek culture adopted and reinterpreted the Minoan culture of 1,000 years earlier, which was inherited through the Mycenaeans. As Harrison has conclusively shown, this was a process of revision that ran through many if not all of the Greek myths, where the original goddess-oriented cultures have been modified or inverted to create a new kind of significance more in accord with the god-oriented culture of the Greeks.[39] The original spirit in many of the myths, however, is still visible in the images.

Reading through the narrative to the image, it seems clear that this legend of Theseus contains within it two separate stories with two quite distinct points of view. The ruling story is the Greek hero myth, in which Theseus the hero slays the monster in the dark underground labyrinth and wins freedom for his country. There may well be some historical truth in this story, even though it is glimpsed through the perspective and values of a different culture. Frazer surmises that 'the tribute of seven youths and seven maidens whom the Athenians were bound to send to Minos every eight years had some connexion with the renewal of the king's power for another octennial cycle.'[40]

If we look at the bull as the Minoans would have done, we see the sacred embodiment of the life-force, which the king also embodied in his person as the son–lover of the goddess. At the end of eight years the king's sacred powers needed to be renewed, and whereas in certain other places and times this required that the king himself should be sacrificed at the height of his powers, here the bull could take the king's place. If political prisoners from Athens were involved in some way in this ritual, it would explain their revulsion towards the bull-man of death.

Frazer, who first put forward this idea, explains that

> an octennial cycle is the shortest period at the end of which sun and moon really mark time together after overlapping, so to say, throughout the whole of the interval. Thus, for example, it is only once in every eight years that the full moon coincides with the longest or shortest day.[41]

The significance of this special conjunction of sun and moon was that solar and lunar time were brought into harmony in the image of a sacred marriage between them. Frazer concludes:

> The tradition plainly implies that at the end of every eight years the king's sacred powers needed to be renewed by intercourse with the god-head, and that without such a renewal he would have forfeited his right to the throne. We may surmise that among the solemn ceremonies which marked the beginning or the end of the eight year cycle the sacred marriage of the king with the queen played an important part.[42]

Frazer argues that, here as elsewhere, the king was ritually sacrificed to ensure that the fertility of human, animal and plant life did not diminish with his failing powers. At a certain point in time the bull was substituted for the king and sacrificed in his place. The prominence of the bull in Cretan ritual suggests that by the Minoan period this momentous evolution in human consciousness had already taken place, although it is possible that this practice was not uniform throughout the ancient Near East.

It is most probable that the ritual slaying of the bull by a priest (Fig. 49) took place at the same time as the sacred marriage between the priestess-queen and the priest-king of Knossos, since both were connected with the renewal of life. Perhaps a ritual leap over the bull or a ritual combat with the bull was necessary to bestow the right to rule. The bull would have then been slain as the embodiment of the old cycle, allowing the sacred marriage to take place. The marriage ceremony was undoubtedly enacted in the costume and masks of a bull and cow, as it was in Egypt.[43] Pasiphae, the priestess-queen, uniting with the priest-king – she inside the cow and he inside the bull – would answer to this description, as would the Minotaur, with the body of a man and the head of a bull. When the priestess-queen 'married' the priest-king, she became the goddess and he became the son–lover, and through this union the earth was regenerated. This marriage of the priest-king and the priestess-queen was also an imitation on earth of the marriage in heaven, when the sun and moon returned after eight revolving years to 'the same heavenly bridal chamber where first they met'.[44]

The bull used to be related to the moon through the crescent shape of its horns as the male form of the lunar goddess. By now, it seems as if the fertilizing principle embodied in the bull is related to the vital power of the sun, rather than to the nightly fructifying dew of the moon, as in earlier times.[45] The bull personifying the sun rather than the moon reflects the growing to independence of the male generative power of the once androgynous goddess. This generative power, imaged first as a horned animal and then as the son of the goddess, can now encounter her as her lover. After the sacred marriage between them, the lover must be sacrificed to be reborn from her as her son in the image of continuous renewal. All over the Near East this sacrifice was enacted as the ritual slaying of the bull. The sacrifice of the bull was an act of propitiation to the dark phase of moon, sun and year, which guaranteed the return of the light in heaven and fertility on earth.

The seals and frescoes at Knossos suggest that before the ceremony of the bull slaying, the bull's magical power was invoked by young men and women vaulting over its back. The risk of death seems as nothing to the joy of the dance, suggesting that these were priests and priestesses under-going an initiation rite into the service of the goddess who presided over the ritual. The women in the fresco at Knossos (Fig. 50) have white skin and the men have red, as they do in Egyptian frescoes. One woman is about to vault the bull, her two hands straining to grasp its left horn, while another waits to receive the body of the male vaulter who has half completed his 'mortal leap'. The unique ivory and gold figure in Figure

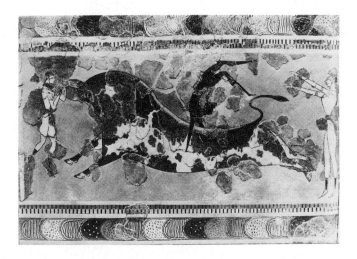

Figure 50. Male and female bull-vaulters; fresco, *c.* 1500 BC. Knossos.

Figure 51. (*Left*) The Goddess as vaulter of the bull; chryselephantine,
c. 1600 BC, height 7 in. (17.5 cm). Said to have been found at Knossos,
Crete.
Figure 52. (*Right*) The Sacred Marriage (Theseus and Ariadne?); vase
painting, c. 700 BC. Herakleion.

51, which is only 7 in. (17.5 cm) tall, shows the goddess or her high
priestess dressed ceremonially as the vaulter of the bull, her expression
one of rapt concentration, as though poised for the acrobatic leap over the
horns.

It seems, then, highly plausible that the ultimate focus of the rituals at
Knossos was the sacred marriage (Fig. 52), and this underlying meaning
is implicitly conveyed in the story of the Minotaur through the symbolism
of the names. What happens in the legend mythologically is a cycle of
sacred marriages between the sun as the bull and the moon as the princess
or priestess. All five 'marriages' – Zeus, the bull, with Europa; Minos,
son of the bull, with Pasiphae; the bull from Poseidon with Pasiphae;
Theseus, son of Poseidon the bull, with Ariadne; and later Dionysos, the
bull, with Ariadne – symbolize the marriage of sun and moon as an
unending cycle. Even when this cycle appears to be interrupted, as when
Theseus abandons Ariadne, Dionysos the bull takes his place and completes the ritual.

All the female names in the tale carry overtones of the moon and all the
male names carry overtones of the sun. Europa's name means 'she of the
wide eyes'. Her mother was called Telephaessa, 'the far-shining one', or
Argiope, the 'white-faced'; her father was King Phoenix, which means the

reddish colour of the sun. Kerenyi comments: 'In other words, the face of both mother and daughter was that of the moon.'[46] In Crete, Europa married King Asterios, whose name means 'king of the stars'. The name Minos is interesting because it recalls King Menes, the first dynastic king of Egypt (2850 BC), and also Min, the Egyptian god of fertility and growth, who was represented in processions by a white bull, which preceded the ithyphallic image of the god. Min also carried a flail used for separating the seed from the husk, as did Osiris, whose resemblance to Minos as judge of the dead is striking. It is possible also that Minos was the name of a dynasty: his grandson is called Idomeneus, which carries the same root of Minos in the centre. The name Min may have meant 'bringer of fertility', after the Egyptian fertility god Min, possibly following the Egyptian custom of pharaohs, who added the name of their gods to their own: as, for example, Tut Ank Amun. Pasiphae, the wife of Minos, has a name that means 'she who shines for all', and is herself the daughter of Helios, the sun, and of Perseis, one of the names of the moon goddess in Hesiod's genealogy who was the mother of Hecate and who gave her name to Persephone. In some versions of the tale the Minotaur was also called Asterios ('star'), the name of Europa's husband, the King of Crete. Ariadne, originally Ariagne, meant 'holy and pure', a superlative form of Hagne, which was an appellation of Persephone in her role as Queen of the Underworld, from which we get the word 'hag'. Ariadne's other name was Aridela, the 'one visible from afar', a name that referred to her transformation into a wreath of stars in heaven beside her husband, Dionysos, the bull.[47]

Taking the tale symbolically, as one of the stories that illumine an understanding of the psyche of any age, Theseus becomes an image of the questing consciousness (the 'archetypal masculine' in everyone) that must journey into the unknown regions of the psyche to seek the treasure at the heart. Ariadne's thread is then the intuition (the 'archetypal feminine' in everyone) that guides the conscious mind through the labyrinthine turnings leading to the source, and which can be trusted to lead us safely back.

This essential relationship between the masculine and feminine modes of being is perhaps the most fundamental aspect of what is being explored through the stories of goddesses and gods. But returning to the historical stage on which this archetypal drama is set, we can say that Theseus of the heroic deed leaves behind Ariadne of the moon to the embrace of the latest incarnation of the bull god, while he sails away unencumbered to the land of freedom, not knowing that he carries fast within him the lunar thread. For there in Athens he will find the goddess Athena of the shield and serpent, Artemis of the animals and Demeter of the golden corn. There, also, will be Persephone, Demeter's daughter, who holds the torches of the underworld, Aphrodite riding upon her goose and swan, and 'cow-eyed' Hera with her husband, Zeus the bull. And finally, Gaia, Goddess of Earth, who gave birth to them all.

Crete has left us with a unique vision of life as a celebration of being alive and an image of death as the same, so that life and death are experienced as one sacred whole. It is as though life were lived on the intake of a breath of wonder and delight, where, as in childhood and moments of epiphany, nature and the divine ground of being are one. Can it be a coincidence that for thousands of years the people of Crete lived in harmony with the rhythms of nature experienced as a great goddess and also lived in peace? The myth of the goddess reached its culmination here before its gradual decline in the Bronze Age cultures of the Near East and then its nearly total extinction in the Iron Age. For Crete was the direct inheritor of the Neolithic vision, which had persisted relatively undisturbed upon the earth for many millennia, and with the ending of Minoan and Mycenaean civilization a unique insight is lost into how human consciousness might have continued to evolve. Within the island it seems clear that human nature was not war-like. In other parts of the world, on the other hand, attack and defence were becoming the norm. Nomadic tribes, who worshipped tribal gods of storm, wind, thunder and volcanic fire, fought their way into other peoples' lands with no feeling for the subtle harmonies of agricultural life and the religious rituals they destroyed. Now the god and his divine representative on earth, the warrior-king, begin to take the centre of the stage. It is no wonder that, many centuries later, Classical Greece looked back to Crete as to a lost Golden Age and found there the inspiration of its goddesses and gods.

4

THE BRONZE AGE:
THE MOTHER GODDESS
AND HER SON-LOVER

Eternity is in love with the productions of time.

William Blake

The Bronze Age, which begins about 3500 BC and lasts until 1250 BC, seems to have been named in the image of conquest, commemorating not its culture but its technology. For the invention of bronze – an alloy of copper and tin – made possible not only more flexible and durable tools, but also weapons that would not break in battle. So, in the river valleys of the earliest civilizations bronze was moulded not just to the shape of the plough, but also to the shape of battle-axe and sword.

Yet the momentous discovery of the Bronze Age was the art of writing. Now, for the first time, massive stone columns and walls of temples are carved with images and hieroglyphs, which tell the stories that had been handed down through countless generations by word of mouth. On tablets of clay and strips of papyrus so fragile that their survival seems miraculous, pictures and words appear together, bringing to life the soul of long-forgotten peoples.

Now we read everywhere of goddesses and gods who take their being from one Primordial Goddess who is the origin of all things. We can recognize her as the Great Mother Goddess of the Palaeolithic and Neolithic eras. At last, in the Bronze Age, we can hear the hymns sung to her, and can follow the story of a goddess who is one yet becomes many, who has a sister or a brother, a daughter or a son. She is single yet she marries; she is virgin and mother; and sometimes her son becomes her consort. As before, she gives life and she takes it away. The goddess has many names and many different tales are told about her, but one story is unvarying throughout the Near East. The goddess becomes separated from the one she loves, who dies or seems to die, and falls into a darkness called 'the Underworld'. This separation is reflected in nature as a loss of light and fertility. The goddess descends to overcome the darkness so that her loved one may return to the light, and life may continue.

In Sumeria the name of the goddess is Inanna, and she goes down to the world below to meet her sister, Ereshkigal, Queen of the Underworld.

Figure 1. (*Left*) Sumerian cuneiform writing; black basalt foundation stone of the Ziggurat of Ur-Nammu, founder of the Third Dynasty of Ur, *c.* 2100 BC. Inscribed 'For Inanna, Lady of Eanna, His lady, Ur-Nammu, powerful male, King of Ur, King of Sumer and Akkad, built and restored her temple for her.'

Figure 2. (*Right*) Egyptian hieroglyphic writing showing husband (Shery) and wife (Kherta) with offerings; Old Kingdom cornice of false tomb door, Fourth Dynasty, *c.* 2575–2467 BC. Saqqara.

Returning to the world above, she sends back Dumuzi, her consort, 'Lord of the Abyss', to take her place. In Babylonia her name is Ishtar, and yearly she journeys to awaken her son–lover, Tammuz, from his sleep in the darkness below the earth, and to bring him up into the light. In Egypt the goddess Isis, married to her brother–husband, Osiris, loses him through death at the hands of their brother, Seth. The whole earth is barren until she finds him and brings back together the dismembered pieces of his body. In Canaan the god Baal enters into the Underworld to confront the power of death personified by his brother, Mot. Mot defeats him, and Baal's sister, the goddess Anath, goes down to fetch his body for burial. She herself kills Mot, scattering him like grain in the fields. In Greece the goddess Demeter loses her daughter, Persephone, to the god of the underworld, Hades, who seizes her away from the light to be his bride in the darkness below. Demeter's mourning leaves the earth without food, and only when her daughter is returned to her in spring does the earth grow fruitful and offer up the life-giving corn.

Later on, the myths of the Iron Age tell a similar story of Cybele and Attis, and of Aphrodite and Adonis. The goddess Cybele loves a shepherd boy who is a king's son, but he falls in love with a nymph. Driven insane by the jealous goddess, Attis castrates himself with a stone. As the goddess mourns him, a pine tree springs from his body and flowers rise from his blood. The Greek goddess Aphrodite loses her lover, the beautiful Adonis, Lord of Vegetation, who is gored to death by a boar while hunting in the woods. Now the goddess no longer rescues him herself, but has to ask the god Zeus to allow him to return to life from spring to autumn, the fertile season of the earth. Finally, Jesus, son of the Virgin Mother, Mary, dies and descends into Hell for three days, the number of days of darkness when the moon is gone. In the Christian myth Christ is 'rescued' by his Father in Heaven, but, like the others, his return coincides with the date of the earth's regeneration. Easter is celebrated on the Sunday following the first full moon after the spring equinox, so that Christ's resurrection, like those before him, also reflects the turning of winter into spring.

The pattern of this story may have been inspired by humanity's relationship to the moon. For countless thousands of years human beings had seen the light growing to fullness, then giving way to the darkness and being reborn from it again and again in a continuous rhythm that must have felt eternal. In the Palaeolithic era the moon gave people time: sequence, duration and recurrence. In the Neolithic, the cycles of the moon were experienced in the cycle of the crops, where the light and dark phases of the moon were reflected in the fertile and barren phases of the earth. Now, in the Bronze Age, the moon's phases are given dramatic form in the great myths that have come down to us from Mesopotamia, Egypt, Anatolia, Syria and Greece. They become a story that is lived by goddesses and gods in their changing relation to each other and to humanity on earth.

The moon was an image in the sky that was always changing yet was always the same. What endured was the cycle, whose totality could never be seen at any one moment. All that was visible was the constant interplay between light and dark in an ever-recurring sequence. Implicitly, however, the early people must have come to see every part of the cycle from the perspective of the whole. The individual phases could not be named, nor the relations between them expressed, without assuming the presence of the whole cycle. The whole was invisible, an enduring and unchanging circle, yet it contained the visible phases. Symbolically, it was as if the visible 'came from' and 'returned to' the invisible – like being born and dying, and being born again.

The great myth of the Bronze Age is structured upon the distinction between the 'whole', personified as the Great Mother Goddess, and 'the part', personified as her son–lover or her daughter. She gives birth to her son as the new moon, marries him as the full moon, loses him to the darkness as the waning moon, goes in search of him as the dark moon, and rescues him as the returning crescent. In the Greek myth, in which the daughter plays the role of 'the part', the cycle is the same, but the marriage is between the daughter and a god who personifies the dark phase of the moon. The daughter, like the son, is rescued by the mother. In both variations of the myth, the Goddess may be understood as the eternal cycle of the whole: the unity of life and death as a single process. The young goddess or god is her mortal form in time, which, as manifested life – whether plant, animal or human being – is subject to a cyclical process of birth, flowering, decay, death and rebirth.

This essential distinction between the whole and the part was later formulated in the Greek language by the two different Greek words for life, *zoe* and *bios*, as the embodiment of two dimensions co-existing in life. *Zoe* is eternal and infinite life; *bios* is finite and individual life. *Zoe* is infinite 'being'; *bios* is the living and dying manifestation of this eternal world in time. The Classical scholar Carl Kerenyi explains: '*Zoe* is the thread upon which every individual *bios* is strung like a bead, and which, in contrast to *bios*, can be conceived of only as endless' – as 'infinite life'.[1]

Relating this to the moon, *zoe* becomes the totality of the cycle of the moon's phases, and *bios* becomes the individual phases. *Zoe* is then both transcendent and immanent, and *bios* is the immanent form of *zoe*. In this way *bios* is contained in *zoe*, as the part is contained in the whole. *Zoe* contains *bios*, but *bios* cannot contain *zoe*. Similarly, we suggested that the Palaeolithic myth of the Goddess contained the myth of the hunter, but the myth of the hunter could not contain the myth of the Goddess.

The Great Mother Goddess can be recognized as the totality of the lunar cycle – as *zoe* – and her daughter and son–lover, who emerge from and return to her, can be seen as the moon's phases – as *bios*. Together they image the two 'faces' of life: eternal and transitory, unmanifest and manifest, invisible and visible. The son and daughter personify the ever-dying and ever-renewed forms of life, whether human, animal or plant. Related to the cycles of the earth's seasons, the son and daughter incarnate the life of vegetation. The transitional moments in the agricultural cycle are commemorated with festivals of mourning and rejoicing, and in the great mythic dramas that express the mysterious analogy between the life of the moon, the life of plants and the life of human beings. Participating in these rituals created a trust that as darkness is always followed by light, so death is followed by rebirth. All life, therefore, holds a promise of renewal. The sacred marriage, in which the Mother Goddess as bride is united with her son as lover, reconnects symbolically the two 'worlds' of *zoe* and *bios*, and it is this union that regenerates the earth.

THE GODDESS CULTURE IN THE EARLY BRONZE AGE

The myth and rituals of the goddess and her son–lover underlie the life of all the agricultural communities in the Bronze Age. Three areas of Bronze Age culture play a principal role in the transmission of goddess imagery from the Neolithic era to the Iron Age, and eventually to Western civilization. These are Crete, Sumeria and Egypt. The Sumerian goddess Inanna will be discussed in Chapter 5, and the Egyptian goddess Isis in Chapter 6. In this chapter the aim is to give an overall view of what happened to the goddess culture during the Bronze Age.

The myth of the goddess extended all the way from Old Europe to the Indus Valley, and a comprehensive study of the imagery would have to include the Indus Valley and India as a whole. The civilization of the Indus Valley, with its two great cities of Mohenjo-Daro in the south and Harappa in the north, was flourishing before 2500 BC. It had many features in common with Sumeria and Egypt, but seems to have had a higher standard of living. There is evidence of close trade contacts between the Indus Valley cities and Sumeria during the fourth and third millennia BC, which were interrupted during the period of the Aryan invasions, and identical seals have been found there and in Eshnunna in Mesopotamia, as well as in ancient Elam (Iran), dating from before 2300 BC.[2] Campbell draws attention to the universality of the mythic imagery that evolved from Western Europe to Asia, for, as he writes, we find the same symbolic images in the Aegean and in India: the goddess as cow and lioness, the Tree of Life, and the god, consort to the goddess, whose animal is the bull and whose fate is linked to the waxing and waning phases of the moon. The evidence suggests there was one focal mythology whose matrix was the Near East, which was carried in both directions across the land and sea probably in the course of trade.[3] The two striking images in Figures 3 and 4 – one from the place where eastern Anatolia touches Syria and the other from the Indus Valley – show a continuity not only with the earliest goddess images of the Palaeolithic, but with the Neolithic bird and serpent goddesses of Old Europe.

In the fourth millennium BC nature was still experienced as numinous, that is, as an overwhelming mystery that is both sacred and alive.[4] Campbell evokes this quality of consciousness when he says that 'it is not that the divine is every*where*: it is that the divine is every*thing*.'[5] It was the

Figure 3. (*Left*) Snake goddess figurine; *c.* 5000 BC.
Anatolia (northern Syria).
Figure 4. (*Right*) Goddess figure; *c.* 3000 BC, height 3⅔ in. (9.3 cm).
Mehrgarh, Indus Valley.

sun's rays, the river's rise and fall, the luminosity of the stars, the violence of flood water, the great bud of the date palm, the green shoots of corn, the fruit-bearing tree, the grapes of the vine. It was the attraction of male and female, the thunderous roar of the storm, the life-giving rain and the devouring terror of the beast of prey. It was health and disease, life and death. The numinous energy of all these powers was 'named' by the Sumerians and Egyptians as goddesses and gods, who became manifest as these different forms of life.

At the same time a tremendous explosion of knowledge took place as writing, mathematics and astronomy were discovered. It was as if the human mind had suddenly revealed a new dimension of itself. These discoveries began with the priesthood, but as the pace of life accelerated to integrate them, no member of society was left untouched. Humanity in these cultures seemed on the brink of a new age, yet during the next 2,000 years Sumeria was shaken to its foundations by some cataclysmic event. What happened?

In the early Bronze Age people lived in small villages, cultivating the land around them, where the animals also grazed. In Egypt and Sumeria the temple came to be the focus of the rites that renewed the earth's fertility, as well as being the safest place of storage for the produce of the

Figure 5. (*Left*) The goddess Ishtar holding a vase of the waters of life;
c. 1800 BC. Palace of Mari, Mesopotamia.
Figure 6. (*Right*) Seti I receiving the sacred collar from the goddess Hathor;
bas-relief, Nineteenth Dynasty, *c.* 1300 BC.

land. In Sumeria the temple and the produce belonged in the first instance to the goddess, who was known by various names in different cities. Here the priestess or priest who took care of the rites of the deity was also the custodian of the land, the *En*, who organized the people of the village to look after it. The earliest Sumerian kings were the shepherds of their people and the caretakers of the land on behalf of the goddess and, later, the god. Everyone served the deity, working on the land, tending the animals or building the temples.

Above all else, it was the astounding synthesis of astronomy, mathematics and writing that created an inspirational vision of the relationship between the Above and the Below. Astronomical calculations were, as we have seen, more advanced than anyone suspected, but they were not written down so as to contribute to a continually expanding system of knowledge. Campbell writes:

> The most important and far-reaching cultural mutation of this kind in the history of the human race was that which occurred in Mesopotamia about the middle of the fourth millennium BC, with the rise . . . of a constellation of city-states governed by kings according to a notion of cosmic order and law derived from a long-continued, systematic observation of the heavens. Towering temples symbolic of a new image of the universe made their appearance at that time – the first examples of monumental architecture in the history of civilization; and it was within the precincts of those sanctuaries that the members of a new type of highly specialized, heavenward-gazing priesthood invented, *ca.* 3200 BC, writing, mathematical notation (both sexagesimal and decimal), and the beginnings of a true science of exact astronomical observation . . . This life-transfiguring concept of a celestially based political and social order reached Egypt *ca.* 2850 BC with the founding of the First Dynasty; Crete on one hand, India on the other, *ca.* 2500 BC.[6]

The images of the constellations, the months of the year, the hours and seconds that still mark the passage of time in the twentieth century are the inheritance of the Sumerian discoveries some 5,500 years ago.

THE SEPARATION FROM NATURE

The greatest social change in the Bronze Age was the transition from the village to the town, the town to the city, city to city-state and, eventually, city-state to empire. Many thousands of people were drawn together to live in much closer proximity to each other than ever before. The accumulation of a food surplus, due to better methods of cultivating soil, released energy for developing many new skills and crafts. This led to a new division of the population into various 'castes' or groupings: priests, farmers, craftsmen and – for the first time – warriors. In addition, constant invasion by alien peoples meant that the community had to be reorganized for defence. Gradually, during the course of the third millennium BC, the atmosphere of Bronze Age culture changes. Instead of villages clustered around a temple-mound and focused on agricultural and pastoral activities, there is the city, and then the city-state ruled by a king, who had increasingly to use his powers to defend his land. The temple was no longer the concern of the headman of the village but of a body of priests, who also organized the life of the community and were responsible for keeping accounts, taxation, apportioning land and distributing food. In Sumeria the movement from the countryside to the city became irreversible, as the population was continually threatened by attack.

Towards the middle of the Bronze Age the Mother Goddess recedes into the background as father gods begin to move to the centre of the stage. Erich Neumann, in his *Origins and History of Consciousness*, discusses this movement as an inevitable and lawful development in the history of human consciousness.[7] However, this 'natural' progression was undoubtedly accelerated and frequently distorted by the suddenness of the impact of people coming into the Near East who had a totally different vision of life. The imagery of the goddess begins to lose its capacity to inspire; gradually the male principle assumes an increasingly dynamic role. It is as if the energy released during this time of tumultuous change leads to the discovery of many new kinds of skills, which in turn extend the imagery of the 'powers' from which they derive. Each aspect of human activity comes to be under the governance of a particular goddess or god; their help is invoked as new activities are added to old ones. 'Mother' and 'Father' goddesses and gods engender 'sons' and 'daughters', and an elaborate system of divine relationship and intermarriage connects the new discoveries in the human realm with the original deities of the source of life, ultimately with the Mother Goddess. However, new creation myths, in which the Father God plays the central role, now begin to overshadow the old ones.

Sumeria and Egypt provide the first record of the myth of the separation between Earth and Heaven that was to become the foundation of Iron Age theologies. The emphasis is no longer on creation emerging from a mother goddess, but on a god separating his parents and so initiating the 'process' of creation. The earliest Sumerian creation myth tells the story of Nammu, Goddess of the Primordial Waters, who brought forth the cosmic mountain An-Ki, Heaven and Earth. An and Ki brought forth a son, Enlil (God of Air or Breath), who separated Heaven from Earth and carried off Earth, his mother, to be his bride.

> The lord whose decisions are unalterable,
> Enlil, who brings up the seed of the land from the earth,
> Took care to move away Heaven from Earth
> Took care to move away Earth from Heaven.[8]

Enlil begins to take the place of the goddess as the supreme creator and his home is now the temple that was once her body, the primordial mountain. With the appearance of Enlil, creation is no longer imagined as a birth from the mother, but as 'the word' that speaks all things into being.

> Your word – it is plants, your word – it is grain,
> Your word is the floodwater, the life of all the lands.[9]

In Egypt the Primeval Waters were common to all cosmologies as the origin of the universe from which all life emerged. Unlike Sumeria, these primordial waters – Nun – were imaged as the father rather than the mother, just as earth was male and sky was female. In Heliopolis the god Atum rose out of the waters as the Primeval Mound. Then Atum created Shu and Tefnut – male and female – either through masturbating or spitting them into being, complementary images of nature as a union of matter and spirit, terms whose differentiation was only now beginning: the spitting signified the entry of the breath of life into the substance of the sperm. Shu was Air, and Tefnut, Moisture; later Shu became Life, and Tefnut became Order. Shu and Tefnut in turn gave birth to Nut, Sky (female), and Geb, Earth (male). However, Shu is both Light and Space as well as Air. He speaks to Atum-Re:

> I am that space which came about in the waters
> I came into being in them, I grew in them,
> but I was not consigned to the abode of darkness.[10]

Shu, like the Sumerian Enlil, is the instigator of the next stage of creation, which is the separation of Earth and Sky. As Light, Shu separates the Earth from the Sky, and as Air, he holds the Sky away from the

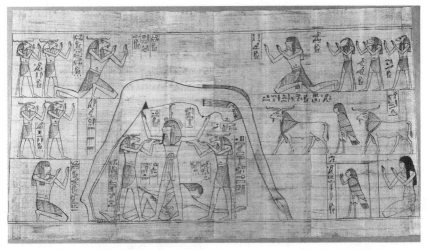

Figure 7. The Egyptian god Shu (Air) separating Nut (Sky) and Geb (Earth); Egyptian painting, detail of the Greenfield Papyrus, *c.* 1000 BC.

Earth, creating the space between them. This can be understood as an image of the birth of consciousness, which brings duality into being and sets free the process of creation (Fig. 7).

In Memphis the creation myth focuses on the god Ptah, whose divine essence was believed to enter into all creation, in the analogy of the mind and heart giving life to the body: he 'thought in his heart' everything that exists, and his tongue gave the word to the thought in his heart:

> The seeing of the eyes and the breathing of the nose bring messages to the heart . . . It is the heart which causes all decisions to be made, but it is the tongue which reports what the heart has thought out . . . All is in accord with the command which the heart has devised and which has appeared upon the tongue. Thus is determined the peculiar nature of everything.[11]

The separation of heaven and earth is an image of the birth of consciousness in which humanity is set apart from nature. The self who perceives and values is separated from that which is perceived and evaluated. Creation myths that show the division of the primal unity into two halves portray the human capacity to act reflectively rather than instinctively, which inevitably involves an initial dissociation from the instinctive life of nature. This new development of consciousness finds expression in the god who orders from beyond rather than the goddess who moves from within. The difficulty of this dissociation is the temptation to call the goddess (nature) 'lower' and the god (spirit) 'higher', assuming that consciousness can evolve only through making the distinction between what is wanted and what is not wanted, striving to reach the one and avoid the other. Another respect of this separation from nature is the emergence of the individual from the tribal group through ceasing to act 'collectively', that is, with the immediate, unreflective response of a member of the tribe.

In the Bronze Age, for the first time, we learn the names of individual men and women, what they say and do. We hear King Gudea of Lagash recounting a dream that inspired him to build a temple,[12] and a high priestess, Enheduanna, lamenting her enforced exile from her temple.[13] We listen to the scribe who finds his priestly master difficult to please, and a man like Job who has suffered terrible afflictions and cannot understand what he has done to offend his god.[14] We become aware not only of the personality of men and women, but also of the individuality of goddesses and gods, whose characters are defined and whose creative acts are named. All these differentiations reflect the growing awareness of the individual's power to shape events. The challenges of many different kinds of activity give rise to the myth of the 'hero' – the person of greater wisdom, power or strength who will be able to respond to a whole new dimension of endeavour, and who offers a model for the rest of the tribe to emulate: how, for example, to stop a mighty river flooding the land, how to govern a city with many thousands of people, how to defend the city against a barbarous enemy.

Here the ancient hunting instinct is diverted away from the animal to the new demands of survival. The heroic action of the gifted individual was needed in every sphere of life, and the heroic individual becomes the 'forerunner of mankind in general', as Neumann says,[15] defining the task that will eventually have to be accomplished by all individuals. The appearance of the myth of the hero shifts the focus of attention from the great round of nature, expressed as the myth of the goddess, to 'the world as the centre of the universe, the spot upon which man stands'.[16] It is possible to see that what we referred to as the myth of the hunter in the Palaeolithic age has now become the myth of the hero.

THE ARYAN AND SEMITIC INVASIONS

We can only wonder how the goddess cultures of the Bronze Age would have continued to evolve had they not been disrupted by the arrival of migratory warrior tribesmen who imposed their mythology and their patriarchal customs on the agricultural peoples whose territory they invaded. Wherever sky gods – of lightning, thunder, fire, air and storm – are found, together with the mace, the battle-axe and the glorification of the warrior, we are in the presence of the Indo-European (Aryan) and Semitic inheritance. The impact of these tribal peoples on the Bronze Age goddess cultures from Europe to India was, as Campbell writes, dramatic:

> Towards the close of the Age of Bronze and, more strongly, with the dawn of the Iron Age (*c.* 1250 BC in the Levant), the old cosmology and mythologies of the goddess mother were radically transformed, reinterpreted, and in large measure even suppressed, by those suddenly intrusive patriarchal warrior tribesmen whose traditions have come down to us chiefly in the Old and New Testaments and in the myths of Greece. Two extensive geographical matrices were the source lands of these insurgent warrior waves: for the Semites, the Syro-Arabian deserts, where, as ranging nomads, they herded sheep and goats and later mastered the camel, and, for the Hellenic-Aryan stems, the broad plains of Europe and south Russia, where they had grazed their herds of cattle and early mastered the horse.[17]

The destruction wrought on the culture of Old Europe by the Kurgan tribes has been explored in Chapter 2, and the same pattern of disruption is apparent in the Near East as early as the fifth millennium BC. From the fourth millenium BC onwards, Indo-European tribes, in ever-increasing numbers, force their way into Mesopotamia, Anatolia, and lands stretching eastwards to the Indus Valley. At the same time Semitic tribes move into Mesopotamia and Canaan from the Syro-Arabian desert. The descendants of the old Palaeolithic hunters in their tribal homelands of the vast grassy steppes north of the Caspian and Black Seas have now become warriors, and we can trace their path of conquest as they appear as Hittites in Anatolia and Syria; Mittani, Hurrians and Kassites in Mesopotamia; Achaeans and then Dorians in Greece; and Aryans in the Indus Valley.[18] Wherever they penetrated, they established themselves as the ruling caste and their appearance is marked by a trail of devastation: in Anatolia alone some 300 cities were sacked and burned, among them Troy (*c.* 2300 BC), and this pattern was repeated from Greece to the Indus Valley.[19] There is little trace of the goddess myth to mitigate the barbarism of this ethos or to reunite the parts with the whole. Rather, the whole is violently fragmented and the parts set in opposition to each other, a situation of conflict that has endured to the present day. The echo of the mythology of war, which resounds in the *Mahabharata* as it does in the *Iliad* and the Old Testament, descends from these Bronze Age migrations.

The Aryans were predominantly a society of warriors: 'They were polygamous, patriarchal, proud of their genealogies, tent dwellers, filthy, and tough.'[20] They herded cattle, rode horses and invented the spoked wheel and light chariot about 2000–1750 BC.[21] They buried their tribal leaders beneath a mound, together with sacrificed attendants and horses, as the Kurgans had done before them. They worshipped sky gods, particularly the gods of lightning, storm, wind, sun and fire. Their mythological traditions were transmitted orally, a feature of their culture on which they placed great emphasis, prohibiting writing.[22] They esteemed the warrior above even the priest who performed their rituals of sacrifice, where the chief victim was the horse. A Sumerian scribe, writing about 2100 BC, may have described them when he wrote of the devastation wrought by 'a host whose onslaught was like a hurricane, a people who had never known a city'.[23] The sight of these men welded to their horses must have terrified the people they swept down upon, perhaps giving rise to the image of the centaur or man-horse.

The Aryans were not the only tribes to threaten the goddess culture. To the west of Mesopotamia is a vast desert, reaching from Syria in the north to the southern tip of Arabia in the south. It was this region, contrasting so radically with the fertile upland valleys and the lands nourished by great rivers, that was the matrix from which emerged all the Semitic tribes known and named during the Bronze and Iron Ages. Among these were the Akkadians, who established themselves in northern Sumeria and, eventually, under their king Sargon (2300 BC), gained control of the southern cities as well; also the Amoritic Babylonians, whose King Hammurabi (1800 BC) is famous for his code of laws. Another group of Amorites conquered the city of Jericho about 1450 BC, leaving it in ruins; they were succeeded by the Canaanites, who followed them into Palestine and Syria. The Hebrews in their turn conquered the Canaanites but succumbed to the Assyrians (580 BC), who had seized Babylon in 1100 BC and extended their huge empire over their terrified neighbours.[24]

But long before we know of them by their tribal names, the Semites had migrated into Mesopotamia, bringing with them their herds of sheep and goats, and perhaps merging with the inhabitants in earlier times more peacefully than their successors. The gods of the Semites dwelt in clouds and on mountain tops, and hurled thunderbolts like the gods of the Aryans. But they also had more the character of tribal gods, each protective of a specific tribal group and, later, of a city.

Both invading peoples introduced the idea of an opposition between the powers of light and darkness, imposing this polarity on the older view in which the whole contained both light and darkness in an ever-changing relationship. In both mythologies there is evidence of a desacralization of nature and of human life, which is starkly contrasted with the attitude of the Neolithic farmer, living close to the soil and to the rhythmic laws of the goddess as immanent in all life. The belief in the absolute separation between humanity and the deity is contrary to the Neolithic agriculturalist's vision, and neither is it Sumerian, so that we have to ask what can have given rise to it? Did the harshness of existence in the desert and the steppes call forth from the nomadic tribes the feeling that humanity was condemned to stand against the powers of nature and be forever defeated by them? The Semitic view of life gained ascendance in Mesopotamia as the desert tribes established themselves in the north of Sumeria and eventually achieved political dominance over the south as well. They brought to the literature of the Bronze Age a deep sense of the futility of life, the finality of death and a fundamental conviction of human guilt.

As a result of the Aryan and Semitic invasions, attitudes to life and to death were radically altered, as life was experienced as untrustworthy, and violent death became the norm rather than the exception. A relationship with nature many thousands of years old was disrupted as people no longer felt safe in villages, and sought refuge first in towns and then in cities girdled by immense walls. A new social group – that of the warrior – came into being and the former close-knit group of farmers became little more than serfs.[25] Indeed, the whole character of the mythology changes as goddesses as well as gods are infected by the warrior ethos, ratifying the barbaric actions of kings whose territorial ambitions draw them ever more deeply into the compulsion to conquer and enslave other peoples. Eliade writes that now 'the pursuit and killing of a wild animal becomes the mythical model for the conquest of a territory and the founding of a state'.[26]

The tribal migrations changed the character of the early Bronze Age and had a lasting effect on the evolution of consciousness in the civilizations that followed them. Their legacy lives on in pervasive attitudes and structures of response to life that have not been questioned and still have a controlling influence on the psyche today. Since this was a profound change for the worse, it is essential to make a distinction between the vision and values of the Aryan and Semitic tribes and those of the people who had been settled agriculturalists for thousands of years, apparently more or less peacefully. No less a question than our vision of human nature is involved here. Are we to regard the values of these nomadic tribes as specific to their own experience of life or as representative of the human race as a whole? If we see the ethos of conquest that they brought with them as specific to tribal consciousness only, then we do not need to generalize this vision of life and conclude that human nature itself is innately aggressive and war-like.

As the inheritors of both the Neolithic and Bronze Age experience – in what proportions relative to each other is inevitably unknowable – we have two 'historical souls' in us, one with the vision of life that prevailed before the Bronze Age and the other with the vision that was forged in the crucible of that terrifying age. We may have accepted uncritically only one of these visions as being intrinsic to human nature – the paradigm of 'the victors' – rather than asking whether it was something imposed upon us so long ago that it now seems 'natural'.

THE ORDER OF THE PATRIARCHY

This picture of continuous infiltration, both from the Syro-Arabian desert and the Central Asian steppe, helps us to understand how and why the goddess culture was fundamentally changed. The cosmology of the settled agriculturalists was eventually totally undermined and a pattern of war and conflict was established in the Near East that has endured to the present day. This change was reflected in a cosmology in which sky gods predominated and the order of society was correspondingly patriarchal in character. The moral order of the goddess culture, inherited from the Neolithic, was based on the principle of the relationship of the manifest to the unmanifest, where the manifest was the epiphany, or 'showing forth', of the unmanifest. Human, animal and plant life were all part of this epiphany. The moral order of the god culture, derived from the Aryan and Semitic tribes, was based on the paradigm of opposition and conquest: a view of life, and particularly nature, as something 'other' to be conquered. The manifest world was seen as intrinsically separate from the unmanifest world, which was now placed outside or beyond nature in the realm of the transcendent gods. 'It is now perfectly clear', writes Campbell,

> that before the violent entry of the late Bronze and early Iron Age nomadic Aryan cattle-herders from the north and Semitic sheep-and-goat-herders from the south into the old cult sites of the ancient world, there had prevailed in that world an essentially organic, vegetal, non-heroic view of the nature and necessities of life that was completely repugnant to those lion hearts for whom not the patient toil of earth but the battle spear and its plunder were the source of both wealth and joy. In the older mother myths and rites the light and darker aspects of the mixed thing that is life had been honored equally and together, whereas in the later, male-oriented, patriar-

chal myths, all that is good and noble was attributed to the new, heroic master gods, leaving to the native nature powers the character only of darkness – to which, also, a negative moral judgment now was added. For, as a great body of evidence shows, the social as well as mythic orders of the two contrasting ways of life were opposed. Where the goddess had been venerated as the giver and supporter of life as well as consumer of the dead, women as her representatives had been accorded a paramount position in society as well as in cult. Such an order of female-dominated social and cultic custom is termed, in a broad and general way, the order of Mother Right. And opposed to such, without quarter, is the order of the Patriarchy, with an ardor of righteous eloquence and a fury of fire and sword.[27]

These political changes were reflected in the changing position of certain goddesses and in the position of women. It seems that in early Sumeria, as in early Egypt and Crete, women played a public role in society, particularly the priestesses. They owned property, transacted business, and their interests were protected in the law courts. Sisters and brothers inherited property on equal terms from the family estate. Daughters who married took a dowry with them, which they kept in the event of a divorce.[28] In the centuries after 2300 BC the status of women in Sumerian society deteriorated. Although they still owned property, their husbands had to be consulted before buying and selling. Concurrently with these changes, the female deities in the Sumerian pantheon also lost their former position.[29]

Moreover, in the Akkadian north of Sumeria, which later became known as Babylonia, the Semitic tribes regarded women as possessions of men. Fathers and husbands claimed the power of life and death over daughters and wives. Sons inherited from their fathers, whereas daughters inherited nothing, and could be sold into slavery by their fathers and brothers. The birth of a son was hailed as a blessing, while a daughter could be exposed to die. Although the Semitic state of Babylonia ratified, in Hammurabi's famous code (1800 BC), the earlier Sumerian laws relating to the position of women, there is a marked deterioration after the third millennium BC, which suggests the strengthening of the Semitic over the Sumerian attitude. This was given added impetus by the customs of the Aryan people, who had no priestesses and treated women as servants or chattels.

Another crucial change in consciousness took place in Bronze Age Sumeria. A new attitude to death appeared about 2500 BC: death came to be regarded as the absolute end and opposite of life. The old lunar concept of death and rebirth no longer prevailed in Sumerian consciousness, although it did in Egypt to some extent. Darkness was now associated with what was *not* light or life, rather than, as in the lunar mythology, with the disappearance of manifestation and the place from which new life was born. Death became something final, terrifying, remorseless and without the promise of rebirth.

The profound implications of this cosmology were reflected in the astonishing increase of incidents of bloodshed and war, where it seems that the constant *celebration* of the killing of the enemy can be explained psychologically only through the ancient idea of ritual sacrifice. From this perspective, the 'sacrifice' of 'the other' in war would serve as a substitute for one's own death, and the annihilation of the opposing tribe would guarantee the renewal of life for one's own tribe. Sacrifice had been practised for millennia in different ways, but what was new was that the containing framework in which this idea 'made sense' as a restoration of the divine order was now missing. To try to understand war as ritual sacrifice and (which may be the same question) how indiscriminate slaughter could be justified, it may be helpful to pause and attempt the very difficult task of making some sense of the purpose and practice of sacrifice in earlier times, and even now.

THE RITUAL OF SACRIFICE

At an early stage of humanity's development, Frazer writes, human beings have a natural instinct of immortality. This may arise, he continues, from

> the sense of life which every man feels in his own breast ... Arguing apparently from his own sensations he conceives of life as an indestructible kind of energy, which when it disappears in one form must necessarily reappear in another, though in the new form it need not be immediately perceptible by us; in other words he infers that death does not destroy the vital principle nor even the conscious personality, but it merely transforms both of them into other shapes, which are not the less real because they commonly elude the evidence of our senses.[30]

One image of this energy that never dies was captured in the figure of the mother perpetually giving birth, as we saw in the Neolithic sculptures at Çatal Hüyük, where the idea behind continual renewal is the unity of life.

The great problem for human beings was how not to 'break' this unity in their need for food; for life lives on life, and taking life from one part of the whole allows another part of the whole to stay alive. In killing an animal, disturbing the soil and pulling up crops from the earth, people must have felt they were violating what was originally 'given', so they devised rituals that would magically restore what was lost. This is the experience of an Indian of the last century:

> You ask me to plough the ground! Shall I take a knife and tear my mother's bosom? Then when I die she will not take me to her bosom to rest. You ask me to dig for stone! Shall I dig under her skin for her bones? Then when I die, I cannot enter her body to be born again.[31]

The 'killing' and 'eating' the divine body of Mother Earth was felt to be a sacrilege, which needed rituals of atonement to invoke her goodwill and avoid her wrath. Neumann writes that rituals of sacrifice arose out of the need to restore a disrupted unity:

> Because the unity of life is the central phenomenon of the situation of psychic origination, every disturbance of this unity – the felling of a tree, the killing or eating of an animal, and so on – must be compensated by a ritual offering, a sacrifice. For early man all growth and development depend on man's sacrifice and ritual activity, precisely because man's living bond with the world and the human group is projected upon nature as a whole.[32]

The meaning of the word 'sacrifice' in Latin is 'to make whole or sacred' – *sacer facere* – and this seems to have been interpreted in the sense of restoring to the whole something that has been lost in order to allow life to continue. The renewal of life was associated with the shedding of blood as far back as Palaeolithic times, when red-ochre covered the bodies for burial as a substitute for blood, and was painted on the sculptured bodies of goddesses, as on the Goddess of Laussel. This was because blood was regarded as the life-force itself, and also because blood was centrally involved in the birth mysteries of women. The rites of primitive hunting tribes also work on the assumption that there is no such thing as death. Campbell explains:

> If the blood of an animal slain is returned to the soil, it will carry the life principle back to Mother Earth for rebirth, and the same beast will return next season to yield its temporal body again. The animals of the hunt are regarded in this way as willing victims who give their bodies to mankind with the understanding that adequate rites are to be performed to return the life principle to its source.[33]

In Neolithic times the blood of the sacrificed victim that soaked into the ground was believed actually to fertilize it, making the crops grow. Similarly, the striking or beating of the victim with branches in bud or leaf, often on the generative organs, was believed to transfuse vital energy from him to the earth or specific crop for whose growth he was sacrificed. In other rituals the beating of the victim was thought to banish malevolent influences from the community.

The Bronze Age myth of the mother goddess and her son–lover may offer an insight into the rationale behind the idea that death is necessary to renew life. But what does the son–lover signify in this context? The gradual separation of human consciousness from the original matrix (a term deriving from the Latin word for mother, *mater*) is characteristically expressed in the appearance of a young god, who comes to symbolize this emerging consciousness. The rise of the god in the Neolithic parallels humanity's growing discovery of the laws of natural life and how best to cooperate with them in order to survive. By the Bronze Age the generative principle of creation is separated from the mother goddess and identified with the god, so that both goddess and god are necessary for creation.

The god, who is firstly born from the goddess and then unites with her on equal terms as her consort, is then the living and dying aspect of the timeless whole, the matrix. Where the child of the goddess is female, the daughter is the new life inherent in the old. In the myths the son–lover or daughter is invariably lost to the underworld through an enforced death, and subsequently found or resurrected, at least on partial terms. What does this mean as an expression of the perennial attempt to understand how particular lives seem to come and go, whereas Life itself never, as it were, runs out?

Returning to the model suggested at the beginning of this chapter, the gradual 'swallowing' or 'dismemberment' of the moon during its dark phase may have offered an image of the idea that death was necessary to renew the principle of life. By 'imitating' the moon's apparent death, people would themselves assist in restoring fertility to the earth. In the myth of the Great Mother, the loss and finding of her son–lover or daughter appeared to be necessary for regeneration to continue. If the Great Mother is identified with the cycle of the moon, which is permanent and unchanging, and the son or daughter with the individual phases that wax and wane, then their disappearance could have been interpreted as a 'sacrifice' back into the Mother that allowed the cycle to begin again. Enacting the dark phase *literally*, the tribal practice would be to kill and dismember a 'sacred' victim who personified the dying moon as an image of dying life, burying the parts of the body in the earth, the Mother, to ensure that the life principle would persist and the crops would reappear. It is significant that in the myth of Osiris the body is dismembered into fourteen parts, the number of days of the waning moon. Similarly, the myth of the descent into the belly of the whale (Jonah) or hell (Jesus) – often pictured as the gaping jaws of a great monster – invariably takes three days, the number of days the moon is gone and the sky is black.

If we try to understand what has gone wrong in the thinking that leads to human or animal sacrifice, we might put it in the context of humanity's irrevocable disorientation on becoming aware of the fact of mortality. That is the moment when spirit is born. Up to that moment there is not a union of spirit and nature; there is simply unity that is unconscious of itself. Thus nature and spirit arise together in the hope that spirit will redeem the nature that is lost in the very act of perceiving it. Humanity's act of becoming aware that it is a creature distinct from animal and plant ruptures the wholeness of the divine order by splitting consciousness into a duality of perceiver and perceived. As Hesiod puts it: 'When gods and men parted, sacrifice was created.'[34] This separation from nature, the condition of the birth of human consciousness, is experienced as a wound that continually challenges us to understand our relation to nature, and to heal the separation in ourselves between our 'human' and our 'animal' natures.

One of the illusory ways of trying to heal the wound is to look *outside* for the image of the whole that reunites the parts. As long as this wound is unconscious, both the original wholeness and the dismembered part are projected on to external images that carry the two aspects of humanity's total being. The Great Mother served as the image of humanity's original wholeness and her son as the image of the part separated from the totality that once was all. When the cycle of the moon is experienced mythically, the part, which is the son, dies and is reunited with the whole, and a new part is born from their union. The myth gives reassurance that death is not final, simply one phase of a greater cycle. This myth and all the imagery of the goddess can be seen as arising from the human need to belong to the whole and the fear of becoming irrevocably cut off from it. The rituals of sacrifice, whether animal or human, then served the purpose of restoring the lost feeling of unity, but they could never accomplish the permanent healing of the wound; for, as the experience of Depth Psychology indicates, so long as the images were projected and the rites literally enacted, the wound would remain unrecognized, and no true healing could take place.

In rituals of sacrifice, human beings, as *bios*, performing the sacrifice themselves on a chosen victim, are in danger of unconsciously identifying themselves with *zoe*, which is the greatest risk of any approach to the numinous. The terrifying lions that guard the entrance to the inner chamber of the Palaeolithic cave, and later stand at the gates of temples, are expressly there as a warning: do not cross the threshold with a literal mind. As long as the lions, sphinxes, griffins and other fierce and enigmatic beasts still have the power to terrify, the transition from literal enactment to symbolic understanding has not been made. When this warning is not heeded, an identification of *bios* with *zoe* takes place, in which the part forgets it is only a part and, assuming the mystery of life can be solved in its own terms, appropriates to itself the ordering of life. Here, the human being is apparently released from the complexity of the human condition by playing the role of the deity.

While this sacrifice was undoubtedly experienced in a state of mythic seizure as a sacred act in which people 'assisted' goddess or god, it can be recognized instead as a compensation for the feeling of impotence in the face of forces that they could not comprehend or control. Consequently, the act of sacrifice, in which one human being kills another, might be best understood as a symptom of a radical disorder of the psyche in which the person or tribe has claimed for itself the powers of the deity. In the language of psychology, this is an unconscious defence against fear, expressed in the dual reflex of 'denial' and 'inversion': 'I am not afraid and I am powerful.' With Campbell, we will call this 'mythic inflation',[35] and consider the practice of sacrifice to be the earliest collective expression of what has come in this century to be called 'psychosis'. Psychosis is the ultimate defence against *unconscious* terror.

In the ritual of sacrifice human beings project and focus their fear of death on a specific human or animal, so that the slaying of this particular living being is at the same time a slaying of their fear, for the death of the other substitutes for their own. If, on the other hand, the fear is made conscious, it becomes clear that it is their own creation and does not exist in the nature of things, so it is the fear itself that must be 'sacrificed'. If this can be done, they are then reunited with the whole from which their fear has separated them. Obviously, as a warning instinct, fear is essential for the preservation of life, but when the object of fear is not a specific danger but the *idea* of death, the original signal is distorted so that a particular death and 'Death itself' are confused.

Sacrifice of the God–King: Ritual Regicide

The myth of the divine being whose body is 'given' as creation and as food for the human race is found all over the world as an image of the mysterious process whereby the One becomes the Many while still remaining the One.[36] It also explains how the Many – as the temporal manifestation of the One – can die, while the One is without end. In some agricultural rituals when the crops were cut down, a victim was selected to personify the dying corn, the waning moon and the old year's passing away; his sacrifice allowed the renewal of the life force. At one time, Frazer suggests, this role was played by the king, who in turn played the role of the god.[37]

Frazer, in his *Dying God*, has shown how the desire to restore the unity disrupted by the need for food was translated into rituals in which the king, high priest or sometimes a young girl or child was sacrificed at the end of a fixed period, as well as in times of special adversity. The king or high priest personified the life energy that was both divine and human. Any sign of illness or weakness in the king threatened the course of nature and the continuity of life. The sacrifice of the 'old' king then ensured that the forces of decay would be arrested, just as the installation of a 'young' or 'new' king would renew life for the whole community. So long-lasting were these rites of death and resurrection that they are still enacted in various guises all over the world. Even in this century, spring festivals took place in which 'death', in the figure of an old man, was 'carried out', and another figure, dressed in leaves, bark and moss, symbolizing spring and the renewal of life, perhaps the 'Green Man' of many legends, was 'carried in'. As Frazer says, these rituals suggest that 'the killing of the god, that is, of his human incarnation, is . . . merely a necessary step to his revival or resurrection in a better form'.[38]

In Christian ritual this archaic rite has been continued for centuries at the end of each winter, in Lent, the time of mourning that precedes the death and resurrection of Jesus with the advent of spring. It is celebrated in the Easter procession of penitents in Seville, together with the flower-decked floats that carry images of the Virgin Mary and Jesus. The same ritual month of mourning is observed by Islam during Ramadan, and in the Jewish religion at Passover. These ceremonies are the legacies of a time when human sacrifice was enacted in reality, as in the practice of regicide and the offering of first-born children, together with the sacrifice of finger joints and foreskins. At various points in the history of different cultures animals began to replace human beings in religious ritual. The bull, the boar and the ram were eventually sacrificed in the king's place as the animal in whom his powers were concentrated and embodied.

What is most interesting, as Frazer points out, is that the king, man, woman or animal selected for sacrifice could also be regarded as a scape-goat who would carry away with his death all the afflictions of the com-munity – disease, famine and malevolent influences. These were first ritually transferred to the sacrificial victim and then banished or exorcized by his death. Frazer suggests that there may once have been two separate rituals and that at some time they were combined:

> On the one hand we have seen that it has been customary to kill the human or animal god in order to save his divine life from being weakened by the inroads of age. On the other hand we have seen that it has been customary to have a general expulsion of evils and sins once a year. Now if it occurred to people to combine these two customs, the result would be the employment of the dying god as a scapegoat. He was killed, not originally to take away sin, but to save the divine life from the degeneracy of old age; but since he had to be killed at any rate, people may have thought that they might as well seize the opportunity to lay upon him the burden of their sufferings and sins, in order that he might bear it away with him to the unknown world beyond the grave.[39]

Frazer explains that the custom of 'killing a god' is so archaic that its legacy in much later customs is not recognized:

> The divine character of the animal or man is forgotten and he comes to be regarded merely as an ordinary victim . . . When a nation becomes civilized, if it does not drop human sacrifices altogether, it at least selects as victims only such wretches as would be put to death at any rate. Thus the killing of a god may sometimes be confounded with the execution of a criminal.[40]

The degenerate practice of sacrificing another in order to vindicate an idea and implicitly save oneself can be seen to lie behind the witch 'hunts' and the burning of heretics, as well as in contemporary acts of terrorism. From the ease with which human barbarism can be justified in these terms it must once have required – and often still does – a decisive struggle even to perceive the act of taking life from another person as morally wrong.

Sacrifice in the Bronze Age

In Sumeria, Egypt, Crete and other Bronze Age cultures, including the Indus Valley, the older agricultural rituals connected with the earth's fertility continued to be practised. The king was both the personification of the life of the community and the divine life of vegetation. In his ritual role as the incarnation of the principle of fertility – the 'son–lover' of the goddess – the king was held to be half divine and half human. His 'wholeness' was given new definition as perfect health, knowledge, wisdom and strength against adversity.

In the early Bronze Age it seems that the death of the king was required to renew the fertility of life. Later, from the evidence of the ritual burials in the Sumerian city of Ur, it seems as if the natural death (or maybe still the sacrifice) of the king or queen required the further sacrifice of their courtiers (a sentiment that persisted in the ritual of *suttee* in India). The sixteen burials at Ur, and the numerous burials in Egypt, bear witness to a ritual that to the people of that time, living in a state of mythic identification with their king, was probably felt to be essential to their security.

The astounding burials discovered by Sir Leonard Woolley at Ur, the Sumerian city sacred to the moon god, Nanna, have left an image of a Bronze Age sacrificial ritual in all its splendour and barbarity. Here lay the bodies of priest-kings, or their substitutes, together with those of priestess-queens and many court or temple servants, including charioteers, musicians and soldiers. In the most elaborate of these graves the king, whose name was A-bar-gi, had sixty-five people who died with, or soon after, him, and the queen, whose name was Shub-ad, had twenty-five:

> We found five bodies lying side by side in a shallow sloping trench . . .
> Then below them . . . another group of bodies, those of ten women carefully arranged in two rows; they wore head-dresses of gold, lapis lazuli, and carnelian, and elaborate bead necklaces. At the end of the row lay the remains of a wonderful harp . . . and from the front of it projected a splendid head of a bull wrought in gold with eyes and beard of lapis lazuli; across the ruins of the harp lay the bones of the gold-crowned harpist . . .
> At one end, on the remains of a wooden bier, lay the body of the queen, a gold cup near her hand, the upper part of the body was entirely hidden by a mass of beads of gold, silver, lapis lazuli, carnelian, agate, and chalcedony, long strings of which, hanging from a collar, had formed a cloak reaching to the waist and bordered below with a broad band of tubular beads of lapis, carnelian, and gold . . .[41]

Figure 8. Reconstruction of the king's harp; *c.* 2500 BC. The Royal Graves at Ur.

Woolley writes that human sacrifice was confined to the funerals of royal personages. There was no sign of anything similar in the graves of commoners, however rich. Neither the kings, queens nor the courtiers appear to have suffered in these royal graves, or to have gone unwillingly to their death. They must have been given a soporific drink before being buried alive.

War as a Ritual Sacrifice

It may have been as a result of the Aryan and Semitic invasions of Sumeria that a variation of the archaic idea of ritual sacrifice began to evolve, the sacrifice of victims of war. The apparently endless and otherwise gratuitous conquest of territory must have come to serve the ritual purpose of securing the surrogate sacrifice of 'the other' in place of oneself or one's group. This was an ominous extension of the Neolithic idea that ritual sacrifice would ensure the continued life of the community and the renewal of the world order. On this hypothesis the wholesale extermination of other people – now designated the 'enemy' – became a new way magically to avoid death, and the blood of the enemy shed in battle was thought to 'fertilize' the life of one's own tribal group, and even increase the 'divine potency' of the king himself. Since fear lies at the heart of sacrificial rituals, it follows that communities that feel threatened, either by natural forces or by attack from outside, will experience relief from fear in the sacrifice of others. As the Bronze Age progressed, the incidence of war and the victims of war increased incalculably, until the time when the barbarism of Assyria extinguished what was left of the civilization of Mesopotamia.

Figure 9. The stele of Naram Sin; *c.* 2300 BC. Susa. Naram Sin of Agade, wearing the horned crown of a god, stands in victory over the Lullubians. One captive in the centre appears to have been hurled downwards.

THE DEGENERATION OF THE MOTHER GODDESS

The image of unity, incarnated in the goddess of life-and-death, did not survive the bitter experience of the carnage of war, and a radical transformation took place in the image of the goddess. The Great Mother gradually assumed two separate roles: life and death were no longer regarded as two complementary aspects of her divine totality, but as opposites excluding each other. One brought hope and joy, the other terror and despair. The waters beneath the earth that were once filled with the generative power of the goddess now shrank to a single river of death, or a barren underworld of dust and darkness. Neumann, in his book *The Great Mother*, has described the Mother Goddess as separated into two opposing functions from the beginning: 'positive' and 'negative' – the 'good' mother, who gives life, and the 'terrible' mother, who takes it away.[42] But this differentiation of role is not truly felt in earlier millennia, when there seems to have existed an experience of a totality prior to these distinctions. It is important not to read back into the Palaeolithic and Neolithic ages those distinctions that we unthinkingly accept because we have inherited them ourselves from the Bronze Age. The radical difference in feeling between the 'good' mother and the 'terrible' mother belongs rather to the oppositional paradigm of the Aryan and Semitic tribes, which was imposed upon, and gradually accepted by, the people they conquered. The evidence now available from the Neolithic shows that this opposition had not always existed. Gimbutas insists that 'there was no isolated image of a Mother Terrible; the aspects of death and life are inextricably intertwined . . . The (Old) European Great Goddess, like the Sumerian Ninkhursag, gave life to the Dead.'[43]

From about 2000 BC the Babylonians and the Assyrians portrayed the underworld in horrifying detail. The dead consigned to its regions become impotent spirits, condemned to the most minimal existence the human mind can imagine. In the *Epic of Gilgamesh*, Enkidu tells his dream of the underworld:

> There is the house whose people sit in darkness; dust is their food and clay their meat. They are clothed like birds with wings for covering, they see no light, they sit in darkness. I entered the house of dust and I saw the kings of the earth, their crowns put away for ever; rulers and princes, all those who once wore kingly crowns and ruled the world in the days of old.[44]

This description, from the second-millennium-BC *Epic of Gilgamesh*, is the earliest text that gives this despairing vision of death. It anticipates the image in the *Odyssey* of the dead as 'the disembodied wraiths of men'.[45] When Penelope's suitors are led away, they are described as 'gibbering like bats that squeak and flutter in the depths of some mysterious cave when one of them has fallen from the rocky roof, losing his hold on his clustered friends'.[46] An Assyrian tablet tells of a dark apocalypse in which the angels are all demons. The sphinx, the lion and the griffin all entered the human imagination at this time, and survived through medieval religious iconography and heraldry into the modern world.[47] The dead are no longer the ancestral guides and counsellors of the living, as they once were in the Neolithic and early Sumeria. With this transformation of attitudes to death, there seems to be a fundamental rupture of continuity with the past.

On the other hand, in Egypt the old Neolithic view continued, which must have had something to do with the fact that Egypt did not suffer mass invasion. Egyptians were not filled with terror and despair at the prospect of death, but with the hope that they might enter the fields of paradise. One Egyptian says: 'I know the field of reeds of Re ... the height of its barley ... the dwellers of the horizon reap it beside the Eastern Souls.'[48] This rebirth was not for the king alone, nor the priests or nobles, but for all souls who leave the earth: 'There is not one who fails to reach that place ... as for the duration of life upon earth, it is a sort of dream; they say "Welcome, safe and sound" to him who reaches the West.'[49]

THE GODDESS OF WAR

It may be precisely because the image of 'goddess of death' is split off from the original image of the goddess of life-and-death that a new image appears: the goddess of war, that is, the goddess of death to others. This is the goddess Ishtar as she once was:

> Reverence the queen of women, the greatest of all the gods; she is clothed with delight and with love, she is full of ardour, enchantment, and voluptuous joy, in her lips she is sweet, in her mouth is Life, when she is present felicity is greatest; how glorious she looks, the veils thrown over her head, her lovely form, her brilliant eyes.[50]

And this is who she becomes: 'lady of sorrows and of battles'.[51] A Babylonian hymn addresses her with the words: 'Oh star of lamentation, brothers at peace together you cause to fight one another, and yet you give constant friendship. Mighty one, lady of battles who overturns mountains.'[52] The goddess now brings fear to the heart and destruction to those named as enemies; she drinks the blood of the victims who were formerly her children.

The Sumerian Inanna says:

> When I stand in the front line of battle
> I am the leader of all the lands,
> When I stand at the opening of the battle,
> I am the quiver ready to hand,
> When I stand in the midst of the battle,

Figure 10. Inanna–Ishtar
as goddess of war;
c. 2000 BC.

> I am the heart of the battle,
> The arm of the warriors,
> When I begin moving at the end of the battle,
> I am an evilly rising flood . . .[53]

The Babylonian Ishtar proclaims: 'I will flay your enemies and present them to you'[54] – a chilling evocation of the degenerated goddess. The king offers her sacrifices to invoke her help in the seizure of the territory of others. The goddess has effectively become the servant of the king's will to power, and so the figure who in totality used to inspire a reverence for the sanctity of life, now, fragmented, justifies the profane disregard of it.

In Egypt also a terrifying image of the goddess emerges in a story of the killing of humanity. The Egyptian goddess Sekhmet was imagined as a lioness, whose 'mane smoked with fire, her back had the colour of blood, her countenance glowed like the sun, her eyes shone with fire'.[55] A document from *c.* 2000 BC tells the tale of how the goddess could not be halted in her slaughter of the human race. The gods, to save humanity, ordered the brewing of 7,000 jars of beer, to which was added a red powder so that it resembled human blood, and then this liquid was poured out over the fields. With the coming of morning the goddess gazed at her reflection in it, drank it all and returned to her palace intoxicated. So it was that humanity was saved.

MYTHIC INFLATION

The potentiality to 'mythic inflation' of tribal leaders – whether of the Bronze Age, Iron Age or twentieth century – is, perhaps, the one aspect of the human character that offers most grounds for concern about the future of the species. Campbell defines the state of mythic inflation as 'the exaltation of ego in the posture of a god'.[56] Individuals take upon themselves the powers and attributes that, they believe, belong to a deity, even to the extent of believing the deity is incarnated in their own persons or that they are enacting the will of the deity. In the Bronze Age it happened with King Sargon, 'the mighty king, Monarch of Agade'. Legend said he was born of a temple priestess and an unknown father and was raised to the rank of king and son–lover by the goddess Inanna–Ishtar, so coming to rule over the 'black-headed people':

> My mother, an *enitum* [temple priestess], conceived me,
>   in secret she bore me.
> She set me in a basket of rushes,
>   with bitumen she sealed my lid.
> She cast me into the river, which
>   rose not over me.
> The river bore me up and carried
>   me to Akki, the drawer of water.
> Akki, the drawer of water, lifted me
>   out as he dipped his bucket.
> Akki, the drawer of water, took me
>   as his son and reared me.
> Akki, the drawer of water,
>   appointed me as his gardener.
> While I was a gardener, Ishtar
>   granted me love.
> And for four and . . . years I
>   exercised kingship,
> The black-headed people I ruled, I governed.[57]

This formula is the first of many legends of divine origin in which the old imagery of the goddess culture is transferred to the king in order to legitimize his rule. The focus of interest has now shifted from the goddess to her 'son', the king. The myth of the goddess is then literally interpreted so that the king as her son takes himself to be divine. Here is the continuing story of Sargon, who in 2350 BC extended his rule from Akkad in the Semitic north of Sumeria to the south, and eventually ruled over the immense territory extending between the two seas – the Persian Gulf and the Mediterranean:

Sargon, king of Agade, Viceregent of Inanna (Ishtar), King of Kish, pashishu of Anu (the god of the heavens), King of the Land, great ishakku of Enlil (the air god): the city of Uruk he smote and its walls he destroyed. With the people of Uruk he battled and he routed them. With Luggalzaggisi, King of Uruk he battled and he captured him and in fetters he led him through the gate of Enlil. Sargon of Agade battled with the man of Ur and vanquished him; his city he smote and its wall he destroyed. E-Ninmar he smote and its wall he destroyed, and its entire territory, from Lagash to the sea, he smote. And he washed his weapons in the sea. With the man of

Figure 11. Head of Sargon I; *c.* 2300 BC.

Umma he battled and he routed him and smote his city and destroyed its wall. Unto Sargon, King of the Land, Enlil gave no adversary; from the upper sea to the lower sea, Enlil subjected to him the lands.[58]

THE 'GREAT REVERSAL'

As the Bronze Age progresses, a new thread enters the great tapestry of human evolution. It is terror: not the terror of nature, but the terror of death by the hand of other human beings. The lamentations that begin to appear during the third millennium BC, rising to a crescendo during the second and first millennia BC, bear witness to an ever-rising tide of barbarism, which battered the walls of the cities in the valleys and flowed over their inhabitants, bringing death and slavery to many thousands and mortal fear to all.

These calamitous events brought about what Campbell calls the 'Great Reversal', when death came to be welcomed as a rescue from this terror and was no longer viewed as 'a continuance of the wonder of life'.[59] The Sumerian scholar Jacobsen confirms this, writing here of Sumeria:

> With the beginning of the third millennium BC, the ever present fear of famine was no longer the main reminder of the precariousness of the human condition. Sudden death by the sword in wars or raids by bandits joined famine as equally fearsome threats ... As far as we can judge, the fourth millennium and the ages before it had been moderately peaceful. Wars and raids were not unknown; but they were not constant and they did not dominate existence. In the third millennium they appear to have become the order of the day. No one was safe ... queens and great ladies like their humble sisters faced the constant possibility that the next day might find them widowed, torn from home and children, and enslaved in some barbarous household.[60]

A queen's lament speaks for itself:

> Alas! that day of mine, on which I was destroyed.
> Alas! that day of mine, on which I was destroyed.
>
> . . . . .
>
> For on it he came hither to me in my house,
> for on it he turned in the mountains,
> into the road to me,
> for on it the boat came on my river toward me,
> for on it, (heading) toward me,
> the boat moored at my quay,
> for on it the master of the boat came in to me,
> for on it he reached out his dirty hands toward me,
> for on it he yelled to me: 'Get up! Get on board!'
> For on it the goods were taken aboard in the bow.
> For on it I, the queen, was taken on board in the stern.
> For on it I grew cold with the most shivering fear.
> The foe trampled with his booted feet into my chamber!
> That foe reached out his dirty hands toward me!
> He reached out the hand toward me, he terrified me!
> That foe reached out his hand toward me,
> made me die with fear.[61]

Enormous walls were built round every city, like the ones Gilgamesh built round Uruk in about 2700 BC. The former network of small villages vanished as people took refuge within the city. The new conditions required a ruler of superior strength and courage, a defender of his city with the limitless powers of emergency. With the rise of the powerful king, the epic came into being, celebrating the heroic exploits of the warrior-ruler. The destruction of a city in war was experienced by the conquered people as the anger or hatred of a god, and likened to a hurricane-force wind.

From Egypt in *c.* 2200 BC comes this lament of a man, in dialogue with his soul, who longs for death as a release from the horror of life:

> To whom can I speak today?
> Brothers are evil
> and the friends of today are unloving.
> Hearts are full of greed
> and everyone clings to his neighbour's goods.
> The gentle man has perished
> and the man without scruples goes everywhere.
>
> To whom can I speak today?
> The wrongdoer is a close friend
> and the former brother in action is become an enemy.
> None remember the past
> and he who used to do good has no help.
> Faces are turned away
> and every man looks sideways at his brethren.

Death is before me today,
like the coming of health to a sick man,
like going into a garden after a sickness.
Death is before me today
like the wafting of myrrh,
like swaying under a sail on a windy day.

Death is before me today,
like the clearing of the sky,
like a man who looks for something he does not know.
Death is before me today,
as when a man longs to see his home
after many long years in captivity.[62]

As the image of death becomes increasingly terrifying and without redemption, the need to achieve immortality while living becomes more urgent. Heroism – the extraordinary act that elevates the idea of human nature – was one response to the power of death, which was thereby vanquished by immortal fame. The myth of the hero was a solar myth in that it was an imitation on earth of the sun's conquest of the powers of darkness in heaven, as the coming of dawn was now perceived. The emphasis fell therefore on conflict and mastery, and the target of the solar hero on earth was characteristically some dimension of the old order of the lunar goddess culture that the hero sought to change. In the new myth the hero stands alone against the opposing force, supported by his father in heaven, in striking contrast to the old myth of the goddess and her son–lover, where the drama was one of the ever-changing phases of relationship. The focus has now shifted from the goddess to her son, from the cosmos to humanity.

In the Sumerian *Epic of Gilgamesh*, for instance – the first story of the hero – and in all the hero myths of the Bronze and Iron Ages, it is the great individual who takes on the challenge of changing forces and powers that may lie visibly in external life but are ultimately limitations of the inner life. It is as though this era in human evolution represents a stage where people must strive to know rather than to be, where they have to lose their sense of relationship with the whole in order to discover themselves as individuals beyond their roles as members of a community or tribe. Mythologically, this transition can be expressed as the movement from a goddess to a god. The gradual process of this movement will be followed through the goddesses Inanna and Isis in Chapters 5 and 6, and in Chapter 7 through the total deposition of the Mother Goddess Tiamat in the Iron Age.

5

INANNA–ISHTAR:
MESOPOTAMIAN GODDESS
OF THE GREAT ABOVE
AND THE GREAT BELOW

An eye is meant to see things.
The Soul is here for its own joy.

Rumi

In Figure 1 Inanna wears the horned and tiered crown enclosing a cone –
image of the sacred mountain – which is worn by all the major Sumerian
deities, and also the flounced and tiered dress worn by Sumerian goddesses. An eight-rayed star is near her, the image of the planet we now
call Venus; for in the mythology of this goddess the crescent moon and
the evening star, as the 'daughter' of the moon, belonged together. She
carries a staff of intertwined serpents[1] and stands or rests her foot upon
lions. Shoots ending in buds spring from her left shoulder, and ray-like
maces, emblems of her power, emerge from her right shoulder, since by
the time this cylinder seal was made Inanna's original nature had changed
and she was invoked as goddess of war. Sometimes these buds and maces
alternate with formalized images of the serpent. Both the serpents and the
wings springing from her shoulders show her descent from the Neolithic
Bird and Snake Goddess, and announce that she was once the source

Figure 1. Inanna as Queen of Heaven and Earth; cylinder seal, Akkad
period, *c.* 2334–2154 BC.

of the Upper and the Lower Waters, Queen of Heaven, Earth and Underworld.

Inanna, or Ishtar as she was called in northern Sumeria, was one of the three great goddesses of the Bronze Age, the others being Isis of Egypt and Cybele of Anatolia. All three reflect the image of the Great Mother who presided over the earliest civilizations that arose between Europe and the Indian subcontinent. Inanna relates the Neolithic Great Mother to the Biblical Eve, Sophia and Mary. Her imagery is the foundation of Sophia (the Hebrew Hokhmah, or Wisdom), the Gnostic Great Mother and even the medieval Shekhinah of the Jewish Kabbalah. Sumerian civilization offers an essential perspective on later Hebrew and Christian culture, which inherited so much from it, and is the source of many stories and images in the Old Testament, including the Garden of Eden, the Flood, the Wisdom tradition and the Song of Songs. With Inanna, as with Isis in Egypt, the image of the archetypal feminine is given a defini- tion in mythology that has endured – however obscured, fragmented and distorted it has become – for over 5,000 years.

The image of Inanna reaches from earth to heaven: she is 'clothed with the heavens and crowned with the stars';[2] her lapis jewels reflect the blue of the sky and the blue of the fathomless waters of space that the Sumer- ians named 'The Deep'. She wears the rainbow as her necklace and the zodiac as her girdle. But Inanna is also named 'The Green One', 'She of the springing verdure',[3] after the rippling green corn that the earth wears as her mantle in spring. She carries on her head the lunar horns, which proclaim her to be the descendant of the ancient goddess who originally was the sky, earth and underworld. As early as 3500 BC, perhaps far earlier, Inanna was worshipped as the Great Goddess of Sumeria and named as Virgin Queen of Heaven and Earth. Amazingly, 3,000 years later, she was still worshipped at Uruk – the early Sumerian city that was the centre of her cult – and was still driving a chariot harnessed with the lions that had always been one of her epiphanies.[4]

Through the cuneiform script that has miraculously preserved them, her many titles resound: 'Queen of Heaven and Earth', 'Priestess of Heaven', 'Light of the World', 'Morning and Evening Star', 'First Daugh- ter of the Moon', 'Loud Thundering Storm', 'Righteous Judge', 'Forgiver of Sins', 'Holy Shepherdess', 'Hierodule of Heaven', 'Opener of the Womb', 'Framer of All Decrees', 'The Amazement of the Land'.[5] Her sacred number is the lunar fourteen or fifteen. Roses or rosettes adorned her temples. A Sumerian hymn addresses Inanna as the Great Lady of Heaven:

> I say, 'Hail!' to the Holy One who appears in the heavens!
> I say, 'Hail!' to the Holy Priestess of Heaven!
> I say 'Hail!', to Inanna Great Lady of Heaven![6]

The hymns and prayers offered in southern Sumeria to Inanna, Virgin Queen of Heaven and Earth, and in northern Sumeria to her counterpart,

Ishtar, anticipate those offered today to Mary, Virgin Queen of Heaven. Their images were, like Mary's, the crescent moon and the morning and evening star we call Venus, after the Roman goddess of love. Inanna's dying and resurrected consort annually descended into the underworld, slain by the burning rays of the July sun, which parched and shrivelled the land, and ascended again as the young shoots of corn that proclaimed the renewal of the earth's fertility. Mary, like Ishtar, has a son who dies a sacrificial death, descends into the underworld and is resurrected from the dead. The mourning goddess and the suffering god accompany each other in the lunar myth, which has endured intact throughout this immense span of time, enshrined in the rituals of a Church that still greets the birth of a mother's son at Christmas, mourns his death on Good Friday and celebrates his resurrection on Easter Sunday.

The rare cylinder seal depicted in Figure 2 – there are only five of a goddess and her son (see also Fig. 12) – shows the goddess holding her child above her lap. In front of him and slightly above him, over a ritual vase, are the eight-rayed star and lunar crescent, which suggest the goddess is Inanna–Ishtar. To the left, two figures approach the mother and child. This image anticipates the story of the Nativity and the brilliant star that illuminated the birth place of the divine child at Bethlehem. It is possible that the story of the Nativity at the beginning of the Gospels of Luke and Matthew, and the story of the trial, crucifixion and resurrection at the end of the four Gospels, actually retrace the lineaments of the far older story that belonged to the mythology of the goddess Inanna and her son–lover Dumuzi. Even the star that hovered over the manger at Bethlehem reflects the luminous planet that was Inanna's star 3,000 years earlier. Inanna, as Holy Shepherdess and Keeper of the Cow-byre, gave birth then to the son who was named 'the Shepherd', 'Lord of the Sheepfold', 'Lord of the Net' and 'Lord of Life'.[7]

This pattern of resemblance invites the question: was the archetypal story, which is presented as a 'revelation' by Christianity, once part of the lost or destroyed Wisdom literature of the Hebrew people, and was

Figure 2. The Sumerian goddess and her son; Akkad period,
c. 2334–2154 BC.

its original 'model' Sumerian? Babylon during the Captivity (586–538 BC) was the meeting place of Sumerian and Hebrew culture, and many thousands of Jews stayed in Mesopotamia after the years of exile and established thriving communities there. It may be that this myth of the goddess and her son was preserved and cherished by certain of them until it was retold in the form it was given in the Gospels. Once the older imagery of the goddess is discovered, her long-obscured role in the Christian story becomes apparent. Moreover, the reappearance of the old myth in an unbroken sequence from 3000 BC to the present day suggests that the psyche needs, indeed insists on, a continual restatement of these archetypal images.

SUMERIA

The composite image of the Sumerian goddess Inanna and her Semitic counterpart in Babylonia, the goddess Ishtar (who later becomes the great goddess of Assyria), emerges from the poems and hymns that have been so laboriously translated in the course of this century, drawing upon the vast quantity of material excavated during the last one. One hundred and fifty years ago no one had heard of Sumeria and few people today know of the brilliance of Sumerian culture, which flourished in the fourth and third millennia BC. There now exist some 30,000 lines of Sumerian writings, mostly in poetic form, which have been translated during the last forty years, and these include some 29 epic tales and 200 or so hymns, together with collections of proverbs.[8] Yet all this is only a fragment in relation to what remains to be discovered from untranslated tablets still buried in the vaults of museums and beneath the sands of the Iraqi desert. There are tantalizing hints of myths still unknown. It is from this fragment, however, that our knowledge of Inanna is drawn. 'The Descent of Inanna to the Nether World' – telling perhaps the most interesting of all Sumerian myths – pre-dates a similar poem describing Ishtar's descent by over 1,000 years. It was only when tablets were discovered at Nippur, one of the northern Sumerian cities that later belonged to the Babylonian and then the Assyrian Empire, that the existence of the older myth was revealed.

Why is Sumeria so important? The Old and New Testaments are saturated with images that came originally from Sumeria and reached Judaic culture through the medium of Babylonian, Assyrian and Canaanite culture. Only Egypt can rival Sumeria's pervasive influence. Much later, and farther to the west, the mythology of the Greeks and the Romans bears witness to the legacy of Sumerian images. To the east, the rich mythology of Hinduism and Mahayana Buddhism reveals a common ground with Sumerian mythology. Although the details are not yet fully clear,[9] the discovery of Sumeria is like a revelation. No one has conveyed

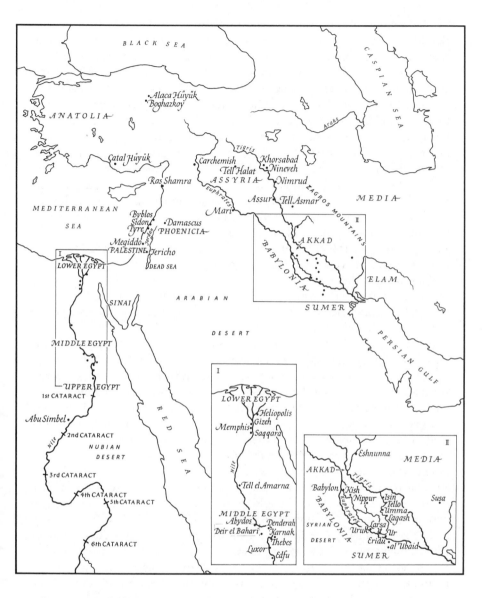

Map 5. Principal Mesopotamian and Egyptian cities, *c.* 2500–1000 BC.

the excitement of the archaeologists exploring the buried cities of Mesopotamia more graphically than Smith, who discovered the tablets at Nippur telling the story of the Flood; Layard, who excavated Nineveh; and Woolley, who uncovered the treasure of the burials at Ur.

The origins of the Sumerians and their language, which is neither Semitic nor Indo-European, are still a mystery. However, the fusion of their energy and intellect with the mythology and technical skills of the indigenous peoples already established in southern Mesopotamia created an explosion whose effect accelerated the development of every aspect of cultural life in the Near East. The system of writing they invented and their cosmology were so revolutionary that wherever their influence reached, it precipitated the growth of literature, law, mathematics, astronomy and the careful keeping of records and accounts. The area around Basra, where Iran and Iraq meet, once witnessed the genesis of this prodigious civilization, whose influence extended to Anatolia, Egypt and the Indus Valley. Woolley remarks on the strength of Sumerian influence on Egypt early in the fourth millennium BC.[10] Sumerian culture, which was already flourishing at this date, evolved predominantly in southern Mesopotamia, in the cities of Ur, Uruk, Lagash, Larsa and Eridu – the last was the most venerated because it was the oldest of the five believed to date to a time before the Flood. The remains of seventeen temples were discovered beneath the Third Dynasty ziggurat at Eridu, and radio-carbon testing has established a date of 5000–4900 BC for the earliest temple built at Uruk, which became Inanna's city.[11]

Farther to the north of Sumeria were the cities of Nippur, Akkad, Babylon, Sippar and Kish, which were inhabited mainly by the Semitic peoples, who were already established there and who at first accepted the supremacy of their southern neighbours, but then engaged in a long struggle for power with the cities where the Sumerians were dominant. Ultimately, *c.* 1750 BC, the northern cities seized control under the leadership of Hammurabi, and the Sumerian south was eclipsed. The transition from peaceful coexistence to rivalry and war, at first confined within the boundaries of Sumeria, then extending beyond them to a time when Assyria took the centre of the stage (*c.* 1100 BC) and descended on her neighbours 'like a wolf on the fold',[12] is a chronicle of terror, devastation and the eventual exhaustion of people and resources.

The Babylonians, as Hammurabi's followers came to be called, retained the language, mythology, literature and educational system of the Sumerians, translating them into their own Akkadian language, and transmitted them all over the Near East, so diffusing Sumerian culture through Anatolia, Assyria and Canaan during the following two millennia. Therefore, many of the myths, hymns and stories seeming to belong to Assyrian or Canaanite culture may in fact be 3,000 years older, and these are only a fraction of what still remains to be deciphered and discovered.

So it was that Ishtar, the great goddess of Babylonia, inherited the imagery and ritual dramas of her Sumerian predecessor and contemporary, Inanna; the story of the Flood, until recently believed to be unique to the Old Testament, was discovered to be first Assyrian, then Babylonian and finally Sumerian. Astonished archaeologists read how Assurbanipal, the last king of Assyria, who ruled in the seventh century BC, had these words inscribed on the clay tablets they found in the ruins of Nineveh, the capital of his empire: 'I understand the enigmatic words in the stone engravings from the days before the Flood.' It was in this way that the treasure of Sumerian culture was restored to a world that learnt for the first time of its goddess Inanna, and listened to the unknown epic of its hero Gilgamesh, a story that may have been sung in the Greek courts at the time of Homer, 2,000 years after Gilgamesh lived.

The mythology of the Sumerian goddesses and gods seems to reflect the uneasy fusion of at least four different cultures. It draws imagery that belongs to a people worshipping the Great Mother, who are closely concerned with earth and water, together with imagery that reflects mountain and sky gods who rule the sky, air and storm. The imagery of the mother goddess can be traced to the Al 'Ubaid culture of the unknown people who settled in this area as early as the sixth millennium BC, and who were highly gifted potters and craftsmen.

Then there was the culture of the Sumerians themselves, who called themselves the 'black' or 'dark-headed' people, and who are believed to have arrived sometime during the second half of the fourth millennium BC from an area that has still not been precisely identified.[13] Thirdly, there were the Akkadian-speaking Semitic peoples, who established themselves mainly in the north of Sumeria, as well as other Semitic tribes, who continually infiltrated Mesopotamia from the Arabian and Syrian desert to the south and west. Lastly, Sumeria was invaded by Indo-European (Aryan) tribes, descending from the north, who introduced the horse-drawn war chariot and the devastating power of the mounted warrior, and inflicted on Sumeria in the third millennium BC, or even earlier, the same destruction they wrought on Old Europe and on cultures as far west as Anatolia and Greece and as far east as the Indus Valley.

All these different tribes brought with them their own deities, and we can listen to the different resonance of the goddess and god imagery in the Sumerian pantheon as it reflects both the marriage and the tension between them. The arrival of tribes worshipping sky gods goes far to explain the strong trinity of gods in Sumeria – An, Enlil and Enki – and the gradual rise to supremacy of Enlil, the god of air, whose city was Nippur and whose power as creative word lies behind the image of the biblical father god Yahweh. These gods were superimposed on an equally strong goddess tradition, descending from the settled Neolithic Al 'Ubaid people. It does not seem unreasonable to draw a comparison between Sumeria and India, where the Aryan invaders suppressed but did not extinguish the goddess culture or the genius of its artists and visionary poets. After the initial devastation, a new civilization arose in which elements of both cultures were integrated in a cosmology and philosophy that were grounded in the images of unity belonging to the older one.[14]

The high position of women in Sumeria in the fourth and early third

Figure 3. Enthroned Sumerian goddess wearing horned crown, with sacred trees and birds; *c.* 1800 BC. Ur.

millennia BC suggests that Indo-European and/or Semitic influence began to gain ground only in the second half of the third millennium BC. The Sumerian scholar Dr Samuel Noah Kramer writes that about 2400 BC 'there is evidence to demonstrate the Sumerian woman was man's equal, socially and economically, at least among the upper classes'.[15] But after this, at the time when the Akkadian Semitic influence of the north becomes paramount, the position of goddesses in relation to gods and of women in relation to men is down-graded.[16] It seems most likely that in Sumeria a prior goddess tradition descending from Neolithic times was continually overlaid and reinterpreted by the tradition of male gods which the various newcomers brought with them. This would explain why there seem to be two 'layers' of mythology: an older one, where the goddess is primary; and a newer one, where the god begins to dominate.

Kramer comments that Ki, Mother Earth, 'could no longer be worshipped and adored as the mother of Enlil, the god who gradually became the leading deity of the Sumerian pantheon. Instead she was conceived by the theologians (*c.* 2400 BC) as Enlil's "big sister".' It seems as if Ki's role as Mother Earth was usurped by Enlil.[17] Much research still needs to be done before it becomes clear how and at what date the god as son evolved into the god as father. At one time the goddess seems to give birth to everything as the primordial mother; at others she is the wife, sister or daughter of a god, even being raped by the gods or 'walking in fear' of them,[18] situations that would have been inconceivable in the older mythology but which are understandable in the light of an alien sky god mythology being imposed on a goddess mythology. This may explain the difficulty of trying to discover a consistent identity and genealogy for the many goddesses and gods. Their dates and names are still muddled and obscure, partly because every city in Sumeria had its favourite deity and sometimes gave a special name to a god or goddess who may have played the same role in different places; partly because older goddesses evolved into new ones and were given new names. Moreover, they have Sumerian names in the south and Semitic names in the north, even though they may be contemporary with each other.[19]

Whatever will ultimately be discovered about the origin of the Sumerians and the inversion of the mythology of a goddess culture, the most important event at this time was the movement in human consciousness from participation in the cyclical round of the earth to ever more precise observation of the cyclical round of the stars in the sky. It was this that gave Sumerian culture in the fourth millennium BC its particular character and led to the cultivation of its mathematical genius. The Sumerians did not invent the idea of the transcendence of the gods or of an immutable heavenly order that governed the earthly one, for the relation of the earth to the moon and the sun had always been the foundation of this idea, but they gave it a mythological framework that influenced all subsequent cultures, and married this to a mathematical structure breathtaking in its scope and precision. The cycles of heavenly time were minutely aligned with the passage of time on earth, even with the pulse rate of the human body, so that humanity, by 'attuning' the cycles of its own life and the life of the earth to the immensely greater cycles of cosmic time, could not only discover its place and role in the universe but could cooperate with the unseen 'powers' of nature that ordered their hidden relationship.

Campbell comments on this revolutionary development:

> A decisive, enormous leap out of the confines of all local histories and landscapes occurred in Mesopotamia in the fourth millennium BC, during the period of the rise of the ziggurats, those storied temple towers, symbolic of the *axis mundi*, which are caricatured in the Bible as the Tower of Babel. The leap was from geography to the cosmos, beyond the moon . . . The priestly watchers of the night skies at the time were the first in the world to recognize that there is a mathematical regularity in the celestial passages of the seven visible spheres – the sun, the moon, Mercury, Venus, Mars, Jupiter, and Saturn – along with the heaven-way of the Zodiac. And with that, the idea dawned of a cosmic order, *mathematically* discoverable, which it should be the function of a governing priesthood to translate from its heavenly revelation into an order of civilized human life . . . A vast concept took form of the universe as a living being in the likeness of a great mother, within whose womb all the worlds, both of life and of death, had their existence.[20]

Looking at the desert-like country of modern Iraq, it is hard to imagine the immense garden that once covered this land before creeping salinization and war ravaged it: the vineyards, cornfields, orchards of date palm, olive and fruit trees; the pasturelands for cattle, sheep and goats; the abundance of fruit and flowers, barley, wine and beer. It is in poetry above all that Sumeria speaks to us. Through it we discover the imagery of mythological and daily life that were so closely interwoven in the lives of its people. Sumeria, in the first 1,000 years, was felt to be the garden, the orchard and the sheepfold of the gods, in which humanity, as their servant, laboured to fulfil their will. We learn of the feelings of the people of Sumeria through the love, delight, passionate eroticism, anger, hatred, vindictiveness, cruelty and sorrow of their goddesses and gods. There is an exultation in the richness and delight of the physical world reflected in the following poem, yet it already carries within its lines the inversion of the Neolithic imagery of the goddess culture:

> The great Earth-crust was resplendent, its surface was jewel-green,
> The wide Earth – its surface was covered with precious metals and lapis-lazuli,
> It was adorned with diorite, nir-stone, carnelian, and antimony,
> The Earth was arrayed luxuriantly in plants and herbs, its presence was majestic,
> The holy Earth, the pure Earth, beautified herself for holy Heaven,
> Heaven, the noble god, inserted his sex into the wide Earth,
> Let flow the semen of the heroes, Trees and Reed, into her womb.
> The Earthly Orb, the trusty cow, was impregnated with the good semen of Heaven.[21]

The Sumerian Temple

Crowned with the crescent horns of moon and bull, the Sumerian temple (Fig. 4) was designed to encompass the three dimensions of heaven, earth and underworld. In the early centuries of Sumerian civilization the invisible and visible worlds were experienced as a unity. But with the discovery of distant patterns in the heavens, the dimension of invisible causality appeared to be further and further removed from the world of human activity. The ziggurat was a symbolic way of connecting earth to heaven, the visible to the invisible. At its summit was the place where the two dimensions met, where a sacred marriage was celebrated that reunited them and so released the generative powers that renewed life. Human beings (as priestess or priest) ascended to the summit and the goddess or god descended to it, the steps or spiralling pathway becoming a new image of the path between earth and heaven. The temple evolved from the cow-byre and sheepfold as the body of the goddess: the sanctuary for her sacred herd, where the great mysteries of fertility took place. It slowly developed into the spiralling, towered ziggurat, which, as the sacred mountain, was still symbolically the body of the goddess. As in Hindu mythology, the temple symbolized the primordial cosmic mountain that existed before the creation of earth and heaven.[22]

At Nippur, as Levy observed:

> The temple was called the House of the Mountain, but also the Bond of Heaven and Earth (Dur-an-ki) . . . This bond, like the tree pillar, connected Heaven and Earth, and the ziggurat was thus conceived as a kind of Jacob's ladder whose pathways were external, a stairway later mounting in a spiral

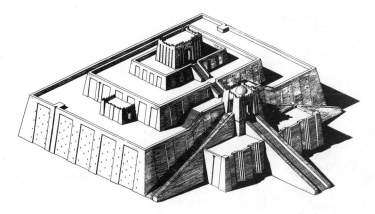

Figure 4. The Ziggurat of Ur-Nammu (restored); *c.* 2100 BC.

from stage to stage, the Megalithic way of approach to the divine state here lifted towards the sky.[23]

Throughout the Neolithic world a mound or mountain was symbolic of the goddess, and in the Bronze Age the beehive tomb and the omphalos belong to this imagery, as does the sacred enclosure, whether temple precinct or walled city or garden. The focus of the temple was the sanctuary at the summit, where the sacred marriage rite was enacted.[24]

Like the Palaeolithic cave and the Megalithic temple, the Sumerian temple was both womb and tomb. The hollow sanctuary beneath the temple, the 'underworld', symbolized the womb of the goddess, where the processes of gestation and regeneration mysteriously took place, and where the sacrificed god rested during his winter sleep 'in the mountain'. Mythic dramas enacting these mysteries, such as 'The Descent of Inanna', may have been performed in the temple precinct by priestesses and priests, as they were in Egypt.

THE GODDESS INANNA

Before Inanna's story can be told, it is necessary to mention two other goddesses. The first of these is Nammu, goddess of the primordial ocean or sea, whose cult endured for millennia; for the greatest and wisest of the late Sumerian kings, Ur-Nammu (*c.* 2100 BC), takes her name, calling himself 'Servant of the goddess Nammu'.[25] (The Babylonian mother goddess Tiamat seems to have been a later or alternative name for Nammu, for she also was the primordial waters, the First or Great Mother, the Great Deep.) Nammu is important not only for Inanna's story, but also for an understanding of the later biblical passages that derive from her imagery and for a comparison of Sumerian with Hindu mythology.

Figure 5. Alabaster head; *c.* 3100 BC. Uruk. Inanna's temple precinct was called *Eanna*, or 'House of Heaven', and in it was found this magnificent and life-like alabaster head which may be an image of the goddess or of a queen who was her high priestess.

The Sumerians believed that the primeval sea was the source from which all creation emerged. Nammu, whose ideogram or hieroglyph was the sea, may originally have been portrayed as a serpent goddess, in the manner of the early goddess with a serpent's head, from Ur, in Figure 6.

Nammu may be compared with the Hindu image of Ananta, 'the Endless', the great serpent of the cosmic abyss, on whose coils the god Vishnu 'rested' between avatars. The image of the goddess as a great serpent reappears in Mahayana Buddhism, where the serpent goddess Mucalinda provides a throne for the Buddha and raises her seven hoods to offer him

Figure 6. (*Left*) Goddess with a serpent's head, holding her child; *c.* 4000–3000 BC. Ur.
Figure 7. (*Right*) The Buddha seated on the coils of the great serpent goddess Mucalinda, protected by her hoods; Srivijaya period, *c.* thirteenth century AD. Thailand.

a protective canopy as he confronts the destructive powers of the universe on the night of his awakening (Fig. 7). She is at once serpent and tree. This beautiful image of the relationship of the mother goddess as *zoe* to her son as *bios* may offer a perspective on the Sumerian image of Nammu as the great serpent goddess of the abyss, and her son, Enki (Fig. 8).

In the Sumerian myth of creation Nammu, as the cosmic waters, gave birth to the cosmic mountain, An-Ki, Heaven-and-Earth. These two, her son and daughter, who were still one, gave birth to a son, Enlil, the Air, who separated his parents and carried off his mother, Ki, the Earth, to be his wife. In this new creation myth An and Ki, Heaven and Earth, had to be separated before gods, plants, animals and human beings could be created. From the union of Earth (Ki) and Air, or Breath (Enlil), came all the other gods. The story of Enlil as the 'word' or power of his father, An, the god who personified heaven, carrying off his mother as his wife seems to be a modification of the older mythology in which the goddess is the mother of all life and her son becomes her consort. The emphasis is moving from the birth-giving capacity of the Great Mother to the initiative of her son, who seizes her as his wife. 'Seizing' or 'carrying off' is not an act characteristic of the goddess culture. It is interesting that this myth of Mother, Father and Son is one of the earliest formulations of the concept of the Trinity; the other, still earlier, is the image of the triune lunar goddess in her aspects as daughter or maiden, mother and old woman. In both mythologies the three emerge from the primal source, the One, which reveals the constancy of the lunar myth underlying both images.[26]

In Mesopotamia, Professor Frankfort writes, 'the source of life is female'; for 'life comes forth from a goddess' and 'the universe is conceived rather than begotten'.[27] When the writer of the Apocryphal Book of Ben Sirach (Ecclesiasticus) said of Wisdom that 'her thoughts are more than the sea, and her counsels profounder than the great deep' (24:29), he could not have known that this imagery came originally from Nammu, the primordial mother goddess of the watery abyss, whose ideogram was the sea; yet the echo of this Sumerian goddess reverberates through the biblical verses describing the nature and attributes of Wisdom. It is as though the Bible were missing a whole layer of mythology, which, if recovered, could point to the original heritage of its Wisdom books. The imagery of the feminine archetype is there, but there is no actual image of the goddess herself. Only fragments remain of what was once a definitive cosmology deriving from the mother goddess and from the cosmic union of goddess and god. We have to look to Indian mythology, Gnosticism and Kabbalism to provide the image of the missing goddess together with the sense of the primordial unity between goddess and god that once existed in Bronze Age Sumeria and Egypt, but is not intrinsic to the mythology of Judaeo-Christian culture.

Kramer writes that Nammu's 'vast powers as goddess of the sea were turned over to the male deity Enki, who was then designated by the

Figure 8. The god Enki, son of Nammu; cylinder seal, *c.* 1800 BC.

theologians as the son of Nammu'.[28] It is most likely that Enki (Ea in Akkadian) was at one time her consort, as he may also have been the son and consort of Ki, the earth goddess, for his name means 'Lord Earth'. He was the personification of wisdom, apparently inheriting this title because he was Nammu's son. Later, Enki becomes one of the three principal gods of Sumeria, the dynamic 'organizer' of Sumerian civilization.

A most interesting carved bowl (Fig. 9), found at Khafaje, north-east of Baghdad, and now in the British Museum, shows all the imagery relating to the Neolithic goddess. The strange fact is that although the forms of the goddess are Sumerian in character, the hump-backed bull was not native to Mesopotamia. The images show, from left to right, a goddess holding streams of water in each hand with a star and a crescent moon to her left and a hump-backed bull on either side of her. In the background are what look like ears of corn or wheat and plant forms nourished by the water flowing through the goddess's hands. Further along, the same goddess, wearing a similar skirt with a net-like pattern, holds a serpent in each hand, while two lionesses or leopards with tails upraised lie at her feet. The star motif is repeated. There is also a scene with a lion and a vulture attacking a bull. Every one of these images belongs to the Neolithic goddess and the mythology of regeneration. Copies of the bowl, used perhaps for ritual purposes, were found north of Sumeria at Mari and south of it at sites in the Persian Gulf, and as far to the east as the Indus Valley,[29] indicating how widespread the myth of this goddess had become; for, with her animals, she instantly evokes the great goddess of Çatal Hüyük seated between leopards, and the Cretan goddess who holds a serpent in each hand. This goddess belongs chronologically roughly half-way between them and may be related to the cult of a Sumerian goddess, possibly Ki-Ninhursag.

Ki (Nammu's daughter), or Ninhursag as she was later named, was the goddess of life and fertility, and she is extremely important for tracing the transmission of goddess imagery from the Neolithic to the Bronze Age. In the Akkadian north she was called Aruru. Her titles suggest that she was

Figure 9. Carved steatite bowl showing the serpent goddess and the goddess
of regeneration; *c.* 2700–2500 BC. Khafaje, Iraq.

originally the Great Mother of an agricultural people who were skilled in
craftsmanship, and that, like Nammu, she had been revered as creator
before the gods An, Enlil and Enki. She was called:

> The Builder of that which has Breath
> The Carpenter of Mankind
> The Carpenter of the Heart
> The Coppersmith of the Gods,
> The Coppersmith of the Land,
> The Lady Potter.[30]

The earliest temple known to have been dedicated to Ninhursag, built
on a mound in the settlement of Al 'Ubaid near Ur, dates to 3000 BC; but,
as with all Sumerian temples, it was built on the site of many older,
demolished temples. Two bronze lions guarded its entrance. It had two
friezes decorating its walls, one showing doves on white limestone against
a black ground, the other showing a procession of cows with priests
milking them and pouring the milk into stone jars (Fig. 10). The great
lintel over the doorway of the same temple shows a lion-headed eagle
between two stags (Fig. 11), an epiphany scene of the goddess that reveals
her descent from the Neolithic Goddess of the Animals and the Bird
Goddess.

Figure 10. Frieze from the temple of Al 'Ubaid, showing priests and the
sacred cattle of the goddess Inanna by the gate to her temple; *c.* 3000 BC.

Figure 11. Lintel from the temple of Al 'Ubaid, showing lion-headed bird
and stags; *c.* 3000 BC.

Ki-Ninhursag was one of the principal Sumerian deities, 'the mother of
all living': mother of the gods and of humanity; mother of the earth itself,
the soil and the rocky ground, and all the plants and crops it brought
forth.[31] But she was also the mother of the wild animals and of the herd
animals, of cow, sheep and goat. As she presided over birth in all these
different orders of creation, her ideogram was an inverted U, or horseshoe
(like the Greek letter omega, Ω), which symbolized the birthplace, womb,
sheepfold or cow-byre from which new life came into being. She was the
generative power that gave shape to the life in the womb, the dynamic
power that released the foetus for birth, and the divine midwife of gods,
kings, mortals and animals, the 'Opener of the Womb'. There is a suggestion that a lying-in place for women to give birth was associated with the
temple, housing the sheepfold, cow-byre and granary within its precincts.
All the produce and animal life belonged in the first instance to the
goddess as the Great Mother and therefore to her temple, and from there
was distributed by the priestesses and priests to her people and her
animals. It is interesting that the Sumerian word for sheepfold, vulva,
womb, loins and lap is the same.[32] The milk of Ninhursag's sacred herd,
kept in the temple precincts and fields, nourished the people of the village.
Later, this same milk was given to the kings, who became her 'sons' when
they assumed the kingship of a city.[33] As in Egypt, the goddess was
portrayed as the Great Cow,[34] offering her milk to all people.

The life of the corn, vine and fruit tree, imaged as a dying and resurrected god, symbolically emerged from and re-entered Ninhursag's
womb, which was also the underworld or dwelling place of the dead. In
her role as Great Mother of Life-and-Death her title was Nintinugga,
'She Who Gives Life to the Dead'.

Figure 12. Mother goddess with her child; cylinder seals, *c.* 2300–2000 BC.

The rare cylinder seals shown in Figure 12, of which only five exist (see also Fig. 2), may portray Ki-Ninhursag in her role as Great Mother of all life, but, as Ninhursag's imagery was also shared by Inanna, they may portray her or another goddess with the son who as king is to take the role of the life of the vegetation. The crescent moon is clearly visible on one of the seals, the Tree of Life on another.

The Goddess Inanna as the Great Mother

Inanna is often spoken of as a young goddess but she also assumes or shares many aspects of Ki-Ninhursag's role as Great Mother; she is far more the living incarnation of a myth than is the earlier goddess, and her mythology includes the sky as well as the earth. Her title 'Queen of Earth and Heaven' reveals the lineaments of the Neolithic Great Mother whose being was Life-and-Death, and in this role she is reflected in the other great goddesses of the Bronze Age – Isis and Cybele – who share her lunar character. For Inanna is, above all, a lunar goddess who gives life as the waxing moon and then withdraws it as the waning moon. Although she is incarnated in the morning and evening star and in the star Sirius, all the myths about her are woven with this lunar thread. The light and dark dimensions to her power, the horned head-dress and serpent staff, her dying and resurrected son–lover, who annually descends to the under-world and rises again from it – all suggest a lunar mythology.

As holder of the *me*, the Sumerian Tablets of the Law, she incarnates the principle of justice, derived from the idea of the duality of the lunar power that can balance the giving of life with the taking away. She

Figure 13. Inanna standing on two lions and holding the caduceus of entwined serpents in her right hand; cylinder seal, *c.* 1850–1700 BC.

embodies the cyclical aspect of time, both as goddess of life-and-death, and as goddess of fertility. Her mythology revolves around the connection made between the light and dark lunar phases and the rhythmic alteration of the earth's fertility and barrenness. She is alternately virgin creatrix and sorrowing mother or consort, alternately the bringer of life and the bringer of death. Virgin, she carries within herself the totality of life, the totality of the moon's cycle. The triune character of the goddess as mother, bride and sister of the young god shows the trinity of the light lunar phases. The fourth, dark phase in Sumerian mythology is personified by Inanna's sister, Ereshkigal, Queen of the Underworld. In Hebrew mythology Lilith inherits the role of the dark aspect of life's power to withdraw the forms it has created; in Greece, Hecate, Queen of Night.

Virginity has always been an image belonging to the Great Mother as the lunar goddess. The Virgin Goddess is Life itself, and Life, like the cycles of the moon, appears out of itself without union with anything external to itself. The virginity of the goddess had nothing to do with sexual 'purity' in the sense that has been given to it in our culture. The goddess is virgin because she carries within herself her own fertilizing power; and life pours into manifestation from the 'sea' of her womb in a never-ending stream. Virginity has to be understood as a symbol that describes a metaphysical dimension – *zoe* – where the two aspects of the goddess, the fertilizing male phallus and the gestating female womb, are united in perpetual, life-giving embrace. The life that was born out of herself and taken back into herself is everlastingly her 'child' – *bios*. A poem suggests that the goddess is the inner aspect or hidden face of the male gods who give form to her invisible being:

Begetting Mother am I, within the Spirit I abide and none see me.
In the word of An I abide, and none see me
In the word of Enlil I abide, and none see me
In the word of the holy temple I abide, and none see me.[35]

Foremost among the magisterial symbols of Inanna's power as Great Mother are the caduceus and the double-headed axe, which, as in Crete, symbolized the power to bestow and withdraw life.[36] As sorrowing consort and mother, Inanna, as the dark aspect of the lunar Great Mother, weeps for her son–lover, the life that is going to wane. As the Great Mother, Inanna is both the radiance of the luminous dew-bestowing moon and the diminishing and vanishing of that radiance in the darkened moon. The white lunar bird, the dove, and the swallow image her in the role of bestowing life and fertility; the scorpion and viper in the role of withdrawing it. She incarnates both generous and wrathful feeling, both love and rage. She is ever-changing yet ever the same; by turns 'radiant, thundering, destructive, defiant, judgmental, kind, generous, peaceful, healing, erotic, decisive, discerning, wise, transcendent, loving, fertile, joyous and ever youthful',[37] all modes of being that were 'seen' in the moon. She is the implacable Law of Life, experienced by humanity as fate. Men and women prayed to her for compassion, as today some do to Mary:

> To thee I cry, O lady of the gods,
> Lady of ladies, goddess without peer,
> Ishtar who shapes the lives of all mankind,
> Thou stately world queen, sovereign of the sky,
> And lady ruler of the host of heaven –
> Illustrious is thy name . . . O light divine,
> Gleaming in lofty splendour o'er the earth –
> Heroic daughter of the moon, oh! hear . . .[38]

In the great poem of her 'Descent into the Nether World' Inanna as the moon is the life principle that seeks its own sacrifice and is reborn from its own darkness. In the later Akkadian myth Ishtar descends to the underworld to awaken her son–lover, Tammuz, and brings him forth as the new cycle of life. When Ishtar is in the underworld, the impulse for fertility disappears: 'The bull does not spring upon the cow, the ass does not bow over the jenny . . . the man sleeps in his chamber, the woman sleeps alone.'[39] Inanna, in the person of her son–lover, is again the life principle that dies as the corn and is regenerated as the seed that holds the promise of nourishment for human and beast.

Her temples were adorned with the great crescent horns that imaged the moon's power to fertilize the earth and, like the cow, to feed her young. As the Great Mother, she was the cow who nourished her children with the milk that was the same whiteness as the moon, and with this milk she suckled the kings of the land, who were her 'special' sons. In a land where the burning rays of the sun brought death to the vegetation, the cool lunar rays brought the refreshing, and, so the Sumerians believed, fertilizing dew. Ishtar was called the 'All-Dewy-One'. Milk, water, semen, rain and dew were all connected with the life-giving aspect of the moon. There was a Sumerian tradition, Neolithic in its imagery, that saw the sky as the goddess and the clouds heavy with rain as her breasts, which were like the udders of the cow. Like the Neolithic sky goddess, Inanna as the Queen of Heaven was the goddess of the rain that caused the grain to sprout:

> I step onto the heavens, and the rain rains down;
> I step onto the earth, and grass and herbs sprout up.[40]

Whereas the goddess Ki-Ninhursag seems gradually to decline, Inanna seems to grow in stature – her cult enduring 4,000 years – perhaps because she is far more the living incarnation of a myth than the other goddesses, and her mythology includes the sky as well as the earth. But it is important to remember her role as Queen of Earth because it is this aspect of the goddess that has been lost in the Judaeo-Christian tradition. Named as Queen of Earth, Inanna is goddess of fertility: the lunar mother who gives birth to the solar god of vegetation, the bride who weds him and the sorrowful wife who mourns him. As Holy Shepherdess, Inanna is the guardian, like Ki-Ninhursag, of the domesticated animals, including the sheep and cow, and the wild animals, particularly the stag and the lion. The lions that draw Inanna's chariot, and the lion by her side, beneath her throne or under her foot[41] show her as the Goddess of the Animals and indicate her descent, like Ki-Ninhursag, from the Neolithic goddess.

The entrance to Inanna's byre or sheepfold was the entrance to the womb whence all living things came forth, over which she presided as shepherdess and cowherd. The entrance was marked by a special gate, symbolically the vulva of the goddess. In earliest times two bundles of reeds with curved ends stood at the entrance to the cow-byre of the goddess Ki-Ninhursag. Later, they become one of the principal images that mark the presence of Inanna. They stood on either side of the temple entrance, or with the flocks and herds of the goddess or on her crescent-shaped reed boat. As shown in Chapter 3, they carried the same significance in Sumeria as the sacred knot did in Crete. The reed bundle was sometimes stylized into a single pole with loops and then became the sacred tree that was planted on the precinct of the goddess's temple.[42] This is one of the earliest images of the Tree of Life. Between the reed bundles there was a connecting rope, which took the shape of a curve, and this, once a natural part of the cow-byre, became stylized into the crescent. The crescent was originally the image of the goddess herself, and remains so, but it also becomes associated with her consort, the bull of heaven, whose crescent horns adorn the head-dress of the god as well as the goddess.

Figure 14. Seal showing Inanna's face, her flower or star image in the shape
of the eight-petalled rosette and the gateposts of her temple; *c.* 3000 BC.
Tell Agrab.

As Queen of Earth, Inanna was the goddess of the grain and the vine,
the date palm, cedar, sycamore fig, olive and apple tree, all of which were
her epiphanies.[43] One of these trees was always planted in her temple as a
symbol of her life-bestowing power. Her principal animal images were
the lion and the cow; her bird images, the dove and the sparrow, relating
her once again to the Neolithic Bird Goddess. The viper and scorpion,
whose bite or sting bring death, as the serpent and the dragon, reveal her
connection with the underworld aspect of the Neolithic goddess and with
Nammu, the serpent goddess of the abyss. As goddess of fertility, 'The
Green One', 'She of the Springing Verdure',[44] Inanna was the shepherdess, 'Queen of Stall and Fold', who watched over the sheepfold and
cow-byre – her 'womb' – and the sacred herd of her temple.[45]

The intricate system of canalized waterways came under her protection
because all crops and animals depended upon them. Whatever grew in the
fields or was harvested from fruit tree and vine came under her jurisdiction. A particular kind of bread was baked on her altars and made into
cakes called 'the baked cakes of the goddess Inanna'.[46] The cakes were an
offering of herself as the fruits of her body for the feeding of her children.
Wheat or barley and the bread that was made from the ground flour,
wine, beer, dates and all fruits were the actual substance of the goddess,
and were harvested with rituals that, like the baking of the sacred cakes,
celebrated this imagery of nourishment and transformation through assimilating the 'body' of the goddess. Because the reeds at the water's edge
were also part of her fertility, and because these were made into the stylus
used by the Sumerian scribes to write on their clay tablets, she over-
shadows the goddess Nidaba, patroness of the art of writing, literature
and the interpretation of dreams.

One of the oldest ritual vases of carved stone, the Uruk Vase from
Inanna's temple there (Fig. 15), shows Inanna standing at the gate of her
temple, marked by the two stylized reed pillars,[47] to receive the sacrificial
horned animals, the clusters of dates and the sheaves of corn which are
her own substance: the offering, as Gertrude Levy writes, of 'herself to

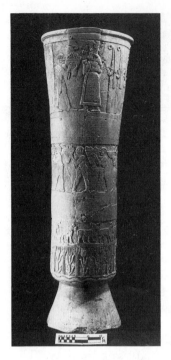

b

a

Figure 15. (a) The Uruk Vase, and (b) detail showing man offering a vase of produce to high priestess; *c.* 3000 BC.

herself'.[48] The frieze begins at the bottom with the stream of water without which there is no life. It moves on to the luxuriant growth of wheat and barley and then to the flocks of sheep. After them comes a procession of men carrying the produce of the land, which is to be stored in great jars inside the temple. Their leader approaches Inanna's high priestess, standing in front of the reed pillars, and offers her a vase of produce. Behind him, unfortunately destroyed, is the figure of a man, possibly the king or high priest, whose magnificent tasselled belt is held up by an attendant.

The imagery of Inanna as the Great Mother suggests that in the Bronze Age nature was not yet split off from spirit. The life of the earth and everything she produced was sacred. Plant and animal, sexuality and fertility were all the epiphanies, or the 'showing forth', of the being of the goddess, as Figure 15 suggests. Whatever existed was the life of the goddess manifested as the life of plant, animal and human being. One divine life was incarnate in the life of each and all, one mother was the source of everything. The lion beneath Inanna's foot, the dragon – half lion, half bird, which unified in one image the life of heaven and earth – the Tree of Life that grew in her temple, all expressed this insight, which may have been given metaphysical expression in temple teachings of which only fragments remain, suggesting the existence of a cosmology that may have been as intricate as it was profound. With the differentiation of the original concept of the unity of life into a multitude of goddesses and gods, and finally with the image of the single transcendent god that evolved with Judaism and Christianity, this understanding of the unity of life was lost.

Inanna as Hierodule

Inanna and Ishtar were the goddesses of sexual love and fertility and one of their titles was 'Hierodule of Heaven'. *Hierodule* is a Greek word that means 'sacred work' or 'servant of the holy'. The word 'harlot' or 'prostitute', which is often used to describe the priestesses of Inanna and Ishtar, no longer conveys the original sacredness of their service to the goddess, although the original meaning of the word 'prostitute' was 'to stand on behalf of'. The priestesses who served in the temples of Inanna and Ishtar were the vehicles of her creative life in their sexual union with the men who came there to perform a sacred ritual.

The image of Inanna's and Ishtar's role as the Hierodule of Heaven goes back to the Neolithic idea that the characteristic mode of being of the Great Mother was procreation. Both are called the Virgin, yet their virginity did not suggest a physical condition, but rather that the creativity of the goddess was a constant state, brought about by herself in union with herself, and that the fertility of all aspects of creation was her epiphany. At this time metaphysical ideas were embodied in the sexual intercourse performed ritually in the temple precinct itself, for the fertility of human, animal and plant life depended upon the enactment of this ritual in a sacred place where men and women participated magically in the generation of the life of the goddess.

It is difficult for our fragmented consciousness to comprehend this act of participation. Sexual intercourse and giving birth were two channels through which the divine energy of the goddess poured into life. Ishtar proclaimed: 'I turn the male to the female. I am she who adorneth the male for the female; I am she who adorneth the female for the male.'[49] Sexuality was the vehicle of bringing life into the world and was a sacred act. It was also sacred because the ecstasy that accompanied it was the nearest experience to the state of bliss associated with the divine existence of the goddesses and gods.[50] For this reason, sexual intercourse in early cultures was a ritual of participation, a magical act of fertility. It was an expression of the divine because, in their total abandonment to the sexual instinct inspired by the goddess, men and women offered themselves as the vehicle of her generative power. The priestesses of Inanna and Ishtar, through their union with the men who came to the temple, bestowed on them an ecstatic experience that was, so to speak, the 'life' of the goddess. A girl's sacrifice of her virginity to the goddess brought sexuality within the realm of the sacred both for the woman and the man who sought intercourse with the goddess through her priestess, for the sexuality of

Figure 16. Ishtar as goddess of fertility; *c.* 2000 BC.

neither was 'their own', but was received from the goddess.[51] As Woolley explains, 'The devotee gave to the service of god the virginity which as plenty of clauses in the law prove was no less precious to the Sumerian woman than to others.'[52] The castrated men, who also served the goddess as her priests, offered their sexuality to her as a sacrifice to promote new life, a practice later to be transmitted to the priests of Cybele and those of the Canaanite goddesses. This sacrifice is reflected in the vow of celibacy of the Roman Catholic priesthood.

One of the functions of the high priestess, known as the *Entu*, was to take the role of the goddess in the ritual union of the sacred marriage. In this, the king took the role of her bridegroom, personifying the son–lover of the goddess. It is possible that the temple unions were the source of the belief that the children born of them were of half divine and half human parentage, as was Gilgamesh. Sargon I was the son of a high priestess and an unknown father, whom he calls a 'gardener'. 'Gardener' was an epithet given to the kings who played the role of the son–lover in the sacred marriage rite. Sargon's story suggests that Sumerian kings were literally the sons, consorts and fathers of the high priestesses, who personified the goddess and presided over her temple.[53]

The role of a high priestess is illustrated by a remarkable series of poems written in the middle of the third millennium BC by a woman who was a priestess, princess and poet. Her name was Enheduanna, the daughter of the first King Sargon of Akkad (*c.* 2350 BC). Her hymn to Inanna, called *The Exaltation of Inanna*,[54] is the earliest record of the poetry of a woman who was also a high priestess, and it is interesting that she addresses her great cycle of poems to Inanna rather than to the gods An or Nanna. Enheduanna's influence is revealed by the fact that, long after she had died, copies of her hymns were made and sung in the temples of Inanna and Ishtar. Her literary style is so distinctive that other poems by her hand may eventually come to light. Her poem as a whole shows a new emphasis on the degenerate function of the goddess in human war rather than drawing the goddess in her original role as life-giver, and also reveals how the gods An and Enlil have strengthened their hold over the Sumerian pantheon at the expense of the goddess.

Inanna as Queen of Heaven

The Sumerians and Babylonians were fascinated by the stars, in the way, perhaps, that we now respond to the idea of exploring the universe. Nightly from the roof terraces of their houses they must have watched the great constellations wheeling around them, as they came to identify the most brilliant stars and gave the zodiacal belt the names and images that have endured to this day. Both Inanna and Ishtar were worshipped as Queen of Heaven. Their principal images were the moon and Venus, the morning and evening star, which may have given rise to the image of the eight-pointed star as well as the stylized rosette with eight petals as symbolic of their presence. Eight was the number sacred to the morning and evening star, addressed as the 'Radiant Star', 'The Great Light' in a Sumerian poem.[55] Eight was the number of years it took for the planet to return to the same point of the zodiac while at greatest brilliancy.[56] It is also the number of the sacred year, celebrated not only in Sumeria but in Egypt, Crete and Greece, when the full moon coincided exactly with the longest or shortest day, so reconciling lunar and solar time.[57] Ishtar in later seals is often shown with a circle of stars around her, as she

Figure 17. Cylinder seals showing Inanna–Ishtar as Queen of Heaven.

personified the zodiac. Indeed, the zodiac was called 'Ishtar's Girdle'.[58] Sirius, the star that held great significance for Bronze Age civilizations, in Egypt and Crete as well as Sumeria, was also specifically associated with Inanna and Ishtar, as were certain constellations, such as Virgo and Scorpio.[59]

The story of how Inanna became a moon goddess derives from Enlil's second marriage to a goddess called Ninlil, whose name means 'Lady Air'. After having been raped by Enlil, she gave birth to Nanna, the moon god, who in turn married Ningal, goddess of the moon, and they had two children, Inanna, whose name means Queen Moon or Lady Moon, and Utu, the sun god. So in this genealogy, which seems to be a later rationalization of her existence, Inanna is the great-great-granddaughter of Nammu, and the great-granddaughter of Ki-Ninhursag. In this mythology Inanna takes more of an individual character, and she is the first goddess or god we know of who suffers as though she were human, and who can, therefore, express the mysterious drama of the human condition. A hymn addresses her as the Moon Goddess and the Morning Star:

> She made the night come forth like the moonlight,
> She made the morning come forth like the bright daylight,
> When in the bed-chamber sweet sleep had come to an end,
> When all the lands and the black-haired people had assembled –
> Who had slept on the roofs, who had slept in the walls –
> And uttering orisons approached her, brought their words to her,
> Then did she study their words, knew the evildoer,
> Against the evildoer she renders a cruel judgment, destroys the wicked,
> She looks with kindly eyes on the straightforward, gives him her blessing.
>
> My Lady looks on in sweet wonder from heaven's midst,
> They parade before the holy Inanna,
> The Lady who reaches heaven, Inanna, is lofty,
> The Maid, Inanna, I would praise as is fitting.[60]

Inanna as Goddess of the Storm

In early Sumeria, as in Old Europe, there was no separate image of a 'terrible' goddess of death and destruction. Life and death were intertwined like the strands of a rope, two aspects of a whole. Inanna was identified with the unpredictable, chaotic and destructive powers of nature as well as with the nurturing and life-bringing powers. It was she who presided over the thunderous roar of the storm and the raging flood water that could erase years of labour in a few months, sweeping away human lives, dwellings and crops like so many lumps of mud. The Sumerians greatly feared the power of the storm to inflict devastating floods on the land by the sudden rising of the river waters. Inanna as sky goddess in her dark aspect was portrayed as the thunderstorm whose terrifying roar issued from the lion-headed thunder bird, Imdugud. Imdugud appears on cylinder seals with Inanna and is carved in stone between two great stags on the lintel of the temple of the goddess Ki-Ninhursag at Al 'Ubaid, near Ur. However, Imdugud is also associated with Ninurta, god of thunder and storm, who was a son of Enlil, the air god, and with Ishkur, who was a brother of Inanna. It seems likely that this attribution of the bird to gods derives from the later Indo-European or Semitic influence over the more ancient Neolithic imagery.[61] Cylinder seals showing a goddess holding the thunderbolt in her hand and standing on a dragon may portray Inanna, for she is often addressed in hymns as 'the dragon'. The venom flowing from the dragon's mouth may be the destructive power of the storm or flood.[62] The dragon and the torrential flood water also appear in poetry as metaphors for the devastating power of war, for, from the third millennium BC onwards, Inanna and Ishtar became goddesses of war.

Figure 18. Inanna, wearing the horned crown, with crescent moon and Morning Star, riding her storm dragon.

In the seal in Figure 18 Inanna rides on the back of her winged dragon. The dragon vomits the torrent of storm or flood, or possibly the ravages of war. She is crowned and clothed in her usual flounced robe as she gestures towards the crescent moon and the star. A lion follows behind the dragon.

Many centuries after all memory of Sumeria had vanished, the Gnostic literature of the first centuries of Christianity contains a poem called 'The Thunder, Perfect Mind' (see Chapter 15, pp. 630–1). The old image of the Sumerian and Babylonian goddess, whose archetypal power was expressed as the thunder's roar, is here integrated with the iconography of the goddess as the personification of wisdom that had evolved during the intervening millennia. How had it been preserved intact over such an immense stretch of time?

Inanna–Ishtar was also identified with Sirius, the 'Bow Star'. The beautiful Assyrian seal in Figure 19 shows her holding the bow that signified her epiphany as Sirius. Stars tip the arrows and quiver she holds, and one rests on her crown. Beneath her feet is her lion. The rising of Sirius in conjunction with the sunrise in the month of July heralded the parching drought and death-bringing heat of the summer months, when everything visible withered and died and the people of Sumeria were struck by the arrows of the twin scourges of hunger and disease. As Sirius, Inanna was the power who, through drought, disease, war and death, destroyed the earth and her children. Yet her power to bring death is balanced by the palm tree, the Tree of Life. This was the time when her 'son', the earth's vegetation, was sacrificed and descended into the underworld to await the time of regeneration.

Figure 19. Inanna–Ishtar, crowned with a star and holding the bow, the image of Sirius, with the Tree of Life; neo-Assyrian cylinder seal, *c.* 700 BC.

Inanna as Goddess of War

As suggested in Chapter 4, perhaps because the original image of the goddess begins to be split apart by the ravages of war and new attitudes to death towards the end of the third millennium BC, the former goddess of life-and-death assumes the mask of the goddess of war. The old relationship between death and regeneration vanishes or is assimilated to the increased power of the king victorious over his enemies. One of the most significant aspects of Bronze Age Sumeria is that as it developed, so did the practice of war. Small villages grew into towns, and towns into great cities with large populations. The territory serving one city began to touch that belonging to another and so rivalry between cities exploded. Sumerian society became increasingly disrupted by wars between kings who were obsessed with the drive for power and renown, or who were intent on establishing the power of the south against the north, or vice versa, and it is this process that seems to have given birth to the image of the goddess of war. Invaders from outside Sumeria, ravaging the river valleys from the north and east, added to the terrifying experience of its inhabitants, who could know no lasting peace, but might at any moment be slaughtered, widowed, orphaned or carried off into slavery.

Consequently, the massive walls of Uruk erected by Gilgamesh in the third millennium BC testify to the need for defence against enemies both within and without Sumeria. They were over 8 miles (13 km) long, nearly 20 feet (6 m) high and 15 feet (4.5 m) thick, with some 900 turrets placed

Figure 20. Inanna–Ishtar as goddess of war, with Anubanini, king of the Lullubians; rock sculpture, *c.* 2300 BC. Zohab, in the Zagros mountain region of Iran.

Figure 21. Ishtar as goddess of war,
standing on her lion; Assyrian relief,
c. 800 BC. Tell Asmar.

at intervals of 39 feet (12 m). They had only two gates, one to the north
and one to the south. War was increasingly extolled as a way of life for
kings and heroes. The goddess was invoked as 'patroness' of war, and this
role was transmitted to the goddesses of later cultures: those of Assyria,
Canaan, and Greece and even the Christian Mary.

The image of Inanna as goddess of war is surely the origin of the verse
in the Song of Songs: 'Who is she that looketh forth as the morning, fair
as the moon, clear as the sun, and terrible as an army with banners?' (S.
of S. 6:10) One of Inanna's names was Labbatu, meaning lioness.[63] In
Figure 21 Ishtar as goddess of war rides on the back of a lion. It is
interesting to compare her with the Indian goddess Durga, who also rides
on a lion, showing the parallel imagery between the two goddesses, but in
India Durga is defeating a mythological being, the Titan Buffalo, not the
worldly enemies of kings. In Inanna's role as the fearful goddess of war,
the archaic image of the lion, like the dragon and the thunderous roar of
the storm, is given a new context as the bringer of destruction and terror:
'Like a lion you roared in heaven and earth';[64] 'Like an awesome lion you
annihilated with your venom the hostile and disobedient.'[65]

The portrayal of Inanna–Ishtar as the goddess bringing death and
destruction like the flood makes clear how profound a change has been
wrought in the conception of the goddess. A late Babylonian text says: 'In
battle I fly like a swallow, I heap up heads that are so many harvested
rushes.'[66] She who incarnated the power of nature has now become the
inciter of deadly *human* action that destroys her creation. Yahweh in the

Old Testament inherits her bloodstained mantle, for by then no tribal group that wished to establish itself in the turbulent climate of the Iron Age could manage without a war god. From now on, the power of the goddess is invoked by kings to help them overcome their enemies, a subtle shift of emphasis that reveals a diminution of numinosity in the figure of the Great Goddess and an ominous rise in the king's appropriation of that numinosity to himself. Ishtar truly becomes the goddess of death as she speaks to Esarhaddon, King of Assyria, 'I am Ishtar of Arbela. I will flay your enemies and present them to you.'[67]

INANNA AND THE LAWS

As in Egypt and later in Greece, justice and the right ordering of Sumerian society were believed to derive from the goddess who, as the lunar deity, the Great Mother, 'ordered' all forms of life. In the story given below Inanna brings to her city the *me*, or Laws of Civilization. The *me* seem to have the same character and durability as the later Hebrew Tablets of the Law, yet they are more in the nature of archetypes than moral precepts. The *me*

> are described in the literary documents as 'good,' 'pure,' 'holy,' 'great,' 'noble,' 'precise,' 'innumerable,' 'eternal,' 'awesome,' 'intricate,' 'untouchable'; they could be 'presented,' 'given,' 'taken,' 'held,' 'lifted,' 'gathered,' 'worn' (like a garment), 'fastened at the side,' 'directed,' 'perfected'; deities could sit upon them, put their feet upon them, ride upon them; they could even be loaded on a boat and carried off from one city to another.[68]

With the wisdom derived from her possession of the *me*, Inanna incarnates the principle of justice. She comforts the widow and punishes the wrong-doer, as does the goddess Nanshe of the city of Lagash. Compassion is one of the qualities appealed to in hymns to Inanna and Ishtar: 'Thy ways are just and holy; thou dost gaze on sinners with compassion, and each morn leadest the wayward to the rightful path.'[69] The unhappy, the destitute, the oppressed, all appeal to the goddess. Again, because of the *me* and her earlier identification with the serpent wisdom of the underworld, the goddess is the bestower of wisdom and the gift of prophecy. In later Babylonian times Ishtar in her temple at Arbela was concerned with prophecy and with the interpretation of dreams: 'To give omens do I arise, do I arise in perfectness.'[70]

In the story of Enki giving the *me* to Inanna, the priestly inversion of older imagery is transparent, although the story may be a dramatization of a new political alliance between the cities of Uruk and Eridu. Inanna journeys to Enki's city, Eridu, banquets with him and is offered the *me*. Having given them to her, Enki regrets his decision and tries to get them back, without success. Inanna is presented as if she were Enki's daughter, yet the manner in which she resists Enki's attempts to regain the *me* suggests that she intends to keep what may rightfully belong to her as the lunar goddess. Six times Enki sends his emissary with fearsome monsters to bring back the *me* to Eridu and six times Inanna, with the help of her companion Ninshubur, manages to sail in on her 'Boat of Heaven' with her precious cargo. Indignantly she cries:

> 'My father has changed his word to me!
> He has violated his pledge – broken his promise!'[71]

But Inanna reaches her city, Uruk. As the *me* are unloaded on the White Quay of Inanna's city, it is found that there are more *me* than Enki had actually given her, among them, the art of women, musical instruments, as well as 'the perfect execution of the *me*', as though she invented them herself in her own right. Enki concedes defeat.

Other poems tell of the same rivalry between goddesses and gods, perhaps reflecting the rivalry between the cities over which they presided. At some stage in the course of the third millennium BC Inanna seems temporarily to have lost her position as Great Mother. There is a poem in which Enki, now one of the three principal male gods, glorifies himself as the god responsible for the earth's fertility: supreme among the gods (the *Annunaki*, or powers of heaven and earth) to whom he allocates different functions and prerogatives. Inanna, perhaps through the voice of her high priestess, complains that she has been neglected, that she has lost her 'prerogatives'. Enki is now her 'father':

> Inanna to her father Enki,
> Enters the house, and humbly weeping, utters a plaint,
> 'The Annunaki, the great gods – their fate
> Enlil placed firmly in your hand,
> Me, the woman, why did you treat differently?
> I, the holy Inanna, – where are my prerogatives?'[72]

Enki attempts to soothe her by telling her that her powers are by no means negligible, but the feeling is that Inanna is not comforted and that the powers that were once hers have been divided up by Enki among many other goddesses and gods.

However, in a late myth called the 'Elevation of Inanna', she seems to have restored to her the powers that once belonged to her as Great Mother. An, Enlil and Enki, the Sumerian trinity of male gods, give her their respective powers and she becomes goddess of the heavens, the air and the waters. She becomes Queen of the Universe. But this cannot disguise the fact that the inversion of her powers is complete: instead of the powers being naturally hers because she is life itself, she now receives them as the gift of her father, An, the god of heaven:

> My father gave me heaven, gave me earth,
> I, the Queen of Heaven am I,

Is there a god who can vie with me?
Enlil gave me heaven, gave me earth,
I, the Queen of Heaven am I!
He has given me lordship,
He has given me queenship,
He has given me battle, he has given me combat,
He has given me the Flood, he has given me the Tempest,
He has placed heaven as a crown on my head,
He has tied the earth as a sandal at my foot,
He has fastened the holy garment of the *me* about my body,
He has placed the holy scepter in my hand.[73]

THE GODDESS AND HER SON–LOVER

The Bronze Age myth of the goddess and her half-divine, half-human son and consort comes to life in the poetry of Sumeria because, for the first time, we can listen to the words and visualize the images that tell the story of the death and resurrection of the god, and the goddess's search for him in the underworld. The name of the consort of Inanna and Ishtar was Dumuzi in southern Sumeria and Tammuz in northern, Akkadian-speaking Sumeria. Both names mean the 'Faithful Son'.[74] Both gods carried, like their mothers, the title of 'the Green One' (*Urikittu*), an image that reappears millennia later in the faces that gaze from the carved foliage of the Gothic cathedrals, and in the Grail legends of Gawain and Parsifal, who release the waters and so restore the wasteland to verdant life. The goddess was the vine (Geshtinanna) or the rootstock of the vine, and her son was the fruit of the vine, the grape cluster.[75] The goddess was the palm tree – the Tree of Life – and her son, Dumuzi, was the son of The Lady of the Date Clusters. He was called Amaushumgalanna, 'the one great source of the date clusters', and was personified by the great date bud.[76] The young son–lover of the goddess was associated not just with vegetation in general but also with specific crops in different parts of Sumeria: for example, the fruit tree of the north and the date palm of the south, the vine that bore its fruit in autumn and the corn that ripened in late spring. He was also Lord of the Sheepfold and Cattlestall, and his life was identified with the fecundity of cattle, sheep and goats. Sometimes he appears in the person of Enki as the son and perhaps the consort of Nammu, the great serpent-mother, and in this aspect he is the fecundating life of the waters, sometimes drawn with a serpent coiled around the lower limbs or emerging from each shoulder. The caduceus, with its intertwining serpents, was a symbol shared by both mother and son, as was the double-headed axe. Dumuzi–Tammuz was sometimes portrayed as a fish god, the 'True Son of the Deep' – the source of wisdom.

In the magnificent cup of the Sumerian King Gudea of Lagash (Fig. 22) two winged dragons hold back a pair of opening doors to reveal a caduceus

Figure 22. Detail of the Cup of Lagash, showing the image of the god Ningizzida; *c.* 2025 BC.

of uniting serpents, incarnation of the god Ningizzida, one of the names given to the consort of the mother goddess, and to whom the cup is inscribed: 'Lord of the Tree of Truth'. A hymn from Eridu gives the sense of the son–lover's relation to his mother–spouse and speaks of a great tree whose roots reached towards the Deep:

> Its seat was the central place of the earth; its foliage was the couch of the primeval mother. Into the heart of its holy house which spreads its shade like a forest hath no man entered; there (is the home of) the mighty mother who passes across the sky; in the midst of it was Tammuz.[77]

In the rich cosmology of Eridu, the oldest Sumerian city and the nearest to the Persian Gulf, the Deep was the hieroglyph of the Mother Goddess and the primordial waters of space. Eridu was the origin of all the later images of Wisdom as the goddess herself, and also of her sons who came forth, like Enki, Tammuz or the Babylonian Oannes, from these great waters.

The return of the god brought the renewal of life and fertility to the earth. The cylinder seals in Figures 23 and 24 show the goddess with her consort, the grain god. Both scenes show the god in the process of becoming the new life of the earth as he sprouts branches of corn while the goddess sits enthroned, holding branches in her hand.

Figure 23. (*Left*) The goddess and her consort, the grain god; cylinder seal, *c.* 2300 BC.
Figure 24. (*Right*) The goddess receiving the grain god; cylinder seal, *c.* 2300–2000 BC.

Figure 25. Dumuzi as the Shepherd; cylinder seal, *c.* 3200–3000 BC. Dumuzi
is standing between two sheep. The stylized reed pillars of Inanna – her
asherim – frame the scene, and the rose tree grows from a
massive stone vase.

Whoever these figures may actually represent, it is as Dumuzi and
Tammuz that we know them. In the mythology that tells their story they
are primarily named as shepherds, which was also the title of the kings of
Sumeria in their role as servant of the gods and custodian of the land and
its produce. Dumuzi and Tammuz had many titles: 'Lord of Life', 'Lord
of the Net' and 'Lord of the Flood'. As 'Lord of the Net' they wore the
ritual skirt with a net-like pattern (Fig. 25). They were the 'Keeper of the
Sheepfold' and the 'Shepherd of the People', titles that came originally
from their relationship to the Mother Goddess as 'Holy Shepherdess'.
When sacrificed, they were the lamb. One may speculate as to how some
of these titles descended to Jesus as the Good Shepherd and the sacrificed
Lamb. Even the miracle of the loaves and the fishes carries overtones
of the older mythology, for the 'Lord of Life' brought abundance and
increase.

The magnificent image of a golden and blue ram resting its front legs
on the golden Tree of Life (Fig. 26) was found in the royal graves at Ur
and represents the consort of the goddess caught in the rose tree, which
symbolized the goddess herself.[78] The son–lover could also be represented
by a goat – usually Enki's sacred animal – as well as by the ram and the
bull.

The image of the bull was most important in Sumerian mythology, as
in all Mediterranean and Near Eastern cultures. Dumuzi and Tammuz, as
the brother, husband or son of Inanna and Ishtar, are repeatedly called
the 'Bull of Heaven'. Enlil, who may also have been originally the son–
lover of Ki, his mother, 'set his foot upon the earth like a great bull'.[79] A
poem illustrates the mysterious triune relationship between mother and
son; Inanna is the mother, wife and sister of the god, imagery that derives
originally from the phases of the moon:

> In heaven there is light, on earth there is light,
> In the bosom of his mother in his childhood she gave him rest.
> In (his) childhood, the mother, mother compassionate, compassion spoke.

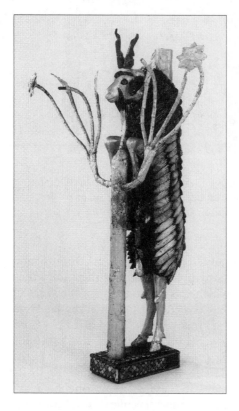

Figure 26. *The Ram in the Thicket*; *c.* 2500 BC. The Royal Graves at Ur.

In (her) bosom his sister, sister compassionate, compassion spoke.
In (her) bosom his wife Ininni (Inanna) gave him rest.[80]

The poems telling of the courtship of Inanna and Dumuzi are among the loveliest in Sumerian literature. They have humour as well as tenderness, and their imagery animates the story so that it is as vivid now as it must have been then. In the love of Inanna for Dumuzi and in his love for her, the poets seem to express the love of men and women for each other, which was exalted in the myth of the goddess and her consort into a cosmic relationship. In one of the courtship poems Inanna opens the door of her house to Dumuzi:

> Like a moonbeam she came forth to him
>   Out of the house,
> He looked at her, rejoiced in her,
> Took her in his arms and kissed her.[81]

Inanna said to him:

> 'What I tell you
> Let the singer weave into song.
> What I tell you,
> Let it flow from ear to mouth,
> Let it pass from old to young.'[82]

THE SACRED MARRIAGE

The cylinder seal in Figure 27 may portray the union of the goddess with her consort in the ritual of the sacred marriage. Beneath the nuptial bed is a scorpion, sacred to Inanna, which symbolized her power to destroy life as well as to give it, and hints, therefore, at the sacrifice of her consort, the vegetation god. The sacred marriage symbolized the union of the moon and the sun, of heaven and earth. It was celebrated in spring, after the return of the god from the underworld, and took place in the bridal chamber at the summit of the temple or ziggurat, where the high priestess or queen took the role of the goddess. The role of the newly risen vegetation god Dumuzi–Tammuz was enacted by the high priest or king of the city, who in the earliest times was one and the same person and may have actually replaced the previous sacrificed king. A poem tells us how central this ceremony was to the people, and how carefully the Sumerian rituals were attuned to the phases of the moon, as Easter still is to this day:

> The people of Sumer assemble in the palace,
> The house which guides the land.
> The king builds a throne for the queen of the palace.
> He sits beside her on the throne.
>
> In order to care for the life of all the lands,
> The exact first day of the month is closely examined,
> And on the day of the disappearance of the moon,
> On the day of the sleeping of the moon,
> The *me* are perfectly carried out
> So that the New Year's Day, the day of rites,
> May be properly determined,
> And a sleeping place be set up for Inanna.[83]

Milk, water, semen, dew and honey are all at this time images of the moon's nourishing and fertilizing power. The sacred marriage rite was celebrated at the New Year ceremony to consecrate the king of the city as the 'bridegroom' and 'son' of the goddess, even perhaps to deify him. At

Figure 27. The Sacred Marriage; cylinder seal showing a couple on a bed, with a scorpion under the bed, Early Dynastic Period, *c.* 2800 BC.

the same time it was the most important ritual for the renewal of the fertility of the land, bringing together in union the goddess and the god, who, as king, personified the 'life' of the earth. Throughout, the goddess or her priestess takes the initiative. The king comes to her temple, bearing the appropriate offerings, hoping for her favour. He waits for her embrace. This poem celebrates the marriage *c.* 2250 BC of Inanna and the deified king Isin-Dagan, her 'consort'.

> She embraces her beloved husband.
> Holy Inanna embraces him.
> The throne in the great sanctuary is made glorious
> Like the daylight.
> The king like the Sun-god,
> Plenty, happiness and abundance before him prosper.
> A feast of good things they set before him,
> The dark-headed people prosper before him.
>
> . . . . .
>
> The king with food and drink is fitly provided.
> The divine mother, fearful dragon of heaven, with food
> and drink is fitly provided.
> The temple gleams, the king rejoices.
> Daily the people are satisfied with abundance,
> The divine mother, fearful dragon of heaven, rejoices.[84]

The seal image in Figure 28 may be one of the oldest and rarest images of the sacred marriage to survive the passage of time and the ravages of the Sumerian climate. The serpent rises on its coils next to the figure of the goddess, who sits facing her consort, the god, across the Tree of Life. The imagery of this scene anticipates the scene in the Garden of Eden that was to be given so different a meaning in Genesis. Many poems celebrating the sacred marriage ritual have come down to us intact, and it is these, recited in the temple courts for literally thousands of years, infused with a sense of magical participation and delight, that evoke the scene. In words that anticipate those in the Song of Songs, Dumuzi says:

Figure 28. Goddess and god seated beside the Tree of Life, with serpent;
cylinder seal, *c.* 2500 BC.

> 'My sister, I would go with you to my garden.
> Inanna, I would go with you to my garden.
> I would go with you to my orchard.
> I would go with you to my apple tree.
> There I would plant the sweet, honey-covered seed.'

And Inanna says:

> 'He brought me into his garden.
> My brother, Dumuzi, brought me into his garden.
> I strolled with him among the standing trees,
> I stood with him among the fallen trees,
> By an apple tree I knelt as is proper.
> Before my brother coming in song,
> Who rose to me out of the poplar leaves,
> Who came to me in the midday heat,
> Before my lord Dumuzi,
> I poured out plants from my womb.
> I placed plants before him,
> I poured out plants before him,
> I placed grain before him,
> I poured out grain before him.
> I poured out grain from my womb.'[85]

The imagery of fertility permeates other poems:

> At the king's lap stood the rising cedar.
> Plants grew high by their side.
> Grains grew high by their side.
> Gardens flourished luxuriantly.
>
> . . . . .
>
> 'O Lady, your breast is your field.
> Inanna, your breast is your field.
> Your broad field pours out plants.
> Your broad field pours out grain.
> Water flows from on high for your servant.
> Bread flows from on high for your servant.
> Pour it out for me, Inanna.
> I will drink all you offer.'[86]

And Inanna said:

> 'Bridegroom, dear to my heart,
> Goodly is your beauty, honeysweet,
> Lion, dear to my heart,
> Goodly is your beauty, honeysweet.
>
> 'You have captivated me, let me stand tremblingly before you,
> Bridegroom, I would be taken by you to the bedchamber,
> You have captivated me, let me stand tremblingly before you,
> Lion, I would be taken by you to the bedchamber.

Bridegroom, let me caress you,
My precious caress is more savory than honey,
In the bedchamber, honey filled,
Let us enjoy your goodly beauty,
Lion, let me caress you,
My precious caress is more savory than honey.'[87]

These beautiful words, reverberating long after Sumeria has vanished, speak to us in the voice of the high priestess of Inanna's temple. It may be

Figure 29. Marriage bed with embracing couple; clay plaque,
c. 2000 BC. Elam.

that our 'honeymoon' – the honey month – descends from this ceremony. Clay plaques have survived from this time showing a woman and a man in embrace (Fig. 29) and caressing, holding the image for a wife and husband of the sacred marriage in the temple. Another poem celebrates the return of fertility to the land. Inanna sings:

> 'He has sprouted; he has burgeoned;
> He is lettuce planted by the water.
> He is the one my womb loves best.
>
> 'My well-stocked garden of the plain,
> My barley growing high in its furrow,
> My apple tree which bears fruit up to its crown,
> He is lettuce planted by the water.
>
> 'My honey-man, my honey-man sweetens me always.
> My lord, the honey-man of the gods,
> He is the one my womb loves best.
> His hand is honey, his foot is honey,
> He sweetens me always.
>
> 'My eager impetuous caresser of the navel,
> My caresser of the soft thighs,
> He is the one my womb loves best,
> He is lettuce planted by the water.'[88]

Another poem, equally rich in sexual imagery, shows the close bond between priest, shepherd and king and the symbolism of the bull:

> 'I bathed for the wild bull,
> I bathed for the shepherd Dumuzi,
> I perfumed my sides with ointment,
> I coated my mouth with sweet-smelling amber,
> I painted my eyes with kohl.
>
> 'He shaped my loins with his fair hands,
> The shepherd Dumuzi filled my lap with cream and milk,
> He stroked my pubic hair,
> He watered my womb.
> He laid his hands on my holy vulva,
> He smoothed my black boat with cream,
> He quickened my narrow boat with milk,
> He caressed me on the bed.
>
> 'Now I will caress my high priest on the bed,
> I will caress the faithful shepherd Dumuzi,
> I will caress his loins, the shepherdship of the land,
> I will decree a sweet fate for him.'[89]

THE DESCENT OF INANNA

In this story of Inanna and Ishtar we come finally to what, apart from the *Epic of Gilgamesh*, was the greatest and most influential of Bronze Age myths, the poem known as 'The Descent of Inanna'. In this oldest ritual dramatization of a lunar myth, at least 2,000, if not 3,000 years older than the Christian myth of the crucifixion, descent into hell and resurrection of Jesus, Inanna makes her descent into the dark realm of her sister, Ereshki-gal, removing, piece by piece, the regalia of her office at each of the seven gates of the underworld. Ereshkigal fastens on Inanna 'the eye of death', and for three days she hangs like a carcass on a hook. Her faithful companion, Ninshubur – whose name means 'Queen of the East' – whom she warns to go in search of help for her if she does not return, appeals to the god Enlil, then to the moon god, Nanna, and finally to Enki. Enki, the god of wisdom, responds to her and sends two creatures to plead with Ereshkigal for Inanna's release. They find Ereshkigal in the process of giving birth. Inanna is restored to life and ascends like the moon after its three days' 'death' to assume her place once more as Queen of Heaven. But she is forced to appoint someone as a sacrifice in her place and, refusing to allow Ninshubur to be sacrificed, or her sons, she chooses her husband, Dumuzi. This great lunar drama, telling the story of the darkening of the moon and the appearance of the new crescent after the three days of darkness, was probably already very old when it was first written down about 1750 BC, and may have been altered from its earliest version.

It is probable that the terracotta image in Figure 30 is that of Inanna in her role as goddess of sky, earth and underworld, Queen of the Great Above and the Great Below. It is perhaps the most important image of her to have survived from Sumerian times. Its authenticity does not seem to be in doubt and it has been dated by Frankfort, who comments on its exquisite modelling, to the last third of the third millennium BC.[90]

The goddess is sculpted to face the approaching worshipper, as are the lions and the owls standing sentinel to her left and right. She wears a crown with four horned tiers, and her hair frames her face and is drawn into a bun at the back. She wears a necklace round her throat. She is winged, showing her relationship to the sky and heaven, and her wings, as well as the wings of the owls to her left and right, are painted alternately black and red. Her body shows traces of red ochre paint all over it. Her taloned feet rest on lions, and the lions in turn rest upon the sacred mountain, which is identified by the design of scales along the bottom of the sculpture.

The Sumerian word for owl is *ninna* and the name Nin-ninna given to the goddess in her owl form meant 'Divine Lady Owl'.[91] The ancient texts also give the Akkadian word *kilili* for Nin-ninna, and this name was one shared by Inanna and Ishtar. (Perhaps *kilili* is the original derivation of Lilith, who, much later, in biblical times, is called 'night-owl' or

Figure 30. The Burney Relief; terracotta plaque of Inanna–Ishtar, with lions, owls and the rod and line of measurement; *c.* 2300–2000 BC, height 19½ in. (49.5 cm), width 14½ in. (37 cm).

'screech-owl'. It seems as if the Lilith in Hebrew mythology may be a distorted image of the Sumero-Akkadian goddess, for the emphasis in the stories about her is always on her death-bringing powers.) Throughout Neolithic civilization the owl is an image of the goddess of the world beyond death. Lions and birds are the oldest epiphanies of the goddess, discovered first in the Palaeolithic era, and then in Çatal Hüyük and Old Europe, and the Sumerian plaque is striking for bringing them together in a magnificent statement. In the light of the Neolithic imagery from which Bronze Age mythology evolved, this figure suggests rather a climate of belief in which the image of the goddess was not yet split into heavenly and demonic, light and dark aspects. On the contrary, it unifies the upper world and the underworld; Inanna does not terrify but inspires with the majesty of her presence.

The imagery of regeneration is striking in the poem of Inanna's Descent; we hear Ereshkigal about to give birth in the underworld – and to whom does she restore life but Inanna? It is as if Inanna, as goddess of life, requires this passage through her own depths in order to be reunited with her underworld aspect. Behind these powerful images is the lunar myth, where the light has to descend into darkness in order to reappear in the next cycle. The two sisters together represent the whole, the unified 'faces' of the Great Mother, the one imaging the light, the other the dark that 'kills' it, yet restores it in the new cycle to its place in heaven. Ereshkigal is the dark moon, who 'kills' her younger sister, disrobing her as she descends into the underworld through the seven stages or days of the waning moon, impaling her on a nail or stake during the three days of darkness when the moon is gone. Inanna is restored to her full splendour as she ascends from the dark regions through the stages or days of the waxing moon, and in this way life is shown to emerge from darkness.

The Babylonian story of Ishtar's Descent has a few different features, which are of great interest. Tammuz, her son–lover, is mortally wounded by a wild boar and Ishtar descends into the underworld to awaken him from the sleep that holds him spellbound. Her manner is more imperious than Inanna's as she demands entrance at the gates of the underworld.

Ishtar, like Inanna, descends through the seven gates, is divested of her robes and comes naked into the presence of the goddess of the underworld, and later has restored to her in seven stages the glorious apparel of her office as Queen of Heaven and Earth. While she is there, during the three days of darkness, it is as though a spell has been cast on the upper world. Fertility is suspended; everything falls asleep. The imagery of the Sleeping Beauty comes irresistibly to mind, although in the story of Ishtar and Tammuz it is the 'prince' who falls asleep and the 'queen' who awakens him and breaks the enchantment. Was this story the origin of the fairy-tale whose lunar princess, together with her parents and the court, falls asleep on her fifteenth birthday and is awakened by the prince, who restores her and the whole court to life?

THE SACRIFICE OF THE SON–LOVER

Just as the sacred marriage ritualized sexuality and the ecstatic experience of life, so the sacrifice of the son–lover ritualized the counter-pole of human experience, the loss of life. The sacrifice of the young god embodied the dark phase of the lunar myth of the goddess in which he had to descend into the underworld for the sake of the earth's regeneration, yet always with the promise of return in the new cycle of life. The son–lover of the goddess plays a passive role in both the Sumerian and the Babylonian versions of the Descent. In the Sumerian version Dumuzi is seized by the emissaries of the underworld on Inanna's orders and against his will, as a substitute for herself. In the Babylonian version of the myth Ishtar goes down into the underworld to rescue Tammuz and awaken him from his sleep. The theme of the sleeping god is found in another version of the myth in which the god – this time Enki – is asleep in the underworld and has to be awakened by his mother, Nammu. In the myth of Inanna's Descent, when she returns to the upper world, the *galla*, or 'demons' of the underworld, demand that they be given another in her place. She comes to her city, Uruk, and finds her husband, Dumuzi, sitting on a throne by the sacred apple tree in her temple. Inanna fastens the eye of death on him, and appoints him to take her place.[92] The *galla* beat Dumuzi with axes and blows, and he prays for help to the sun god, Utu, Inanna's brother, who turns him into a snake, and so he escapes from his persecutors. He calls to his sister, Geshtinanna, and tells her of a dream he has had. The dream foretells his death and Geshtinanna weeps as she listens to it. The seven *galla* approach once more, and once more Dumuzi appeals for help to Utu, who now changes him into a gazelle, which runs to his sister's sheepfold for refuge. Geshtinanna, knowing his fate, weeps, and 'her grief covered the horizon like a garment'.[93] The *galla* find Dumuzi and the first one strikes his cheek with a nail. They seize him:

> The churn was silent. No milk was poured.
> The cup was shattered, Dumuzi was no more.
> The sheepfold was given to the winds.[94]

Figure 31. Sacrifice of a king or son–lover; cylinder seal, *c.* 2330 BC.

A lament is raised in the city and three women mourn the young king, anticipating the three women who mourn at the grave of Jesus. Inanna weeps bitterly for her young husband. Dumuzi's mother, Sirtur (Ninsun), also weeps:

> 'My heart plays the reed pipe of mourning.
> I would go to him,
> I would see my child.'[95]

And Geshtinanna wanders through the city, weeping for her brother. The story tells how Inanna, seeing Geshtinanna's grief, goes to her and expresses a wish to take her to Dumuzi, but she (Inanna) does not know where he is. Then a fly appears and directs them to Dumuzi. Inanna takes Dumuzi by the hand and says that he will go to the underworld for half the year and Geshtinanna the other half and, with that, she 'placed Dumuzi in the hands of the eternal'.[96]

The cylinder seal in Figure 31 may be a portrayal of the ritual sacrifice of Dumuzi. Priests attired in the skins of animals seize the king by his beard and raise their arms as if to strike him. A gazelle is seen to his left, a bird to his right. The kneeling king or god seems about to be dispatched to the underworld, the abyss of the *Kur*. In the adjoining scene the king or god seems to be returning from the underworld, as the vegetation sprouts from his body and from an altar nearby.

The royal tombs discovered at Ur give us some idea of the elaborate ceremonial and rich costume that must have been part of this seasonal ritual drama of sacrifice, which was performed in the courts of the temple. Here were found magnificent bull- and cow-headed lyres, the golden ram with his feet caught in a rose tree, and exquisite head-dresses of priestesses or queens, some adorned with gold beech and willow leaves.[97] It is a remarkable fact that nearly seventy years after these tombs were excavated at Ur by Sir Leonard Woolley, nothing has been found in Mesopotamia that compares with their wealth or their cultural brilliance. Woolley originally dated them to 3500 BC, but the date is now set at 2500 BC . They feel far older, partly because they are unique and partly because there is no reference to them in any known text. The only context in which they can be placed is the myth of the sacrificed god. We do not know when this tradition of ritual sacrifice began or when and why it ended. We know only that later, in the temple of Marduk in Babylon, the sacrifice of the king was still enacted symbolically in a ritual in which the priest struck the king's face, removed his regalia of office and forced him to make a 'negative confession' of the evil deeds he had not done.[98] If tears came to the king's eyes from the force of the blow, it was taken as an omen that the land would give good yield, revealing once again the lunar symbolism of dew or moisture. The ritual of striking the king may have been a vestige of the ritual drama of Inanna's Descent to the Nether World, where the *galla* pursuing her son–lover, Dumuzi, strike his cheek with a nail.[99]

Sumerian scholars have searched for evidence of human sacrifice and for references in the literary texts to the archaic ritual of immolating the king's court at his death (again an image of the court 'falling asleep'), but most of the texts do not date to this early period. By the time of King Ur-Nammu, about 2100 BC, we know that the king's wife, children and servants did not accompany him to the Nether World; as a poem tells us, the wailing of his mourning relatives reached him there, and he in turn set up a long and bitter lament.[100] However, Campbell brings evidence to support the thesis, based on Frazer, that before 2500 BC kings were ritually sacrificed every octennial Great Year in their role as the vegetation god, together with the high priestess or queen who personified the goddess.[101]

Many of the beautiful laments in Sumerian and Babylonian literature are inspired by the sorrow of Inanna–Ishtar, the mother, wife and sister of Dumuzi–Tammuz. The rites of mourning and of greeting the risen god are virtually the same in both cultures. From here they seem to have spread all over the Near East and the Mediterranean. Everywhere the same myth of the virgin goddess whose son–lover dies a sacrificial death and is reborn after she goes in search of him in the underworld was ritually celebrated.

In 3000 BC the spring equinox, which began the Sumerian year, was in the sign of Taurus, the Bull. The great star Sirius set in conjunction with the sun about 1 May, when vegetation was at its most luxuriant. Sirius then disappeared from view until it rose once again in conjunction with the sun in mid-July. The month of mourning sacred to the sacrificed son of the goddess – the sixth month of the year, known as the month of wailing for Tammuz – took place after the corn and other crops had been harvested from mid-June to mid-July.[102] The reappearance of Sirius with the sunrise announced the death of the vegetation god, who was struck by its 'burning rays'. It is possible that the return of Sirius also marked the time for the descent of the goddess into the underworld in search of her son–lover. When the apple tree, date palm, vine and corn showed signs of renewed life, the god returned. There were many hymns for the wailing of the god and these were accompanied by the flute. The earliest form of temple music was the flute and the earliest temple hymns were called 'songs to the flute' (*Irshemma*). Sometimes it was the goddess as mother, sometimes as wife and sometimes as sister, who lamented the sacrificed god. Here, Inanna laments the death of her husband, Dumuzi:

> 'Gone is my husband, my sweet husband.
> Gone is my love, my sweet love.
> My beloved has been taken from the city,
> O, you flies of the steppe,
> My beloved bridegroom has been taken from me
> Before I could wrap him with a proper shroud.

★

'The wild bull lives no more.
The shepherd, the wild bull lives no more.
Dumuzi, the wild bull, lives no more.'[103]

Another lament of Inanna, which may refer to the loss of Dumuzi or to the loss of her rightful place in the pantheon of deities, or even to the destruction of her temple due to war, is addressed to Enlil, the god of air:

Tell me where is my house, my mute, silent house,
My house in which a spouse no longer lives, in which I no longer greet a son,
I, the queen of heaven, am one in whose house a spouse no longer lives, in whose house I no longer greet a son.

The bird has its nesting place, but I – my young are dispersed,
The fish lies in calm waters, but I – my resting place exists not,
The dog kneels at the threshold, but I – I have no threshold,
The ox has a stall, but I – I have no stall,
The cow has a place to lie down, but I – I have no place to lie down,
The ewe has a fold, but I – I have no fold,
The beasts have a place to sleep, but I – I have no place to sleep.[104]

The women of the city participated in the ritual mourning for the lost god,[105] perhaps intoning the words of lament sung by his mother and wife. When he was 'lost' to life, the god was called 'the Shepherd who had left his sheep'.[106] As with the rites at the death of Adonis much later in Syria and Greece,[107] a wooden effigy of the god was laid in a boat or raft and set afloat on the waters. As it sank, Dumuzi–Tammuz descended into the underworld. Perhaps the women placed little rafts holding green lettuce or cress upon the waters.[108] The following lament of Ishtar strangely anticipates the Virgin Mary's sorrow for her dead son:

Him of the plains why have they slain?
The shepherd,
The wise one,
The man of sorrows why have they slain?
The Lady of the vine stalk with the lambs and calves languishes.
The lord shepherd of the folds lives no more,
The husband of the heavenly queen lives no more,
The Lord of the cattle stalls lives no more.
When he slumbers the sheep and lambs slumber also,
When he slumbers the she-goat and kids slumber also.[109]

The difficulty of awakening the god from sleep and bringing him back to life was part of the ritual drama of the myth of the goddess. It is most interesting to discover that this imagery reappears in Gnosticism in the early centuries of Christianity, where the soul has to be 'awakened' from its sleep in the 'underworld' of earth in order to return to its 'home' in the celestial world. The imagery of the archaic myth is there transposed to the context of the human soul.[110]

THE UNDERWORLD

Where did the sacrificed god go when he died? Transported along the river in his 'moon' boat, bearing the 'sacred bough' of the goddess, he passed the Horned Gate that marked the entrance to the Nether World.[111] He entered the mountain, the *Kur*, the abyss of the Deep, where Ereshkigal, Inanna's sister goddess, ruled as the dark counterpart of her luminous brilliance. He also made the journey of return in his boat, whose prow sprouted the leaves that signalled the renewal of life (Fig. 32).

In the Sumerian creation myth the separation of An and Ki – the son and daughter of Nammu – seems to have coincided with the creation of the underworld or nether world[112] and the seizure of the goddess Ereshkigal by underworld powers. Sometimes it seems as if Nammu, as serpent goddess of the Deep, was the original goddess of the underworld and that Ereshkigal is a later substitution. The name Ereshkigal means the 'Lady of the Great Earth' and suggests that she may have been the underworld aspect of the goddess Ki, the daughter of Nammu. The Greek myth in which Persephone, similarly carried off into the underworld, was the daughter of the corn goddess, Demeter, may be a later version of a Sumerian myth.

The later Sumerians, but more particularly the Babylonians and Assyrians after them, came to regard the underworld as a fearful place, inhabited by demons and evil spirits that only too easily could seize upon and inhabit the souls of men and women. A river separated the dead from the living, and the dead had to cross this expanse of treacherous water by ferry, and go:

> On the road from which there is no way back,
> To the house wherein the dwellers are bereft of light,
> Where dust is their fare and clay their food,
> They are clothed like birds, with wings for garments,
> And see no light, residing in darkness.[113]

Figure 32. The journey to or from the underworld; *c.* 2300–2150 BC.

The image cannot have inspired hope and trust in the dying, and it is in strong contrast to the burials at Ur, which seem much closer to the Egyptian trust in life after death.

The underworld in later Sumerian and Babylonian mythology seems to personify everything that has become most terrifying to human conscious-ness as it moves farther and farther away from a sense of the wholeness and sacrality of life. A dimension of existence that cannot be seen or perceived through the senses, which is invisible and therefore in-comprehensible, is filled with the fear of death which is projected into this 'space' as demonic forms or beings. Death begins to be treated as something final and absolute, rather than a rite of passage between two dimensions in the sense that the Egyptians imagined it. The more the known and unknown, light and dark phases of life are split apart and associated with good and evil, the more terrifying the dimension beyond death becomes, and the more demonic is the activity of its rulers and emissaries. The ultimate legacy of this fear is reached in the Hebrew Lilith and the Christian image of hell and the devil.

All the more significant, then, is the Sumerian myth of Inanna's De-scent, for she, Queen of Heaven and Earth, a young and radiant goddess adorned with all the 'powers' of her office, wishes to experience that unknown dimension of the underworld. 'Opening her ear' to the Great Below, she makes the shamanic journey to the hidden face of life in order to achieve a deeper understanding of its mysteries. Inanna's journey seems to mirror the need of a culture for a ritual that would reconnect it with its psychic roots – the underworld. Her descent is not only a dramatization of the ancient rituals associated with the moon cycle that had influenced human consciousness for so many thousands of years; it also dramatizes an initiation into a feared dimension that was conceived as *geographically* remote from the 'upper' light world of everyday life and practical concerns.

There is no reason to suppose that the priestesses and priests who ritualized this myth as drama were unaware of its significance as a *rite d'entrée* into a dimension already becoming remote and terrifying to human consciousness. It was an initiation into the realization that death is not inimical to life but an essential aspect of its totality and, indeed, the passageway to a 'new' cycle of life. Inanna's descent into the underworld and her return from it after her submission to her sister offered Sumerian culture the paradigm of the 'Great Below' as the essential counterpart of the 'Great Above'.

6
ISIS OF EGYPT:
QUEEN OF HEAVEN, EARTH AND
UNDERWORLD

'O let me teach you how to knit again
This scattered corn into one mutual sheaf,
These broken limbs again into one body . . .'

William Shakespeare, *Titus Andronicus*, V, iii

Isis was the greatest goddess in Egypt and was worshipped for over 3,000 years, from pre-dynastic times – before 3000 BC – until the second century AD, when her cult and many of her images passed directly on to the figure of Mary. Her sphere was not confined to Egypt, for during that time she crossed boundaries of culture, race and nation, reaching Greece in the third century BC and spreading throughout the Roman Empire, even to the borders of the Danube and the Rhine. She lasted so long that the evolution of consciousness can be seen reflected in the different ways she was conceived and honoured.

The immense range of thought and feeling focused through the figure of Isis appears in the diversity of her images or epiphanies. She was, variously, the milk-giving cow goddess; goddess of the serpents of the primeval waters; the star goddess Sirius, who brought about the inundation of the Nile; the fertile pig goddess; the bird goddess; goddess of the underworld, whose breath gave life to the dead; goddess of the Tree of Life, offering the food and water of immortality; goddess of the words of power; the tender, caring mother of Horus, her son; and goddess of the throne upon whose sovereign lap the king sat as her infant child in the image of all humanity. To the playful logic of the mythic mind it was no contradiction that Isis was the Great Mother Goddess of the Universe, from whom all gods, goddesses, worlds and humanity were born, and, at the same time, one of four children of the Sky Goddess, Nut, and the Earth God, Geb, belonging, in this guise, to the fourth generation of gods and goddesses who came forth from the formless waters in the beginning.

In the beginning everywhere was water and water was everywhere, and the name of the waters was Nun. And out of the primordial waters of the dark abyss a hill began to rise up; it was the 'mound of the first time', and it was the first time of light. And the name of the High Hill was Atum, the 'Complete One'.

Figure 1. Isis, wearing a head-dress of the sun-disc between cow's horns
and holding the sistrum of regeneration before the Osiris-king; Nineteenth
Dynasty, *c.* 1300 BC. Temple of Seti I, Abydos.

This happened in the beginning, and it happened every day in the birth
of the sun from the primordial abyss of night, and every year in the rising
of the land from the inundating waters of the Nile. When the great flood
receded, tiny hills of mud rose up out of the dark water, growing higher

and higher, and then plants began to sprout from them, insects crawled and flew over them, birds and animals alighted and walked over them, and humans could find 'somewhere to stand or sit'. So all life came from the rich brown teeming waters of the Nile, as had happened in the first time.

Every year the Nile dies and is reborn, and the whole of Egypt with it. In mid-June, around the summer solstice, the Nile appears to be going away for ever, evaporated into earth and air, shrunk to half its size. But just as life reaches its lowest ebb, the fields dusty and dry, the cattle thin and thirsty, and the people wasting with hunger, then the Nile begins to stir and swell, slowly at first but gathering force until it races along with tumbling waters and suddenly bursts its banks and water spills over the miles of flat and shrivelled land lying on each side of the river. From July to October all things sink into the state of the beginning of the world from which all life came and will come forth again. In the autumn the waters drop, the inundation recedes and the fertilized fields are pregnant with life, ready for seeding in November.

Ancient Egypt took its orientation from the Nile, flowing north towards the sea, bringing water for the whole world to drink; where it did not reach there was death, for on either side of the black fertile soil lay the arid desert: rocky wastes of dry sands, burnt bare by the sun, where nothing grew. Yet the sands were always moving, moving towards the wet land, ready to encroach on the cultivated fields. The contrast between life and death was ever-present. It was a dynamic drama of conflicting forces, and life was poised as an art between contraries: too great an inundation and the canals and dams capsized; too little, and the people went hungry.

This feeling for the waters as the origin of life, mirrored in the constantly flowing Nile, was common to all stories of creation in Egypt. Then different places diverged: Memphis, Heliopolis, Hermopolis, Thebes, Edfu and Denderah, all imagined the ordering of the universe in a slightly different way, giving their gods and goddesses a variety of names, overlapping, merging and separating with no contention between them.[1] There were two main centres of official religious doctrine, one at Memphis with the god Ptah bringing creation forth as the Word (see p. 154) and the other at Heliopolis, the City of the Sun. Isis belonged originally to the cosmology of Heliopolis, generally taken as the orthodoxy, and inscribed in the Pyramid Texts, but not held to be exclusively correct except in Heliopolis itself.

Atum, who comes into being as risen land and light, generates the male Shu (Air, Life, Space, Light) and the female Tefnut (Moisture, Order), who gives birth to Nut (Sky) and Geb (Earth). Shu then lifts his daughter Nut (the sky goddess) away from his son Geb (the earth god), supporting her so she can give birth to the stars and, 'taking them up into her', let them sail across her watery body as the sky. (Alternatively, it is written that the sun god, Ra, gave birth to Shu and Tefnut, and this refers not to a separate being but to the visible manifestation of Atum as Ra.) Now that the primordial elements of the universe are in place, it remains to relate them to the human world. It is here that this story begins.

THE STORY OF ISIS AND OSIRIS

Now (once upon a time) Nut and Geb gave birth to Osiris, and at the hour of his birth a voice issued forth saying 'The Lord of All advances to the light'. On the second day was born Arueris (called the elder Horus); on the third day, Seth, but not in due season or manner, who with a blow broke through his mother's side and leapt forth; on the fourth day Isis was born in the regions that are ever moist; and on the fifth day, Nephthys. With their parents and grandparents and Atum, they were called the Ennead, the Nine Gods and Goddesses. They were born in sacred time, in the interval of five days that were left over between one year (of 360 days) and the next, which Thoth had won playing at draughts with the moon. Nephthys became the wife of Seth, but Isis and Osiris loved each other even in the darkness of their mother's womb before they were born.

Osiris became the first king of Egypt and the creator of civilization, teaching his people the art of cultivation and the honouring of the gods, 'establishing justice throughout both banks of the Nile'.[2] He taught the Egyptians how to plant wheat and barley, how to gather the fruit from the trees and to cultivate the vine, and before their time the races of the world had been but savages. When he travelled to teach other nations, Isis ruled vigilantly and peacefully in his absence.

But Seth, the wicked brother of Osiris, was jealous of his virtue and his fame. So he constructed a chest the size of his brother, and one night at the palace, in the midst of the feasting, he had the richly decorated chest brought into the room and promised as a jest to give it to the one it would fit exactly. When Osiris laid himself inside it, seventy-two conspirators immediately leapt forward and nailed the lid on the chest, sealed it with molten lead and flung it into the Nile. Then it floated down to the sea.

Isis, overwhelmed with grief, cut off her hair, put on mourning clothes and searched everywhere, up and down the Nile, asking everyone she met whether they had seen the chest. It so happened that some children, playing by the river, had seen which mouth of the Nile had carried it out to the sea. Isis learnt that the chest had been carried by the waves to the coast of Byblos in Phoenicia. There it had gently lodged itself in the branches of an erica tree, which had quickly grown up around it, enclosing it on every side so it was completely hidden. So beautiful and fragrant was the tree that the local king and queen had the tree felled and fashioned into a pillar at the palace.

So Isis came to Byblos and she placed herself by a well of the city, veiled and in mourning, her divinity disguised, speaking to no one. When

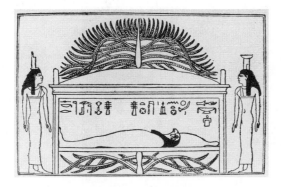

Figure 2. Osiris in the erica tree, with Isis and Nephthys; bas-relief,
c. first century BC. Denderah.

some of the queen's maidens came to the well, she greeted them kindly
and began to braid their hair, breathing on them such wondrous fragrance
that when they returned to the palace Queen Astarte smelled the perfume
on the braids and, sending for the stranger, took her into her house and
made her the nurse of her child.[3]

Now the great goddess gave the infant her finger to suck instead of the
breast, and at night she placed him in a fire to burn away all that was
mortal in him. And then, transforming herself into a swallow, she flew
around the pillar, mournfully singing. But it happened that one night
Queen Astarte, seeing her little son lying there in the flames, shrieked
dreadfully, and in that one moment deprived her child for ever of the
treasure of immortal life.

Isis then revealed her true nature and asked that the pillar that held up
the roof be given to her. She took it down and, cutting away the wood of
the tree, revealed the sarcophagus of Osiris hidden inside. When Isis saw
it, she fell upon it with such a piercing cry that the younger of the
Queen's sons was frightened out of his life. Then, taking the elder son
with her, Isis set sail with the chest for Egypt (though, finding the river
too rough and windy, she grew angry and dried up its stream). As soon as
she arrived at a desert place where she was alone, she opened the chest
and, laying her face on the face of her brother, she kissed him and wept.
(Suddenly, though, she caught sight of the boy watching her, and gave
him a look of such gravity that he died of fright on the instant.)

Now, according to some, it was when Isis fluttered round the pillar as a
swallow that she conceived her son, Horus, from Osiris. But according to
others, when Isis lay upon her husband in the boat she conceived their
child, for, taking the form of a kite, she hovered lovingly over him,
bringing him back to life with the beating of her great wings:

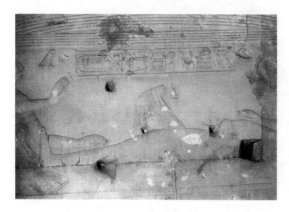

Figure 3. Isis as a kite conceiving Horus; Nineteenth Dynasty, *c.* 1300 BC. Temple of Seti I, Abydos. The hieroglyph for her name – the throne – is written before the head of the bird.

> It is she, Isis, the just, who protects her brother,
> Who seeks him without wearying,
> Who in mourning traverses the whole land
> Without respite before finding him,
> Who gives shade with her feathers,
> And wind with her wings.
> It is she who praises her brother,
> Who relieves the weakness of him who is tired,
> Who receives his seed and gives birth to his heir,
> Who nurtures the child in solitude,
> Without anyone knowing where she is.[4]

Isis then hid the chest enclosing the body of Osiris in the remote marshes of the delta, while she went to Buto to take care of her son, Horus.

One night Seth was hunting wild boar in the light of the full moon when he discovered the chest hidden among the reeds. He tore the body into fourteen pieces and scattered them up and down the country, each in a different place, and he may even have thrown the phallus of Osiris into the Nile. When Isis learned of this, once again she had to search for her husband, sailing through the swamps in a boat of papyrus. This time her sister Nephthys, sister-bride of their wicked brother Seth, helped her and so did Nephthys' son, Anubis, who had the head of a jackal. Anubis had been fathered by Osiris, who, one night when it was very dark, mistook Nephthys for Isis. Some people say this is why Seth bore such malice towards Osiris. Little Horus, who had the head of a hawk, was now old enough to help too, and they were joined by Thoth, the moon god, who had the head of an ibis, and could take the form of a baboon.

So, with Thoth's powers of discrimination and Anubis's intuitive nose, together they found all the parts of Osiris except for the genital member, which had been swallowed by a fish. Wherever Isis found a piece of Osiris's body she buried it with all the ritual due to a god, rites that were to be performed in Egypt ever afterwards. She made a replica of the missing phallus to take its place, consecrating it with great ceremony.

Some say that the funeral rites were only formal, and that Isis carefully brought all the parts back together again and reassembled them as a mummy, swathed tightly in linen bandages, through the transforming magic of Anubis in the role of embalming priest. Then Isis fanned the dead body again with her wings and Osiris revived to become the Ruler of Eternity. He now sits in the underworld with all power and majesty, in the Hall of Two Truths, where he judges the souls of the dead, which are weighed in a balance against the feather of truth of the goddess Maat, she in whose care are the laws of the universe.[5]

> Osiris! You went away, but you have returned,
> you fell asleep, but you have awakened,
> you died, but you live again.[6]

The conflict with Seth was not over, however, and the story continues with Horus growing up to take his father's place and avenge his death.

During the 'Contendings of Horus and Seth' (a New Kingdom compilation of different texts, which may point to the late arrival of this part of the story) Horus lost his left eye, which Thoth healed, and Seth his testicle. Their battles took place over three days and three nights, the figure of gestation as the time of the moon's darkness, which appears in every culture when the issues of life and death hang in the balance. Horus finally overcame Seth and gave him in chains to Isis to put to death, but

Figure 4. Horus protected by Isis sets out to avenge his father; *c.* 600 BC.

she released him. Horus, enraged with his mother, cut off her head but
Thoth replaced it with the head of a cow.

Seth (in an abrupt but familiar politicization of the mythic dimension)
then accused Horus of being illegitimate, and the issue between them
changed as to which one had the right of inheritance. Formerly inheritance
came through the mother, which would have given Seth, as brother to
Isis, precedence over Horus; but now, the council ruled, it was to be
through the father. Horus was judged the rightful heir, the patrilineal
principle was assured and Horus was crowned the new king. The time of
the confusion past, Seth was made to serve the new order: the unregulated,
chaotic powers of the universe were now mastered and, further, brought
into relation with the new order by being required to help sustain it. In
the festivals of Osiris along the Nile, Seth was the boat that carried his
effigy, just as he carried the sun through the watery abyss of night.

> This is Horus speaking, he has ordained action for his father,
> he has shown himself master of the storm,
> he has countered the blustering of Seth,
> so that he, Seth, must bear you –
> for it is he that must carry him who is again complete.[7]

Horus then journeyed to the underworld to tell the news to Osiris and
to awaken him and 'set his soul in motion'. He presented him with the eye
that was torn out in the struggle, which restored Osiris to eternal life and
became known as the *Wedjat*-eye, the Eye of Eternity, called the 'whole
one', which protected against all harm (Fig. 5). As Osiris revived, the
spirit of life and growth awakened, and the new year began.

It is strange that nowhere in Egypt was there a complete text of the
story of Isis and Osiris. Over the 3,000-year period in which the tale was
told texts refer only to isolated episodes as though a knowledge of the
whole myth was assumed as part of the culture. This may point to an oral
tradition (to which originally Homer's *Odyssey* and *Iliad* belonged); for
where a myth was at the centre of a culture, there would have been no
need to record it in writing. The drama of the death and rebirth of Osiris
was enacted every year in the Mystery plays at Abydos, so the story may
have been handed down, in the manner of an art or a skill, from one
generation to another. The most sequential and composite story comes
from Plutarch alone, a second-century-AD Greek writer, who is known to
have visited Egypt at least once. Since the Egyptian sources all corroborate
Plutarch's version, it may be taken as true to the original, though they
also make it clear that Greek and Egyptian speak a different mythological
language.

This story is, on one level, a myth of the invisible reality that underlies
and makes intelligible the workings of what we would call Nature, which
is also, ultimately, for the Egyptians, the drama of human nature. It is
essentially a myth of immanence, for the gods and goddesses in Egypt

Figure 5. Osiris as the guardian presence of eternity, holding crook and flail, with two *Wedjat*-eyes of Horus; Twentieth Dynasty, *c.* 1190–1085 BC. Tomb of Sennejem, Deir el Medina, Thebes.

were manifest in and as creation, with many different and also mutual spheres of manifestation. In this way the manifold dimensions of the phenomenal world were brought into relation with human feeling, and the mystic bond that unified humanity with nature could be explored.

Osiris, for instance, comes alive in the rising Nile, the growing grain, the waxing moon, and in everything that is affirmative in nature and in human beings. He dies in the falling Nile, the withering grain, the waning moon and in all that succumbs to ignorance and violence and destruction. The rising Nile was also seen as the tears of Isis; for when the goddess was mourning for the lost Osiris, the tears dropped from her eyes and swelled the waters of the Nile, giving their moisture to the parched, inert body of her brother-husband. Isis was said to make the Nile swell and overflow, 'to swell in his season', and the Greek writer Pausanias explains: 'The Egyptians say that Isis bewails Osiris when the river begins to rise; and when it inundates the fields they say that it is the tears of Isis.'[8] She was manifest as the star Sothis, also called Sirius and the Dog Star, whose rising on the eastern horizon brought Osiris back to life and freed the inundation. The image unites the human and the natural world, for it is Isis's compassion, her continual searching for and then finding Osiris that restores him to life and swells the waters. According to Plutarch, Sothis in Egyptian signifies 'pregnancy', so Isis is pregnant with the rebirth of Osiris, which is Horus, his son, the new year: 'Osiris is yesterday; Horus is today.'[9]

> It is Horus the intrepid that will come forth from you
> (Osiris), in his name of Horus who is within Sothis.[10]

'Thou art the Nile ... gods and men live from thy outflow,' says Rameses IV in a hymn to Osiris.[11] But Osiris did not exist alone. After his death he was fundamentally passive and hidden; in his helplessness he had to be rescued by Isis, and not just once, but twice. In the myth she is always searching for him, finding him and awakening him from his sleep. The 'finding' of Osiris (which was to have a striking Greek counterpart in 'the finding of Kore' in the Eleusinian Mysteries) was central to the rituals that celebrated the rising of the Nile, for, even in Plutarch's time, the pouring of sweet water from the Nile into a golden casket on the occasion of the flooding was accompanied by the cry 'Osiris is found'.[12]

Osiris has to be distinguished from Min, god of the harvest, whose gift was the vitality of growth. The gift of Osiris is revival or resurrection, though, as the corn must die to live again, the two are obviously connected. The plants begin to grow when the soul of Osiris rises; they are the soul of Osiris 'speeding upwards' (Fig. 6). Osiris is the lunar mystery, the cyclical round where darkness is followed by the resurgence of light and life; whereas Min is the solar mystery, the vital force that is there or not, often pictured as a white bull or an ithyphallic man, having more in common with Horus. It was to Min that the harvest festival was dedicated, his statue drawn along the streets in procession, accompanied by a box of lettuce plants (which were later to become the plant belonging to the rites of the Greek Adonis). Similarly, Hapi, the Nile god with female breasts, who pours out his Nile water from two vases, was often identified with Osiris, but was not himself a figure through whom the cyclical drama of the Nile was reflected. Osiris, on the other hand, waxed and waned.

The helplessness of Osiris as the dead land waits to be revived is the subject of one of the most moving Coffin Texts, in which Isis and Nephthys, the two sisters who speak with one voice, call him back to life:

Figure 6. Cow-headed Isis as the star Sothis bringing the inundation that makes the plants grow. The soul bird rises above the corn as the released soul of Osiris. The Temple of Isis, Philae.

Ah Helpless One!
Ah Helpless One asleep!
Ah Helpless One in this place
   which you know not – yet I know it!
Behold I have found you (lying) on your side –
   the great Listless One.
'Ah, Sister!' says Isis to Nephthys,
'This is our brother,
Come let us lift up his head,
Come, let us (rejoin) his bones,
Come, let us reassemble his limbs,
Come, let us put an end to all his woe,
that, as far as we can help, he will weary no more.
May the moisture begin to mount for this spirit!
May the canals be filled through you!
May the names of the rivers be created through you!
Osiris, live!
Osiris, let the great Listless One arise!
I am Isis.'

      'I am Nephthys.
It shall be that Horus will avenge you,
It shall be that Thoth will protect you
   – your two sons of the Great White Crown –
It shall be that the Company will hear.
Then will your power be visible in the sky
and you will cause havoc among the (hostile) gods,
for Horus, your son, has seized the Great White Crown,
seizing it from him who acted against you.
Then will your father Atum call "Come!"
Osiris, live! . . .'[13]

Isis and Nephthys become one character in this hymn, and they are usually shown helping Osiris together, one on either side of him as he lies on his bier, making the swathings for his mummy and assisting his resurrection. Symbolically, Isis is the light moon and Nephthys is the dark moon, or, in a solar image, Isis is the dawn and Nephthys is the twilight, or Isis is the morning star and Nephthys is the evening star; or, more widely, in Plutarch's terms, Isis is the visible part of the world and Nephthys is the invisible. Together they form a completeness, complementing the duality of Osiris and Seth, their brother-husbands. But Nephthys, though wife to Seth, invariably takes the part of Isis against him (as the face of dark perpetually turned toward the light), lamenting for Osiris and conceiving Anubis from him, he who can see in the dark. The 'throne', the name of Isis and the hieroglyph she wears on her head, is the outward form of the 'Lady of the House', the name of Nephthys and the hieroglyph she wears on her head, sometimes the only distinguishing feature between them.

Figure 7. Isis, with the throne on her head, guarding Rameses III at one
end of his sarcophagus; Twentieth Dynasty, *c.* 1194–1163 BC.

The living king became Horus and the deceased king took on the role of
Osiris, or 'became Osiris' (as did all the deceased from the beginning of
the Middle Kingdom), and so many sarcophagi were painted and engraved
with Isis and Nephthys protecting the pharaoh with their outstretched
wings, as in Figures 7 and 8. Here they are seen kneeling one at each end
of the sarcophagus of Rameses III, enclosing his earthly body between
them, cradling him into eternity, as they had done for Osiris and as they
do for the sun (Ra, Horus), also reborn from the dark each dawn.

The bond between Isis and Osiris is one of the creative forces of life,
for together they are the universal soul of growth. If he is the flooding of
the Nile, then she is the earth that the Nile covers, and from this union,

Figure 8. Nephthys, with the house on her head, guarding Rameses III at the other end of his sarcophagus; Twentieth Dynasty, *c.* 1194–1163 BC.

as Plutarch said, the Egyptians make Horus to be born.[14] The new life in the grain is the child of both, Osiris renewed as Horus through Isis. Where Osiris is manifest in the grain, Isis is manifest in the crops. As the power of growth manifest in the water Osiris is called 'the Great Green Thing', and as the power of growth manifest in the earth he is called 'the Great Black Thing', the moisture that generates the corn. In Memphis it was said that Osiris 'becomes earth',[15] and, in consort, Isis is called 'Queen of Earth', the 'Green Goddess, whose green colour is like unto the greenness of the earth', 'Creator of green things', 'Lady of bread', 'Lady of beer', 'Lady of abundance'. In a Coffin Text, 'Spell for becoming Barley', the poet calls on Osiris as the life-force of the corn:

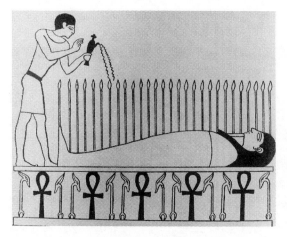

Figure 9. Osiris with wheat growing from his body, watered by a priest, with the *ankh* life-sign and the *was*-sceptre of divine prosperity beneath him; bas-relief. The Ptolemaic Temple of Isis at Philae.

I am the plant of life
which comes forth from Osiris,
which grows upon the ribs of Osiris,
which allows the people to live,
which makes the gods divine,
which spiritualizes the spirits,
which sustains the masters of wealth
and the masters of substance,
which makes the *pak* cakes for the spirits,
which enlivens the limbs of the living.
I live as corn, the life of the living,
I live upon the rib of Geb (the God of Earth),
but the love of me is in the sky, on earth,
on the water and in the fields.
Now Isis is content for her son Horus her god,
she is jubilant in him, Horus her god,
I am life appearing from Osiris.[16]

The phases in the life of the corn were also understood as the god in the grain dying and coming to life again. When the first ears of corn were cut, there was weeping and wailing, as though the body of the god in the corn were being dismembered, and the reapers invoked Isis to lament with them. 'Come to thy house, beautiful one!' For as the oxen threshed the barley, so Osiris was 'beaten' by Seth, 'hacked to pieces'. In the New Kingdom, *c.* 1550–1070 BC, models of Osiris were filled with silt and planted with barley, and placed in the burial chambers of royal tombs. These 'Osiris-beds', as they were called, sprouting with barley, implied that the deceased would be resurrected in the same way that Osiris was reborn in the grain. The same custom reappears in the Greek rituals of Adonis when shallow beds of fast-growing plants are thrown into the sea along with his effigy.

Late Classical writers tell of an ancient custom in which Isis collected the scattered limbs of Osiris in a winnowing basket, and certainly in Roman times throughout the empire a basket was carried in processions of Isis. A Pyramid Text compares the king to Osiris as the grain that flies to heaven in the clouds of chaff that rise when the grain is winnowed:

> Osiris is Unas in the mounting chaff . . .
> He has not entered Geb to perish.
> He is not sleeping in his house upon earth
> So that his bones may be broken . . .
> Unas is up and away to heaven
> With the wind, with the wind![17]

The loss and finding of Osiris were also manifest in the waning and waxing of the moon. Plutarch writes that the years of Osiris's life were twenty-eight, and in 'the dismemberment of Osiris into fourteen parts they refer allegorically to the days of the waning of that satellite from the time of the full moon to the new moon'.[18] Osiris was also found in the star Orion, with Isis as Sothis nearby. On a Ptolemaic text Isis addresses Osiris: 'Thy sacred image, Orion in heaven, rises and sets every day; I am Sothis following after him, and I will not forsake him.'[19] Plutarch adds that the Apis Bull, which was the animate image of Osiris in his visible form, comes into being when a 'fructifying light thrusts forth from the moon and falls upon a cow in her breeding season'.[20] But when the moon is swallowed up by the sun, then Seth has shut Osiris up in his coffin.

Seth is the opposing principle to Osiris; he is the perpetual antagonist. Where Osiris is moisture, Seth is aridity and dryness; where Osiris is the Nile, Seth is the desert that threatens to cover it over, or the winds that scatter the burning sand, or the scorching heat of the sun that evaporates the waters. Seth is the salt sea into which the Nile waters are dissipated and lost, he is the drought that parches the crops and bakes the ground hard, he is the darkness that engulfs the sun each night. He is the one 'great of strength', and he even has red hair like the desert, the 'Red Land'. His animals are the ass, the crocodile and the hippopotamus. He is the earthquake, the storm, thunder, death; he is blind force, unregulated, unpredictable, ungovernable; in humans he is, as Plutarch puts it, a truculence of soul.[21] He is, in short, everything harmful and destructive that threatens to diminish life or take it away.

Yet Seth is not so much evil as the inevitably opposing element in the universe that has to be mastered, continually brought into the rule of the good. When he carries the coffin of Osiris and bears the boat of the sun god, Ra (just as the ass, Seth's animal, carries Christ in his journey from Bethany to Jerusalem), he is an image transformed through awareness, a model of how to relate to whatever is antagonistic in life. At first, Osiris did not know his brother's nature and so fell into his trap (as, in *King Lear*, Edgar did not know Edmund). When Horus revived Osiris, he gave him the power of knowing Seth and so creating a right relation to him:

> Horus has seized Seth, he has put him beneath you so that he can
> lift you up. He will groan beneath you as an earthquake . . .

Horus has made you recognize him in his real nature,
let him not escape you;
he has made you hold him by your hand,
let him not get away from you.[22]

In this drama of conflict Isis plays the role of the mediator. Without her, it is implied, in the first contest Seth would win: Osiris would be vanquished and anarchy would prevail. Yet in the resumption of the contest, when Horus is winning, she lets Seth go. Thoth also keeps the dynamic of opposites alive, assisting the side that is losing so that a creative equilibrium will be maintained. Campbell comments: 'Mythologically representing the inevitable dialectic of temporality, where all things appear in pairs, Horus and Seth are forever in conflict; whereas in the sphere of eternity, beyond the veil of time and space, where there is no duality, they are at one.'[23]

Isis here reconciles the opposites without dissolving their opposition. But, earlier, when the story dramatizes the universal sorrow for Osiris and the falling, this side of the veil, of all things into their dissolution, then Isis personifies the loving power in the universe, which resurrects life from death, and the act of loving in human nature, which bestows beauty upon the lover and the beloved alike:

Behold now, Isis speaketh, –
Come to thy house, oh An! [sun god as risen Osiris]
Come to thy house for thine enemies are not!
Behold the excellent sistrum-bearer – come to thy house!
Lo, I thy sister, love thee – do not thou depart from me!
Behold Hunnu [name of the sun god], the beautiful one!
Come to thy house immediately – come to thy temple immediately!
Behold thou my heart, which grieveth for thee;
Behold me seeking for thee – I am searching for thee to behold thee
Lo, I am prevented from beholding thee –
I am prevented from beholding thee, oh An! . . .
I love thee more than all the earth –
And thou lovest not another as thou dost thy sister!

Behold now, Nephthys speaketh, –
Behold the excellent sistrum-bearer! Come to thy house!
Cause thy heart to rejoice, for thy enemies are not!
All thy sister-goddesses are at thy side and behind thy couch,
calling upon thee with weeping – yet thou art prostrate upon thy bed!
Hearken unto the beautiful words uttered by us
and by every noble one among us!
Subdue thou every sorrow which is in the hearts of us thy sisters,
Oh thou strong one among the gods, – strong among men who behold thee!
We come before thee, oh prince, our lord;
Turn thou not away thy face before us;
Sweeten our hearts when we behold thee, oh prince!
Beautify our hearts when we behold thee!

I, Nephthys, thy sister, I love thee:
Thy foes are subdued, there is not one remaining.
Lo, I am with thee; I shall protect thy limbs for ever, eternally.[24]

Because Isis loves Osiris she searches for him, and because of her power she brings him back to life, becoming thereby, mythologically, his mother. In one of the Pyramid Texts she says:

> Thy mother has come to thee, that thou mayst not perish away,
> The great modeler she is come, that thou mayst not perish away.
> She sets thy head in place for thee,
> She puts together thy limbs for thee;
> What she brings to thee is thy heart, is thy body.
> So dost thou become he who presides over his forerunners,
> Thou givest command to thy ancestors
> And also thou makest thy house to prosper after thee,
> Thou dost defend thy children from affliction.[25]

So the pattern of the myth of the mother goddess and the son–lover becomes visible through the symbolism of the story, as a variation on the universal theme. The boar, which slays Tammuz (in one version), Adonis and Attis, as an image of the dark moon, the abyss of death, turns up here, as though incidentally, in Seth's hunting at the full moon, significantly at the point where the moon is about to wane. The fourteen pieces into which Osiris's body is dismembered are, of course, an image of the dismembered light of the moon, which Isis reassembles as the crescent moon, the day of resurrection, symbolized by the raising of the *Djed* column. Here again she is the essential 'mother' of his rebirth, taking her place, symbolically, as the perpetual cycle of the moon and the everlasting source of the forms of life, *zoe*, while the role of the living and dying phases of manifestation of the source, *bios*, is shared in the Egyptian myth by Osiris and Horus as two aspects of the same principle. Osiris, like all the gods of the myth of the goddess and the son–lover, is incarnate in the bull, as is his son Horus, who, in an 'adjacent' myth, is called the 'bull of his mother'.

The raising of the *Djed* pillar or column from the supine horizontal to the upright vertical position (Fig. 10) was the culmination of the rites of Osiris celebrated on the day before the new year began, which was also the day of the Sed festival when the periodic rites of kingship were renewed and the king 'became Horus'. The word *Djed* meant 'stable' or 'durable', and as a symbol of Osiris its uplifting meant that the god, the life-force, had endured over the inert forces of decay that lie lifeless on the ground. Seth had 'laid the *Djed* on its side',[26] but Osiris had prevailed; his backbone, another meaning of the pillar, had stood up again. Isis calls:

'Come to thy house, come to thy house, thou pillar! Come to thy house, beautiful bull, Lord of men, Beloved, Lord of women.'[27]

Figure 10. Isis helping Seti I to raise the *Djed* pillar of Osiris; Nineteenth Dynasty, *c.* 1300 BC. Temple of Seti I, Abydos.

In relation to the harvest, the raising of the pillar meant that the spirit of the corn had not been killed in the cutting down of the corn. For Osiris, as the animating principle of all vegetation, is everlasting, and because of this the corn would grow upwards towards the light again. Sometimes the pillar is drawn as a tree with lopped off branches (as later is the Christian cross, see Chapter 14, Fig. 30), recalling the erica tree that enclosed Osiris's coffin at Byblos and signifying the Tree of Life as the Axis of the World. Certainly, as the illustrations show, the pillar was as heavy and difficult to erect as an actual tree would have been. The four horizontal lines, which may originally have been the uppermost branches of the tree, refer to the four quarters of the horizon, which the goddesses Hathor and Nut also encompass. After the *Djed* column was raised, a knot of cloth or leather, called a *Tit*, was tied around it, and the column was clothed in the manner of a statue in a ceremony called 'the Offering of Cloths'. The *Tit* was an emblem of Isis, and so the combination of the *Djed* and the *Tit* meant the union of Osiris and Isis, a restoration of harmony as it was in the beginning. The image of rising up also recapitulates the first time when the High Hill (Atum) rose up out of the waters of Nun as the first 'island' of consciousness, and this original event, enacted every day the sun (Ra) rises up out of the night (Atum-Ra), can be represented as coming out of the pillar itself.

In Figure 11 the sun rests between arms forming the sign of the *Ka* – the divine embrace in which each thing, person and god is held – coming from the *ankh* of imperishable life, itself coming from and generated by

Figure 11. Isis (left) and Nephthys (right), kneeling, assisting the sun to rise from the *Djed* column, with six baboons celebrating; Papyrus of Ani, Eighteenth Dynasty, *c.* 1250 BC.

the *Djed* pillar, whose life-force is nurtured into being by the guardian presences of Isis and Nephthys, themselves making the *Ka* gesture of epiphany, embracing the rising of the sun. The baboons, more simply, greet the sun as it comes up, as they still do, chattering excitedly in the African bush. In a characteristic Egyptian merging of characters and identities the sun was Ra or Re, the sun god, the visible manifestation of Atum (often known as Atum-Ra), and Horus, the sunlight, piercing the sky like a falcon, was sometimes elided into Horus-Ra, and so the sunrise was also the resurrection of Osiris. The *Book of the Dead*, as it is translated, meant, more exactly, 'The Chapters of Coming Forth by Day':[28]

> Yesterday is Osiris and Today is Ra on the day when he shall destroy the enemies of Osiris and when he shall establish as prince and ruler his son Horus.[29]

Consequently, when Isis and Nephthys stand with their outstretched wings across the shrine in Figure 12, they are not only protecting Tutankhamun's mummy, they are nurturing his resurrection as the reborn sun –

Figure 12. Isis and Nephthys on the inner face of the doors of the third
shrine of Tutankhamun, *c.* 1325 BC. In the spaces around their bodies is
inscribed their promise of everlasting life for the king to accompany the sun
god Ra in his boat across the sky.[30]

helping him to come forth by day – in the same way that they do for
Osiris and the sun at dawn, and for all those who become Osiris and are
'found' by Isis and Nephthys; an image of the soul's transformation.

   In one of the old Pyramid Texts this stanza is addressed to the deceased
king who now takes part in the order of the universe:

> Thou risest and settest; thou goest down with Re,
>   sinking in the dust with Nedy.
> Thou risest and settest; thou risest up with Re
>   and ascendest with the Great Reed Float.
> Thou risest and settest; thou goest down with Nephthys,
>   sinking in the dust with the Evening Boat of the Sun.
> Thou risest and settest; thou risest up with Isis,
>   ascending with the Morning Boat of the Sun.[31]

ORIGINS OF ISIS

It is one of the paradoxes of Egyptian mythology that while the drama of religious life is focused on Osiris, the constant presence of Isis is so essential to the resolution of Osiris's story that she becomes involved in all the other unresolved stories of life at one time or another. And so her sphere of manifestation extended beyond even his and eventually beyond that of any other goddess, whose attributes she absorbed or could absorb when necessary. Another way of looking at this is to say that Isis discloses the unity of creation.

Long before the Pyramid Texts were written (before 2500 BC) Isis was already a precisely imagined figure, and she entered the cosmology of the priests of Heliopolis with her care of the dead clearly defined.[32] Even in the second century AD Plutarch still portrays her as a universal principle:

> Isis is, in fact, the female principle of Nature, and is receptive of every form of generation, in accord with which she is called by Plato the gentle nurse and the all-receptive, and by most people has been called countless names, since, because of the force of Reason, she turns herself to this thing or that and is receptive of all manner of shapes and forms. She has an innate love for the first and most dominant of all things, which is identical with the good, and this she yearns for and pursues; but the portion which comes from evil she tries to avoid and reject, for she serves them both as a place and means of growth, but inclines always towards the better and offers to it opportunity to create from her and to impregnate her with affluxes and likenesses in which she rejoices and is glad that she is made pregnant and teeming with these creations. For creation is the image of being in matter, and the thing created is a picture of reality.[33]

The images that clothe Isis throughout this almost unimaginable span of time show that she comes out of a living tradition already rooted in the Neolithic sensibility of a unified world. The fourth-millennium-BC Bird Goddess from pre-dynastic Egypt, whose arms are raised upwards like wings (see Chapter 3, Fig. 32b), is reflected in the all-enveloping wings with which Isis shelters her son, her husband, kings and subjects. In the Pyramid Texts the deceased is said to 'breathe the breath of Isis',[34] an image arising out of the story in which she took the form of a kite and, with the beating of her wings, created the wind – the breath of life – to awaken her dead husband, Osiris, back into life, conceiving a child from him as he lay resting there, breathing her breath and so suspended from death. So, for all those whose soul has left their bodies through the mouth, breathed out as the last breath, Isis hovers with her life-giving wings offering the first breath of eternal life.

In a parallel image, the *Ba*-soul – the individual, personal soul – also hovers over the deceased person in the form of a bird, and once they are unified, they greet the *Ka*-soul – the universal soul, the vital essence of the life force out of which they were made: 'When Atum spat forth Shu

Figure 13. Gold pectoral in the form of winged Isis; Third Ethiopian
Dynasty, *c.* 710–663 BC. Kushite tomb of King Amarinataki-lebte, Nuri,
Sudan.

and Tefnut, he put his arms around them with his *ka*, so that his *ka* was
in them.'[35] The *Ka* often appears to the deceased in the form of a blue
phoenix, and is here imagined greeting the deceased as a mother: 'Behold
I am behind thee, I am thy temple, thy mother, forever and forever.'[36] To
die is to rejoin one's *Ka*.

In the Neolithic the bird goddess of the Upper Waters and the serpent
goddess of the Lower Waters were conceived as one Great Goddess of the
circular abyss of waters enclosing the earth. This primordial unity is
reflected in Bronze Age Egypt in the relation between the goddesses of
Lower and Upper Egypt, one of whom was a serpent goddess – Wedjat of
the Delta and Lower Egypt – and the other was a vulture goddess –
Nekhbet of Upper Egypt, also sometimes pictured as a serpent. The
serpent and the vulture (or serpent) often framed the entrances to temples,
one on either side, symbolizing the union of the two lands and, more
generally, the union beyond duality required in the heart for contemplation. Wedjat was also found as the royal uraeus, the rearing and spitting
cobra centred in the foreheads of gods, goddesses and kings, and known
as the 'eye of Ra', the sun god. So close was the ancient association of
goddess and serpent that one of the hieroglyphs for goddess was the
serpent, drawn as this rearing cobra and registering the self-renewing
character of divinity (the other hieroglyph was an oval egg). Wedjat was
often assimilated to Isis in her character as serpent and as the 'eye of Ra',
as she was sometimes called; and, in Figure 14, the crowns of Lower and
Upper Egypt are carried by Isis and her sister Nephthys respectively, as
the inscription shows, pointing to the immanence of the goddesses in the
two crowns with which the king was crowned.

Between the Neolithic Egyptian pig goddess (Chapter 2, Fig. 29) and
the image of Isis with legs outspread as though to give birth upon the

Figure 14. Isis and Nephthys as serpent goddesses, their names inscribed in front of them, carrying the crowns of Lower and Upper Egypt respectively; Nineteenth Dynasty, *c.* 1300 BC. Tomb of Seti I, Valley of the Kings, Thebes.

back of a pig (Fig. 15) is a time span of at least 1,000 years, yet both belong to the same spectrum of feeling, where the perpetually renewing powers of nature become luminous in the constant fertility of the pig. Isis holds a ladder in her hand, suggesting levels of transformation and recalling the ladders painted on the sides of the tombs for the soul to climb to heaven. To reach forward, the Virgin Mary is addressed as the 'Gate to Heaven', and the image of the ladder reappears in the myth of Sophia.

Figure 15. Isis giving birth on the back of a pig.

As well as the kite, the snake and the pig, divine being was manifest in the cow, the bull, the jackal, the crocodile, the cat, the hawk, the falcon, the vulture, the heron, the scorpion, the ram, the toad and the dung beetle among many others, as well as composite creatures and imaginary animals and birds. The great Egyptian scholar Henri Frankfort points out that this wondrous variety suggests 'an underlying religious awe felt before all animal life', such that '*animals as such* possessed religious significance for the Egyptians',[37] arising possibly from a feeling for the animals' sacred *otherness*: 'The animals never change, and in this respect especially they would appear to share – in a degree unknown to man – the fundamental nature of creation.'[38] Frankfort has shown how pervasive was the Egyptian belief that the universe was unchanging in the sense that the one great event happened in the beginning, when the world emerged, so that all cosmic and social order take their reference from the 'First Time'.[39]

The animals' otherness was observed with minute particularity, and we cannot understand how the creative force that is Isis can be manifest in a pig, a serpent and a cow – or Egyptian mythology generally – without entering into the ancient Egyptians' feeling for the animals around them. To give just one example: the French Egyptologists R. A. Schwaller de Lubicz and his wife, Isha, explain that the god Anubis (son of Nephthys and Osiris), who leads the dead down into the underworld and who is called 'the Judge' and the god of transformation, has the head of a jackal (or the whole body of the jackal) precisely because the jackal is the animal who saves the rotting flesh of other animals from falling out of the life-cycle because he can eat it when no other animal can. The jackal tears his food into pieces and buries them, digging them up at just the right moment to eat them. So the jackal transforms putrified flesh into life-giving nourishment: 'What would be poisonous for almost all other creatures in him becomes an element of life through a transformation of elements which are bringing about this decomposition.' [40]

Anubis is the one who adjusts the scales at the weighing of the heart of the deceased to decide whether the soul is worthy to enter the presence of Osiris; he is the judge of the weighing because, in eating, the jackal discriminates exactly between those elements that are capable of transformation and those that are not. For the same reason, the intestines of the deceased in embalming rituals are placed under the care of Anubis, whose image is painted on the jar that holds them after death. The same principle obtains when Isis takes the form of a kite to rejuvenate Osiris. The kite appears to the modern traveller as a scavenging predator with huge wings, but this means that the kite is able to eat food that other birds and animals cannot, and so can redeem the soul of the life-cycle from its farthest point of incarnation, such that the wind created by the flapping of its great wings in the moment of holding its prey becomes the breath of life. The vulture as the goddess of death and regeneration in Çatal Hüyük makes sense also from this perspective. So in all manifesta-

Figure 16. The lion-headed goddess
Sekhmet seated, with sun disc and
uraeus on her head; black granite
statue, Twenty-second Dynasty,
c. 930 BC. Temple of Mut, Karnak.

tions of goddesses and gods as animals, birds, reptiles and insects, this
precise and practical reverence for the sacred drama of nature must be
remembered.

Consequently, the stories and images that bring these manifestations to
life have much to teach us about the nature of symbolism. The goddess
Sekhmet, for instance, has the magnificent head of a lioness and carries
on it the sun circled by the uraeus, the cobra that spits fire, as an image of
powerfully concentrated energy – which we see in a lion, the fierce sun,
the spitting cobra and potentially in human beings – and, the images
imply, the very force of its focus can become destructive if the aim misses
the mark (as in the tale mentioned in Chapter 4, p. 170). Sekhmet was
inevitably used by bloodthirsty kings to justify their wars, but it is interesting that she was also invoked as a healer, on the assumption that she could
slay pestilence as well as bring it.[41] In Memphite theology Sekhmet is the
consort of Ptah as the one who gives power to the word that he speaks
from his heart. In Thebes she merged with Mut, wife of Amun, and as
many as 600 statues of Sekhmet stood at the entrance to the Temple of
Mut (Fig. 16). Many goddesses of other cultures stand or sit upon lions
and even give birth between them or, more tamely, have them beneath
their thrones, but here lion and goddess became one.

ISIS AS THE THRONE

The image of a high-backed throne was both the hieroglyph of the name Isis and rested upon the head of the goddess, often as her only distinguishing feature. As an ancient image, the throne recalls the primal order of the beginning, for in its shape lies the original mound, the 'High Hill', which first emerged from the waters as habitable land, and in many other cultures the hill was the image of the goddess as earth. In Sumeria the mountain was also the underworld – *Kur* – the womb of the Mother, and in Crete the goddess stands upon her mountain, flanked by lions and holding her sceptre of rule. Since the mountain, then as now, seemed the closest place to heaven and so the first place on which a divinity, descending, would land, the Mesopotamian temple – the ziggurat – where the sacred marriage of heaven and earth was enacted between a priestess as the Mother Goddess and a priest as her king-consort, was modelled as a mountain. In Egypt the pyramid also symbolized the primeval hill.

In an extension of this symbolism the lap of the goddess Isis became the royal throne of Egypt, so that ascending the throne was to sit upon her lap, and to suckle from her breast was to receive the divine nourishment that would give the king the qualities of kingship and guarantee his

Figure 17. Isis, painted gold, with the golden throne upon her head, kneeling on the emblem of gold, holding the ring of eternity; sarcophagus of Amenhotep II, *c.* 1427–1401 BC. Tomb of Amenhotep (Amenophis) II, Valley of the Kings, Thebes.

Figure 18. (*Left*) Isis with King Seti I on her lap as the throne; Nineteenth Dynasty, *c.* 1300 BC. Temple of Seti I, Abydos.
Figure 19. (*Right*) Isis suckling Seti I; Nineteenth Dynasty, *c.* 1300 BC. Temple of Seti I, Abydos.

right to rule: 'The throne "makes" the king', as many of the texts say, and already in the First Dynasty a pharaoh was calling himself 'son of Isis'.[42] So Isis is the mother of the king, who rules the land as her son in her place. This was how the cosmic order in the universe was perceived as related to the social order of human beings – 'the divine right of kings', as we know it. But, Frankfort reminds us, offering an important insight into mythic thinking, we cannot say that

> Isis was originally the throne personified, nor that the throne acquired a transcendental quality because it was conceived as a mother. The two notions are fundamentally correlated, and mythopoeic thought expresses such a bond as identity. The throne made manifest a divine power which changed one of several princes into a king fit to rule. The awe felt before this manifestation of power became articulated in the adoration of the mother-goddess.[43]

In the New Kingdom, almost 2,000 years later, King Seti I sits upon the lap of the goddess Isis, whose body and the throne of Egypt are one and the same (Fig. 18). In Figure 19 she nurses him from her breast, giving the term 'son–lover of the goddess' an unusually precise image.

ISIS AND HATHOR

No other goddess took this precise relation to pharaonic sovereignty, but in many other of her images Isis merges in and out of other goddesses, as though the feminine principle were so all pervasive, its absence so inconceivable, that it could come into manifestation at any point as any character under any name. For, alternating with the throne, Isis also wears upon her head a crown of cow's horns with the sun's disc resting between them (see Fig. 1), which is the head-dress belonging to Hathor (see Chapter 4, Fig. 6). When Isis wears the horns, it would have been understood as the creative force that manifested in the goddess Hathor also manifesting in Isis, where Isis assimilates the qualities of Hathor into herself or blurs the line (we make) between them. The sistrum Isis carries in Figure 1, the musical rattle that she shakes before the king as a blessing and whose sound frightens away Seth, has Hathor's face upon it, a female face with the ears of a cow.

There was another tradition, which is likely to have been much older, in which the Primeval Waters and the High God were not conceived of as masculine or androgynous, but feminine, and the heavenly ocean was imagined as a 'great flood', which was manifest in the form of a great cow nourishing the world with her rain-milk, an image familiar from the Neolithic. Her four legs standing upon the earth fixed the four cardinal points of the universe, and her star-spangled belly formed the sky through which the sun travelled in his daily and nightly passage – a conception also expressed in the sky goddess Nut, who can be embodied as a cow (Fig. 21). Sometimes the king is drawn suckling directly from the cow, Hathor, as when the young Amenophis II kneels beneath her drinking her milk.[44] In the very old and celebrated Narmer Palette (c. 2850 BC), it is Hathor's face that frames the four corners of the palette as an image of the ordered structure of creation, bounded on all sides by the mother goddess, who brings forth the life within it, upholds, sustains and nourishes it with her eternal milk.[45]

A further parallel between Isis and Hathor is suggested in the fact that both goddesses have a son called Horus, in each case an apparently different figure yet with an arrestingly identical name (sometimes distinguished as Horus the Elder and Horus the Younger). Hathor's name meant the 'House of Horus', and expressed the feeling that the golden solar falcon, the sun god Horus, flying from east to west, flew each evening into the mouth of Hathor and was reborn from her each day as her son. He was, therefore, her new-born son in the morning, when the red of the dawn signified the blood of his birth from his mother, and, gaining in strength throughout the day, became her full-grown consort in the evening, when the black night of her starry body swallowed him up. In a characteristically abrupt change of metaphor Horus, the sun, the bird of prey, was also called 'the Bull of his Mother', for, like all son–lovers of the mother goddess, he was lover to his mother and so became his own father.

Reading this as an expression of the relation of the phenomenal and visible *bios* to the invisible and eternal *zoe*, it offers a glimpse into the symbolic life of ancient Egypt, when each sunrise was an epiphany to which the whole universe bore witness. The visible sun, *bios*, is here born from the invisible ground of being, *zoe*, whose infinite potentiality to create the world is imagined as a cow continuously giving birth and giving milk, that is, sustaining the life she has brought forth from herself. It is significant that *bios* contributes also to the eternal *zoe* by dying into her, impregnating her and helping to bring about a rebirth.[46]

Hathor is, then, one of the oldest deities in Egypt, worshipped from predynastic times in many forms, including the human form of a woman with horned head-dress carrying the sun between her horns, and she was identified with numerous local goddesses. In some myths she is also called the star Sothis, the 'second sun' (as well as Isis), and so is related to the rising of the Nile and the inundation, suggesting why Isis has the head of a cow in Figure 6. When the sun god is called Re or Ra, Hathor becomes his female counterpart; at other times she is his daughter. In another myth the sun and the moon are called the eyes of Hathor, and she is called the 'mother of the light'.[47] In her aspect as goddess of the night and the underworld she feeds the dead from her sycamore tree, often

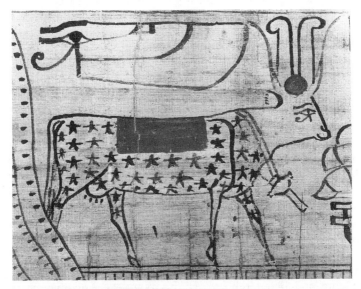

Figure 20. Hathor emerging from the western mountain, where a tomb chapel is built inside, the stars of night upon her body and the *menat* hanging from her neck; she stands before a bowl of lotuses, the flower out of which the sun rose the first time; the winged *Wedjat*-eye of Horus protects from above; painting on papyrus, *c.* 1000 BC.

wearing the *menat*, the sacred necklace of healing, around her neck – a necklace with a loop or knot at the back that recalls the knot of Inanna and the Minoan goddess (see Chapter 3, Figs. 23, 24, 25). She frequently stands as a cow coming out of the mountain of the dead, welcoming the deceased person home.

For this reason, the royal coffins were made from the sycamore tree, in which the goddess and her life-giving milk were incarnated, so that dying was conceived as a return to the womb to be reborn: 'Take my breast that you may drink, so that you may live again', says Hathor to her son in one of the Pyramid Texts.[48] There is a drawing on the face of a column in the burial chamber of the tomb of King Tuthmosis III showing the tree of Hathor or Isis with arms and a breast, from which the king is drinking the milk of rebirth (see Chapter 13, Fig. 6). Hathor was called the 'Golden One' and the golden cliffs of western Thebes, which catch the last rays of the setting sun, were regarded as the domain and even the actual body of Hathor, with her children lying inside the mountains in her womb.

When Isis wears the horns of the heavenly cow, she gathers, as it were, the story of Hathor to herself, so that everything she is or does resonates with the feelings and images ascribed to Hathor. It is a process of assimilation, not discrimination, to which an analytic interpretation only adds confusion. Frankfort observes that ancient thought 'admitted side by side certain *limited* insights, which were held to be *simultaneously* valid, each in its own proper context, each corresponding to a definite avenue of approach'.[49] Few goddesses and gods were confined to a single mode of manifestation, since they were immanent divinities and could appear in any context that called them forth.

None the less, one is still tempted to ask, is this the *same* Horus that was the son of Isis and Osiris? Or, more tempted, did the little boy Isis suckled in the marshes grow up to be the falcon who flew across the sky as the sun and then was Hathor's little boy in the morning? Perhaps we could talk of parallel stories that cross over at points of great intensity. Taking the images as primary, one story tells of Isis and Osiris, who was called the bull; their son was called Horus, who did grow up to be the golden falcon of the sun. Now, Osiris, 'chief of the westerners', was identified with the setting sun in the west, evening, yesterday and all the past, in turn identified with the dead father of the living pharaoh; while Horus, the son, was identified with the rising sun in the east, morning, today, the present and the living pharaoh on the throne. This almost painfully complex picture becomes clearer when it is realized that Osiris and Horus are substantially one figure in two aspects: the old and the new, dying and being reborn. At this point we can imagine the story expanding, as it were, into the sky, which is Hathor, and so now she 'becomes' the mother through whom the old is renewed, and her 'House of Horus' is then the vessel of transformation into which the sun dies and out of which he is reborn. So, in the evening, when the day is gone,

Horus, as Osiris, is the bull of Hathor, and in the morning Osiris, as Horus, is reborn into the light of the coming day. At this point we can say that Hathor and Isis have also become one.

The interchangeable nature of Hathor and Isis appears in this hymn of creation, in which the light child or the sun god is called, not Ra, not Horus, but Ihy:

> My majesty precedes me as Ihy, the sun of Hathor.
> I am the male of masculinity,
> I slid forth from the outflow between her thighs
> in this my name of Jackal of the Light.
> I broke forth from the egg, I oozed out of her essence,
> I escaped in her blood. I am the master of the redness.
> I am the Bull of the Confusion, my mother Isis generated me
> though she was ignorant of herself
> beneath the fingers of the Lord of the gods.
> I broke free from her on that day that the deep was uplifted as the . . .
> I took shape, I grew, I crawled about, I crept around, I grew big,
> I became tall like my father when he rose to his full height . . .
> The flood it was that raised me up while the waters gave me . . .
> My mother Isis suckled me, I tasted of her sweetness . . .
> I am the babe in the Primeval Waters . . .
> I sought an abiding place in this my name of Hahu
> and I found it in Punt. I built a house there on the hillside
> where my mother resides beneath her sycamores.[50]

The reunion of Hathor and Horus that took place, then, each evening, when the son flew into the mouth of his mother, was also celebrated every year at the time of the first fruits of the harvest. From the temple of Hathor in Denderah there set out a procession of ships accompanying the golden barque of Hathor, which carried her statue up the Nile to the temple of Horus at Edfu. She arrived, and they were reconciled in the ceremony of the sacred marriage at the time of the new moon, when new life is born. The festival lasted till the fourteenth day, when, as the moon began to wane, the ships started their journey upstream to the sound of singing and cheering, with the rowers chanting to the rhythm of their oars:

> All hail, jubilation to you, O Golden One . . .
> Sole ruler, Uraeus of the Supreme Lord himself!
> Mysterious one, who gives birth to the divine entities,
> forms the animals, models them as she pleases, fashions men . . .
> O Mother! . . . Luminous One who thrusts back the darkness,
> who illuminates every human creature with her rays,
> Hail Great One of many names . . .
> You from whom the divine entities come forth
>   in this your name of Mut-Isis!
> You-who-cause the throat to breathe, daughter of Re,
> whom he spat forth from his mouth in this your name of Tefnut!

O Neith who appeared in your barque in this your name of Mut!
O Venerable Mother, you who subdue your adversaries
   in this your name of Nekhbet!
O You-who-know-how-to-make-right-use-of-the-heart,
   you who triumph over your enemies in this your name of Sekhmet!
It is the Golden One . . . the lady of drunkenness, of music, of dance,
   of frankincense, of the crown of young women,
   whom men acclaim because they love her!
It is the Gold of the divine entities, who comes forth at her season,
   in the month of Epiphi, the day of the new moon,
   at the festival of 'She is Delivered' . . .
Heaven makes merry, the earth is full of gladness,
   the Castle of Horus rejoices.[51]

ISIS AND NUT

The other goddess often elided with Isis and Hathor was Nut, goddess of
the sky, mother (also) of sun, moon and stars, often called 'she who bore
the gods'. The image of the cosmic mother as a cow could also take the
name of Nut as well as Hathor, as in Figure 21. Here, in the tomb of Seti
I, Nut stands impassive as an immovable force, with the sun boats of
night and day sailing just beneath her belly, the lighted one near her

Figure 21. Nut as the heavenly cow, supported by Shu, bearing the boat of
the sun; Nineteenth Dynasty, *c.* 1300 BC. Tomb of Seti I, Valley of the
Kings, Thebes.

forelegs bearing the sun god standing with the sun above his head as day. In what looks like a symbolic gesture a diminutive Shu supports her great sky-belly marked with stars.

In hieroglyphics the water jar is the symbol of Nut, she who gathers and pours down rain from heaven, even as she rises from the sycamore tree holding vases of the water of eternal life, offering drink and food to the souls of those who have died (see Chapter 13, Fig. 7). As the sky goddess, Nut was more often drawn in the image of a woman arching over the body of the earth god, her husband, Geb (sometimes called 'the Bull of Nut'), with her fingers and toes touching the earth as the east and west points of the horizon. In Chapter 4, Figure 7 shows the god Shu separating Nut as the sky from Geb as the earth. Here, in Figure 22, the drama of the next stage of creation – the birth, growth and death of the sun – is shown re-enacted each day through the body of Nut, his mother, while (in this version of the myth) the face of Hathor in the centre becomes the horizon, which reflects the first rays of the sun at dawn. The pattern is the same, suggesting that the names and identities are ultimately ephemeral. The body of the goddess Nut here composes time and space, the laws structuring the incarnate universe. As a morning hymn sings:

> Thy mother Nut has borne thee,
> How beautiful art thou, Re-Harakhte.[52]

Neumann observes that 'in the matriarchal sphere, the daytime sky is the realm where the sun is born and dies, not, as later, the realm over which it rules.'[53] From the matriarchal perspective, Nut is the all-encompassing feminine form of the primeval ocean, Nun; she is the fixed and enduring one, the fundamental containing form, and the sun, moon and stars are her transient and perishable children, who rise and fall

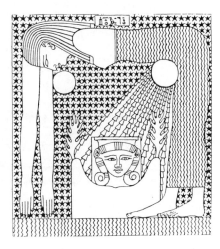

Figure 22. The sky goddess Nut swallowing and giving birth to the sun god, whose rays fall on Hathor as the horizon; painted ceiling relief, *c.* 116 BC – AD 34. Temple of Hathor, Denderah.

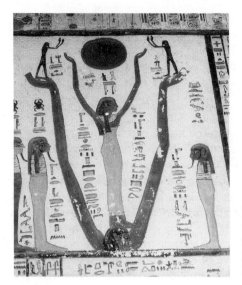

Figure 23. Birth of the Sun; detail of north wall, burial chamber of tomb of Rameses VI; Twentieth Dynasty, *c.* 1150 BC. Valley of the Kings, Thebes.

within the tides of her body (Fig. 22). From the patriarchal perspective, on the other hand, the sun god is the focus, the primary being, and he travels in his boat across the 'watery abyss of heaven' rendered as the body of the heavenly cow who bears him rather than generates him (see Fig. 21). Or he is the epiphany to whom all creation bears witness, as expressed in Figure 23 in this joyful gesture of the arms raised in offering to his renaissance.

In this vision of the ordering of creation Nut is no longer formally the mother of the sun god, Ra, the visible manifestation of Atum, the

Figure 24. Seth spears Apophis, serpent of darkness, with the sun god, Ra, seated in his boat; from the *Book of the Dead of Lady Cheritwebeshet,* *c.* 1085–950 BC.

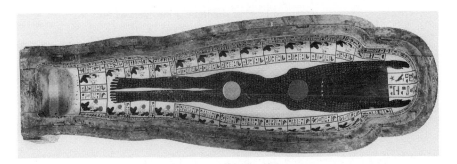

Figure 25. The sarcophagus as the womb of the goddess Nut, with the soul of the deceased passing through her body to be reborn like the sun; base of sarcophagus, *c.* seventh century BC.

Complete One, but his granddaughter – a reversal of role familiar from Sumeria and Babylonia, though in Egypt the two roles co-exist without a choice having to be made between them. Rundle Clark suggests that the matriarchal view was the one deeply embedded in the folk, while the patriarchal view was the one held primarily by the priests who formulated the religious teachings.[54] The story of sunrise changes quite radically in the patriarchal view: the reddening of the dawn is seen no longer as the birth-blood of the mother, but as the blood of the serpent of darkness, Apophis (or Apep), who has been heroically slain by the sun. Like Seth, he may be wounded but never entirely vanquished; each night he is reborn, even as the sun is reborn each dawn. In Figure 24, in an image of achieved equilibrium, Seth spears Apophis, another dimension of himself, while the sun is seated in his boat. This image of conflict is well-known from other late Bronze and Iron Age cultures, and passed into Greece and Rome as the myth of the slaying of the powers of darkness by the god of light.

However the sun was conceived, Nut, as the night sky, never relinquished her central role in the care of those whose day is ended. She is found everywhere in coffins, often one image of her on the base, facing upwards, and another on the inside of the lid, facing downwards so that the deceased may lie truly enfolded in the loving embrace of the heavenly mother, taken back into her body like the sun at evening, to be reborn into the dawn of eternity:

> O my mother Nut,
> stretch your wings over me.
> Let me become like the imperishable stars,
> like the indefatigable stars.
> May Nut extend her arms over me
> and her name of
> > 'She who extends her arms'
> > chases away the shadows

and makes the light shine everywhere.
O Great Being who is in the world of the Dead,
At whose feet is Eternity.
In whose hand is the always,
Come to me,
O great divine beloved Soul,
who is in the mysterious abyss,
Come to me.[55]

ISIS AND MAAT

The goddess Maat (or Mayet) and the principle she embodies are perhaps
of the essence of Egyptian mythology, binding divine beings and human
beings within one universal law, for they all live 'by Maat, in Maat and
for Maat'.[56] The goddess wore upon her head a single ostrich feather,
which was put in the balance beside the heart of the deceased, and these
combined notions of weighing and weightlessness refer us to the meaning
of equilibrium, balance and harmony as the structure of the laws of the
universe. This was imagined through the figure of the goddess. She was
in the boat of Ra – along with Thoth, her male counterpart, who played
the balancing role in the conflict of Seth with Osiris and Horus – when, in
a slight variation of the myth, the sun god rose above the waters of the
primeval abyss for the first time. Like Sophia, she was 'there' in the
beginning as the one who brings the heart of the supreme being alive.
When, before creation had 'begun', Atum wished that his heart might
live: 'Nun said to Atum: Breathe in thy daughter Maat, bring her to thy
nose in order that thy heart may live. That she be not removed from thee,
that thy daughter Maat be with thy son Shu whose name is Life.'[57]

Maat is often pictured giving the breath of life to the pharaohs by
holding the *ankh* to the nose, as also are Hathor (see Chapter 11, Fig. 1)
and other gods and goddesses, but here she breathes life into the beginning
of everything.

Atum says, 'When the heavens were sleeping, I lived with my daughter
Maat, one within me, the other around me',[58] disclosing the meaning of
the 'double Maat': at one level, the union of the South and the North
(Upper and Lower Egypt), and, at another, the union of individual and
universal or cosmic consciousness, which creates harmony. Schwaller de
Lubicz writes:

> The principle of Harmony is a cosmic law, the Voice of God. Whatever be
> the disorder that man or fortuitous natural accident may provoke, Nature,
> left to herself, will put everything in order again through affinities (the
> Consciousness in all things). Harmony is the *a priori* Law written in all
> of Nature; it imposes itself on our intelligence, yet it is in itself
> incomprehensible.[59]

Figure 26. The goddess Maat on the lintel framing the entrance to the tomb
of Nefertari, wife of Rameses II, with Anubis on the walls on either side;
Nineteenth Dynasty, *c.* 1290–1224 BC.

Maat was, then, the goddess through whom the fundamental laws of
the universe became visible. She embodies truth, right order, lawfulness
and justice. In a sense she is not separate from the other goddesses and
gods, but is the principle enacted in all of them as divinity. Seated on his
throne, the pharaoh would hold in his hand a tiny doll-like figure of the
goddess, also seated, which was offered up to the gods as a sign that the
king represented the divine order, which 'had not been disturbed since
the day of its creator'.[60] Similarly, the judges wore a lapis lazuli emblem
of Maat on their breasts. Social order was then a reflection of divine
order, and the rulership of each day re-enacted the primordial time when
Ra, the sun, 'put order (Maat) in the place of Chaos'.[61] Here, the state of
being that is the goddess appears to be abstracted from the figure of
the goddess herself; but it is rather that this distinction (between goddess
and idea) did not exist for the Egyptians, any more than the distinction
between ethics and metaphysics, in life or in death.

In Figure 27 the king makes the offering of Maat to Osiris, while the
words of the incantation were chanted:

> I have come to you, I am Thoth, my two hands united to carry Maat.
> ... Maat is in every place that is yours ... You rise with Maat,
> you live with Maat, you join your limbs to Maat, you make Maat
> rest on your head in order that she may take her seat on your forehead.
> You become young again in the sight of your daughter Maat,
> you live from the perfume of her dew.
> Maat is worn like an amulet at your throat, she rests on your chest,

Figure 27. (*Left*) King Seti I makes the offering of Maat; Nineteenth
Dynasty, *c.* 1300 BC. Temple of Seti I, Abydos.
Figure 28. (*Right*) Osiris with Isis and Nephthys behind him;
Book of the Dead of Hunefer, c. 1310 BC.

the divine entities reward you with Maat, for they know her wisdom . . .
Your right eye is Maat, your left eye is Maat . . .
your flesh, your members are Maat . . .
your food is Maat, your drink is Maat . . .
the breaths of your nose are Maat . . .
you exist because Maat exists,
and she exists because you exist.[62]

So it was that the feather of Maat was placed in the scales of justice to
be weighed against the heart of one who had died. If the heart was heavier
than the feather, the scales would tip and the heart would fall into the
open jaws of Ta Urt, the monster with crocodile head, hippopotamus
body and lion feet, crouching beneath. 'Make me light'[63] was the understandable plea to Ra (light as a feather, we might say). If the deceased
had indeed lived 'with Maat in his heart',[64] then he would be conducted
by Thoth, the god of wisdom, into the presence of Osiris, lord of the
underworld and eternal life, with Isis and Nephthys standing behind him.
In Figure 28, the winged eye of Horus holds in its bird's talons the
feather of Maat towards Osiris, who embodies Maat in the underworld.
The primordial waters of Nun lie beneath the throne of Osiris, and give
birth to the lotus (which blossoms in the rays of the morning sun, and so

becomes the original cosmic flower whose petals opened to reveal the sun, which, on the instant, rose up and flew across the sky). The four sons of Horus, who support the four cardinal points of the universe, rest in the face of the flower, themselves ultimately supported by Nun.

Maat, as an idea, parallels the *me* in Sumeria, and later the *Tao* in Chinese philosophy, the *Dharma* in Indian, Sophia in the Wisdom literature of the Old Testament and the Gnostic Christian tradition, and also, perhaps, 'the Kingdom of Heaven' as Jesus uses it in the Synoptic Gospels and 'the Kingdom' in the Gnostic Gospels. All these terms refer in different ways to an image of cosmic order – archetypal harmony or universal law – which human social order and, in Egypt, even the principles of musical harmony derive from and reflect.[65] Our orthodox tradition, which understands this idea under the masculine term Logos – 'In the beginning was the Word' (Greek *Logos*), John I:1 – might find it difficult to conceive of this idea as being originally embodied as a goddess. Yet 'in the beginning' it was an inherently feminine conception expressing the spiritual order of the whole and the law of incarnation governing the principles whereby unity became manifest as diversity. This was experienced as the continuous birth of all creation from the divine Mother.

When, sometimes, Isis wears on her head the ostrich feather of the double crowns of the South and North, Upper and Lower Egypt, with the ostrich feather of the goddess Maat rising from the back, the principles of Maat are transferred to her in feeling, as they are also to Hathor.

Figure 29. Isis greets Rameses III, while an attendant holds the feather of Maat; tomb of Amenhirkhopshef, son of Rameses III, Twentieth Dynasty, *c.* 1163–1156 BC. Valley of the Queens.

THE GODDESS OF A THOUSAND NAMES

Nut, Hathor and Isis are often spoken of as a unity, and all three are at times called the 'Goddess of the Sycamore Tree', 'Mother of Heaven', 'Queen of all gods and goddesses'. Isis was also called 'Queen of Earth and Heaven', 'Maker of the Sunrise', 'Sothis, the Opener of the Year', 'the God-mother', 'the Lady of Life', the 'Green Goddess', 'Lady of Bread and Beer', 'Lady of Joy and Abundance', 'Lady of Love', 'the Maker of Kings', 'Lady of the Shuttle', 'Benefactress of the *Tuat*' (the Underworld), 'the Creatrix of the Nile Flood', and the 'Wife of the Lord of the Inundation, Osiris'. Yet, especially by the New Kingdom (1550 BC) (when the national god changed from Atum to Amun, now based in Thebes), Isis surpassed all other goddesses who came and went, or began locally and merged eventually into the figure of Isis, keeping their names but losing their roles. Why, then, was she alone the 'goddess of a thousand names'?

There is a paradox in Isis, for she was adored as the Great Mother of Life, Death and Regeneration yet she also suffered trial and loss like human beings, and this may explain her lasting appeal. Of all the Egyptian goddesses, only Isis has an individual character and a personal story. As an identifiable 'person', as well as a sister, wife and mother, she brings to the image of the universal mother an entirely new dimension. Like Inanna in Mesopotamia, so Isis in Egypt *relates* humanity to the unknowable face of divinity by becoming personal, we might almost say human. She is the mediator between the two realms, as the Virgin Mary was to be for many people thousands of years later.

In the story of Isis and Osiris, the Mother of All becomes so like a human mother, sister and wife that she becomes flesh and dwells among us. She lives happily with her brother–husband Osiris, but then he is taken from her and, mourning, she goes everywhere in search of him. Like humanity, she feels pain and anguish, is defeated but will not give in, and recovers not all she had lost but some part of it; some dignity is found, some assent is made. But, unlike the people who identified with her, her human qualities of courage and persistence break through, as it were, to the divine realm, transforming tragedy into myth. Her husband dies, but she brings him back to life; she is childless but then conceives a child from him; her child, Horus, is stung by a scorpion but she restores him from death; she outwits her enemy, Seth, with her grown child's help and, though Osiris can live only in the underworld, she continues to live with him as his wife, standing behind him as he sits on his throne. Isis, then, both suffers and transcends the trials of the human condition and so can serve as an image of reconciliation to the conditions of human life.

GODDESS OF THE WORD OF POWER

There are two further stories of Isis that explore this paradox of human vulnerability and divine power. In fact, in one of the myths about her Isis begins by being a woman and ends as a goddess with power over even the sun god, Ra, 'the self-created being'. This ambivalence as to the status of Isis also discloses the co-existence of the goddess and the god tradition of worship. The goddess tradition, inherited from the Neolithic, persisted as a living tradition throughout the ages, especially among the people close to the soil, reappearing in provincial places and wherever the official religion lost its central hold, until finally, in the second and third centuries AD it almost superseded the god-orientated official religion in the expansion of the Mysteries of Isis. In these two much earlier myths the ancient and supreme power of goddess worship breaks through the orthodox position.

In Heliopolis, the orthodox position was that Ra, the visible manifestation of Atum, was great-grandfather to Isis and creator of all. In what seems to be a fusion of two mythic systems, there is a story of Isis winning from Ra the secret of his name and so gaining supremacy over him by her knowledge of the 'word of power'.

> Now Isis was a woman who possessed words of power, but she was weary with men and loved gods, but she loved best the realm of the spirits. She meditated in her heart, saying, 'Cannot I by means of the sacred name of God make myself mistress of the earth and become a goddess of like rank and power to Ra in heaven and upon earth?' Ra had grown old and dribbled, and his spittle fell to the earth. So Isis kneaded some of the spittle and formed a sacred serpent, setting it on the ground in the great god's path, and as he passed by, the serpent bit him. He cried aloud, and the poison spread through his flesh just as Nile rushes through his land. 'Who could have done this to me?' he asked. 'I have multitudes of names and multitudes of forms, and my being is in every god.' Then the children of every god came to him, grieving. Isis also came, bringing her words of magical power, and her mouth was full of the breath of life; for her talismans vanquish the pains of sickness, and her words make to live again the throats of those who are dead. 'I will heal you,' she said, 'but tell me your name, holy Father, for whatsoever shall be delivered by your name shall live.' And Ra said, 'I have made the heavens and the earth, the mountains, and the water. I am he who, if he opens his eyes, makes the light, and if he closes them, darkness comes.' Isis said, 'But what you have said is not your name. Tell it to me and the poison will go.' Now the poison burned like fire, and the great god said, 'I consent that Isis shall search into me, and that my name shall pass from me into her.' So Isis said, 'Poison, depart, go forth from Ra. Let Ra live and let the poison die.' These are the words of Isis, the mighty lady, the mistress of the gods, who knew Ra by his own name.[66]

Here the serpent is the active power of Isis, an aspect of herself in relation to Ra, to which she gives form. Also, the mystery surrounding the secret name of the 'Most High' anticipates the unpronounceability of the Holy Name of Yahweh in the Hebrew tradition. At times Isis was called the wife of Ra or the mother of Ra, or, still more comprehensively, the female counterpart, like Nut, of the primeval abyss of water, source of all life. Her magical potency entered into all the regions of the imagination – life on earth, life above in heaven and life below in the underworld.

MOTHER AND CHILD

The infant lying alone and helpless, cradled only by nature in a wild place far from human company, is a constant motif in the myths of the world, which reappears every time a hero is born. Horus was born in secret in a thicket full of poisonous snakes, scorpions and insects in the swampy marshes of the Delta, but there was no other place to hide. He was safe as long as Isis looked after him, but then she had to go begging for food, so she left him in the care of the marsh nymphs and all the goddesses of the Delta. Many legends grew up about the mother and child, as they did about Mary and Jesus, drawing on that heightened feeling of hope and fear when affairs of great moment, and here the saviour of the world, seem poised upon the whim of hazard. Isis had been away and what happened, she said, was this:

> 'All day, while I was caring for his needs, I was longing for my little boy. When I returned, expecting to embrace him, I found my beautiful golden Horus, my innocent, fatherless child, lying on the ground with water streaming from his eyes and saliva dropping from his lips. His body was limp, his heart was weak, the pulses of his body did not beat. I cried out saying, "Here I am, here I am!" but the child was too weak to reply.'[67]

She appealed for help to the dwellers of the marshes and they told her that Horus had been poisoned. So Isis cried out to Ra in his Boat of Millions of Years, and when it drew level with her, the sun stopped. Then Thoth came down and when he learned what had gone wrong he said:

> 'Do not fear, Divine Isis! and you, Nephthys, lament not! I have come down from the sky with the breath of life to cure the child – to his mother's

Figure 30. Isis suckles Horus in the Delta swamps.

Figure 31. (*Left*) Isis seated on a lion throne suckling Horus; bronze statue, *c.* 600–400 BC.

Figure 32. (*Right*) Isis suckling the youthful Horus; *c.* 30 BC–AD 14. Outer wall of Temple of Hathor, Denderah.

delight.' Thoth utters the magic words of power, Horus recovers, and then he has to leave. 'But they are waiting for me to push off in the Evening Boat and, thereafter, to set sail in the Morning Boat.'[68]

In a similar tale Isis herself cures the sting of the scorpion and though the story dramatizes someone else's child stung instead of her own, the feeling of loss is common to them both. After Osiris's death, Isis is imprisoned by Seth and set to work in a spinning-mill (significant in the light of the Great Mother's role of spinning destiny out of herself), but Thoth helps her escape, telling her to hide herself in the marshes. So, accompanied by seven scorpions, she sets out for the Crocodile Town that lies at the edge of the marshes. On the way a certain rich lady shuts the door in her face, whereas a poor little girl from the fisher folk invites her into her humble home. Now the scorpions, her companions, were exceedingly grieved at this and one crept under the door and stung the rich lady's child. Distraught, the lady regrets what she did and Isis forgives her:

> So Isis cried to her saying: 'Come to me! Come to me who have the secret of restoring to life. I am a daughter, one well known in her town, who can expel poison with her spell . . .' So Isis laid her hands on the child to soothe him as he lay panting for breath. 'O Poison of Tefen, come, flow to the ground! . . . May the child live and the poison die . . .'[69]

The image of a vulnerable mother, alone and facing dangerous forces, which she finally overcomes with the help of greater powers, either outside of her or within, was one of the most enduring images, and countless mother and child statues were made to celebrate this divinity who could yet invite compassion from humanity:

'Ah, Horus, my son! Lying in a fever in a lonely place! There is no water there, nor am I there. May there be brought me water between the banks of a stream to quench the fire.'[70]

'Ah, baby boy! Ah, my son! Are you burning, O my nestling? Are you over-hot, there in the bush? Your mother cannot be by you, nor is there a sister there to fan you, nor a nurse to give you succour.'[71]

THE HELLENISTIC ISIS

When Alexander the Great conquered Egypt in 332 BC, Egypt was suddenly opened up and became part of the Greek world, though Greek philosophers had been coming to Egypt for centuries.[72] Alexander's successors, the Ptolemaic kings, encouraged the merging of Egyptian and Greek religions, and Isis became the wife of the new god of the Ptolemies, who was called Serapis, the old bull god in a new form. Traders from Egypt brought the cult of Isis and Serapis to Greece, where Isis was linked with Demeter, and the parallels between Isis searching for Osiris and Demeter searching for Persephone were obvious to an intellectual climate that sought to find similarities rather than emphasize differences. Plutarch identified Osiris with Dionysos, who was related to Demeter in the Eleusinian Mysteries (see Chapter 9, Fig. 16), and others allied Osiris with Pluto and Hades as well. Athens was an important centre of the Egyptian Mystery rituals and Isis had a shrine on the south slope of the Acropolis, and Serapis also had a temple there. On Delos a temple to Isis stood beside temples to the Greek goddesses and gods.

A hymn to Isis, composed in Greek in Cymi as late as the second century AD, conceives Isis as the bearer of those qualities (among others) more usually attributed to Maat, such as the right ordering of the universe, the ordaining of law (the role also given to the Greek Demeter) and the seeding of moral perception in human beings: 'I ordained that the true should be thought good.' It is written narratively as though Isis were speaking and, as in Plutarch, some of the Egyptian divinities have been changed to their Greek parallels; it is at least 3,000 years after the first mention of her name in the First Dynasty.

I am Isis, the mistress of every land, and I was taught by Hermes [Thoth],
   and with Hermes [Thoth] I devised letters, both the sacred (Hieroglyphs)
   and the demotic, that all things might not be written with the same
   (letters).
I gave and ordained laws for men, which no one is able to change.
I am the eldest daughter of Kronos [Shu].
I am wife and sister of King Osiris.

I am she who findeth fruit for men.
I am mother of King Horus.
I am she that riseth in the Dog Star.
I am she that is called goddess by women.
For me was the city of Bubastis built.
I divided the earth from the heaven.
I showed the paths of the stars.
I ordered the course of the sun and the moon.
I devised business in the sea.
I made strong the right.
I brought together woman and man.
I appointed to women to bring their infants to birth in the tenth month.
I laid punishment upon those disposed without natural affection towards
    their parents.
I made with my brother Osiris an end to the eating of men.
I revealed mysteries unto men.
I taught (men) to honor images of the gods.
I consecrated the precincts of the gods.
I broke down the governments of tyrants.
I made an end to murders.
I compelled women to be loved by men.
I made the right to be stronger than gold and silver.
I ordained that the true should be thought good.
I devised marriage contracts.
I assigned to Greeks and barbarians their languages.
I made the beautiful and the shameful to be distinguished by nature.
I ordained that nothing should be more feared than an oath.
I have delivered the plotter of evil against other men into the hands of the
    one he plotted against.
I established penalties for those who practice injustice.
I decreed mercy to suppliants.
I protect (or honor) righteous guards.
With me the right prevails.
I am the Queen of rivers and winds and sea.
No one is held in honor without my knowing it.
I am the Queen of war.
I am the Queen of the thunderbolt.
I stir up the sea and I calm it.
I am in the rays of the sun.
Whatever I please, this too shall come to an end.
With me everything is reasonable.
I set free those in bonds.
I am the Queen of seamanship.
I make the navigable unnavigable when it pleases me.
I created walls of cities.
I am called the Lawgiver [*Thesmophoros*, like Demeter].
I brought up islands out of the depth into the light.
I am Lord of rainstorms.
I overcome fate.

Fate hearkens to me.
Hail, O Egypt, that nourished me![73]

The rhythms of the poem evoke those of both the Akathistos Hymn to
Mary (see Chapter 14, pp. 575–6), composed or written down in the fifth
century AD – only 300 years later – and the Gnostic hymn to Sophia, 'The
Thunder, Perfect Mind' (see Chapter 15, pp. 630–1), all of which at one time
may have been contemporary with each other.

Not surprisingly, Isis was known as 'the goddess of a thousand names'
even by the philosopher Apuleius, writing in the second century AD,
following the tradition from Plutarch, who died the year Apuleius was
born.

A college of the servants of Isis was founded in Rome about 80 BC, but
the worship of Isis was proscribed after a few years and temples to her
were pulled down from 58 to 48 BC. In 43 BC, in a fine register of how the
people felt, the triumvirs, wanting the people's vote, built temples in
honour of Isis and Serapis and publicly sanctioned their use. The worship
of Isis was again banned temporarily after the conquest of Egypt in 31 BC
by Octavian, but subsequently flourished all over the Roman Empire
until the general introduction of Christianity. Apuleius, writing in Latin,
identifies Isis with Ceres, Venus and Proserpine as goddess of the wheat
and crops, and tells how the sistra were still shaking until the sun had
risen at her temple in Rome during her festivals. Pausanias also tells of
festivals to Isis at Tithorea, where anyone who watched them profanely
did not live long to tell the tale.[74]

Apuleius was a barrister and an initiate of the Mysteries of Isis. Here,
in his book *The Golden Ass*, Isis appears to Lucius, whom, in a precise
metaphor of initiation, she is to transform from an ass to a human being:

You see me here, Lucius, in answer to your prayer. I am Nature, the
universal Mother, mistress of all the elements, primordial child of time,
sovereign of all things spiritual, queen of the dead, queen also of the immortals, the single manifestation of all gods and goddesses that are. My nod
governs the shining heights of Heaven, the wholesome sea-breezes, the
lamentable silences of the world below. Though I am worshipped in many
aspects, known by countless names, and propitiated with all manner of
different rites, yet the whole round earth venerates me. The primeval Phrygians call me Pessinuntica, Mother of the gods; the Athenians, sprung from
their own soil, call me Cecropian Artemis; for the islanders of Cyprus I am
Paphian Aphrodite; for the archers of Crete I am Dyctynna; for the trilingual
Sicilians, Stygian Proserpine; and for the Eleusinians their ancient Mother
of the Corn.

Some know me as Juno, some as Bellona of the Battles; others as Hecate,
others again as Rhamnubia, but both races of Aethiopians, whose lands the
morning sun first shines upon, and the Egyptians, who excel in ancient
learning and worship me with ceremonies proper to my godhead, call me by
my true name, namely, Queen Isis. I have come in pity of your plight, I

Figure 33. Isis with snakes; coin, first century BC. Egypt.

have come to favour and aid you. Weep no more, lament no longer; the hour of deliverance, shone over by my watchful light, is at hand.[75]

The Mysteries in Egypt from the earliest dynasties to the later ones of the New Kingdom – enacted in secret in the inner rooms of the temples, which the ordinary people were forbidden to enter – dramatized the Passion of Osiris, his life, the manner of his death, his need for protection in the underworld, the assistance of Isis and Nephthys and the other goddesses and gods, and his resurrection in which the whole universe participated. As a festival that marked the passage of one year, his drama must have offered inspiration to many for any kind of liberation. An inscription on one of the tombs says: 'This will be useful for a man here on earth as well as when he has died.'[76]

But in Apuleius's account of the Mysteries, many hundreds if not more than 1,000 years later, the focus has shifted on to Isis. The story in *The Golden Ass* is told from the point of view of an initiate (unlike the stories of the Eleusinian Mysteries, which came from Christian priests), and so the magnificence of the ceremonies is here unobscured. Lucius, whose name means 'light', had been turned into an ass; when 'the sun shone at midnight', the hidden inner light of his own true nature was revealed and he was transformed. First, he had undergone a voluntary death – the condition of mystic illumination everywhere – in his case extending even to the death of the sense of being human. In a moving culmination to his trials, after dipping himself seven times beneath the waves while a dazzling full moon was rising from the sea, he prays to the Goddess, with 'tears running down my hairy face'. He had scarcely closed his eyes when

the apparition of a woman began to rise from the middle of the sea with so lovely a face that the gods themselves would have fallen down in adoration of it. First the head, then the whole shining body gradually emerged and stood before me poised on the surface of the waves . . .

Her long thick hair fell in tapering ringlets on her lovely neck, and was crowned with an intricate chaplet in which was woven every kind of flower. Just above her brow shone a round disc, like a mirror, or like the bright face of the moon, which told me who she was. Vipers rising from the left-hand and right-hand partings of her hair supported this disc, with ears of corn bristling beside them. Her many-coloured robe was of finest linen; part was glistening white, part crocus-yellow, part glowing red and along the entire hem a woven bordure of flowers and fruit clung swaying in the breeze. But what caught and held my eye more than anything else was the deep black lustre of her mantle. She wore it slung across her body from the right hip to the left shoulder, where it was caught in a knot resembling the boss of a shield; but part of it hung in innumerable folds, the tasselled fringe quivering. It was embroidered with glittering stars on the hem and everywhere else, and in the middle beamed a full and fiery moon.

In her right hand she held a bronze rattle, of the sort used to frighten away the God of the Sirocco; its narrow rim was curved like a sword-belt and three little rods, which sang shrilly when she shook the handle, passed horizontally through it. A boat-shaped gold dish hung from her left hand, and along the upper surface of the handle writhed an asp with puffed throat and head raised ready to strike. On her divine feet were slippers of palm leaves, the emblem of victory.[77]

The Queen of the Night, the original for many renditions of *The Magic Flute*, is visible as the epiphany of Nature, who is the Mother of all.

It was the vision of the Goddess Mother and her child saviour that caught the imagination of the new manifestation of the myth that was Christianity. The magnificence of nature and the immanence of divinity as nature were to be veiled in the formal Judaeo-Christian reinterpretation of the ancient myth, but the beauty of the images of Isis suckling her child and the feelings of compassion evoked by the stories of Isis and Horus were not lost, and continued to inspire the people under their new names.

Figure 34. Isis nursing Horus on her lap; copper statue, 2040–1700 BC.

7
TIAMAT OF BABYLON:
THE DEFEAT OF THE GODDESS

You yourself are even another little world and have within you the sun and the moon and also the stars.

Origen

The *Enuma Elish* – the Babylonian epic of creation – tells the story of the conquest and murder of the original mother goddess, Tiamat, by the god Marduk, her great-great-great-grandson. In this moment of drama a new myth is born:

> Then joined issue Tiamat and Marduk, wisest of the gods.
> They struck in single combat, locked in battle.
> The lord spread out his net to enfold her,
> The Evil Wind which followed behind, he let loose in her face.
> When Tiamat opened her mouth to consume him
> He drove in the Evil Wind that she close not her lips.[1]

The Iron Age (beginning *c.* 1250 BC) saw the completion of the process begun in the Bronze Age in which numinosity was transferred from the Mother Goddess to the Father God. The *Enuma Elish* is the first story of the replacing of a mother goddess who generates creation as part of herself by a god who 'makes' creation as something separate from himself. All the myths of the Iron Age in which a sky or sun god or hero conquers

Figure 1. The conquest of the mother goddess Tiamat by the god Marduk; cylinder seal, *c.* ninth–eighth century BC.

a great serpent or dragon can be traced to this Babylonian epic, in which humanity was created from the blood of a sacrificed god and no longer from the womb of a primordial goddess. Its influence can be followed through Hittite, Assyrian, Persian, Canaanite, Hebrew, Greek and Roman mythology.

In the goddess culture the conception of the relation between creator and creation was expressed in the image of the Mother as *zoe*, the eternal source, giving birth to the son as *bios*, the created life in time which lives and dies back into the source. The son was the part that emerged from the whole, through which the whole might come to know itself. As the god 'grew up' during the course of the Bronze Age, he came to be the consort of the goddess and sometimes co-creator with her. But in the Iron Age the image of relationship enacted in the sacred marriage disappears, and the emerging balance between the female and male divine images is lost.

Now a father god establishes a position of supremacy in relation to a mother goddess, and he is gradually transformed into the consortless god of the three patriarchal religions known to us today: Judaism, Christianity and Islam. The god is then the sole primal creator, where before the goddess had been the only source of life. But the god becomes the *maker* of heaven and earth whereas the goddess *was* heaven and earth. The concept of 'making' is radically different from 'being', in the sense that what is made is not necessarily of the same substance as its maker, and may be conceived as inferior to him; while what emerges from the mother is necessarily part of her and she of it.

In this way the essential identity between creator and creation was broken, and a fundamental dualism was born from their separation, the dualism that we know as spirit and nature. In the myth of the goddess these two terms have no meaning in separation from each other: nature is spiritual and spirit is natural, because the divine is immanent as creation. In the myth of the god, nature is no longer 'spiritual' and spirit is no longer 'natural', because the divine is transcendent to creation. Spirit is not inherent in nature, but outside it or beyond it; it even becomes the source of nature. So a new meaning enters the language: spirit becomes creative and nature becomes created. In this new kind of myth, creation is the result of a divine act that brings order out of chaos.

We can see these myths as stories told by humanity at different stages of its evolution, both of which explore different ways of being in the universe. But our Judaeo-Christian tradition, which has inherited only the myth of the god, implicitly presents the duality of spirit and nature as 'given'; inherent in the way things are. Yet this dualism, as we have seen, was not always there. Furthermore, its origin in *human history* has been lost to consciousness because, in the patriarchal cultures in which the father god was worshipped as unique creator, no memory of the earlier imagery of the mother goddess as creator survived in recognizable form.

THE BABYLONIAN EPIC OF CREATION

The mythological roots of all three patriarchal religions descend from the *Enuma Elish*, which was known all over the ancient world. The oldest story in which a hero-god conquers a dragon is Sumerian, but the Babylonian epic, with its greater ferocity, is the one that caught the imagination of the Iron Age. Originally, as Frazer suggests, it may have been the mythical celebration of the coming of the Babylonian spring, where the sun god conquered the great serpent or dragon that was the image of the winding rivers and the fierce, inundating floods of winter, which turned the Babylonian plain into a watery chaos.[2] The god embodied the powers of creation, and the serpent goddess, the powers of destruction. The great battle between them was re-enacted every spring, when the creative and destructive powers engaged with each other and the outcome of their conflict hung in the balance. The people waited anxiously for the appearance of the dry land amid the waters, and for the confirmation of the god's victory in the freshly sprouting grain. The *Enuma Elish*, which means 'From on High', was recited annually to 'assist' the victory of the lord god Marduk in his defeat of the great serpent-dragon Tiamat.[3]

The *Enuma Elish* was not to remain a local 'nature myth', for its immense popularity carried it far beyond its original boundaries. The violent image of conquest in the *Enuma Elish* set the paradigm of the Iron Age as one of conflict between the older mythology of the mother goddess and the new myths of the Aryan and Semitic father gods. The father gods struggled for supremacy in Mesopotamia, Persia, India, Anatolia, Canaan and Greece and, less obviously, in Egypt. But Marduk was the first god to vanquish the mother goddess and take her place as creator of life.

This epic offers the earliest evidence of the complete inversion of the mythology of the earlier era. Instead of the goddess sacrificing her son–lover, the goddess is herself sacrificed by a being of her own creation: the young god, her great-great-great-grandson. We know of the epic only from tablets unearthed in AD 1848 from the library of Assurbanipal, the last king of Assyria, who immolated himself in the flames of his burning palace in 626 BC, but it dates to the era 1,000 years earlier, when the

Figure 2. Marduk pursuing Tiamat; Assyrian seal, *c.* 800 BC.

Semitic Amorite Hammurabian dynasty came to power in Babylonia about
1750 BC. The first mention of the epic comes in a tablet of about 1580 BC.
It is a myth created by a young people, newly come to the experience of
political power. The language and imagery are abrasive, not yet enriched
or mellowed by insight and wisdom, and contrast stridently with the tone
of the older Sumerian myths.

The epic tells the story of how the gods are brought into being by the
primal mother and father, Tiamat and Apsu; how conflict arises between
the older and younger generations; and how the older generation is eventually overthrown by the younger, whose leader is Marduk. Marduk then
initiates a new order of creation. It begins with imagery that still recalls
the earlier poetry of Sumeria:

> When the heights of heaven and the earth beneath had not been named, and
> when Apsu, their father [the waters that fell from heaven and the sweet
> river waters], and Tiamat, their mother [the salt waters of the sea], still
> mingled their waters; when no field or marsh was formed and no gods had
> been called into being, then were the great gods created within the primal
> pair. The first gods were Lahmu and Lahamu, then Anshar and Kishar
> were created [probably the Sumerian An and Ki, Heaven and Earth], and
> then Anu and Ea. But these new generations of gods disturbed Apsu with
> their clamour, and he consulted his minister, Mummu. Together they went
> to Tiamat to tell her of their decision to destroy them, so that once again
> there could be peace and quiet. Tiamat protested at their plan: 'Why destroy
> what we ourselves have brought into being?' she cried, but Mummu counsel-
> led Apsu to proceed, and together they plotted the downfall of the younger
> gods.

Now these younger gods became aware of the plan to destroy them, so
Ea drew a magic circle around them to protect them. Then, while Apsu
and Mummu slept, he killed Apsu and took Mummu prisoner, 'holding
him by a nose rope'. Then Ea established his residence over the waters of
Apsu and with his wife, Damkina, created Marduk, who was nursed by
the breasts of goddesses and so filled with awe-inspiring majesty:

> His figure was enticing, flashing the look of his eyes, manly his going forth.
> He was a leader from the start. And when Ea, his father, beheld him, he
> rejoiced and bestowed on him double equality with the gods. Marduk was
> exalted beyond them in all ways: in all his members marvellously arranged:
> incomprehensible and difficult to look upon. He had four eyes and as many
> ears, and when his lips moved, fire blazed forth. Each of the ears grew large;
> each of the eyes, also, to see all. He was prodigious and was clothed with the
> radiance of ten gods, with a majesty to inspire fear.[4]

Ea's elder brother, Anu, then created great winds that disturbed the
waters of Tiamat. It was this apparently small incident that created a
rupture in the order of being and turned Tiamat from a life-giving mother
to a death-dealing dragon, bringing forth trouble into the world. She

Figure 3. Marduk slaying Tiamat; Assyrian relief (later called *Ninurta and the Demon*), *c*. ninth century BC.

becomes more and more agitated and gives birth to a monster brood of serpents, 'sharp of tooth and merciless of fang', whose bodies were filled with poison instead of blood. Whoever beheld them was transfixed with terror. Eleven kinds of monster were created. All these were Tiamat's sons and the chief of them was Kingu, whom she took as her husband, appointing him to lead her host to defend her and affixing the Tablets of the Law to his breast.

The gods set up a throne for Marduk, and said: 'We give thee sovereignty over the whole world. Thy weapon shall never lose its power, it shall crush thy foe.' To test his power, they spread the starry garment of the night sky before him, telling him to command it to disappear and reappear. When they saw he could do this, they said, 'Marduk is king!' and they gave him the sceptre, throne and ring, and an invincible weapon, the thunderbolt. Marduk took his bow, his spear and mace, and 'set lightning before him, with burning flame he filled his body'. He made a net to enclose the inward parts of Tiamat and summoned the seven winds to obey him, including the tempest, whirlwind and hurricane, and 'the wind which had no equal'. Seizing his thunderbolt, he mounted his chariot, and as he approached her a brilliant halo shone round his head.

Marduk now conquers Tiamat, Kingu and their host, and takes the Tablets of the Law for himself:

> The lord spread out his net to enfold her,
> The Evil Wind, which followed behind, he let loose in her face.
> When Tiamat opened her mouth to consume him,
> He drove in the Evil Wind that she close not her lips.
> As the fierce winds charged her belly,

> Her body was distended and her mouth was wide open.
> He released the arrow, it tore her belly,
> It cut through her insides, splitting the heart.
> Having thus subdued her, he extinguished her life.
> He cast down her carcass to stand upon it.
>
> The lord trod on the legs of Tiamat,
> With his unsparing mace he crushed her skull.
> When the arteries of her blood he had severed,
> The North Wind bore it to places undisclosed.
> On seeing this, his fathers were joyful and jubilant,
> They brought gifts of homage to him.
> Then the lord paused to view her dead body,
> That he might divide the monster and do artful works.
> He split her like a shellfish into two parts:
> Half of her he set up and ceiled it as sky . . .

The other half of Tiamat's lifeless body became the earth. A greater contrast between this harsh myth and the poetry of early Sumeria can hardly be imagined. The goddess no longer brings forth heaven and earth as the cosmic mountain: now heaven and earth are made from her carcass by a god. No longer is the net an image of the interweaving of all life but a trap for the one who wove it into being. And so a new creation myth is born.

Marduk then, as it were, creates creation again: he establishes the year with its twelve months, makes the constellations, giving the pole star a specific location in the sky, and he appoints the sun and moon to their heavenly places. The powers of nature are experienced no longer as goddesses and gods but as elements subject to this one god. Now, this master of the primordial goddess turns his attention to the earth:

> He heaped up a mountain over Tiamat's head,
> pierced her eyes to form the sources of the Tigris and Euphrates,
> and heaped similar mountains over her dugs,
> which he pierced to make the rivers
> from the eastern mountains that flow into the Tigris.
> Her tail he bent up into the sky to make the Milky Way,
> and her crotch he used to support the sky.[5]

Marduk then has a further inspiration, and the story is told on the sixth tablet:

> Opening his mouth, he addressed Ea (his father)
> to impart the plan he had conceived in his heart:
> 'Blood I will mass and cause bones to be.
> I will establish a savage, "man" shall be his name.
> Verily, savage-man I will create.
> He shall be charged with the service of the gods
> that they might be at ease!'

. . . . .

> Ea answered him, speaking a word to him,
> Giving him another plan for the relief of the gods:
> 'Let but one of their brothers (the defeated gods) be handed over;
> He alone shall perish that mankind may be fashioned
> (out of his blood).
> Let him be handed over who contrived the uprising.
> His guilt will I make him bear.'
>
> . . . . .
>
> They bound him (Kingu), holding him before Ea.
> They imposed on him his guilt and severed his blood vessels.
> Out of his blood they fashioned mankind.[6]

In this myth heaven and earth are made from the dismembered body of the goddess, and the human race from the murdered body of her son–lover, for Kingu was both the son and the consort of Tiamat.

This epic of the conquest of the primordial Mother Goddess by the sky, wind and sun god, Marduk, coincides with the final stage of the Sumero-Babylonian civilization, which was marked by the decline of its culture and an ever-increasing emphasis on war and conquest, leading to the growth of an empire. Perhaps it tells and vindicates the actual story of the Babylonian conquest of Sumeria. In the *Enuma Elish* Marduk, who describes himself as the son of Ea, god of wisdom, is set up as the new ruler of the gods, which effectively symbolizes the transfer of power from the old Sumerian 'Mother' kingdom to the new Babylonian kingdom of the 'Son' who becomes the 'Father'.[7] It certainly registers the final end of the earlier cultural phase in which the religion of the Mother Goddess prevailed. The primordial Mother Goddess, known as Nammu or Ninmah, whose image in Sumeria was both the sea and a great serpent, has now become Tiamat, the demoness-mother. The defeat of Tiamat may have served to discredit the Sumerian 'Mother' land, which is now portrayed as threatening and evil in the image of a dragon worthy of destruction. Marduk takes the Tablets of the Law from Tiamat, and this may signify the transfer of political control from Sumeria to Babylonia, and of religious power from the mother goddess to the young god.

Creation, as the myths of other cultures suggest, does not have to be imagined in only one way. Fragments of other creation myths exist in which the creation of the world and humanity is not associated with the death of a dragon, and takes place by the act of a goddess, or a goddess and a god, or by all the goddesses and gods acting in concert. In the Sumerian *Epic of Gilgamesh* the father god, Anu, calls to the goddess of creation, Aruru, to create Enkidu as a companion to Gilgamesh:

> You made him, O Aruru, now create his equal; let it be as like him as his own reflection, his second self, stormy heart for stormy heart . . . So the goddess conceived an image in her mind, and it was the stuff of Anu of the firmament. She dipped her hands in water and pinched off clay, she let it fall in the wilderness, and noble Enkidu was created.[8]

Here, we note, the breath of life, or spirit, did not have to be added to the inert clay, as it did later with Adam. The image of life in the mind of the goddess and the pinching of the wet clay bring Enkidu alive.

The following fragment of an alternative creation myth shows quite a different Marduk, much closer to his earlier prototype, the Sumerian Enlil, and offers another conception of the creation of humanity. Here, the same goddess Aruru is co-creator with Marduk:

> Marduk laid a reed upon the face of the waters
> He formed dust and poured it out beside the reed.
> That he might cause the gods to dwell
> in the habitation of their hearts' desire,
> He formed mankind,
> The Goddess Aruru together with him
> created the seed of mankind.
> The beasts of the field and living creatures
> in the field he formed.
>
> . . . . .
>
> The grass, the rush of the marsh, the reed,
> and the forest he created,
> The lands, the marshes, and the swamps,
> the wild cow and her young, the wild calf;
> the ewe and her young, the lamb of the fold;
> plantations and forests . . . he brought into existence.[9]

None the less, the *Enuma Elish* was the creation myth that prevailed over all others, and its popularity endured through Babylonian, Assyrian and even Hittite civilizations. It strongly influenced the Hebrew myth of creation. From about 1700 BC, for over 1,000 years, it was recited in Babylon at the time of the spring equinox, on the fourth day of the eleven-day festival known as Zagmuk. The dragon myth existed in early Sumeria in the legend of Enki defeating the dragon of the *Kur* (the mountain, abyss or underworld), but not until this epic did it appear as part of a creation myth, where it is conceived in terms of the god defeating the dragon-serpent goddess and making heaven and earth from her carcass.

The *Enuma Elish* is the earliest example of what might be called priestly politics, whereby the mythology of an earlier age and culture is completely inverted, so that the divinities of the previous era are named demons and the divinities of the new order are exalted to a position of supremacy. The *Enuma Elish* replaces the old lunar goddess image with the sky and solar god so radically that it prevents any possibility of relationship with the older order of consciousness. The defeat of the serpent goddess marked the end of a culture, and also the end of the Neolithic way of perceiving life, which very soon becomes almost inaccessible; for the victory of a solar god creates a new way of living, a new way of relating to the divine by identifying with the god's power of conquest, the victory over darkness that the sun wins each dawn. The myth validates, as Campbell says, not only a new social order but also a new psychology . . . a new structure of human thought and feeling, overinterpreted as of cosmic reach . . . We have now entered a theatre of myth that the rational, non-mystic mind can comprehend without aid, where the art of politics, the art of gaining power over men, received for all time its celestial model.[10]

THE NEW PARADIGM OF CONSCIOUSNESS

The effects of this split in consciousness between the old and the new orders, expressed here as a conflict between a goddess and a god, can be traced through the Iron Age down to our own culture. The mythic model of the older goddess culture was one of relationship between every aspect of creation, and this expressed the way the people of that time experienced the universe. From now on, the mythic model of the new culture ruled by a male deity is one of mastery and control, expressing the desire to shape and order what has been created. The increasing power to influence the environment was matched by the power to extend tribal territory through war and conquest, assisted by the horse and the war chariot. The new paradigm of the Iron Age reflects what had become primarily a warrior's experience of life: it was heroic, combative and aggressive, since the emphasis was on victory in battle and acquisition through conquest. At the same time, the new image also reflects a growing sense of individuality as men (but not women) discovered a greater ability to determine their fate and to win the acclaim and devotion of other men. The king or leader – the outstanding individual – personified this new sense of identity, which had begun to manifest itself in the Bronze Age, but reaches a clear definition in the Iron Age. The experience and voice of the women of that time are not so audible nor so distinctive as they had been in the Bronze Age.

These changes were reflected in the new interpretation given to old images. One of the most archaic images of the awesome creative and destructive force of the goddess was the lion, whereas the bull was the image of created life that had annually to be sacrificed for its own renewal. The image of the lion killing the bull was an image of this perennial necessity. The lion's relation with the goddess has persisted through the ages down to the lion throne of Mary, though by this time its fearful dimension has fallen away and the image points only to the strength of unvanquishable life that continually renews itself.

Often the goddess is shown standing on a lion, like the Egyptian and Syrian Qetesh and the Hindu goddess Durga; or she sits in a chariot drawn by lions, like the Anatolian and Roman Cybele. However, with the rise of the god culture, the lion's power was co-opted by the god, who is also imaged in the sun. The king, who in his turn incarnated the power of the god, then assumes the images of lion and sun in his own person and

Figure 4. Lion-headed eagle
on the back of a human-headed
bull; Sumerian limestone
plaque, *c*. 2500 BC. Ur.

role. At this point the image of the lion killing the bull takes on a different
meaning. It signifies the solar religion of the sky gods overcoming the
lunar religion of the goddess, a symbolic re-enactment of Marduk's conquest of Tiamat. Implicitly, therefore, in the language of imagery, the
new solar lion appropriates the mastery of creation. More generally in the
mythology of the Iron Age, sky becomes exalted over earth, and the
paradigm of opposition and conflict grips the consciousness of humanity.

Warrior kings, like Hammurabi (1728–1686 BC), were not slow to identify themselves with the new solar imagery:

> At that time Anu and Bel (Marduk) called to me, Hammurabi, the pious
> prince, worshipper of the gods, summoning me by name, to bring about the
> rule of righteousness in the land, to wipe out the wicked and evil, to prevent
> the strong from oppressing the weak, to go forth like the sun over the
> human race, to illuminate the land, and to further the welfare of mankind.[11]

In the *Enuma Elish* there is already the germ of three principal ideas
that were to inform the age to come: the supremacy of the father god over
the mother goddess; the paradigm of opposition implicit in the deathly
struggle between god and goddess; and the association of light, order and
good with the god, and of darkness, chaos and evil with the goddess. This
was also expressed as the polarization of spirit and nature, mind and body,
the one divine and good, the other 'fallen' and 'evil'. This opposition was
extended to the categorization of gender in all aspects of life, which then
polarized into conflicting opposites, instead of following the earlier model
of differentiation and complementarity. When this opposition was crudely
oversimplified, as it often was, the 'male' aspect of life became identified
with spirit, light, order and mind, which were good, and the 'female'
aspect of life became identified with nature, darkness, chaos and body,

which were evil. This divinely sanctioned opposition led, in turn, to the related idea of the 'holy war', the war of the forces of 'good' against the forces of 'evil'.

As the position of the father god in the Iron Age became everywhere secure and supreme, the mythologies based on the imagery of the sky and solar god were interpreted by the various priesthoods as divine revelation, and so they have remained to this day. As there was one sun, so there would be one saviour, who is the supreme god, the god of gods – not the One that is an image of unity, but the One who stands above and alone. Marduk's desire for his word alone to prevail would find its historical legacy in Yahweh's words: 'I am the first and I am the last; and beside me there is no God' (Isa. 44:6). Few people are aware of the disparate influences that combined to create the Judaic and Christian 'revelations', and the historical pressures that led to the evolution of a monotheistic religion with a supreme Father God. It is not generally known, for instance, that Babylonia provided the seminal ideas that shaped the mythic imagery of Persian Zoroastrianism, Judaism, Christianity and Islam. Consequently, the fact that there was an earlier understanding that assumed the essential identity of nature and spirit was eventually forgotten.

The importance of this change of imagery cannot be overemphasized, for it has influenced the Judaeo-Christian view of nature, matter and whatever else has been defined as feminine, and it has structured our paradigm images in mythology, religion, literature, science and psychology. Here, in its earliest formulation, the idea is precisely articulated and embodied in myth: that what is feminine is chaotic, destructive, demonic, and is to be feared and mastered. This complex of ideas was reinforced in early Christianity, particularly by Paul and the early Christian Fathers, and can be found today in the doctrinal reluctance to ordain women as priests (compounding the confusion by identifying 'the feminine' with 'women'). More widely, it may go some way to explain the characteristic twentieth-century disregard of the Earth, our 'Mother Nature'.

When the values of an ancient culture are overlaid by those of another, the despised values do not, as we used to think, vanish into the past and, as it were, cease to be. They fall rather into the unconscious of the race, where they continue to influence the conscious psyche, but not as finely or effectively as when there is a constructive dialogue held in full consciousness. Because the rejected values are now unconscious, the tendency is rather to obstruct: to be either too weak to have any effect or to exaggerate, so at either extreme there is distortion.

As suggested in Chapter 1, Jung's important hypothesis of the Collective Unconscious has shown that 'nothing in the psyche is ever lost'[12] and, further, that what seems lost must be found if it is to function at the highest level of which it is capable. In our culture there still exists a prejudice against the deeper instinctive layers of the psyche on the grounds that they are non-rational, chaotic and uncontrollable – qualities that have been designated as 'feminine' – together with the assumption that the only ordering principle in the psyche comes from the 'masculine' exercise of 'reason', which can formulate the laws of consciousness capable of intellectual definition. The idea that spontaneity has its own order – that there is in the personal as well as the collective unconscious an innate and inherent lawfulness, an 'intelligence' that is more comprehensive than, and so includes, the intellect – is not one that belongs to our cultural paradigms, and so we do not explore it to discover if, when and how it is true.

The terms 'feminine' and 'masculine', 'female' and 'male' have been given so many different nuances of meaning down the ages and have been the repository of so much unconscious projection that they are now utterly ambiguous until a context is provided. Although, in a sense, this whole discussion is about opening up the possibilities of meaning of these ideas, and to mention them only briefly here risks trivializing them, it none the less seems necessary at this point to emphasize that we intend the terms 'feminine' and 'masculine' to refer to a way of being or a mode of consciousness available to *both* men and women. Yin and yang, receptive and active, would be, perhaps, their most generic formulation. As ideas, they are in themselves descriptive terms, not evaluative: sometimes one mode is more appropriate, sometimes the other. Any way of being or mode of consciousness can be evaluated, of course, but it is the context that enables us to do so, not some inherent quality in the terms themselves. Jung's idea of archetypes is invaluable here, for it allows us to talk about the archetypal feminine in men and the archetypal masculine in women, often as a way of getting beyond the conceptual language of gender at either the abstract or the personal level.

The archetypal feminine is rendered in mythology as the figure of the goddess who was originally androgynous, that is, she was both female and male in the metaphorical sense that she was both the womb and the generative force that seeded new forms of life within it, which she brought forth as the universe. In the Neolithic metaphor the goddess was heaven, earth and the waters beneath the earth. In a later Mesopotamian metaphor, when the archetypal masculine image of generation had separated from the archetypal feminine vessel, the goddess was earth and the god was heaven. In Egypt, possibly for the reasons suggested in Chapter 6, the goddess was heaven and the god was earth. In modern Germany and Japan the moon is masculine and the sun is feminine, whereas in most other places the sun is masculine – *le soleil* – and the moon is feminine – *la lune*. Their countries are also thought of as 'fatherlands' rather than 'mother' countries. (There has never yet been a 'Father Nature', however!) While these differences are significant for an understanding of different cultural orientations,[13] they are mentioned here mainly to point out that the terms feminine and masculine, female and male are highly evocative, and it is very important to be clear as to when, how and why they are being used.

In the Iron Age, as suggested above, these terms became fixed and absolute, and were assigned definite values. What was feminine was the dragon-mother, the earth and moon, darkness, chaos, confusion, nature as emptied of spirit; and what was masculine was the sky-father, the heaven and sun, light, order, clarity, spirit as freed from nature. That these simplistic assignations of value, originating 4,000 years ago, are only recently being challenged on a wide scale indicates how deeply they have entered into our culture without our noticing. When we come to the hero myth, for instance, the original stories undoubtedly meant the hero to be masculine in the rewardingly simple sense of being a man. The symbolic significance of the hero myths for us, on the other hand, is that the hero is the embodiment of the archetypal masculine in *all* human beings – the questing consciousness in search of a goal.

WAR AS THE ETHOS OF THE IRON AGE

Returning, with the relentless spear of Rameses II, to the Iron Age, wherever the hero myth of the solar hero and dragon has been interpreted literally, in terms of a warrior confronting a powerful and dangerous enemy, it has led to polarization and endless strife. The *Enuma Elish* offered a paradigm of divine behaviour that was inevitably used to justify the violation of life that was the hallmark of the Iron Age. The rise of the Babylonian cult of Marduk coincided with the glorification of war and conquest that plunged the different peoples and races of the Near East into a struggle for supremacy or survival, whose legacy of conflict has still not come to an end after 4,000 years – presumably because the beliefs formulated then still govern human consciousness. What, in the history books of the early part of this century, used to be *admired* as the 'great

Figure 5. Rameses II destroying Libyans; *c.* 1260 BC. Abu Simbel.

age' of the Babylonian and Assyrian Empires was marked by the most barbarous cruelty: the flaying alive of bodies, gouging out of eyes and cutting off of limbs, the murder of thousands of enemy prisoners, practices that are not extolled in the early centuries of Sumerian civilization. The emotional climate of the Iron Age is one of acute anxiety and fear of disaster. This, more than anything else, created a compulsion to aggression. The majority of men *had* to be warriors. They defended the community, avenged the dead, brought glory to the family name. The king, in particular, had to be a 'mighty' warrior, one like David, of whom they sang one to another in dances, saying, 'Saul hath slain his thousands, and David his ten thousands' (1 Sam. 18:7).

The Iron Age is dominated by a mythology of war, in which the hero is seen politically as the mighty warrior. The ideal of the king was no longer to be the shepherd of his people, as it was in early Sumeria, but the mighty conqueror, on the model of Hammurabi, Darius, Agamemnon or Alexander. Cruelty became a virtue and barbarism a way of life. War was regarded as natural and right, the royal road for a man to follow if he were to serve his gods, his king and his country (the rhythms are familiar). Like the Palaeolithic hunt, war brought men together in a shared aim and a shared heroic purpose whose intensity was such that no tilling of the soil or herding of animals could emulate it. The ideal of conquest forged the bond of a tribal consciousness, pre-empting the otherwise universal reflections of art, as can be seen in the seemingly endless lines of identical warriors carved on Assyrian tablets dedicated to destruction. Campbell wryly observes that the two greatest works of war mythology in the West are the *Iliad* and the Old Testament,[14] an alliance that places these books firmly in the context of their age, whose focus was war. One immediate difference between them is that in the *Iliad* the sympathies and assistance of the many gods are offered to both sides, so that neither is designated as intrinsically wrong or evil, which means that both sides are ultimately bound by a common humanity. In the Old Testament, on the other hand, with its single and omnipotent god, there is only rare evidence of respect for the enemy or sympathy with his fate.

In the course of the Iron Age five great empires – Babylonian, Assyrian, Persian, Greek and Roman – imposed themselves successively on an immense area of land, which at one time extended from Greece to India and from the Caspian Sea to the Sudan. To the north-west of Mesopotamia, the Hittite Empire was established in Anatolia, extending its influence southwards into Syria and Canaan. Further to the south Egypt pursued the same pattern of imperial expansion after the invasions of the Hyksos in 1500 BC.

During this time the organic growth of the psyche was abruptly cut off as the close relationship of people with a specific soil, established over many millennia, was irrevocably broken. Whole tribal groups were uprooted or taken into slavery, since the agricultural prosperity of these empires depended upon the labour of slaves. Women and children were often seized as slaves when their fathers or husbands were killed, or when pirates raided foreign shores in search of loot. The Greek writer of the *Iliad* imagines the feelings of the Trojan Andromache as she remonstrates with her husband, Hector, on the walls of Troy:

> Hector, you are possessed. This bravery of yours will be your end. You do not think of your little boy or your unhappy wife, whom you will make a widow soon. Some day the Achaeans are bound to kill you in a massed attack. And when I lose you I might as well be dead. There will be no comfort left when you have met your doom – nothing but grief. I have no father, no mother, now . . . I had seven brothers too at home. In one day all of them went down to Hades' House. The great Achilles of the swift feet killed them all.

But Hector replies as a hero:

> If I hid myself like a coward and refused to fight, I could never face the Trojans and the Trojan ladies in their trailing gowns. Besides, it would go against the grain, for I have trained myself always, like a good soldier, to take my place in the front line and win glory for my father and myself. Deep in my heart I know the day is coming when holy Ilium will be destroyed . . . yet I am not so much distressed by the thought of what the Trojans will suffer, as by the thought of you, dragged off in tears by some Achaean man-at-arms to slavery. I see you there in Argos, toiling for some other woman at the loom, or carrying water from an alien well, a helpless drudge with no will of your own.[15]

Andromache's fears were realized, and her little son, once dazzled by his father's brilliant helmet with its horsehair plume, was thrown to his death from the walls of Troy.

The beautiful sculpture in Figure 6 is carved in the iconographic tradition of a son–lover parting from the Mother Goddess, his consort. The relation between the man with the staff or spear and the seated woman with the tiny child at her feet recalls the scene in which Hector bids farewell for the last time to Andromache. The artist has given the 'dog' beneath the woman's chair the features of a lion, suggestive of the goddess on her lion throne, an image that would have been well known to the culture of ancient Greece.

The Assyrian king Tiglath Pileser III (745–727 BC) was the first to institute the wholesale transplantation of populations; in Babylonia, which was conquered by Assyria in 745 BC, as many as thirty-five different tribal groups were broken up and transferred elsewhere. Shalmaneser V followed his father's example when he dispersed the ten tribes of Israel throughout the Assyrian Empire in 721 BC. Many thousands of people journeyed away from lands that for centuries had been their home only to arrive at places totally unknown to them, where they were forced to live among strangers. Wherever a population was deported, another was trans-

Figure 6. Husband parting from wife and family; marble sculpture, *c*. fifth century BC.

ferred to the vacated lands. If it happened to be the policy of particular kings to leave no living thing in the cities they conquered, then the whole people were put to death. The politics of massacre can be followed from the late Babylonian monarchs, through the Assyrian Empire, to the Persians and then the Hebrews as they conquered the land of Canaan. The 'lost' ten northern tribes of Israel were among the many thousands of people who were transplanted by the Assyrians to areas unfamiliar to them, where they were forced to settle or die.[16] Countless were the men and women who must have lamented their fate in a strange land, as the Hebrews did in Babylon during their exile there from 586 to 538 BC:

> By the rivers of Babylon, there we sat down, yea, we wept, when we remembered Zion.
> We hanged our harps upon the willows in the midst thereof.
> For there they that carried us away captive required of us a song; and they that wasted us required of us mirth, saying, 'Sing us one of the songs of Zion.'
> How shall we sing the Lord's song in a strange land? (Ps. 137:1-4)

The Persian king Cyrus, who restored the exiled Jewish people to their lands in 538 BC, stands out like a saviour from the general pattern of cruelty, and was gratefully praised by Persian, Jew and Greek alike for his clemency and tolerance of different religious beliefs. Isaiah saw Cyrus as the agent of a divine historical intention whom Yahweh would reward for his righteousness: 'And I will give thee the treasures of darkness, and hidden riches of secret places, that thou mayest know that I, the Lord, which call thee by thy name, am the God of Israel' (Isa. 45:3). Under the great majority of rulers, however, the climate in which people struggled to survive and bring up their children was one not of trust but of fear.

Brutalized people create brutal gods and goddesses, or, in Harrison's phrase: 'Man makes his demons in the image of his own irrational passions.'[17] The increasing barbarism that reached a crescendo as Assyria came down upon its neighbours – 'like the wolf on the fold'[18] – was reflected in the fate of some of the ancient gods. An, once the supreme god of Sumeria, is flayed alive. Enlil, who had once overshadowed even An in power, has his eyes put out. Ishtar, now primarily a goddess of war, says to Esarhaddon, ruler of Assyria, 'I am Ishtar of Arbela. I will flay your enemies and present them to you.'[19] Brutal gods and goddesses in turn endorse the brutality of men: Sennacherib, King of Assyria (704–681 BC), recording his conquest of Babylon, wrote without shame:

> I left not a single one young or old, with their corpses I filled the city's broad streets . . . The belongings of that city: silver, gold, precious stones, effects, belongings, I counted as my people's share and they took them for their own. The gods living in its midst the hands of my people seized and smashed, taking their effects and belongings.[20]

Erra, the Assyrian god of death, riot and indiscriminate slaughter, unheard of in earlier times, becomes supremely important in the later pantheon. There is even a new epic composed about him with the chilling words:

> Respect no god! Fear no man!
> Put to death young and old alike,
> the suckling and the babe – leave not anyone![21]

Sennacherib's grandson, Assurbanipal (668–626 BC), who was so justly proud of his library, could yet celebrate Erra's devastation with the words:

> . . . I now – as a funerary offering to him (Sennacherib) – ploughed those people under alive. Their flesh I fed to the dogs, pigs, vultures, eagles – the birds of heaven and the fish of the deep . . . I took the corpses of the people whom Erra had laid low and who had laid down their lives through hunger and famine; . . . those bones (I took) out of Babylon, Kutha and Sippar and threw them on heaps.[22]

He was later to immolate himself with his books rather than be taken captive alive by the conquering Babylonians and Medes, for with the conquest of the Assyrian capital, Nineveh, the Assyrians, who had lived by the sword, also died by the sword. Eduard Meyer sounds their epitaph: 'Practically the entire people who for centuries had been the scourge and horror of the nations was annihilated . . . No people has ever been more completely wiped out than the Assyrians.'[23]

Not surprisingly, the Babylonian, Assyrian and some aspects of the Hebrew religion became deeply fatalistic and a host of demons haunted the minds of the people by day and by night, obliging the continuous offering of propitiatory rites to different deities in order to be saved from their malice. The more people lost touch with the values that had instinctively guided them in an earlier era, the more they became possessed by the passion of the *furor bellicus*, the rage to kill, and the bloodthirstiness of their gods corresponds to this possession.

THE HERO MYTH

Everywhere in Iron Age art and literature there appears the same myth of the solar hero conquering the dragon or serpent, who is the embodiment of chaos, evil and death. This suggests that there has been a fundamental change of consciousness from the earlier era, when death and life were perceived as phases of a lunar totality. Eliade comments on this change:

> The moon confers a religious valorization on cosmic becoming and re-conciles man to death. The sun, on the contrary, reveals a different mode of existence. The sun does not share in becoming; although always in motion, the sun remains unchangeable; its form is always the same. Solar hiero-phanies give expression to the religious values of autonomy and power, of sovereignty, of intelligence. This is why, in certain cultures, we witness a process of solarization of the supreme beings . . .
>
> Many heroic mythologies are solar in structure. The hero is assimilated to the sun; like the sun, he fights darkness, descends into the realm of death and emerges victorious. Here darkness is no longer, as it is in lunar myth-ologies, one of the modes of being of divinity; instead, it symbolizes all that the god *is not*, hence the adversary *par excellence*. Darkness is no longer valorized as a necessary phase in cosmic life; in the perspective of solar religion, it is opposed to life, to forms, and to intelligence. In some cultures the luminous epiphanies of solar gods become the sign of intelligence. In the end *sun* and *intelligence* will be assimilated to such a degree that the solar and syncretistic theologies of the end of antiquity become rationalistic philos-ophies; the sun is proclaimed to be the intelligence of the world.[24]

Hero myths may have had their origin in the constant observation of the ceaseless passage of the sun through the heavens and its disappearance at night.[25] Sometimes the journey of the sun god was conceived as a boat crossing the great sea of the sky, just as the moon was once imagined as a lighted boat crossing a sea of darkness. As shown in Chapter 6, Figure 24, the Egyptian sun god, Ra, is drawn in his barque through the sky, and every night he must defeat the huge serpent-demon Apophis, image of the darkness of the darkest hour of night, which threatens to swallow up the sun at the furthest point of his journey.

The new mythic image of the Iron Age is that of the solar hero god who confronts and kills the devouring dragon of darkness and chaos.[26] As suggested in Chapter 4, this seems to appear as primarily a warrior myth at the time when Indo-European (Aryan) culture established itself in Mesopotamia, Persia, India and Greece. It is also found in Canaan, which was predominantly settled by Semitic rather than Aryan peoples. Hebrew, Persian and Greek culture were all deeply influenced by the oppositional paradigm of the *Enuma Elish*.

The Canaanite Baal, son of 'the Bull El', father of the gods, was the slayer of the serpent, but he was also a fertility god, who brought rain from heaven. Like Marduk, the lightning bolt was his weapon, and the bull was the animal that embodied his creative power on earth.[27] Drought was the great natural enemy of the Canaanites, as flood was of the Sumerians. Baal's descent into the underworld caused the death of the crops, and his rescue by Anat, his sister and consort, regenerated them. Like Tammuz, who also goes into the underworld, Baal continued to be the dying and resurrected son–lover of the goddess. Anat, his sister–wife, goddess of the dew, went in search of him, 'desiring him as a cow doth her calf or a ewe her lamb'. His rescue involved a fierce battle between Anat and Mot, the god who personified drought, like the Egyptian Seth, and more generally sterility and the underworld. (The Hebrew word for death is *mot*.) Embedded in the tale is the image of the dragon-fight in which life battles against death, and light against darkness. But it is set here in the context of the annual regeneration of the earth's fertility. Baal's return from the underworld depends upon Anat's defeat of Mot. Mot, fighting back, says to Baal:

> Though thou didst smite Lotan the Primeval Serpent,
> And didst annihilate the Tortuous Serpent,
> The Close-coiling One of Seven Heads,
> Thou shalt wilt, ennervated, desolate,
> Eaten up; I myself shall consume thee.[28]

But when Anat found Mot, she winnowed him in a sieve, scorched him, ground him in a mill, scattered his flesh over the fields and gave him to the birds to eat, just as though she were sowing the seed. When Baal returns to life as the sprouting corn, 'the skies rain oil, the waddis run with honey',[29] and all the earth rejoices. Here, the hero myth abstracts part of the son–lover myth, isolating the image of life overcoming death.

The dragon fight is also found in Greece as the gods of light confront the dragons of dark. Zeus, who hurls thunder and lightning, has to overcome the dragon Typhaon, the monster with a hundred serpents' heads, youngest son of Gaia, Earth, before he can establish himself as the father of all the gods. Similarly, Zeus's youthful son, Apollo, the archer god with the golden bow, becomes oracular god of Delphi only after slaying the dragon of Earth, who ruled before him:

Whoever went to meet the she-dragon,
the day of death would carry him off,
until the lord Apollo,
who works from afar,
let fly at her his strong arrow.
Then, heavily, she lay there,
racked with bitter pain,
gasping for breath
and rolling about on the ground.
An unspeakable scream
came into being,
a more than mortal sound.
All over the wood
she writhed incessantly,
now here, now there,
and then
life left her,
breathing out blood.[30]

In the Old Testament Yahweh inherits much of the mythic structure of contest from Baal as well as from Marduk. His role in delivering his 'people' Israel out of Egypt is cast in the heroic model of the conquest of the forces of darkness by the light. So is his overcoming of 'Leviathan, the piercing serpent, even Leviathan that crooked serpent . . . the dragon that is in the sea' (Isa. 27:1). The raw imagery of physical struggle and ferocious combat dominates these passages, in which Yahweh is ostensibly 'stilling' Tehom, the Deep, whose name significantly comes from Tiamat:

Figure 7. Zeus slaying Typhon; Greek vase painting, *c.* 550–500 BC.

Thou dost rule the raging of Tehom;
When its waves rise, thou stillest them.
Thou didst crush Rahab like a carcass,
Thou didst scatter thy enemies with thy mighty arm. (Ps. 89:9–10)

Thou didst divide the sea by thy might;
Thou didst break the heads of the dragons on the waters.
Thou didst crush the heads of Leviathan,
Thou didst give him as food for the creatures of the wilderness.
  (Ps. 74:13–24)

The imagery of the dragon fight was transmitted through the Old Testament to Christianity, where it is re-enacted in the familiar story of the Saints Michael and George with their Dragons of Evil. The Babylonian sources of Michael's battle with Lucifer in the Apocalypse can be seen by substituting Marduk for Michael, Tiamat for the Devil, and her demonic host for the fallen angels:

And there was war in heaven: Michael and his angels fought against the dragon; and the dragon fought and his angels,
  And prevailed not; neither was their place found any more in heaven.
  And the great dragon was cast out, that old serpent, called the Devil, and Satan, which deceiveth the whole world: he was cast out into the earth, and his angels were cast out with him. (Rev. 12:7–9)

Who would now be able to recognize in the dragon the image of the old Mother Goddess? Few traces are left of the historical process through

Figure 8. St Michael and the Dragon; *c.* AD 1140. Tympanum of the Church of Saint-Michel d'Étraignes, Angoulême.

which she was transformed from creator into the enemy of her own creation. In the Anglo-Saxon epic *Beowulf*, in which the hero kills the great she-dragon of the depths and her son with her, the origins are still more obscure.

One way of interpreting the hero myth is historically, in terms of a sky god culture overcoming the mother goddess culture. But the myth suggests another level of meaning, more directly related to the psyche of that time. Symbolically, the struggle between hero and serpent-dragon represents the power of human consciousness to gain mastery of instinctual and unconscious patterns of behaviour, to rise 'out of nature' and, at the same time, out of tribal, collective attitudes and patterns of behaviour that endlessly repeat the unquestioned beliefs of the past. It symbolizes the need for individuals to separate from these collective responses by challenging the tribal values with their own vision. Where the hero myth is perceived in terms of the growth of consciousness, it becomes an inner quest for illumination. Here the conflict is not so much between good and evil, but rather one between a greater or a lesser understanding. The 'dragon' is then ignorance or unconsciousness, not so much chaos as the fear of it. This is one meaning of the 'conquest' of darkness by the light, where the aim of the hero is to master his own inner darkness – his fear, or the limitations of his knowledge, both, ultimately, the same thing. This idea is expressed in Persian Zoroastrianism, in which humanity's role was conceived as one of helping the light to establish itself against the power of darkness.

The heroic image of the solar god defeating the serpent-dragon stands as the creation of the human psyche at a time when this image of authority and power was required to establish order and meaning in an increasingly complex and disturbed society. The impact of Aryan gods on the goddess culture was in some respects catastrophic, but, in others, where the culture was able to some extent to assimilate them, it became intensely creative, especially where the new gods married the older goddesses, as happened in Greece. This fusion gave birth to a powerful sense of individuality and purpose articulated in the myths of heroes like Theseus, Jason, Hercules, the shining Perseus and the wily Odysseus. The solar hero sets out on a quest for a treasure: the golden fleece, the golden apples of the Hesperides, or, with Odysseus, the journey to 'home', all ultimately treasures of the soul, symbolized in *Gilgamesh* by the herb of immortality. But first, the quest involves overcoming a challenge: slaying the Minotaur, beheading the Medusa, bypassing a dragon – guardians of the threshold. Yet these heroes cannot reach the treasure with their rational minds, which sunder everything into opposites, but only with the help of the deeper instinctual levels of the psyche. These are characteristically personified as female – the ambiguous figures of Medea, Ariadne, Circe – that complexity of feeling and intuition often symbolized as the maiden tied to the dragon, so that both have to be encountered at once. In the legend of Jason and the Golden Fleece, Medea, the priestess, lulls the dragon to sleep, rather in the way that trusting the voice of intuition charms away fear:

> The monster in his sheath of horny scales rolled forward his interminable coils, like the eddies of black smoke that spring from smouldering logs and chase each other from below in endless convolutions. But as he writhed he saw the maiden take her stand, and heard her in her sweet voice invoking Sleep, the conqueror of the Gods, to charm him. She also called on the night-wandering queen of the world below to countenance her efforts. Jason from behind looked on in terror. But the giant snake, enchanted by her song, was soon relaxing the whole length of his serrated spine and smoothing out his multitudinous undulation, like a dark and silent swell rolling across a sluggish sea. Yet his grim head still hovered over them and the cruel jaws threatened to snap them up. But Medea, chanting a spell, dipped a fresh sprig of juniper in her brew and sprinkled his eyes with her most potent drug; as the all-pervading magic scent spread round his head, sleep fell on him. Stirring no more, he let his jaw sink to the ground, and his innumerable coils lay stretched out far behind, spanning the deep wood. Medea called to Jason and he snatched the Golden Fleece from the oak.[31]

In this legend it is only with the help of Medea that the hero can overcome the serpent coiled around the tree that holds the golden fleece, just as Theseus can overcome the Minotaur and return from the labyrinth only with the help of Ariadne. So, also, Perseus can vanquish Medusa only with the help of the eye of the three ancient wise women, the Graeae. Odysseus, throughout his long journey back to Ithaca, is guided by the goddess Athena, whose presence is fully revealed only when he is finally reunited with Penelope, his wife. His 'initiations' are given by two semi-divine women, Calypso and Circe. Historically, the hero may have been a

Figure 9. Jason seizing the Golden Fleece, protected by the goddess Athena; detail of vase painting by the Orchard painter, *c.* 470–460 BC.

king, who, in the older goddess culture, held the throne as the son–lover of the goddess. But now this imagery is extended. The hero becomes the son–lover who can accomplish his task only with the help of his 'mother', the goddess, who in many tales becomes his bride. In Medea, Ariadne, Athena and also Penelope, who nightly unweaves what she has woven by day, the lineaments of the ancient goddess are revealed. These female figures personify the older layers of consciousness that have to be sought out by the hero, who cannot reach his goal without them. Where the image of the feminine is dramatized only as evil, as in the Old Testament, the transforming power of the wisdom stored in the archaic experience of the psyche – the 'mother' – is unavailable, and the 'hero-son' is left without guidance or inspiration. Only his fragile rationality remains to confront the terrifying image of the father who demands to be obeyed. The natural response to this image is fear, which obstructs understanding and change.

Turning to the many images of the hero slaying the dragon, it is the dragon who is ultimately the hero's own fear, just as the hero personifies the state of mind that can overcome fear. The hero myth as a symbolic drama of inner conflict is then valid in any age, for men and women, whenever and wherever the situation of unconscious bondage to fear prevails. Jung writes:

> In myths the hero is the one who conquers the dragon, not the one who is devoured by it . . . Also, he is no hero who never met the dragon, or who, if he once saw it, declared afterwards that he saw nothing. Equally, only one who has risked the fight with the dragon and is not overcome by it, wins the hoard, the 'treasure hard to attain.' He alone has a genuine claim to self-confidence, for he has faced the dark ground of his self and thereby has gained himself. This experience gives him faith and trust, the *pistis* in the ability of the self to sustain him, for everything that menaced him from inside he has made his own . . . He has arrived at an inner certainty which makes him capable of self-reliance, and attained what the alchemists called the *unio mentalis*.[32]

THE GREAT FATHER GOD

The drive for power as well as the ever-present fear of being attacked goes far to explain the need for an ever more powerful – eventually a 'supreme' – god who would unite his people in a common cause of defence or attack. This god was everywhere a sky-father, ruling from the heights of heaven, where all things can be seen, foreseen and overseen, and where the minute particulars of earthly life are diminished before the vast planetary scope of space.

The rise of sky gods with solar powers can be followed in Babylonia, Anatolia, Persia, Canaan and Greece, and the same rise to power of father gods may have taken place in Vedic India. These gods were originally the sky gods of the Aryan invaders. Their weapons were fire, wind and storm, the lightning bolt and the thunder's roar. Marduk, Assur, El, Baal, Yahweh and Zeus probably personify those very forces that the Palaeolithic hunters held in awe. But now the hunter has become a warrior and his gods, accordingly, have become the mightiest warriors, armed with the great sky powers of nature. The supremacy of sky gods is assured by a male priesthood, in India, Persia and Hebrew Canaan, as later in Christian and Islamic cultures.

Possibly as a result of the predominance of the sky-father god, there appeared in Persian mythology (*c.* 600–400 BC) a different idea of time. No longer was time conceived as cyclical on the lunar model of the mother goddess, who received the dead back into the darkness of her womb for rebirth in the next crescent. Since the father god could not take the dead back into himself nor return them to the earth for rebirth (though, in Egypt, he could take them with him into the heavens as stars), time for humanity became linear: it had a beginning with birth and an end with death. Similarly, when raised to cosmic proportion, creation itself had an absolute beginning and would have an absolute end, and this would coincide with the final triumph of light over dark, an ultimate statement of the original victory that had brought the universe into being.

These ideas may have been absorbed by the Hebrews who remained in Babylon and so came under the influence of the Persians after the end of the Babylonian captivity. History was seen as a linear unfolding in time of the intention of the creator god, who was necessarily outside or beyond time and creation. These ideas were in strong contrast to the immense aeonic cycles conceived in the goddess cultures, but they were the inevitable corollary to the new idea that human life had a beginning and a final end, and that death did not ultimately lead 'round' again to rebirth. (This linear model may still underlie the twentieth century's scientific 'creation myth' of a 'big bang' as the beginning of life and may also inform contemporary dread about an apocalyptic 'big bang' at the end.)

Iron Age mythology follows the transformation of the young god, once the son–lover of the goddess and himself god of fertility, into the sky-father god. As the solar image of the god brightens, so the lunar image of the goddess is eclipsed. The gods become the bearers of Light, Authority, Law and Justice. Like the terrible goddess of the Bronze Age, they also wage war. They are the progenitors of humanity, their servant, 'making' it from blood, dust, clay and breath, according to their word. The myth of the father god in the later Iron Age is explored chiefly through two gods, Zeus and Yahweh, whose mythic images have surprisingly little in common. Zeus, the father god of Greek mythology, is known and loved for his relationships with his goddess wife, his divine and mortal lovers, and his daughters and sons. The god of Hebrew mythology, Yahweh–Elohim, on the other hand, has no formally recognized relationship with any goddess whatever, and so no relation with nature even as a force with which to deal. The dragon-monster who was Tiamat is distanced and abstracted in Genesis into Tehom, a formless void. So while much of the mythic imagery of Marduk, El and Baal, and especially their habitation in mountain top, cloud, lightning and thunder, is inherited by the Hebrew god, their relationships with mothers, wives, sisters and brothers are not.[33] Yahweh is a tribal god and rules his tribe alone. Yet it is he who gradually becomes the only, the supreme and universal father god of Judaism, Christianity and Islam.

The continuing myth of Marduk's conquest of Tiamat in many lands shows that people no longer feel themselves to be the child of the Mother but the child of the Father. Nature is no longer experienced as source but as adversary, and darkness is no longer a mode of divine being, as it was in the lunar cycles, but a mode of being devoid of divinity and actively hostile, devouring of light, clarity and order. The only place where the voice of the old order breaks through, though so disguised as to be barely recognizable, is where the inspiration of poetry re-animates the old mythic images. John Phillips, in his book *Eve: The History of an Idea*, comments:

> The Old Testament cannot suggest that there are other divinities with whom humanity might have to deal; there is only God. Nevertheless, what is not permissible as doctrine is allowed to be expressed in the poetry of ancient liturgy, where it serves to remind us of Yahweh's power. Yahweh continually struggles against evil personified as female forces and powers: Tehom (Tiamat), Rahab, and Leviathan (Lothan), all names for the chaotic dragon in Mesopotamian and Canaanite tradition.[34]

It is upon this foundation that the Levite priesthood of Israel con-structed its doctrine of pure monotheism with the image of the sole Father God, King of kings and God of gods. No apparent trace of the goddess and her son–lover remained to challenge it, although in other cultures this myth continued to live, however obscurely. Doctrinally (but only doctrinally), the drama of conflict with the goddess is finished: the supreme Father is One.

GODDESSES OF GREECE:
GAIA, HERA, ARTEMIS AND
ATHENA

What, with us, crops up only in dreams and fantasies was once either conscious custom or general belief. But what was once strong enough to mould the spiritual life of a highly developed people will not have vanished without a trace from the human soul in the course of a few generations. We must remember that a mere eighty generations separate us from the Golden Age of Greek culture. And what are eighty generations? They shrink to an almost imperceptible span when compared with the enormous stretch of time that separates us from Neanderthal or Heidelberg man.

C. G. Jung

Returning to Bronze Age Crete, the myth of the goddess managed to survive the revisioning and diminishing that took place all over the mainlands of the Near and Middle East, perhaps because Crete was an island, perhaps because the goddess had been the inspiration of the whole culture. For the Great Goddess of Minoan and Mycenaean Crete was not lost with the final disintegration of Minoan and Mycenaean culture in 1200 BC, and after a 'dark age' of some 400 years she re-emerges in Greece – not as the supreme power she once was, but as an underlying reality whose presence in many spheres of life could not be ignored. Goddesses and gods, with their hands raised in the Minoan epiphany gesture, began to appear in Greece from the eighth century BC, and even a serpent goddess surfaced in Athens, as though for the human psyche 400 years had been but a day.

Indo-European tribes had been invading the land of Greece from as early as 2500 BC, but according to Egyptian records the destruction of Minoan and Mycenaean culture in Crete and mainland Greece was the work of an unknown people, whom they called the 'Sea Peoples'. The Ionians, Achaeans and, finally, the Dorians followed in their wake, eventually gaining supremacy over the whole of Greece and, much later, the islands. They brought with them a patriarchal social order, a cosmology of sky, sun and storm, whose ruler was the Great Father God Zeus, who hurled the Lightning and Thunderbolt. What they found was a deeply rooted religion of goddess worship that had evolved peacefully over the millennia from the Neolithic past.

Figure 1. Enthroned Mother Goddess holding child; *c.* 700 BC. Boeotia, Greece.

During the Dark Age – between 1200 and 800 BC – there were no new stone buildings of any size, no pictures or sculptures, not even simple clay figures, but much was preserved, particularly in Crete and Cyprus and in Boeotia on the mainland, where many Mycenaeans emigrated. Boeotia lies between Delphi and Athens, and some of the earliest and most eloquent images of the goddess come from there, recalling instantly the art and vision of Minoan and Mycenaean Crete, as in Figure 1. The bird-beaked face and the falling and zigzag lines down the front of her robe and throne – perhaps the currents of rainfall – are reminiscent, too, of Old Europe.

It must have been the oral tradition of songs and story-telling that kept the tradition alive, as it had done for countless thousands of years before that, and this is one of the reasons why the original goddess culture has to be pieced together from later fragments, relying on implications, juxtapositions, contradictions and allusions to a different kind of order. As in the Classical Greek myth of Theseus and the Minotaur, the older and much longer-lasting pre-Hellenic civilization can be glimpsed beneath the surface of the Olympian myths, at once informing, complicating and disrupting them. The earliest songs of the goddesses and gods that were written down in the eighth century BC are called the Homeric Hymns, a name reflecting the absence in contemporary knowledge of any name but Homer, while recognizing a common source of mythic inspiration between the hymns and the *Odyssey* and the *Iliad* (though the *Odyssey* has an orientation quite different in feeling from the *Iliad*, most particularly in the dignity and authority it accords to the older goddess culture).

The hymn to Pythian Apollo, for instance, tells how he searched all over the earth looking for a place to build a temple for his oracle, and could not find one. When he reaches Telphusa, the place of the goddess of the flowing waters, and at last begins to lay out his stone foundations, she is outraged in her heart and persuades him to move on. But once he has slain the she-dragon (see Chapter 7, pp. 291–2), he realizes Telphusa has tricked him and heaves a mountain top over her sacred streams, and his stone temple covers them up. The sacrifice of the old to the new order is registered here, and, ironically, the people Apollo chooses to be his priests and announce his laws are Cretans from Minoan Knossos, whose understanding of the laws of life is born of the goddess culture Apollo has replaced. In this way, access to the past is kept open. As the Greek scholar Walter Burkert comments: 'Greek religion is rooted in the Minoan-Mycenaean age and yet not to be equated with it.'[1] Another hymn, entitled simply 'To the Mother of the Gods', directly recalls Minoan mountain rituals: the goddess addressed loves the sound of drums, flutes and castanets all echoing in the hills to the howling of wolves and the crying of bright-eyed lions, testimony to the older stratum of thought whose ancient rhythms still sounded recognizably through the measured steps of the Olympian dance (see Chapter 10, pp. 393–4).

The myths in Homer and Hesiod characteristically place the origins of Greek goddesses and gods in Crete: either they were born there, as Zeus and Dionysos, or came from there, as Demeter, or lived there all the time under a different name, as Diktynna and Britomartis for Artemis. This, in the language of legend, is the evidence of a cultural transmission that must have occurred over many centuries, as Minoans and Mycenaeans sailed across the wine-dark sea, landing at Cyprus, Rhodes, Kos, Delos, Boeotia, and many other shores, bringing the old life to the new place.

Tracing the continuity from Minoan and Mycenaean culture, the original Great Mother Goddess has become many separate goddesses related to each other, as though they each personify a different aspect of her totality. As always, the images tell the story: the snakes fall to Athena, Demeter, Hera and Hygeia, the corn and poppies to Demeter and Persephone, the birds to Athena, Demeter and Aphrodite, and the dove in particular to Aphrodite and Persephone. The lions, stags and animals of the wild belong to Artemis, and the dog to Hecate. The olive tree is Athena's gift to the people of Athens, and the fruit-bearing trees and the corn are the province of Demeter. All the Greek goddesses are moon goddesses: Persephone the maiden and Artemis the virgin personify the new moon, Demeter and Hera, as mother or fulfilled wife, personify the full moon, and Hecate of the underworld personifies the waning and dark moon. The Minoan bee goddesses are found in the three bee maidens, the seers who taught Apollo to prophesy, and the grape and the vine are taken over by Dionysos. The Mycenaean helmet and shield become Athena's as patron of the city, also a moon goddess, as is Selene with her white arms and flashing horses. The Minoan sacred marriage ceremonies of the lunar cow and the solar bull are re-enacted in 'cow-eyed' Hera with her consort, Zeus, the bull. The distinctive difference is made by Zeus, who is no longer the child upon the mother's knee or the young god saluting the goddess, but is now the Great Father of all the goddesses and gods.

At its finest, Greek mythology can be seen as the working out of a right relationship between the dynamic sky and sun gods of the invading Indo-Europeans and the older lunar agricultural stratum of the pre-Hellenic goddess culture that had been established for many millennia. At its less fine, however, as Jane Harrison has consistently argued, Classical mythology, with its emphasis on conquest and war, displays a debasement and trivialization of the vision of the conquered culture, which does no justice to a way of life that was founded on an innate harmony with nature.[2] At a superficial glance, for instance, the great goddess Hera becomes a jealous vengeful wife; Aphrodite, the awesome goddess of fertility, becomes the frivolous winner of a beauty contest; Athena, goddess of the snake and shield, becomes the masculinized daughter of intellect, born through the forehead of Zeus as though she were exclusively the product of his own creative mind; Pandora, who rose from the earth with gifts for all, becomes (like Eve) the source of human toil, pain and death; and Artemis, untameable goddess of the wild animals, shrinks in stature beside her brother, Apollo, whose golden arrows of light slay the shadows from far away. But, looking more closely, the powers of the goddesses were not to be dismissed so easily. Although inevitably much of the indigenous culture was lost with the successions of invasions, the spirit of that culture, woven into new cloth, tells of a tradition that endured in spite of a change of form. So to restore the balance between the pre-Hellenic and the Olympian mythic visions it is essential to discern the different layers of thought that compose the finished version of the stories we know.

GAIA

Hymn to Gaia

Gaia
mother of all
foundation of all
the oldest one

I shall sing to Earth

She feeds everything
that is in the world

Whoever you are
whether you live upon her sacred ground
or whether you live along the paths of the sea
you that fly

it is she
who nourishes you
from her treasure-store

Queen of Earth
through you

beautiful children
beautiful harvests
come

The giving of life
and the taking of life

both are yours

Happy is the man you honour
the one who has this
has everything

His fields thicken with ripe corn
his cattle grow heavy in the pastures
his house brims over with good things

These are the men who are masters of their city
the laws are just, the women are fair
happiness and fortune richly follow them

Their sons delight
in the ecstasy of youth

Their daughters play
they dance among the flowers
skipping in and out

they dance on the grass
over soft flowers

Holy goddess, you
honoured them
ever-flowing spirit

Farewell
mother of the gods
bride of Heaven
sparkling with stars

For my song, life
allow me
loved of the heart

Now
and in my other songs
I shall remember you[3]

As though in answer to our present crisis of environment (a term describing nature that means merely 'round about'), the name of Gaia is now everywhere heard. There is the 'Gaia Hypothesis' of the physicist James Lovelock, which proposes that the planet Earth is a self-regulating system; there is 'Gaia Consciousness', which urges that the Earth and her creatures be considered as one whole; and there is simply the term 'Gaia', which expresses a reverence for the planet as a being who is alive and on whom all other life depends. Underlying this phenomenon is the idea that only a personification of the Earth can restore a sacred identity to it, or rather, her, so that a new relationship might become possible between humans and the natural world we take for 'granted'.

It is no coincidence that the twentieth century returns to the Greek mind to formulate this experience, for in the West the last Goddess of Earth was Gaia. And although in Classical mythology the goddess no longer held the status of the supreme mother of all living, as she did in Minoan, Sumerian and Neolithic times, Earth remained, even in philosophy, a living being – *zoon* is Plato's term. This is the consciousness that was to be lost with the Judaeo-Christian heritage, which can be seen most obviously in the way in which we treat the Earth as if 'it' were dead matter. Less obvious, but none the less crucial, is the fact that Mary, the unrecognized mother goddess of the Christian Church, has formally acquired all the attributes of the old mother goddesses *except* that of Goddess of Earth.

However, by the eighth century BC the reality of the one mother goddess had become historical; the original unity of earth and heaven was lost in the legend of the beginning. Hesiod, writing, like Homer, close to the end of the Dark Age in *c.* 700 BC, evokes this time as a memory of his mother's, suggesting, perhaps, how the goddess culture was remembered in stories told for generations, as it were, at the mother's knee: 'Not from me, but from my mother, comes the tale of how earth and sky were once one form.'[4] But now, because the one goddess had differentiated into many goddesses, and because the gods now ruled beside them and often in their place, a different way of relating to the universe had begun.

In the Homeric Hymn above, Gaia is still invoked as 'Mother of all', but she has also become 'bride of starry Heaven', and no mention is made of the fact that in other myths Ouranos, Heaven, was once her child, as was everyone else whom she brought forth from herself. Here, she is the one who feeds everything in the world; she gives life and she takes it away. Aeschylus echoes the hymn:

> Yea, summon Earth, who brings all things to life
> and rears and takes again into her womb.[5]

Although formally she was now subject to the law of Zeus, in practice her oracles were persistently consulted through her priestesses, sitting in the hot sun beside cracks in the earth. And the later gods of Delphi – Poseidon, Dionysos and Apollo – never forgot that she was 'there' first. The priestess of Apollo, the Pythia (named after Python, the he-dragon Apollo slew), would always open the Delphic rituals with an invocation to Gaia:

> I give first place of honour in my prayer to her
> who of the gods first prophesied, the Earth.[6]

In the face in Figure 2 the distinction of character is subsumed in the idea of origin; in modern terminology, the very absence of particularity makes her seem the most 'archetypal' of all the goddesses. The flat and heavy stillness of her face evokes the Indo-European name for the goddess Earth, *Plataea*, 'the Broad One', and, despite the slow curls of the hair, there is an androgynous feeling, drawing us back to the pre-Hellenic sensibility and also into the land of beginnings, which is, of course, nowhere. Following a tradition historically, it is easy to lose the balance between the two perspectives of what happens and what always is. Myths are not history, yet they manifest in time and create history and so are clothed in the language of becoming and change. Myth, in Joseph Campbell's evocative phrase, 'is the secret opening through which the inexhaustible energies of the cosmos pour into human cultural manifestation'.[7]

Returning to this particular moment on the cultural continuum, the time is one in which the direction of energy has shifted from Gaia to her great-grandson, Zeus, the cloud-gatherer, who, with muscular tautness and undeviating purpose, aims his lightning bolt (see p. 317). As had happened when Babylonian culture met the older Sumerian one, stories of the origin of the world and of humanity also changed in relation to the new order of priorities. In Greece this resulted in four main myths of creation

Figure 2. Gaia, Goddess of Earth; late third–early second century BC.
Paleokastro, Crete.

– the Pelasgian, the Homeric, the Orphic and the Olympian – and they all, in different ways, reflect the transition from the great goddess to the god.

The Pelasgian creation myth (named after the indigenous people of north Greece, the Pelasgians) begins with the Goddess of All Things, called Eurynome, a name that means 'wide-wandering' like the moon. She rose naked out of Chaos, but found nothing substantial for her feet to rest upon, so she divided the sea from the sky, and, lonely on the waves, she danced the world into being. She danced towards the south and the wind was set in motion behind her, like something new and apart with which to start the work of creation. Catching hold of this north wind, she rubbed it between her hands and it became a great serpent, Ophion, who, made lusty by her dancing, coupled with her, making her pregnant with Life. Then, taking the form of a dove, she laid the Universal Egg on the waters. At her bidding, Ophion, the serpent, coiled seven times round the egg until it hatched and split into two, letting out her children, who are everything that exists: sun, moon, planets, stars, the earth with its rivers, mountains, trees, herbs and living creatures. Then she created the seven planetary powers, putting a male and female Titan over each of them. The first man was called Pelasgos, who sprang from the soil of Arcadia, and was the ancestor of the Pelasgians.[8] In the words of the poet Asius:

> Divine Pelasgos on the wood-clad hills
> Black Earth brought forth, that mortal man might be.[9]

The Homeric creation myth in the *Iliad* is similar to the Pelasgian, but the order of coming into being is reversed. It begins with Oceanus, the stream that girdles the world (as did Ophion), and names Tethys as the 'mother of his children', who, like Eurynome, reigns over the sea. This resembles the Babylonian Apsu and Tiamat as the original pair.[10]

In the Orphic myth the goddess and the wind are again the primary images of the archetypal feminine and masculine principles. Here, the goddess of black-winged Night united with the Wind and laid a silver egg in the womb of Darkness. Out of this egg came golden-winged Eros (Love) – whom some call Phanes, the 'revealer' – who then set the universe in motion. Eros lived in a cave with the goddess Night, who was also Order and Justice. Outside the cave sat Rhea, drumming, calling to humanity to listen to the oracles of the triple goddess. Though Eros or Phanes created earth, sky, sun and moon, the triple goddess ruled the universe until her sceptre passed to Ouranos.[11]

In Hesiod's *Theogony*, in which the Olympian version of creation is found, Gaia is only the first to emerge from Chaos, together with Eros, and so Chaos, not the Mother, is implicitly named as the source. Chaos produced Night and Erebos (the Underworld), and from the union of Night and Erebos came Day and Space. As though independent of these structuring principles, Gaia gives birth to what is visible, to what we call Nature:

> Chaos was first of all, but next appeared
> Broad-bosomed Earth, sure standing place for all
> The gods who live on snowy Olympus' peak,
> And misty Tartarus, in a recess
> Of broad-pathed earth, and Love, most beautiful
> Of all the deathless gods. He makes men weak,
> He overpowers the clever mind, and tames
> The spirit in the breasts of men and gods.
> From Chaos came black Night and Erebos.
> And Night in turn gave birth to Day and Space
> Whom she conceived in love to Erebos.
> And Earth bore starry Heaven, first, to be
> An equal to herself, to cover her
> All over, and to be a resting-place,
> Always secure, for all the blessed gods.
> Then she brought forth long hills, the lovely homes
> Of goddesses, the Nymphs who live among
> The mountain clefts. Then without pleasant love
> She bore the barren sea with its swollen waves,
> Pontus. And then she lay with Heaven, and bore
> Deep-whirling Oceanus and Koios; then
> Kreius, Iapetos, Hyperion,
> Theia, Rhea, Themis, Mnemosyne,
> Lovely Tethys, and Phoebe, golden-crowned.
> Last, after these, most terrible of sons,

> The crooked-scheming Chronos came to birth
> Who was his father's vigorous enemy.[12]

Only after Gaia has created the sea does she unite with Ouranos, Heaven, her first son, and together they bring forth the forms of nature with precise and familiar names, those who have become goddesses and gods. After this, a fascinating variation of the mother goddess and son–lover myth can be glimpsed. In Crete, as we have seen, the sacrifice of the son–lover, or his substitute the bull or sometimes the tree, was required for the renewal of seasonal fertility. Here, the process of creation is arrested until the son–lover, Ouranos, is castrated, and it is this act of genital sacrifice that inaugurates the rule of Chronos, the beginning of time – the meaning of his name. In other words, the myth is here an exploration of how time, as it were, got going; in the primitive way in which thinking still happens, this is the perennially unanswered question: how did it begin?

What happened was this. Gaia and Ouranos gave birth to three mighty and violent giants, who were insolent and ugly, with fifty heads and a hundred arms. Ouranos, their father, hated them as soon as they were born and hid them in a secret hiding-place so that they would not see the light. This strained and stretched Gaia, vast as she was, and she groaned mightily. So she thought of a clever 'evil' plan. She brought forth grey iron and formed a huge sickle with great teeth, and then she urged her sons to repay their father's crime. It was Chronos who took up the challenge on his mother's behalf, and carried out the plot she had devised:

> Great Heaven came, and with him brought the night.
> Longing for love, he lay around the Earth,
> Spreading out fully. But the hidden boy
> Stretched forth his left hand; in his right he took
> The great long jagged sickle; eagerly
> He harvested his father's genitals
> And threw them off behind. They did not fall
> From his hands in vain, for all the bloody drops
> That leaped out were received by Earth; and when
> The year's time was accomplished, she gave birth
> To the Furies, and the Giants, strong and huge,
> Who fought in shining armour, with long spears,
> And the nymphs called Meliae on the broad earth.[13]

This story is amazingly similar to the *Enuma Elish*, where Apsu, the original father, once the son and now the husband of Tiamat, is disturbed by the clamour of their children and plans to destroy them. Apsu is subsequently overthrown by Ea, one of the younger gods, just as here Ouranos is overthrown by Chronos. Yet there is a further echo from the ancient Babylonian past that circles around the same perplexing question:

how, and why, did ugly and destructive things come into being? In the *Enuma Elish* the elder brother of Ea, for no reason that is given, creates great winds that agitate Tiamat and she gives birth to a monster brood of poisonous serpents. The chief of these starts a war against the gods, who then themselves, under the leadership of Marduk, destroy Tiamat, their mother of origin; and creation, as it were, starts again.

In the Greek myth, similarly, no reason is offered for the fact that after creating so many beautiful things Gaia and Ouranos bear three violent sons with a terrible and ugly strength. However, in both myths their arrival signifies the end of the old order, with the significant difference that, probably in part because of the Minoan influence, the Mother Goddess Earth is not herself destroyed but, even in Olympian times, is still honoured as the source and the daily giver of food to everything living.[14]

It was Gaia who, in Hesiod's version, assisted Rhea, the mother of Zeus, to outwit Chronos, and so to inaugurate the next stage of Creation, when Time, it seemed, had stopped. For if Chronos (Time) were to swallow all his children, who would succeed him? She it was also who gave Zeus the thunderbolt and the lightning flash, which had never before left the inside of the Earth. So Earth was never forgotten as the source of all things, even of the sovereignty of Zeus. In this way the Greek mind, unlike our own, continued to honour Gaia as a living and sacred presence whose laws were written in the lives of all creation.

Consequently, Gaia's law – or Nature, as we might say – is related in Greek thought to the moral life of human nature. In other words, the order of nature was for the Greeks a moral order, and as such could be disturbed by the immoral behaviour of human beings. Hesiod, in his *Works and Days*, for instance, writes that when people are just, their city flourishes and they are free from famine and war: 'For them the earth brings forth food in plenty, and on the hills the oak tree bears acorns at the top and bees in the middle.'[15] In Sophocles' *Oedipus Rex* it is the protest of Nature that begins the drama of Oedipus's awakening to his killing of his father and his unconscious incest with his mother. The land of Thebes he rules begins to die:

> A blight is on the fruitful plants of the earth,
> A blight is on the cattle in the fields,
> A blight is on our women that no children
> are born to them.[16]

This was the original meaning of pollution. A human crime against the divine order had been committed. At the Delphic Oracle of Apollo:

> King Phoebus in plain words commanded us
> to drive out a pollution from our land,
> pollution grown ingrained within the land.[17]

'Redeem the debt of our pollution that lies on us because of this dead man',[18] Oedipus tells the blind Teiresias with inner sight, and when he discovers he is himself the unknown murderer of his father and leaves the city, the land starts to live again.

The symbolic relation of this story to the plight of our Earth must be obvious. Perhaps the Greek conviction that Nature is a moral being, suffering under human ignorance, is one that the return of Gaia to our language will help us to reconsider.

HERA

In Classical times Hera was known primarily as the wife of Zeus, to whom she came second; but in the sculpture in Figure 3 she stands over him in the manner of a great goddess with her arm raised, while he, clasping her wrist, leans backward and away from her, seated in the pose of the supplicant son–lover, as befits the younger brother that he is. In Olympia the temple to Hera existed long before the temple to Zeus, and there, reminiscent of Minoan seals, he stands in the form of a bearded and helmeted warrior beside the goddess enthroned.[19] As in Figure 3, the Olympic scene suggests that the god is the chosen one of the goddess, rather than the other way round, and also that the goddess was originally the Mistress of the Games. Though Hera and Zeus, sister and brother in

Figure 3. Hera and Zeus; metope, fifth century BC.
Temple of Hera, Sicily.

the Olympian pantheon, were officially 'married' in the Bronze Age – probably before the thirteenth century BC, since both names appear side by side in the Linear B tablets – her origins are far older than Zeus's.

Her name, which means the mistress, is not, like his, Indo-European, and the images of snakes, lions and water-birds that accompany her give her a more ancient lineage. Herodotus thought that Hera was taken over by the Greeks from the indigenous Pelasgians in northern Greece,[20] which would restore to her an original creative unity. Gimbutas suggests that, like Athena, with whom she frequently appears in legend, Hera may reach back to the Neolithic Snake Goddess who ruled the heavenly waters, and Homer and Plato both connected her name with the air.[21] In the *Iliad* she is called 'Queen of Heaven' and 'Hera of the Golden Throne'. She is also called the 'white-armed goddess', a romantic image of moonbeams spreading out through the night sky, as is Selene, who is herself formally described as the moon goddess. In fact, the three phases of the once Great Goddess of the Moon are still accorded to Hera (though now understood in patriarchally proper relation to her wifely role) in the form of three temples built to her in Stymphalos: the Girl, the Fulfilled and the Separated. The same lunar myth informs the ritual in which her statue was bathed in a spring every year, at the actual time of the new moon, to renew her maidenhood, so that she went to meet Zeus as it was in the beginning, symbolically virgin, one-in-herself like the reborn moon.

On the other hand, the epithet given Hera by Homer – *boophis*, meaning 'cow-eyed' – suggests that she was also a Goddess of Earth, who was everywhere personified from earliest times as a cow: the Sumerian Ninhursag and the Egyptian Hathor, for example, not to mention the nameless consorts of the great succession of fertilizing bulls, whose horns were shaped to the crescent moon. The demonic character of some of her children – the dragon Typhaon and the monster Hydra, to which monsters, in the manner of earth goddesses as seen by sky gods, she gives birth autonomously – tells the same tale. For once, in anger against her husband for producing Athena without her, Hera smote the Earth and called to Gaia and Ouranos. As she did so, Gaia, the source of life, quivered. Hera knew her wish was granted and, a year later, Typhaon was born. The name of Hera's dragon, who was sent to Delphi to the care of the dragoness Delphinus – later to be slain by Zeus's son of light, Apollo – is too similar to Typhaon, Gaia's youngest son, whom Zeus killed, not to speak of some essential connection between Gaia and Hera, presumably in their capacity as Goddesses of Earth. Again, fertile plains with herds of cattle were her home, and oxen were sacrificed at her temples. Goddess of Argos as well as Samos, she took over the Mycenaean temples and her cult spread throughout Greece, where she was worshipped as 'goddess of the yoke' and 'rich in oxen'. Ears of wheat were called the 'flowers of Hera' and sprinkled over the altars when cattle were sacrificed.

Figure 4. Hera as the Great Goddess, crowned, between two lions;
Cycladic clay relief pithos, *c.* 680–670 BC. Thebes.

In Figure 4, a pithos 4 feet (1.2 m) tall, the majestic Hera wears the crown of the Queen of the Gods, from which come snake-like branches hanging with grapes. Hera lifts up her arms in the gesture of epiphany, while two lions rise up towards her in the pose of the Minoan mountain goddess and the Mycenaean Gate, and two priestesses attend to her net-like robe, covered with dots that suggest at once seed sown in fields and stars sprinkled over the heavens. Beneath the neck of the vase is a procession of dappled deer with exquisitely fine heads. This is a figure who is queen in her own right, far from the portraiture of the petty wife in the *Iliad*.

In Boeotia a number of cities led by Plataea, the Earth Goddess, set up a special festival every sixtieth year as a marriage festival, complete with wooden figures of bride and bridesmaid, and had as its central sacrifice a cow for Hera and a bull for Zeus, all of which were finally burnt.[22] The sacred marriage rituals of Knossos come instantly to mind. Marriage ceremonies between Hera and Zeus were held in many places in Greece, re-enacting the old ritual marriage of Heaven and Earth, which blessed and regenerated life. Memories of the original Mystery Ritual of Sacred Marriage, rather than the quarrelsome couple that was so often depicted, are visible still in the description of their reunion in the *Iliad*, for when they are reunited all the earth flowers. And when Zeus takes Hera in his arms, a golden mist too thick for the sun to see through hides them:

> So speaking, the Son of Chronos caught his wife in his arms. There
> underneath them the divine earth broke into young, fresh
> grass, and into dewy clover, crocus and hyacinth
> so thick and soft it held the hard ground deep away from them.
> There they lay down together and drew about them a golden
> wonderful cloud, and from it the glimmering dew descended.
>   So the father slept unshaken on the peak of Gargaron
> with his wife in his arms, when sleep and passion had stilled him.[23]

It is as though this divine event, which once drew together the complementary principles of the universe, was secularized in patriarchal Greece to serve primarily as a model for the right ordering of society through due observance of the ceremony of marriage. (Greek women, it may be remembered, were, like slaves, excluded from democracy, with no right to vote, and rarely a right to the same education as their brothers and husbands.) Hera became the goddess of weddings and marriage, while love, beauty and desire fell to Aphrodite, the tending of the home to Hestia, goddess of the hearth, and childbirth and motherhood as well as maidenhood, to Artemis. 'You lie in the arms of Zeus'[24] became the emblem of Hera's authority, an ambivalent source of satisfaction for one who used to be goddess in her own right, as the tales of her rage at Zeus's freedom imply; for taken out of their marital context, and rendered back into the historical moment when those who were bound together in wedlock represented different and even mutually inconsistent ways of living in the universe, Hera's sense of injustice becomes clear as a refusal to submit to Zeus's terms of the merging of the two cultures. Though Hera often shared an altar with Zeus, the memory of her former independence was always present: he was not to forget that she was his elder sister, and even saved him as a tiny infant from the jaws of Chronos, since, in some tales, she brought him to Crete herself. All these stories, read symbolically, contribute to the sense of *mythological* protest at the yoke of marriage to an unequal partner. Otherwise, as Harrison asks: 'Is the tyrannous mistress really made by the Greek housewife even of Homeric days in her own image? The answer is clear: Hera has been forcibly married, but she is never really wife.'[25]

In one story even her marriage comes by subterfuge: during a thunderstorm in which Hera was separated from the other goddesses and gods, sitting alone on the mountain where her temple was later to be built, Zeus transforms himself into a cuckoo, wet and bedraggled from the rain, and settles in Hera's lap. Taking pity on the poor bird, she covers him with her robe, and Zeus reveals himself. Here, Zeus is drawn as the intruder who steals marriage, not the great god who claims it. Kerenyi comments: 'By this unique mythological creation Zeus is *precisely fitted into the history of the Hera religion of Argos*' [his italics].[26]

Figure 5. The Sacred Marriage of Hera and
Zeus; wood carving, *c.* late seventh century
BC. Possibly from Samos. The cuckoo, seen
from behind, is set between the heads of
Zeus and Hera as an image of their union,
while Zeus holds out Hera's breast rather in
the way that the goddess used to offer her
breast herself for the nourishment of the
world.

In the Olympianization of Hera, however, this is not the official story,
which was, instead, that she had two children by Zeus – Hephaestos and
Ares (according to Homer) – or one child – Ares (according to Hesiod) –
neither of whom was a success. Their offspring are not, in any case, what
one might expect from so divine a couple: the one ugly, misshapen and
vindictive (Hephaestos, the smith, hurled by Hera into the mountain,
who in turn imprisons her in a mechanical throne), and the other a
lawless, brazen coward (Ares, hated above all the gods by Zeus). Her
implacable pursuit of Zeus's liaisons and the children that were the fruit
of them turn her, in some parts of the *Iliad*, into a comic parody, the
model for the wicked stepmother, manipulating wife and the terrible
mother as seen by the dominant consciousness of an errant 'son', who in
turn revenges himself upon her.

To turn back to the unofficial story, the images of Zeus's rage against
her (reading beyond the secular 'Go to Hell') betray her ancient role as
Goddess of the Underworld:

> 'This is the way it is fated to be; and for you and your anger
> I care not; not if you stray apart to the undermost limits
> of earth and sea, where Iapetos and Kronos seated
> have no shining of the sun god Hyperion to delight them
> nor winds' delight, but Tartaros stands deeply about them.[27]

The slight allusion to a journey through the underworld becomes more
resonant in relation to Hera's role as goddess of the waning moon, the
stage of her relationship to Zeus called the 'separated', 'solitary' or

'widow'. Virgil's Juno, closely modelled on Hera, clarifies this: 'If I cannot bend the gods to my will, I shall move the underworld,'[28] she says, a sentiment echoed in a sculpture of her holding a pomegranate, like Persephone.[29] Between the lines of the Homeric passage, the missing dimension of the Great Goddess of the three realms of Heaven, Earth and Underworld is implicitly acknowledged.

Another hint of her former role as great goddess is made through her relation to the hero Heracles. His name means 'Glory to Hera', and the twelve labours she sets him symbolize the twelve months through which the sun 'labours' in his annual round. Though Heracles in the narrative undertakes these tasks unwillingly at the insistence of Hera (in her role as the Dark Goddess of the Waning Moon), yet the image of the servant or son–lover of the goddess implied in his name suggests that the old ritual of the sun uniting with the moon when she is full – when he has won her through his service – may lie behind the eventual tale. The image of Heracles as a grown man suckling at the breast of Hera, as is found in a picture on an Etruscan mirror, for instance,[30] recalls the pharaohs suckling at the breast of Isis in their role of son–lover to the goddess. The legend around this was that Zeus lulled Hera to sleep, and Hermes put Heracles to her breast, but – hero that he was – he bit it and awoke her, and as she thrust him off her milk spilled out over the heavens as the Milky Way.

ZEUS

By the time of Olympian mythology the picture of Hera cannot be brought fully to life without a separate consideration of her brother–husband Zeus: for though they were wedded, it was his rule that prevailed and she who belonged to him, while her virginal precedence receded into the distant pre-Olympian past. This is true of most of the Greek goddesses (except perhaps Gaia and Demeter), since their relationship to him is central for who they are and what they mean. Brother to Hera and Demeter, Zeus was father to Artemis, Athena and Persephone (Demeter's daughter), while Aphrodite is, in one myth, his daughter and, in another, daughter to his grandfather, Ouranos.

It was by marrying or fathering the goddesses that Zeus annexed or appropriated their powers to himself. As the Great Father, he was the undisputed head of the Olympian family, though the goddesses continued to be honoured in their own particular right. But the structuring of the world had become patriarchal. Zeus and his two brothers, Poseidon and Hades – like An, Enlil and Ea in Sumeria – now ruled the three dimensions of sky, sea and underworld that had always been the province of the Mother Goddess. The once lunar division into the three phases is now shared by the three sons of Chronos. Kings take their sovereignty from Zeus, as before they had done from the goddess. But although Zeus became a universal god, he never lost his distinctive and dramatic personality – falling into rages, lusting, feeling compassion for mortals, hurling the gods around the palace – and so the distance from the human and the divine was not as great as it was in Judaism: 'Zeus was, Zeus is, Zeus will be: O great Zeus,' the priestesses at Dodona sang, followed, significantly, by the chant, 'Earth sends up fruits, so praise we Earth the Mother.'[31]

In the figure of Zeus the transformation from son–lover to great father can be seen in the legends about his childhood, and in the epithets that attached themselves to his name. We have to ask, what is the significance of the stories that set his childhood in Crete? The Minoan seal with the child upon the mother's knee greeting his worshippers (Fig. 6) tells of a divine birth, and the added coincidence of Zeus's Cretan birth would seem too great to draw no connection between them. The child acknowledging with raised hands the greeting of his worshippers wearing the shield was most likely the child who grew to become the divine *Kouros* (young god), whose birth and death were celebrated in Crete as the renewal of life.

In Hesiod's tale Rhea goes to Crete to give birth to Zeus, giving him into the care of Gaia, who hid him in a vast cave. A tradition was handed down that this was an actual cave deep in the Dictaion mountain. Zeus was called *Dictaios*, and it was here that the unique 'Hymn of the *Kouretes*', addressed to him, was discovered. The cave that was imagined for this epiphany, which can still be visited, is haunting enough to house a vision of the Earth in labour and giving birth to a son, and many models of bulls and young saluting gods were found wedged into the walls, as the Minoans waited, perhaps, for the god himself to appear. In the Greek story the infant Zeus was fed by doves, bees and goats, and a group of young men, the *Kouretes*, beat their shields so that their noise would drown the infant's

Figure 6. The Mother Goddess and the Child; Minoan seal, *c.* 700–600 BC. Boeotia, Greece.

cries and Chronos would not hear him. Rhea gave Chronos a stone instead, and in due time he disgorged all his other children and was flung by Zeus down to Tartaros.

In another myth Zeus was born in a cave sacred to bees, who nursed him on honey, suggesting that this rite was linked to the Bee Goddess of the Minoan seals, and to an annual ritual of the death and rebirth of the year and vegetation god; for every year (the story went) at a precise moment of the annual round, a great glare of fire streamed from this cave, announcing that the blood from the birth of Zeus had fallen upon the earth. The older origins of the god are suggested here, and reappear in some of the tales; when, for instance, Zeus appears as a snake to unite with Persephone as she sits weaving the threads of destiny in a cave. The result was the birth of Dionysos, the god who in Crete, it so happens, was synonymous with Zeus himself.

None the less, both the son–lover of the goddess in a Cretan cave and the awesome serpent who was worshipped in shrines dedicated to Zeus are far from the Classical Greek Father God in the heavens, who in the *Iliad* proclaims his supremacy from on high:

> Let down out of the sky a cord of gold; lay hold of it
> all you who are gods and all who are goddesses, yet not
> even so can you drag down Zeus from the sky to the ground, not
> Zeus the high lord of counsel, though you try until you grow weary.
> Yet whenever I might strongly be minded to pull you,
> I could drag you up, earth and all and sea and all with you,

Figure 7. (*Left*) Zeus Meilichios; inscribed relief on votive tablet, fourth century BC. Piraeus, Greece.
Figure 8. (*Right*) Zeus hurling a thunderbolt; statuette, *c.* 460 BC, height 6 in. (15 cm). Dodona.

then fetch the golden rope about the horn of Olympos
and make it fast, so that all once more should dangle in mid air,
so much stronger am I than the gods, and stronger than mortals.[32]

The relation between the old and the new orders is worked out initially
through the metaphor of combat in Zeus – as it is in Marduk and Yahweh
– firstly against the Titans, then a dragon and lastly the giants. After he
had defeated the Titans, though only with Gaia's help, Zeus had to
overcome Typhon, the youngest child of Gaia, who was a gigantic half
man, half beast, and from whose shoulders grew 100 serpents. Zeus's
weapons were the lightning bolt and the steel sickle, but here he needed
the help of the goddesses of Fate, the Moirae. In Zeus's last battle for
supremacy, the fight against the giants, Gaia is significantly not his saviour
but his opponent, and so finally the rule of Heaven was established over
and against the rule of Earth.

The name Zeus is Indo-European, coming from the word *deiwos*, meaning sky, and the same name is found in the Roman Diespiter (Jupiter), the
Indic sky god Dyaus Pita, and the Germanic Tuesday (Thor's day); the
same root is found in the Greek *eudia*, fair weather, the Latin *deus*, god,
and *dies*, day. Zeus appears here with the others as the Sky Father in the
image of the luminous day sky, to which are added the storm images of
cloud-gatherer, lover of thunder and lightning. All his epiphanies are
dramatic: he shines like the sun, falls as a shower of golden rain, hurls his
thunderbolts, flashes his lightning, and draws the black clouds together in
an angry scowl. The soaring eagle manifests his presence, as the falcon
did for Horus. It was this dramatic quality of 'lighting up' that, for the
Greeks, connected Zeus not with the beginning of the world but with the
beginning of their own time, the new time that defined them as Greek.[33]
Zeus's defeat of the Titan giants, for instance, is a setting of limitation
upon vastness, an image of the human mind drawing boundaries around
unnameable spaces as a condition for a particular civilization to gather
and grow.

On the other hand, when he marries the many different goddesses
whose rule preceded him, he does not extinguish their powers but brings
them under his ordinance. This is to say that the human experiences that
the goddesses have so long enacted and rendered sacred are now articulated in the psyche in a new way. Zeus's many sons and daughters
conceived of those goddesses – Apollo, Artemis, Hermes, Persephone,
Dionysos, Athena and Ares – reflect, again, a further capacity for ordering
in the psyche of that time, which was not possible before.

James Hillman proposes that Zeus should be seen in relation to the
Titans as 'the ordering power of the differentiated imagination',[34] which
keeps excess at bay and makes possible measure, right timing and exact-
ness. The word 'titan' means 'to stretch, to extend, to spread forth';
Ouranos, their father, said 'they strained in insolence',[35] and their hugeness
contrasts distinctly not just with the rule of law that Zeus inaugurates,

but also with the precision of imagination that his relationships of marriage and fatherhood with the different goddesses symbolize. In this sense, a new era came into being with Zeus, which is potentially as significant a fact as his dispossession of the goddess's roles and spheres of influence. Male and female giants in fairy-tales signify the sweeping emotions that threaten to crush everything underfoot, which the new order of consciousness (usually tiny by contrast, like the figure of Jack the Giant Killer, or David against Goliath) has to outwit by cunning, foresight and strategy. Hermes, called *argophontes*, slayer of the many-eyed giant Argos, is the prototype of this art in the realm of the gods, as is his protégé Odysseus among mortals, when he tricks the one-eyed giant Polyphemus by calling himself 'Nobody'.[36]

But 'excess' – the giants and dragons conceived by a detached and differentiated consciousness as inimical to itself – was not, in the Greek sensibility, to be mistakenly identified with the feminine, as it was in the Judaeo-Christian tradition. For unlike Marduk and Yahweh–Elohim, Zeus never entirely lost his relation with the old order of the goddess culture or with the feminine mode of being in the psyche, as his stormy marriage to Hera discloses.

The difficulties of the relationship between Hera and Zeus may be understood as symbolizing at the deepest level the labour of uniting the lunar and the solar traditions within the human psyche; for even when both are honoured as valid metaphors for distinct ways of being in life, the task still remains as to how they are to co-exist in harmony and, further, how their union may bear fruit. This is the question of what new kind of consciousness is made possible when the realities they symbolize are experienced as belonging to each other in one greater whole. It is important to remember that, as mentioned in Chapter 7, the lunar and the solar modes of being or seeing are not invariably personified as goddess and god in every culture, since in Germany and Japan, for instance, the sun is conceived as feminine and the moon as masculine, so that these metaphors are ultimately beyond the classification of gender. However they are conceived, they point to the challenge of reconciling two existential possibilities or styles of consciousness that are not, once truly experienced, opposed to each other. The solar heroic mode, with its clarity, direction, particularity, and will for change, and the lunar cyclical mode of transformation of the whole through the phases of feeling and intuition are only apparent polarities in the soul. Rather, their right relation is inherently creative in the sense that it has to be continually sought and found, lost, mourned and then glimpsed anew and recovered in new form.

ARTEMIS

Hymn to Artemis

Artemis I sing
with her golden arrows
and her hunting cry
the sacred maiden
deer-huntress
showering arrows
sister of Apollo
with his golden sword.

In mountains of shadow
and peaks of wind
she delights in the chase,
she arches her bow
of solid gold

she lets fly
arrows
that moan

Crests
of high mountains
tremble,
the forest
in darkness
screams
with the terrible howling
of wild animals

the earth itself shudders,
even the sea
alive with fish

But the heart of the goddess
is strong,
she darts everywhere
in and out, every way
killing
the race of beasts.

And when she has had enough
of looking for animals,
this huntress
who takes pleasure in arrows,
when her heart is elated,
then she unstrings
her curved bow

and goes
to the great house

of Phoebus Apollo,
her dear brother,
in the fertile grasslands
of Delphi
and there she arranges
the lovely dance
of the Muses and Graces

There she hangs up
her unstrung bow
and her quiver of arrows,
and gracefully
clothing her body
she takes first place
at the dances
and begins

With heavenly voices
they all sing

they sing of Leto
with her lovely ankles,
how she gave birth
to the best children
of all the gods,
supreme
in what they say
and do.

Farewell
children of Zeus and Leto,
she of the beautiful hair.
Now
and in another song
I will remember you.[37]

Artemis, the huntress, with her golden bow and moaning arrows, who leaves in her trail howling animals and a shuddering earth, is goddess of the wild, virgin nature, all the inviolate places of the earth where humans dare not enter.

Lovely you are and kind
to the tender young of ravening lions.
For sucklings of all the savage
beasts that lurk in the lonely places you have sympathy.[38]

So sing the chorus to 'Artemis the undefiled' in Aeschylus' *Agamemnon*. The remote, lonely places – the solitude of the forest, grove and mountain, the tumbling stream down the mountain side, the meadow with unpicked flowers, the rough, bare land far from the tilled husbandry of crops – all these belong to Artemis. 'Lady of the wild mountains', as Aeschylus calls her,[39] for it is she who loves clear streams and turns warm springs into healing waters.

She understands the nature of wild animals and birds: the soaring eagle and the shy, nimble deer, the tenderness of ravening lions to their young, the independence of bears, the swift stag, running hare, the boar, goat and bull. She could be seen racing across the mountains with her nymphs, playing and dancing and showering her arrows, exulting in the chase, just like the animals she loves. In the *Odyssey* the sight of Nausicaa of the white arms playing with her maidens makes the poet think of Artemis:

> It was just such a scene as gladdens Leto's heart, when her Daughter, Artemis the Archeress, has come down from the mountain along the high ridge of Taygetus or Erymanthus to chase the wild boar or the nimble deer, and the Nymphs of the countryside join with her in the sport. They too are heaven-born, but Artemis overtops them all, and where all are beautiful there is no question which is she.[40]

The nymphs are the divinities that dwell in brooks and flowers, and so here the living soul of nature clothes itself in maiden form, dancing and singing as the murmuring voices of streams, the rustling of breezes and whispering flowers. Artemis was called 'the sounding one', *keladeine*, evolving out of the music of the wild, the spirit of the place, the language of animals, birds, fish, insects – the immanent presence of the whole of nature as a sacred reality. In Figure 9 she is not yet the goddess Artemis herself, but the original figure still almost wholly contained in the form of the wild, whose later forms were called Artemis. At this point, she is, as Harrison remarks, 'all bird'.[41]

Artemis became the Goddess of Wild Animals, a title she was given in the *Iliad* – *Potnia Theron* – inheriting her role from the Palaeolithic Goddess of the Wild Animals of the Hunt. As the least civilized of all the

Figure 9. Winged Bird Goddess, later known as Artemis, with birds; ivory plaque from dress-pin, mid-seventh century BC. Sanctuary of Artemis Orthia, Sparta.

Greek goddesses, with the oldest lineage, she reflects backwards into the ancient time before the cultivation of land and the construction of cities. To a twentieth-century sensibility, she embodies a wisdom that has been largely lost, both of outer nature and of that untamed animal region of human nature, and of the necessary relation between them.

In the passage of the centuries many traditions of experience converged on her, and the figure whom the Greeks knew as Artemis carried memories from Neolithic Old Europe, Anatolia and Minoan Crete. The Old European Bear Goddess, Bird Goddess and the Weaving Goddess of the spindlewhorls can be rediscovered in the stories and images that surround her, and in the kind of festivals that were held in her honour. Spindles and loom weights were found in many of her shrines, and on Corinthian vases she holds the spindle of destiny as the weaver of the interlocking web of animal and human life.

The name 'Artemis' is not Greek, though it is known from Greek, Lydian and Etruscan inscriptions. It first occurs in Linear B tablets in Pylos, old Nestor's home, linking her through the Mycenaeans with the old Minoan goddess of Crete, where legends of the goddesses Diktynna, 'She of the Net', Britomartis, the 'Sweet Virgin', and Eileithyia, goddess of childbirth, are transferred to her. At the springtime festival at Ephesus in Anatolia her sacrificial rites included a kind of bullfight, reminiscent of the Minoan bull festivals.

Figure 10. Artemis as Goddess of the Animals; Etruscan vase painting, sixth century BC.

In Figure 10 Artemis has evolved from the divinity of the animals to the divine figure to whom the animals belong. She grasps the necks of the lion and the stag as her children, and the lion's body goes limp, as though he were a kitten held in his mother's mouth. The image of a goddess, often winged and standing between two wild animals or birds, usually symmetrically positioned, is eventually called by her name all over Greece and Asia Minor.

Goddess of the Hunt

Artemis is also the goddess of hunting and hunters, and so the myth asks us to understand how she who is mother to her animals is also the one who slays them. The Homeric 'Hymn to Artemis' quoted on pp. 320–1, written *c.* 700 BC, draws her as a deer-huntress, with golden bow and moaning arrows, leaving in her wake dark forests screaming with the howling of animals in pain – imagery that captures the savagery of the hunt. Homer says of one hunter that

> . . . Artemis herself had taught him
> to strike down every wild thing that grows in the mountain forests.[42]

The fortunate hunter would hang the skin and horns of his prey on a tree or pillar sacred to Artemis in gratitude, and in the temple of Despoina in Arcadia her statue was clothed with a deer skin.

Yet as Goddess of the Animals she often walks with a stag or a doe, or she rides on a chariot drawn by two stags, or even appears herself as a doe or she-bear, since the wild animals are the goddess herself incarnate in animal form. It seems, then, as if the figure of Artemis is structured on a paradox, for she is both hunted and huntress, the prey and the arrow that brings them down. What can it mean that, as huntress, she showers her golden arrows upon herself?

In Palaeolithic times the killing of an animal was a disruption of a sacred bond, and the primal unity had to be restored for the people to be able to live in harmony with nature, which was at the same time a harmony with their own being. The purity of the hunter is a very ancient hunting ritual, as is the ritual of restitution for the life taken, either through sacrificing some part of the animal killed or through reconstituting the animal through art. The bear on the cave wall of Les Trois Frères, covered in arrows, could be read in this light. However, if both hunted animal and the person who hunts it are under the protection of the goddess – or, at a deeper level, are two aspects of the goddess herself as two necessary dimensions of life – then the sacred order cannot be truly violated. It is ultimately she who gives and she who takes away, so in the last instance human animals can take away only on her behalf and with her consent.

But this dependence on the grace of the goddess brings with it fear:

Figure 11. Artemis and her lion, with swastikas; vase painting, *c.* fifth century BC.

that the hunter may not be pure enough to engage in her rituals, that the sacrifice of restitution may not be sufficient, that her gift may be withheld or that the hunters themselves may end up her prey. And this fear is extended beyond the strict ritual of the hunting of beasts:

> Zeus has made you a lion
> among women, and given you leave to kill any at your pleasure[43]

Hera says to Artemis, in her capacity to 'hunt' or to spare women as they give birth to their young.

Virgin Goddess of Childbirth

Reflecting on the act of childbirth, wondering, as it were, which goddess you would want with you, it seems inevitable that it would be Artemis, with her knowledge of the animal purposes and instinctive drives that relate mother and baby in the drama of birth. Artemis was, of course, the ruler of childbirth, teaching the woman in labour to give up her cultural identity and allow the deeper wisdom of the body to lead: 'Once I felt this thrill of pain in my womb. I cried out for Artemis in heaven, who loves the hunt and whose care relieves those giving birth. She came to me then and eased me.'[44] So the chorus in Euripides sings. The lion-like image of Artemis again expresses that fear of abandon to the forces of nature, which – especially in childbirth, with its necessary moment of surrender – can feel like a gift or a curse. 'This savage cry from afar announces the advent of Artemis', Ginette Paris writes, beautifully articulating the place and meaning of Artemis in the birth of a child.[45] In recognition of this, the clothes of women who died giving birth, hunted down like the animals by her golden arrows, were offered to Artemis at Brauron.

As the 'Bear-Mother', so tenderly depicted in the Neolithic mother bear and her cub (see Chapter 2, Fig. 30), she also nursed the new-born infant, since the suckling of the young of all species belongs also to this region where the instincts of nature take over. The bear mothering her young is the fiercest animal in the world and, in all but human animals, this act of suckling makes the difference between life and death. Young girls danced to Artemis as bears, wearing masks of bears on their faces and costumes of bears on their bodies, exploring the freedom of their own bear nature, and were accordingly called *Arktoi*, 'She-bears'. In modern Crete Mary is still worshipped in her mothering role as 'Virgin Mary of the Bear'.[46]

Yet Artemis was herself no mother, but the inviolate virgin whose short tunic and practised strength gave her the aspect of a young boy, and nine-year-old girls in their 'tomboy' phase were her favoured companions. At her festival dances girls often wore phalluses to celebrate her containment of her masculine nature within herself. There was a purity, an uncompromising autonomy, about Artemis that related the uncharted empty spaces in nature to the solitude required by every human being to discover a single identity.

As the goddess of unmarried girls and of mothers in childbirth, Artemis again unites in herself two otherwise opposing principles by mediating between them. This may be an expression of a genuine ambivalence at reaching a turning point in life, from the untamed and unaccountable freedom of the girl to the constant dedication required to care for a child. To have one and the same divine presence ruling over both aspects of life may have made the transition from one state to the other easier to contemplate. It may also have been a reminder that the independent autonomous girl is present also even in relationship, and even with a child. Certainly, young girls considering marriage came to dance at her festivals, and on the night before marriage girls consecrated their tunics to Artemis. No wedding took place without her.[47]

Euripides' *Hippolytus* dramatizes the antithetical relationship of Artemis and Aphrodite, the one embodying what D. H. Lawrence calls 'free proud singleness',[48] and the other the longing for union. The play opens with Aphrodite's pledge of punishment to Hippolytus, a hunter who has dedicated himself too entirely to Artemis, and this frames the whole action of the play, so from the beginning his love for Artemis is doomed. He lays a garland of flowers on her altar, and prays:

> My Goddess Mistress, I bring you ready woven
> this garland. It was I that plucked and wove it,
> plucked it for you in your inviolate Meadow.
> No shepherd dares to feed his flock within it:
> no reaper plies a busy scythe within it:
> only the bees in springtime haunt the inviolate meadow.[49]

His old servant tries to warn Hippolytus not to ignore Aphrodite: 'for men hate the haughty of heart who will not be the friend of every man', and so it is with gods.[50] 'Men make their choice,' Hippolytus replies, 'one man honours one god, and one another.'[51] But Aphrodite's punishment results in his death. The myth suggests that it is impossible to be completely faithful to both realities at once, and also that too exclusive a devotion to one or the other is a sacrifice of some kind of possibility of wholeness. It is not that Aphrodite is the stronger of the two, for Artemis is one of the three goddesses over whom her power fails. It is rather the extremes that fall over into the opposite.

Artemis and Sacrifice

Artemis, of all the Greek goddesses, was the one who received the bloodiest sacrifices. Pausanias tells of a yearly sacrifice to Artemis at Patrae, among many other places, where all kinds of wild animals were thrown on to a fire and burnt – birds, deer, fawns, wolf cubs, bear cubs, boars. The same happened at Messene near to a temple of Eileithyia, the old Cretan goddess of childbirth often associated with Artemis.

It would seem that the goddess who personifies the wildness of nature evokes the most primitive fear of dependence on forces that are beyond the control of human beings, and whose law they can, therefore, violate without knowing it. Propitiation of the goddess may then appease her revenge upon their ignorance. The central Greek epic of the Trojan War begins with a mistake of this kind. Agamemnon killed a stag in a grove sacred to Artemis, and as retribution she demands the sacrifice of his daughter Iphigeneia. Through the cunning of her brother, Orestes, a doe is substituted in her place, but the image of Artemis still requires human blood. So Orestes takes the statue away from the land of the Tauroi to the festival of Artemis Tauropolos, where blood was drawn from a man's throat. Burkert comments: 'In the context of the epic this sacrifice has the

Figure 12. Artemis with
Gorgon's Head; terracotta plate,
c. 630 BC. Rhodes.

function of opening war; in reality, goat sacrifices to Artemis Agrotera are made before battle is engaged. Hunting and war are shown as equivalent.'[52] In the plate shown in Figure 12 Artemis, holding her birds by the necks, wears the implacable face of a gorgon, with tongue outstretched in defiance of human codes.

Artemis and Hecate: Goddesses of the New and the Dark Moon

When Aeschylus speaks of 'the glance of her starry eye'[53] he means that Artemis and the pale gleaming light of the new moon are one and the same. When she who was called 'the goddess who roves by night' went hunting through the mountains, she gave off a 'brilliant blaze' of light. As virgin, Artemis personified the new moon, the goddess Hecate personified the dark moon, and Selene, or sometimes Demeter, was the full moon.

Hecate – 'Queen of Night', as the poet Sappho calls her – wears a bright headband and carries two torches in her hands as the brilliant eyes of the dark, an image, perhaps, of intuition that sees the shapes of things not yet visible. This would explain why, together with Hermes, god of imagination, she is guardian of the crossroads where the 'right' way is not yet known. Dogs were her companions, animals who follow a scent 'blindly', recalling the jackal Anubis of the Egyptian underworld, who could distinguish good from bad, and the three-headed dog Cerberus, who guarded the underworld of Greece. In Figure 13, Hecate has three heads, like Cerberus, as well as six arms, and appears in this Roman gem as a formidable figure, reminiscent of the Hindu goddess Kali.

Hecate is often identified with Artemis as her dark aspect, the underworldly being she might become if she were offended and withdrew her light. Sophocles draws Artemis in Hecate's image when he calls her the 'smiter of the deer, goddess of the two-fold torch',[54] and at Aulis there were two stone statues of Artemis, one with bow and arrow and one with torches. It seems as though the original goddess of the moon contained both the light and dark aspects in one whole, and this sense of a totality underlies these images of Artemis but is no longer fully present. It is as if the dark moon has now split off from its original unity and has taken on a

Figure 13. Hecate with torches and snakes; engraved gem. Rome.

separate personality as Hecate, in common with the Iron Age tendency for the dark aspect to separate from the cyclical pattern and come to stand against the light. By Christian times Hecate was looked on as very menacing, though in the Homeric 'Hymn to Demeter' she is helpful to Demeter – 'tender-hearted' – and the only one who heard Persephone raped into the underworld.

Artemis of Ephesus

At Ephesus in Asia Minor, where the Great Anatolian Mother Goddess once gave birth leaning on her leopards, there stood a magnificent temple with an immense statue of Artemis, a huge blackened figure covered with the heads of animals and massive egg-like breasts all over her body (Fig. 14). What is curious is why she is given the name of Artemis, for this fecund figure of overwhelming fertility looks nothing like the angular Artemis of the Greek tradition. It is likely that she was originally a local manifestation of Cybele who was renamed Artemis by the Greeks. Since mythical images last for many millennia, it is not without significance

Fugure 14. Artemis of Ephesus; bronze and alabaster, second century AD. Rome.

that, over 1,000 years later, Ephesus was also to be the place where Mary, mother of Jesus, was declared to be *Theotokos*, 'Mother of God'.

Artemis and Apollo

The Olympian version of the ancient lineage of Artemis makes her the daughter of Zeus and Leto, sister to Apollo. The story went that, because of the jealousy of Hera, Leto suffered the pangs of childbirth for nine days and nights before she gave birth to her twins: Artemis, first and without pain, and then Apollo. They became, in some tales, the moon and the sun.

The relation between Artemis and Apollo may not always have been the simple one of brother and sister who shared the bow and arrow, the lyre, and the purity of distance and wide open spaces. In their birthplace, Delos, which later became Apollo's sanctuary, the earliest and largest temple, constructed about 700 BC, belonged to Artemis, as did the horned altar. Apollo's temple stood only on the periphery, though at Delphi, which Apollo took over from the earth goddess in the eighth century BC, Artemis is not present. Harrison sees this exclusion of Artemis as significant: 'What happened,' she says, 'is fairly obvious':

> Artemis, as Mother, had a male-god or son as subordinate consort, just as Aphrodite had Adonis. When patriarchy ousted matriarchy, the relationship between the pair is first spiritualized as we find it in Artemis and Hippolytus; next the pair are conceived of in the barren relation of sister and brother. Finally the female figure dwindles altogether and the male-consort emerges as merely son of his father or utterer of his father's will.[55]

Figure 15. Artemis, standing with her stag, greets Apollo in his chariot; painting on amphora, *c.* 650 BC. Melos.

In Figure 15, Artemis, probably as Mistress of Delos, greets Apollo who, despite his two Muses and his spoked-wheel chariot of winged horses, appears diminutive in size and authority beside the considerably larger and more imposing figure of the goddess and her guardian stag. The prancing stag, as well as the swastikas, spirals, rosettes and the frieze of birds along the top would make this Artemis's sanctuary.

The Goddess and Her Son–Lover

The myth of the great mother who unites with and then sacrifices her consort in the rite of sacred marriage can be more clearly seen in the familiar Classical tale of Actaeon, in which the older myth is still visible in the imagery. Actaeon was himself a hunter, so the story goes, and he caught sight of Artemis while she was bathing, gazing at her perhaps with eyes more appropriate to Aphrodite. Artemis, profaned by this human intrusion on her sacred rites, punished him by turning him into a stag, whereupon his hounds, not recognizing their master, tore him to pieces. His mother, Autonoe, took the role that Isis performed for Osiris of reconstituting his dismembered body, by reassembling the bones of her son.

Kerenyi suggests that 'it must have been an older tale in which Actaeon clothed himself in a stag's pelt and approached Artemis in this disguise'.[56] A still older tale, however, may have been the union and subsequent dismemberment of the mythical marriage between Artemis as the doe and her son–lover as the stag. In the painting in Figure 16 Artemis has a doe's skin hanging from her back, so she effectively transforms Actaeon into a male version of herself, that is, into her consort. The union of doe and stag, either between goddess and son–lover or enacted in a human ceremony in the wearing of their skins, recalls the Minoan festival of the

Figure 16. The death of Actaeon;
Attic Red Figure Krater by the
Pan painter, *c.* 470 BC.

sacred marriage between bull god and cow goddess, celebrated by the king and queen or priestess at the reunion of sun and moon. The bathing of Artemis has resonances of the ritual bath of the goddess, which, Tacitus tells, in Germania could be seen only by 'men doomed to die'.[57] The hounds that dismember Actaeon are also Artemis's sacred animals, and her priestesses wore the masks of hunting dogs,[58] suggesting the dismemberment could have been enacted or mimed by the priestesses.

The difference between the old and the new myth is instructive for evaluating the importance of what has been lost, for much more is involved in the change from matriarchy to patriarchy than the fact that men took power from women and gods from goddesses. What was lost, more importantly, was a story that is true in the sense that it articulates an intuitive perception of the psyche, and so restores to the psyche its inherent harmony. Cassirer's observation that 'man can apprehend and know his own being only in so far as he can make it visible in the image of his gods'[59] implies that any diminution in the images of the gods works to diminish still further the ability of human beings to know themselves. The story of the sacred marriage of goddess and god, which is the story of the union of *zoe* and *bios*, dramatizes the relation between infinite and finite life, and so between the divine and human portion of the psyche, in such a way that the conflicting forces within may be more profoundly understood.

Artemis, as the soul of the wilderness, gives expression to the place in the psyche where humanity feels itself to be free from human concerns, and so at the same time open to the immense untameable powers of nature. The figure who came alive in the Greek imagination conferred an absolute sacrality upon the wilds of nature and the wild places of the human heart that reflected them.

ATHENA

In Classical Greek art there are two quite different images of Athena. The more familiar figure is the severe, helmeted and girdled goddess, with firm stride and massive shield, the unvanquished virgin warrior as guardian of the city, she who 'cares for the work of war, the destruction of cities and the shouts of battle'.[60] However, there is an older image of a wild and awesome goddess, wreathed in snakes, as in Figure 17, where snakes wind round her head as hair and crown, their heads fringe the folds of her robe, and she holds a rearing head firmly in her left hand. The two images are usually alternative conceptions of the goddess, but are found together as two sides of one cup in Figure 18.

But even when the goddess as warrior is found on her own, she still carries the archaic memory of her origins in the design of her shield – the head of the gorgon hissing with snakes, also known as the aegis, the

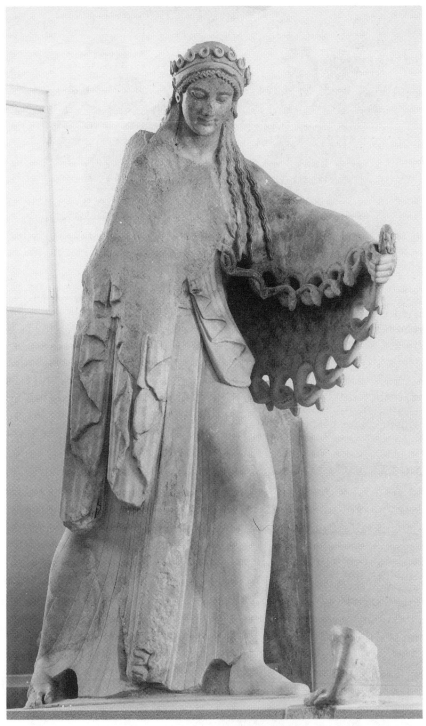

Figure 17. Statue of Athena; *c.* 520 BC. From the Gigantomachy pediment
in the Archaic temple on the Acropolis.

Figure 18. (a) Athena, winged, with snake robe; and (b) Athena with shield;
painting on two sides of black-figured cup.

goatskin. One story tells how this shield was once a goat, which the
goddess herself killed and skinned. Another tells how this gorgon was a
monster slain by Perseus with Athena's help, and the head given to her as
tribute, a later tale in which the goddess's primitive nature has been
masked. Either way, the gorgon's head remains a testament to an earlier
time, and looking through the Classical myth of the daughter who sprang
fully armed from the head of her father, Zeus, we can see the direct
descendant of the Minoan snake goddess of over 1,000 years earlier, who,
with rapt gaze, held the snakes of life and death in both her hands.[61]

Figure 19. Athena with snakes, shield,
swastikas and gorgon's head; vase
painting by the Andokides painter,
c. 525 BC.

The Birth of Athena

Bearing these antecedents in mind, the Classical tale of Athena's birth takes on another dimension of meaning. Hesiod, in his *Theogony*, tells of a goddess, Metis, daughter of Oceanus and Tethys, the primal couple in the Homeric creation myth, counterparts of the Mesopotamian Apsu and Tiamat. Metis became Zeus's first wife, but he learned that if her second child were born, he would lose his power:

> Now Zeus, king of the gods, first took to wife
> Metis, wisest of all, of gods and men.
> But when she was about to bear her child
> Grey-eyed Athene, he deceived her mind
> With clever words and guile, and thrust her down
> Into his belly, as he was advised
> By Earth and starry Heaven. In that way
> They said, no other god than Zeus would get
> The royal power over all the gods
> Who live for ever. For her fate would be
> To bear outstanding children, greatly wise.
> First a girl, Tritogeneia, the grey-eyed,
> Equal in spirit and intelligence
> To Zeus her father . . .
> But Zeus, forestalling danger, put her down
> Into his belly, so that the goddess could
> Counsel him in both good and evil plans . . .
> But Zeus himself produced, from his own head,
> Grey-eyed Athene, fearsome queen who brings
> The noise of war and, tireless, leads the host,
> She who loves shouts and battling and fights.[62]

From one point of view this myth can be seen as the record of that moment in history when what the German philosopher of history Johann Bachofen calls 'Father-right' was established over the older order of 'Mother-right',[63] and as such it stands as a warning against so complete a victory; for the swallowing of the pregnant mother and birth through the head of the father has the same uneasy dissonance as does the birth of Eve from Adam's rib. Interestingly, both Athena and Eve are centrally associated with the serpent: sometimes the serpent could even stand instead of Athena, and in Genesis the serpent often has the face of Eve, though the meaning given to the two images in the two traditions is very different. But in both myths 'Mother' Nature is depotentiated, and her birth-giving powers are taken over by the male. As Harrison protests of Athena's birth: 'It remains a desperate theological expedient to rid an earth-born Kore of her matriarchal conditions', which 'does not impress', for 'through it all we feel and resent the theological intent . . . We cannot love a goddess who on principle forgets the Earth from which she sprang.'[64]

Homer does not refer to this myth at all, calling Athena only 'the daughter of the powerful father'.

In Aeschylus' second play of the Oresteia trilogy, *The Eumenides*, Apollo advances the manner of Athena's birth as the sole reason why all children are related only to their fathers. It is at this point that the claims of patriarchy-against-matriarchy become not merely absurd but alarming:

> The mother is no parent of that which is called
> her child, but only nurse of the new-planted seed
> that grows. The parent is he who mounts. A stranger she
> preserves a stranger's seed, if no god interfere.
> I will show you proof of what I have explained. There can
> be a father without any mother. There she stands,
> the living witness, daughter of Olympian Zeus,
> yet who was never fostered in the dark of the womb,
> yet such a child as no goddess could bring to birth.[65]

Figure 20. Athena as warrior; Archaic statue, *c.* 480 BC. Temple of Aegina.

And Athena, about to cast the decisive vote that absolves Orestes for the murder of his mother, confirms Apollo's line of argument:

> There is no mother anywhere who gave me birth,
> and, but for marriage, I am always for the male
> with all my heart, and strongly on my father's side.[66]

In this obviously deliberate revisioning of an older inheritance there is no trace left of the goddess who, with Demeter, is the closest link to the old Great Goddess of Crete. In the Linear B script in Knossos there is an explicit reference to Athena in a close approximation to her name as it appears in Greek: *Atana Potinija* means 'Mistress of At(h)ana'. A further link with Mycenae is suggested by the temple of Athena that stood in the palace of Mycenae near the sanctuary of the shield deity, where there was also a fresco painting of a helmeted goddess. The olive tree of the Mycenaean seals is also Athena's particular gift to the Athenians, people who live in the city that bears her name. In Greek her name is simply *A Thea*, the goddess, which suggests that the city of Athens was named after the goddess, rather than the other way round.

Everywhere in Greece she is the pre-eminent goddess of the city, the armed maiden who guards the city from enemies without and organizes it from within. Pallas, her other name, means 'maiden', as does Parthenon, the maiden's chamber that still stands as her temple on the Acropolis. She is never a natural mother to god, goddess or human, rather a foster-mother, friend and counsellor of male heroes; though she is in a sense mother to the city as the patron of civilized life. She is the personal protectress of the king, as was the Cretan goddess.

Still more ancient is her association with the diver-bird and the owl. On a sixth-century-BC Corinthian vase Athena sits in her chariot while, just behind her, perched on the horses, is a woman-headed bird, established as a diver-bird.[67] Such an archaic image reveals Athena's descent from the Neolithic Bird Goddess, who had as her counterpart the cosmic snake, and also the Minoan and Mycenaean bird goddess. Yet this inevitably raises the question, how does Athena come to be a goddess of war when the Old European Bird Goddess was not, and why was the chief war deity of the Greeks female? Gimbutas answers that 'Athena, as a direct descendant of the Minoan palace goddess and as the distant heir of Old Europe, became Indo-Europeanized and Orientalized during the course of two millennia of Indo-European and Oriental influence in Greece. The protectress of a city naturally became engaged in war.'[68]

Athena as 'Goddess of Wisdom'

The two more recent strands of historical influence that come together in Athena are symbolized in the central polarity between the serpent and the helmet, for there is a fundamental inner tension in the figure of Athena that complicates any simple reading of what she embodies. Through the image of Athena the matriarchal character of the Minoan goddess is brought into relation with the patriarchal ideals of Aryan and Dorian Greece, and their consequent fusion transforms them both. The result is a new relation to instinct, a disciplining and organizing of nature that can make possible what Hillman calls an 'imagination of civic order',[69] but, alternatively, can result simply in repression and apathy. At its finest, though (that is, when undertaken consciously), this is the 'wisdom' of Athena, and it is this that unites her divergent spheres of influence: she teaches weaving, wool-working, carpentry and all manner of handicrafts whose success depends upon holding in the mind an image of the end.

In the Greek imagination Athena invented the bridle and the chariot for the horse, she helped construct the Wooden Horse that defeated Troy, and she built the first ship. The antithesis on which Athena is structured can be historically traced, yet, at a deeper level of the image, there is an inherent rightness about the depiction of civilized action as a balance between expressing an impulse and restraining it. The *initial* moment of controlling an instinct might well be experienced as opposing its urgency the more effectively to channel it, so the union of helmet and snake has here an inner meaning. One can imagine the contemplation of such an image as actually assisting the process it embodies: 'In league with Athena set your hand to work', as the proverb has it. Kerenyi comments that 'the image of Athena contains a polarity and an inner tension which one cannot assert a priori was an accidental product of history'.[70] In Figure 21 Athena leans on her staff, in mourning for the dead whose names are recorded on the upright stone, also an image of intense inward reflection.

Walter F. Otto, in his book *The Homeric Gods*, calls Athena the 'goddess of nearness'.[71] In significant contrast, the province of the gods becomes the untamed elemental forces where might is right. Poseidon provides the horse, while Athena bridles it and builds the chariot; Poseidon rules the waves, while Athena constructs the ship that rides them. Again, her gift to Athens is not the salt spring gushing upwards from the depths of the earth, as is Poseidon's, but the carefully cultivated olive, whose oil was the prize at her festival. By this gift she, and not Poseidon, won rulership of Attica, later the country of the Athenians.

Even in war she is controlled, in contrast to Ares' savage and indiscriminate rage, and she easily defeats him in combat. She comes to the side of Achilles when he needs self-discipline, and to Odysseus when he needs strategy and foresight. Here, in the *Iliad*, Achilles is deliberating whether to reach for his sword in his quarrel with Agamemnon:

Figure 21. Athena mourning; marble bas-relief, *c.* 480–450 BC. Acropolis.

Now as he weighed in mind and spirit these two courses
and was drawing from its scabbard the great sword, Athene descended
from the sky. For Hera the goddess of the white arms sent her,
who loved both men equally in her heart and cared for them.
The goddess standing behind Peleus' son caught him by the fair hair,
appearing to him only, for no man of the others saw her.
Achilles in amazement turned about, and straightaway
knew Pallas Athene and the terrible eyes shining.[72]

Significantly, it is in a moment of reflection occasioned by his conflicting impulses that Athena appears, as the epiphany of his victory over unbridled instinct. Similarly, she comes to Odysseus when he is sunk in sad thoughts, advising him to curb the rush home by engaging in shared discussion. The quality of restraint is the value she embodies, and her 'flashing eyes' are the emblem of a lucid intelligence that can see beyond the immediate satisfaction. She once planned to make a man called Tydeus immortal, but when she sees the dying hero split his enemy's skull and swallow his brains, she leaves him in disgust.

It is good counsel, thinking through or practical foresight – the capacity to reflect – that she offers to her protégés. This is called *metis*, after her mother of the same name, translated as 'counsel' or 'practical wisdom', but sometimes with the overtones of shrewdness and craftiness, of thinking too much upon the event. In Sophocles' *Ajax* old Nestor teaches his son about *metis*: 'Through *metis* a man is a better cleaver of wood than through strength; through *metis* the pilot steers his swift ship through the storms in the dark; through *metis* the charioteer gains the upper hand over his fellows.'[73]

Athena is most bound to Odysseus, who is called *polymetis*, 'he of many counsels', the praise accorded to her in the Homeric Hymn even before her warrior qualities are celebrated. She is for this reason the inspiration and guide of Odysseus, along with Hermes, from beginning to end.

Athena and the Medusa

The older snake origins of this ubiquitous goddess are betrayed in the legend of the Medusa, whom Perseus slays, and whose head Athena wears on her shield. Medusa was the Queen of the Gorgons, her hair was of snakes and the look of her eyes turned men to stone. Originally, Medusa was one of the many granddaughters of Gaia, the goddess Earth, and Medusa's name actually means 'mistress' or 'queen'. Her face, however, is not Greek so much as Melanesian, and in her squatting pose, with her tongue falling over her chin, eyes widely staring and arms raised, she resembles the guardian of the other world in the pig cults of Melanesia, to whom a pig had to be offered in order to pass through the gates.[74] The terrifying effect of her gaze is the same as that of all guardians whose task is to scare away the uninitiated, beginning possibly with the Palaeolithic lions. In Greek legend, also, Medusa lives at the limits of life, in a cave beyond the edge of day, guarding the tree of golden apples called the Hesperides, a name taken from the west, where the sun sets. Campbell suggests that

Figure 22. Gorgon with caduceus on her belly; marble relief, *c.* sixth century BC. Corfu.

Medusa and the other Greek goddesses of the old Titan generation (before Zeus) were established in Greece and the islands long before the Dorians came, and in fact exhibit every possible sign of an original relationship to an extremely early neolithic – perhaps even mesolithic – lunar-serpent-pig context that is represented in the myths of Melanesia and the Pacific and also Celtic Ireland.[75]

The Medusa may originally have been simply a masked head attached to the entrance of shrines. The fact that a gorgon's head is found on the Mistress of the Wild Animals at the temple of Artemis in Ephesus as well as in Demeter's shrines suggests that the gorgon was once the nature of a *function* for all the goddesses, and was only later identified exclusively with Athena. Here, for instance, the gorgon in Figure 22, with winged feet and a caduceus on her belly reminiscent of the Minoan goddess, is sculpted in Athena's temple. As Harrison writes: 'The ritual object comes first; then the monster is begotten to account for it; then the hero is supplied to account for the slaying of the monster.'[76] Yet we can still ask why Athena is the one to inherit the head, and what does this say about the particular quality of consciousness she embodies? Is it perhaps the quality of self-disciplined awareness in Athena that can transform the terrifying face of instinct into a protective shield? This may be the meaning of the detail in which Perseus is saved from being petrified by the Medusa's gaze (literally, 'turned to stone': Greek *petros* means 'stone')

Figure 23. Perseus slaying Medusa with a gorgon's head and the body of a horse; detail of neck of pithos, seventh century BC. Boeotia, Greece.

through the device of a mirror that Athena gives him, by which he avoids looking at the Medusa directly but sees her reflected in the glass. Reflection – the perception of the image in the mind's eye rather than an immediate instinctive identification with what is outwardly seen – is thereby suggested as the way to face and master the object without; and the outer object of fear is then still further suggested as being ultimately a fear within.

The Medusa contains more than one layer of mythic association, and the earliest stratum connects her with the horse, as in Figure 23. Poseidon, god of the sea and brother to Zeus, himself called Hippios (Greek, 'horse'), took the form of a horse and mated with Medusa as mare (as he did with Demeter also), and she conceived a winged horse, Pegasus, and his human twin, Chrysaor. This tale must have been added some time after 2000 BC, for the horse was brought to Greece between 2100 and 1800 BC, probably by the invading Indo-Aryans from Anatolia. In the Mycenaean Linear B tablets of *c.* 1400–1200 BC offerings are made to a god with the name of Horse, who most likely became Poseidon in Classical times. The winged horse, destined to draw the chariot of Zeus, is released when the head of the gorgon is struck off by Perseus' gleaming sword, as though the hero (whose name means 'shining', in the same solar tradition as his father, Zeus) had struck off for ever the terrors of the dark. As such, it becomes another solar tale of unnecessary combat and illusory victory. It is difficult to find a perspective on the story that does not, snake-like, twist and coil into the opposing point of view, and this may reflect a genuine ambivalence in the original myth.

In Figure 24, a later reading of the myth, the Medusa has lost her half-horse body but gained the snakes on her head and on her body, and has great wings and winged feet, suggesting how a myth changes in the course of 100 years.

Figure 24. Perseus slaying Medusa with caduceus on her belly, with Hermes helping; vase painting by the Amasis painter, *c.* 560–525 BC.

In any event, the Medusa, at once terrifying and sympathetic, does not really die. Blood from her veins, on the left side and on the right, was given to Asclepius, god of healing. With blood from the left he slays, and with blood from the right he heals, an early instance of the left as sinister (in Latin *sinister* means 'left', and in French *sinistre* retains the dual meaning of 'left' and 'sinister'). The two bloodstreams of life and death, allied to the crown of serpents in her hair and the copulating serpents in her belly, return us to the two snakes of life and death of the Minoan goddess, who is thereby brought into the new order as the dark, paradoxical place from where healing comes.

Perseus as a historical figure may have been the founder of a new dynasty around 1290 BC, in which case the myth may also be the recording of a decisive change in religious and political organization. Robert Graves reads the myth as saying: 'The Hellenes overran the goddess's chief shrines, stripped her priestesses of their gorgon masks, and took possession of the sacred horses – an early representation of the goddess with a gorgon's head and a mare's body has been found in Boeotia.'[77]

Zeus, as the embodiment of the new order, is also validated politically through the myth of Athena's birth through his head, since it is on her shield that the severed head of the gorgon finally comes to rest. The Homeric 'Hymn to Athena' registers the magnificence of this goddess:

> Pallas Athena
> I shall sing,
> the glorious goddess
> whose eyes gleam,
> brilliantly inventive,
> her heart relentless,
> formidable maiden,
> guardian of cities,
> the courageous Tritogeneia.
>
> Wise Zeus gave birth to her himself
> out of his majestic head.
> Golden armour clothed her,
> warlike, glistening.
> All the gods who saw her
> were overcome with awe.
>
> Suddenly she was there
> before Zeus who holds the aegis.
> She sprang from his immortal head,
> shaking her sharp spear.
>
> Great Olympos trembled terribly
> at the power of the goddess
> with the gleaming eyes.
> And all around her the earth
> screamed awfully

and then the sea
started to move, frothing
with dark waves, and salt
foam suddenly
spurted up.

The brilliant son of Hyperion,
the sun,
stilled
his swift-footed horses
for a long time until
Pallas Athena, the maiden,
unclasped the god-like armour
from her immortal shoulders.
Wise Zeus was delighted.

Greetings, daughter of Zeus
who holds the aegis.
Now, and in another song,
I will remember you.[78]

The Goddess and the Son–Lover

There is one further resonance of meaning, suggested by a variation of
the birth myth, when Hephaestos splits Zeus's skull with an axe in order
to release Athena. He is often shown fleeing with his axe after the deed is
done, as though he has committed some punishable crime, implying that
literally or metaphorically he has killed Zeus to allow Athena to be born.
Burkert says that 'Axe blow and flight was a cultic reality in the ox
sacrifice for Zeus which took place on the Acropolis', concluding that
'this – never expressed – element of patricide in the birth myth leads back
to the apocryphal Pallas Myth'.[79] In this myth Athena slew and skinned a
human giant called Pallas, clothing herself in his skin. In this version of
the origins of her name she is like the snake who emerges from the dead
skin of the old form.

Is it fanciful to wonder if this tale and the birth myth alluded not just
to patricide but to a very archaic remnant of the goddess and son–lover
myth? The one sacrificed could have been the local hunter or the king, or
some other ritual figure of the year god, in which case the ox or bull (the
form Zeus took in the Cretan tale) may have been his ritual substitute.
The wearing of the skin of an animal is known from the tale of Artemis
and Actaeon, as well as from the Cretan ceremonies. The vision of the
goddess arising anew from the death of the old consort or king is precisely
the form of renewal that the ancient rituals took. Zeus, once the son–lover
in Crete, would in patriarchal Greece become the mighty father, and the
positions of supremacy would be reversed. In that case, Athena would,
somewhat surprisingly, join the other goddesses – Gaia, Hera, Artemis

Figure 25. The birth of Athena from the head of Zeus, with Hephaestos
assisting; vase painting by the Phrynos painter, *c.* 560 BC.

and Aphrodite – in whom the ancient mythic theme of mother goddess
and son–lover is implicitly re-enacted.

Recalling that goddesses and gods are potentialities available to every
human being, it would seem that the myth of Athena explores above all
the quality of reflection, and her stories often compose a meditation on
the value of thinking something through or seeing beyond the immediate
response to an event. She assists so many heroes that this quality is
thereby recommended for those on the heroic journey for self-mastery
and understanding.

PART II
THE SACRED MARRIAGE

9

GODDESSES OF GREECE:
APHRODITE, DEMETER
AND PERSEPHONE

. . . for beauty is nothing
but the beginning of terror, which we are still just able to bear

Rainer Maria Rilke

APHRODITE

Hymn to Aphrodite

Golden crowned, beautiful
awesome Aphrodite
is who I shall sing,
she who possesses the heights
of all
sea-wet Cyprus
where Zephyros swept her
with his moist breath
over the waves
of the roaring sea
in soft foam.

In their circles of gold
the Hours joyously
received her
and wrapped
the ambrosial garments around her.
On her immortal head
they laid a crown of gold
that was wonderfully made
and in
the pierced lobes of her ears
they hung
flowers of copper
from the mountains
and precious gold.

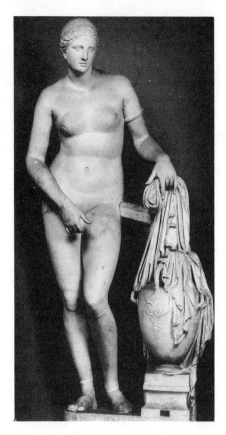

Figure 1. Aphrodite of Knidos;
marble, *c.* 350–330 BC. Graeco-
Roman copy of lost original by
Praxiteles.

Round her delicate throat
and her silvery breasts
they fastened
necklaces of gold
which they,
the gold-filleted Hours,
wear themselves
when they go
to the lovely dances of the gods
in their father's house.

And when they had arranged
all these decorations
on her body
then they led her
to the immortal gods
who saw her
and welcomed her
and reached out their hands
towards her
longing,
every one of them,

to take her home
to be his lawful wife,
so enraptured
were they all
with the beauty of the Cytherean
crowned in violets.

Farewell
quick-glancing
sweet-smiling goddess.
Grant me victory
in this contest.
Favour my song
and in another song also
I shall remember you.[1]

In this poem the birth of Aphrodite is imagined as the act of love – born of the soft sea foam. Later, the clothing and decorating of her by the Hours and the leading of the goddess to the gods gathers the naked act of physical union into the world of relationships and time. As an image arising in the human heart, Aphrodite comes alive when the animal nature of humanity is experienced as divine.

She is there whenever life sparkles with beauty and joy. The Graces who attend her, weaving her robes, plaiting her crown of violets, are called Joyous (*Euphrosyne*), Brilliance (*Aglea*) and Flowering (*Thalia*) – all that makes for sweetness in life. When she steps out of the waves on to the shore, grass and flowers spring up beneath her feet. Desire (*Himeros*) and Love (*Eros*) follow her wherever she goes. As she walks up her mountain, the animals are filled with longing for each other:

So she came to Ida with its many springs,
the mother of the wild animals,
and she went straight up the mountain
to the sheepfolds. Behind her moved
grey wolves, fawning on her,
and fierce-eyed lions and bears
and swift-footed leopards,
ravenous for deer.
She felt joy in her heart to see them,
and she filled their hearts with longing,
so that they all went in twos
into the shade of the valley
and made love with each other.[2]

It is the same with goddesses and gods. Only Athena, Artemis and Hestia, goddess of the hearth, can withstand her power – those with sharply defined spheres of action – and even Zeus cannot resist her when she has made up her mind. Hera knows this, and when she wants to beguile Zeus into sleep to help the Trojans, she dresses herself in her most lovely gown and goes to ask Aphrodite for her favour: 'Give me Love and Desire,' she says, 'the powers by which you yourself subdue mankind and gods alike.' In answer, Aphrodite takes from her breast 'the curiously embroidered girdle in which all her magic resides, Love and Desire and the sweet bewitching words that turn a wise man into a fool'. Accordingly, when Zeus saw her,

> ... desire was a mist about his close heart
> as much as on that time they first went to bed together
> and lay in love, and their dear parents knew nothing of it.[3]

Aphrodite's embroidered girdle (reminiscent of Inanna's, which, later, though with fervently transformed meaning, is to become Mary's) was one of the irrevocable forces in life, and whoever was given it to wear became irresistible.

Aphrodite, the 'golden one' and 'lover of laughter', was known in Greece as the goddess of love, she who intensifies and transforms the settled custom of the world: 'Ever on her hair she wears a garland of sweet-smelling roses, and ever she sends the Loves to assist in the court of wisdom. No good thing is wrought without their help.'[4] So writes Euripides in his *Medea*. The Greeks made a verb from her name: *aphrodizein* means to 'make love', and by a pun her attribute of 'lover of laughter' was also 'lover of genitals'.

This atmosphere of playful affection and exhilarating joy, mixed with awe and respect, contrasts profoundly with the Judaeo-Christian attitude to what would be called Aphrodite if it had not already been reduced to sex. Where is the association with sin, we might wonder, or death? We should perhaps remember that in our culture the divinity of Aphrodite has been so long sacrificed to what Erich Neumann describes as the patriarchal sexualization of the feminine[5] that we have probably forgotten who she is.

The Greek myth of her birth accords to her a dignity belonging to the structure of creation beyond what we might initially see as the place of physical love. To redress our cultural imbalance, it might be more open-minded to explore the Greek idea that love belongs to the original nature of things, for Aphrodite is born of the moment when Heaven is separated from Earth, and creation, arrested till then by the weight of Heaven, is suddenly set free.

The Birth of Aphrodite

In Hesiod's tale, Ouranos (Heaven) would not let the children of himself and Gaia (Earth) – now his wife, once his mother – see the light. Heaven and Earth, that is to say, were still bound together as one. Light, or the space between Heaven and Earth, is here, as in Egyptian myth, the image of consciousness that sets in motion the changing forms of time. When Heaven lay around Earth at night, Chronos, with the sickle given him by his mother, Earth, 'harvests' his father's genitals and throws them behind. They fall into the stormy sea and are carried along by the waves for a long time:

> And their immortal flesh stirred a white foam
> around them, and in it grew a girl. At first
> it floated to the holy Cythera, and from there
> it came to Cyprus, circled by the waves. And there
> came forth a goddess, beautiful and feared,
> and grass grew up beneath her delicate feet.
> Her name is Aphrodite among men and gods
> because she grew up in the foam.[6]

Aphrodite is then the daughter of Heaven and Sea – the original mother goddess in many traditions – and the first fruit of the separation of Heaven and Earth, carrying as her birthright, as it were, the memory of their union. By imagining Aphrodite at the very beginning of the process of creation when Heaven and Earth are parted – as the Orphic myth does with Eros – love is drawn in the greater perspective of humanity's longing for reunion with the whole. Aphrodite is no longer the one Great Mother Goddess who is the origin of all things, but, as daughter of the sea, she is the child of the beginning. Consequently, she is the figure who, in the likeness of the original goddess, brings back together the separate forms of her creation. In this sense Aphrodite is 'born' when people joyfully remember, as a distinct and sacred reality, the bonds that exist between human beings and animals and, indeed, the whole of nature. The myth proposes that this happens through love. Union is then reunion, for love that begets life resounds with the mystery of life itself.

Nature was the vision of the interrelatedness of all creation, and, as in Sumeria, the union of Heaven and Earth was felt as an actual physical experience. This was the domain of Aphrodite, drawing back together what has been sundered, bringing the eternal memory back into time. Here is Aeschylus:

> The great and amorous sky curved over the earth,
> and lay upon her as a pure lover.
> The rain, the humid flux descending from heaven
> for both human and animal, for both thick and strong,
> germinated the wheat, swelled the furrows with fecund mud
> and brought forth the buds in the orchards.
> And it is I who empowered these moist espousals,
> I, the great Aphrodite . . .[7]

As union is reunion, so fertility is rebirth. This understanding was rendered in the annual ritual bathing of Aphrodite in the spring, which

Figure 2. *The Birth of Aphrodite* (sometimes called *The Return of the Maiden*); marble, *c.* 470–460 BC. Ludovisi Throne.

renewed her virginity and the virginity of the earth. The Hours, who first clothed Aphrodite when she was born, are also the goddesses of the seasons – the hours of the year – and in spring, when the year is born, they clothe her again, assisted by the Graces. Every year, in her temple at Paphos in Cyprus, Aphrodite in legend was bathed, and maybe, like Hera, her statue was also washed clean of winter, carried down by her priestesses to the waves. In the late archaic sculpture in Figure 2 the birth from the sea and the sacred bath are related through the wavy folds of the garments, the weight of her arms on the shoulders of the Hours and their covering of her nakedness as she rises. Her arising is like the *anodos* (coming up) of the Earth Goddess in Crete and Persephone in Greece, for in all these epiphanies the moment of drama is the return of the maiden from the depths as a rebirth: so she is again virgin. Harrison comments: 'Virginity was to these ancients in their wisdom a grace not lost but perennially renewed, hence the immortal maidenhood of Aphrodite.'[8] The song of Demodocus in the *Odyssey* tells that after the crude exposure of Aphrodite to the jesting gods (Hephaestos, her husband, had captured her and Ares together in a net of his making and showed them lying in bed together to the gods), she fled away to her sanctuary to be restored:

> And away she fled, Aphrodite, lover of laughter,
> quickly over the sea to Cyprus,
> to the pleasant shores of Paphos

Figure 3. *The Birth of Venus*; Sandro Botticelli, *c.* 1485.

and her fragrant altar stone, and there
the Graces washed her body and anointed her
with the ambrosial oil that the immortals use.
And when they had wrapped her in her lovely garments,
she was truly a wonder to behold.[9]

Aphrodite's name comes from the manner of her birth – *aphros* means
'foam' in Greek – but not until the fourth century BC was the womb of
the sea, which gathered and nurtured the semen of heaven, conceived as a

shell, the image immortalized by Botticelli. (*Kteis*, the Greek word for a scallop shell, also meant the female genitals.) Perhaps the most beautiful rendering of her birth comes in the first Homeric Hymn to her, given in full above, which was discovered only in the fifteenth century AD in a manuscript in Florence, and was first translated by the poet Poliziano, a friend of Ficino, when it became the inspiration of Botticelli's *Birth of Venus*. In the Neoplatonic tradition in which Botticelli painted, the beauty of Aphrodite was an image of the union of the dual nature of love, the sensuous and the chaste, of which her attendants – the passionate Zephyros blowing her to shore, breathing roses upon her, and the modest Hour clothing her – represent the separate aspects. Similarly, in his *Primavera* (1477) Venus is the figure who reconciles the earthly and the heavenly. Through her 'what descends to the earth as the breath of passion returns to heaven in the spirit of contemplation', as Edgar Wind writes,[10] drawing our eyes from Zephyros to Mercury (and back) through the mediation of the goddess, whose commanding presence enfolds the whole drama of transformation, both in nature and in human nature.

Stories and images of Aphrodite portray her as a synthesis of nature and culture: natural beauty and the art that celebrates the beauty of life. As Ginette Paris shows in her book *Pagan Meditations* (essential reading for the reinstatement of Aphrodite as a serious divinity), Aphrodite 'cultivates the ephemeral beauties', reflecting the divine in its daily aspect.[11] But this is not intrinsically a less civilizing value than the enduring works of Apollo, cast in stone, marble and bronze, and made to last. Both are necessary, and require a continual dialogue with each other to prevent trivialization at one pole and a barren formal perfection at the other. The difference, Paris argues, 'is in the attitude of each towards time. Aphrodisiacal art is a matter of making everyday life more beautiful and more "civilized". Certainly this latter beauty is ephemeral rather than lasting; it fades quickly, and in this there is a certain sadness.'[12]

One way in which the Greeks understood this presentiment of death-in-the-midst-of-life was through the image of Aphrodite in the guise of a bee, inherited from the bee goddesses dancing on the golden seals in Crete, and linked to prophecy and knowledge of a hidden destiny as teachers of Apollo. Golden Aphrodite brings the honey of life to all she touches; she renders the person, the occasion, luminous, incandescent, she gives it the blessing of timelessness, but she is not bound to stay:

> For her breath is on all that hath life, and she floats in the air
> Bee-like, death-like, a wonder.[13]

Aphrodite as Queen of Heaven and Earth

Aphrodite came to Greece from Cyprus and, before that, from Mesopotamia, and so she was a goddess who was very old – as old as time – and, in Olympia, very new, inhabiting a diminished role. As Harrison diagnoses, she is in Homer 'a departmental goddess, having for her sphere one human passion. The earlier forms of divinities are of larger import, they tend to be gods of all work.'[14] But when she is sculpted and painted with her animals and birds – the dolphin, goat, goose, swan and dove – her older lineage shines through. As Goddess of the Sea, she skims through the waves on the backs of dolphins; as Goddess of the Animals, she moves them with longing, drawing them to each other; and as Goddess of Earth in her aspect of fertility, she gathers Heaven to Earth as falling rain and she impels the seeds of the moistened earth to open into roots and shoots. As Goddess of Heaven, she rides through the air on chariots of swans and geese, and she sits upon a throne of swans. In Figure 4, standing upon a flying goose, she holds in her arm a casket of her gifts, and in Figure 5, her body rises from the bodies of two swans, their backs creating her throne and their curving necks and heads forming the arms her swathed body conceals.

Figure 4. (*Left*) Aphrodite standing on a swan or goose, holding a casket; terracotta, sixth century BC. Boeotia, Greece.
Figure 5. (*Right*) Aphrodite seated on a swan throne; terracotta, sixth century BC. Greece.

Like Inanna–Ishtar, Aphrodite was embodied in the brightest star in heaven, the morning and evening star we call by her Roman name of Venus. The twelfth-century-BC Mycenaean temple on Cyprus dedicated to Aphrodite was decorated with a star and the crescent of the moon; and also the dove. In the fourth century BC, in recognition of her range of rulership – but also unyoking what she exists to unite – a distinction arose in Platonic philosophy between a heavenly and an earthly Aphrodite, which was intended to express the different kinds and intensities of love: Aphrodite *Ourania*, Heavenly Aphrodite, was the figure who inspired the possibility of a comprehensive love, including the passion for ideas and suggesting ultimately the passion of the soul wherever it might fall. Aphrodite *Pandemos*, literally, 'Aphrodite of the people', who relates all humanity in the common bond of nature, was the image of a more direct earthly kind of loving in which everyone can share. This expression of Aphrodite also involved the ritual of temple 'prostitution', a service offered freely on behalf of the goddess, for which there were always long queues. Aphrodite's animal here is the goat, affectionately known for its amorous nature.

Figure 6. Aphrodite holding her goat; terracotta relief, *c.* 500 BC.
Gela, Sicily.

Although Aphrodite inhabits our imagination as essentially Greek, the Greeks in their turn inherited her from Cyprus via Crete, Anatolia and Mesopotamia. Yet Aphrodite is primarily a descendant of the Mesopotamian goddess Inanna–Ishtar, who became Astarte in Phoenicia and was called Atargatis by the Philistines, and Ashtoreth by the Hebrews. Inanna's consort, Dumuzi, and Ishtar's Tammuz became, in the Greek tradition, Aphrodite's Adonis, the dying and resurrected son–lover of the goddess in a new form. The Homeric Hymn, in which she walks up to Mount Ida, connects her also to Cybele, since Ida lies in Anatolia within sight of Troy, and Anchises, the mortal man she loves in the hymn (from which union Aeneas was born), was also called Agdistis, Cybele's other name.

In all the Greek myths about her, Aphrodite is 'born' in Cyprus, where the Mycenaeans also emigrated. Phoenicia is only 60 miles (96 km) from Cyprus at the nearest point – a day's sail away – and in the second millennium BC the Phoenicians spread along the Palestine coast, trading their purple dyes and cloths along with their customs and beliefs. The oldest city of Phoenicia was Byblos, and here the rites of Adonis were celebrated, as they were also in Cyprus. Now Byblos was where Isis went to look for her Osiris, whose body was enclosed in the erica tree, a tree also sacred to Adonis. In fact, the actual celebration of the rites of Osiris and Adonis so closely resembled each other that even in Cyprus the two figures were identified.[15]

Cyprus was the meeting place for many different traditions: Phoenician, Phrygian and Mycenaean. Mycenaean Achaeans came to Cyprus as early as the twelfth century BC, and built in Paphos a monumental temple to Aphrodite, which was one of the wonders of the ancient world.

These different traditions merged to create a figure who was not simply the Greek version of the old myth, but a totally new image of life in which the original feeling is transformed. Perhaps the image common to all the cultures is the dove, which is sacred to Aphrodite as it was to Inanna–Ishtar, and recalls the dove resting on the top of the crown of the goddess in Crete (see Chapter 3, Fig. 30). Remembering Aphrodite's rulership of Heaven and Earth, and her mediation between them, it is significant that the dove is pre-eminently the image of relationship in the Christian tradition as the missing feminine aspect of the godhead: the Holy Spirit who *relates* humanity to the deity, descending at the baptism of Christ and at Pentecost.

Aphrodite in Relationship

Aphrodite's own relationships suggest a convergence of ideas from different sources. In late Olympian myth she was married to Hephaestos, the lame, misshapen god who, like the volcano, makes fire deep within the earth, as the smith god, son of Hera, who forged the thunderbolts for Zeus. The very implausibility of this alliance – the moment of recoil at its very existence – is eloquent of the impossibility of restraining the dimension of the psyche that Aphrodite embodies within a legal bond.

This Olympianized figure had an alternative tale of her origins, one more in accord with her reduced status. Homer calls her the child of Zeus and Dione – herself the daughter of Oceanus and Tethys, the original couple in Homeric myth – or of Air and Earth. But the names tell an older story, for Dione is simply the feminine form of Zeus, in which case Aphrodite is the child of a sacred marriage of sky and earth, or again sky and sea. Zeus, here Aphrodite's father, would in Hesiod belong to two generations later, as the son of Chronos, himself the fateful son of Aphrodite's father, Ouranos. As Harrison says, 'Hesiod, if later in date, is always earlier in thought than Homer.'[16]

Aphrodite's liaison with Ares, the alternately courageous and cowardly but always undisciplined god of war, riotously discovered by Hephaestos, resulted in the birth of a girl, called Harmony, and two boys, called Fear and Terror. This exploration of passion and its ambivalent implications invokes the spectre of the Trojan War, of which Aphrodite was the prime mover. When, in the late tale of what came to be called the 'Judgement of Paris', the Trojan Paris chooses Aphrodite over Athena and Hera (granting her the 'apple of discord' due to the fairest one, while she promises him that Helen will love him), he discovers he has 'chosen' the passion for Helen that drives him to take her away from the Greek Menelaus. This, in turn, leads Menelaus, Agamemnon and their armies to travel across the sea to Troy to avenge the dishonour on their house by winning her back. The original meaning of this tale before inversion set in, as Harrison brilliantly demonstrates, was that Paris, standing before the three Fates or Goddesses of Destiny and prevented from running away by Hermes, is himself chosen by Aphrodite and cannot escape the destiny of his own nature, that unfathomable depth of longing we call 'god-given' (or, as moderns, archetypal) because it comes upon us whether we will or no.[17] The chorus of maidens in Euripides' *Hippolytus* sing:

> I pray that love may never come to me
> with murderous intent,
> in rhythms measureless and wild.
> Not fire nor stars have stronger bolts
> than those of Aphrodite sent
> by the hand of Eros, Zeus's child.[18]

Hephaestos and Ares are Olympian lovers, but a much older pre-Hellenic relationship is suggested in the myth of Eros, who, in Hesiod's *Theogony*, is named as the fourth to appear in creation, after Chaos, Gaia and Tartaros, though, curiously, nothing further is told of him. In the Orphic myth Eros is hatched from the egg of night as the force separating

Figure 7. Aphrodite riding on her goose; Attic cup by the Pistoxenos
painter, *c.* 470 BC. Camirus, Rhodes.

the two halves of the cosmic egg, which became Heaven and Earth,
significantly similar to Aphrodite's own appearance at the birth of creation. Aphrodite's resemblance to Eurynome, who, in the Pelasgian creation
myth, rose from chaos and danced upon the waves, is also resonant here.
(This placing of Aphrodite and Eros at the moment of disunion is echoed,
albeit somewhat ironically, by Aristophanes in Plato's *Symposium*. There
the hermaphrodite beings, descended from the moon, are sliced in half by
Zeus, after which each half yearns and searches for the 'other half' to be
complete.)[19] The point is that all these stories name Aphrodite and Eros
as equals, consorts in parallel, an unusual balance of feminine and
masculine images. When Eros turns up later as Aphrodite's child – a young
god who aims her arrows of love where she directs them – it would be
surprising if that were all there were to it. (Euripides calls Eros 'Zeus's
child' above, but generally he is just called 'son of Aphrodite'.) The
chorus in *Hippolytus* here mourns the fate of Theseus' son whom Aphrodite punished for disdaining her:

> Aphrodite, you guide the hearts of humans
> and the inflexible gods and with you
> comes Eros with the flashing wings,
> comes Eros with the swiftest of wings.
> Over the earth he flies and the loud-echoing salt sea.
> He bewitches and maddens the heart of the victim

he swoops down upon.
He bewitches the race of mountain-hunting lions
and the beasts of the sea and all the creatures
that earth feeds and the blazing sun sees –
and human beings too.[20]

Eros is here the hunter of hearts, as Adonis is a hunter of wild animals, offering to the idea of affinity a very ancient image. (In Bushman ritual the boy makes a tiny bow and arrow and aims it at the girl he loves, and if she does not throw it away, he knows she has accepted him.) So in the hiatus of the story of Eros and Aphrodite – the curious doubling of names of the old god and the young child, and the strange lack of any connection made between them – we might surmise that once Eros played yet another character in the perennial role of dying and resurrected son–lover to the goddess, giving over his part, when the season was ended, to Adonis, a god, by all accounts almost as beautiful as himself.

Aphrodite and her son–lover Adonis

The living marriage celebrated in the imagination of Classical Greece was between Aphrodite and Adonis. The name Adonis means simply 'Lord', and was originally a title of honour conferred on the earlier deity Tammuz by the Semites who worshipped him in Babylonia and Syria. In the Old Testament, similarly, the name Adonai, Lord, is often given to Yahweh. By the seventh century BC the Greeks had converted a title of honour into a proper name, and the great consort of Inanna–Ishtar became the beautiful youth Adonis whom Aphrodite loved.

Adonis was born from a myrrh tree, so the story goes, transforming the old Semitic ritual of burning myrrh at the ceremonies of Tammuz into a tale of mythic proportion in which the balm tree of the Great Mother gives birth to a son. 'Historically', Adonis, in his human guise, comes from the incestuous union of Myrrha and her father, Kinyras, King of Paphos. To protect her from her father's wrath, for she had deceived him into impregnating her, she was changed by divine dispensation into a myrrh tree, so her pregnancy became the pregnancy of the tree. Ten months later the tree opened and Adonis was born. The son–lover is then both divine and human together.

So beautiful was the baby that Aphrodite hid him in a chest and gave it to Persephone for safe-keeping. But when the goddess of the underworld opened up the chest, she decided to keep the child for herself, even though, like Inanna–Ishtar, the goddess of love went down into the underworld to plead with her to give him back. Aphrodite then appealed to Zeus, who, adjudicating between the claims of life and death, allowed Adonis to spend part of the year with Persephone in the darkness below and the other part above with Aphrodite in the golden sunlight. The dove, which both goddesses hold, relates them to each other.

Adonis grows into a beautiful young man, who is loved and protected by Aphrodite, but one day, against her advice, he goes hunting and a wild boar gores him to death. Aphrodite hears him groaning and goes in search of him in her bird-drawn carriage, only to find him lying dead in a pool of blood. The blood is so bright she transforms it into a flower – the anemone, which grows on the hillsides in spring.

Putting the stories together, the resemblance of Aphrodite to Inanna–Ishtar is suggestive, for Aphrodite, as it were, lends Adonis to death as soon as he is born. The Sumerian goddess sacrifices Dumuzi herself, requiring him to take her place in the underworld, though he is only doomed when he, like Adonis, is hunted down as a gazelle. The boar that kills Adonis (and Tammuz in some versions) may owe something to Egyptian myth also, for it was the boar of Seth that, in the marshes at the full moon, hunted down the casket that held the body of the dead Osiris. Furthermore, the pig, like the ass (Seth's animal), was employed in all these countries to thresh the corn, grinding it into the ground to release the seeds from the cut plant. As such, the boar is the agent of change as one phase of life succeeds another.

Adonis, as the god of vegetation and the corn, and of all visible, growing and dying life, must suffer his particular death that the life of the whole may continue, just like Osiris and Attis (also killed by a boar in some stories). Here the boar embodies the male aspect of the great mother as the fertile pig – like Isis and Demeter, for instance – where she sacrifices the lover that he may be reborn as the son. But at the deepest level the import of all the stories would seem to belong again to the familiar drama of *zoe* and *bios*, in which the son–lover must accept death – as the image of incarnate being that falls back, like the seed, into the source – while the goddess, here the continuous principle of life, endures to bring forth new forms from the inexhaustible store.

In the annual rituals that attended this ceremony – held in summer in Greece and Alexandria and in spring in Syria – effigies of Adonis, and sometimes Aphrodite as well, were carried through the streets and then, to the sound of weeping and wailing, Adonis was thrown into the rivers or the sea. In Alexandria a sacred marriage was mimed by displaying the lovers on two couches strewn with flowers and fruit, and, on the day after, the people cast the image of Adonis beneath the waves, singing of rebirth. Mostly, his revival was celebrated the following day. At Byblos in Syria, the River Adonis, which, to a secular mind, is coloured red by the earth it flows through, was seen by the mourners as streaming with Adonis' blood. Here, the mourners shaved their heads, as did the Egyptians on the death of the bull Apis (a later form of Osiris), expecting him also to rise the next day.

Another ritual involved the 'gardens of Adonis', as they were called. These were fast-growing, fast-dying plants – lettuce, fennel, barley and wheat – that were sown in little baskets filled with shallow earth, heated by the sun and tended for eight days, chiefly by women; but then, having no deep roots, they soon withered and were sent into the water along with the effigies – images, together, of his vegetable and human form.

It is easy to see these ceremonies simply as 'fertility rites', a term (along with cult and idol) that habitually dismisses the religious customs of cultures other than our own. But this is to forget that to a closely participating consciousness the magical element (of 'assisting' the corn to grow and 'bringing' the rain down) was at one with what we might call the religious dimension because the whole world was a sacred reality. Indeed, it is doubtful if the magical element is ever truly absent from religious ritual, since even now the symbols of, say, bread and wine become, at the moment of epiphany, real as the body and blood of the resurrected Christ. Similarly, sharing in the drama of Adonis and acting out his destiny, which is the destiny of plants, creatures and themselves, the hearts and minds of the mourners might be for that moment released from identification with the mortal body that suffers the fate of Adonis and be reunited with the principle that is ever reborn, transforming, in this way, sorrow into joy.

Some such recognition of a common heritage is offered by no less a personage than St Jerome, who translated the Holy Scriptures into Latin. He remarked that Bethlehem, the birthplace of our 'Lord', was shaded by a grove of the Syrian Lord Adonis, and that where the infant Jesus had wept, the lover of Venus was bewailed.[21] The Virgin Mary and Aphrodite the Virgin, two figures often opposed in the Christian tradition, are hereby brought together in unholy alliance as a promise of things to come; for, in the Catholic faith, the persistent call for Mary to have a place in the Christian story of the divine is, we shall suggest in Chapter 14, at one level a plea to reinstate the divine as immanent in human life and in the life of nature. In Greece this image of immanence was pre-eminently realized in the figure of golden Aphrodite.

DEMETER AND PERSEPHONE

Demeter is the Corn Mother, goddess of the golden harvests and the fertility of the ploughed earth, and Persephone, her daughter, is the Corn Maiden, the seed in whom the corn, her mother, is continually reborn. Like Inanna, Demeter is called 'the green one', 'the bringer of fruit' and 'she who brings the seasons'. She appears in a wreath of ears of corn or she holds corn in her hands (see Chapter 3, Fig. 15), as did the Mycenaean goddess before her, in the millennial tradition of the Old European Neolithic goddess of the grain, who sat beside the god with the sickle to cut down the dying stalks when the season was ended. The name for food was hers – the 'groats of Demeter' it was called – and her blessing was invoked

Figure 8. The Mother Goddess Demeter, seated; sculpture, possibly by Leochares, who built the Mausoleum, late fourth century BC. Asia Minor.

at harvesting and seed time. She is the one who 'fills the barn', and in Cyprus the word for harvesting takes her name, *damatrizein*. Her festivals were celebrated at the changing of the seasons, in spring and autumn, the time of the dying and the rebirth of the grain. In the *Iliad* Demeter is drawn in the colour of the ripened corn:

> when golden Demeter, blowing with the wind, sifts the chaff from the grain on the sacred threshing-floor.[22]

Demeter's name was once thought to mean Mother Earth, from *Da* or *Ge*, an alternative for *Gaia*, Earth, and *Meter*, Mother; but it more likely comes from the Cretan word for barley grains, *dyai*. For Demeter is not goddess of the whole earth, as is her great-grandmother Gaia, but only that aspect of the earth which gives food, or which human beings can transform into food. She is goddess of the fruits of the earth, and especially the earth that is cultivated, when her help above all others is needed.

Demeter arrived in Greece in the Mycenaean age sometime in the fifteenth century BC, probably bringing her name with her.[23] In the Homeric 'Hymn to Demeter', when she comes to Eleusis disguised as an old woman, she tells the people she came across the sea from Crete. Hesiod, in his *Theogony*, written the same time as the hymn in about 700 BC, describes a sacred marriage that took place in Crete:

> Demeter, shining goddess, joined in love
> With Iasion the hero, on the rich
> Island of Crete. They lay on fallow land
> Which had been ploughed three times, and she gave birth
> To Ploutos, splendid god who travels far
> Over the land, and on the sea's broad back;
> And everyone who meets or touches him
> Grows wealthy, for great riches come from him.[24]

Significantly, in the Homeric Hymn, the King of Eleusis, to whom she teaches her mysteries and who becomes thereby her foster-son, is called Triptolemos, which means 'thrice-ploughed', and the great riches that come from him in Eleusis are both the art of agriculture and the fruits of the spirit. Harrison comments, 'Triptolemos is the Eleusinian Iasion.'[25] Calypso's tale in the *Odyssey* tells of the death of Iasion in the tradition of lovers who have to die after a sacred marriage with the goddess:

> But not for long she loved him, for Zeus high overhead
> Cast on him his white lightning and Iasion lay dead.[26]

The similarity between Ploutos, whose name means wealth, and Hades, Olympian god of the dead, whose Latinized name is Pluto, is also interesting, particularly since, in the older view, what was buried beneath the

Figure 9. Demeter with her son, Ploutos; votive tablet,
c. fifth century BC. Eleusis, Greece.

earth was the great treasure of regeneration. According to Ovid, Demeter's lover was a hunter, which is also significant since the great hunter in Crete was Zagreus, Lord of the Underworld, who catches mortals 'in his net', and was later identified with Dionysos. Demeter's daughter, Persephone, was also born in Crete, and the archaic legend of Zeus uniting with his daughter as a serpent (see p. 317) took place in Crete as well, and the child of their union was Dionysos. The coincidences become too great to suppose there is no connection between the Demeter who is documented in Crete and the Demeter of Greece. She was obviously brought to Eleusis by the Mycenaeans, and her ancient origins were registered when the songs that became the Homeric Hymns were finally written down.[27] The entire middle section of the hymn is taken up with describing how Demeter came to Eleusis, as a place specially favoured, when she was angry with the gods for withholding her daughter, and how she initiated the kings of Eleusis, including Triptolemos, into her mysteries and into the art of agriculture, which they then imparted to the rest of the world.

In the later Olympian myth Demeter was the daughter of the Titans Rhea and Chronos, and sister to Zeus, Poseidon and Hades, the three brothers who took over the three realms of Heaven, Sea and Underworld, which belonged, in Mycenaean, Minoan and Neolithic times, to the Great Mother Goddess. Zeus was also father to Demeter's daughter, Persephone. Yet the customs and images surrounding Demeter disclose a goddess established far longer than those who became her brothers in the new order. As mother of the corn that falls beneath the earth in order to grow again, Demeter was also Mother of the Dead, and Plutarch says that the dead were known as 'Demeter's people' – *Demetrioi*. This puts Demeter much closer in feeling to the Neolithic agriculturalists, for whom death was a taking back into Mother Earth and not a cavernous place where souls flit about in the dark like homeless bats, separated from the living community.

In the olden days, when the earth loosened and new life was beginning to sprout, the custom was for the ancestors to come back up to earth, where they were festively received until their visit had to end.[28] By Homer's time, the connection between the living and the dead has been severed and the sphere of the dead has lost its sanctity. The dead inhabit a shadowy, ghostly realm, with limited awareness and no power, and can be summoned only by a sacrifice of blood. In the *Iliad* and the *Odyssey* Homer ignores Demeter's homely association with death, referring only to the 'dread Persephone' as 'Queen of the Dead', together with her husband, Hades, but without mentioning Hades' rape of Persephone, or that she is Demeter's favourite child.

Demeter's archaic origins persist in some of her darker images, for finally her grief and rage are such that Zeus has to grant her the return of her daughter, as the famine on earth is annihilating the race of humans and depriving those who live on Olympos of 'the glorious honour of

Figure 10. (*Left*) Persephone holding a torch; plate from Boeotia, *c*. fifth century BC. The shining light of the torch in the dark underworld quickens the grain and the poppies she holds in her hand. A casket of treasure stands before her while behind her is a bird, which, like the winged Hermes, can escort her back to the upper world.
Figure 11. (*Right*) Persephone with two companions and a flower; drawing on a cup, *c*. 2000 BC. Minoan. See Chapter 3, Fig. 16.

offerings and sacrifices'. So ultimately, like Inanna in the *Epic of Gilgamesh*, who threatened to mix up the dead with the living if she was not revenged on Enkidu, Demeter draws upon some of her ancient power in her dispute with Zeus.

The story of Demeter is inseparable from that of her daughter. Persephone is often called simply Kore, which means 'maiden', and is also the feminine form of *koros*, 'sprout'. Both mother and maiden are referred to as 'the two goddesses', or the *Demetres*, as though Kore, the sprout, were the new form of the plant, the mother. There was an inscription in Delos, beside a temple of Isis, that said: '(Property) of Demeter the Eleusinian, maiden and woman.' In vase paintings of the two together it is often difficult to find any distinguishing feature between them other than the hair – long and loose for the maiden, coiled around the head for the mother. Sometimes Demeter holds corn or fruit and Persephone holds flowers or torches. In fact, the bond between mother and maiden is imagined so closely and so ideally that their union suggests, rather, a union of principles, that is, one figure in two guises. Is this, then, the one great goddess in her dual form as mother and maiden, the older and younger aspect of the one figure, mother of the living and the dead? Dramatically, the maiden, like the sons of Inanna, Isis, Aphrodite and Cybele, is the image of the new – the seed of corn, the seed of life – born from, lost, mourned, found, and reborn out of the old – the mother – in a cycle as continuous as the revolving of the moon.

The story of Demeter and Persephone inevitably recalls earlier stories: the two goddesses of Çatal Hüyük in ancient Anatolia and the Sumerian goddess in her dual role as Inanna of the Upper World and Ereshkigal of the Lower World. On the Mycenaean seal on which the goddess is seated beside the Tree of Life a younger daughter figure emerges from the earth as the spirit of the new life (see Chapter 3, Fig. 11). Demeter also continues the tradition of Cybele from Asia Minor, who lasted so long she was both an Anatolian and a Roman deity; according to Harrison, 'Demeter and Cybele were but local forms of the Great Mother worshipped under diverse names.'[29]

As the Great Mother of life and death, and specifically of agriculture, Demeter contains within herself both the upper and the lower worlds, and her story explores the paradoxical relation between them, for what dies above the earth falls below and comes back new, different yet the same. In the figures of Demeter and Persephone, the one goddess is divided into the two aspects of above and below, living and dead; though, since these generally opposed states of being are imagined as mother and daughter, they are here not polarized, but joined at the root. It is this fact that expresses the idea of rebirth. As a nature myth, Persephone is the seed that splits off from the body of the ripened grain, the mother, when, sinking beneath the earth, she returns in spring as the new shoot. The etymology of her name – 'she who shines in the dark' – suggests that the seed does not actually die but continues to live in the underworld, even though it cannot be seen above. This is mystery enough, perhaps, but what is meant by the Mystery Tradition is that the analogy between the life of vegetation and the life of humanity is explicitly addressed, in such a way that the truth of the former is revealed to be, at the same time, a truth of the latter.

The Homeric 'Hymn to Demeter' comprehends both kinds of myth, for in the centre of the story of Demeter's search for her daughter there is a long passage, taking up one-third of the whole poem, that describes the attempt and failure of the goddess to render a human child immortal. When human ignorance, in the person of the child's mother, interrupts the goddess's purpose, she imparts to the household the secret of her mysteries, as though this is the next best thing. Only then does her search for Persephone continue. The conclusion, in which her daughter, tricked by Hades into eating a seed of the red juicy pomegranate, must spend one-third of the year underground with him and the remaining two-thirds above with her mother, returns to the structural analogy between the cycle of the seasonal grain and the cycle of human life. Upper and lower worlds are reunited in the idea of continuous regeneration.

The beauty of the poem is such that in the rape of Persephone it is difficult not to share her horror at being forced to leave the world of light and life, just as Demeter's impassioned search for her daughter expresses a human longing for an assurance of rebirth.

Hymn to Demeter

Demeter, thick-haired Demeter, awe-inspiring goddess,
she it is I shall now sing, she and her daughter
with the slender feet whom Aidoneus seized away,
and loud-thundering, far-seeing Zeus sanctioned it.
Far away from Demeter, with her golden sword
and her glorious harvests, the daughter was playing
with the deep-breasted daughters of Oceanus,
they were gathering flowers, roses and crocuses
and beautiful violets in a soft meadow,
there were irises and hyacinths and a narcissus
which Gaia grew as a snare for the flower-like girl,
for Zeus willed it and He Who Receives So Many
wanted it, and the flower shone wondrously.

Everyone who saw it was amazed, immortal gods
as well as mortal men. From its root there grew
a hundred blooms which had a scent so sweet that all
the wide heaven above and all the earth and all
the salt swelling of the sea laughed aloud.
And then the girl too wondered at it, she reached out
her hands to take this thing of such delight,
but the earth with wide paths gaped in the plain of Nysia,
and He Who Accepts So Many, the lord, sprang upon her
with his immortal horses, that son of Chronos with many names.

He caught hold of her, protesting, and he took her away,
weeping, in his chariot of gold.
Then she screamed in a shrill voice, calling for her father,
son of Chronos, the most powerful and best.
But no one, not the immortal gods nor mortal men,
no one heard her voice, not even the olive trees
heavy with fruit. Only the daughter of Persaeus from her cave,
Hecate of the bright head-band, always tender-hearted,
and the lord Helios, shining son of Hyperion,
they heard her crying for her father, son of Chronos.
But he was sitting apart, far away from the gods,
in his temple of many prayers, accepting fine offerings
from mortals. So although she resisted,
the Ruler of Many and Receiver of Many,
the brother of her father – for Zeus
had advised it – drove his immortal horses on,
that son of Chronos with many names.

Yet the goddess, as long as she could see the earth
and the sparkling sky and the fast-flowing sea
full of fishes and the light of the sun,
and as long as she still hoped to look upon
her dear mother and the tribe of gods who live for ever,
then that hope charmed her great heart in spite of her grief . . .

And the peaks of the mountains and the depths of the sea echoed
with her immortal voice, and her queenly mother heard her.
A sharp pain seized her heart. With her lovely hands
she tore the veil from her long ambrosial hair,
she let fall her dark blue cloak from off her shoulders,
and like a solitary wild bird she streaked out
across dry land and sea, searching

But no one wanted to tell her the truth,
neither the gods nor mortal men, and not even one
true messenger of the birds of omen came back to her.
For nine days queenly Deo circled over the earth,
with flaming torches in both her hands, and she never once
tasted ambrosia and the sweet drink of nectar, nor sprinkled
water on her skin, so deep in grief was she.
But when the tenth luminous dawn had already come,
Hecate met her face to face, holding a torch in her hands
and offering her news, she spoke to her and said:
'Queenly Demeter, bringer of seasons, giver of splendid gifts,
who of the heavenly gods or of mortal men
has carried away Persephone, and brought sorrow
to you dear heart? For I heard her voice,
though I did not see with my eyes who it was.
But I tell you quickly and truly all I know.'

So Hecate spoke. And the daughter of thick-haired Rhea
answered her nor a word, but darted swiftly away with her,
flaming torches in both her hands. So they reached Helios,
he who watches gods and men, they stood
before his horses and the sacred goddess asked him:
'Helios, will you give me, the goddess, honour, if ever
I have warmed your heart and soul by word or deed?
The girl I bore, that sweet young shoot, lovely to look upon,
I heard her sobbing in the empty air
as if she were being forced against her will
though with my eyes I saw nothing.
But you with your rays, you look down from the luminous air
on all the earth and all the sea,
tell me your infallible truth about my dear child,
if you saw her anywhere, who it was, far away from me,
who seized her violently against her will and was gone,
who of the gods or mortal men?'

So she spoke. And the son of Hyperion answered her:
'Queen Demeter, daughter of thick-haired Rhea,
you shall know. For greatly do I respect and pity you,
grieving for your daughter with the slender feet.
There is no other god to blame but Zeus
who gathers the clouds, he gave her to Hades,
his own brother, to be called his fair wife.

He carried her off on his horses and he led her down
into mist and darkness, screaming loudly.
But, goddess, calm your mighty weeping.
It is not fitting to persist in vain
with your insatiable rage. He is not unseemly
as a son-in-law among the gods, Aidoneus,
Ruler of Many, your own brother and your own blood.
Also he received his share of honour in the beginning
when division was made in three ways, and he
was made lord of those in the place where he lived.'
Saying this, he called to his horses.
At his shout quickly they whirled
his swift chariot along like long-winged birds.

Pain sharper still and yet more savage came into her heart.
Outraged with the son of Chronos, shrouded in dark clouds,
she withdrew from the company of gods and from high Olympos,
and she went to the cities of men and their rich fields,
disguising her form for a long time. And no one who saw her
knew her, no man or deep-breasted woman, until she came
to the house of Celeus, lord of fragrant Eleusis.
Saddened in her heart she sank down near the wayside
of the Maiden Well, where the citizens came to draw water.
She sat in the shade, and branches of an olive tree
grew overhead. And she was like an old, old woman,
full of her years, cut off from child-bearing
and the gifts of Aphrodite, lover of garlands,
like the nurses of the children of kings who deal justice,
or like the house-keepers in their echoing halls . . .[30]

The mourning passage in which Demeter tries to make a human child
immortal by burning him in the fire is virtually the same as the mourning
interlude in Isis, as told by Plutarch. What is interesting is that this
middle passage lacks the poetry of the passages preceding and following
it, in which human life is not mentioned. So, poetically at least, this
central passage – where Demeter's failure to make a boy a god results in
the institution of those rites that became the Eleusinian Mysteries – has
the feeling of an interpolation. Since Plutarch held Isis and Demeter to be
two versions of the same goddess, as he took Osiris and Dionysos to
be two versions of the same god, it is possible that he read the Greek tale
back into his version of the tale of Isis; but it is much more likely that
elements of the Mystery cult at Eleusis originated from Egypt, as did
much of Greek philosophy, including Plato, Pythagoras and Orpheus,[31]
and that these were merged with other elements from Minoan and Mycenaean Crete. At the least, a common tradition is undeniable. Herodotus,
in the fifth century BC, looked to Egypt for the origin of the Mysteries,
but links between Egypt and Crete were well established by the second
millennium BC. Harrison comments that 'in Cretan "Mycenaean"

Figure 12. Persephone and Hades in the underworld; votive plaque,
c. 480–450 BC. Locri, Italy.

civilization, and only there, is seen that strange blend of Egyptian and "Pelasgian" that haunted Plutarch and made him say that Osiris was one with Dionysus, Isis with Demeter.'[32] Whether Egypt or Crete was the greater influence on the Mysteries, it is certain that in Eleusis they lasted for almost 2,000 years, until the fourth century AD, when they were proscribed by the Christian Theophrastus, and later the temples were sacked by the Goths.

The Thesmophoria

The Mysteries at Eleusis grew out of a much older autumn festival dedicated to Demeter at the time of the sowing of the seed. Herodotus places the origin of the festival long before the 'upset of the whole of the Peloponnesos by the Dorians', attributing it to the Egyptians, who 'taught it to the Pelasgian women'.[33] However, the connection between corn and pig is made as early as the Neolithic era, long before Isis was drawn riding on a pig.[34] The rites were attended only by women, who were for that time sexually abstinent, and the essential feature was the pig sacrifice. *Thesmoi* means 'laws' and *thesmos* means 'what is laid down', while *phoria* means 'carrying', and the festival celebrated the attribute of Demeter as law-bearer or law-giver: Demeter *Thesmophoros*. Yet what was actually laid down in deep chasms beneath the earth were the pigs, so the meaning of the rites must have combined the notion of pig and the notion of law. The two ideas come together in a new understanding of the lawfulness of the earth's fertility, an idea that was essential to a culture that depended on agriculture as the chief source of food.[35] Demeter was the goddess who gave the law that transformed Greece from a nomadic into an agricultural community. This is one of the meanings of Triptolemos receiving the ear of corn from Demeter and Persephone, and travelling in his snake-drawn chariot to teach the art of agriculture to the rest of Greece. With agriculture came the beginnings of settled life and civilized law. In Figure 13 the woman or priestess holds the pig over the dark chasm lit by the three torches of the underworld (recalling the lunar number three heads of Cerberus and Hecate), holding in her other hand a basket containing something sacred also involved in the ritual.

The festival, held in the month of October, lasted three days and was widespread throughout Greece. The first day was called the *Kathodos* and the *Anados* – 'The Way Down' and 'The Way Up' – when pigs were let down into deep clefts of chasms filled with snakes, called *megara*, and the decomposed remains of the pigs sacrificed the previous year were brought up. The main witness to these rites was the Scholiast Lucian, who gives a fascinating account of the way ritual and myth are intertwined:

> According to the more mythological explanation (the Thesmophoria) are celebrated in that Kore when she was gathering flowers was carried off by Plouton. At the time a certain Eubouleus, a swineherd, was feeding his

swine on the spot and they were swallowed down with her in the chasm of Kore. Hence in honour of Eubouleus the swine are thrown into the chasms of Demeter and Kore. Certain women who have purified themselves for three days and who bear the name of 'Drawers Up' bring up the rotten portions of the swine that have been cast into the *megara*. And they descend into the inner sanctuaries and having brought up (the remains) they place them on the altars, and they hold that whoever takes of the remains and mixes it with his seed will have a good crop. And they say that in and about the chasms are snakes which consume the most part of what is thrown in; hence a rattling din is made when the women draw up the remains and when they replace the remains by those well-known images, in order that the snakes which they hold to be the guardians of the sanctuaries may go away.[36]

Lucian's identification of Plouton and Hades is significant in the light of the common Cretan tradition. Harrison comments: 'The myth of the

Figure 13. Woman or priestess sacrificing a pig before the three torches of the underworld; vase painting, *c.* fifth century BC.

Figure 14. Demeter and Persephone reunited; marble bas-relief, *c.* early
fifth century BC. Eleusis, Greece.

rape of Persephone of course really arose from the ritual, not the ritual
from the myth', adding that the real object was 'the impulsion of nature'.[37]
The second day was called *Nestia* – 'Fasting' – and then the women
fasted, sitting on the ground, ritually as an imitation of the processes of
nature, and mythologically as a re-enactment of Demeter's grief for the
loss of Persephone, when she sat desolate by the well. The mood was
gloomy and no garlands were worn. Plutarch writes that the Boeotians
called the Thesmophoria the 'Festival of Sorrow'.[38] On the third day, a
banquet of meat took place, the rotten flesh was scattered on the fields
and the goddess of beautiful birth – *Kalligeneia* – was invoked. Only a
secular culture would make a distinction between the 'fair birth' of the
crops and the 'fair-born' goddess, the daughter of earth's renewal; in
cultures that live in a sacred world the human-like goddess 'daughter' and
the earth's plant 'daughter' are felt to belong to the same reality and
emerge, therefore, as one. In the earlier Minoan seal (see Chapter 3,
Fig. 12) the goddess and the plants return together, and here, in Figure

14, Demeter and Persephone are reunited, lovingly recognizing each other, both holding flowers.

Eleusis

Demeter in her capacity as *Thesmophoros* is not mentioned in the hymn, which focuses solely on the rites of Eleusis, though this festival appears to be a more spiritualized version of the earlier one. The purpose and meaning of the Mysteries was initiation into a vision. 'Eleusis' itself means 'the Place of Happy Arrival', from which the 'Elysian Fields' take their name. The term 'Mysteries' comes from the word *muein*, which means 'to close' both eyes and mouth, and referred both to the secrecy surrounding the ceremonies and to the 'closure' required of the initiate – that he or she allow something to be done to him or her – and so takes on the meaning 'to initiate'. The culmination of the ceremony was a showing forth of sacred objects in the inner sanctuary by the high priest or hierophant – *o iera phainon*, 'he who makes the sacred objects appear'. Nothing but allusions to what took place were permitted, of which the central one was simply that Demeter found and met with her daughter at Eleusis. Only Christian writers violated these rules, and while their testimony had its own bias, a Gnostic writer describes the high point of the ceremony as the cutting of an ear of corn in silence.

Anyone could attend the Mysteries provided they could speak Greek and had not shed blood, indicating the moral dimension of the festival. The Lesser Mysteries, which took place towards the end of winter in the month of flowers, the *Anthesterion*, were a condition for entry into the Greater Mysteries, which took place in the autumn. The first stage of the initiation at the Lesser Mysteries was the sacrifice of a young pig, the animal sacred to Demeter, which was symbolically to take the place of the initiate's own death. This, as in the *Thesmophoria*, follows the Orphic variant of the myth, mentioned by Lucian, which associated the death of the pig with the rape of Persephone.

The second stage of the initiation was a ceremony of purification in which the initiate was blindfolded. Heracles is shown in reliefs veiled and sitting on a ram fleece, following the example of Demeter in the hymn, while a torch is brought up close to him from below, or a winnowing fan is held over him. This must have been very frightening and a trial of the initiate's courage to prepare him for what was to come. The successive stages of the initiation rites are again described in allusive terms, such as would have been intelligible to fellow initiates, but not to outsiders. Clement of Alexandria quotes an initiate as having said: 'I fasted, I drank from the *kykeon*, I took out of the *kiste*, worked, placed back in the basket and from the basket into the *kiste* (chest).'[39] What was hidden in the basket has been the subject of much Christian speculation on the nature of genitals, symbolic or otherwise, but the Greek writer Theophrastus

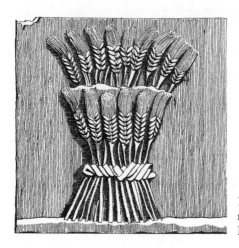

Figure 15. A sheaf of corn;
marble relief, *c.* fifth century BC.
Eleusis, Greece.

alludes to the idea that corn-grinding tools were held to be sacred, so it
may have been a mortar and pestle that were hidden in the basket, the
means of preparing the *kykeon*, the barley drink.[40]

The Greater Mysteries were held originally every five years and, later,
every year in autumn, beginning on the fifteenth of the month of *Boedromion* and lasting nine days. Initiates came from all over the Hellenic
and Roman world, and a truce between the Greek city-states was declared
for fifty-five days, from the month preceding to the month afterwards.
On the day before the opening, the sacred objects, or *hiera*, of Demeter
were taken by procession from Eleusis to Athens. The first day was the
summoning and preparation of the initiates, and the second day was the
cleansing of the initiates in the sea – called the 'banishing' – together with
the sacrifice of the piglets by the initiates themselves, possibly by drowning them in the sea. The third day seems to have been an official sacrifice
on behalf of the city of Athens. The fourth day, called the *Asklepeia* in
honour of Asclepius, the god of healing, was a further day of purification.
The fifth day (19 *Boedromion*), known as *Iacchos*, was the day of celebration, when a great procession from Athens to Eleusis took place along the
sacred way, a distance of some 20 miles (32 km). Priestesses carried the
hiera in closed *kista*, chests or baskets, surrounded by crowds dancing and
shouting ecstatically the name of Iacchos, whose statue, crowned with
myrtle and bearing a torch, stood upright in a carriage.

Iacchos was another name for Dionysos, who, according to Orphic
legend, was the child of Persephone by her father, Zeus, conceived that
night when he approached her in an underground cave in the form of
a serpent. This was not Dionysos as the wine and bull god (whose
counterpart is the Cretan Zagreus), the god who is dismembered and yet

Figure 16. Demeter and Dionysos; marble relief, 470–460 BC. Locri, Italy. Dionysos, with vines falling from his shoulder, hands the cup of transformation to the seated Demeter, holding up her corn. Comparing this sculpture to Persephone and Hades (Fig. 12), also from Locri, the resemblance of the figures is such that it is almost as though Persephone and Hades portrayed a marriage in the underworld, while Demeter and Dionysos celebrate a marriage in the upper world of fruits and feasting. This would relate all four figures as mirror images of each other, the life of corn and vine as a cyclical image of transformation, connecting the above with the below.

lives again. But it was Dionysos as the mystical child at the breast, the image of perpetual renewal, and the sign that the Eleusinian and the Dionysian Mysteries had come together.[41]

At the boundary between Athens and Eleusis the procession was mocked by masked figures, enacting the myth that Iambe or Baubo had cheered up Demeter and, as many another festival of renewal (like the later Roman Saturnalia, for instance), making way for the birth of the new by mocking the old. When the stars came out, the *Mystai* (singular: *Mystes*) broke their fast, as the twentieth day of the month had arrived; according to Aristophanes' *Frogs*, the rest of the night was spent in singing and dancing. The temples of Poseidon and Artemis were open to all, but behind them lay the gate to the sanctuary, which none but the initiates might enter on pain of death.

The sixth day was a day of resting, fasting, purification and sacrificing, following the myth of Demeter's fast and enacting the ritual of winter's barrenness; and the fast was broken by the same drink she had requested: meal mixed with water and soft mint. Then the initiates were allowed into the closed sanctuary. The celebration took place in the *Telesterion*, so called because here *telos*, 'the goal' (from which the word *teleo*, 'to initiate', was derived) was achieved. This was a huge building, which could hold several thousand people, all watching the demonstration of the sacred objects at the same time. It had a skylight for letting out the smoke that came from the enormous fire under which the hierophant stood. In the centre was the *Anaktoron*, a rectangular stone construction with a door at the end, which only the hierophant could pass through.

What happened in this, the beginning of the actual initiation? It seems to have taken place in three stages: the *Dromena*, the things done; the *Legomena*, the things said; the *Deiknymena*, the things shown. There followed a special ceremony known as the *Epopteia*, the state of 'having seen', only for those initiated the previous year.

In the *Dromena* the initiates participated in a sacred pageant that re-enacted the story of Demeter and Persephone, living through the feelings of sorrow, rage and rejoicing, probably carrying torches in the darkness to the sound of music and singing. Clement of Alexandria writes that 'Demeter and Kore have come to be the subject of a mystic drama, and Eleusis celebrates with torches the abduction of the daughter and the sorrowful wanderings of the mother.'[42] Foucart believed that the *Mystai* also experienced a journey to the underworld through wandering in the dark in the lower part of the *Telesterion*, and that the initiates suffered the terrors of death as a condition of initiation.[43]

In Apuleius' tale, initiation into the mysteries of Isis involved a voluntary death before the other life was possible. Similarly, the Mysteries of Cybele included the sacrifice of a ram and a bull, after which the candidates had to lie in a grave and the blood of the animals, sacrificed on a platform above, poured down over them. The blood of the animals that drenched them would have symbolized their own death. Objections to Foucart's interpretation have focused on the fact that excavations of the sanctuary revealed no underground chambers in which the *Mystai* could ritually descend to the underworld, but this seems to be an unnecessary concretization of what could be achieved through sensitivity to atmosphere – darkness, sound, flame and the terror of the unknown.

There was a cave – a temple of Hades – which signified the entrance to the underworld, and probably also an omphalos there.[44] Plutarch writes that 'to die is to be initiated', which, though a play on words (*teleutan* = *teleisthai*), has the force of tradition behind it. Only after this did the light return, and it is more than likely that now the *Mystes* passed upward to a vision of the joyous meadows of the Elysian Fields, lit by a brilliant light. Clement and Foucart are actually in agreement here, for enacting Demeter's search and identifying with Persephone is precisely to wander in the underworld of death, just as the finding of Kore is a return from death to life.

The *Legomena* consisted of short ritual invocations, more like comments accompanying the pageant and explaining the significance of the drama. The *Deiknymena*, the showing of the sacred objects, culminated in the revelation by the hierophant, which was forbidden to be told. The *Epopteia* also contained the showing of *hiera*, though we do not know what these sacred objects were.

Imagine the great hall of mysteries shrouded in darkness, thronged with people, waiting in stillness. Dim figures of priests move in the darkness, carrying flickering torches. In the centre of the darkness some secret drama is being performed. Suddenly a gong sounds like thunder, the underworld breaks open and out of the depths of the earth Kore appears. A radiant light fills the chamber, the huge fire blazes upwards, and the hierophant chants: 'The great goddess has borne a sacred child: Brimo has borne Brimos.' Then, in the profound silence, he holds up a single ear of corn.

Now is the time for celebrations. There is singing and dancing in the courtyard, a great bull is sacrificed, and all the people break their fast together. Finally, the priest fills two vessels and, lifting one to the west and the other to the east, he pours the contents of the vessels on to the ground. The people, looking up to heaven, cry 'Rain!' and, looking down to earth, cry 'Conceive!': *hye, kye*. So end the Mysteries at Eleusis.

'Thrice-blessed are those mortals who have seen these rites and thus enter into Hades: for them alone there is life, for the others all is misery.'[45] So Sophocles writes, following the idea in the hymn, and Pindar also says, 'Blessed is he who has seen this and thus goes beneath the earth; he knows the end of life, he knows the beginning given by Zeus.'[46] It is impossible not to ask the question: what did they see? Did they see apparitions – *phasmatata*? When Heracles says, 'I have seen Kore', does he mean that he saw a goddess rise up from beneath the earth? Or was there a miraculous sudden growth of the wheat out of season in autumn, which was then cut to yield the ear of corn, revealing the transcendence of natural law? Or perhaps the question we should be asking is not *what* did they see, but *how* did they see? The fasting, the drinking of a special potion, the communion in the darkness and then the final revelation can also be understood as a preparation for a change of mind in which, whatever the participants saw, they saw with such intensity that they united with what was seen, and so they experienced a totally different level of the psyche.

We have to ask, then, how was this revelation made possible? It is significant that the two central features of religious ceremony, possibly from Neolithic times onwards, are present here at Eleusis also, namely, the sacred marriage and the birth of the child. Harrison writes that 'the rite of the Sacred Marriage and the Birth of the Holy Child . . . were, I believe, *the* central mystery'.[47] The ceremonies concluded with the symbolic marriage of the heavenly rain with the receptive earth, which was to conceive the child of the grain, but a sacred marriage may have been symbolically, or actually, enacted between the hierophant and a priestess before the return of Kore took place (or, rather, to bring Kore back). Clement of Alexandria describes the formula whereby the *Epoptes* recognized each other as somewhat different from the one used in the Lesser Mysteries. It included a *pastos*, a bridal chamber: 'I have eaten from the *Tympanon*, I have drunk from the *Kymbalon*, I have carried the *Kernos* (fan), and I have crawled under the *Pastos* (bridal bed).'[48] Asterius, Bishop of Amaseia at the turn of the fifth century AD, speaks with proper Christian horror of the sacred marriage as the crowning rite of the Mysteries:

> Is there not performed the descent into darkness, the venerated congress of the Hierophant with the priestess, of him alone with her alone? Are not the torches extinguished and does not the vast and countless assemblage believe that in what is done by the two in the darkness is their salvation?[49]

Harrison comments that the marriage and the birth were indeed

> . . . the culminating ritual acts, acts by which *union with the divine*, the goal of all mystic ceremonial, was at first held to be actually effected, later symbolized . . . Man makes the rites of the gods in the image of his human conduct. The mysteries of these man-made gods are but the eternal mysteries of the life of man.[50]

How this 'marriage' became 'real' for the initiates is as bewildering a question here as it is of the 'mysteries' of any religious ritual, not least because those who ask it are by definition unmoved by it, and are asking, therefore, questions of the intellect that can be answered only through passion. Only a mystic understands the Mysteries.

The sacred marriage, as the union of *zoe* and *bios*, was held in Mesopotamia, Egypt and Crete as a marriage between mother goddess and son–lover. Here this central myth undergoes certain variations because of the central focus of the mother and maid. Zeus may have been the son–lover of the goddess in Crete, where both he and Demeter originated, but now he has the character of consort and father in his own right. None the less, Demeter was undoubtedly the mother at Eleusis, and no godly consort is mentioned in the myth, so the marriage between the hierophant and the priestess may still have retained its original emphasis, where the male *bios* – the life which begins and ends, whether it be Zeus or the Cretan Iasion – unites with the female *zoe*, the timeless principle of regeneration that does not die, symbolized here as Demeter, the Mother.

However, the Homeric Hymn contains both pre-Homeric and Olympian elements, as though the fusion of two different world views is still in the process of taking place. For instance, Zeus is subtly identified with Hades as the underworld counterpart of himself through the device of calling both Zeus and Hades 'that son of Chronos with many names', at one point rendering us unable to distinguish between them. Zeus even plans the marriage between Hades and Kore, which, in so far as Hades embodies his own darker aspect, parallels his own union with Persephone as a snake. In the Orphic version Eubouleus, the swineherd, is an epithet – 'of good counsel' – sometimes applied to Zeus. On the other hand, Demeter is drawn in her pre-Homeric splendour as an actual bird circling round the earth, and in her power to give or withdraw life from humanity she is still the Great Mother Goddess whose voice has to be heard. So in the end Zeus has to bow to Demeter's rage, which withers the earth and threatens to deprive the gods of their own food from the sacrifices by human beings, so a balance between the two powers, the old and the new, is eventually achieved.

Because the separation and reunion of mother and maid holds the centre of the story, the marriage between Demeter and Iasion or Zeus is displaced, and paralleled or echoed by an underworld marriage between Persephone and Hades, or the underworld Zeus. In a sense, then, there are two marriages, one of light and one of dark, which are brought into relation with each other through the reunion of the mother and the daughter. Persephone's marriage is a marriage of death in which she, not the lover, dies, and so the former pattern of mother goddess with her dying and returning son–lover is here reversed. It does not seem consistent with the antiquity of the dual goddess myth to read this entirely as a late patriarchal inversion. It is even likely that behind the myth lurks an ancient ritual whereby the virgin, like her substitute, the young pig, was forced to go down into the abyss of the underworld to save the fertility of the earth above. On the other hand, as the dynamic principle in a vegetation myth, her descent is necessary in that it is the precondition for the continuation of growth. Perhaps this explains why Gaia assists Zeus by growing the narcissus as a snare for the young girl – a flower herself, as her mother says – instead of supporting Demeter against him, as might have been expected.

In any case, by Olympian times the narrative focuses on the questing and finding of the daughter by the mother. When they are eventually reunited,

Figure 17. The Reunion of Demeter and Persephone; marble, fifth century BC. Eleusis, Greece.

their meeting makes possible a new kind of union between life and death, in which the passage between the upper and the lower worlds is kept open. The Greek myth belongs to the old tradition recorded in the Descent of Inanna, who goes back and forth herself. Here, Persephone, the daughter, is the aspect of the mother who goes below and returns to the mother, forming a new whole. Both myths, with at least 1,000 years between them, probably more, inaugurate a new state of being: life is not felt to be the same as before, but then neither is death. It is more like a perception of continuity and relationship – life-in-death and death-in-life – a 'seeing through' the one into the other, which releases humanity from their opposition. When mother and maid are seen to be one, then birth and rebirth become phases from a common source, and duality is, in that perception, transcended.

The sequence of events in the Mystery celebrations suggests that it is the sacred marriage enacted by hierophant and priestess that makes possible firstly the 'birth' of Kore from the underworld, and then the birth of the child, Brimos. The name Brimo means the 'mighty' or the 'raging one', and is resonant of the anger of Demeter that resulted eventually in the return of her daughter. Brimo was an actual underworld goddess in Thessaly to the north. But apart from suggesting a Thessalian and, later, Thracian influence in the introduction of agriculture and the Mysteries to Greece, the names Brimo and Brimos do not tell us much more than that the mother gives birth to a male version of herself. The question as to who Brimo and Brimos were at Eleusis still remains elusive, though various answers have been suggested: either Persephone gave birth to Iacchos–Dionysos, the ever-dying, ever-living god, or Demeter gave birth to Ploutos. Kerenyi takes Brimo to be 'primarily a designation for the queen of the realm of the dead, for Demeter, Kore, and Hecate in their quality of goddesses of the underworld'.[51] In this case, the child is the spirit of renewal conceived in the underworld as living witness that in death is life, whether this be the 'wealth' of the harvest or the 'treasure' of spiritual insight. The meaning of Ploutos and Iacchos–Dionysos is here the same. However, there may be a further meaning implicit in the very provoking of the question. The 'great goddess' is not named, perhaps because, in the moment of epiphany, the two goddesses have become one and, symbolically at least, it is this momentous union that 'gives birth' to the new vision that is the child.

The Lunar Myth

The myth of loss, searching and finding is a lunar myth, and Demeter's quest for the lost part of herself follows the course of the moon after the full, when it wanders across the heavens in search of its vanishing light until the darkness seizes it completely and it is gone. The new moon that returns after three days is then the light that the old moon has found, so the moon has been restored to itself. In lunar symbolism this is a reunion of mother, the full moon, and maid, the new moon, which now begins to grow again into the mother. Lunar symbolism structured the timing of both the *Thesmophoria* and the Eleusinian festival. The Eleusinian Mysteries were held in the last third of the month, in accordance with the lunar calendar.[52] Also, the three days' celebration of the *Thesmophoria*, timed to the three days' disappearance of the moon, follows exactly the dying and resurrection phase of the lunar story. The number three runs through much of the story of Demeter and Persephone. In the Orphic version of the tale Persephone was playing with Athena and Artemis when the earth opened up (making three maidens, like the three lunar graces and muses, as on the Minoan cup, Fig. 11). Also the dividing of Persephone's year into thirds follows the triple lunar division of waxing, full and waning, rather than any seasonal or agricultural rhythm of measurement. On a lunar analogy, then, both mother and maid are changed by their reunion: the mother receives back the younger version of herself and can begin life again, and the maid can grow to be a mother herself. In that sense the child is also a child of their reunion – the fruit of the regenerative powers of nature and the consequence of the uniting of the upper and lower worlds. In the thirteenth-century-BC Mycenaean ivory in Chapter 3 (Fig. 38) the boy child climbs from the lap of one goddess to the lap of the other, as though he were the child of them both. Certainly, it is after the finding again of Kore that the hierophant proclaims the birth of the male from the female, the great goddess of the living and the dead.

Triptolemos

Triptolemos is characteristically portrayed standing between the two goddesses as though he is the son of both of them. In the relief in Figure 18 the ear of grain (which has broken off) is being handed to him by Demeter, while behind him, level with Demeter, stands Persephone with her hand upon his head as though in blessing. Frequently Demeter holds the grain and Persephone holds the torches, as though encompassing the young man with the continuous cycle of life and death. But who was Triptolemos? Is he a human version of the divine child Iacchos or Ploutos, who has come, in the placing of the figures – Persephone behind and Demeter before him – from death to life?

In the Homeric Hymn, Triptolemos is mentioned as one of four law-givers in Eleusis, and historically he was a local king. Harrison adds that 'it may be that he became young out of complementary rivalry with the child Iacchos'.[53] He is usually shown riding a chariot drawn by two large snakes, sometimes winged, just as snakes also accompany Demeter in other representations. It was on this chariot that he drove around all the people on the earth teaching them the art of agriculture and probably also the meaning of the Mysteries. Sometimes Hermes accompanies him, as

Figure 18. Triptolemos standing between Demeter and Persephone; marble bas-relief, *c.* 440 BC.

Figure 19. Demeter offering an ear of corn to Triptolemos with Persephone standing behind him; early red-figured vase painting, fifth century BC. Boeotia, Greece.

though to suggest that he could travel between the realms of life and death. Sometimes Dionysos is drawn on the reverse side of the vase, suggesting a relation between Triptolemos and Iacchos. Kerenyi remarks that 'Triptolemos could also be a name for the primordial man, since there is a genealogy which represents him as the son of Oceanos and Gaia, the Earth',[54] which would transform the story into a creation myth of the birth of humanity. His name can mean 'threefold warrior', which is close to the meaning of Demophoon, the babe that Demeter placed in the fire, whose name means 'slayer of the people', so the two may be intrinsically related or became subsequently identified. There was a tradition to the effect that the goddess was his nurse, while according to another tradition he was Demeter's lover under the name of Iasion, since his name can also be interpreted as thrice-ploughed field.

Certainly, there is a wondrous confusion of roles and meanings here, all having the effect of linking Triptolemos to the goddess as more than a local hero who happened to be one of four kings of Eleusis when she passed by. From another perspective, Triptolemos follows the tradition of son–lovers of the goddess, such as Osiris, who taught agriculture and the civilizing arts to humanity, as Dionysos taught the art of transforming the grape into wine. Kerenyi concludes that 'there is no doubt that the myth of Triptolemos leads back to early archaic times, preceding the existence of the Homeric Hymn'.[55] Sometimes Triptolemos rests between his two great snakes as a king, resembling Dionysos or Iacchos. Sometimes he stands as the generating principle of life, like the axis between the

Figure 20. Triptolemos in his chariot, as teacher of the Mysteries; Attic
red-figured vase painting attributed to the Troilus Painter, *c.* 490–480 BC.

caduceus, as though he were once the child of Demeter and Persephone
now grown into the lover, articulating the gift of the knowledge of life and
death.

The Ear of Wheat

Euripides, in his play *Hypsipyle*, has one character respond to the death of a child in the image of corn: 'One buries children, one gains new children, one dies oneself; and this men take heavily, carrying earth to earth. But it is necessary to harvest life like a fruit-bearing ear of corn, and that the one be, the other not.'[56]

Although necessarily enacted as separate events, the birth of the child and the epiphany of the ear of wheat could be said to convey the same symbolic meaning. The chief source of evidence is the anonymous author of the *Philosophoumena*, of the third century AD, who speaks of the Athenians initiating people at the *Eleusinia* and showing to the initiates 'the mighty and marvellous and most complete epoptic mystery, an ear of grain reaped in solemn silence'.[57] Significantly, it is just before this that the writer describes the Phrygians as believing that god is 'a fresh ear of grain reaped', adding that the Phrygians also held the 'cut wheat' to be a mystery. Along with the festivals of the death and resurrection of Adonis, this forms a long and constant tradition of the mystery of corn. Ears of wheat are found on the architecture of Eleusis and on the Lesser Propylaea; in fact, the ear of wheat was the emblem of Eleusis, as was, to a lesser extent, the pig. It is impossible not to think of Osiris, from whose prostrate body sprouted shoots of wheat, particularly in the light of the parallel ceremony in both traditions when both Osiris and Kore are summoned from the underworld by the same striking of a gong. Osiris was actually identified with the grain, and in the temple at Philae Osiris in a sarcophagus from which parallel ears of corn are rising, watered by a priest (see Chapter 6, Fig. 9), with an inscription that reads, 'This is the form of the unmentionable, secret Osiris who is speeding upwards.'[58]

The cut wheat is like the cut tree in Crete and Rome, the image of that which dies every year yet returns to life. Like Osiris, Attis and Adonis, and like Persephone, the daughter, the cutting of the wheat did not mean the death of what made the wheat grow; indeed the paradox of the cut wheat is that its death brings life back. In Attica corn was sown on the tombs, and Cicero explains this as taking place 'so that the earth, cleansed by this seed, could be given back to the living'.[59]

The question, then, is how did the initiates see the ear of wheat? When the hierophant harvests the ear of wheat and holds it up in the silence, he must have made it appear translucent with an essential truth of human life. In the terms we have tried to establish so far, might they not have had a vision of *bios* united with *zoe*, in which the individual life and the source of all life are reconciled as one and the same? Ordinarily, wheat, when it is cut, is seen as ended, about to die and be nothing – as *bios* separated from *zoe* – the state of death as generally conceived. But the vision of the *Mystai* was, perhaps, to experience the cut wheat as both *bios* and *zoe* together, death and eternal life as a unity. In this way, a simple farming ceremony becomes a symbol of human destiny.

This symbolism is well known to us from the Christian tradition whose rituals also culminate in an offering of a wafer of corn. Jesus said:

> Verily, verily, I say unto you, Except a corn of wheat fall into the ground and die, it abideth alone; but if it die, it bringeth forth much fruit.
>
> He that loveth his life shall lose it; and he that hateth his life in this world shall keep it unto life eternal. (John 12:24–5)

10

CYBELE:
GREAT GODDESS
OF ANATOLIA AND ROME

For O, I know, in the dust, where we have buried
The silenced races and all their abominations,
We have buried so much of the delicate magic of life.

D. H. Lawrence

In the Iron Age, which began *c.* 1250 BC, the Bronze Age myth of the mother goddess and her son–lover did not die out in spite of the formal worship of the great father god. It persisted in various forms in Egypt, Anatolia, Syria, Palestine, Greece and Rome, until it found a new expression in the Mystery cults of Egypt, Greece and Rome and, ultimately, in Christianity. As spirit and nature were driven further and further apart in the religions of the Iron Age, this myth continued to hold them together in their original relationship. It is no coincidence that Anatolia and Syria, as well as Alexandria and Rome, were the areas most receptive both to the Orthodox and the Gnostic tradition of Christianity. The long-standing cult of the Great Goddess and her son–lover in these places, together with the Mysteries celebrated there, goes far to explain why this was so. Wherever Cybele's cult was most strongly established, from Anatolia and Syria to Western Europe, there also the adoration of Mary flourished.

Cybele is far less familiar to us than other goddesses, and the liturgies and hymns addressed to her in the pre-Roman era are very sparse in comparison with the many poems and songs arising from the worship of Inanna and Isis. Nevertheless it is through her, as well as through the Sumerian or Egyptian goddesses, that the myth of the goddess can be traced from the Neolithic era through the Iron Age and far into the Christian era, for, amazingly, it hardly changes throughout this immense period of time.

The lion is inseparable from the image of the goddess and in Anatolia this relationship can be traced as far back as Çatal Hüyük, where the mother goddess in the act of giving birth sits between two felines (see Chapter 2, Fig. 45). Millennia later, lions flank the central pillar of the goddess over the gateway of Mycenae (1500 BC) (see Chapter 3, Fig. 28) and a miniature lion or leopard rests on the head of the Minoan goddess

Figure 1. Cybele enthroned, holding her lion on her lap;
fourth century BC. Greece.

(1600 BC) (see Chapter 3, Fig. 7), who may have come originally to Crete
from Anatolia. Leopards or lionesses form a frieze on the seventh-
century-BC temple of the goddess at Prinias, in Crete. In Greece statues of
Cybele show her with a lion resting on her lap (Fig. 1). After the cult of
Cybele moved to Rome early in the third century AD, her chariot, harnessed to lions, was drawn through the streets in her yearly procession. A
hymn to her from Pergamum in the second century AD describes her
seated in this chariot and occupying the central throne in the cosmos and
the earth – ruler of the rivers and the seas.[1] A thousand years later the
Christian Mary sits between the lion-headed arms of a great throne (see
Chapter 14, Fig. 21), as did Isis and Cybele before her.

Cybele was 'the Lady of Ida', a great mountain in western Anatolia, and 'the Goddess of the Mountain', images that may have influenced the formation of the Cretan goddess. Much later, Anatolia and Crete are still related through legends of Mount Ida in Anatolia, where the gods watched the battle over Troy, and Mount Ida in Crete, where Aphrodite walked and Zeus played as a child.

Like all the great goddesses, Cybele was guardian of the dead and goddess of fertility and wild life. Her connection with the goddesses of Greece is clear, for Artemis, the great goddess of wild, untamed nature, was one of her names, and Aphrodite, in the Homeric Hymn, also comes to Mount Ida with its many springs, followed by the wild animals. Another Homeric Hymn, to the nameless 'Mother of the Gods', sings of her in these words:

> Mother of all the gods
> the mother of mortals
>
> Sing of her
> for me, Muse,
> daughter of mighty Zeus,
> a clear song
>
> She loves
> the clatter of rattles
> the din of kettle drums

Figure 2. Cybele, crowned with a crescent moon, standing before her lion throne with serpents and between two goddesses, one of whom is Demeter.

>and she loves
>the wailing of flutes
>
>and also she loves
>the howling of wolves
>and the growling
>of bright-eyed lions . . .[2]

In Greek and Roman times Cybele is called 'Mother of the Gods', ranking with Demeter and Gaia, and Sophocles calls her the 'All-nurturing One', the 'All-Mother'.[3] The clash of cymbals belonged to the rituals of both Cybele and Demeter, and sometimes she and Demeter are sculpted side by side in adjacent niches. But in one image, at Thasos, Cybele receives the respects of other deities, including Demeter and Persephone.[4] Figure 2 shows a similar scene of Cybele between two goddesses.

A hymn of praise addresses her with the words:

>Mother of *all* that exists
>For Thou and for Rhea, goddess of origin,
>For Thou, highest Attis, that spanst *all* creation,
>That at all times makest *all* thrive . . .[5]

Another hymn of the second to third century AD addresses Cybele as the source of all life and mother of the gods:

>The food of life
>Thou metest out in eternal loyalty
>And, when life has left us,
>We take our refuge in Thee.
>Thus everything Thou dolest out
>Returns into Thy womb.
>Rightly Thou art called the Mother of the Gods
>Because by Thy loyalty
>Thou hast conquered the power of the Gods.
>Verily Thou art also the Mother
>Of the peoples and the Gods,
>Without Thee nothing can thrive nor be;
>Thou art powerful, of the Gods Thou art
>The queen and also the goddess.[6]

The cult of Cybele spread from Anatolia to Greece. In the fifth century BC a magnificent seated statue of Cybele flanked by lions and with a tambourine in her hands, sculpted by Phidias or Agoracritas, was placed in her temple, the Metroon, in Athens. She appears on the frieze of the Treasury at Delphi (550–525 BC) riding in her lion-drawn chariot as she defends Olympus against the Giants. The great frieze from the temple of Athena at Pergamum, now in the Pergamum Museum in Berlin, shows a similar scene. The image of justice belongs with Cybele, as it does with Inanna in Sumeria and Maat in Egypt, for the legal archives of Athens were housed in her temple. Like Inanna, Isis and Demeter, she was regarded as the founder of agriculture and law. The Emperor Julian in the fourth century AD told the story of how Cybele's temple was first established in Athens:

> The Athenians are said to have insulted and driven away the gallus [priest of Cybele] as an innovator in religion, not understanding how important the Goddess was, and how she was the Goddess honoured amongst them as Deo, Rhea and Demeter . . . From that followed the wrath of the deity and the attempt to appease it . . . The prophetess of the Pythian god bade them propitiate the wrath of the Mother of the Gods. The Metroon, they say, was set up for this purpose – the place where all the official documents of the Athenians used to be kept.[7]

THE ORIGINS OF CYBELE'S NAME

The earliest form of Cybele's name may have been Kubaba or Kumbaba (*Kybebe* in Greek), which sounds strangely like Humbaba, the guardian of the forest in the *Epic of Gilgamesh*. The cult of Kubaba appears at Carchemish, at the eastern end of the Hittite Empire, on the Euphrates. It seems to develop in this area, then to move westwards to Hittite Bogazkoy, later to Pessinus, Pergamum and Rome.[8] However, if the earlier Neolithic roots of the Anatolian goddess are borne in mind, it is just as likely that

Figure 3. Head of the goddess Kubaba; basalt relief, *c.* 1050–850 BC. Carchemish, Syria.

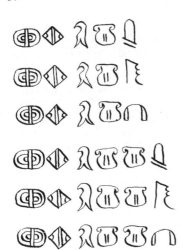

Figure 4. Ideograms of the name Kubaba in the Hittite alphabet.

her cult spread eastwards towards the Euphrates or that it was indigenous throughout this vast area of land. The root of the name Kubaba may be *kube* or *kuba*, meaning a cube, which suggests the connection with the meteorite or cube-shaped stone worshipped as the goddess in Anatolia.[9] This image relates also to the cube-shaped black stone at Petra and to the other meteorite stone of the Ka'aba at Mecca, which was worshipped as an image of the goddess until the rise of Islam. The priests who tended the shrine even after the rise of Islam were known as 'the sons of the Old Woman'. Kubaba may also mean a hollow vessel or cave, which again evokes the imagery of the Neolithic, and her shrines, like Cybele's, were often situated in a cave or near a rock. Kubaba or Kumbaba may be a Hittite name for the goddess, and a statue of her at the city of Carchemish (Fig. 3) shows her wearing a high cap embellished with roses and what appears to be a snake emerging at the front of it, over her forehead. In her hand she holds a pomegranate. Roses and pomegranates still belong to her in Rome 1,000 years later. An Akkadian inscription found at Ugarit on the Syrian coast, and dating to the fourteenth–thirteenth century BC, has the words, 'The Lady Kubaba, mistress of the land of Carchemish'.[10] Kubaba's temple has been found at Carchemish, and there are over forty mentions of her as 'Queen of Carchemish'.[11]

The five ideograms of Kubaba's name were a lozenge or cube, a double-headed axe, a dove, a vase and a door or gate (Fig. 4), all of which were images of the goddess in the Neolithic Old European civilization, though at Çatal Hüyük only the lozenge is found. The lozenge inscribed on the body of the vegetation goddess in Old Europe may have had the same significance in Anatolia and may stand for the cultivated field, but this shape may also represent the sacred black stone that was the testimony of her presence on earth. The second image, which has been called a clasp decoration, is likely to be a double axe with rounded blades and central

Figure 5. Minoan stylization of double axe;
1450 BC. Palace of Minos, Knossos, Crete.

shaft (Fig. 5). Precisely the same style of rounded double axe made of electrum was found in one of the largest of the royal tombs at Ur. It is also found in Crete on vases, and is illustrated in Evans's work *The Palace of Minos*.[12] The dove is the familiar descendant of the Bird Goddess, and the vase evolved from the image of the containing womb and the cave. The last image on the right suggests a door or gate and this, once again, recalls the imagery of the Neolithic, where the goddess was the door or gateway into the hidden dimension through which the dead passed on their way to rebirth.

THE HITTITE AND PHRYGIAN INVASIONS

Anatolia endured a devastating series of invasions by Indo-European (Aryan) tribes between 2300 and 1700 BC. At least 300 cities and villages were sacked and burned during this time. The most powerful of these tribes were the Hittites, who conquered Anatolia about 1740 BC and, overthrowing the dynasty of Hammurabi in Babylon around 1600 BC, established an empire that lasted until about 1170 BC, shortly after the Trojan War. It stretched from the west coast of Anatolia to the Euphrates, and southwards into what is now Syria, with the northern capital at Bogazkoy. The southern capital has not yet been discovered. Documents recently deciphered from Bogazkoy have shown that the court of the Hittite king was in constant communication with Egypt, Greece and Babylonia, and that eight languages were understood by the scribes working for the king.

At the great rock temple of Yazilikaya, 2 miles (3.2 km) from Bogazkoy, many figures of goddesses and gods have been sculpted, among them a goddess standing on a leopard or a lioness. She holds a staff in one hand, and in the other she offers gifts in the form of hieroglyphic signs, which may denote her name. True to the tradition of the son–lover, a young god stands near her on a leopard or panther, with a pointed hat on his head, holding a double axe in one hand. It is believed that this shrine may have been the place where the Hittite king and queen celebrated the sacred marriage in the manner of the Sumerian ceremony.[13] As in Sumeria, the queen mother or queen consort was high priestess; the king was high priest. In a later sculpture (Fig. 6) the goddess holds an apple or a pomegranate in her hand and wears a high crown, perhaps symbolizing the heavens, and a fluted skirt. On either side of her stands a musician, one playing a double pipe and the other a tambourine, for the image of Cybele brought music and dance wherever she was worshipped.

Figure 6. Cybele standing between musicians; *c.* 1050–850 BC.
From the post-Hittite citadel of Buyuk Kale at Bogazkoy, Anatolia.

The Hittite Empire was concentrated in eastern Anatolia, but another group of invaders came from Thrace (Bulgaria) in the twelfth century BC, from the area that Gimbutas has named as Old Europe. The power of the Hittite Empire was broken, and these people settled in a part of western Anatolia that came to be known as Phrygia and which was to become one of the focal areas for the cult of Cybele and her son–lover, Attis. Only the narrow straits of the Dardanelles separated Old Europe from Anatolia, and as there was known to be trade between different areas around the Black Sea in Neolithic times, there is no reason why the imagery of the goddess should not have spread from Old Europe to Anatolia or vice versa during this era. There may, indeed, have been continuous relations between the two lands over many thousands of years. Statues of Cybele have been found as far away as the Ukraine, the Crimea, Romania and Bulgaria, and this goddess may have been worshipped at the shrines of the older, Neolithic one, in the same way that Mary was worshipped at shrines once sacred to Cybele and Isis.

The Phrygians established themselves in central and western Anatolia during the second millennium BC. One of their kings was Midas – he of the ass's ears – whose capital was at Gordion, and he built a great temple to Cybele at Pessinus, which today is a small village south-west of Ankara. The Phrygian language is extremely difficult to decipher, so that, as Vermaseren writes, 'Much concerning Cybele and Attis [her son–lover] in their mother country still remains a closed book.'[14] An interesting image to follow through different civilizations is the 'Phrygian cap', which was worn by Attis and the priests of Cybele. This distinctive cap first appears in Crete, worn by the Minoan goddess, who is accompanied by her lion (Fig. 7). It is next discovered worn by the young Hittite god sculpted

Figure 7. Minoan seal of a goddess with lion; *c.* 1500 BC. Crete.

from the rock near the figure of a goddess in the shrine at Yazilikaya, near Bogazkoy. Later, in Greece, it is worn by Hermes, messenger of the gods, and throughout the Roman Empire where the rites of Cybele or Mithraic ritual were celebrated it is worn by Attis and by Mithra. Today a similar cap is worn by the Sufi dervishes, whose central shrine in Turkey is Konya – once perhaps a Phrygian town – not far from Çatal Hüyük.

After Alexander's conquest of the Persian Empire in 336 BC, Anatolia became part of the Greek Empire and many splendid cities were built, of which Ephesus was one of the greatest. In Vienna there is a statue of Cybele that is very like the many-breasted Artemis that once stood in her temple at Ephesus, sculpted with lions, bulls and griffins. The Greek Artemis, like Demeter and Aphrodite, has strong associations with the Anatolian Cybele. Artemis, also goddess of the wild animals, was an alternative name for Cybele in Anatolia.

CYBELE AND THE ROMAN EMPIRE

With the growth of the Roman Empire, Anatolia was transformed into the Roman province of Asia Minor and Cybele became 'Mother' to the Romans, as she had been to the Greeks. In 204 BC Rome was in dire straits in its war with Hannibal. A delegation was sent to the prophetess at Delphi for an interpretation of the prophecy in the Sibylline books that said that 'whenever a foreign enemy has invaded Italy, he can only be driven away and vanquished, if the Mother of Mount Ida is transferred from Pessinus to Rome'.[15] The prophetess confirmed the written prophecy and envoys were sent to the king of Pergamum in Asia Minor to request that the sacred black meteorite stone, which embodied the presence of the goddess in her temple, be moved to Rome. It is not clear whether this stone was in her temple at Pessinus or Pergamum or at a shrine on Mount Ida, but Lucretius and Ovid recorded its historic journey from one sanctuary to another on a ship made from the pine trees of her mountain, Mount Ida. A year after her arrival in Rome, Hannibal left Italy, and from then on the lion-drawn chariot and the strange, ecstatic rites of Cybele, otherwise alien to the Roman temperament, animated the streets of Rome (Figs. 8, 9).

A description by Lucretius (99–55 BC) of the goddess's procession through the streets of Rome suggests that her statue rather than the stone was carried in the chariot:

> Borne from her sacred precinct in her car she drove a yoke of lions; her head they wreathed with a battlemented crown, because embattled on glorious heights she sustains towns; and dowered with this emblem even now the image of the divine mother is carried in awesome state through great

Figure 8. Cybele enthroned in her lion-drawn chariot; bronze sculpture,
second century AD. Roman.

countries. On her the diverse nations in the ancient rite of worship call as the
Mother of Ida, and they give her Phrygian bands to bear her company,
because from those lands first they say corn began to be produced throughout the whole world.[16]

No Roman was allowed to become her priest or to take part in her
processions until, under the Empire, the cult of Cybele became part of the
Roman state religion. It existed side by side with the cult of Isis, which
was still very popular in Rome, and both spread all over the Roman
Empire. The language of Cybele's cult remained Greek, both in Rome
and throughout the Empire. Her temple, built in Rome in the short space
of thirteen years to house the black stone, was to stand on that site until
the fifth century AD, although it was destroyed several times by fire. The
stone, not surprisingly, has never been found.

Greek continued to be spoken throughout the Roman Empire by all
educated people, much as the Sumerian language was still used long after
Sumeria ceased to exist. The Romans renamed the different areas of Asia
Minor, among them Galatea and Colossia, known to us from the New
Testament letters of Paul. During the Roman period three cities in particular venerated Cybele: Troy, Pergamum and Pessinus. Throughout the
Roman epoch, Vermaseren writes, 'there was no citadel, village or hamlet
that did not remain true to the worship of Cybele'.[17] In the *Aeneid* Virgil
shows how the goddess has become the support of the hero Aeneas, son of

Figure 9. Cybele enthroned with her lions; second–third century AD. Roman.

the goddess Venus (Aphrodite's Roman counterpart). In the epic one senses the familiar presence of the old myth: once again, it is the half-divine, half-human hero who is the son–lover of the goddess, and who, following Gilgamesh and Odysseus, descends into the underworld to over-come death, and bring back the 'golden bough' of immortality. Here, the Trojan Aeneas appeals to Cybele for help in his struggle to gain possession of Italy:

> Generous goddess of Ida, you, Mother
> of Gods, who take delight in Dindyma
> and towered towns and lions yoked in pairs,
> now guide me in this coming battle; goddess,
> make this sign favourable, stride beside
> the Phrygian squadrons with your gracious step.[18]

The continuity of the imagery of the mother goddess is disclosed in a passage written by the Neoplatonist Roman Emperor Julian in AD 363. Stopping at Pessinus on his way to a campaign against the Persians, and inspired by the star-strewn beauty of the night, he wrote:

Who is then the Mother of the Gods? She is the source of the intellectual and creative gods, who, in their turn guide the visible gods: she is both the mother and the spouse of mighty Zeus; she came into being next to and together with the great creator; she is in control of every form of life, and the cause of all generation; she easily brings to perfection all things that are made; without pain she brings to birth, and with the father's aid creates all things that are; she is the motherless maiden, enthroned at the side of Zeus, and in very truth is the Mother of all the Gods. For having received into herself the causes of all the gods, both intelligible and supra-mundane, she became the source of the intellectual gods.[19]

This, and the following prayer to Mother Earth from the second or third century AD, gives some idea of the place Cybele held in the Roman imagination:

Holy Goddess Earth, Nature's mother, who bringeth all to life, and revives all from day to day. The food of life Thou grantest in eternal fidelity. And when the soul hath retired we take refuge in Thee. All that Thou grantest falls back somewhere into Thy womb.[20]

The Romans assimilated the images and the roles of the Greek goddesses and gods to their own pantheon: Hera becomes Juno; Athena, Minerva; Aphrodite, Venus; Artemis, Diana; Demeter, Ceres; Persephone, Proserpine. And of the gods, Zeus becomes Jupiter; Hermes, Mercury; Ares, Mars. Apollo was adopted by the Romans and keeps his Greek name. Tellus Mater (Mother Earth) seems to share something of the older imagery of Demeter: she watched over the seed through all the stages from when it was sown in the soil until it grew to fruition. The cult of all these goddesses and gods travelled throughout the Roman Empire. As late as the twelfth century in France castles were named after Minerva and the ancient rituals whereby Tellus Mater brought blessing to the soil and the seed were still honoured.

Cybele belongs to the Roman pantheon but seems to stand apart from it, assuming more the mantle of the universal mother, as Gaia does in Greece. The Romans adorned her statues with roses, as they did those of Venus, and it may have been at the time her Mysteries were celebrated in Rome that the symbolism of the rose began to evolve as an image of resurrection, and the rose garden as the sacred world or hidden dimension of the goddess.

Roses and lions may seem strangely aligned, yet Cybele's lion-drawn chariot was probably heaped with roses thrown by her devotees as it passed through the streets of Rome. A silver dish from Parabiago, in northern Italy, shows Cybele in her chariot drawn by four magnificent lions, while above her the four diminutive horses of the sun god gallop across the sky (Fig. 10). Beside her sits Attis, holding his shepherd's crook. Facing her a serpent entwines itself around an obelisk, image of regeneration. Nearby are two salamanders, suggesting the same symbolism. Vermaseren comments:

It is not only Nature that the Goddess rules: her power reaches much further. She stands in the centre of the Universe of Time, Sun and Moon, Earth, Water, the Sea and the Seasons. In front of her chariot stands the Tree of Life, stylized as an obelisk and entwined by a serpent. The young

Figure 10. Silver dish showing Cybele in her lion-drawn chariot. Roman, from Parabiago, Italy.

man standing beside it, his right hand grasping the oval ring of the Zodiac, is the youthful god of time, or Aion. Time is further symbolized by the rising chariot of the Sun god, preceded by the torch-bearing light-bringer, Lucifer, and by the descending Moon goddess in her ox-car, guided by the evening star, Vesper or Hesperos. The seasons are also represented, as tiny figures below the chariot: Summer with a sheaf of corn, Spring with a lamb on its shoulders, Autumn with the bunch of grapes and, finally, Winter wrapped in a thick coat.[21]

What resonances there are in this imagery of the Great Goddess of the Bronze Age, whose body was the sky and the earth, and whose epiphany was the Tree of Life and the seasons of the year!

The image of the mother goddess in the Roman Empire seems to bring together Cybele, Ceres and Tellus Mater, and all three watch over the life of the earth and the life of the grain. Many statues have been found that show that the mother goddess had her place in the house as well as in her great shrines, but, with the coming of Christianity, these figures were named as demons, mutilated and thrown into wells. One of the names of Cybele in Gaul was Berecynthia and her image used to be drawn about the fields in a cart, accompanied by men and women dancing and singing, until, from the fourth century AD, the people were 'converted' and abandoned the old religion for the new one.[22]

The story of the loss of a very ancient image of the mother goddess cannot be fully followed in this chapter, but Pamela Berger, in her book

The Goddess Obscured, tells how the mother goddess, whether as Cybele, Ceres or Tellus Mater, who once was mother of the gods and the life of the soil as plants, fruit and golden grain, gradually became 'a mere personification of the earth'; and how, eventually, she was identified with 'the negative principle of materiality' (as opposed to the spirituality implicit in the earth's opposite, air). Finally, by the twelfth century, the goddess iconographically 'came to stand for one of the worst sins of Christendom, female sensuality'.[23]

And so, the image of the goddess as the life of the earth faded in the memory of the people, who transferred their hope and trust and their ancient rituals to the Virgin Mary and the Christian female saints.

THE RITES OF CYBELE

Returning to Rome, the public rites of Cybele in the city streets were orgiastic and ecstatic, and involved self-flagellation and self-castration while in a state of ecstatic trance. They were accompanied by the sacrifice of a bull or ram in a ritual known as the *Taurobolium* or *Crinobolium*, in which the initiate or the high priest or priestess of Cybele stood beneath a

Figure 11. Cybele, holding her tambourine and accompanied by her lion, appears with Attis, while, to the right, a mother and daughter approach; third or second century BC.

platform and was drenched in the blood of the sacrificed animal. The priests and priestesses of Cybele in Greece and Rome were never Greeks or Romans but came from Asia Minor, the place of her origin. Romans were, in fact, forbidden to serve as priests in Cybele's cult or to castrate themselves as her devotees, and they despised the effeminate behaviour of the castrated priests, who had long hair and processed in strange costume through their streets to the sound of flutes, pipes and tambourines.[24]

The Old Testament reveals that the same practices were found in Canaan, for Elijah mocked the priests of Baal who 'cried aloud, and cut themselves after their manner with knives and lancets, till the blood gushed out upon them' (1 Kgs. 18:28), and who identified their flowing blood with the rain that would cause the crops to grow. Some vestige of these archaic ceremonies lingers in the Passion Week processions in Seville, where the flagellants following the flower-bedecked floats that carry the effigies of the Virgin Mary and Jesus reflect the rituals performed in honour of Cybele and Attis. The Christian 'Holy Week' coincides with the week that formerly was dedicated to the rites of Cybele and Attis. The priestesses of Cybele were called *melissae* – bees – precisely the same word as described the priestesses of Artemis and Persephone. They carried the vessels used in the ritual feasts and, like the priestesses of so many other temples, they performed the rituals of mourning for Attis in March.[25] Women as well as men held the position of high priest or priestess.

A late fourth-century-AD epitaph, inscribed on a sepulchral monument, was written by a priestess of Cybele. Expressing gratitude to her husband for initiating her into the rites of the goddess, she says:

> Under your eyes I have been initiated into all the mysteries; you, my pious partner in life, honour in me the priestess of the Goddess of Mount Dindymus and of Attis, while you ordained me with the bull's blood; you teach the threefold mystery to me, priestess of Hecate; you prepare me to become worthy of the mysteries of Ceres, the Greek goddess.[26]

ATTIS

In Figure 12 Attis lies dying beneath the pine and the cypress, which were his sacred trees. His right hand covers his wound and his shepherd's crook rests beside him. The son–lover of Cybele is a figure less clearly drawn than Dumuzi and Tammuz, though this may be because Anatolia has hardly begun to disclose the secrets of its past and the Phrygian language has not yet been deciphered. Attis has strong affinities with Dionysos and Orpheus, as well as with Adonis and the older Dumuzi and Tammuz. The ecstatic passion of the spring festival spread throughout Anatolia during the Greek and Roman era. The myth and its rituals could have originated in Anatolia in Neolithic times or they could have been

Figure 12. The dying Attis; marble relief, second–first century BC.
Hellenistic.

brought from the territory of Old Europe when the Phrygians invaded
Anatolia and overthrew the Hittite Empire. Equally, they may have moved
westward from Mesopotamia, where the myth of the goddess and her
son–lover was long established. So Attis may not have originated in Phrygia, though it was the place where the cult was most concentrated.

Whatever their origin, the relationship between Cybele and Attis confirms once again the image of the sacred marriage between the goddess
and the god or king who once personified the year god and was sacrificed
and dismembered in person or in mime at the spring fertility ritual.
Whether the son–lover is Attis, Dionysos or Zagreus, the imagery of
dismemberment and death followed by resurrection is the same. The
sickle used for the castration of Attis and the flint knife used by the
priests of Cybele point back to the sickle of the Old European male
companion of the Mother Goddess of the Neolithic era (see Chapter 2,
Fig. 39b). The castrated high priest of Cybele was regarded as Attis
himself, and in Rome was called *Archigallus*. The shadowy lineaments of
the old vegetation and initiation rites come into focus: it is more than
likely that castration, like circumcision, was at one time substituted for
the ritual killing of the king or high priest. Originally, Cybele may have
had a single high priest and king, her 'son–lover', who was at first killed
but whose genitals in a later era were offered in sacrifice instead of his life
because their potency was believed to fertilize the earth they fell upon.[27]

The priests of Cybele were not her only attendants. In Phrygia the
Korybantes were the counterparts of the Cretan *Kouretes*, who danced and
set up a great clamour with their voices and musical instruments. It was
believed they could bind and release men from spells, and both induce
and heal madness.[28] In Greece these priests were called *Metragyrtai*.[29]

They did not settle in one place but wandered throughout the country, in the manner of shamans. It may be that this tradition of the wandering *Galloi* of Cybele descends in Asia Minor to the Sufi dervishes, for the ecstatic dance, the trance, and the playing of flute and reed pipe are common to both. The double pipe was a musical instrument used in Cybele's rituals. Throughout her history the image of Cybele is inseparable from music.

Legends abound as to the origins of Attis himself. The oldest story is that Cybele was androgynous, and where her severed male genitals touched the ground an almond tree arose, whose fruits gave birth to Attis by the daughter of the river Sangarios.[30] Some legends said that he was a king's son, or a foundling, like Moses or Sargon of Akkad. Yet again, it was told that Attis was inadvertently killed in the course of a hunt, like Adonis, and that the man responsible for his death was, like Judas, overcome by remorse and took his own life. Sometimes the stories tell of the grief of the goddess when she hears of Attis' death; sometimes her vengeful rage that he has fallen in love with a mortal woman. Other legends emphasized the pine tree under which he lay when he castrated himself, or was castrated with a sickle. It is clear that all these different legends and images point to a very widespread cult in which each district had its own version of the myth. The earliest written mention of Attis appears in a fourth-century-BC Greek comedy in which a young man called Atys is killed by a boar.[31]

Most of the images of Attis belong to Roman times. In these he wears a distinctive costume: a pointed Phrygian cap, a long shirt, sometimes opened to reveal his stomach, a cloak and baggy trousers. He is also shown as a shepherd, like Dumuzi; he usually holds a shepherd's crook and may carry a sheep on his shoulders in the image of 'the good shepherd'. Sometimes he leans against a pine tree or lies beneath one. He may ride a ram or drive a ram-drawn cart. He plays a syrinx, a reed pipe with seven tubes. Sun-rays or ears of corn or fruit emerge from his cap, proclaiming him both a solar god and a god of regeneration; this imagery is shared with the rites of Eleusis. In his rituals he was called 'the cornstalk' or 'the ear of wheat', and his symbols were the pine-cone and the pomegranate. Like Dumuzi and Tammuz, he was lord of cattle, sheep and plants. He sometimes stands on one side of Cybele, with Mercury (wearing a similar cap) on the other; he is also linked with Aion, the god of time, and with the gods of ecstatic rites, Dionysos and Orpheus. Mithra, who was originally an Aryan and then a Persian god, the son–lover of the Persian goddess Atagartis, became the foremost deity worshipped by the Roman soldiers all over the Empire, and was also connected with the rites of Attis.

In Figure 13 Mithra is shown in the act of killing the bull, the life-force of the earth that he himself embodied. A scorpion grips the bull's genitals, and a snake slithers along the ground from the scorpion towards the plant

Figure 13. Mithra slaying the bull; second century AD. Roman.

forms springing from the blood pouring from the bull's wounds. The whole image suggests regeneration through sacrifice. Mithra wears the same pointed Phrygian cap of the initiate of the Mysteries of Cybele, and at times it is difficult to distinguish between Mithra and Attis and their rites, for both involved Mysteries and the sacrifice of a bull. It is thought that the Mithraic rites were reserved for men, while those of Cybele may have been primarily for women. Cumont writes that

> we have every reason to believe that the worship of the Iranian god and that of the Phrygian goddess were conducted in intimate communion with each other throughout the entire extent of the empire . . . The Great Mother . . . had her *Matres* or 'Mothers', as Mithra had his 'Fathers'; and her initiates were known among one another as 'Sisters', just as the votaries of her associate called one another 'Brothers'.[32]

In Rome the Mysteries of Attis were observed from 15 to 28 March, whereas those of Cybele took place in April. On 15 March cut reeds were carried in procession through the city, perhaps in memory of the reeds of the river Gallus, in Phrygia, where as a baby, legend said, Attis was found and brought up by shepherds. Originally, Attis himself would have personified the reeds and their cutting would have symbolized his death. On 22 March a pine tree was cut down from among those in the sacred grove of pines near the temple of Cybele, bandaged like a mummy and decorated with ribbons and violets, because violets were said to have sprung from the god's blood, just as anemones flowered from the blood of Adonis;[33] the pine, an evergreen like the Dionysian ivy, symbolized undying life. In this form Attis was mourned as the dying and resurrected god of vegeta-tion, in the way that Tammuz and Dumuzi and Baal were mourned in an earlier age. On this day the attendants, like the earlier *Kouretes* or *Korybantes*, beat their shields and danced.

On 24 March – the Day of Blood, the day of lamentation for the death of Attis – the *Taurobolium*, or sacrifice of the bull, took place and his genitals were offered to the goddess. This was the day when the priests flagellated and lacerated themselves, sprinkling the altar and the effigy of Attis with their blood, and when devotees castrated themselves. These rites represented the dismemberment of the god, the life-force of the earth, similarly enacted in the Dionysian and Orphic rituals, and most probably also in the Canaanite rituals detested by the prophets. Attis was laid in his grave on the eve of 25 March, four days after the spring equinox, when a nine-day period of fasting and abstinence came to an end. A vigil lasted throughout the 'holy' night until morning, which was greeted by the high priest with the words: 'Be of good heart, you novices, because the god is saved. Deliverance from distress will come for us, as well.'[34] That day was marked by the feast of the Hilaria, the Festival of Joy, which celebrated Attis' return from the dead. For the populace, the Hilaria was a day of carnival, feasting, drinking and general licence. The last day of the festival was one of rest, when the effigy of the goddess, the sacred vessels and ritual instruments were taken to the river to be washed in a ceremony called the *Lavatio*.

Attis and the Green Man

These rituals, and those of Mithra, spread from Rome all over the Empire, carried to its furthest reaches by the Roman army. In 46 BC the Julian calendar, established by Julius Caesar, altered the date of the Hilaria festival of Attis from 25 March to 1 May, and so all over Europe until this century the rites that once coincided with the spring equinox in March were advanced to May. May instead of March became the month sacred to the goddess, and May was later to become the month sacred to Mary. On the first of May, in Christian times, the statue of Mary was, and still is, crowned and garlanded with flowers, and drawn through the streets. The magnificent floats holding the Virgin Mother and her Son, heavy with the scent of thousands of flowers, are carried at Easter through the streets of Seville and other Mediterranean cities, and may be the last vestiges of those effigies that were once borne through the streets of Rome, Alexandria and Babylon. The 'May Magnificat' of Gerard Manley Hopkins enshrines older memories in his words of homage to Mary:

> May is Mary's month and I
> Muse at that and wonder why:
> Her feasts follow reason,
> Dated due to season –
>
> . . . . .

Figure 14. The Green Man; thirteenth–fourteenth century AD.
Sutton Benger Church, Wiltshire.

> Ask of her, the mighty mother:
> Her reply puts this other
>   Question: What is spring?
>   Growth in every thing –.

An echo of the archaic fertility rites is also found in the European spring festival of the first of May, when the May Queen and the Green Man used to be named and the May pole set up and decorated with ribbons and flowers, as once the pine tree of Attis had been wreathed with ribbons and violets. The May pole, a tree sometimes 60 feet (18 m) tall, was carried in a cart drawn by oxen, while the May Queen followed in a cart, or chariot, drawn by young men and women. Her partner or 'consort', the Green Man, descendant of Dumuzi, Tammuz and Attis, also called 'the Green One', was clothed in leaves. In some parts of Europe the couple were 'married'. So May Day celebrated the sacred marriage and the ritual of the regeneration of life, and the morris dancers may be the last descendants of the Anatolian *Korybantes*. All over Europe traces of the Green Man may still be discovered, and he is even found in the name of many British pubs. In Arthurian legend the Green Knight, who rides into Arthur's court demanding that one of Arthur's knights should strike his head from his shoulders, personifies the ancient sacrificed year god, whose rites lead into the deeper mysteries of life and death. However often he lost his head or his life, he could never die. The astonished knights of King Arthur's court watched how the Green Knight, beheaded by Gawain, retrieved his head and, tucking it under his arm, rode from the hall. And Gawain, responding to his challenge, had to go through the initiation of overcoming his fear of death at the hands of the man who was both his host and his executioner.

The face of the Green Man gazes out from the midst of carved foliage on Gothic cathedral screens, pulpits, vaulted naves and choir stalls, redeeming nature from the pall of sin that had descended on her with the idea of the Fall, and invoking that more ancient knowledge of the relationship of the goddess to her son, incarnate through him as the life of the earth. William Anderson, in his book *The Rise of the Gothic*, writes of the Green Man that 'he seems to declare to us that the love we feel for nature is reflected back to us in measure for our appreciation and that the source of this love is the same for us as is the driving force of sap in leaves and branches'.[35] He concludes:

Even if one were to regard him, at the lowest level, as a mascot of the masons, his presence in so many regions and over so long a period indicates that he had a particular meaning for them. Did he sum up for them the energy they had to transform, the energy both of living nature and of the past stored in the collective unconscious? Did he at the same time express the spirit of inspiration, the *genius* hidden in created things?[36]

The Green Man appears in the Islamic Sufi tradition as *Khidr* or *Khadir*, 'the Verdant One', who appeared in a vision to Ibn Arabi (1165–1240), one of the greatest Sufi teachers.[37] But the image of the Green Man also pervades the Western alchemical tradition as the figure of Mercurius, the *Lumen Naturae*, whose power for self-generation, self-transformation and self-destruction was described by the alchemists, who understood this energy to be the divine life in all of nature, ever changing, yet ever the same.[38] The old Sumerian and Egyptian image of the son–lover has undergone a profound transformation yet the underlying imagery is the same. In this century Jung describes how the vision of the Green Man appeared to him in 1939, at the point when he was becoming immersed in alchemy and aware that the whole direction of his work was moving towards a reinterpretation of the meaning of the Christian symbols:

One night I awoke and saw, bathed in bright light at the foot of my bed, the figure of Christ on the Cross. It was not quite life-size, but extremely distinct; and I saw that his body was made of greenish gold. The vision was marvellously beautiful, and yet I was profoundly shaken by it.[39]

The green figure changing to gold reflects as much the soul's 'ripening' as it does the image of wheat changing from the green of spring growth to the burnished gold of harvest.

THE RITUAL OF SACRIFICE AND THE MYSTERIES

The rituals of sacrifice in the Iron Age are one of its most striking religious features. The sacrifice of the bull is the one that is common to all the cultures considered in this book, and was offered for the regeneration of life. Harrison has shown how deeply established this ritual was in Greece.[40] Later, it becomes an act of propitiation or thanksgiving and in this form it is continually referred to in the *Iliad*. The last desacralized vestiges of it – perhaps once part of the rites of Cybele and Mithra – are to be found in the bullfights of Spain and south-western France. The bull or ram sacrifice replaced human sacrifice, but human sacrifice was still practised on occasions where the community felt itself to be particularly threatened, as is clear from Greek writers (in the *Iliad*, for instance). Even in the modern bullfight, the occasional sacrifice of the matador on the horns of the bull is accepted as part of the ritual, as it must have been in Minoan Crete. Similarly, Semitic peoples once sacrificed the first-born child or first-born animal as part of religious observance.

With the Mysteries, we move into a totally new concept of sacrifice. In the Roman Empire, as in Greece, the Mysteries or secret rites, together with the philosophical teaching that infused them, attracted many men and women who were drawn to them by their search for a deeper meaning to existence than that offered by the official state religion. While the fearful sacrificial rites of the Roman arena drew the masses to participate in an orgy of blood-lust, and the rituals of flagellation and castration attracted many in the hysteria of the annual processions of Cybele, others found their way to a different experience of sacrifice. The old sacrament of the ritual feast described by Harrison in relation to the Dionysian and Orphic rites – when the participants ate the raw flesh of the god in the form of a sacrificed bull in the belief that they were absorbing the mana of the god – was replaced by another, no longer 'red and bleeding'.[41]

The public ceremonies of Cybele and Attis were quite distinct from these other rituals, which were shared by relatively few people, who never divulged their secret, as with the Eleusinian Mysteries in Greece. In what little is known of the Mysteries of the Great Mother and her son–lover the transformation of the ritual of sacrifice can be followed most closely. The Mysteries were the root of the Gnostic sects that came to prominence before and after the beginning of the Christian era (whose ideas will be explored in Chapter 15). It seems as if the old Neolithic vision of life somehow survived the Bronze and Iron Ages to re-emerge in these Mysteries, so that, with a new phase in the evolution of consciousness enshrined in this new level of insight, a sacrament of communion could be celebrated with the divine life, whose image at this time was the goddess. The initiate himself becomes the son–lover, whose old beliefs and way of life are sacrificed to his or her new understanding of the Mysteries, and who is 'reborn' from the death-like state of his former level of understanding.

The 'Day of Blood' (*Dies Sanguinis*) symbolized the death or sacrifice of the former state. The *Hilaria*, or day of rejoicing, celebrated the return or ascent of the soul to its source.⁴² The child 'born' of the sacred marriage between the initiate and the goddess was at once the image of regenerated life on earth and the initiate's own spiritual regeneration. In the fourth century AD the Neoplatonist Emperor Julian expressed this understanding with the words:

> But him whom I call Gallus or Attis I discern of my own knowledge to be the substance of the generative and creative Mind which engenders all things down to the lowest plane of matter and comprehends in itself all the concepts and causes of the forms that are embodied in matter.⁴³

The fundamental experience of these Mysteries, ritually enacted in an initiation ceremony that involved the 'death' of the initiate, may have been that death was an illusion, and the soul immortal. The inner and symbolic 'sacrifice' of the fear of death released the initiate from the conception of life and death as irreconcilable opposites, and opened his or her consciousness to the wonder of being. Here *bios*, the individual life in time, was reunited with *zoe*, the ground of all life, and the finite perspective was transcended in a living experience. Such was the true meaning of *sacer facere*, to make whole. 'I am a child of Earth and Starry Heaven; But my race is of Heaven alone'⁴⁴ the Orphic initiate proclaimed, and by this understood that the body might return to earth, but the soul belonged to a life that was paradoxically both beyond and also manifest *as* natural life. The initiates of the Mysteries of Cybele and Attis would have known themselves to be both human and divine, but have seen no essential separateness in that duality. Immortality was certain because humanity, like all creation, was divine. They had 'fallen from' or forgotten this knowledge, but through the rituals of the Mysteries they could remember it.

The Mysteries that took place during the 'holy' night before the return or resurrection of Attis are still exceedingly obscure and, like the Mysteries of Eleusis, are, unfortunately, recorded only by prejudiced Christian sources.⁴⁵ It is known that a ritual feast and a sacred marriage ceremony were part of them, as they were in the Dionysian and Orphic Mysteries of Greece. A tablet dedicated to Cybele has a fish and cup inscribed on it, and it is possible that fish, as well as wine and bread, was the food shared by the initiates, and that it was laid in the sacred cup or vessels which symbolized the goddess herself. The fish, as the spirit of the waters, is one of the oldest images of regenerated life, and fish and cakes were offered to the goddess by her devotees and eaten as her sacred 'body' in Mesopotamia and Syria. Fish is still the ritual meal eaten on Friday, the day once sacred to the goddess. (Our word Friday comes from the name of the Norse goddess Freia, and in Italy, fish is eaten on the day named after Venus, *Venerdi*.)

The sacrality of fish and bread, and the image of fecundity associated with them because of their original connection with the goddess, are strangely reflected in the miracle of the loaves and fishes of the New Testament. Clement of Alexandria writes contemptuously of the Attis ritual where the initiate says: 'I have eaten from the timbrel, I have drunk from the cymbal [these were musical instruments], I have carried the *kernos*, I have gone down into the bridal chamber.'[46] The first three *tokens*, as Harrison observes, 'are practically identical with the *tokens* of Eleusis and relate to the solemn partaking of first-fruits; the last is a manifest avowal of a Sacred Marriage. The word *pastos* here used by Clement means a "bridal chamber or bridal bed".'[47] To eat these foods would have been to partake of *zoe*, divine life, and to realize that all life was *that* life. It seems that the initiation involved a symbolic descent into the underworld into the sacred cave or crypt beneath or beside the temple of Cybele, and here the ceremony of the sacred marriage took place, and from here the initiate was 'reborn' as a 'son' or 'daughter' of the goddess.

As to the origin of these Mysteries, according to a Greek writer, Diodorus, they came originally from Crete, where they had been an open festival:

> The Cretans, in alleging that they handed on from Crete to other peoples the dues of the gods, their sacrifices, and the rites appertaining to mysteries, bring forward this point as being to their thinking the chief piece of evidence. The rite of initiation at Eleusis, which is perhaps the most celebrated of all, and the rite of Samothrace, among the Cicones, whence came Orpheus, its inventor, are all imparted as mysteries; whereas in Crete, at Knossos, from ancient days it was the custom that these rites should be imparted openly to all, and things that among other peoples were communicated in dead secrecy, among the Cretans, they said, no one concealed from anyone who wished to know such matters.[48]

The Mysteries took the imagery of fertility and transposed it from the literal to the symbolic level, an alchemy that worked a profound transformation of consciousness. The sacrality of nature was not discarded but, on the contrary, honoured by bringing the natural images to life in relation to the soul's own life. The analogy was experienced as a revelation. An inscription at Delphi declares that Athens, by establishing the Mysteries, brought humanity from barbarism to civilization.[49] Perhaps the Mysteries of Cybele and Attis did the same.

11

THE IRON AGE:
THE GREAT FATHER GOD
YAHWEH-ELOHIM

Man lives, not directly or nakedly in nature like the animals, but within a mythological universe, a body of assumptions and beliefs developed from his existential concerns. Most of this is held unconsciously, which means that our imaginations may recognize elements of it, when presented in art or literature, without consciously understanding what it is that we recognize. Practically all that we can see of this body of concern is socially conditioned and culturally inherited. Below the cultural inheritance, there must be a common psychological inheritance, otherwise forms of culture would not be intelligible to us. But I doubt if we can reach this common inheritance directly, by-passing the distinctive qualities in our specific culture. One of the practical functions of criticism, by which I mean the conscious organizing of a cultural tradition, is, I think, to make us more aware of our mythological conditioning.

Northrop Frye, *The Great Code: The Bible and Literature*

I pray to God to keep me from 'God'.

Meister Eckhart

In the beginning God created the heaven and the earth.
And the earth was without form, and void: and darkness was upon the face of the deep. And the Spirit of God moved upon the face of the waters.
And God said, Let there be light; and there was light.
And God saw the light, that it was good: and God divided the light from the darkness.
And God called the light Day, and the darkness he called Night. And the evening and the morning were the first day.
And God said, Let there be a firmament in the midst of the waters, and let it divide the waters from the waters.
And God made the firmament,
And divided the waters which were under the firmament from the waters which were above the firmament: and it was so.
And God called the firmament Heaven. And the evening and the morning were the second day.
And God said, Let the waters under the heaven be gathered together unto one place, and let the dry land appear: and it was so.

And God called the dry land Earth;
And the gathering together of the waters called he Seas: and God saw that it was
good. (Gen. 1:1–10)[1]

With the Old Testament, we come to our own particular mythological universe, the cultural inheritance whose assumptions we are most likely to hold unconsciously and be least able, therefore, to challenge directly. Northrop Frye, in the passage quoted above, asks us to consider the question of 'mythological conditioning', where we may not even realize that we have certain beliefs about the nature of the world, and that there could be, quite legitimately, alternative ways of looking at things. Even if we do not accept the Bible as 'the Written Word of God', we may have taken on the most fundamental of its premises: that divinity is transcendent in the sense of being, necessarily, *beyond* nature. When we look around us we may see a fallen world more easily than we see a world divine, even though that divinity is often obscured, perhaps even by the way we perceive it. And if we grant a soul to humanity, we may not grant a soul, or even consciousness, to nature.

Turning, then, to Hebrew mythology on its own terms, the Great Father God Yahweh–Elohim created heaven and earth in the beginning, and what he said was so, and he saw that it was good. Unlike any earlier god, this god creates and rules alone: he has no lineage, no family, no mother, wife or child. The world he makes and looks upon comes not from his body but from his word. The transubstantial and unrepresentable deity comes to the human beings he has made in his own image as a disembodied voice.

In Hebrew mythology all the various male deities of earlier cultures – Enlil, Ptah, Marduk and El – coalesce into the one image of the Great Father God, who enters the stage of the Bible as though he were the first and only deity. As suggested in Chapter 7, the elevation of the god begotten of the mother goddess into the father god was finally achieved in Babylonian mythology; but now it becomes supreme, as though the idea of a mother goddess had never existed in the human psyche. Yet the Old Testament did not arise in the beginning out of a formless void, and echoes of a rich historical past sound throughout the stories, telling of people who travelled, were transported, exiled, dispersed, influenced and inspired, though answerable finally to their own poetic vision.

There is no doubt that, as poetry, the first three chapters of Genesis are incomparably more beautiful than the Babylonian myth of creation, the *Enuma Elish*. Both myths have many images in common, but in Genesis these images have been transformed into a new way of perceiving the world, one in which creation is seen as the linear unfolding of an intelligible divine plan. None the less, it is vital to remember, as Campbell does, that wherever the poetry of myth is interpreted as biography, history or science, it is killed. The living images become only a remote fact of a distant time or sky; furthermore it is never difficult to demonstrate that as science and history mythology is absurd . . . When a civilization begins to reinterpret its mythology in this way, the life goes out of it.[2]

The living images of the Old Testament are understood here, with Campbell, as 'poetic readings of the mystery of life from a certain interested point of view', and so 'a product, like every other piece of ancient literature, not of God's literary talent but of man's . . . not of eternity but of time, and specifically an extremely troubled time'.[3] The Old Testament reflects the vision of a people, wonderfully gifted as poets, living in a particularly violent age. However, to interpret mythology solely in terms of the historical events that may have given rise to it is to undervalue the numinosity of the image that still has the power to inspire and to heal. The beauty of the verse does much to explain the lasting appeal of what 'happened' in the beginning, even when the happening is finally placed, for some, within the human psyche.

When we read the word 'God' or 'the Lord' in the English Bible, we are perhaps not aware that these words come from two Hebrew names for the Hebrew deity, Elohim and Yahweh. The name 'Elohim' comes from the body of writing known as the Elohim, or 'E', texts, which belonged originally to the mythology of the northern kingdom of Israel, and here the sacred mountain is called Horeb. These texts date to the eighth century BC. Elohim is the plural form of the word El (which was also the name of the Canaanite father god) and is translated as 'god', although the more accurate translation would be 'gods'. The name 'Yahweh' (translated as 'the Lord') comes from the body of writings known as the Yahwist, or 'J', texts, which belonged to the mythology of the southern kingdom of Judah and date to the ninth century BC; in these texts the sacred mountain is called Sinai.

The mythology of Genesis 1 belongs to the later of these two, the 'E' texts, and Genesis 2 and 3 to the earlier, 'J' texts. However, the Elohim text was reworked at least twice, once in the seventh century BC by an editor who brought the two mythological traditions together, and then again after the Babylonian Exile during the fifth and fourth centuries BC. This last reworked text is known as the Priestly, or 'P', text. When we read Genesis, we need to bear in mind that the creation myth in Genesis 1, and in verses 1–4 of Chapter 2, belongs to the Elohim text originating in the eighth century BC and reworked after the Exile; and that the creation myth in Genesis 2:4–25 is drawn from sources from the southern kingdom dating to the ninth century BC, also reworked after the Exile in Babylon. Both stories were finally placed together at the beginning of Genesis. If this seems confusing, it is! Why was the later, Priestly version put first? It is a complicated story.

It is not surprising to discover that there are many parallels between the myth of creation in Genesis 1, which took seven days, and the earlier Babylonian creation myth – the *Enuma Elish*, which means 'When on High'. Significantly, it was on seven tablets that Marduk's war against Tiamat was recorded as the seven stages of his defeat of chaos upon which creation was predicated. Because of the immense popularity of the Babylonian epic of creation, the Hebrews would have been familiar with its theme long before they were in Babylon, and during their exile in Babylon (586–538 BC) they would have had the opportunity of hearing the tablets recited every year in the great temple of Marduk at the spring festival.

As in earlier creation myths, the first event in Genesis 1 is the creation and separation of heaven and earth, which Elohim accomplishes more lyrically than Marduk's crude splitting of Tiamat's corpse. In both myths there is an abyss of waters at the beginning denoted by almost the same Semitic word. The Hebrew *Tehom*, the Deep, is the equivalent of the Semitic-Babylonian *Tiamat*. This, together with the image of the formless void, *tohu wa-bohu*, reveals the image of the conquered Babylonian Mother Goddess, whose name is also related to *tohu wa-bohu*. The placing of the firmament and the dividing of the waters above from the waters below recall Marduk's construction of heaven from one half of Tiamat's lifeless body and his 'fixing' of the upper waters: he 'shot a bolt across, and placed watchers over it to prevent Tiamat from letting out her waters'.[4] But what was drama in Babylon has become merely an abstraction in the Hebrew myth.[5] Graves and Patai, in their book *Hebrew Myths*, observe that:

> The monotheistic editor of the cosmogony in Genesis 1 and 11 could assign no part in Creation to anyone but God, and therefore omitted all pre-existing elements or beings which might be held divine. Such abstractions as Chaos (*tohu wa-bohu*), Darkness (*hosekh*), and the Deep (*tehom*) would, however, tempt no worshippers: so these took the place of the ancient matriarchal deities.[6]

The Babylonian image of cosmic conflict is formally obliterated in the biblical myth of the sole creator god. However, it breaks through in poetic tributes to Yahweh's power, where he continually struggles victoriously against the great primordial forces that threaten his rule, characteristically personified as female. These, in turn, are identified with the Canaanite religion and with the political enemies of the Hebrews, particularly the Babylonians, Assyrians and Egyptians. Here, Yahweh vanquishes chaos personified by Tehom (Tiamat), Rahab and Leviathan. Tohu, in the phrase *tohu wa-bohu*, becomes Tehom and Tehomot. Bohu becomes Behom and Behomot, a variation of Job's Behemoth, 'the dry-land counterpart of the sea-monster Leviathan'.[7]

All these monsters personify the waters that were originally imaged as the mother serpent-dragon, and all refer back to Tiamat, the prototype of the terrible Babylonian Mother Goddess Ishtar, who 'devoured' the people of Judah by taking them into captivity.[8] In the Book of Job, Behemoth is associated with the hippopotamus and Leviathan with the crocodile. Both these animals were sacred to Seth, the Egyptian god who personified the destructive forces of nature. If the Tehom–Tiamat parallel had not been discovered, no one would have known that behind Tehom, Leviathan and Rahab stands the serpent-dragon image of the formidable Babylonian Mother Goddess – she who gave birth to the gods, offended them and was finally murdered by them. Her body was used by her great-great-great-grandson Marduk to create the 'matter' of the universe.[9] With this understanding of the hidden presence of the Babylonian myth in the Old Testament, many passages, like those quoted in Chapter 7, take on a new meaning. Here, the imagery of the older contest is clearly seen:

> In that day the Lord with his sore and great and strong sword shall punish Leviathan the piercing serpent, even Leviathan that crooked serpent; and he shall slay the dragon that is in the sea. (Isa. 27:1)[10]

The mythic defeat of the Mother Goddess by a god is not, of course, unique to Babylonian mythology or to the Old Testament, but is enacted in the myths of every culture where the new rule of sky-gods is super-imposed on the older goddess religion.

YAHWEH–ELOHIM AS THE 'MAKER' OF CREATION

The first image of a creator god appears in both Sumeria and Egypt before the second millennium BC. Enlil gradually came to eclipse the other three creator goddesses and gods of the Sumerian pantheon – Ninhursag, the 'Mother of the gods', An and Enki. Enlil's role in Sumeria is later assumed by Marduk in Babylonia. Ninhursag held various titles that show that she was once revered as creator before An, Enlil and Enki, and that she must have been the earlier prototype of the goddess Aruru, who created Enkidu from clay. Ninhursag was called the 'Lady Potter'.

Unlike Enlil or Marduk, Yahweh–Elohim in Genesis 1 and 2 is the son of no Mother Goddess. He is primary to, and distinct from, his creation. Unlike the goddess Nammu, the primal creator in Sumerian myth, he does not bring creation forth from his body as the great mountain of Heaven-and-Earth, An-Ki. On the contrary, the mountain is his home. Yahweh is even described as making the things of the earth before they are there: 'And every plant of the field before it was in the earth, and every herb of the field before it grew' (Gen. 2:5).

Elohim in Genesis 1 makes creation like a craftsman. Alternatively, he 'says' or 'calls' it into being and 'tells' it what to do. He 'sees' that it is good. So also did the Mesopotamian craftsman when his work was complete, as he was required by law before his goods left the shop.[11] Similarly, the Sumerian god Enlil was himself the 'word' that spoke all things into being:

> Your word – it is plants, your word – it is grain,
> Your word is the floodwater, the life of all the lands.[12]

The Egyptian god Ptah, worshipped as the architect of the universe 2,000 years before Genesis was written, also created the world through the word: Ptah 'spoke on his tongue the utterances of his heart'.[13] In all these images the creative word alone has the power to manifest the divine will as creation.

Like these earlier myths of how the world came into being, Genesis is also a story of the coming into being of consciousness, when consciousness becomes aware of itself. In particular, the image of a god ordering the creation from which he himself has emerged may reflect that stage of human experience when the skill of recording speech was achieved. The 'creation of the word' in the form of writing arose in Sumeria about 3500 BC. Phillips, exploring the background to the story of Eve, writes:

> Creation, unlike procreation, depends on conceptualizing. There thus appears to be a more than coincidental relationship between the beginning of history – the writing of epic creation myths as the religious foundation of civilization – and the notably anti-feminine plot of such myths. The beginning of civilization seems to require a seizure of religious power by male gods, in order to break the ties of humanity to blood, soil, and nature.[14]

Both the Babylonian and the biblical creation myth in Genesis I took the lunar number seven to be sacred, following the seven planets, which were seen as the ordering principle of the universe. The order of creation followed the order of the planetary gods in the Babylonian week: for example, Nergal was a pastoral god and came third in the week, whereas Nabu, the god of astronomy, came fourth in the week, so, in the Babylonian order of creation, pasture came before stars. Similarly, in the biblical creation of Genesis I dry land, grass and trees are created before the 'luminaries' – the stars and planets in heaven – in both cases reflecting the prior human experience of agriculture before astronomy. The seven branches of the Menorah, the sacred candelabrum, also derive from these seven planetary gods.[15]

In the Neolithic era sun, moon and stars were the epiphany of the Mother Goddess, and by the time of the Bronze Age they had become deities in their own right. However, in the *Enuma Elish* they are no longer divine beings, but objects set in space, created by a god. Together with plants, animals and humanity, they owe their creation to Marduk, who was superior to them and not related to them in any other way. The first chapter of Genesis develops this imagery, and there the supreme creator also 'makes' the 'greater' and 'lesser' lights of sun and moon, together with the firmament, the dry land, the seas, animals, plants, and man and woman.

In the Genesis 1 story of creation there are other features that resemble the earlier epic. The actual creation of plants and animals is missing from the Babylonian epic, but Marduk is described as 'the Bestower of Planting, the Founder of Sowing, the Creator of Grain and Plants' and 'He who caused the green herb to spring up'. In Genesis, Elohim says: 'Let the earth bring forth grass, the herb yielding seed, and the fruit tree yielding fruit after his kind, whose seed is in itself, upon the earth: and it was so' (Gen. 1:11). It is clear that the abundant life of vegetation is Babylonian in origin, and that, as Campbell observes:

> The ultimate source of the Biblical Eden, therefore, cannot have been a mythology of the desert – that is to say, a primitive Hebrew myth – but was the old planting mythology of the peoples of the soil.[16]

THE TWO CREATION MYTHS

Mysteriously, as we have seen (p. 418), there are two creation myths in Genesis. In about 458 BC, eighty years after the Exile in Babylon ended, the priest Ezra and a group of priestly scribes arrived in Jerusalem from Babylon and, with the prophet Nehemiah, began the work of compiling and editing the sacred stories and legends of the people of Israel, giving them the form that led ultimately to the Old Testament as we know it now. Ezra was in the service of the Persian Empire, dispatched by the Persian king to Jerusalem to restore the temple there to its former glory.

Graves and Patai draw attention to the fact that Genesis 1 – the later (Priestly) myth, in which the earth emerges from a primeval watery chaos – resembles Babylonian creation myths, which celebrated the annual emergence of dry land from the winter floods of the Tigris and Euphrates. In Mesopotamia, therefore, the creative moment is the spring. By contrast, in Canaan the creative moment is in the autumn, when the rain comes. Genesis 2 – the earlier myth (J), in which 'there went up a mist from the earth' – reflects the parched and barren land of summer in Canaan before the first hint of coming rain in the dense white morning mist that rose from the valleys.[17] These two different 'New Year's days' were observed in the two Jewish feasts, one of which took place in spring, following the precedent of the Babylonian spring festival, and the other in autumn, following an older Canaanite festival.[18]

The Creation of Man and Woman

There are significant differences in the two creation myths in Genesis. In Genesis 1 (P) the animals are created before man and woman; in Genesis 2 (J), in striking contrast, they are created after Adam but before Eve. In Genesis 1 (P) man and woman are created together in the image of Elohim, which suggests that Elohim is imagined as both male and female; but in Genesis 2 (J), where the story of the Exile from the Garden is told, the man is created first, and when no suitable companion for him can be found among the animals, a woman is then created from the man's body. There is yet another version of the creation of man and woman in Genesis 5, which echoes the Priestly version in Genesis 1. Yet it is usually the Yahwist creation myth in Genesis 2 (written first and placed second) that is given great emphasis and portrayed in art, rarely the later story placed at the beginning as Genesis 1.

Version 1: Priestly

And God said, Let us make man in our image, after our likeness: and let them have dominion over the fish of the sea, and over the fowl of the air, and over the cattle, and over all the earth, and over every creeping thing that creepeth upon the earth.

So God created man in his *own* image, in the image of God created he him; male and female created he them. (Gen. 1:26–7)

Version 2: Yahwist

. . . and there was not a man to till the ground.

But there went up a mist from the earth, and watered the whole face of the ground.

And the Lord God formed man of the dust of the ground, and breathed into his nostrils the breath of life; and man became a living soul. (Gen. 2:5–7)

Version 3

This is the book of the generations of Adam. In the day that God created man, in the likeness of God made he him;

Male and female created he them; and blessed them, and called their name Adam, in the day when they were created. (Gen. 5:1–2)

The human race is no longer made from the blood of a slain demon, but does it share in the divinity of Elohim and Yahweh? The first and the third story suggest that male and female – made in 'our image, after our likeness', as Elohim says – do partake of the divinity of the creator. In the second story Adam, but not Eve, is formed of the dust of the ground and has his nostrils breathed into by his creator, who passes the 'breath of life' from himself to the man, to make him 'a living soul'. This is exactly how

Figure 1. The goddess
Hathor holding the
ankh to the nostrils
of the Pharaoh
Amenhotep II; tomb
painting, *c.* 1425 BC.
Thebes.

the Egyptian goddesses and gods gave life to the living and the dead, by
holding the symbol of eternal life – the *ankh* – to their nostrils.

The myth of humanity's creation from earth, clay or dust had long
existed in the Near East. In the Sumerian *Epic of Gilgamesh* the goddess
Aruru made Enkidu by pinching off a piece of clay from the earth that

Figure 2. The god Ptah throwing the
cosmic egg on to the potter's wheel.

was her own 'body' and breathing life into him. The god Enki and the goddess Ninhursag made human beings from clay, and in Egypt the gods Knum and Ptah threw the forms of men and women on the potter's wheel.

In Genesis 2 the creation of human beings is told somewhat differently. Before humanity was created, 'the Lord God had not caused it to rain upon the earth' (Gen. 2:5). Once the decision to create human beings was made, '. . . there went up a mist from the earth, and watered the whole face of the ground. And the Lord God formed man of the dust of the ground' (Gen. 2:6–7) so that the mixture of dust and water could become clay. It is as though the man and the mist had to be made together to bring the earth to life. It is clear that Yahweh takes over the imagery of the Egyptian Ptah and the Sumerian Ninhursag and Enki. Like the goddess Aruru before him, he breathes life into creation. The image of the god as divine potter is later extended to his shaping of the destiny of Israel: 'Behold, as the clay is in the potter's hand, so are ye in mine hand, O house of Israel' (Jer. 18:6).

Immediately after he made man, Yahweh 'planted a garden' and put the man into it to 'dress it and keep it' (Gen. 2:15). There is still no sign of woman. Significantly, however, in the light of subsequent events, it is Yahweh's first mention of death which brings the idea of a 'help-meet' to mind. Yahweh forbids the man to eat of the tree of knowledge of good and evil, 'for in the day that thou eatest thereof thou shalt surely die'. After this disconcerting intrusion of the images of evil and death, Yahweh sees the man all alone in the garden of the world.

In the first story Elohim saw that what he (the gods) had made was good. In the second story Yahweh does not delight in his creation. Good is not his appraisal of what is made, but enters only as a disembodied opposite to 'evil' on a tree called the 'Tree of Knowledge', strangely contrasted with another tree 'in the midst of the garden' called the 'Tree of Life'. Yahweh's first idea of a 'help-meet' for the man was the beast of the field and the fowl of the air. It is only when Yahweh brings to him the animals to see what he would call them that the man receives his own name, Adam, from the name for the soil, *Adamah*, actually a noun of feminine gender that could be interpreted as 'mother'.[19]

The Creation of Eve

'But for Adam there was not found an help-meet for him' (Gen. 2:20). In the second story (J) Eve appears only as an afterthought, after Yahweh had made Adam and Adam had named all the animals, 'every beast of the field and every fowl of the air':

> And the Lord God caused a deep sleep to fall upon Adam, and he slept: and
> he took one of his ribs, and closed up the flesh instead thereof;
> And the rib, which the Lord God had taken from man, made he a woman,
> and brought her unto the man.

> And Adam said, This is now bone of my bones, and flesh of my flesh: she
> shall be called Woman, because she was taken out of Man. (Gen. 2:21–3)

Unlike the animals, Eve is named only *after* the curse of Yahweh: 'And
Adam called his wife's name Eve; because she was the mother of all
living' (Gen. 3:20).

So at last woman comes into being. She is not made from the substance
of earth and does not have the breath of life breathed into her, yet Adam
gives her, apparently unwittingly, the title of the old Mother Goddess,
'Mother of All Living'. It seems that the first story, in which Elohim
makes man and woman in 'our' own image – which suggests that 'he' is
both god and goddess, or at least more than one god – has been changed,
so that the creation of woman becomes different from, and secondary to,
that of man.[20] The prophets blamed the two calamities of the dispersal of
the ten tribes of the northern Hebrew kingdom of Israel in 721 BC and the
Exile in Babylon upon the people's worship of the Canaanite goddess and
her son, Baal. Their defamation of the goddess may well be reflected in
the tone of the second creation story, in which Eve is blamed for the exile
of humankind from the Garden.

In the first chapter of Genesis the man and the woman are told:

> Be fruitful and multiply, and replenish the earth, and subdue it: and have
> dominion over the fish of the sea, and over the fowl of the air, and over
> every living thing that moveth upon the earth. (Gen. 1:28)

This bestowal of power is amplified later when Yahweh speaks to Noah:

> Be fruitful and multiply, and replenish the earth.
> And the fear of you and the dread of you shall be upon every beast of the
> earth, and upon every fowl of the air, upon all that moveth upon the earth,
> and upon all the fishes of the sea; into your hand are they delivered.
> Every moving thing that liveth shall be meat for you; even as the green
> herb have I given you all things. (Gen. 9:1–3)

No one before was ever told to subdue and have dominion over the
earth, so what does this mean? Are human beings now to be intrinsically
superior to the other orders of creation, with unlimited powers over
them? The metaphor is one of ownership and possession with the re-
ciprocal relation of fear and dread on the part of those so treated. The
martial image of subduing and having dominion over the other – whether
that be earth, fish, fowl and every living thing that moves, or as it was
eventually extended to mean, the opposing tribe, religion, or even wife –
not only embodied the prevailing war-like ethos of the Iron Age, but,
worse, ratified it as divine instruction.

THE BIBLE AS MYTH AND METAPHOR

For someone coming to the Old Testament for the first time, it is helpful to bear in mind Frye's proposal, in his book *The Great Code: The Bible and Literature*, that the Bible can be read as a gigantic and complex metaphor, and that this 'metaphor is not an incidental ornament of Biblical language, but one of its controlling modes of thought'.[21] It is, he explains, one of the greatest examples of mythical or poetic thinking, as opposed to historical thinking, and the controlling metaphor is one of descent and ascent. This is a metaphor very different in feeling from that of cyclic renewal, though ultimately the same mythic image informs both kinds of story. The people of Israel are enslaved in the 'underworld' of Egypt, and cry out to Yahweh for help. They are 'delivered' by an emissary sent from Yahweh, but fall again into slavery, this time in Babylon. Again, they are delivered. The theme is repeated once more in the New Testament, where the myth of the Fall and Descent in Genesis is completed by the myth of Ascent and Resurrection. In the Old Testament the society of Israel is the focus of the myth; in the New Testament an individual lives out the myth. The ever-repeated cycle of the former mythologies has become one Great Cycle, with the Hebrew experience standing as the prototype for the whole of humanity, as though, indeed, history 'began' with Adam. In every scene of this drama, as Frye says, 'priority is given to the mythical structure or outline of the story, not to the historical content'.[22] This means that 'what is true is what the writer thinks ought to be true'.[23] And not one writer, but many.

The Old Testament asks to be comprehended as an integrated whole, but, studied historically, it inevitably shows itself to be a compendium of many different stories by many different hands, themselves changed and reworked by many other and different hands. One of the last of these was the priest Ezra, who, above all, set his stamp on what the truth should be. Structurally, at any rate, the Book of Genesis forms an introduction to the first five books of the Old Testament, called the Pentateuch, and the Book of Joshua. These tell the story of the deliverance of the people of Israel from Egypt and the Hebrew settlement of Canaan, which transformed a disparate group of Semitic clans into a nation. Genesis, then, provides the mythological background to the heroic theme of conquest that follows, endowing this people with the ancestors which give them an historic role and an identity as a tribe.

Canaan was a strip of land that is today divided into Syria, Lebanon, Jordan and Israel. It was the great highway between the Mediterranean and the Persian Gulf, the vital corridor that connected the two great centres of civilization, Egypt and Mesopotamia. People had settled in Canaan from Neolithic times; Jericho was already building defensive walls in the seventh millennium BC, and the cities of Ugarit (Ras Shamra), Tyre, Sidon and Byblos were thriving ports by the time of the Hebrew settlement in Canaan. During the Bronze and Iron Ages a variety of Semitic tribes from the Syro-Arabian desert and from Mesopotamia established themselves in Canaan, and adopted or assimilated the religion of the people already settled there, and also of neighbouring Sumeria and Babylonia. Although geographically closer to Egypt, these tribes had a greater affinity with the Semitic peoples who were already living in northern Mesopotamia. Canaanite mythology shares many stories and images with Mesopotamia and Egypt.

It was these people, Semites like themselves, whom the Hebrews found – living in great cities and cultivating the land – when they entered Canaan, the land 'flowing with milk and honey' (Exod. 33:3). The Book of Joshua describes the conquest of Canaan, presenting the destruction of Canaanite civilization as a work of divine cleansing, one of the best documented examples of the phenomenon known (by those who start it) as a 'holy war'. One way in which this war is portrayed is through the story of the long and relentless struggle between the god of the Hebrews and the goddess of the Canaanites, who was called, variously, Asherah, Anath and Ashtoreth (whose other name was Astarte).

THE INFLUENCE OF SUMERIA, BABYLONIA AND EGYPT ON THE OLD TESTAMENT

Though the influence of Sumeria, Babylonia, Egypt and Persia on the Bible has long been documented by scholars, it is only recently that the implications have become more widely considered. Without this awareness, the transmission of imagery from one culture to another passes unnoticed and the gradual evolution of consciousness is ignored. From a reading of the Old Testament alone it would be hard to appreciate that the goddess culture existed for many thousands of years before the appearance of the monotheistic father god. Consequently, the effects of the Iron Age repression of the goddess culture, and its implications for our own culture, have not yet been fully evaluated.

The imagery of many of the stories in Genesis is unmistakably Sumerian and Babylonian. In Sumeria there was the story of a mythical place where wild animals did not kill or ravage, and where old age, sickness and death did not exist. The name of this Sumerian paradise was Dilmun, a word that can mean both 'land' and 'mountain'.

> In Dilmun the raven utters no cry,
> The *ittidu*-bird utters not the cry of the *ittidu*-bird,
> The lion kills not,
> The wolf snatches not the lamb,
> Unknown is the kid-devouring wild dog,
> Unknown is the grain-devouring (boar) . . .[24]

The resemblance to Isaiah's prophecy is remarkable:

> The wolf also shall dwell with the lamb, and the leopard shall lie down
> with the kid; and the calf and the young lion and the fatling together . . .
>
>   . . . . .
>
> They shall not hurt or destroy in all my holy mountain . . . (Isa. 11:6, 9)

The Sumerian deities and the Babylonian Marduk had created the
human race to 'serve the gods'. Yahweh created the man to 'till the
ground' of the earth, to 'dress and keep' the garden: 'And the Lord God
took the man, and put him into the garden of Eden to dress it and to keep
it' (Gen. 2:15).

The story of the first gardener comes from Sumeria, the first 'garden'
in the world, where human beings were to work to provide food for the
gods to save the gods having to till the ground themselves. Later the king,
as the son–lover of the goddess, took the official title of 'gardener', personifying the life of vegetation and the fruitfulness of the earth, and
enacting the role of husbandman and shepherd. He held his throne by
virtue of this covenant with the goddess: 'I am he', says the Sumerian
king, Ishme-Dagan, 'whom Inanna, Queen of Heaven and Earth, has
chosen for her beloved husband.' The Hebrews entered the fertile land of
Canaan from the desert, where the oasis, with its trees and water, signified
resurgent life – in Frye's words, 'a garden directly created and sustained
by God . . . the visible form of the invisible divine creation'.[25] In Genesis,
Adam, the first man, is also the gardener, but now, in a patriarchal
culture, he becomes the 'son' of the Great Father rather than the son and
consort of the Great Mother.

Both cultures had a tradition of sacred stone tablets. The Babylonian
seven tablets of creation, on which the *Enuma Elish* was written, parallel
the seven days of creation in Genesis. The Tower of Babel refers to the
ziggurat, possibly Marduk's or Ishtar's temple in Babylon, which many
Hebrews would have seen for themselves during the Exile. The image of
Moses going up to the top of Mount Sinai to receive the tablets of the law
from Yahweh recalls the stone relief of the Babylonian King Hammurabi
(*c.* 1730 BC) receiving his code of laws from Shamash, who is quite clearly
seated on a mountain, with flames emerging from his shoulders (Fig. 3).
One difference, of course, is that there is no image of Yahweh:

> And the Lord came down upon mount Sinai, on the top of the mount: and
> the Lord called Moses up to the top of the mount; and Moses went up . . .
>
> And all the people saw the thunderings and the lightnings, and the noise of
> the trumpet, and the mountain smoking . . . (Exod. 19:20; 20:18)

Many people do not know that there are two earlier versions of the
Flood – Sumerian and Babylonian. The story of the Flood in Genesis
derives its quality of tone, in particular the piety of Noah, directly from
the Sumerian myth of the Flood. This formed part of the *Epic of*

Figure 3. Hammurabi receiving the Tablet of Laws from the god Shamash, seated on a mountain; engraved stone, *c.* 1730 BC.

Gilgamesh, where Gilgamesh, like Eve and Adam, aspired to attain to the immortality of the gods. In the Sumerian version humanity was destroyed because the noise rising up from earth disturbed the gods. In Genesis humanity is destroyed because it is 'wicked' (Gen. 6:5). With the Flood, the fertilizing waters of the sky god have turned demonic and destructive; the Father who creates has become the Father who destroys what he has made. Yet Yahweh warns Noah of the coming catastrophe, just as Enki warned Ziusudra in the Sumerian version, and as Ea warned Utnapishtim in the Babylonian version.

Significantly, the one image missing in the Genesis version of the Flood story is the goddess. The creators of human beings, animals and plants in the Sumerian story were goddesses and gods – Anu, Enlil, Enki and Nintu or Ninhursag, also called Inanna. In both the Sumerian and Babylonian stories Inanna and Ishtar lament the destruction of the people they had brought into being. The Sumerian lament precedes the coming of the Flood: 'The holy Inanna lamented on account of her people'. In the Babylonian version the goddess Ishtar, 'the sweet-voiced Queen of Heaven', cries out as the great storm approaches:

> Alas the days of old are turned to dust because I commanded evil; why did I command this evil in the council of all the gods. I commanded wars to destroy the people, but are they not my people, for I brought them forth? Now like the spawn of fish they float in the ocean.[26]

After the Flood, the gods in the Sumerian version 'smell a sweet savour' rising to heaven, as does Yahweh in Genesis: 'And the Lord smelled a sweet savour' (Gen. 8:21). In *Gilgamesh* Ishtar joins the sacrifice and blames the Flood on Enlil's lack of reflection:

> She lifted her necklace with the jewels of heaven that once Anu had made to please her. 'O you gods here present, by the lapis lazuli round my neck I shall remember these days as I remember the jewels of my throat; these last days I shall not forget. Let all the gods gather round the sacrifice, except Enlil. He shall not approach this offering, for without reflection he brought the flood; he consigned my people to destuction.'[27]

Another version says that Ishtar placed her many-jewelled necklace, which encircled her neck like the rainbow, in the sky to prevent Enlil receiving the sacrificial offerings on earth, 'since rashly he caused the flood-storm, and handed over my people to destruction'.[28] When Enlil arrived, he was furious and 'swelled with anger at the gods, the host of heaven, saying, "Has any of these mortals escaped? Not one was to have survived the destruction."' But Ea, god of wisdom, 'opened his mouth and spoke to the warrior Enlil', and counselled him to be merciful:

> Lay upon the sinner his sin,
> Lay upon the transgressor his transgression,
> Punish him a little when he breaks loose,
> Do not drive him too hard or he perishes;
> Would that a lion had ravaged mankind
> Rather than the flood,
> Would that a wolf had ravaged mankind
> Rather than the flood,
> Would that famine had wasted the world
> Rather than the flood,
> Would that pestilence had wasted mankind
> Rather than the flood.[29]

Enlil relented and, taking Utnapishtim and his wife by the hand, blessed them both.

In Genesis there is no vestige of the goddess except her birds, the raven and the dove, though in *Gilgamesh* a swallow – another bird sacred to Ishtar as well as to Inanna and Isis – is sent out too. In the Babylonian story Ishtar swears by her jewelled necklace, the rainbow, that she will remember those awful days. In Genesis the rainbow becomes the symbol of Yahweh's covenant that he will no longer destroy humankind by a flood. And Noah is promised the regular cycle of the seasons, which is the foundation of farming life: 'While the earth remaineth, seedtime and harvest, and cold and heat, and summer and winter, and day and night shall not cease' (Gen. 8:22).[30]

The priestly compilers of the Flood story in Genesis seem to have drawn considerably on the image of Enlil for the character of Yahweh, so we might ask why did they leave out the image of the goddess in their portrayal of the Creation and the Flood? Was it because of the humiliation of the Exile and the prophets' contempt for Ishtar, the 'Great Whore of Babylon', as they called her?

Certain stories besides the Flood are paralleled in Sumerian stories; for instance, the theme of the rivalry between two brothers: Cain, the tiller of the soil, and Abel, the herdsman; or Esau, 'the hairy man', and Jacob, 'the smooth man'. Both of these stories have echoes of the Sumerian tale that compares the virtues of the shepherd and the farmer. Here Inanna is urged by her brother Utu, the sun god, to marry the shepherd Dumuzi:

> O my sister, let the shepherd marry you,
> O maid Inanna, why are you unwilling?
> His cream is good, his milk is good,
> The shepherd, everything his hand touches is bright . . .

Inanna is not beguiled by the image of the shepherd drawn by her brother and she wants to marry the farmer Enkimdu.

> Me, the shepherd shall not marry,
> In his new garment he shall not drape me,
> His fine wool shall not cover me,
> Me, the maid, the farmer shall marry,
> The farmer who makes plants grow abundantly,
> The farmer who makes grain grow abundantly . . .[31]

Dumuzi, the shepherd, then offers a long list of qualities that show his produce to be superior to that of the farmer Enkimdu, whose name is too similar to that of the 'wild' man Enkidu to be a coincidence. In *Gilgamesh* Enkidu is also described in the image of a hairy man:

(Enkidu's) body was rough, he had long hair like a woman's; it waved like the hair of Nisaba, the goddess of corn. His body was covered with matted hair like Samuqan's, the god of cattle.[32]

Dumuzi picks a quarrel with Enkimdu, who refuses to respond and offers to let Dumuzi pasture his flocks anywhere on his territory. Somewhere in the course of this story Inanna changes her mind and agrees to marry Dumuzi, who now invites Enkimdu to their wedding.

In Genesis the outcome is less agreeable. Inanna is replaced by Yahweh, who prefers Abel's offering to Cain's. The outcome is a murder rather than a reconciliation, and a curse instead of a wedding. Through the figures of the farmer and the shepherd in the earlier Sumerian story we can discern the Bronze Age conflict between the nomadic Semitic tribes from the Syro-Arabian desert and the sedentary agriculturalists of the river valleys whose land they entered. Behind the warring brothers in Genesis lies the Hebrew conquest of Canaan and, if the Book of Joshua is an accurate record, the subjugation of the agriculturalist by the shepherd: it was Abel's offering of the lamb that Yahweh received, not the fruit of the ground offered by Cain (whose name carries an echo of Canaan). The Canaanite agriculturalists and the nomadic, sheep-herding Hebrews were both Semites, and it is possible that they looked upon each other as elder and younger 'brothers'. In Genesis, Yahweh always prefers the younger son, the shepherd, to the elder, the farmer, whose hairiness implies that he is closer to the beasts.

There was also a Babylonian practice at the New Year festival, when two men smeared the shrine of Marduk's son with the blood of a sheep, so defiling themselves, and fled into the wilderness until the festival was over.[33] In the Hebrew ritual of the Day of Atonement the two men were replaced by two goats, one of which was sacrificed to Yahweh, while the other was driven into the desert, carrying the sins of the community that had been ritually transferred to it. From this ritual came the expression 'scapegoat'. Having driven out the 'evil' with the goat, the community felt restored to its at-onement with Yahweh, just as in an earlier time the ritual sacrifice of the king or a substitute drove out the ills, actual or anticipated, and restored a right relationship with the unseen powers of life.[34]

Egypt and Mesopotamia are concealed beneath the surface of the Old Testament more often than might be expected. The Middle Eastern scholar James Pritchard points to such parallels as, for instance, sayings in the Egyptian 'Instruction of the Vizier Ptah-Hotep' (a text that dates to *c.* 2450 BC), which are found in the Book of Proverbs as well as those of the Prophets.[35] Lines from Egyptian as well as Sumerian sacred marriage hymns, composed for the celebration of the annual union of Isis and Osiris or Inanna and Dumuzi, find their way into the Song of Songs.[36] Finally, in Isaiah, there is the passage (possibly written about 545 BC, before the end of the Exile) that describes the suffering servant. These lines have been interpreted as a prophecy of the coming of Jesus, but also evoke the Sumerian and Babylonian liturgies that spoke of the one who, as Dumuzi and Tammuz, gave his life for the life of the community and was mourned:

> He is despised and rejected of men; a man of sorrows, and acquainted with grief . . .[37]
> Surely he hath borne our griefs, and carried our sorrows: yet we did esteem him stricken, smitten of God, and afflicted.
> But he was wounded for our transgressions, he was bruised for our iniquities: the chastisement of our peace was upon him; and with his stripes we are healed. (Isa. 53: 2–5)

When this is interpreted as a prophecy of the coming of the 'Anointed', it is not always realized that this was a title that was given to earlier saviours of the community in their role as the sacrificed god.

YAHWEH–ELOHIM AS THE TRANSCENDENT GOD

Not surprisingly for a work of art assembled over a long period of time by many different people, there are many different images of Yahweh–Elohim in the Old Testament. Some of them are related, but many of them are incompatible and even contradictory, and it is a vain task to try to gather them under one heading, as though, on the monotheistic model, they should be One. About the only thing they invariably have in common is that they are all, at the last, male, even though the notion of gender is inconsistent with the other images of universality and transcendence.

In the first chapter of Genesis the word Elohim means 'the gods', though, following the singular verb, it has always been translated as 'God'. But in Exodus 22:28 in the Masoretic text of the Old Testament Elohim has the meaning of 'the Judges', which calls to mind the Sumerian alliance of 'gods' and 'judges' called the *Annunaki*, the divine judges of the underworld who later became the seven Babylonian planetary gods. El was also the name of the Canaanite father god.

Yahweh is firstly the ancestral father god of the nomadic tribe. The Semites, like the Aryans, were a patriarchal people, who honoured their male ancestors. There is continual reference in Genesis to the 'God of the Father', the God of Abraham, Isaac and Jacob, and this is the way Yahweh introduced himself to Moses. The idea must have originated in the tribal ancestor, the 'Great Father' who guided the tribe and helped it in times of adversity. 'He is a god of nomads,' Eliade writes, 'not tied to a sanctuary but to a group of men, whom he accompanies and protects.'[38] In Genesis Yahweh says to Abraham that he must leave his country and his family for a strange land that will be revealed to him. He makes a covenant with him: 'I will make of thee a great nation, and I will bless thee' (Gen. 12:2). His descendants will be as numberless as the stars (Gen. 15:5). Gods had spoken to the kings of Sumeria and instructed them, but this god has different and greater plans conceived for Abraham than anything envisaged in the past.

Yahweh, in this relation, is a personal god with a distinctive character: it is not so much that he is their god; rather, they are 'his people'. Like the head of a clan, he will look out for them, give them lands, see that they prosper; he will, as it were, make himself responsible for them. In return, they must love and obey him and keep his commandments: they must have no other gods before him – 'for I the Lord thy God am a jealous god' (Exod. 20:5) – and, further, they must make no image of him that would limit his personality in a human way:

> Thou shalt have no other gods before me.
> Thou shalt not make unto thee any graven image or any likeness of any thing that is in heaven above, or that is in the earth beneath, or that is in the water under the earth. (Exod. 20:3–4)

In this radically new conception of the deity all image-making is forbidden. It is this innovation, above all, that marks this as a new stage in the evolution of consciousness; for the sacred essence, which is the organizing principle of the tribe and of the world, is conceived as *not* in nature: it is unrepresentable to the eye, though not, significantly, to the ear. God (unlike children) can be heard but not seen. This is how Yahweh 'appears' to Elijah:

> ... And, behold, the Lord passed by, and a great and strong wind rent the mountains, and brake in pieces the rocks before the Lord; but the Lord was not in the wind: and after the wind an earthquake; but the Lord was not in the earthquake:
> And after the earthquake a fire; but the Lord was not in the fire: and after the fire a still small voice. (I Kgs. 19:11–12)

A new kind of focus is demanded here: that human beings should, as it were, look through the world to the invisible source that called it into being. The divine, or the numinous, is no longer to shine in the beauty of nature and all created things; people can only point to the numinous, which is beyond them. Yet it is not suggested that contemplation of these phenomena would convey the mind to the contemplation of their invisible maker. Rather, the instruction is to detach the mind from appearances, so that worship of the divine cannot be confused with worship of nature or anything in the world ('this world', as it was later to become in Christianity, inevitably invoking the glory of 'the next').

Owen Barfield, in his crucially important book *Saving the Appearances*, has called the earlier way of living in nature 'original participation', which he defines as 'the sense that there stands behind the phenomena, *and on the other side of them from man*, a represented, which is of the same nature as man' (his italics).[39] Barfield's definitions are often as difficult as the thing he is defining, but, with some persistence, it becomes likely that he is describing what we have called the consciousness of the goddess culture, where the substance of creation is divine because it comes from and, ultimately, is the 'body of the goddess'. This is 'immanence', in that the visible appearance and the invisible source are one and the same. In Barfield's language, 'Nature [is] apprehended (as later also in myth and poetry) as female.'[40] There is, then, a bond between humanity and nature, and numinosity clothes them both – in the sense of binding human nature to the phenomenal world (the sense that Yahweh forbids) and in the sense that nature is wondrously alive with the same life as humanity (the sense that is sacrificed by obeying Yahweh's instruction). Barfield points out that this kind of original participation with nature is now lost to us, and we can understand it only in rare moments of union with nature, though (as will be discussed in Chapter 16) it can be re-created at a higher level through the Imagination. It is the vision of Romantic poetry, for instance, and is often portrayed in our age (2,000 years on from the Old Testament) as a lost vision. Shakespeare casts the dark misshapen Caliban as the memory of this way of perceiving nature:

> Be not afeard: the isle is full of noises,
> Sounds, and sweet airs, that give delight and hurt not.
> Sometimes a thousand twangling instruments
> Will hum about mine ears; and sometimes voices,
> That, if I then had waked after long sleep,
> Will make me sleep again; and then, in dreaming,
> The clouds, methought, would open and show riches
> Ready to drop upon me: that, when I waked,
> I cried to dream again.[41]

At this time, Barfield argues, human consciousness needed to detach itself from participation with nature, in order to gain more space, more play between itself and its world. Then consciousness could expand inwards and learn to name and control those outward phenomena whose beauty would otherwise tempt it away from the moral law:

> In every other nation at that time there prevailed unquestioned the participating consciousness which apprehends the phenomena as representations and naturally expresses itself in making images. For the Jews, henceforward, any dealings with those nations were strictly forbidden. Everywhere throughout the world original participation was in full swing. For the Jews, from that moment on, original participation, and anything smacking of it, became a deadly sin. And what is the Old Testament but the tale of their long struggle against that very sin, their repeated relapses and their final victory?[42]

Divinity is thus drawn away from nature, and the consequent loss of the numinous power in things that can be perceived and felt leaves humanity both more free to shape and 'dominate' its surroundings and more alone in the midst of them. Into this space comes the Word, the voice of the Law. For this dimension of Yahweh is primarily a voice, resounding from 'on high', or emerging 'still and small' out of the disappearance of all appearances. It speaks from that place where the visible dissolves into the invisible and the invisible flows into the visible but cannot yet be seen, so is without form or image. The idea is that if an image were to be beheld, it would by definition be too close to humanity to contain divinity, for no specification is possible without reduction. And Moses said to his people:

> And ye came near and stood under the mountain; and the mountain burned with fire unto the midst of heaven, with darkness, clouds, and thick darkness.
> And the Lord spake unto you out of the midst of the fire: ye heard the voice of the words, but saw no similitude: only ye heard a voice.

. . . . .

Take ye therefore good heed unto yourselves; for ye saw no manner of similitude on the day that the Lord spake unto you in Horeb out of the midst of the fire:

Lest ye corrupt yourselves, and make you a graven image, the similitude of any figure, the likeness of male or female.

The likeness of any beast that is on the earth, the likeness of any winged fowl that flieth in the air.

The likeness of any thing that creepeth on the ground, the likeness of any fish that is in the waters beneath the earth:

And lest thou lift up thine eyes unto heaven and when thou seest the sun, and the moon, and the stars, even all the host of heaven, shouldest be driven to worship them, and serve them, which the Lord thy God hath divided unto all nations under the whole heaven. (Deut. 4:11–12, 15–19).

As Yahweh is to have no form, so he is to have no name. When Moses came to the 'mountain of God' he saw a flame of fire coming out of a bush, but, as the bush was not consumed, he turned aside in wonder. It is this act of turning aside that makes the relationship possible. Then the Lord calls him by name, 'Moses'. But when Moses asks how he shall answer his people who say to him of the Lord 'What is his name?', Yahweh replies: I Am That I Am ... Thus shalt thou say unto the children of Israel, "I Am hath sent me to you" ' (Exod. 3:13–14). Here Yahweh has no predicates, so Yahweh is that which is beyond prediction: both the totality of being and its total transcendence.

The Name (called the Tetragrammaton after its four letters, YHYH) was regarded as too holy to be communicable, so other names such as 'Adonai' (Lord) or 'Elohim' were substituted when speaking aloud, at least by the third century BC. Only the high priest on the Day of Atonement or the priests when blessing the people could pronounce it. Typographically, the Name is represented by four Hebrew consonants, but etymologically it is a modification of the verb 'to be', which also means 'to breathe'. (In the English form Yahweh is made sayable by inserting between the consonants the vowels appropriate to the words Adonai and Elohim.) Barfield comments:

The Hebrew word for 'Jew' may similarly be rendered YHWDI; the texture of the language hints that a devout Jew could hardly name his race without tending to utter the Tetragrammaton. Written, as all Hebrew words were, without vowels, when any true child of Israel perused the unspoken Name, יהוה may have seemed to come whispering up, as it were, from the depths of his own being![43]

Yahweh may have a Semitic root derived from *Hwy*, the Semitic word for wind, and wind is related both to air and to breath. A god named Jw, a son of El, the Canaanite father god, has been discovered in the Canaanite Ras Shamra texts.[44] As Merlin Stone has pointed out in her book *The Paradise Papers*, Yahweh is also closely related to the Sanskrit word *Yahveh*, meaning 'everflowing':[45]

> And mount Sinai was altogether on a smoke, because the Lord descended
> upon it in fire: and the smoke thereof ascended as the smoke of a furnace,
> and the whole mount quaked greatly. (Exod. 19:18)

So for all Yahweh's ontological transcendence, the language of magnificent physical epiphany is close by, testimony, perhaps, to the difficulty of
preventing the tribe from identifying divinity with nature. But what once
was sacred in itself is now defined as the place from which Yahweh
speaks. He speaks from the mountain tops, out of clouds, fire, lightning,
storm, wind and thunder, much as the Semitic and Aryan gods before
him: the Sumerian Enlil, the Babylonian Marduk and the Canaanite gods
El and Baal. The primordial mountain in Sumeria, as in Neolithic
cultures, was the womb of the goddess herself. In the Bronze Age it
became the 'home' of all the goddesses and gods. Then, in Iron Age
Canaan it became, as Mount Saphon, El's 'holy' mountain, as it was his
son Baal's. In Greece, as Mount Olympos, it was the home of Zeus and
the other gods and goddesses. In the Old Testament it is the holy place
where the voice of the Lord can be heard.

Elsewhere, Yahweh rides upon a cloud. Isaiah sees Yahweh 'riding on
a swift cloud' on his way to Egypt (Isa. 19:1). The Psalmist addresses
Yahweh as the one:

> ... who maketh the clouds his chariot: who walketh upon the wings of the
> wind:
> Who maketh his angels spirits; his ministers a flaming fire. (Ps. 104:3–4)

Sometimes the cloud as the mount of the god is personified as a cherub:
'And he rode upon a cherub, and did fly; yea, he did fly upon the wings
of the wind' (Ps. 18:10). Or when Moses and Aaron had set up the
tabernacle in the desert:

> Then a cloud covered the tent of the congregation, and the glory of the
> Lord filled the tabernacle.
> . . . . .
> And when the cloud was taken up from over the tabernacle, the children
> of Israel went onward in all their journeys:
> But if the cloud were not taken up, then they journeyed not till the day
> that it was taken up.
> For the cloud of the Lord was upon the tabernacle by day, and fire was
> on it by night, in the sight of all the house of Israel, throughout all their
> journeys. (Exod. 40:36–8)

As Barfield concludes: 'Everything proclaims the glory of God, but
nothing represents Him.'[46]

The problem, however, is that Yahweh's transcendence was not consistent; or, to put it another way, there were many images of Yahweh when
his transcendence was, as it were, added on. When he appears to be only
too human – vengeful, jealous, angry or kind, protective, reassuring – the

particular attributes of human nature that he embodies are then elevated to the divine model, confusing thereby both humanity and divinity.

THE IMAGE OF YAHWEH–ELOHIM AS EXCLUSIVELY MALE

Although the image of the deity had become transcendent, it yet retained several very human characteristics, the most obvious of which was gender: it was, in fact, male. But it was male without any of the partiality that otherwise attaches to just one of two genders, because this male god was also 'one' in the sense of both and, indeed, all. This fusion – or confusion – of the oneness and maleness of the deity has, until lately, passed unquestioned in the orthodox Jewish conception of divinity, as it has also in the Christian conception that derived from it. In his book *The Hebrew Goddess* Patai writes that 'this credo had its complementary corollary in the denial of the very possibility of other gods'.[47] God is, he says:

> eternal, omnipotent, omnipresent, omniscient, aphysical (and therefore invisible), inscrutable and incomprehensible, as well as just, good, compassionate, merciful and benevolent. Since, being pure spirit, he is without body, he possesses no physical attributes and hence no sexual traits. To say that God is either male or female is therefore completely impossible from the viewpoint of traditional Judaism.
>
> . . . . .
>
> Yet one factor, a linguistic one, defied all theological repugnance to the attribution of bodily qualities to God. It is in the nature of the Hebrew language that every noun has either the masculine or the feminine gender (except a very few which can take either). The two Biblical names of God, *Yahweh* (pronounced out of reverence for its great holiness as 'Adonai,' and usually translated as 'the Lord') and *Elohim* (or briefly *El*, translated as 'God') are masculine. When a pronoun is used to refer to God, it is the masculine 'He'; when a verb describes that he did something or an adjective qualifies him, they appear in the masculine form (in Hebrew there are male and female forms for verbs and adjectives). Thus, every verbal statement about God conveyed the idea that he was masculine ... No subsequent teaching about the aphysical, incomprehensible or transcendental nature of the deity could eradicate this early mental image of the masculine God ... The Biblical prophets, psalmists, moralists and historians, as well as the sages, scribes, theologians, rabbis and teachers of the Talmudic period, constantly use unmitigated anthropomorphisms in referring to God. He is a 'Man of War,' a 'Hero,' 'Lord of Hosts,' 'King,' 'Master of the Universe,' and 'Our Father in Heaven,' to mention only a few expressions. Needless to say, these appellations all carry a pronouncedly masculine connotation, and, together with the words of the prayer, 'We are Your sons, and You are our

Father,' or 'Have mercy upon us as a father has on his sons!' indelibly impressed all Jews not only with the Kingship and Fatherhood, but also with the Manhood of God.[48]

. . . . .

The Biblical God-concept [he concludes] intuitively grasped by the prophets and gropingly reached by the people, reflects the strictly patriarchal order of society which produced it; this patriarchal society gave rise to a religion centered around a single universal deity whose will was embodied in the Law, but who was abstract, devoid of all physical attributes and yet pronouncedly male, a true projection of the patriarchal family-head.[49]

The old imagery of the god as the son, lover and consort of the goddess has apparently vanished forever as if it had never existed. There is nothing to modify the exclusive and unrelated maleness of god. This absence of feminine symbolism in the image of God, as Pagels has pointed out, is to mark Judaism, Christianity and Islam in striking contrast to the world's other religious traditions.[50] The contradiction between the universality and transubstantiality of Yahweh and his exclusive masculinity has regrettably entered the unconscious of the West, so that it is now extremely difficult to speak of 'God', in the impersonal sense of 'Creative Source' or 'All That Is', without wrestling (usually unsuccessfully) against the urge to say 'He'; for the 'graven image' that Yahweh, as the transcendent god, forbids to be made, would have been unmistakably male.

YAHWEH AS A TRIBAL WARRIOR GOD

Again, a truly transcendent and universal deity cannot, ontologically, take sides, least of all order the slaughtering of one race by another. However, in Exodus Yahweh leads the people of Israel through the desert to the Promised Land of Canaan, a land 'flowing with milk and honey'. Here he speaks as a tribal god, who guides and directs his people to the land he has selected for them. But this god is also a warrior god in the Aryan mode, whose people are first and foremost warriors:

> And the Lord spake unto Moses . . . saying,
> Speak unto the children of Israel, and say unto them, When ye are passed over Jordan into the land of Canaan:
> Then ye shall drive out all the inhabitants of the land from before you, and destroy all their pictures, and destroy all the molten images, and quite pluck down all their high places:
> And ye shall dispossess the inhabitants of the land, and dwell therein: for I have given you the land to possess it. (Num. 33:52–3)

The spirit of the Iron Age informs this war imagery, which pervades the books of the Pentateuch as well as those of the prophets. In Joshua, also, Yahweh speaks as an ancestral warrior spirit, instructing his people and, particularly, their 'heroic' warrior-leaders how to wage war:

> And when the Lord thy God hath delivered it into thine hands, thou shalt smite every male thereof with the edge of the sword,
>
> But the women and the little ones, and the cattle, and all that is in the city, even all the spoil thereof, shalt thou take unto thyself; and thou shalt eat the spoil of thine enemies, which the Lord thy God hath given thee.
>
> Thus shalt thou do unto all the cities which are very far off from thee, which are not of the cities of these nations.
>
> But of the cities of these people, which the Lord thy God doth give thee for an inheritance, thou shalt save alive nothing that breatheth,
>
> But thou shalt utterly destroy them, namely, the Hittites, and the Amorites, the Canaanites, and the Perizzites, the Hivites, and the Jebusites, as the Lord thy God hath commanded thee. (Deut. 20:10–17)

True to divine command, the Book of Joshua records that at Jericho:

> ... they utterly destroyed all that was in the city, both man and woman, young and old, and ox, and sheep, and ass, with the edge of the sword ...
> And they burnt the city with fire, and all that was therein. (Josh. 6:21, 24)

Yahweh assumes the mantle of the goddess of war as he wallows in the blood of his enemies, as did Sekhmet, Ishtar and Anath, the Canaanite goddess of war, who herself 'plunged knee-deep in the blood of soldiers, neck-high in the gore of their companies'.[51] Isaiah asks:

> Wherefore art thou red in thine apparel, and thy garments like him that treadeth in the winevat?

and receives the chilling answer:

> I have trodden the winepress alone; and of the people there was none with me: for I will tread them in mine anger, and trample them in my fury; and their blood shall be sprinkled upon my garments, and I will stain all my raiment. (Isa. 63:2–3)

Graves and Patai comment on the similarity between the massacres in honour of the goddess Anath and those in honour of Yahweh, adding that 'the crucial question was: in whose honour these prophecies and hymns should now be sung or these rites enacted. If in honour of Yahweh–Elohim, not Anath, Baal or Tammuz, all was proper and pious.'[52] The 'morality' of Yahweh in his tribal aspect is, therefore, a perplexing matter! Jung, writing about Yahweh, comments:

> The absence of human morality in Yahweh is a stumbling block which cannot be overlooked ... We miss reason and moral values, that is, two main characteristics of a mature human mind. It is therefore obvious that the Yahwistic image or conception of the deity is less than that of certain human specimens: the image of a personified brutal force and of an unethical and non-spiritual mind, yet inconsistent enough to exhibit traits of kindness and generosity besides a violent power-drive. It is the picture of a sort of

The Myth of the Goddess

nature-demon and at the same time of a primitive chieftain aggrandized to a colossal size, just the sort of conception one could expect of a more or less barbarous society – *cum grano salis*.[53]

Harrison adds her voice to this:

The morality of a god is not often much in advance of that of his worshippers, and sometimes it lags considerably behind. The social structure is also, it is allowed, in some sense reflected in the god: a matriarchal society will worship a Mother and a Son, a patriarchal society will tend to have a cult of the Father.[54]

The tribal Yahweh is here like a patriarch with unlimited power, unchecked by any alternative point of view, and this reflects the organization of the priesthood at the time. The Levite priesthood enforced patriarchal custom as tribal law, with the result that any infringement of sexual taboos was punished out of all proportion to the 'offence'. Women belonged to one of two men, their father or their husband. The morality of the earlier era, whereby children could be born to temple priestesses and be supported by the temple, was suppressed. So also, although with great difficulty, was the ritual of sexual intercourse on special occasions, which was believed to contribute to the earth's fertility.[55] Husbands could have several wives and could discard their wives without obligation to support them, but wives might have only one husband and adultery was punished with death by stoning. Every woman who was betrothed or married could be stoned to death if she was raped, unless the rape took place in the countryside where her calls for help went unheard (Deut. 22:26–7). The injunction: 'Do not prostitute thy daughter to cause her to be a whore; lest the land fall to whoredom, and the land become full of wickedness' (Lev. 19:29) was a directive to stop the Hebrews following the Babylonian, and probably also the Canaanite, custom whereby a girl before marriage offered her virginity to the goddess or became a temple priestess. There were to be no Hebrew priestesses. Any Levite priest whose daughter was discovered following the old customs was to burn her. Any Israelite who 'gave his seed to Molech' (Baal) by having intercourse with a temple priestess in a Canaanite temple was to be put to death (Lev. 20:2).[56]

Whether or not the Book of Joshua, with its fierce tribalism, describes what actually took place when the Hebrews entered Canaan, it must reflect the values of the Hebrews who recorded it. The deficient morality of Yahweh becomes more understandable when his commands are taken not as divine revelation, but as 'revelations' of Iron Age values and patriarchal customs reflected in the behaviour of kings, priests and prophets. Jehu, for example, was praised by Yahweh for having murdered the remnant of the former king Ahab's household and for ridding Israel of the entire priesthood of Baal – inviting them to celebrate their rites in a temple and then ordering their massacre (2 Kgs. 10:30). Elijah (*c.* 860 BC) supervised the murder of the 450 priests of Baal:

> Take the prophets of Baal, let not one escape. And they took them and Elijah brought them down to the brook Kishon and slew them there. (1 Kgs. 18:40)

Episodes like these were used, consciously or unconsciously, to justify the brutality of wars waged against an 'evil' enemy. Not surprisingly, this model of conduct has greatly influenced both Christianity and Islam, which look upon the Old Testament as divine revelation. Wherever a teaching did not agree with the 'law of God', its exponents could be persecuted. The Levite priests apparently exempted themselves, as later did the Christian and Islamic priesthood, from the commandment they believed to be sent by God: 'Thou shalt not kill'. The law of life's sacrality was not observed when it was a question of the infringement of religious doctrine or the threat of a tribal enemy. New kinds of ritual sacrifice in which murder was justified, such as the stoning and crucifixion of prophets or the torturing and burning of heretics, appeared wherever these archaic values went unchallenged. The idea of the 'holy war' waged in Yahweh's name against unbelievers and 'the wicked' has echoed down the ages in the Christian Crusades, the persecution of 'heretics' and 'witches', and 'enemies of God'. The image of Marduk's 'holy war' against the goddess Tiamat and Yahweh's war against the living Canaanites has endured a long time, and still persists today whenever a tribal image of the divine is thought to sanction a murder.

THE EVOLUTION OF YAHWEH

A deity that is only a tribal deity reflects the moral values and cultural attitudes of a specific people at a particular historical time – in this case those of the Iron Age Hebrews. On the other hand, the image of the divine is transformed as the moral consciousness of a people evolves, and so it is in the Old Testament when the tribal image is challenged through the passion, and often the suffering, of the individual. Mythology in this sense reflects the evolution of consciousness.

The history of the evolution of consciousness, reflected in the divine images formulated by all peoples, shows how images of divinity gradually change and evolve over many millennia. It could be that the individual's personal experience of the numinous, together with the pressure of historical events, urges the psyche to search for a new image of the divine or to press the old image into a new form. The sense of being called to a destiny, or a revelation through dreams and visions and the search for

444 *The Myth of the Goddess*

their meaning, urges the individual, often against his or her own will, into a confrontation with the collective image of the time, contributing, in this way, to the transformation of the image of the divine.

Gradually, in the inspired voice of the prophets of the Old Testament, there emerges an image of Yahweh as personal *and* ethical, a universal conscience that can never be fully understood but has to be related to and honoured. Yahweh becomes someone to be communed with, respected, feared and challenged, who becomes someone to be loved. Abraham, Moses, Jonah, Esdras, Job and many others, in living dialogue, argue with Yahweh, question his judgement, dispute his harshness or (as with Jonah) his clemency. Job protests not from arrogance or fear, but from love – the one he trusted has let him down. The relationship between these protagonists and the image of Yahweh was wrought out of commitment, and often disillusionment and bewilderment, and through this experience the image of the divine was brought closer to the human heart. Job, for instance, is reconciled to Yahweh only when he knows of him no longer through doctrine and hearsay, but has 'seen' him face to face: 'I have heard of thee by the hearing of the ear: but now mine eye seeth thee' (Job 42:5). This is the inner seeing (which Judaism makes possible), the image that can be seen and known within, but does not have to be represented to the outer eye.

As Judaism develops, most particularly through the Wisdom Books – Job, Psalms, Proverbs, Ben Sirach (Ecclesiasticus) and the Song of Solomon – the idea evolves that humanity has a destiny to discover and fulfil, entrusting the individual with a responsibility towards the divine order of life.

In the third century BC the image of Hokhmah, or Sophia, the feminine counterpart or 'aspect' of the deity, comes into being, and this begins to temper the ethical discipline of the father with the healing compassion of the mother. It may, indeed, be worth wondering more generally to what extent Yahweh's claim to universality depends upon the kind of relation he has to the feminine principle. When, for instance, Yahweh is in conflict with the goddesses of the Canaanites, we find him speaking with all the limitations of a tribal god. When Wisdom is present in the Wisdom Books, in the image of Sophia, then we find him articulating a universal vision that someone of any race could understand. In between these two extremes there are many more subtle stages, as when Israel figures in the imagery as the earthly bride of Yahweh, or when the female cherubim cast their wings upon the walls of the Inner Temple.

But from our knowledge of other cultures we can say that the *relation* of masculine to feminine, as expressed in the sacred marriage of goddess and god, or god and goddess (depending on the culture), was always the culmination of religious ritual. And this must tell us something about a universal need to reconcile these two polarities of human experience. The next chapter explores the possibility that the divine image of the masculine principle requires a complementary divine image of the feminine principle

Figure 4. Christian portrait of the 'Author of Genesis'; stone sculpture,
c. AD 1200. Chartres Cathedral.

if the image of divinity is to inspire and heal. The Ethical Word of the
Law and the Loving Compassion of the Heart may not have to be represented as divine figures – as god and goddess – as long as both conceptions

or principles are present in the divine image. The archetypal masculine quality of Transcendence and the archetypal feminine quality of Immanence may both be necessary in the image of divinity for the sacred marriage to take place within the human soul.

12
THE HIDDEN GODDESS
IN THE OLD TESTAMENT

Man is constantly inclined to forget that what was once good does not remain good eternally. He follows the old ways that once were good long after they have become bad, and only with the greatest sacrifices and untold suffering can he rid himself of this delusion and see that what was once good is now perhaps grown old and is good no longer. This is so in great things as well as in small. The ways and customs of childhood, once so sublimely good, can hardly be laid aside even when their harmfulness has long since been proved. The same, only on a gigantic scale, is true of historical changes of attitude. A collective attitude is equivalent to a religion, and changes of religion constitute one of the most painful chapters in the world's history. In this respect our age is afflicted with a blindness that has no parallel. We think we have only to declare an accepted article of faith incorrect and invalid, and we shall be psychologically rid of all the traditional effects of Christianity and Judaism. We believe in enlightenment, as if an intellectual change of front somehow had a profounder influence on the emotional processes or even on the unconscious. We entirely forget that the religion of the past two thousand years is a psychological attitude, a definite form and manner of adaptation to the world without and within, that lays down a definite cultural pattern and creates an atmosphere which remains wholly uninfluenced by intellectual denials. The change of front is, of course, symptomatically important as an indication of possibilities to come, but on the deeper levels the psyche continues to work for a long time in the old attitude, in accordance with the laws of psychic inertia.

C. G. Jung, *Collected Works*, Vol. 6, *Psychological Types*

Ah, whom can we ever turn to in our need?
Not angels, not humans, and already
the knowing animals are aware
that we are not really at home in our interpreted world.

Rainer Maria Rilke

There is no word for goddess in the Hebrew language. Anyone reading the Old Testament without knowing the mythology of Sumeria, Babylonia and Egypt – and particularly the importance of the goddess in these cultures – would receive the impression that the Hebrews worshipped no goddess at all. Even with some awareness of these earlier civilizations, it still seems as if the god of the Hebrews is a primary revelation that owes nothing to the past. Only the voice of the solitary god Yahweh–Elohim is heard.

So why do the prophetic and historical books have running through them a continual diatribe against the abomination of 'foreign gods' and the worship of images in high places? And why is much of Hebrew mythology cast in the framework of a battle between Yahweh and the goddess of the Canaanites? When disaster struck Israel, as when the ten tribes of the northern province were dispersed throughout the Assyrian Empire, or when the captivity in Babylon was imposed on the people of Judah, the fault was found in the regression of the Hebrews to the Canaanite religion. Responsibility was laid at the feet of the goddess, but why? Did the people then worship a goddess before they were converted to the religion of the monotheistic Yahweh? One interesting point of this story is that, even after the Exile, as much as half of the population of Palestine did not participate in orthodox Judaism. It was these people – the poorer sections of the community, who had not been deported to Babylon – who actually continued in the old beliefs and, as Halevi writes, 'limited and threatened the legalistic vision of the priests'.[1]

Many passages in the Old Testament that refer to Yahweh's anger against foreign gods are perplexing if the existence of shrines, temples and statues of the goddess is not taken into account. When the Hebrews entered Canaan, they did not find a sparsely populated land with primitive people, but a country with a powerful religion and cultural tradition in which queens took the role of high priestesses, and ordinary women were priestesses. Strong and wealthy cities had long been established in Canaan that had trading connections with Egypt, Babylonia and the Hittite kingdom in Anatolia. Canaanite rulers had often married princesses from these foreign courts, and the early Hebrew kings followed this tradition.

Whatever the origin of the Canaanite goddesses, they had many features in common with the contemporary goddesses of Babylonia, Egypt and Anatolia. These goddesses were adopted by the Hebrew tribes when they settled in Canaan, for, like the Semitic invaders who had preceded them, they took over the mythology and the cult sites as well as the seasonal feasts and ritual customs of the Canaanite people.[2] Despite the efforts of the prophets to eradicate the old beliefs, the image of the goddess survived. In Canaan, as in the surrounding countries, the mythology of the goddess and her son–lover was the most deeply rooted aspect of religious belief because it was closely associated with the seasons of the agricultural year, and, more widely, with the archaic rituals of fertility and regeneration.

Patai's study *The Hebrew Goddess* reveals the hidden image of the goddess in the Old Testament. His meticulous unravelling of her story is one of the most interesting contributions to a deeper understanding of this era, for it traces the continuity of the goddess image throughout the history of the Jewish people. With his help, it is possible to listen to the biblical passages that refer to 'foreign gods', 'groves' and 'high places' with a completely new ear. In the introduction to his book he observes that a study of comparative religion suggests that humanity seems to have need of the image of the divine mother as well as the divine father. Then he asks whether Judaism alone failed to fulfil this need: 'Is it conceivable that the human craving for a divine mother did not manifest itself at all in Judaism?'[3]

His question is answered by the historical and archaeological evidence he brings, which shows not only that a Hebrew goddess existed, but that she was deeply established in the lives of the Hebrew people in various forms from the conquest of Canaan to the Babylonian Exile. From about 400 BC – after the post-Exilic reforms of Ezra – she seems to vanish, although, curiously, her image still remains in the Holy of Holies of the Second Temple. Some 1,500 years later, the goddess image subtly reappears in the medieval Kabbalistic literature of the Jewish communities in Spain and south-western France as the Shekhinah and as the Matronit: the Matron, Lady or Queen. Conceived as intercessor between humanity and the deity, she is related, in this role, to the Christian Mary. Patai writes:

> In view of the general human, psychologically determined predisposition to believe in and worship goddesses, it would be strange if the Hebrew-Jewish religion, which flourished for centuries in a region of intensive goddess cults, had remained immune to them. Yet this is precisely the picture one gets when one views Hebrew religion through the polarizing prisms of Mosaic legislation and prophetic teaching. God, this view maintains, revealed Himself in successive stages to Adam, Noah, Abraham, Isaac and Jacob, and gave His law to Moses on Mount Sinai. Biblical religion, in this perspective, is universal ethical monotheism, cast in a ritual-legal form.
>
> Historical scrutiny, however, shows that for many centuries following the traditional date of the Sinaitic revelation, this religion, idealized in retrospect, remained a demand rather than a fact. Further study indicates that there were among the Biblical Hebrews other religious trends, powerful in their attraction for the common people and their leaders alike, in which the worship of goddesses played as important a role as it did anywhere else in comparable stages of religious development.[4]

THE CHERUBIM

The most hidden of all the images of the goddess in Canaan were the cherubim. In spite of the prohibition against graven images in the Hebrew religion, Patai observes, there was an exception to this rule. The cherubs, or cherubim, were indeed 'graven images', yet they were a most important

Figure 1. *(Left)* Female cherub with Tree of Life; ivory plaque, late ninth century BC. From the bed of Hazael, King of Damascus.
Figure 2. *(Right)* Winged female cherub with palm tree as Tree of Life; ivory plaque. Arslan Tash, northern Syria.

part of temple ritual, from the setting up of the Ark in the desert tabernacle to the destruction of the Second Temple in AD 70. Patai explains that the term cherub is derived from the Hebrew noun *K'rubh*, which is related to the Akkadian *Karibu*, an intermediary between humanity and the gods, who presents the prayers of humanity to the gods.[5] In Genesis cherubim were placed by Yahweh east of the Garden of Eden 'to keep the way of the tree of life' (Gen. 3:24) – that is, to stand between the human and the divine realm. The cherubim of the Ark may have the same meaning: they may be guardians of the Mysteries, in just the way that the two winged beings on either side of King Gudea's Lagash cup were guardians of the Mysteries of the Serpent Lord (see Chapter 5, Fig. 22). Patai writes that even from the beginning there were two images of divinity in the Ark: both Yahweh *and* his consort – possibly the Canaanite goddess.[6] These were represented by the most archaic image of divinity: two stone slabs. Later, this dual image was transformed when all images of the divine were forbidden. Yahweh's image disappeared, and the image of the goddess became the two cherubim who covered the Ark with their wings. After the destruction of the First Temple and the building of the Second Temple, the cherubim in the Holy of Holies were believed to reflect the male and female aspects of Yahweh. Later still, before the destruction of the Second Temple, figures of the male and the female cherubim embrac-

Figure 3. Winged female guardians of the Tree of Life; Assyrian relief, ninth century BC. Palace of Assurnasirpal II.

ing, which stood in the Holy of Holies, reflected the union of Yahweh with the Community of Israel, his bride.[7]

The image of the cherubim shielding the Ark is strangely reminiscent of the two winged figures from Syria, which are so similar that they seem to belong together (Figs. 1, 2). These seem to reflect the protective gesture of the Egyptian sister goddesses Isis and Nephthys (see Chapter 6, Figs. 7, 8). But if we turn to Assyria, there also is the image of winged beings, whether female or male, protecting the Tree of Life (Fig. 3). In Figure 4 Isis and Nephthys embrace the sarcophagus of Tutankhamun with their outstretched wings. Patai refers to a pair of guardian figures on a relief from Karnak (c. 1500 BC), whose wings overshadow the Egyptian *ankh*, which they hold in their hands.[8] So there are two sources, one Egyptian, the other Assyrian, for the image of the cherubim guarding the Ark. Another image is found on a plaque from the palace of King Ahab of Israel (873–852 BC), which shows two feminine beings with outstretched wings kneeling facing each other, holding in their hands what seems to be a flower (Fig. 5).

Whether the cherubim of the Temple resembled the Mesopotamian or the Egyptian guardians of the Mysteries, they must have been awe-inspiring. In the desert tabernacle there were twelve pairs of cherubim: one over the Ark, one embroidered on the veil and ten on the curtains. The figures of the cherubim in the early desert tabernacle

were made of beaten gold, and, together with the ark-cover, formed a single piece. Their faces were turned to each other, and downwards toward the

Figure 4. Isis and Nephthys guarding the sarcophagus of Tutankhamun; *c.* 1330 BC.

Figure 5. Ivory plaque from the Palace of King Ahab; *c.* 870 BC.

ark-cover, which was shielded by their outspread wings. It was upon the ark-cover, from between the two Cherubim, that God was believed to speak to Moses.[9]

In the tenth-century-BC Temple, which Solomon built, there were two immense cherubim over the Ark, made of olive wood and covered in gold leaf. They were 15 feet (4.5 m) tall and their wing-span stretched the entire 30 feet (9 m) of the Holy of Holies, the name for the sanctuary where the Ark was kept. The walls were also covered with their image, which alternated with the palm tree: 'And he [Solomon] carved all the walls of the house round about with carved figures of cherubims and palm trees and open flowers, within and without' (1 Kgs. 6:29).

The description given in 1 Kings 7:29 says that there were lions, oxen *and* cherubim, which suggests that the cherubim did not have the shape or faces of lions or oxen.[10] Whatever form they took, the same motif of cherubim alternating with palm trees was carved on the door to the innermost sanctuary and the outer door of the Temple. The veil that protected the Holy of Holies was also woven with the same image.

The First Temple, destroyed in 586 BC, was not rebuilt until 515 BC. When Ezra travelled to Jerusalem in *c.* 458 BC, he undertook to restore it to its former glory, bringing with him the great treasures that had been held in Babylon. Patai suggests that he would probably have restored the old image of the Solomonic cherubim. The cherubim in the Holy of Holies of the Second Temple symbolized the male and female aspects of Yahweh, the one and only god. Later, however – the exact date is not

Figure 6. Rare image of a seated goddess wearing horned crown and net-patterned robe with serpent-like form coiled around her neck and body; ivory, Phoenician, 1800–1700 BC. Ugarit (Ras Shamra), northern Canaan.

certain but it could have been in the third century BC – the form of the cherubim was changed and they were portrayed as a man and woman embracing. At this time, the male cherub was conceived as Yahweh, while the female cherub was no longer the female aspect of Yahweh but the personification of the Community of Israel. It is an amazing story and but for Patai's book it would not be known to anyone outside the world of biblical scholarship.

THE CANAANITE GODDESSES

In comparison with the surrounding Iron Age cultures very few cult images of the Canaanite goddesses have survived; they stood in the great temples of Canaan and the sacred groves of the 'high places', draped in the robes woven for them by the temple priestesses. These goddesses, with their families, lineage, rituals and festivals, were a vital presence in the lands that the Hebrews invaded and settled. The Canaanite pantheon of goddesses and gods can be compared to their Sumero-Babylonian or their later Greek counterparts, although there were fewer of them. Of the many Canaanite deities, the major ones were the mother goddess Asherah, the father god El, their daughter Anath–Ashtoreth and their son Hadd or Hadad, the 'Thunderer', usually known as Baal.

Asherah

The goddess Asherah was probably the oldest. As early as 1750 BC a Sumerian inscription refers to her as the wife of Anu, who can be identified as El, the father god of the Canaanite pantheon, whose role was closely modelled on that of the Sumerian god An. Asherah was called 'the Lady of the Sea', which links her to the Sumerian Nammu, and to the Egyptian Isis, 'born in the all-wetness'. Asherah may have become the wife of Yahweh in the eyes of the Hebrew people when the Hebrew god assimilated to himself the father god imagery of El. Her other title was the 'Mother of the Gods', as was the Sumerian Ninhursag's, and among her seventy children were her sons Baal and Mot and her daughter Anath. Kings were nourished from her breasts, as they had been by the goddess in Sumeria and Egypt.[11]

In the exquisitely worked ivory box in Figure 7 the Mother Goddess Asherah takes the place of the Tree of Life between her animals, who depend upon her for food. As the image of the Tree of Life, she stood in the temples and groves of Canaan and was worshipped as the Giver of Life. Many of her images, called *asherim*, were made of carved wood and were set up next to the altar in the temples, or in a grove of trees nearby, or on shrines on hill-tops or 'high places', sacred to the goddess here as they were in Crete. One image stood for many centuries in the great Temple of Solomon in Jerusalem. Perhaps it resembled the one in Figure

Figure 7. Lid of a Mycenaean ivory unguent box showing mother goddess holding sheaves of corn and seated between two goats; *c.* 1300 BC. Ugarit (Ras Shamra), northern Canaan.

8, where the goddess holds her breasts with the same gesture as the Babylonian image of Ishtar, suggesting the offering of nourishment flowing from them (see Chapter 5, Fig. 16). The *asherim* may also have been actual trees, most probably the sycamore fig or black mulberry, with its rich, dark fruit and milky sap, which belonged to the goddess in Egypt and in Crete. It was the *asherim*, whether tree or effigy, that provoked the fury of the prophets and the orgies of destruction by certain kings, who, from time to time, at the instigation of the prophets, ordered their

Figure 8. Image of the goddess Asherah or Astarte; unglazed earthenware, seventh century BC. Tell Duweir, Palestine.

immediate removal. The word 'Asherah' in the Bible can refer both to the goddess herself and to her carved wooden image, though none of these wooden images of Asherah has survived. However, many small naked figures made of clay have been found inside houses, and, instead of a torso and legs, they have a cylindrical column ending in a flared base like the one in Figure 8. These may have been small models of the larger images that stood in the groves and temples, although the artistry of Figure 7 suggests that the latter were more elaborate. In every major archaeological excavation in Palestine female figures have been found, dating to between 2000 BC and 600 BC. Women may have used these tiny images to appeal to Asherah to help them in childbirth or to grant them fertility.

Asherah was the goddess of both Tyre and Sidon at an early date – at least as early as 1200 BC – and it was most probably a Sidonian wife of Solomon who introduced her into the court of the Hebrew king. Later, King Ahab (873–852 BC) married Jezebel, daughter of a king of Sidon, and once again the worship of Asherah was established at the court, together with that of her son Baal. The many priestesses and priests who attended upon their temple or temples are referred to in the story of Elijah's successful contest with the 450 'prophets' of Baal to produce rain. But whereas Elijah's wrath seems to have fallen on the priests of Baal (whom he had murdered), for some reason the 400 'prophets' of Asherah escaped his wrath (1 Kgs. 18). The worship of Asherah in the northern Kingdom of Israel endured until 721 BC, and even then it lingered in one corner of it, Beth-el, for we hear how Josiah, King of Judah (639–609 BC), destroyed the altars that had been set up by Jeroboam 300 years before and how he 'burned Asherah' (2 Kgs. 23:15).

There are many veiled references by the prophets to the practices in the Canaanite temples, and also to the interpretation of dreams. Eliade writes that 'Israelite ecstatic prophecy has its deep roots in the Canaanite religion',[12] for the Canaanite priestesses and priests were skilled in the shamanic arts. The priestesses and priests of Asherah and Baal were called prophets, but the practice of their calling was increasingly threatened and ultimately suppressed by the Hebrew prophets, who inveighed against anyone who dared to usurp their role as interpreter of the divine word:

> If there arise among you a prophet, or a dreamer of dreams, and giveth thee a sign or a wonder,
> And the sign or the wonder come to pass, whereof he spake unto thee, saying, Let us go after other gods, which thou hast not known, and let us serve them;
>
> . . . . .
>
> ... that prophet, or that dreamer of dreams, shall be put to death ... So shalt thou put the evil away from the midst of thee. (Deut. 13:1–2, 5)

Anath

Anath, the daughter of Asherah and El, and sister–wife of the god Baal, is not referred to at all as a goddess in the Old Testament, although her name appears as a place name, even as Jeremiah's birthplace, Anathoth. Anath is primarily a goddess of the hunt, whose image degenerated to a goddess of war. It seems that, as in Sumeria and Babylonia, this goddess of hunting and fertility was also used to pursue the tribal aims of the leaders of the tribe. In Figure 9 she wears the same lion head as Sekhmet, who, in one myth, wallowed in the blood of humans. As Patai comments: 'No Near Eastern goddess was more blood-thirsty than she.'[13]

Anath has yet another side to her nature. Two of her titles were 'Lady of Heaven, Mistress of all the Gods' and 'Lady of the Mountain', which link her to the Sumerian Ninhursag and suggest that she was also the goddess of the dead, a role confirmed by the ease with which she descends into the underworld to rescue her brother Baal. Anath was also called 'the Maiden' which aligns her image with the old lunar mythology of the two goddesses, mother and maiden. In Canaanite mythology it is the daughter, Anath, who, like Persephone, descends to the underworld, but her mission is, like Ishtar's, to rescue her consort, the god Baal, from his brother Mot. She is a goddess whose life is bound up with the sowing of the seed and the sprouting grain, for when she rescues her brother–consort Baal from his dark brother Mot, who personifies the scorching drought, the corn begins to sprout and the whole earth rejoices. Interestingly, in the light of the persistent motif of the son–lover and the bull, Anath is said to have taken the shape of a heifer to lie with her husband, Baal, and the fruit of their union was a wild bull.[14]

In Canaan the seasons are starkly defined and Canaanite mythology followed the rituals that marked the safe 'ingathering' of the crops in

Figure 9. Anath as goddess of war. Egyptian relief.

autumn after the long anxious months of drought in the summer. The harvesting of the crops of corn, oil, wine and figs was celebrated by a ritual of thanksgiving. This was the Canaanite New Year festival and the Hebrews, in their turn, retained the ancient ritual. A second festival of rejoicing marked the safe harvesting of the spring corn, and as the summer drought approached (and with it the image of conflict between the light and dark powers in nature), it was time for Baal's descent into the underworld. Then Anath descended into the underworld to bring Baal back to life as the fertilizing rain, as Ishtar did in Mesopotamia. With his return came the regeneration of the earth and the promise of abundance.[15]

Astarte

Astarte (Ashtoreth in Hebrew; plural Ashtaroth) is mentioned only nine times in the Old Testament (Asherah has forty entries); this gives no indication of the importance of Astarte's cult, which was, if anything, even more widespread in Canaan than that of Asherah.

It is still not certain whether Anath and Astarte (Ashtoreth) were two separate goddesses or one and the same. Astarte, like Inanna and Ishtar, was called 'Queen of Heaven'. There is also some confusion as to whether Astarte was one of the names or aspects of Asherah, or whether she was a daughter of Asherah along with Anath, or was another name for Anath herself.[16] It may be that one and the same goddess was known by two different names in different places, or that Astarte and Anath were two separate goddesses who performed complementary functions, like Isis and Nephthys in Egypt. Insofar as these two goddesses are polarized, Astarte is the light, heavenly aspect and Anath the dark, chthonic aspect of the former Bronze Age goddess who contained both aspects within herself. In an Egyptian twelfth-century-BC papyrus Astarte and Anath are called the

Figure 10. The Canaanite goddess Qetesh standing on a lion; Egyptian relief, *c.* 1300 BC.

Figure 11. The goddess Astarte or
Ashtoreth standing on a lion, girdled
with serpents and holding lotus flowers
in her hands; gold pendant, fifteenth
century BC. Ugarit (Ras Shamra),
northern Canaan.

'two daughters' of Neith, the mother of the gods. They both had the title
'Lady of Heaven', along with another goddess from the Canaanite pantheon called Qetesh (who was also worshipped in Egypt), who is typically
drawn standing on a lion, and holds the lotus flower in one hand and
serpents in the other (Fig. 10). The gold image of a naked goddess, most
probably Astarte or Ashtoreth, shows her standing on a lion with serpents
encircling her waist (Fig. 11). She wears a crown and a necklace and holds
a lotus flower in each hand. Her hair is arranged in the stylized manner of
the Egyptian goddess Hathor.

By the fourth century BC Astarte had replaced Asherah as the goddess
of Sidon, although the transition from one goddess to another may have
taken place several centuries earlier. It may have been these people, living
close to the sea, who originally gave her the titles of 'Virgin of the Sea'
and 'Guardian of Ships'.[17] A magnificent temple existed in Sidon but
Astarte was worshipped not only in the north, but also in the cities of
Israel and Judah, down to Egypt in the south. Other great temples stood
in the cities of Hieropolis and Byblos in northern Canaan, and at Askalon
in southern Canaan. (In Plutarch's version of Isis and Osiris the coffin of
Osiris becomes a pillar in Queen Astarte's palace at Byblos, suggesting a
coincidence of stories and meanings.) Like Mary many centuries later, she
was the guardian of ships and a prayer appeals to her as goddess of the
sea: 'O Virgin of the Sea, blessed Mother and Lady of the Waters'.[18] The

moon and the morning and evening star were her images, as they were Inanna's and Ishtar's in Mesopotamia. Some figures of Astarte have two horns emerging from her head – 'Astarte of the Two Horns' was one of her names – linking her to Ishtar and to Isis–Hathor in Egypt, for both wore the horned head-dress. The original meaning of the name of Astarte was 'womb' or 'that which issues from the womb',[19] suggesting that Astarte was primarily a goddess of fertility, but also a goddess of every-thing that governed the generation of life. There is also an identity with Cybele, for a stone was the epiphany of her presence and a cone-shaped stone or obelisk stood in all her temples.

Treating Anath and Astarte as essentially one idea, their gentler aspect emerges in the title Queen of Heaven, where it is found in Jeremiah. The people of Judah in exile with him in Egypt (*c.* 586 BC) tell him that they will continue to worship her and to bake cakes to her; so this tale links the hidden goddess of the Hebrews with Inanna, Demeter and Artemis, who were also offered cakes on their altars. These cakes may have been moulded in the form of 'Astarte–Anath' herself, as a stone mould found in Israel and dating from *c.* 1600 BC suggests. They may have been eaten in a ritual in the same way that the wafer of bread is eaten today in the Christian ritual of communion. These rituals descend from a time when the body of a man or woman was sacrificed for the continued life of the tribe, and was actually eaten, just as in later times the flesh of the sacrificed bull – the body of the god – was eaten.

THE DEFAMATION OF THE GODDESS

It is hardly surprising that many of the Hebrew prophets held it to be their religious task to turn their people from the worship of the Canaanite goddesses, both on the grounds of political expediency and following Yahweh's instruction to worship no idols. Furthermore, the way these idols, or goddess images, were actually worshipped was, in the deepest sense, contrary to the whole feeling of the Hebrew religion, which was engaged in withdrawing participation from the images themselves in order to inspire consciousness to focus more deeply on the dimension beyond appearance, that is, beyond anything that can be represented in nature. To restate again Barfield's central contribution to this difficult question, Israel's face was set against the belief that the images were themselves filled with numinosity, that they were, in his phrase, 'stopping-places for *mana*'. This was 'original participation', the 'graven image' that was now proclaimed to be gravely wrong: not, of course, in the later Western sense that they were only matter, but in the sense that 'Thou shalt not bow down thyself to them nor serve them' (Exod. 20:5), thereby mistaking the image for the godhead itself.[20]

The Psalmists insisted that these idols were not filled with anything, they had no 'within', but were mere hollow pretences of life:

Their idols are silver and gold, the work of men's hands.
They have mouths, but they speak not: eyes have they, but they see not.
They have ears, but they hear not: noses have they, but they smell not.
They have hands, but they handle not: feet have they, but they walk not: neither speak they through their throat.
They that make them are like unto them; so is every one that trusteth in them. (Ps. 115:4–8)

This is an interpretation that we, as inheritors of this tradition, understand only too well, even though the dangerous consequences of withdrawing numinosity more widely from the whole field of appearances – that is, ultimately, from the whole of nature itself – are only now being recognized. At this time, however, 2,000 and more years ago, the prophets' wrath was fully intelligible as a way of transferring sovereignty from the outward form to the inward heart, where the voice of divinity could be personally heard and an ethical dialogue could take place.

The point here is that these two religious positions would require no more than a historical comment on the evolution of consciousness if Yahweh's 'holy war' against 'the goddess' had not entered the values of the succeeding centuries as the holy war of masculine *against* feminine. Still worse, the paradigm of opposition, of good against evil, was also bequeathed down the centuries as, implicitly, the only way to progress. (Even now the military metaphor is still the conventional way to view disease.) This will be explored in Chapter 16, but it is worth considering here whether the fact that the oppositional paradigm in general, and the opposition of masculine and feminine in particular, has been accepted so uncritically owes something to the sacred nature of its origins: Yahweh, the Good God, fighting and overcoming the Evil Goddess; for, whatever the virtues of doing without the graven image, the actual form this took then was identifying the sin of the people of Israel as their worship of the goddesses represented in images: Asherah, her daughter Astarte–Anath (Ashtoreth), together with her son Baal. (El, the father god, seems to have been exempted from condemnation, perhaps because his name and father image were assimilated to Yahweh–Elohim.)

Levite laws were designed to eradicate not only the images of the older religion, but also their cult practices, such as the custom of intercourse with temple priestesses and the caring for the children born of these unions by the women. Metaphysics and politics frequently merge so subtly that it is difficult to decide which need is being met at any one time. For instance, the matrilineal line of descent was abolished, and the certainty of patrilineal descent was established by ensuring that no Israelite seed was lost in the seasonal fertility rites of Anath and Baal. Patrilineal descent was guaranteed under threat of death by requiring daughters to be virgin before marriage and wives to 'belong' exclusively to their husbands. The bitter struggle between the Levite priesthood and the Canaanite customs is reflected in the story of Genesis 2–3 in the pejorative image of Eve. The only curious vestige of the former custom of matrilineal descent is the fact that Jewish descent is to this day still inherited through the mother.

From the time that Aaron encouraged the people to make an image of the golden calf, enacting the old sacrificial and sexual rites before it, the form of the struggle was established.[21] The 'golden calf' was the bull form of the son–lover of the goddess, the embodiment of his fertilizing power. In Egypt the bull was Osiris and Serapis; in Sumeria, it was Dumuzi; in Babylonia, Tammuz; and in Canaan, Baal. But it was to return later, after the institution of the monarchy, when Jeroboam, who ruled after Solomon, set up two statues of bulls, one in the north, at Bethel, and one near Jerusalem, saying, as Aaron had said before him: 'These be thy gods, O Israel, which brought thee up out of the land of Egypt.' (Exod. 32:4 and 1 Kgs. 12:28)

Solomon (*c.* 1000 BC) may have been the first King of Israel to introduce the worship of Asherah to Jerusalem. Solomon 'loved Yahweh', but he also 'sacrificed and burnt incense in high places' (1 Kgs. 3:3) and 'did evil in the eyes of the Lord, and went not fully after the Lord as did David his father' (1 Kgs. 11:6). It was the custom in Canaan, as elsewhere at this time, for kings to have many wives. Solomon was reputed to have 700 wives and these 'turned away his heart' (1 Kgs. 11:3). He took princesses from Egypt, Sidon and Anatolia as his wives, as well as from his Canaanite vassals, most probably to establish his sons' title to rule these places through matrilineal descent. All of these princesses would have brought to his court their own goddesses and gods. 'There can be little doubt', writes Patai, 'that it was the worship of Asherah, already popular among the Hebrews for several generations, which was introduced by Solomon into Jerusalem as part of the cult of the royal household, for his Sidonian wife.'[22]

The Kingdom of Israel was divided in two after Solomon's reign, according to the prophets because Solomon had forsaken Yahweh and worshipped Asherah or Astarte (Ashtoreth) instead. There were now two kingdoms, the northern one of Israel and the southern one of Judah, whose capitals were Samaria and Jerusalem respectively. They were constantly at war with each other until the deportation of ten of the twelve tribes of Israel from the northern kingdom by Shalmaneser V, king of the Assyrians, in 721 BC. Until that time, the goddess was worshipped by the Hebrews in both kingdoms, and this continued in the southern kingdom, Judah, after the dispersion of the tribes of the northern kingdom. The melancholy chronicler in 2 Kings interpreted this worship as the cause of the punishment of Israel:

And the children of Israel did secretly those things that were not right against the Lord their God, and they built them high places in all their cities . . .

And they set them up images and groves in every high hill, and under every green tree:

And there they burnt incense in all the high places, as did the heathen whom the Lord carried away before them; and wrought wicked things to provoke the Lord to anger.

. . . . .

Therefore the Lord was very angry with Israel and removed them out of his sight; there was none left but the tribe of Judah only. (2 Kgs. 17:9–11, 18)

In Judah, King Hezekiah (727–698 BC) 'removed the high places, and brake the images [the *asherim*] . . . and brake in pieces the brasen serpent that Moses had made: for unto those days the Children of Israel did burn incense to it' (2 Kgs. 18:4). The serpent was so much a part of the goddess culture that it seems likely that, in spite of Moses' experience on Sinai, it was still integral to the old religion in the eyes of the people. Otherwise, why would Hezekiah need to destroy it? Some 100 years later, in the reign of King Josiah, the discovery of the Book of the Law in Solomon's Temple by the priest Hilkiah in 621 BC led to one of the most complete dissociations from the older culture in the history of Israel (2 Kgs. 23). Yahweh's command seemed once and for all to have been carried out:

'But ye shall destroy their altars, break their images and cut down their groves,

For thou shalt worship no other god: for the Lord whose name is Jealous is a jealous God.' (Exod. 34:13–14)

Yet the old practices returned under the next king, and it fell to the prophet Ezekiel in his vision of the sins of Israel to predict that the worship of false gods would bring about another catastrophe. The vision is believed to date to the year 592 BC, and gives 'the most detailed account of idolatrous practices in the Jerusalem Temple found in the entire Bible'.[23] In the manner of shamanistic experience, Yahweh seizes Ezekiel by a lock of his hair and transports him to the Temple, pointing out one by one the images and practices that he abhorred. Ezekiel is shown the 'Image of Jealousy', most probably the statue of Asherah that had been restored to the Temple by Manesseh (698–642 BC) after Hezekiah's removal of it. There he was also shown the 'women weeping for Tammuz', the sun-worshippers and all kinds of 'creeping things and beasts and all kinds of idols' being worshipped by the seventy elders of Israel (Ezek. 8). Ezekiel's vision of the destruction that is to fall upon Judah is one of the most terrifying in the Old Testament:

Behold, I, even I, will bring a sword upon you, and I will destroy your high places.

And your altars shall be desolate and your images shall be broken: and I will cast down your slain men before your idols.

And I will lay the dead carcases of the children of Israel before their idols; and I will scatter your bones round about your altars. (Ezek. 6:3–5)

The catastrophe of the Exile came to pass only a few years later, and Jeremiah, addressing the remnant of the Judaean people in exile in Egypt, placed the blame for their troubles on their worship of the Queen of Heaven. The goddess mentioned here is evidently not a war goddess, but a mother goddess who was invoked to provide the people with food, peace and well-being. However, Jeremiah met with strong resistance, particularly from the women, for they felt that the calamity had been inflicted on them because they had deserted the Queen of Heaven, not Yahweh:

Then all the men which knew that their wives had burned incense unto other gods, and all the women that stood by, a great multitude, even all the people that dwelt in the land of Egypt, in Pathros, answered Jeremiah, saying,

As for the word that thou has spoken unto us in the name of the Lord, we will not hearken unto thee.

Figure 12. The Gate of Ishtar, with the sacred trees and animals of the goddess; *c.* 600 BC. Babylon.

But we will certainly do whatsoever thing goeth forth out of our own mouth, to burn incense unto the queen of heaven and to pour out drink offerings unto her, as we have done, we, and our fathers, our kings, and our princes, in the cities of Judah, and in the streets of Jerusalem: for then had we plenty of victuals, and were well, and saw no evil.

But since we left off to burn incense to the queen of heaven, and to pour out drink offerings unto her, we have wanted all things, and have been consumed by the sword and by the famine. (Jer. 44:15–18)

The final humiliation and downfall of the detested Babylonian goddess Ishtar at the hand of Yahweh was prophesied by Isaiah:

Come down, and sit in the dust, O virgin daughter of Babylon, sit on the ground: there is no throne, O daughter of the Chaldeans: for thou shalt no more be called tender and delicate.

. . . . .

Thy nakedness shall be uncovered, yea, thy shame shall be seen: I will take vengeance, and I will not meet thee as a man.

. . . . .

Let now the astrologers, the stargazers, the monthly prognosticators, stand up, and save thee from these things that shall come upon thee.

Behold, they shall be as stubble; the fire shall burn them; they shall not deliver themselves from the power of the flame . . .

Thus shall they be unto thee with whom thou hast laboured . . . none shall save thee. (Isa. 47:1, 3, 13–15)

The idea that the Law is more important than the 'sympathetic magic' of soothsayers and astrologers emerges clearly from this passage. The prophets' aim was to demythologize nature by exorcizing the image of divinity from it, so breaking the hold of 'nature worship'. As Barfield says: 'The killing out of participation was the end, in itself, and imagery of all kinds was the quarry marked out for destruction.'[24] Logically, the numinous power of the fertility rituals could be eradicated only by eliminating the goddess, together with the god who was her son, lover or sacrificial victim, 'depending on the phase of the cycle of growth and death that is being stressed'.[25]

An extraordinary story is alluded to here, and one that has marked the Jewish, Christian and Islamic psyche with the image of a fearful, vengeful father god who will tolerate no deviation from his Law. It is one version of the great Bronze and Iron Age battle that was fought in every culture from Greece to India, and which has transmitted its legacy of a fragmented and barely recognizable image of the goddess to future generations, as well as a deeply held belief in the 'divine' polarization of good and evil. It seems undeniable that the image of Yahweh called out in relation to the Canaanite goddesses is that of the tribal god, not the universal god, and, accordingly, the tribal 'morality' and the language of hatred in which it is expressed diminish the conception of divinity to human proportions. It results, then, in a confusion of 'divine' and human, which needs to be radically distinguished from the other images of Yahweh.

MOSES AS A SON–LOVER OF THE GODDESS

In Moses, the chosen leader of the Hebrews, a residual and symbolic form of the old myth of the goddess and her son–lover still survives, despite its transformation by the Hebrew priesthood. The story of Moses found in the bulrushes by the pharaoh's daughter echoes the Sumerian story of Sargon, the Akkadian king beloved of Ishtar, also discovered in the rushes of a Mesopotamian river bank. Campbell points out that the roots of the Egyptian story can be traced to the Sumerian one, not only in this imagery but also in the mention of bitumen and pitch, for these were not known in Egypt until Ptolomaic times.[26] The relationship of the patriarchs Abraham and Joseph to their wives, as well as the relationship of David to Bath-sheba and of Solomon to his royal Egyptian bride, suggests a deep memory of the mythological relationship between the pharaoh as Osiris and his sister–wife as Isis. This theme has been explored by Edmund Leech in his discussion of the relationship of Moses to his sister, Miriam.[27] The fact that there may have been a tradition that recognized the goddess in the 'mother' and sister of Moses is implied in the third-century-AD mural in a synagogue at Dura Europos in Syria: Moses as an infant is shown as having emerged from a sarcophagus, held in the arms of a woman whose nakedness (in contrast to all the other female figures) suggests that she is a goddess (Fig. 13).

Patai believes that this is the image of the Jewish Shekhinah, who is first mentioned by this name in the first century AD.[28] The Shekhinah was known variously as the manifest aspect, or 'presence', of Yahweh, as the bride of Yahweh, or as the Holy Spirit – the intercessor and binding

Figure 13. Moses in the arms of the Shekhinah; third century AD. Dura Europos Synagogue, Syria.

link between the divine and human dimensions. The image of the Shekhinah from the first century AD through the Middle Ages will be considered in Chapter 15.

In the Middle Ages the legend of this relationship was to culminate in the statement made in Kabbalah – the mystical tradition of Judaism – that Moses, and he alone of all men, not only became the husband of the Matronit (the name later given to the Shekhinah), but united with her while still in the flesh.[29] In the earlier Talmudic and Midrashic sources this idea is implicit in the saying that, of all men, Moses was the only one to whom the Shekhinah spoke 'every hour without setting a time in advance', and that, therefore, in order to be always in a state of ritual purity to receive a communication from the Shekhinah, Moses separated himself completely from his wife. Patai describes a legend that said:

> When Moses died, the Shekhina took him on her wings and carried him from Mount Nebo to his unknown burial place four miles away. The Shekhina's function at the death of Moses is paralleled by her administration to him at his birth. When the daughter of Pharaoh, we read in the Babylonian Talmud, found the ark of bulrushes into which his mother had placed Moses, and opened it, 'she saw the Shekhina with him.'[30]

THE PEOPLE OF ISRAEL AS THE BRIDE OF YAHWEH

None the less, the banished imagery of the goddess mysteriously reappears, but now displaced and disguised in a new and unlikely context: as the people of Israel. Somehow, presumably unconsciously, the former mythological image was re-created. The Levite priests and prophets of the Hebrews had employed the rhetoric of war, placing Yahweh and the people of Israel side by side as partners in the heroic role of fighting the powers of chaos embodied in political opponents and the goddess religion. In the course of this battle the father god, who was married to no goddess, took instead the people of Israel as his earthly 'bride'. That is to say, the language in which this relationship was expressed took the form of the relation between bridegroom and bride, or, perhaps, father–husband and child–wife. The fertility of the land and well-being of the people were now dependent upon the 'fidelity' of Israel to her divine bridegroom, no longer on the annual union of the priest-king with the priestess of the goddess. Israel then assumed the imagery of the former goddess, both virgin and harlot, alternating between them as to whether 'she' obeyed her patriarchal husband or not: her harlotry was her regression to worshipping the Canaanite goddess and Baal; her virginity was her faithfulness to Yahweh. Yahweh's divine vengeance fell upon her because of her infidelity to him. Here, in the book of the prophet Hosea, Yahweh is speaking of 'Israel' as his wife:

Plead with your mother, plead: for she is not my wife, neither am I her
husband: let her therefore put away her whoredoms out of her sight, and
her adulteries from between her breasts.

Lest I strip her naked, and set her as in the day that she was born, and
make her as a wilderness, and set her like a dry land, and slay her with
thirst.

. . . . .

Therefore, behold, I will allure her, and bring her into the wilderness,
and speak comfortably unto her.

And I will give her her vineyards . . . and she shall sing there, as in the
days of her youth, and as in the day when she came up out of the land of
Egypt.

And it shall be at that day, saith the Lord, that thou shalt call me Ishi [my
husband]; and thou shalt call me no more Baali [my Baal]. (Hos. 2:2–3, 14–16)

Though the old myth of the goddess culture has died, it is here resurrected in a new form, one in which the earthly principle of divine life is
incarnated in a 'chosen' people, the bride of the father god, rather than in
the life principle of the earth, embodied in the king, the 'chosen' consort
of the goddess. The emphasis in the sacred marriage has been reversed.
Where once the king held his throne and the welfare of his land and
people by virtue of his marriage to the goddess of heaven and earth, now
the prosperity and well-being of a nation depends upon *her* faithfulness to
Yahweh.

The crucial distinction is that formerly the feminine principle in the
form of the goddess was a category of the divine. Now, the feminine
principle in the form of Israel as bride has become secular: it is excluded
from divinity, taking its value solely from its relation to the divine masculine. Inevitably, therefore, the principles of masculine and feminine, as
they are played out in the lives and thoughts of the Judaeo-Christian
tradition, are related to each other hierarchically – the one with the divine
model is superior. In turn, the man, reflecting this model, himself offers
the model to the inferior woman, as, most obviously, in the story of Adam
and Eve.

From a different perspective, Campbell draws attention to one of the
anomalies of allotting to a portion of humanity a role that was formerly
divine, even though here he is talking about Israel not as bride but in its
other mythological role of hero redeemed from the Egyptian underworld
of death. 'It is highly significant', he writes:

that the later festival of the Passover, which, as we have seen, was first
celebrated 621 BC in commemoration of Exodus, occurs on the date of the
annual resurrection of Adonis, which in the Christian cult became Easter.
In both the pagan cult and the Christian, the resurrection is of a god,
whereas in the Jewish it is of the Chosen People.[31]

It is not difficult to understand why the Old Testament has been often
described as 'intolerably patriarchal'.[32] The Hebrew priests of the Iron

Age could not conceive of the possibility of marriage between god and goddess, for this was the image of the detested Canaanite ritual and, moreover, women in their culture were regarded as inferior to men. In the same way that the head of the patriarchal family demanded the unquestioning obedience of his wife and children, so the Hebrew Great Father required the unquestioning obedience of his 'bride', Israel. Judaic monotheism, as it is expressed in the Old Testament, lacked any divine image of the feminine, so there could not be any sacred marriage between god and goddess, heaven and earth. There was no dialogue, as there was in Greece, between the patriarchal and matriarchal visions of life. Because of this, the people were cut off from the whole past experience personified in the image of the goddess, and in the life of images generally, and so lost their former access to ethical values that came from the experience of participation in life animated by divine presence. A divine image was created that was transcendent only, not transcendent *and* immanent, and this, as was intended, undermined the older sense of the sacrality of earth and human life. Life was sacred because Yahweh had created it, not because Yahweh was incarnate in it.

The commandment in Deuteronomy 'I have set before you life and death . . . therefore choose life' (30:19) offered no compromise. Yahweh's people were forced to stay within very narrow boundaries whose infringement drew upon them divine punishment for disobeying his commands. The meticulous rules concerned with the absolute correctness of rituals, including the preparation of food and the strict control of sexuality, fixed father, as Law, and mother, as Nature, irrevocably against each other. This emphasis could result only in the development of a split in the psyche between the 'spiritual' and the 'natural' self, and between mind and body. While this was inevitable, understandable and, at that time, even in part desirable, it exacted a severe price. In the formal interpretation of Yahweh there was no longer any containing image to inspire spontaneous trust and joy in life and the process of living; there was instead awe and inspiration, but also fear of divine wrath for transgression of the Law.

But, again, in the informal and symbolic imagery of the Bible the picture changes. The transcendent and masculine model of the deity is softened and enriched, even totally transformed, by the feminine image of 'Wisdom'. If Israel was the earthly bride of Yahweh, Hokhmah, or Sophia, was his bride in heaven. And, significantly, when he takes a heavenly bride, his tribal concerns are left behind.

SOPHIA (HOKHMAH): THE HEAVENLY BRIDE OF
YAHWEH-ELOHIM

The first man knew her not perfectly: no more shall the last find her out.
For her thoughts are more than the sea, and her counsels profounder than
the great deep. (Sir. 24:28–9)

As the above passage from the Apocryphal Book of Ben Sirach (Ecclesiasticus) suggests, there is indeed a feminine presence in the Old
Testament that is accorded a status so far-reaching as to evoke the feeling
of the divine. This is Hokhmah, who, in Greek, was called Sophia, the
name for Wisdom. 'She', for so she was called, was invariably personified
as a female being, but (like Yahweh) she cannot be seen. Responding to
the beauty of the words, the imagination reaches for an image of her
'whose counsels are profounder than the great deep', but is unable to find
one. Yet 'she' cannot be replaced by a disembodied and abstract idea –
the idea of wisdom – because the poetry is too physical and too present. If
we did not know better, we might suppose her to be a goddess!

The origins of Wisdom, who was 'set up from everlasting, from the
beginning, or ever the earth was' (Sir. 24:9), can be divined from our
knowledge of the Great Goddesses of the Bronze Age. It seems clear,
from the long tradition of imagery that predated the Old Testament, that
Wisdom, or Sophia as we shall call her in this chapter, is a later image of
zoe – the archetype of the ground of being – now imagined as transcendent,
like Yahweh, and given the name of Wisdom.

In the Old Testament the figure of Sophia as the invisible, unnamed
'consort' of Yahweh is portrayed as the master craftswoman of creation,
and in this sense transcendent. Yet she is also described in the language of
immanence, for she walks the streets of her city, crying out for people to
listen to her. It is only in the later Kabbalistic image of the Shekhinah,
however, that the imagery of immanence is completed, for then the 'dwelling place' of the Shekhinah, the bride of Yahweh, is in creation. Where
are we to trace the origin of this idea if not to the goddess who was once
Queen of Heaven and Earth, and united in her person those dimensions
that, in Judaism, were separated in the name of Yahweh?

The idea that the earthly, visible order of creation participates in the
invisible source of being is the greatest legacy of the goddess culture and
is the foundation of the Wisdom traditions of Mesopotamia and Egypt,
some 2,000 years older than Hebrew or Greek civilization. In Greece,
whose great philosophers visited Egypt, it is the foundation of Plato's
image of the Great Chain of Being. Israel's own 'Wisdom Teaching'
is woven with the thread of these older traditions, although the name,
person and representation of the goddess could find no place.[33] It seems
that the psyche's need for the feminine is honoured in some way in
every age, in spite of any conscious decision on the part of a priesthood to
exclude it.

The Origins of Sophia

A little over 4,000 years ago in Sumeria King Gudea of Lagash went to the temple of the god Ningursu to pray for the relief of his people, because the land was afflicted by drought. There he had a dream that he was unable to interpret, and to discover its meaning he went to the temple of the mother goddess and prayed:

> O my Queen, daughter of Purest heaven, whose counsel is of profit, occupier of the highest celestial place, who makes the land to live: Queen, Mother and Foundress of Lagash! Those whom you favour know the wealth of strength; those whom you regard, the wealth of years. I have no mother, you are my mother; no father, you are my father. In the sanctuary you bore me. O my Goddess, (Gatumdug), yours is the wisdom of all goodness. Mother, let me tell you my dream.
>
> There was in my dream the figure of a man whose stature filled the sky, whose stature filled the earth. The crown on his head proclaimed him a god, and at his side was the Imdugud bird. Storm was at his feet. To right and left two lions lay. And he ordered me to build for him his house. But who he was, I did not know.
>
> Thereupon, the sun rose from the earth before me. A woman appeared – Who was she? Who was she not? – In her hand she had a pure stylus; in the other a clay tablet on which celestial constellations were displayed. She was rapt, as it were, in thought. And there appeared in that dream a second man, a warrior, holding a lapis lazuli tablet on which he drew the diagram of a house. A litter was set before me: upon it, a brick-mold of gold, and in the mold, the brick of destiny. And at the right of my king stood a laden ass.
>
> 'My Shepherd,' said the goddess, 'I shall read for you your dream. The man whose stature filled sky and earth, whose crown proclaimed him a god, and at whose side was the Imdugud bird; storm at his feet, and to right and left two lions, was the god, my brother, Ningursu. His command to you was to build his temple Eninnu. Now, the sun that rose from the earth before you was your guardian god, Ningizzida: like a sun, his serpent form rises from the earth. The woman holding a stylus and tablet of constellations, rapt as it were in thought, was the goddess, my sister, Nisaba, showing to you the auspicious star for your building of the temple. The second man, a warrior, with lapis lazuli tablet, was the god Nin-dub, designing for you the temple's structure. And the ass, laden, at the right of the king; that was yourself, ready for your task.'[34]

It is possible that this earliest record of a dream laid the foundation for the later Wisdom literature of the Bible, in which the feminine image of Wisdom inspired some of its most sublime poetry. Behind the figure of Sophia stands the earlier Great Mother – 'Who was she? Who was she not?' – casting her image forward in time. A goddess in all but name, and the feminine counterpart of the supreme creator, Wisdom speaks as Inanna and Isis did before her.

In some parts of the Wisdom literature Sophia speaks with the full
authority of the former goddess. Elsewhere, she personifies an attribute of
the deity, as the wisdom and creativity out of which emerges the active
power that gives form to life, in the way that a craftsman shapes his wood
or clay. In Ben Sirach, Sophia says:

> I came out of the mouth of the most High,
> and covered the earth as a cloud.
> I dwelt in high places,
> and my throne is in a cloudy pillar.
> I alone encompassed the circuit of heaven,
> and walked in the bottom of the deep.
> I had power over the waves of the sea, and over all the earth,
> and over every people and nation.
>
>   . . . . .
>
> He created me from the beginning before the world,
> and I shall never fail.
> In the holy tabernacle I served before him;
> and so was I established in Sion.
> Likewise in the beloved city he gave me rest,
> and in Jerusalem was my power.
>
>   . . . . .
>
> I was exalted like a cedar in Libanus,
> and as a cypress tree upon the mountains of Hermon.
> I was exalted like a palm tree in En-gaddi,
> and as a rose plant in Jericho,
> as a fair olive tree in a pleasant field,
> and grew up as a plane tree by the water.
>
>   . . . . .
>
> I also came out as a brook from a river,
> and as a conduit into a garden.
> I said, I will water my best garden,
> and will water abundantly my garden bed:
> and lo, my brook became a river,
> and my river became a sea.
> I will yet make doctrine to shine as the morning,
> and will send forth her light afar off.
> I will yet pour out doctrine as prophecy,
> and leave it to all ages for ever.
> Behold that I have not laboured for myself only,
> but for all them that seek wisdom. (Sir. 24:3–6, 9–11, 12–14, 30–4)

In the Book of Proverbs (fourth and third centuries BC) Sophia says:

> The Lord possessed me in the beginning of his way, before his works of
> old.
> I was set up from everlasting, from the beginning, or ever the earth was.

When there were no depths, I was brought forth; when there were no fountains abounding with water.

Before the mountains were settled, before the hills was I brought forth:

While as yet he had not made the earth, nor the fields, nor the highest part of the dust of the world.

When he prepared the heavens, I was there: when he set a compass upon the face of the depth:

When he established the clouds above: when he strengthened the fountains of the deep:

When he gave to the sea his decree, that the waters should not pass his commandment: when he appointed the foundations of the earth,

Then I was by him, as one brought up with him,[51] and I was daily his delight, rejoicing always before him,

Rejoicing in the habitable part of his earth; and my delights were with the sons of men. (Prov. 8:23–31)

Echoes of Sumeria and Egypt play through the beauty of this poetry, particularly in its delight of the flowers, trees, fountains, rivers, hills and fields of nature. If the meaning is transcendent, the poetic presence is irrefutably immanent. This feeling for the wondrous clothing of the earth recalls the fullness of the goddess figures of earlier times, for the Sumerian image of the *me* (the Laws of Wisdom) and the Egyptian Goddess of Wisdom, Maat, contained within their meanings of wisdom many related ideas to which we now give separate names: truth, compassion, insight, knowledge, understanding, justice, divine law expressed in human institutions, and the whole ethical realm of human endeavour.

The images of water and sea, the unfathomable abyss of the Deep, return us to Nammu, the Sumerian goddess whose ideogram was the sea, and to the Babylonian goddess Danuna, mother of Marduk, who dwelt in the depths with her lord, Ea, or Oannes, God of Wisdom. The later association of salt, the distilled essence of the sea, with Wisdom, in the sense that it is used by Jesus in his teaching, and also by Cordelia in *King Lear*, may come originally from the Sumerian identification of Wisdom with the Mother Goddess, which is echoed in Ben Sirach: 'For her thoughts are more than the sea, and her counsels profounder than the great deep' (Sir. 24:29). The many different kinds of tree sacred to the goddess – the cedar, the cypress, the palm, the sycamore fig, the apple and the olive – invoke the courtyards of her temples, where the tree and pillar belonged to her as long ago as Neolithic times. The vine, like the tree, was an image both of herself and her son, and is inseparable from the mythology of Sumeria and Babylonia, where Inanna was goddess both of heaven and earth, 'the Green One'. But it is above all in the imagery of light associated with Wisdom that Inanna's ancient lunar presence gleams through the later figure of Sophia (Hokhmah): 'For she is more beautiful than the sun, and above all the order of stars: being compared with light, she is found before it . . .' (Apocrypha: Wisd. 7:29).

The earliest Wisdom literature of the Bible, the Book of Proverbs, was written down only during the fourth century BC, and was a compilation of older material, which included Sumerian and Babylonian as well as Egyptian sayings. The fifty-year-long exile of the Hebrew people in Babylon ended in 538 BC, yet only one-third returned to Israel. Many Jewish scholars remained in Babylon and established rabbinic schools, where the biblical texts were discussed and interpreted for 1,000 years, in much the same way as the Platonic Academy endured in Athens for 1,000 years. The Babylonian Talmud, or body of rabbinic commentaries on the Bible emerging from these schools, has always been held to be more profound than the Palestinian Talmud. However, a great part of the Wisdom literature that once belonged to the sacred texts of Israel has been lost.

It is hardly surprising, therefore, to discover in the Wisdom literature of Israel that Sophia, like the earlier goddesses, has the same quality of virginity: 'Being but one, she can do all things: and remaining in herself, she maketh all things new' (Wisd. 7:27). Eternally, she renews herself, pouring herself forth, 'from the beginning of the world', generation after generation. To follow her 'way' brings life; to reject it invites calamity and death. It is interesting that the old unity between the light and dark aspects of the goddess can be discerned in the Wisdom literature, but the one image is now divided into two different figures, Wisdom and Folly. The dark aspect of the ancient goddess is personified by Folly, who is portrayed as a prostitute, persuading humanity, with 'many allurements', to forsake the path of Wisdom. Behind the image of both Wisdom and Folly, spoken of as the 'strange' or 'foreign' woman, stands Ishtar, the Virgin Goddess of Babylon, whom the Jewish people left behind when they returned from exile, and whom they named 'the Great Whore'. In the passages on Folly the ecstatic sexuality that was once included in the totality of the goddess as her 'power', and enacted in the fertility rites of her temples, is now the image of evil and death:

> And, behold, there met him a woman with the attire of an harlot, and subtil of heart.
> . . . . .
> So she caught him, and kissed him, and with an impudent face said unto him,
> . . . . .
> I have decked my bed with coverings of tapestry, with carved works, with fine linen of Egypt.
> I have perfumed my bed with myrrh, aloes, and cinnamon.
> Come let us take our fill of love until the morning: let us solace ourselves with loves. (Prov. 7:10, 13, 16–18)

The contrast between this image of the 'strange woman' and Inanna–Ishtar, whose 'folly' was one of her divine attributes, could hardly be greater. Yet, it is worth noticing, in distinction to Yahweh's wrath against the goddesses, that the language of correction is compassionate.

Sophia insists on a struggle for insight and understanding. Her yoke is not light. She is compared to a 'mighty stone of trial' (Sir. 6:21). To begin with:

> . . . she will walk with him by crooked ways, and bring fear and dread upon him, and torment him with her discipline, until she may trust his soul, and try him by her laws.
> Then will she return the straight way unto him, and comfort him, and shew him her secrets.
> But if he go wrong, she will forsake him, and give him over to his own ruin. (Sir. 4:17–19)

Wisdom is to be prized above silver and gold: 'My fruit is better than gold, yea than fine gold; and my revenue than choice silver' (Prov. 8:19), a saying that recalls the second-century Greek hymn to Isis quoted in Chapter 6 (see pp. 268–70), which includes the lines: 'I made the right to be stronger than gold and silver. I ordained that the true should be thought good.'[35] The implacable nature of Wisdom as the Law of Life, a composite blend of love and knowledge, whose workings are inscrutable to humanity and bring suffering as well as joy, is revealed in the following passage, where again Sophia speaks with the power and authority of the goddess, even enacting the dark aspect of Inanna–Ishtar when she destroyed her people with the flood and storm:

> Wisdom crieth without; she uttereth her voice in the streets:
>   . . . . .
> How long, ye simple ones, will ye love simplicity [ignorance]?
>   . . . . .
> Turn you at my reproof: behold, I will pour out my spirit unto you, I will make known my words unto you.
> Because I have called and ye refused; I have stretched out my hand, and no man regarded;
> But ye have set at nought all my counsel, and would none of my reproof.
> I also will laugh at your calamity; I will mock when your fear cometh,
> When your fear cometh as desolation, and your destruction cometh as a whirlwind; when distress and anguish cometh upon you.
> Then shall they call upon me, but I will not answer; they shall seek me early but they shall not find me.
>   . . . . .
> But whoso hearkeneth unto me shall dwell safely, and shall be quiet from fear of evil. (Prov. 1:20, 22, 23–8, 33)

Wisdom, like Ishtar, cries at the gates of the city, 'in the top of high places . . . at the entry of the city, at the coming in at the doors' (Prov. 8:2–3). She also secretly 'sets the gates of the City ajar'. The image of the gate, or gates, together with the phrase 'the top of high places' and the sending forth of her maidens (Prov. 9:3) or priestesses, suggests the temple of the goddess. These passages also anticipate the words of Jesus: 'I am the door; by me if any man enter in, he shall be saved, and shall go in and out, and find pasture' (John 10:9).

In other passages Wisdom is spoken of as a specifically feminine attribute of the Divine. Solomon says:

> ... I prayed and understanding was given me: I called upon God, and the spirit of wisdom came to me.
>
> . . . . .
>
> I loved her above health and beauty, and chose to have her instead of light, for the light that cometh from her never goeth out.
>
> . . . . .
>
> And all such things as are either secret or manifest, them I know.
> For wisdom, which is the worker of all things, taught me; for in her is an understanding spirit, holy, one only, manifold, subtil, lively, clear, undefiled, plain, not subject to hurt, loving the thing that is good, quick, which cannot be letted, ready to do good,
> Kind to man, stedfast, sure, free from care, having all power, overseeing all things, and going through all understanding, pure, and most subtil, spirits.
> For wisdom is more moving than any motion; she passeth and goeth through all things by reason of her pureness.
> For she is the breath of the power of God, and a pure influence flowing from the glory of the Almighty:
>
> . . . . .
>
> For she is the brightness of the everlasting light, the unspotted mirror of the power of God, and the image of his goodness.
> And being but one, she can do all things: and remaining in herself, she maketh all things new: and in all ages entering into holy souls, she maketh them friends of God, and prophets.
>
> . . . . .
>
> For she is more beautiful than the sun, and above all the order of stars: being compared with light, she is found before it.
>
> . . . . .
>
> I loved her, and sought her out from my youth, I desired to make her my spouse, and I was a lover of her beauty. (Wisd. 7:7, 10, 21–7, 29; 8:2)

It is as if the speaker cannot help falling into the language and imagery of the sacred marriage.

In the Wisdom literature as a whole, Wisdom appears as mother and bride, the consort of the father god; the image, like the Sumerian and Egyptian goddesses, of light, truth, law, insight, understanding, compassion and justice. She is the feminine counterpart of the masculine deity, the foundation of the world, the master-craftswoman. She speaks both as the unifying light, which is the ground of creation, and the form that 'clothes' it. She is the hidden law that orders it. She describes herself in language that shows that she is the animating power in nature and human life: rooted in tree, vine, earth and water as well as in the human creation of the city. She is judge (Enoch 91:10) and saviour (Enoch 92:1), interceding to save her people, as Ishtar interceded to save humanity from the Flood. She is transcendent, eternally one with the godhead beyond creation, and immanent in the world as the presence of the divine within the forms of creation. She is the invisible spirit guiding human life, who may be discovered by the person who seeks her guidance and help.

The source of Wisdom sometimes alternates between the image of Sophia and that of Yahweh. Engelsman, in her exploration of Sophia, believes there was tension between the adherents of Yahweh and those of Sophia at the beginning of the Christian era: 'This tension appears to have been resolved by repression . . . At least her power and prestige were radically curtailed at this time, and Sophia does not reappear as a major figure until the rise of Jewish mysticism in the Middle Ages.'[36] As we shall show in Chapter 15, the image of the feminine Sophia, as the personification of Wisdom in both Judaism and Christianity, was replaced by the masculine Logos. The Word as Wisdom became the mediator between the godhead and humanity. In this way, the feminine image of the divine was again lost.

Wisdom is traditionally associated with the number seven, the number that belongs above all to lunar mythology. From Sumeria onwards there were always seven sacred planets, seven gates to the underworld, seven *Annunaki*, or guardians of the underworld. The rainbow with seven colours was 'Ishtar's necklace', and it is this she discards as she descends to the underworld. Inanna and Ishtar had to pass through seven gates to gain access to Ereshkigal's or Allatu's dark kingdom; in the Bible seven pillars support Wisdom's house. This tradition is transmitted to later Gnostic myth, where seven Archons, or planetary lords, rule the aeons, or dimensions, between this world and the source of Light. Here, Sophia as the soul, the daughter of Light and Truth, has to pass through these seven aeons with the help of her brother, Christ, freeing herself from their power, on her journey of return to her Mother and Father and the Pleroma, or Light Source, from which she came.

Many of these images are important later for a deeper insight into the Christian and Gnostic Gospels, and the Book of Revelation, as well as alchemical and Grail symbolism. The imagery of the Great Goddess of Egypt and Sumeria is the foundation of the Wisdom literature of the Old Testament, just as the Neolithic era provided the underlying images that developed into the mythology of the Bronze Age. The fourth-century-BC Book of Proverbs, and the later Books of Ben Sirach (second century BC), the Wisdom of Solomon (first century BC), the Song of Solomon (first century BC) and the Book of Enoch (100 BC) mark the transition from an earlier time when Wisdom was an aspect of the Mother Goddess to the time when she becomes the indwelling Holy Spirit, the guiding light of the soul, personified by the image of Christ, as portrayed in the Christian and Gnostic Gospels. Christ is 'one with the Father' in the pleromatic world, yet participates in the world of human experience. The union of bride and bridegroom, so marvellously conveyed in the Song of Songs, is derived from the sacred marriage rituals of Sumeria and Egypt, and anticipates the later Gnostic teaching of the union between the soul and its heavenly counterpart, or bridegroom: Christ, the son of the Divine Mother Sophia.

In these books the emphasis is moving from unquestioning worship of the deity towards relationship with the deity, as it is realized that what was named 'goddess or god' is both beyond human comprehension and an indwelling consciousness in all human beings that can be awakened, brought to birth or incarnated within them. The imagery of the sacred marriage then becomes internalized as a rite of union that can be experienced by the awakened soul, visualized as the bridegroom, with his 'divine' counterpart, the bride; or conversely, with the awakened soul visualized as the bride, united with her heavenly bridegroom. This momentous transfiguration, reaching from the Bronze Age to the Eleusinian and Gnostic Mysteries and then to the flowering of mystical Judaism and Christianity in the Middle Ages, reflects the deepening insight of human consciousness into its own ground; moreover, this insight is continually reformulated in new versions of the age-old myth of the goddess and her son–lover.

However, in the course of this evolution of the image of the goddess her earthly aspect was lost. Hokhmah, or Sophia, became increasingly identified with the abstract notion of the wisdom of the godhead, and this was split off from the image of the divine feminine. It seems to be the case that as the feminine archetype loses its image in the goddess, who includes both earthly and heavenly aspects, women become increasingly denigrated, as they fall under the shadow of the negative, sinful image of Eve. The author of the Book of Ben Sirach, who could write so lyrically about Wisdom, also wrote: 'Of the woman came the beginning of sin, and through her we all die' (Sir. 25:24) and 'Give me any plague but the plague of the heart: and any wickedness but the wickedness of a woman' (Sir. 25:13). Nowhere is the polarization of spirit and nature more obvious than in the distinction drawn in theology between the heavenly Sophia and the earthly Eve, as later it was drawn in Christian theology between Mary and Eve.

THE SACRED MARRIAGE

From Sumeria and Egypt to the beginning of the Christian era, the ritual of the sacred marriage between the Virgin Mother Goddess and her son–lover, the god, gave the psyche an image of wholeness and relationship, unifying the two dimensions of heaven and earth, spirit and nature, which language separates. The temple ritual was reflected in the secular marriage ceremony that was, as it still is for some, one of the most treasured experiences of human life. The image of human union was anchored in the symbolic union of heaven and earth, celebrated annually in the temple precinct between the king and the high priestess, who personified the goddess. Even now, the resonance of this ceremony is apparent in the intense excitement generated by a royal marriage. The psyche appears to need a 'sacred' image of wholeness to preserve its balance, which depends upon its maintaining an equable and dynamic relationship between the feminine and masculine archetypes.

The Song of Songs, the most beautiful of the sacred marriage texts that have come down to us, was written down about 100 BC. Solomon is believed to have lived and built his great temple in Jerusalem in the tenth century BC. Whether or not this text, said to be his bridal song, descends from this time is impossible to say, but there is certainly much in it that relates to an earlier era and to the imagery of the Mother Goddess, who may have been his 'consort' – mother, sister and bride – in a sacred marriage rite similar to the Sumerian one. The richness of the sexual imagery and the abundance of earth's 'fruits' suggest that its origin is not Judaic, but can be placed in a time when earth and sexuality were not split off from the divine. The fact that, although it was not excluded from the canon of Jewish and Christian scriptures, it really belongs within the mystical tradition of Judaism and Christianity may indicate that the aspect of life rejected by the orthodox tradition 'goes underground' into the unconscious and reappears as mysticism, only to be rejected again by orthodoxy.

Litanies now lost may have been written in Canaan for the sacred marriage ritual between the goddess Astarte and her son–lover, the king of the city, who took the role of Baal, or have found their way from Sumerian and Egyptian temples into Canaanite temples. Because we have no text that gives us the sacred marriage ritual in Canaan, unless it is this poem itself, it may help to read it with the image of Inanna's marriage to a king of a Sumerian city in mind, for the image of Inanna is clearly invoked in the words: 'Who is she that looketh forth as the morning, fair as the moon, clear as the sun, and terrible as an army with banners?' (S. of S. 6:10). In the love poetry of Sumeria, Inanna invites the king into her garden; milk and honey, apples and pomegranates were all the fruits of her garden, images of her fertility and the fertility of the land regenerated by the rite of the sacred marriage. Her priestesses may once have been called the 'Daughters of Uruk'. So, in the 'Daughters of Jerusalem' we may perhaps recognize the priestesses of the goddess in Canaan. In Egypt, also, the same rite was celebrated in the temples of Isis and Osiris; Isis and Nephthys rejoiced in the return of Osiris, their brother and bridegroom, in the same imagery as the Song of Songs.[37]

Blackness is an image that was always associated with the Great Goddess: Isis, Cybele, Demeter and Artemis. It symbolized the ineffable wisdom and mystery of life and its power to regenerate itself, in the sense of Vaughan's words: 'There is in God, some say, a deep and dazzling darkness'.[38] Isis in Apuleius' vision wears a black robe. But during the Iron Age, as the goddess was replaced by the god, blackness came to be a symbol of darkness in the sense of evil. It is clear, however, that the imagery of the Song of Songs belongs to the earlier tradition. The Bride here addresses her 'brother', the Bridegroom, saying:

> I am black but comely, O ye daughters of Jerusalem, as the tents of Kedar, as the curtains of Solomon.
>
> . . . . .
>
> Tell me, O thou whom my soul loveth, where thou feedest, where thou makest thy flock to rest at noon:
>
> . . . . .
>
> I am the rose of Sharon and the lily of the valleys.
> As the lily among thorns, so is my love among the daughters.
> As the apple tree among the trees of the wood, so is my beloved among the sons. I sat down under his shadow with great delight, and his fruit was sweet to my taste.
> He brought me to the banqueting house, and his banner over me was love.
> Stay me with flagons, comfort me with apples: for I am sick of love.
> His left hand is under my head, and his right hand doth embrace me.
> I charge you, O ye daughters of Jerusalem, by the roes, and by the hinds of the field, that ye stir not up, nor awake my love, till he please.
>
> . . . . .
>
> My beloved spake, and said unto me: (1:5, 7; 2:1–7, 10)

The Bridegroom answers her:

> Rise up, my love, my fair one, and come away.
> For, lo, the winter is past, the rain is over and gone;
> The flowers appear on the earth; the time of the singing of birds is come, and the voice of the turtle is heard in our land;
> The fig tree putteth forth her green figs, and the vines with the tender grape give a good smell. Arise, my love, my fair one, and come away.
> O my dove, that art in the clefts of the rock, in the secret places of the stairs, let me see thy countenance, let me hear thy voice; for sweet is thy voice, and thy countenance is comely. (2:10–14)

She speaks again:

Go forth, O ye daughters of Zion, and behold king Solomon with the crown wherewith his mother crowned him in the day of his espousals, and in the day of the gladness of his heart. (3:11)

And he replies:

Thou art all fair, my love, there is no spot in thee.

Come with me from Lebanon, my spouse, with me from Lebanon: look from the top of Amana, from the top of Shenir and Hermon, from the lions' dens, from the mountains of the leopards.

Thou has ravished my heart, my sister, my spouse! thou hast ravished my heart with one of thine eyes, with one chain of thy neck.

How fair is thy love, my sister, my spouse! how much better is thy love than wine! and the smell of thine ointments than all spices!

Thy lips, O my spouse, drop as the honeycomb: honey and milk are under thy tongue; and the smell of thy garments is like the smell of Lebanon.

A garden enclosed is my sister, my spouse; a spring shut up, a fountain sealed.

Thy plants are an orchard of pomegranates, with pleasant fruits, camphire, with spikenard,

Spikenard and saffron; calamus and cinnamon, with all trees of frankincense; myrrh and aloes, with all the chief spices.

A fountain of gardens, a well of living waters, and streams from Lebanon. (4:7–15)

She says:

Awake, O north wind; and come, thou south; blow upon my garden, that the spices thereof may flow out. Let my beloved come into his garden, and eat his pleasant fruits. (4:16)

And he responds:

I am come into my garden, my sister, my spouse: I have gathered my myrrh with my spice; I have eaten my honeycomb with my honey; I have drunk my wine with my milk: eat, O friends; drink, yea, drink abundantly, O beloved. (5:1)

She speaks again:

I sleep, but my heart waketh: it is the voice of my beloved that knocketh, saying: Open to me, my sister, my love, my dove, my undefiled; for my head is filled with dew, and my locks with the drops of the night.

. . . . .

I rose up to open to my beloved; and my hands dropped with myrrh, and my fingers with sweet smelling myrrh, upon the handles of the lock.

I opened to my beloved; but my beloved had withdrawn himself, and was gone; my soul failed when he spake: I sought him, but I could not find him; I called him, but he gave me no answer.

The watchmen that went about the city found me, they smote me, they wounded me; the keepers of the walls took away my veil from me.

I charge you, O daughters of Jerusalem, if ye find my beloved, that ye tell him, that I am sick of love. (5:2, 5–8)

The Daughters of Jerusalem speak in chorus:

Whither is thy beloved gone, O thou fairest among women? whither is thy beloved turned aside? that we may seek him with thee. (6:1)

And the Bride answers them:

My beloved is gone down into his garden, to the beds of spices, to feed in the gardens, and to gather lilies.

I am my beloved's and my beloved is mine; he feedeth among the lilies. (6:2–3)

The Bridegroom says:

Thou art beautiful, O my love, as Tirzah, comely as Jerusalem, terrible as an army with banners.

Turn away thine eyes from me, for they have overcome me: thy hair is as a flock of goats that appear from Gilead.

. . . . .

As a piece of pomegranate are thy temples within thy locks. There are threescore queens, and fourscore concubines, and virgins without number.

My dove, my undefiled is but one; she is the only one of her mother, she is the choice one of her that bare her. The daughters saw her, and blessed her; yea, the queens and the concubines, and they praised her.

Who is she that looketh forth as the morning, fair as the moon, clear as the sun, and terrible as an army with banners?

. . . . .

Return, return, O Shulamite; return, return, that we may look upon thee.

. . . . .

How beautiful are thy feet with shoes, O prince's daughter! the joints of thy thighs are like jewels, the work of the hands of a cunning workman.

. . . . .

This thy stature is like to a palm tree and thy breasts to clusters of grapes. (6:4–5, 7–10, 13; 7:1, 7)

And the Bride says:

O that thou wert as my brother, that sucked at the breasts of my mother! when I should find thee without, I would kiss thee; yea, I should not be despised.

I would lead thee, and bring thee into my mother's house, who would instruct me: I would cause thee to drink of spiced wine of the juice of my pomegranate.

. . . . .

I charge you, O daughters of Jerusalem, that ye stir not up, nor awake my love, until he please. (8:1–2, 4)

There is no other previous text yet discovered that is so rich in imagery as the Song of Songs. Its echoes can be traced through the poetry and mystical literature of the next 2,000 years, and wherever its influence is discerned, as in Dante's great work, it becomes the inspiration of a culture. It was from this poem that the images came that cluster round the Virgin Mary: the Rose of Sharon, the Lily of the Valleys, the Enclosed Garden, the Ivory Tower, the Sealed Fountain. In the Middle Ages it inspired the idea of the dialogue between Christ and his bride, the Church, and between Christ and the human soul as Mary.

An early example of its influence is in a Syrian Gnostic text dating to the second century AD, known as 'The Wedding Song of Wisdom', which discloses a similar ritual and may possibly be derived from an earlier text, perhaps celebrating the marriage of Astarte with her son–lover. It shows that the sacred marriage, once associated with a temple ritual unifying heaven and earth, has now become the image of an inner experience. The poem is addressed to Sophia, Light's daughter, and celebrates the wedding between the soul and her bridegroom, Christ:

> The Maiden is Light's Daughter;
> On her the Kings' radiance resteth.
> Like unto spring flowers are her Garments,
> From them streameth scent of sweet odour.
> On the Crown of her Head the King throneth,
> With Living Food feeding those beneath Him.
> Truth on her Head doth repose,
> She sendeth forth Joy from her Feet.
> Her tongue is like the Door-hanging
> Set in motion by those who enter.
> Step-wise her Neck riseth – a Stairway
> The first of all Builders hath builded.
> The Two Palms of her Hands
> Suggest the Choir of Aeons.
> Her fingers are secretly setting
> The Gates of the City ajar.
> Her bridechamber shineth with Light,
> Pouring forth scent of balsam and sweet-herbs,
> Exhaling the sweet perfume both of myrrh and savoury plants,
> And crowds of scented flowers.
> Inside it is strewn with myrtle-boughs;
> Its Folding-doors are beautified with reeds.
> Her bridesmen are grouped round her,
> Seven in number, whom she hath invited.
> Her bridesmaids, too, are Seven,
> Who lead the Dance before her.
> And twelve are her Servants before her,
> Their gaze looking out for the Bridegroom;
> That at His sight they may be filled with Light.
> And then for ever more shall they be with Him

In that eternal everlasting Joy;
And share in that eternal Wedding-feast,
At which the Great Ones (all) assemble;
And so abide in that Delight
In which the Ever-living are deemed worthy.
With Kingly Clothes shall they be clad,
And put on Robes of Light.[39]

The sacred marriage came to be understood by Jewish and Christian mystics as an image of union between the soul and her luminous, or 'heavenly', counterpart. In Jewish mysticism the sacred marriage was contemplated as an image of the union between Yahweh and his divine consort, the Shekhinah, and between the soul and Wisdom. The imagery of Gnostic myth took the union of the two aspects of the godhead as a metaphor for the union of the awakened soul with her bridegroom. These, as sister and brother, were the 'daughter' and 'son' of the transcendent Mother and Father. In the Middle Ages the poets of the twelfth century transcribed the image of the sacred marriage to the Grail legends. Alchemy, in the marriage of sun and moon, king and queen, made the sacred marriage one of the central realizations of the Great Work, the prerequisite of the birth within them of the priceless philosophical gold, or the divine child, the 'son of the philosophers' who were the lovers of Divine Wisdom.

This historical survey of the image of the deity from the Palaeolithic to the Judaeo-Christian era has shown how it changes and evolves as humanity evolves. In relation to the god image, the goddess image prevailed over an immeasurably longer time span, but our civilization, knowing little of this, easily dismisses the inheritance of the past in which this experience lies embedded. We cannot know or even imagine the nature of the consciousness which is the universe. All we can do is to formulate an image of what we conceive as divine in relation to the limitations of our own consciousness. We do not know how or when the goddess-or-god image first arose, whether from dreaming sleep or from waking vision. All that can be said is that the experience of divinity exists in the soul and that the soul insists on making an image of it because, through that image, it feels itself related to something greater than itself. The image is sacred, for it is this above all that binds that part of the psyche incarnated in time and space to the unseen dimension that enfolds it.

Jung has commented on the need to distinguish between any particular 'God-image' (as he called it) and the unknowable 'prime truth':

The God-image is not something *invented*, it is an *experience* that comes upon man spontaneously ... The unconscious God-image can therefore alter the state of consciousness just as the latter can modify the God-image once it has become conscious. This obviously has nothing to do with the 'prime truth,' the unknown God – at least, nothing that could be verified.[40]

As we have seen, the image of the divine can be feminine or masculine or both together. The greatest danger of any religious belief, including monotheism, is idolatry: that is, identifying any particular image of the deity with the whole of divine truth, and ultimately, therefore, worshipping an image created by the human mind. Given the state of consciousness at the end of the Iron Age, and even its present level of development, no single god or goddess image nor all such images together can possibly represent 'ultimate truth', but must continually be enlarged and deepened as human insight evolves. It seems to be essential that the image of a deity at any particular historical moment be separated in principle and in practice from the unknowable nature of the divine. Only in this way can a space be left for a new image to emerge with the minimum of conflict and suffering; in the way that, in Coleridge's understanding of the nature of symbolism, a chrysalis 'leaves room' for the emergence of the butterfly.[41]

As a result of the long historical process outlined in these last chapters, there was, at the end of the Iron Age, a lack of relationship between the feminine and masculine principles in the image of the deity, and the implicit revelation of the goddess culture was lost. At one level, the invasion of the patriarchal Aryans and Semites into communities presided over by the goddess image made possible the further development of consciousness. The intrusion of the concept of linear time upon cultures where the cyclical pattern prevailed created a sense of direction and goal, breaking apart the eternal recurrence of the old. Nature lost her supreme sovereignty and humanity gathered to itself what she had lost. But this was done only at the expense of sacrificing the old human experience of belonging to a sacred earth and a sacred heaven.

The goddess myth needs to be made known not because it is superior to the god myth, but because it has been lost so long that we have apparently forgotten what it meant. For all the limitations of its over-identification with the natural world, it did at least give expression to the indissoluble relationship, even the identity, that exists between part and whole and between visible and invisible in all orders of being. Above all, it gave emphasis to the wonder and delight of life, because it included all manifestations of life within the sphere of the divine. The question a study of the goddess myth invites us to consider now is whether (and, if so, how) we can participate in this relationship with the whole of life without sacrificing the consciousness for the sake of which we sacrificed the image of the divine in the natural world.

13

EVE:
THE MOTHER OF ALL LIVING

There was a muddy centre before we breathed.
There was a myth before the myth began,
Venerable and articulate and complete.
From this the poem springs: that we live in a place
That is not our own and, much more, not ourselves
And hard it is in spite of blazoned days.

Wallace Stevens

And the Lord God caused a deep sleep to fall upon Adam, and he slept: and he took one of his ribs, and closed up the flesh instead thereof;

And the rib, which the Lord God had taken from man, made he a woman, and brought her unto the man.

And Adam said, This is now bone of my bones, and flesh of my flesh: she shall be called Woman, because she was taken out of Man. (Gen. 2:21-3)

Now the serpent was more subtil than any beast of the field which the Lord God had made. And he said unto the woman, Yea, hath God said, Ye shall not eat of every tree of the garden?

And the woman said unto the serpent, We may eat of the fruit of the trees of the garden:

But of the fruit of the tree which is in the midst of the garden, hath God said, Ye shall not eat of it, neither shall ye touch it, lest ye die.

And the serpent said unto the woman, Ye shall not surely die:

For God doth know that in the day ye eat thereof, then your eyes shall be opened, and ye shall be as gods, knowing good and evil.

And when the woman saw that the tree was good for food, and that it was pleasant to the eyes, and a tree to be desired to make one wise, she took of the fruit thereof, and did eat, and gave also unto her husband with her; and he did eat.

And the eyes of them both were opened, and they knew that they were naked; and they sewed fig leaves together, and made themselves aprons.

And they heard the voice of the Lord God walking in the garden in the cool of the day: and Adam and his wife hid themselves from the presence of the Lord God amongst the trees of the garden.

And the Lord God called unto Adam, and said unto him, Where art thou?

And he said, I heard thy voice in the garden, and I was afraid because I was naked; and I hid myself.

And he said, Who told thee that thou wast naked? Hast thou eaten of the tree whereof I commanded thee that thou shouldest not eat?

And the man said, The woman whom thou gavest to be with me, she gave me of the tree, and I did eat.

And the Lord God said unto the woman, What is this that thou hast done? And the woman said, The serpent beguiled me, and I did eat.

And the Lord God said unto the serpent, Because thou hast done this, thou art cursed above all cattle, and above every beast of the field; upon thy belly shalt thou go, and dust shalt thou eat all the days of thy life:

And I will put enmity between thee and the woman, and between thy seed and her seed; it shall bruise thy head, and thou shalt bruise his heel.

Unto the woman he said, I will greatly multiply thy sorrow and thy conception; in sorrow thou shalt bring forth children; and thy desire shall be to thy husband, and he shall rule over thee.

And unto Adam he said, Because thou hast hearkened unto the voice of thy wife, and hast eaten of the tree, of which I commanded thee, saying, Thou shalt not eat of it; cursed is the ground for thy sake; in sorrow shalt thou eat of it all the days of thy life;

Thorns also and thistles shall it bring forth to thee; and thou shalt eat the herb of the field;

In the sweat of thy face shalt thou eat bread, till thou return unto the ground; for out of it wast thou taken: for dust thou art, and unto dust shalt thou return.

And Adam called his wife's name Eve; because she was the mother of all living.

Unto Adam also and to his wife did the Lord God make coats of skins, and clothed them.

And the Lord God said, Behold, the man is become as one of us, to know good and evil: and now, lest he put forth his hand, and take also of the tree of life, and eat, and live forever:

Therefore the Lord God sent him forth from the garden of Eden, to till the ground from whence he was taken.

So he drove out the man: and he placed at the east of the garden of Eden Cherubims, and a flaming sword which turned every way, to keep the way of the tree of life. (Gen. 3:1–24)

The myth of Eve inaugurates a new kind of creation myth, one that appears, from the perspective of earlier myths, to bear the distinctive mark of the Iron Age. Yet the myth has entered the Western imagination as having something timeless to say about the nature of creation and the nature of the human being, particularly the woman. In the story it is Eve's actions that initiate the change of state from unity and harmony with the divine to separation and estrangement, which, in turn, initiates the specifically human condition of birth and death in time. The figure of Eve, however, has been removed from the framework of the myth, and the myth has been removed from its local and historical context and held up as an eternal statement, as though, indeed, it had actually been written by God and not by somebody human. Later Christian commentators, interpreting the myth literally, generalized from the 'sin of Eve' to the character of woman, which has had serious and far-reaching implications for related attitudes to matter, earth and nature as the rejected feminine principle. On the one hand, putting the myth back into its historical context, what emerges is a different story: the demythologizing of the goddess into a human woman. On the other hand, going beyond history into art and reading the myth symbolically, beyond theologies of gender, this story of exile becomes a story of the birth of human consciousness.

In Christian doctrine, however, this story of exile is known as the 'Fall', a term suggestive of the fall of leaves from their trees in autumn as the first sign of approaching winter; and for humanity also the 'Fall' is read as the entry of death, or awareness of death, into the world. What is missing from the analogy is that the leaf falls seasonally when the life-force of the tree withdraws into itself for *renewal*, disclosing the next year's bud beneath, whereas humanity is deemed guilty for the ending of its life on earth, and may not reach for the fruit of the 'Tree of Life' lest, in the words of Yahweh, it 'live for ever'.

As with all myths of the beginning of historical time, this is one that explores the human response to toil, sickness, ageing and death – the unaccountable ending of that time. But in earlier myths a reflection on the mystery of death leads to further reflection on the mystery of life, and still further to the ultimate mystery of the source of being beyond both life and death, thereby leading the human heart to its own source beyond the opposites of time and eternity. The Genesis myth is unique in that it takes the life-affirming images of all the myths before it – the garden, the four rivers, the Tree of Life, the serpent and the world parents – and makes of them an occasion not of joy and wonder, but of fear, guilt, punishment and blame. And what or who is blamed but precisely the woman and the serpent, incarnations, previously, of the goddess and her power, bestowers then not of death but of life eternal.

As we have seen in the mythologies of Mesopotamia, Egypt and Greece, the tree, with the serpent beside or entwined around it, was the Tree of Life of the Great Mother Goddess, and the serpent was her manifest form in time, ever dying and ever renewed like the moon, which slips from its shadow as the serpent slips from its skin. On either side of this World Tree, the *Axis Mundi*, sit or stand, in numerous works of art, the female and male incarnations of this central mystery, the goddess herself in recognizable human form and her consort, who, like the serpent and the moon, dies her lover and is reborn her son, in a ritual that enacts the continuing process underlying the visible cycles of life and death.

Both Figures 1 and 2 show a female and a male figure, a central tree and a serpent, yet their meanings are completely different. In Figure 1 the

Figure 1. (*Above*) Goddess and god beside the Tree of Life; Sumerian cylinder seal, *c.* 2500 BC.
Figure 2. (*Right*) *The Temptation of Eve*; Codex Vigilianus, Albedense, AD 976. Spain.

seated female is the Bronze Age Sumerian Mother Goddess and the serpent who coils upright behind her is the image of her regenerative power. On the other side of the tree, in identical posture, sits her son-lover, called 'Son of the Abyss: Lord of the Tree of Life', whose role as fertilizing the source of life is given in the bull's horns upon his head. Since the serpent and the bull, on opposite sides of the seal, are both images of the living and dying manifestation of the goddess, a true mirror-image is created of the unification of opposites in a single vision. Further, both goddess and son-lover gesture with outstretched hand towards the hanging fruits of the Tree of Life, offering the gifts of immortality and enlightenment together – she, immortality, and he, enlightenment. Here is the perennial story of the sacred marriage of *zoe* and *bios*, enacted under many guises – Inanna and Dumuzi, Ishtar and Tammuz, Isis and Osiris, Aphrodite and Adonis, Cybele and Attis – and all of them images of reconciliation and affirmation.

In Figure 2 the female on the left, into whose eyes the serpent gazes, is no longer a goddess but a mortal woman, born from the body of the man facing her and now the daughter and bride not even of a father god but of a mortal man. Correspondingly, the man, Adam, no longer wears the horned crown of renewal, but gazes fearfully at his wife's liaison with the serpent, and holds his hand to his ear as though anticipating the dreadful word of Yahweh's curse. The hand of the woman, for she has not yet been named, touches the mouth of the serpent as though, prophetically, she were unable to draw herself away from her act of betraying into death the human race not yet born from her. All that remains of the goddess who was once indeed 'Mother of All Living' is the name she receives only when its sacred meaning has become profane. Yet Adam's own name comes from the name for Earth, *Adamah*, once the body of the mother goddess in whose substance all creatures shared. Similarly, the serpent has lost his immanent divinity as guardian of the tree and lord of rebirth, and has become himself the betrayer of both these roles, which are, in essence, one. The picture is dramatic: as the fig leaves reveal, it holds the moment of appalled awareness, when those who are part of nature are set for ever apart from nature in the perception that they are 'naked'. This is rendered in the picture as the same perception that they have broken the commandment of Yahweh, and that, as created beings, they are thereby for ever separated from their creator. Where is the image of the ever-renewing source of life in which humanity can trust and find repose? Nature, and specifically human nature, is to receive the curse of the one whose Word brought it into being, and for whom no atonement from the 'sin' of longing for knowledge and everlasting life is enough.

In Chapter 11, the significance of this reversal of the former point of view was explored in relation to the needs of a new people in a strange land distancing themselves from the religious beliefs they found all around them. It is curious, though, that the terms of the Hebrew creation myth are not those of a mythology of the desert, from where the nomadic tribes had come, but are more those of the fertile agricultural land they found, the age-old lunar mythology of people who live close to the seasons and the soil. On the other hand, the Garden of Eden, with its four rivers that run to the ends of the Earth, is very like the vision of an oasis to the hot and weary traveller, longing for water and shade. None the less, the question still arises as to what has been achieved by inverting the meaning of those images, which, evidently, could still move the heart even though they could no longer console the mind.

The most fundamental change from earlier myths, as suggested in Chapter 11, is the new and absolute distinction between the creator and creation, with the result that the 'flaw' in creation is rendered equivalent to a flaw in the nature of the creatures: death is 'their' fault; in fact, to be doctrinally specific, it is 'her' fault. Comparing this to other creation myths, it seems as if, instead of wrestling with the ambivalence due to created beings imagining their own creation, the absolute perfection of the deity is insisted on to the detriment of human nature (rather in the way that a child in conflict with a parent creates the omnipotence of the parent, on whom its whole world depends, by blaming itself).

A more general question also arises as to whether images and symbols have an inherent meaning proper to them so that they cannot be simply inverted without violation. For Yeats, images are 'living souls':[1] they have a specific life of their own. For Jung, also, symbols cannot be consciously devised or undevised but are 'spontaneous products' of the Collective Unconscious.[2] Consequently, the images of the myth of Eve have a past

and present life of their own whatever story is woven around them.
Campbell makes the important point that the opposition between image
and word leads to a feeling of what he calls 'nervous discord':

> There is consequently an ambivalence inherent in many of the basic symbols
> of the Bible that no amount of rhetorical stress on the patriarchal interpreta-
> tion can suppress. They address a pictorial message to the heart that exactly
> reverses the verbal message addressed to the brain; and this nervous discord
> inhabits both Christianity and Islam as well as Judaism, since they too share
> in the legacy of the Old Testament.[3]

The abundance of the apple tree, the climbing fruits and the happily
resting animals in Cranach's painting (Fig. 3) convey all the joy of the
Goddess of Fertility with her son–lover and her creatures, and in other
pictures Cranach draws the goddess Venus holding the tree and the apple
with the same gesture as Eve. But responding not to the life of the images
themselves but to their Christian interpretation, we name the scene as
'innocence' before the 'Fall' (noting only now how implausibly the lion lies
down with the lamb, doe and stag), and the feeling of excitement the painting
calls forth has to be tempered with the reminder that it is 'unrealistic'.

Figure 3. *Adam and Eve*,
Lucas Cranach the Elder,
1526.

THE DEPOSING OF THE MOTHER GODDESS

The story of Eve is in part the story of the displacing of the mother goddess by the father god. Both Eve's name, Hawwah, and Yahweh's are taken from a form of the Hebrew verb 'to be', pointing to a common derivation. The meaning of her name is then 'Life' or 'She who gives Life', as Adam's subsequent naming of her as the 'Mother of All Living' registers. The figure of Eve is still transparent to her former role, so that her deposition from mother goddess to human woman – from creator to created – can be clearly seen through the images. Demythologizing a goddess is a subtle process whereby the numinosity that once belonged to her is withdrawn and clothes another figure, in this case Yahweh. By contrast, Eve becomes the opposite of what she was, not a giver of life but a cause of death. In so far as she was formerly also creation or nature herself, this demythologizing process extends to the whole of nature, which becomes, like her, fallen and cursed. Consequently, death, once a phase in the totality of being wherein the dead return to the womb of the Mother Goddess for rebirth, is now a final and absolute punishment that she, or her reduced earthly counterpart, brought upon the world.

To return to Campbell's question, how are 'heart' and 'brain' set against each other in the myth of Eve? How damaging to the unity of the psyche is it, for instance, that when Yahweh forms Eve from Adam's rib, this is

Figure 4. *The Creation of Eve*, Lorenzo Maitani, 1310–30. Duomo, Orvieto. The artist has carved the faces and figures of God and Adam in the likeness of an older and younger brother. Eve slips out of the side of the sleeping Adam with God as 'midwife', while the phallic tree, in line with Adam's genitals, bursts into flower as though he had indeed given birth like a mother.

Figure 5. *The Creation of Eve, c.* twelfth century. West front, Cathedral of Notre Dame. Adam, made in God's image, leans on the Tree of Life, resting his hand upon it in a manner reminiscent of the mother of the Buddha.

an act contrary to the rest of nature, in which birth takes place through the female? This tale of the rib once had the *opposite* meaning as a myth of a mother goddess creating life, for behind the meaning of Eve's name and the manner of her birth lies a Sumerian story that draws them together.

The Sumerian word for 'life' was *ti*, which also meant 'rib'. Ninhursag, the Sumerian mother goddess, once healed the rib of Enki, god of the sweet waters, by creating Nin-ti, a goddess of childbirth, who made the bones of infants in the womb from the ribs of their mothers.[4] The Sumerian name Nin-ti could mean either 'the lady who gives life' (the traditional title for a goddess) or 'the lady of the rib'. The Yahwist writer of Genesis 2 and 3 was undoubtedly aware of this double meaning, since in selecting the rib version of it he still accords to it the magic of birth. But in the Sumerian tale the unity of the mother and child carries the analogy of sharing bones as an image of birth, while in the Hebrew myth nature and the goddess are sacrificed to the miracle of Yahweh's inventive mind. (The Greek tale of the birth of Athena from the head of Zeus has a similar inversion.) Furthermore, the Hebrew word for 'rib', *tsela*, meant 'stumbling', so providing the occasion for a jolly pun, since Eve receives her name immediately after she herself has 'stumbled' on behalf of humanity, the first but not the last fallen woman.

'And Adam called his wife Eve, because she was the mother of all living.' The reduced reference of this ancient title means that Eve will be the mother of all living human beings – the first mother of the human race – not, as was its original meaning, mother of all that lives. So, from the perspective of the mythic tradition, she who was once the giver of all names is now named herself at the moment of exile by the man whose rib she has and whose rib she is. It would not, perhaps, be necessary to emphasize the inversion in the story if it had not been seized on with such literalness by generations of interpreters who found in it the irrevocable signature of divine intention.

The original word for 'woman' in Hebrew was *ishshah*, which meant 'taken out of man'.[5] Echoing this biblical order of priority, even the Old English word 'wo-man' means 'wife to man'. Adam's use of the title of the old mother goddess at this point, only after Yahweh's curse, serves to transfer the curse from this woman, Eve, to all the living to whom she will be mother, so that because of what she 'did' she gives birth ultimately to death: before Eve's 'sin' there was no death; after it and because of it, death, pain and travail came into being.

The story of the rib also suggested that the serpent's subtlety was not misplaced in approaching the woman first, for, with the total loss of the old symbolism, the woman, made from a rib of the man created by Yahweh, is that much less likely to obey the divine commandment not to eat the forbidden fruit. This was a theme expounded with endless elaboration by both Jewish and Christian commentators, who took the tale of the birth of Eve from Adam's rib as a divine statement that woman was a secondary creation, made of inferior substance, further from the image and likeness of God, and less capable, therefore, of moral choice. This will be explored later, but, in the language of the old mythology, it is worth remembering that Adam, her husband, was once her son, and Yahweh (whose first pictorial likeness was of a god with serpent legs; see Fig. 9) is her own son turned father.[6]

While the *images* of Eve place her in the ancient tradition as a mother goddess, her *story* – how she is born, what she thinks and says and does – defines her as a human woman. Yet it is not so simple. For, though a mere woman, the role she is given to play is a mythic one; in fact, a new version of the old role of the Mother Goddess who brings death to humanity, but with a crucial difference. In the former mythologies the Mother Goddess who brought death was also the Mother Goddess who gave birth to all creatures first, so that the two phases of existence could be unified in one goddess who cares for both, the Great Mother. Here, the former unity has been split and the two roles polarized, so that the father god takes over the role of creation while the human woman is responsible for destruction. It is as though an archetypal image – in this case the goddess – cannot be displaced without consequence, as if it has to find expression elsewhere, here in a vessel too frail to hold its numinosity, a human woman. Since Eve can incarnate only one dimension of the original archetype, the bringing of death, humanity is left without an image of reconciliation to the whole, where once birth and death were related mythically through the 'body of the goddess'.

In Genesis the activities of divinely caused birth and mortally caused death set immortal and mortal, eternity and time, against each other where before they could be perceived together in relationship. Now the father god gives birth through the Word, and the mortal mother of the human race gives death because of disobedience to the word of Yahweh. How else could it be understood except as a human betrayal of the divine, as an 'original sin', the sin that was there in the beginning of the race, that is, inherent in the nature of humanity?

John Phillips, in his book *Eve: The History of an Idea*, sums up:

> The history of Eve begins with the appearance of Yahweh in the place of the Mother of All the Living. This shift of power marks a fundamental change in the relationship between humanity and God, the world and God, the world and humanity, and men and women.[7]

What it involved, ultimately, Phillips concludes, was 'the rejection of the Feminine as a sacred entity'.[8]

The Garden

As suggested, the demythologizing of the goddess was a process that extended to the whole of nature in whom she had been embodied. When Eve and Adam are cursed by Yahweh, so also is the earth and her cycles of fertility: 'Cursed is the ground for thy sake; in sorrow shall thou eat of it all the days of thy life; Thorns also and thistles shall it bring forth to thee; and thou shall eat the herb of the field' (Gen. 3:17–18). Where before the man was put into the garden 'to dress it and to keep it' (Gen. 2:15), after the curse he has 'to till the ground from whence he was taken' (Gen. 3:23). It is humanity's relation to nature that is cursed. No more is heard of the 'garden' or 'the cool of the day'; earth is now rendered in the hard image of the 'ground', or the dry, desiccated image of 'dust', which is to be the food of the serpent and the substance into which humanity disintegrates: 'For dust thou art, and unto dust shalt thou return' (Gen. 3:19). Human beings are to imagine themselves on their death as lifeless dust from which the breath of life has gone, no longer to share in the sanctity of all life, visible or invisible, and not even that small breath of life is to return to the Father, whose breath it once was. Yahweh has become the punishing Father, who proscribes the life he has made when he saw that it was not good.

In Hebrew Eden means 'a place of delight', while the term 'paradise', which is of Persian origin, comes later. The precision of the topography of Eden and the garden is interesting because they are obviously not to be thought of as the same. Yahweh planted the garden 'eastward in Eden' and there he put the man he had formed. One river went out of Eden to water the garden, where it 'was parted, and became into four heads' (Gen. 2:10). The garden is then situated in the land of the sunrise, symbolically exact for the dawning of human consciousness, but what of the north, south and west of Eden? Is this, then, to be the world that the man and woman are condemned to wander in, banished for ever from the source? The image of the garden with the four rivers and the one (or two) trees at the centre is clearly an image of totality, with the tree as the pivot or axis of creation, and the four rivers marking the four points of the compass or, more widely, the four points of orientation for the human mind. This image of a garden, dressed and kept by the man, is also familiar from Sumeria, where King Sargon was called the beloved gardener of the goddess Ishtar. But there the garden was the goddess herself, immanent as nature, whereas here the garden is created by the word of Yahweh and can as readily be uncreated by a curse.

The Tree of Life and the Tree of Knowledge

The Tree of Life was one of the primary images of the goddess herself, in whose immanent presence all pairs of opposites are reconciled. Growing on the surface of the earth, with roots below and branches above, the tree was the great pillar that united earth with heaven and the underworld, through which the energies of the cosmos poured continuously into earthly creation. The animating spirit that moved within it was the serpent, guardian also of the fruit or treasure of the tree, which was the epiphany of the goddess, that is, the *experience* of unity.

All over the Near East, Egypt, Crete and Greece the tree was planted in the temples of the goddess, particularly the fig, palm, cypress, apple, sycamore and olive. In Egypt, the goddesses Hathor and Isis were both known as the 'Lady of the Sycamore', and the milky juice of the fruit was drunk as the milk from her breasts, as in the drawing on the face of a column in the burial chamber of the king's tomb (Fig. 6). In the eleventh-century-BC painting in Figure 7 Hathor, Nut or Isis is drawn emerging from the tree, offering food and the water of life.

Figure 6. (*Left*) Hathor or Isis as the Tree of Life suckling Tuthmosis III;
c. 1479–1425 BC. Tomb of Tuthmosis III, Valley of the Kings.
Figure 7. (*Right*) Hathor, Isis or Nut as the Tree of Life offering the water
of eternal life to the deceased; vignette from a Book of the Dead,
Twenty-first Dynasty, *c.* 1000 BC.

The Tree of Life had also been linked with the serpent or dragon (winged serpent) for over 1,000 years before Genesis was written. In 2025 BC the cup of the Sumerian King Gudea of Lagash (see Chapter 5, Fig. 22) showed two winged dragons holding back a pair of opening doors to reveal a caduceus of uniting snakes, the incarnation of the god Ningizzida, one of the names given to the consort of the mother goddess, to whom the cup is inscribed: 'Lord of the Tree of Truth'.

A Greek myth of *c.* 700–500 BC told of a sacred tree called the golden apple tree of the Hesperides. It grew at the edge of the world in the land of the setting sun and its apples were given as a wedding gift to Hera, who then placed them under the protection of a great dragon (Fig. 8). The Hesperides themselves were nymphs born from the goddess Night, shown with urns filled with the waters of life out of which the tree grows. Jason also has to encounter a great serpent guarding a sacred tree over which is hung the golden fleece (see Chapter 7, Fig. 9), so here again the motif of the serpent, the tree and the treasure of the tree reappears. Two serpents intertwined as the caduceus re-emerge as the golden wand or rod of transformation of Hermes, the god who can cross the threshold between life and death, while the single serpent falls to Asclepius, god of healing.

As we have seen in earlier chapters, the serpent was, variously, the guardian of the tree, the life-force of the rising and falling sap and, as the consort of the goddess, an image of the alternating living and dying aspects of the eternal principle embodied in the tree itself. According to which phase of life was enacted, the son–lovers were born from the tree (as Adonis), lived in the midst of it (as Tammuz) or were buried in it (as Osiris in his coffin of cedar enclosed in heather). The Sumerians of Eridu spoke of a wondrous tree with roots of white crystal that 'stretched towards the deep, its seat the central place of the earth, its foliage the couch of the

Figure 8. The Golden Apple Tree of the Hesperides; vase painting, *c.* 700–400 BC.

primeval Mother. In its midst was Tammuz'.[9] The ritual cutting down of the tree signified the dying phase of the totality of being, seasonally celebrated as the 'fall', which, far from preventing rebirth, acknowledged its perennial possibility.

Turning back to Genesis with this in mind, the tree, or the two trees, and the serpent take on a different resonance. Since, on discovering not the water of life but their own nakedness, Adam and Eve sewed fig leaves together and made themselves aprons, this tree also may have been a sycamore fig, with its large leaves, the same tree that was sacred to the goddess Asherah in Canaan, as it was in Egypt and Crete. It was only in the Middle Ages, when Latin texts of the Bible were available, that the tradition grew up that the Tree of Knowledge was an apple tree, since, in another of those puns, the word for apple in Latin, *malus*, is from the same root as the word for evil, *malum*. (*Bonum*, as might be expected, fell by the wayside.)

In northern Babylonia the goddess of the Tree of Life was called the 'divine Lady of Eden' or Edin, and in the south she was called the 'Lady of the Vine', an understandable change of name given that the Sumerian sign for 'life' was originally a vine leaf.[10] However, in the myth of Eden, where there is no unifying image of a goddess, there is significantly also not one tree but two trees, or, it could be said, the one tree has become two, and now the fruit of both of them is forbidden. In earlier mythologies the one tree offered both 'knowledge' and 'life', or 'wisdom' and 'immortality' (as in Fig. 1). Here, knowledge of good and evil is split apart from eternal life, so that a perception of duality is rendered absolutely antithetical to a perception of life's unity.[11] Campbell comments that: 'The principle of mythic dissociation, by which God and his world, immortality and mortality, are set apart in the Bible is expressed in a dissociation of the Tree of Knowledge from the Tree of Immortal Life.'[12]

So once again there is a confusion between the picture as we see it and the story as we hear it. The picture given is of both trees standing in the same place in the centre of the garden, whereas the story takes its meaning from the fact that they are different, and so required, presumably, to stand in two different places:

> And out of the ground made the Lord God to grow every tree that is pleasant to the sight, and good for food; the tree of life also in the midst of the garden, and the tree of knowledge of good and evil. (Gen. 2:9)

This puts the Tree of Life at the centre – 'in the midst' – and the Tree of Knowledge somewhere else. But when Eve talks to the serpent, she tells him: 'But of the fruit of the tree which is in the midst of the garden, God hath said, Ye shall not eat of it, neither shall ye touch it, lest ye die' (Gen. 3:3). Here, the *Tree of Knowledge* is the tree in the midst of the garden, so on the plane of imagery the two trees are, as they always were, one. Significantly, Yahweh does not withhold the fruit of the Tree of Life until after the fruit of the Tree of Knowledge has been tasted, as though the deeper dimension of the tree is only then disclosed. Only when their eyes are opened can they see what they do not have, for then they know the distinction between mortal and immortal, where before these categories did not exist. It is then tempting but primitive logic to infer that (the tree of) knowledge deprives them of (the tree of) immortality, that consciousness of the lack of something actually takes that thing away. But it is rather that, as in all dualisms, the two terms arise together and do not exist without each other. Hence it is only epiphany, a revelation of the source of being beyond both terms, that can dissolve them.

One way of making sense of the separation of the two 'trees' might be to see the life in time, initiated by consciousness, as itself the opportunity to understand the meaning of eternity, the fruit of that other tree, which, now it has been pointed out, is guarded by the cherubim. The image of the cherubim holding a flaming sword that turned every way 'to keep the way of the tree of life' is reminiscent both of the cherubim guarding the Ark of the Covenant and the older mythic imagery of Mesopotamia and Assyria, in which on either side of the Tree of Life also stood two winged beings, in human form or as lion-birds or winged dragons. Only in Christian art were the cherubim depicted exclusively as angels of human form.

The Serpent

The serpent first appears as a serpent mother goddess in the Neolithic era (see Chapter 2, Fig. 18), and is also drawn coiling around the womb and the phallus as the principle of regeneration. In the Sumerian cities of Ur and Uruk, in the lowest level of excavation, were found two very old images of the Mother Goddess and her child, both having the heads of snakes.[13] As the male aspect of the goddess was differentiated, the serpent became the fertilizing phallus, image of the god who was her son and consort, born from her, married with her and dying back into her for rebirth in unending cycle.

As we have seen, in images of the goddess in every culture the serpent is never far away, standing behind her, eating from her hand, entwined in her tree, or even, as in Tiamat, the shape of the goddess herself. Genesis is no exception to this, unless it be that, formally, there is no goddess, only a woman of the same name. However, taking the story, not the image, the serpent, once lord of rebirth, has now turned into his opposite, the instigator of death in league with Eve. There are faint echoes of the *Epic of Gilgamesh* in this reversal, since there the serpent steals the herb of immortality humanity might have had, and in Genesis, from this point of view, the serpent tricks the first parents of the race into death: 'For in the day that thou eatest thereof thou shalt surely die' (Gen. 2:17). But, once the Goddess has become a woman, and the Serpent God has become a reptile, any meaningful union between them is impossible, and the images can no longer serve as a means of metaphysical exploration.

The serpent is the first to receive Yahweh's curse and, notably, in terms that suggest that up to that point he was upright, as he is drawn on the earlier seals: 'Upon thy belly shalt thou go, and dust shalt thou eat all the days of thy life . . .' (Gen. 3:14). No longer is he to be the ever-rising sap of the Tree of Life, supreme among all others; now he is cursed above cattle and every beast of the field. His former vertical posture, as it would seem in the light of later developments, has been appropriated.

There is, therefore, a continuing ambivalence towards the serpent in the Old Testament, which may in part reflect the continuation of the old religion of the Canaanites and the difficulties experienced by the Hebrew priests in turning their people away from it. In the story of Moses and the brazen serpent, for instance, the serpent brings both death and life: when the people complained to Moses and to Yahweh that they had been brought out of Egypt into the wilderness to die, 'the Lord sent fiery serpents among the people, and they bit the people; and much people of Israel died' (Num. 21:6). When they repented, Moses prayed for them.

> And the Lord said unto Moses:
> Make thee a fiery serpent, and set it upon a pole: and it shall come to pass, that every one that is bitten, when he looketh upon it, shall live.
> And Moses made a serpent of brass, and put it upon a pole, and it came to pass, that if a serpent had bitten any man, when he beheld the serpent of brass, he lived. (Num. 21:8–9)

This serpent of brass stood in the temple of Jerusalem, together with the Asherah, or image of the Mother Goddess, for about 200 years, until King Hezekiah 'did what was right in the sight of the Lord' (2 Kgs. 18:3).

Once before, Yahweh had (strictly) not appeared to Moses as a serpent, but rather, in the precise language of transcendence, his appearance had manifested itself in the form of a serpent. Moses asks the Lord for a sign, saying:

> . . . they will say, The Lord hath not appeared to thee.
> And the Lord said unto him, What is that in thine hand? And he said, A rod.
> And he said, Cast it on the ground. And he cast it on the ground, and it became a serpent; and Moses fled from before it.
> And the Lord said unto Moses, Put forth thine hand, and take it by the tail. And he put forth his hand, and caught it, and it became a rod in his hand. (Exod. 4:1–4)

This is the same rod with which Yahweh commanded Moses to tell Aaron to smite the waters of Egypt and turn them to blood, cause frogs to come out of the waters, and make the dust of the earth into lice. But it

Figure 9. (a) Yahweh with serpent legs; inscription on Jewish amulets of
Hellenistic and Roman periods, second–first century BC. (b) Sumerian
serpent god; early Babylonian cylinder seal, *c.* 2300–2150 BC.

was only when Moses himself 'stretched forth his rod toward heaven' to
bring down hail that the hard heart of Pharaoh relented. Later, in the
desert, the Lord commanded Moses to strike the rock with his rod to
release water for his people to drink (Exod. 17:5–6).[14]

The relationship between Yahweh and the serpent is somewhat baffling,
given, firstly, the prohibition against graven images and, secondly, the
unflagging attempts of the prophets to eradicate all trace of the Canaanite
religion, in which serpents belonged to the priestesses as signs of their
power of prophecy. None the less, by the second and first centuries BC
seals of Yahweh appeared in which the Almighty had the legs of a serpent.
'Serpent gods', explains Campbell, 'do not die.'[15]

FROM MYTH TO DOCTRINE

In spite of the inconsistency of this myth's point of view – in which image
and word constantly belie each other – it has haunted the Western imagination for over 2,000 years, and so it is worth asking if this discordance is
itself meaningful in ways other than orthodox doctrine would have it be.
Here we are faced instantly with the radical dichotomy between the story
taken literally as the divine word of God – what 'God thinks' of humanity
– and the story taken symbolically, as an attempt to dramatize a dimension
of human experience in order to understand what cannot be known
through the intellect alone. A story, in other words, like any other story.
But it is easy to underestimate how readily a story written to explore a
complex metaphysical idea becomes, in the minds of those who require
certainties, a concretized doctrine of belief, when, of course, its range of
meanings entirely changes.

When, in the Judaeo-Christian tradition, this story has been taken as
divine revelation, it has fostered a conception of human nature as inherently prone to corrupting and betraying all that is best in itself, as
antithetical to the sacredness of life in which it also, paradoxically, feels

Figure 10. *Eve*; marble sculpture by Auguste Rodin, 1881, $4\frac{1}{2} \times 18 \times 21$ ft ($139 \times 550 \times 642$ cm).

itself held. Read literally, what the story says, in effect, is that Eve and Adam deserve to die because they broke their word to God. Reading, still literally, Eve and Adam as paradigmatic of women and men as a whole, what the story says is that the human race is cursed into life in time, such that the passage from birth to death is and should be an expiation for the sin of their origin. The idea of 'original sin' is a concretization of this position, one that predisposes the race into a posture of justification, and one that is hopeless because it is bound to fail. With an entrance like this, playful, spontaneous being is simply not good enough.

Baldly stated, who would fall for that? Yet, as Frye has reminded us, we do not live directly or nakedly in the universe as (we suppose) other life forms do, but within a mythological universe, that is, a body of assumptions and beliefs most of which are held unconsciously, or at least invisibly.[16] We are at once the beneficiaries and the victims of our mythological tradition as we are of our linguistic and social traditions, one of the differences being that our mythological conditioning is more difficult to perceive since it is shared across frontiers that would otherwise challenge us to question our own assumptions.[17]

The myth of Adam and Eve stands at the beginning of our cultural inheritance, and, whatever our religious background, it is characteristically offered to children at an age when all stories are true. Adam and Eve do not live happily ever after, but neither is God cast in the role of the wicked wizard, so no reason is given for the unhappy ending, unless it is what happens when you grow up.[18] Even if, subsequently, we return to it as a story that tries to comprehend the meaning of suffering and death, then we come immediately upon the fact that it is the first story to introduce the idea that someone is to blame for it. The serpent is to blame for Eve, who is to blame for Adam, who is to blame for taking any notice of either of them. Sorrow and death are a punishment for bad behaviour, a notion Job resisted in spite of his comforters.

Furthermore, the story presents the longing for knowledge and for immortality – 'ye shall be as gods' – as itself wrong. Yet when Gilgamesh journeys to 'the land of Dilmun in the garden of the sun' to seek for everlasting life, he is not censured. He tells Utnapishtim, alone of all the human race to live for ever: 'Because of my brother I am afraid of death; because of my brother I stray through the wilderness. His fate lies heavy upon me. How can I be silent, how can I rest? He is dust and I shall die also and be laid in the earth for ever.'[19] No more than Adam and Eve does Gilgamesh receive what he is hoping for, but it is not his fault, it is 'his destiny'.

Comparing the myth of the 'Fall' with this and other myths of the paradox of the soul 'fastened to a dying animal', as Yeats sees it,[20] we might wonder if the attributions of sin, blame and guilt are proper guides for any journeyers towards understanding to take with them, and still more how these categories lodged in the mind themselves corrupt our earthly business of hurt, pain, uncertainty and loss. Add to this the fact that Eve and Adam are not presented as characters in a narrative, as are Gilgamesh and his friend Enkidu, so we cannot imagine ourselves in their predicament and feel for them, but must see them apart, as a mirror held up to human nature and its flaw.

Eve and her kind, as we shall see below, have borne most of the brunt of this view, taken as a true story of how things are, and she has been doctrinally accused of being a real woman, who committed a real crime, which makes all real women like her capable of behaving in the same way. Why the 'Word of God' is assumed to be without irony, paradox, symbolism and all the other literary excellences available to his creatures is a matter obviously not susceptible of theological debate, since 'He' writes quite plainly in the literal mode of concrete fact. Revelation and literalism go ominously together. The mind that finds fault and blames – especially a blaming of oneself for a 'sin' that has not, in fact, been committed, so cannot be atoned – is inevitably relieved when a scapegoat has been found, for some semblance of order is thereby restored to an incomprehensible situation. Perhaps we could go further and say that someone, or a group, with an unconscious bondage to such an idea tends to look for a scapegoat on whom to project this feeling of guilt and be supposedly freed from it. In literal interpretations of this tale the scapegoat was Eve, and the reason was not hard to find: she was a woman. So runs the patriarchal syllogism of orthodox Christian thought, some centuries after Aristotle gave us the definition of tautology.

It may, indeed, not be too much to claim that this myth, read as factually true, has implicitly shaped or certainly contributed to our cultural assumptions about the relationship between men and women, the place of sexuality in human life, humanity's relation to nature and to the divine, and so our view of human nature itself. Standing for a moment outside our mythological structures of perception, we should expect at least that a whole range of imaginative possibilities has been excluded.

Considering the human psyche as a whole from the perspective of Jung's idea of the Collective Unconscious, it may be said that the deeper layers of the soul were suddenly deprived of a life of participation with creation and of an instinctual perception of the unity of life governed by divine law, which had been understood for thousands of years through the image of the goddess.

THE FALL AS THE MYTH OF THE BIRTH OF CONSCIOUSNESS

If, however, the myth is understood symbolically – not as an incontrovertible statement *about* human nature but as an expression of humanity's *own experience* of itself at the moment of initiation into consciousness – then the meaning changes totally. To bite into the knowledge of good and evil is then to be separated for ever from the state of unconscious unity in which all life is one. Suddenly there are two things, two terms: I and you, I and them, I and it. Division polarizes; discrimination – this is not that – brings with it evaluation: this is better than that; this is good, this is not good (evil). The experience of opposites results in conflict because either both are wanted and only one can be had, or only one is wanted and both are there. Now life comes with death, pleasure with pain, joy with sorrow, or the self comes *without* the other, the man without the woman, spirit without nature, and the human being without the divine being.

The state before this awareness has always been imagined as a golden age of happiness 'before', to be regained in the return to happiness 'ever after', sometimes known as heaven. 'In the beginning' there was no man and woman but both were one, as in Plato's original Round Man and the hermaphroditic Adam, the primary substance of earth from which man and woman both emerged in the image of their androgynous creator. The childhood garden of the four rivers and the central tree has the completeness of a pastoral fantasy in which every wish comes true. When, from the deepest promptings of intuition, a voice appears and asks 'why?', who would know there was so much to lose? 'Why don't you eat that fruit?' 'Oh, we mustn't, we'll die.' 'No, you won't, it'll be even better', and conflict has begun. 'Two souls, alas, are housed within my breast,' cries Faust.[21] Inevitably, the first 'thing' they look upon is themselves, and in that look body and mind come apart – the meaning of 'And they saw that they were naked'. When all the other dualisms follow after, must not the feeling be one of loss, and then regret, and then a longing to return to what can never be again as once upon a time it was? And would not the fruit taste bitter in the mouth? Then, also, consciousness would feel like a curse, and the fatal question 'why?' feel like a crime, as though, Prometheus-like, we had taken something that does not belong to us. And, furthermore, this 'why?' that exiles us from paradise is always with us until we take up the challenge of consciousness – and try to discover some answer. Erich Fromm writes:

> Human existence poses a question. Man is thrown into this world without his volition, and taken away from it again without his volition . . . *He has to live* his life, he *is not lived by* it. He is *in* nature, yet he *transcends nature* . . . The very fact of being born poses a problem. At the moment of birth, life asks man a question, and this question he must answer. He must answer it at every moment; not his mind, not his body, but *he*, the person who thinks and dreams, who sleeps and eats and cries and laughs – *the whole man* – must answer it.[22]

Figure 11. *The Terrestrial Paradise*, from *Les Très Riches Heures du Duc de Berry*, Limbourg Brothers, *c.* 1410. Here the Garden of Eden is imagined as a circle, where the original harmony is rendered in the archetypal image of wholeness, a mandala. This is the state before the separation of consciousness from its ground, symbolized as the Garden, in which Adam and Eve, lingering with nostalgic glances outside the gate, yearn to remain.

In another book, *You Shall Be As Gods*, Fromm addresses the myth of Adam and Eve specifically:

> Adam and Eve at the beginning of their evolution are bound to blood and soil; they are still 'blind'. But 'their eyes are opened' after they acquire the knowledge of good and evil. With this knowledge the original harmony with nature is broken. Man begins the process of individuation and cuts his ties with nature. In fact, he and nature become enemies, not to be reconciled until man has become fully human. With this first step of severing the ties between man and nature, history – and alienation – begins. As we have seen, this is not the story of the 'fall' of man but of his awakening, and thus, of the beginning of his rise.[23]

Perhaps, then, a symbolic reading of the story may restore it to its rightful place at the beginning of our cultural tradition as a myth of the birth of consciousness. (Compare, in Greek culture, the myth of Prometheus.) The guilt Adam and Eve suffer from, which characteristically reappears as any new stage of awareness is reached, must then be seen not as *moral* guilt, in the sense of having done something wrong, but as *tragic* guilt, in the sense that what was done had to be done, because its ultimate roots lie in the very structure of existence itself. In tragedy, forms are shattered out of inner necessity, and out of the dynamic of that tension a new value is won. There is, therefore, no one to blame and nothing to be blamed for. Consciousness entails loss, as Masaccio's picture of the mourning of Adam and Eve expelled from the garden shows (Fig. 12). The drama of Adam and Eve is symbolic of this particular dimension of the human condition.

But tragedy offers only one perspective. The other term of the totality of being is often called comedy; not the comedy that knows nothing of the tragic vision, but the comedy that is born out of it as its ultimately playful resolution. Then follows the restoration of those shattered forms in the joyous participation with the source, sometimes also called the mythic vision. This is the fruit of the Tree of Life, the tree that seems unattainable when first seen as other than the Tree of Knowledge, but whose gift is waiting for the moment when the contentions of life and death are dissolved and the two trees are again one. 'Only through time, time is conquered.'[24] This is the scene of earlier Mesopotamian seals, when the images of infinite life are manifest in their own right, not viewed through the distorting lens of remorse. If 'the god' initiates humanity into duality and the laws of time, then 'the goddess' redeems that vision by releasing the mind from identification with mortality and reuniting it with the universal inexhaustible life out of which all particular lives come and go. In the metaphor that is mythology, this is the sacred marriage, when *bios*, once the son and now the consort, takes his place on the other side of the world tree so that the fruits of immortality and wisdom can, finally, be offered together.

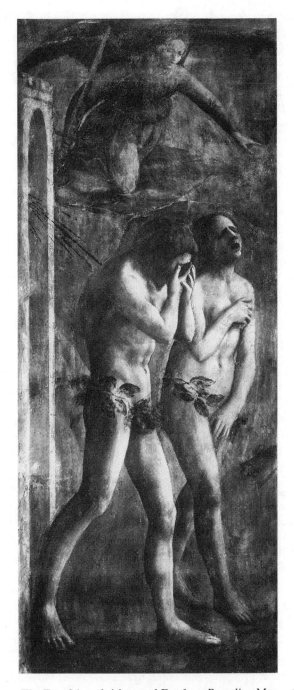

Figure 12. *The Expulsion of Adam and Eve from Paradise*, Masaccio, c. 1425.
Santa Maria del Carmine, Florence.

Figure 13. The Tree of Life and Knowledge in the Garden of Immortality; Sumerian cylinder seal, *c.* 2500 BC.

In the melancholy tale that is to follow, however, we return, with startling change of category, to the literal interpretation of God's holy word, in whose unpronounceable name wars are still waged with presumably holy deaths, and whose first (but not last) curse upon the human race fell upon the woman, Eve.

EVE IN HEBREW CULTURE

'Of the woman came the beginning of sin, and through her we all die' (Sir. 25:24). This interpretation of the biblical story of Adam and Eve, with its subtle generalization from Eve to 'the woman', permeates Judaic literature as well as innumerable theological commentaries on the Bible. A Greek text of the life of Adam and Eve,[25] translated from the Jewish Midrash, or Commentaries on the Old Testament, has the following passage spoken by Eve as Adam is dying:

> Then Eve rose and went out and fell on the ground and said, 'I have sinned, O God; I have sinned, O Father of all; I have sinned against you, I have sinned against your chosen angels, I have sinned against the cherubim, I have sinned against your steadfast throne; I have sinned, Lord, I have sinned much; I have sinned before you, and all sin in creation has come about through me.'[26]

Adam was buried in Paradise and was promised resurrection by God, but when the time for Eve's death came, she was buried with her son Abel, instead of with Adam as she had implored God:

> My Master, Lord and God of all excellence, do not separate me from the body of Adam; for you made me from his members; but rather consider me worthy, even me, unworthy and sinful, to be buried near his body. And just as I was with him in Paradise, and not separated even after the transgression, so also let no one separate us now.[27]

A lighter story, from Ginzberg's *Legends of the Jews*, also taking Eve as the paradigm of woman's nature, makes the point that women are trivial and untrustworthy, like Eve, or, at the very least, good for a laugh. For when the Almighty wished to create Eve he did not know from which part of Adam's body he should fashion her:

> When God was on the point of making Eve, He said: 'I will not make her from the head of man, lest she carry her head high in arrogant pride; not from the eye, lest she be wanton-eyed; not from the ear, lest she be an eavesdropper; not from the neck, lest she be insolent; not from the mouth, lest she be a tattler; not from the heart, lest she be inclined to envy; not from the hand, lest she be a meddler; not from the foot, lest she be a gadabout. I will form her from a chaste portion of the body,' and to every limb and organ as He formed it, God said, 'Be chaste! Be chaste!' Nevertheless, in spite of the great caution used, woman has all the faults God tried to obviate. The daughters of Zion were haughty and walked with stretched forth necks and wanton eyes; Sarah was an eavesdropper in her own tent, when the angel spoke with Abraham; Miriam was a tale-bearer, accusing Moses; Rachel was envious of her sister Leah; Eve put out her hand to take the forbidden fruit, and Dinah was a gadabout.[28]

Expanding on this theme, he adds (more seriously): 'Woman covers her hair in token of Eve's having brought sin into the world; she tries to hide her shame; and women precede men in a funeral cortege, because it was woman who brought death into the world.'[29]

Eve, the demythologized goddess, now the primal ancestress in merely human form, belongs to a whole process of patriarchal revaluation, whose intention is transparently clear in the new myths of the moon and the sun. Here are the words, written as late as the thirteenth century AD, still expressing the way in which moon and sun – symbolically, goddess and god – are redefined in a new relationship more in accord with the Iron Age's changing priorities for women and men:

> God made two great lights. The two lights ascended together with the same dignity. The moon, however, was not at ease with the sun, and in fact each felt mortified by the other . . . God thereupon said to her, 'Go and diminish thyself.' . . . Thereupon she diminished herself so as to be head of the lower ranks. From that time she has had no light of her own, but derives her light from the sun. At first they were on an equality, but afterwards she diminished herself among all those grades of hers, although she is still head of them. When the moon was in connection with the sun, she was luminous, but as soon as she separated from the sun and was assigned the charge of her own hosts, she reduced her status and her light.[30]

Edward Whitmont, in his book *The Return of the Goddess*, points out that it is not only Western cultures that have rejected the feminine. He quotes from the law of Manu, which forms the basis of Hindu culture:

> 'Woman by her nature is always trying to tempt and seduce man . . . The cause of dishonor is woman, the cause of enmity is woman, the cause of

mundane existence is woman – therefore woman must be avoided.' Conversely, 'no matter how wicked, degenerate or devoid of all good qualities a man may be, a good wife must also revere him like a God.'[31]

Lilith

If Eve was charged with the bringing of death, sin and sorrow into the world, Lilith was demonic from the moment of her creation. Lilith arose out of an attempt to make sense of the difference between the two creation myths in Genesis, since in the first story, in Genesis 1, male and female are created equally and together, while in the second story, in Genesis 3, the female is created after the male and out of his body. In the simple logic of legend Lilith was the first wife, who was worse than the second. Yet the figure chosen to play this role in Judaic legend was originally Sumerian, the bright Queen of Heaven, whose name 'Lil' meant 'air' or 'storm'. She was often an ambiguous presence inclined to 'wild, uninhabited places',[32] also associated with Inanna in her dark aspect and her sister, Ereshkigal, Queen of the Underworld. She first appears in a poem about Inanna, when Inanna's tree is cut down by the hero Gilgamesh:

> Gilgamesh struck the serpent who could not be charmed.
> The Anzu-bird flew with his young to the mountains;
> And Lilith smashed her home and fled to the wild, uninhabited places.[33]

Lil was also a Sumero-Akkadian word for a 'dust-storm' or 'dust-cloud', a term that was applied to ghosts, whose form was like a dust-cloud and whose food was supposed to be the dust of the earth. In the Semitic language *lilatu* was then the 'handmaid of a ghost', but this soon became confounded with the word for 'night', *layil*, and became a word of terror, meaning a night-demon. So Lilith, in Hebrew myth, gathered around her all the associations of night and death without repose. The Hebrew image of Lilith could have been based on the images of Inanna–Ishtar, portrayed as the goddess of the Great Above and the Great Below (see Chapter 5, Fig. 30), but understandably debased, seen from the point of view of a people forcibly transported to Babylon.

There is only one reference to Lilith as a night or screech owl in the Old Testament. It occurs in the midst of a prophecy in Isaiah. On the day of Yahweh's vengeance, when the land will be turned into a wilderness, 'the satyr shall cry to his fellow; the screech owl also shall rest there, and find for herself a place of rest' (Isa. 34:14).[34] Inanna and Ishtar were both called 'Divine Lady Owl' (*Nin-ninna* and *Kilili*). This may explain where Lilith came from and why she was described as a screech owl.

One version of Lilith's creation in Hebrew mythology tells that Yahweh made Lilith, like Adam, from earth, but instead of using clean earth, he 'took filth and impure sediments from the earth, and out of these he formed a female. As was to be expected, this creature turned out to be an evil spirit.'[35] In retrospect, Lilith became Adam's first wife, whose original presence is never fully banished from his marriage to the second. What 'went wrong' with the first was obviously Lilith's equality and independence, since that was the matter that was rectified with Eve. Consequently, Lilith's assumption of the role of equal partner is treated in legend as insubordination, as, so the story goes, she would not agree to her 'proper place', which was apparently to lie beneath Adam in sexual intercourse: 'Why should I lie beneath you when I am your equal since both of us were created from dust?' she asks. Adam does not have an answer to that one, so, uttering the magic name of God, she flies away to the wilderness of the Red Sea. There she gives birth to broods of demons to the number of more than 100 a day. God sends three angels after her to bring her back but she will not return. The angels remonstrate with her and even threaten her with drowning, but she warns that she has the power to take the lives of children. In the end she agrees: 'Whenever I shall see you or your names or your images on an amulet, I shall do no harm to the child.'[36] Henceforth, she roams all over the world, searching for the children who deserve to be punished 'because of the sins of their fathers . . . and she smiles at them and kills them'.[37] Death is here conceived as punishment for sin.

Yahweh then tries again to provide Adam with a wife, this time making sure that she is a creation from Adam, and not one in her own right. Eve, however, is no more a success than Lilith, for no sooner is she made than she breaks the only commandment there was. As Phillips comments: 'An independent woman can only represent a fundamental disruption of a divinely ordered state of affairs.'[38]

Consequently, the figure of this lapse of divine order was a focus for all the fearful fantasies of feeling unprotected. Lilith could appear at any moment in the night, when she, or one of her demons, might snatch away a child, striking terror into the hearts of parents of young children. She could also take possession of a man while he slept. He would realize that he had fallen into her power if he found traces of semen when he awoke, for then he would know that Lilith had had intercourse with him. It is hard to escape the conclusion that Lilith became an image of denied sexual desire, repressed and projected on to the female, who thereby becomes the seducer. Amulets guarding against Lilith's 'power' were found everywhere.

In Hebrew culture, in the figure of Lilith, the Iron Age split and polarization of the Great Mother into the life-giving and death-bringing aspects is taken one stage further, for to the terror of inexplicable suffering that can strike without warning is added the new dimension of the demonization of sexuality. The myth in Genesis, even read with earnest doctrinal intention, does not name sexuality but the breaking of Yahweh's commandment as the cause of expulsion into the human condition, nor can the knowledge of good and evil, which they gained by their act of disobedience, be totally explained in terms of sexual knowledge. Yet both the disobedience and the knowledge soon became associated with sexuality

Figure 14. Lilith, winged and
crowned, with serpent's tail,
offers the apple to Eve; after a
woodcut by Holzschmitt, 1470.
Speculum Humanae Salvationis,
Augsburg.

because the first thing Adam and Eve 'saw' when 'their eyes were opened'
was that they were naked. Before that they were naked and unashamed;
afterwards, it is implied, they were ashamed because they knew they were
naked, not because they had broken the word of their Lord God. Shameful
nakedness soon became sinful sexuality, especially when the phallic serpent entered theological speculation. Sometimes the serpent and Lilith
were equated, and the serpent was drawn with a woman's body, which
would have been understood as Lilith. At other times the serpent has a
face like Eve's. For this reason, sexuality, or rather a view of sexuality as
'ungodly', pervades legends about Lilith as the darker aspect of Eve, and
also subtly underpins the character of Eve herself.

In both orthodox and apocryphal literature, Lilith's shadow falls on
women as far forward in time as the fifteenth century AD, when, in the
same imagery as was employed for Lilith, thousands were accused of
copulating with demons, killing infants and seducing men – of being, in a
word, witches. This is a passage from the commentary on the Essenes by
the early first-century-AD Jewish philosopher Philo of Alexandria, whose
philosophy, in this instance, has surrendered to his prejudice, apparently
without protest:

> No Essene takes a wife, because a wife is a selfish creature, excessively
> jealous and an adept in beguiling the morals of her husband and seducing
> him by her continued impostures. For by the fawning talk which she prac-
> tises and the other ways in which she plays her part like an actress on the
> stage, she first ensnares the sight and hearing and then, when these victims
> have, as it were, been duped, she cajoles the sovereign mind.[39]

Philo had a considerable influence on early Christian thought, and in
his account of the Fall it was not simply the fact of Eve's disobedience but
her mere existence that represented the 'fall' of 'man' away from the
higher male spiritual principle. She was the cause of his becoming entrap-
ped in the lower, female, material principle. Eve was, then, not merely the
instigator of the Fall into sin, but herself the paradigm image of materiality
conceived as a state of bondage. Lilith, called in the Zohar 'the ruin of the

world',[40] is drawn as an image of materiality defined in wholly sexual terms.

Sometimes it seems as if Lilith and Eve have become one figure in the minds of their commentators. Jewish literature from apocryphal sources, which were not included in the orthodox canon of the Old Testament, reveals passages like the following:

> Women are evil, my children: because they have no power or strength to stand up against man, they use wiles and try to ensnare him by their charms; and man, whom woman cannot subdue by strength, she subdues by guile. For, indeed, the angel of God told me about them and taught me that women yield to the spirit of fornication more easily than a man does, and they lay plots in their hearts against men: by the way they adorn themselves they first lead their minds astray, and by a look they instil the poison, and then in the act itself they take them captive – for a woman cannot overcome a man by force. So shun fornication, my children, and command your wives and daughters not to adorn their heads and faces, for every woman that uses wiles of this kind has been reserved for eternal punishment.[41]

These examples are enough to show how a myth, if literally conceived and literally understood, can create a prejudice (or sanctify an already existing one) and become a doctrine that declares itself to be divinely revealed truth. The writer of the Apocryphal Book of Ben Sirach, whose devotion to the abstract feminine wisdom of Sophia was correspondingly extreme, must share some responsibility for this process:

> Give me any plague, but the plague of the heart:
> And any wickedness, but the wickedness of a woman.
>
> . . . . .
>
> I had rather dwell with a lion and a dragon,
> Than to keep house with a wicked woman.
>
> . . . . .
>
> All wickedness is but little to the wickedness of a woman:
> Let the portion of a sinner fall upon her.
>
> . . . . .
>
> Of the woman came the beginning of sin,
> And through her we all die. (Sir. 25:13, 16, 19, 24)[42]

It was the idea of Eve's responsibility for the expulsion from the Garden, enshrined in Hebrew text and legend, that became the justification for making Jewish women subject to their fathers and husbands so that they no longer possessed even the small degree of sexual, social, political and religious autonomy belonging to women of the surrounding cultures. As Ginzberg explains: 'And because woman extinguished the light of man's soul, she is bidden to kindle the Sabbath light.'[43] However, it is essential to remember that the myth, and its implications, together with the patriarchal customs regarding women, were *not* endorsed by Jesus – quite the contrary – but they were transmitted from the Old to the New Testament through the writings of Paul, and so they entered formal Christian doctrine.

EVE IN CHRISTIAN CULTURE

John Phillips' book *Eve: The History of an Idea* is a masterly analysis of
the myth of Eve and its legacy: the destructive patterns in our culture that
the myth reflects and supports, most obviously in relation to the feminine
principle. As he says, 'Because Adam and Eve are characterized as they
are, human history and social relationships are set in order in such a way
that certain possibilities are excluded.'[44] He shows how the dispiriting
theme elaborating Eve's and woman's sinfulness can be traced all through
Christian culture, even to the modern theologian Karl Barth. In this
chapter we have been greatly helped by his research, and acknowledge
our debt to him.

Christianity did not heal the wound to the image of woman caused by
the literal reading of the story in Genesis 2 and 3. The inference is that
Adam was perfectly happy by himself in the Garden until Eve came
along. With her appearance his troubles begin. As Luther put it, following
a well-established tradition, if the serpent had assailed Adam, then the
victory would have been Adam's.[45]

In spite of the, one might have thought, crucial fact that in the Gospels
Jesus does *not* refer to original sin *nor* equate sexuality with sinfulness,
this became one of the foundation stones of Christian teaching. The men
who laid it were first of all Paul, and then the Christian Fathers, particularly Augustine, who declared that women have no souls.[46]

Paul does not uphold his great statement that Jew and Greek, bond and
free man, male and female, are 'all one in Christ Jesus' (Gal. 3:28).
Elsewhere, he makes definitive distinctions between men and women's
respective value in the eyes of God. Again, the reason for ruling on God's
creatures is God's holy word in Genesis:

> I will ... that women adorn themselves in modest apparel, with shame-
> facedness and sobriety; not with broided hair, or gold, or pearls, or costly
> array;
> But (which becometh women professing godliness) with good works.
> Let the woman learn in silence with all subjection.
> But I suffer not a woman to teach, nor to usurp authority over the man,
> but to be in silence.
> For Adam was first formed, then Eve.
> And Adam was not deceived, but the woman being deceived was in the
> transgression. (1 Tim. 2:8–14)

Again, in one of his letters to the Ephesians, he writes:

> Wives, submit yourselves unto your own husbands, as unto the Lord.
> For the husband is the head of the wife, even as Christ is the head of the
> church: and he is the saviour of the body.
> Therefore as the church is subject unto Christ, so let the wives be to their
> own husbands in every thing. (Eph. 5:22–4)

The Christian wife followed the role of the Jewish wife, as the Church in relation to Christ took over the role of Israel in relation to Yahweh. In Colossians husbands are enjoined to love their wives, but wives are told, 'submit yourselves unto your own husbands, as it is fit in the Lord' (Col. 3:18). In Paul's letter to the Corinthians, men are allowed to prophesy 'one by one, that all may learn, and all may be comforted' (1 Cor. 14:31) but women must:

> ... keep silence in the churches: for it is not permitted unto them to speak; but they are commanded to be under obedience, as also saith the law.
> And if they will learn any thing, let them ask their husbands at home: for it is a shame for women to speak in the church. (1 Cor. 14:34–5)

In this way Judaic practice was perpetuated, even though Christian men and women were permitted to sit together in church instead of segregated from each other, as they were in the synagogue. The contortions of theology are further expressed in another of Paul's letters, in which he is concerned with the veiling of women in church. As before, he draws his authority from the tale of the rib, with its idea of woman as the secondary creation, arguing that 'the head of every man is Christ; and the head of the woman is the man; and the head of Christ is God' (1 Cor. 11:3). From this it follows that women should cover their heads, even as men should uncover them:

> For a man indeed ought not to cover his head, forasmuch as he is the image and glory of God: but the woman is the glory of man.
> For the man is not of the woman; but the woman of the man.
> Neither was the man created for the woman; but the woman for the man.
> (1 Cor. 11:7–9)

Whether or not these passages are actually from the hand of Paul, they reflect the attitudes of the early Christian priesthood to women, and it is these passages that have been quoted in the past (and present) to keep women in their 'place'.[47]

Eve and Pandora

When the early Fathers were formulating Christian doctrine, they drew on three sources outside the Book of Genesis: the writings of Paul, the non-scriptural Jewish writings – such as the Secret Book of Enoch, the Apocalypse of Moses and the Books of Adam and Eve – and the Greek myth of Pandora. Although it was pagan and so, properly, irrelevant, the parallels between Pandora and Eve proved irresistible.

It is strange that a Greek myth, written down close to the time when the myth of Eve appeared, should carry the same inflection. Hesiod, in his *Works and Days* and *Theogony*, written about 700 BC, tells the story of how Pandora was created by Zeus as a punishment for the human race, because Prometheus had brought them the gift of fire, which he had stolen from the gods:

> 'But I will give men as the price for fire an evil thing in which they may all be glad of heart while they embrace their own destruction.' So said the father of men and gods, and laughed aloud. And he bade famous Hephaestos make haste and mix earth with water and to put in it the voice and strength of human kind, and fashion a sweet, lovely maiden-shape, like to the immortal goddesses in face; and Athena to teach her needlework and the weaving of the varied web; and golden Aphrodite to shed grace upon her head and cruel longing and cares that weary the limbs. And he charged Hermes the guide, the Slayer of Argus, to put in her a shameless mind and a deceitful nature . . . And he called this woman Pandora because all they who dwelt on Olympus gave each a gift, a sorrow to men who eat bread.[48]

Hermes then takes this 'snare' to Epimetheus, whose name means 'hindsight', as a gift from Zeus, and Epimetheus accepts her, forgetting the warning of his brother Prometheus, whose name means 'foresight'. Before this, the human race had no toil, sickness or death, but with the opening of Pandora's mysterious jar or urn, *pithos*, all this was unleashed upon the world:

> But the woman took off the great lid of the jar with her hands and scattered all these and her thought caused sorrow and mischief to men. Only Hope remained there in an unbreakable home within under the rim of the great jar, and did not fly out at the door . . . But the rest, countless plagues, wander amongst men; for earth is full of evils and the sea is full.[49]

Pandora, like Eve, was blamed for human mortality and all the troubles that afflict humanity, though Pandora is not the 'Mother of All Living' but only the Mother of 'the race of women and female kind'.[50] Zeus, like Yahweh, inflicted punishment on the human race through woman. As with the story of Eve, it is not difficult to detect the same inversion as the patriarchal gods established their supremacy in a former goddess culture. A similar inversion is found in the image of the original goddess behind the image of Pandora, where Pandora's name of 'all gifts' (in Greek *pan* means 'all', *dora* means 'gifts') is transparent to the older meaning of 'She who gives all things'. Harrison comments that Zeus 'takes over even the creation of the Earth-Mother who was from the beginning'.[51] This is confirmed by Hesiod's description of the silvery robe and embroidered veil with which Athena clothed Pandora and the exquisite crown that Hephaestos made for her:

> And the goddess bright-eyed Athena girded and clothed her with silvery raiment, and down from her head she spread with her hands a broidered veil, a wonder to see; and she, Pallas Athena put about her head lovely garlands, flowers of new-grown herbs. Also she put upon her head a crown of gold which the very famous Limping God made himself and worked with his own hands as a favour to Zeus his father. On it was much curious work,

wonderful to see; for of the many creatures which the land and sea rear up, he put upon it wondrous things, like living beings with voices: and great beauty shone out from it.[52]

The beauty of this creation was none the less to be a deception to humankind. Hephaestos, having fashioned Pandora from earth and adorned her, brought her before the gods:

When he had made the beautiful evil to be the price for the blessing (of fire), he brought her out ... to the place where the other gods and men were. And wonder took hold of the deathless gods and mortal men when they saw that which was sheer guile, not to be withstood by men.[53]

The Christian Fathers Origen and Tertullian both refer to the myth of Pandora, and Tertullian's association of it with Eve deserves mention:

If ever there was a certain Pandora, whom Hesiod cites as the first woman, hers was the first head to be crowned by the graces with a diadem; for she received gifts from all and was hence called 'Pandora'; to us, however, Moses ... describes the first woman, Eve, as being more conveniently encircled with leaves about the middle than with flowers about the temple.[54]

In Figure 15 the suggestive nakedness of the woman with one hand on the skull of death and the other on the urn of all ills is clearly intended to bring sexuality to mind as the cause of both. The legacy of both myths, combined in the antithetical prose of John Chrysostom in the fourth century AD, shows how taken he was with Hesiod's idea of woman as a 'beautiful evil' (Greek: *kalon kakon*): 'What else is woman but a foe to

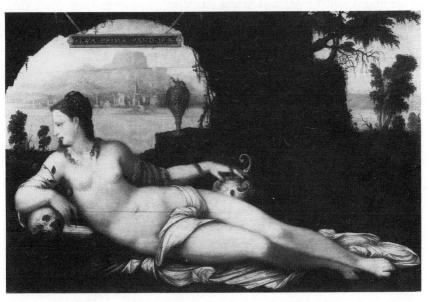

Figure 15. *Eva Prima Pandora*; Jean Cousin, *c.* 1550.

friendship, an inescapable punishment, a necessary evil, a natural temptation, a desirable calamity, a domestic danger, a delectable detriment, an evil nature, painted with fair colours?'[55]

Phillips points out that there is a 'tantalizing hint' that one version of the story that came before Hesiod's story 'presented a man or a woman with two jars, one containing *kalon* – good, and the other *kakon* – evil, and left humanity to choose. By Hesiod's time, or perhaps by his own hand, the two jars had become one and Pandora had become a *kalon kakon*.'[56] The image of the female figure with two jars or urns may carry the same idea as the Minoan goddess with her two snakes, and the urn used for storing oil or wine, and even for burial, was found all over Crete and ancient Greece.[57] The precise contrast of 'hindsight' and 'foresight' in the names of the two brothers supports this further suggestion of a choice between opposites, and indeed Origen explicitly compares the story of the forbidden urn with that of the forbidden fruit.[58] Also Hermes, the guide of souls and trickster god of imagination and divine curiosity, who gives Pandora her name, voice and wily nature, plays a similar role to the serpent in that both disturb the status quo and precipitate change. However, in both cases it is not the initiation into the moral consciousness of choice that is emphasized (though it may have been in the original Greek tale), but the entry of sorrow and death due to the woman.

It was Erasmus who, anticipating quite exactly the notion of a Freudian slip, turned *pithos*, jar or urn, into *pyxis*, box (slang for female genitals), so imposing an indelible sexual innuendo on the original vessel, once the sacred body of the mother goddess containing and conferring all the gifts of life and death.[59] Dora and Erwin Panofsky put forward the interesting idea that Erasmus' 'mistake' was a fusion or confusion of Pandora with Psyche, the bride of Cupid (the Greek Eros), son of Venus (the Greek Aphrodite), in Apuleius' tale of Cupid and Psyche in *The Golden Ass*.[60] Psyche, in the last of the tasks set her by Venus, is given a *pyxis*, which she is to carry down to Hades and fill with a little bit of Persephone's beauty. She obtains the *pyxis*, 'filled and sealed', but cannot resist the temptation of opening it, when she is overcome by the vapours released from it and faints, only then to be rescued by Cupid. The point of the analogy that probably appealed to Erasmus, already steeped in the tradition of Eve, was the capacity of women to succumb to temptation, and so to place subjective desire before objective command. In any case, the movement from the urn of life and death to the box, and the folly of opening it common to both tales, makes again, subtly, that crude analogy between a woman's sex and her moral inferiority. The congeniality of this idea for the Christian Fathers must explain their straying into pagan paths to gather evidence for their case.

Eve as Secondary Creation

The implications of the rib story for Christian thought were, as we have seen, far-reaching: Eve was a secondary creation, not made in God's image, and so of inferior substance, a weaker vessel, less rational, more likely to succumb to the temptation of the serpent; that is, a morally inferior human being. This is Thomas Aquinas, echoing Paul: 'In a secondary sense the image of God is found in man, and not in woman: for man is the beginning and end of woman; as God is the beginning and end of every creature.'[61] From which, on an assumption of God as Supreme Reason, it follows that: 'By a kind of subjection woman is naturally subject to man, because in man the discretion of reason predominates.'[62] As Milton phrases it in *Paradise Lost*: 'He for God only, she for God in him.'[63] This is taken directly from Yahweh's curse to the woman. Firstly she is to suffer the 'sorrow' of childbirth, and secondly she is to relate primarily through Adam: 'Thy desire shall be to thy husband, and he shall rule over thee' (Gen. 3:16). The implication is that her first independent action should be her last. On the other hand, Adam is cursed for two reasons, the first of which is simply stated: 'Thou hast hearkened unto the voice of thy wife' (Gen. 3:17). It is surprising that the second reason does not come first for one with so direct a relation with his creator: that he ate of the tree that God had commanded him not to eat. Again, the implication is that just hearkening – that is, listening and assenting – to his wife is tantamount to breaking the divine commandment.

James Hillman, in his book *The Myth of Analysis*, sums up the psychological history of the male–female relationship as 'a series of footnotes to the tale of Adam and Eve', following the pattern of 'First Adam, then Eve':

> Whatever is divine in Eve comes to her secondhand through the substance of Adam . . . First, the male is prior in time, because he was created first. Second, the male is superior, since he alone is said to be created in the image of God. Third, the male is superior in consciousness, because Eve was extracted from Adam's deep sleep, from his unconsciousness . . . His sleep resulted in Eve; Eve is man's 'sleep.' Fourth, Adam is substantially superior, since Eve is preformed in Adam as part to whole . . . The existence, essence and material substance of Eve depend on Adam. He is her formal cause, since she is made of his rib; and he is her final cause, since her end and purpose is help for him. The male is the precondition of the female and the ground of its possibility.[64]

From this image comes the argument that as Adam and Eve, so man and woman have a fundamentally different relationship with their divine creator. Man's relationship is direct, like Adam's; woman's is indirect and dependent on her 'Adam', like Eve's. (One wonders, parenthetically, what if she doesn't have an 'Adam' to relate through?) Even a modern theologian, Claus Westermann, can write about the fixed order of relationship

Figure 16. *The Creation of Eve*; in *Les Heures de Rohan*, the Rohan Master, *c.* 1415–16.

as if it were 'God-given': 'Woman has always had the fulfillment of her being, her respectability in the community, in belonging to the man, and in motherhood.'[65]

The idea that woman belongs to man rather than to herself and God appears here to be so deeply rooted as to be beyond history, yet it goes back no farther than the Iron Age, specifically to the beliefs and tribal structure of the once nomadic Aryans and Semites.

In the tenderly conceived picture from the *Heures de Rohan* in Figure 16 God draws Eve gently out of the side of the sleeping Adam, yet she is both the diminutive size of a child and also a full-grown woman, an exact image of the imbalance to which Hillman refers.

Eve as Inferior Substance

Because she was created second, out of Adam, the substance of Eve was believed to be inferior. The divine was reflected in her only through reflection from Adam. Secondary creation and inferior substance are then one and the same. This did not extend only to the moral character of Eve, and so to all women, but also to Eve in her function as a female, and so to all females.

The idea of female inferiority, deriving in the Judaeo-Christian tradition from Eve, inevitably biased hypotheses and interfered with empirical observation in that ultimate of nature's mysteries: the creation of new life from old. Woman was therefore considered inferior to man in her capacity to contribute to the birth of a child. This point of view was originally formulated by Aristotle, whose works had reached Europe in the twelfth century and had a great influence on Thomas Aquinas. Aristotle, in his work *On the Generation of Animals*, proposes that 'the female does not contribute semen to generation', merely the blood of the menses, that is, blood that is not transformed. Semen, on the other hand, is blood that has gone through a transformation process called *pepsis*: 'If, then, the male stands for the effective and active, and the female, considered as female, for the passive, it follows that what the female would contribute to the semen of the male would not be semen but material for the semen to work upon.'[66]

For Aquinas, following Aristotle, woman was not the creator of the child but only the passive vehicle that brought it to birth, the active and vital function in procreation being the male. The creation of a female child was, moreover, the result of a flawed process, which could extend even to the weather:

> For the active power in the seed of the male tends to produce something like itself, perfect in masculinity; but the procreation of a female is the result either of the debility of the active power, of some unsuitability of the material, or of some change effected by external influences, like the south wind, for example, which is damp.[67]

The combination of Aristotle and the Genesis myth was decisive for Thomas Aquinas, and in his writings, which were central for Catholic theology, he presented woman as being on a lower plane than man, *ignobilior et vilior*, as he put it. This compares with the Brahmanic teaching in India that woman is destined to reincarnate at a lower level than man because of her innate inferiority.[68] It is also an idea found, astonishingly, in Plato's *Timaeus*.[69] In the West this belief found its expression in the perplexing debate of the Middle Ages: *'Habet Mulier Animum?'* – 'Does Woman have a Soul?'

The residue of these ideas persisted in medicine as late as the nineteenth century, when semen was still regarded as superior to blood, and the male role in procreation superior to the role of the female, who simply provided the womb. On an analogy with the relation of the Virgin Mary to the Holy Spirit, the woman was the vessel to hold the divinely active seed. The female egg was simply not looked for because there was no reason why it should be there; or, more precisely, there was every reason why it was not there. The assumption of female inferiority has been so pervasive that it has structured perception to the point where it can hardly be seen.

In *An Outline of Psychoanalysis*, for instance, one of Freud's last books, the idea of female inferiority is attributed to all female children with a bewildering lack of adult argument. An understanding of feminine psychology, he writes, is to be based on the belief that little girls, comparing themselves to little boys, 'naturally' come to the conclusion that their anatomy is inferior and, unhappily, their subsequent view of themselves never recovers its former innocence:

> A female child has, of course, no need to fear the loss of a penis; she must, however, react to the fact of not having received one. From the very first

she envies boys its possession; her whole development may be said to take place under the colours of envy for the penis. She ... makes efforts to compensate for her defect – efforts which may lead in the end to a normal feminine attitude. If during the phallic phase she attempts to get pleasure like a boy by the manual stimulation of her genitals, it often happens that she fails to obtain sufficient gratification and extends her judgement of inferiority from her stunted penis to her whole self.[70]

As Hillman aptly comments: 'Freud's fantasy *of* the little girl's mind becomes a Freudian fantasy *in* the little girl's mind.'[71] This unique definition of a feminine attitude as the end result of efforts to compensate for a physical 'defect' is even presented as an observed fact, an 'observation' that does not merely assume the superiority of male genitals, but assumes as well a hierarchical model of relationship between the sexes. Perhaps Jung's wry remark that 'one sees what one can best see oneself'[72] is not altogether inappropriate here. As a refreshing contrast, an old African legend goes:

> God made the man and the woman, and put them together.
> When they saw each other, they began to laugh.
> Then God sent them into the world.[73]

Eve, the Serpent and the Devil

If secondary creation and inferior substance are accepted, it follows that there is in Eve an image of a flaw in creation. From the history of scapegoats and sacrifice, we might expect that Eve would receive those accusations of imperfection that human beings with *unconscious* demands for perfection cannot make to themselves, and so project outwards onto a figure who can be blamed instead. The worse the figure can be made out to be, the better the accusers, by contrast, feel themselves to be: 'And why beholdest thou the mote that is in thy brother's eye, but considerest not the beam that is in thine own eye?' (Matt. 7:3).

To put it another way: Eve has been so frequently allied with the serpent and with the devil, as though they were all on the same plane of reference (sitting down, as it were, at table together), that some explanation would seem to be necessary.

The first association between Eve and the serpent comes in the closeness of their names, for the Hebrew *Hawwah* is very close to the Arabic and Aramaic word for serpent, and this was remarked upon by the earliest Jewish commentators. Phillips writes:

The association between Eve and the serpent, and between the serpent and Satan (the *Sammael* of Jewish legend and the *Shaitan* of *Iblis* of the Qur'an) is made again and again in interpretations of the story of the creation and fall of the first humans ... She is held to be the devil's mouthpiece, Satan's

Figure 17. *Adam, Eve and the Serpent*;
Hugo van der Goes, 1460–70.
The serpent is Eve with an animal
body, and even the expression in
their faces is similar.

familiar. At times she *herself* is seen in some way to be the forbidden fruit,
or the serpent in paradise, or even the Fall.[74]

It was probably inevitable that once the association between Eve and
serpent was made in a pejorative sense (whereas, symbolically, the relation
between goddess and serpent had been life-giving), the association of the
serpent with the devil, and of the devil with Eve, would follow sooner or
later. While the serpent often appears to be tempting Eve erotically, Satan
was eventually to appear in European paintings as the serpent with Eve's
head on it, with the suggestion implicit in the image that Eve has assumed
the serpent's tempting role in relation to Adam. The further innuendo
was that Eve's relation with the serpent was not all it should have been.

The alacrity with which some Christian writers of the Faith embraced
this imagery as real calls for some attempt at understanding what happens
when spirituality and sexuality fall into polarity. The sexual instinct, split
off from spirit and depotentiated through repression, appears here to have
found expression in the concrete image of what was simultaneously feared
and longed for: the dissociated genital of the female. As Jung puts it:
'What is unconscious is projected; that's the rule.'[75]

The general premises of theological conviction are admirably parodied
by Milton, when Adam in *Paradise Lost* identifies Eve with the serpent:

> Out of my sight, thou serpent, that name best
> Befits thee, with him leagued, thy self as false
> And hateful; nothing wants, but that thy shape,
> Like his, and colour serpentine may show

> Thy inward fraud, to warn all creatures from thee
> Henceforth; lest that too heavenly form, pretended
> To hellish falsehood, snare them.

concluding that

> . . . all was but a show
> Rather than solid virtue, all but a rib
> Crooked by nature . . .[76]

Phillips summarizes:

The serpent was regarded, consciously or unconsciously, as a powerful symbol for the connection between evil and sexuality. The original transgression was seen from a very early date as having something to do with sexual awareness. Eve thus becomes the vehicle for the intrusion of *lust* into the created order . . . From the genital of Woman all men have come forth, and to the genital of Woman most men return. Psychologically, then, women must be regarded as perpetually confronting men with the threat of nonexistence, and men avoid this terror by reversing the natural course (women are really born from men) or by denying their sexual yearning for the comfort of oblivion (women are seducers). Thus the association of the first woman

Figure 18. *The Temptation and Fall of Eve*; William Blake, 1808.
Illustration for Milton's *Paradise Lost*.

with the devil-snake in legend and art ought not to surprise us. Eve must be the creation of Satan, or created by God out of Satan's substance, or placed on the earth to do Satan's bidding.[77]

Eve as Temptress and the Devil's Gateway

'Woman is like an apple, lovely without, rotten within.' So runs the fifteenth-century York Mystery Cycle. The forbidden fruit, by now the apple, became a symbol of sexual intercourse. Eve was the instigator of the whole affair, for through her beauty and her wiles she seduced Adam to taste of the forbidden fruit. The unquestioned assumption here is one common to most Christian writings, that, due to her secondary creation and inferior substance, Eve was more likely than Adam to give in to temptation because she was a weaker vessel for God's word. So Eve is drawn as morally weak, less rational, less disciplined, vain, greedy, gullible, cunning and wily like the serpent. Being more instinctive and less lawful, she is more sexual. Sexuality was, then, against God, that is, for the devil. It was a short step to find Eve, and those who share her sex, to be a gateway for the devil to enter.

In Figure 19 crossed legs symbolize sexual involvement, and Rubens paints Eve's invitation to eat of the apple as a sexual invitation. A small serpent coils around the trunk of the tree, its tail almost becoming a curl of her hair and its body touching her hand, which also curves, serpentine, around a branch. Eve, here, is the serpent of sex:

> Though the devil tempted Eve to sin, yet Eve seduced Adam. And as the sin of Eve would not have brought death to our soul and body unless the sin had afterwards passed on to Adam, to which he was tempted by Eve, not by the devil, therefore she is more bitter than death.[78]

And again:

> By every garb of penitence woman might the more fully expiate that which she derives from Eve – the ignominy, I mean, of the first sin, and the odium of human perdition . . . Do you not know that you are each an Eve? . . . You are the devil's gateway; you are the unsealer of that forbidden tree; you are the first deserter of the divine law; you are she who persuaded him whom that devil was not valiant enough to attack. You destroyed so easily God's image, man. On account of your desert – that is, death – even the Son of God had to die.[79]

This was Tertullian, writing in the third century AD. Woman is 'each an Eve' and man, then, is each an Adam. Further, Eve is the means through which the devil reaches Adam, and through Adam the human race.

Having polarized God and humanity, Tertullian must find God good and humanity bad. Since, he argues, evil cannot exist in the nature of God, it must have come into existence as a result of something, 'and

Figure 19. *Adam and Eve*; Peter Paul Rubens, 1598.

that something is undoubtedly matter',[80] and the worst of matter is the carnality of the body. Eve and women, with their greater sexuality (as envisaged by the abstinent Christian Fathers), had the power to create evil by luring men into the sin of lust and its practices: 'Man', he continues, was 'solidified in the womb, amongst all uncleanness', and 'issues through the parts of shame'.[81]

The implications of such judgements were not confined to the Church, nor was their purpose limited to a theological reckoning with death. Far more damagingly, they entered a general way of thinking so radically that they could even become a way of expressing love for God. An old Irish lament has all the rhythms of devotion:

> I am Eve, the wife of noble Adam; it was I who violated Jesus in the past; it was I who robbed my children of heaven; it is I by right who should have been crucified. I had heaven at my command; evil the bad choice that shamed me; evil the punishment for my crime that has aged me; alas, my hand is not pure. It was I who plucked the apple; it went past the narrow of my gullet; as long as they live in daylight women will not cease from folly on account of that. There would be no ice in any place; there would be no bright windy winter; there would be no hell, there would be no greed, there would be no terror but for me.[82]

The unconsciousness of these projections is as remarkable as their continued existence in Christian society. Only very recently have people

Figure 20. *The Creation of Adam*; tapestry, *c.* sixteenth–seventeenth century. Florence.

Figure 21. *Adam Accusing Eve*; tapestry, *c.* sixteenth–seventeenth century. Florence.

questioned the law on rape, where the assumption was implicit that a woman was largely responsible for rape attacks, having somehow 'enticed' the man into believing she was inviting his assault, or that (not knowing her own mind) when she said 'no', she did not really mean it. Only recently has a woman's being battered by her husband been treated as an offence against the person, rather than an acceptable punishment from a husband to a wife. The myth of Eve's 'seduction' of Adam's obedience to God and the idea that *she* is 'to blame' for what they both 'did' may lie behind these otherwise incomprehensible phenomena.

The tapestries in Figures 20 and 21 are related. In Figure 20 God greets Adam, just risen from the earth, like a brother, an image of himself. In Figure 21 the primary substance, made in God's image, then self-righteously – and, given his upbringing, most plausibly – blames Eve, with no sense of his own contribution to the breaking of his creator's commandment.

In the fifteenth century two Dominican priests, Sprenger and Kraemer, were empowered by the Pope to set up a commission of inquiry into witchcraft, and to hand over the women they held to be guilty to the Inquisition. Sprenger was the man who, notwithstanding his hatred of women, held the Virgin in utmost veneration, and formed the first lay confraternity for the recitation of the rosary in 1475.[83] The terrifying document these two Dominicans drew up, called the *Malleus Maleficarum* (the Witches' Hammer – literally, the Hammer of the Evil-doers), was published between 1487 and 1489, and became the textbook of the Inquisition, going through nineteen editions and much usage in the next 300 years. It was responsible for the persecution, torture and murder by burning or hanging of thousands of women, including Joan of Arc, who were named as witches who had consorted with the devil.

The Inquisition fused together three categories of persecuted people: witches, heretics and the insane. Many of the accused women were mentally ill, and since at that time the mentally ill were classified as being possessed of the devil, the cause of their possession was, inevitably, pre-occupation with sex. The authors wrote:

> All witchcraft comes from carnal lust, which in women is insatiable. There are three things that are never satisfied, yea, a fourth thing which says not, It is enough; that is, the mouth of the womb. Wherefore for the sake of fulfilling their lusts they consort even with devils.[84]

As with Lilith, who could be warded off with an amulet, these witches also spare those who have been baptized or who wear the sign of the cross. Lilith is no longer a disembodied spirit, but has become 'incarnate' in women and can be recognized by those holy enough to do so.

Zilboorg, in his *History of Medical Psychology*, tracing the history of the treatment of mental illness from Greek to modern times, writes:

The Old World seems to have risen against woman and written this grue-
some testimonial to its own madness. Even after she had been tortured and
broken in body and spirit, woman was not granted the privilege of facing
the world in a direct way. The witch, stripped of her clothes, her wounds
and marks of torture exposed, her head and genitals shaven so that no devil
could conceal himself in her hair, would be led into court backwards so that
her evil eyes might not rest on the judge and bewitch him ... Never in the
history of humanity was woman more systematically degraded. She paid for
the fall of Eve sevenfold, and the Law bore a countenance of pride and self-
satisfaction, and the delusional certainty that the will of the Lord had been
done.[85]

This work was not, however, confined to Catholics, but was taken up
by Luther, Calvin, James I and the Puritans in Massachusetts with the
hanging of the witches of Salem. The last witch was beheaded in Switzerland in 1782. Nor was it only women who were burned, but anyone who
could be 'proven' to be a heretic. Anyone, like Giordano Bruno, who
threatened the established beliefs with a statement that 'contradicted'
scripture, could be destroyed. Compassion for the accused was taken as
proof of complicity with the Devil. Intellect was no protection against the
exigencies of Faith. Calvin was congratulated by Melancthon (known at
the time as a humanist) on the burning of the great physician Servetus,
who had discovered the pulmonary circulation of the blood. His 'heresy'
had been to travel to the Holy Land and describe it as barren instead of
flowing with milk and honey, and for this his tongue was torn out before
he was burnt.

Montaigne must be left the last comment: 'It is', he wrote, 'setting a
high value on one's conjectures, if for their sake one is willing to burn a
human being alive.'[86]

Eve and the Body

Eve came to represent Body and Matter; Adam, accordingly, became
Mind and Spirit, or (with Aquinas) Rational Soul. Eve was Carnality, and
Adam was Spirituality. Because of the long patriarchal inheritance, both
Jewish and Greek, it must have seemed 'quite natural' for the Christian
Fathers to associate man with Mind and woman with Body. This split
between mind and body can be seen as yet another of those oppositions
that follow from the primary separation between creator and creation that
was the mark of Iron Age mythology. The belief that the body must be
controlled, mortified, made to suffer for its desires and in general brought
into a relationship of subjection to the mind is very deeply engrained in
the Christian psyche. Only Alchemy worked on the assumption that spirit
and matter are two aspects of one single matrix of energy. The idea that
body and mind might be two aspects or perspectives of the soul, or that
the body is the temple of the soul and its physical expression, was always

known to alchemists and mystics, and is now advanced by the discoveries of modern physics. The old distinctions have to give way to the idea that all matter, however 'solid' in appearance, is in fact energy, but the relevance of these discoveries to theology and medicine is only now beginning to be explored.[87]

The opposition between mind and body in Christian doctrine took its flavour from the 'sin of Eve', which became the inherent sinfulness of the flesh, in particular all those bodily organs that had to do with excretion of waste matter, sexual intercourse and birth. Marina Warner, in her book on the Virgin Mary, *Alone of All Her Sex*, comments:

> In the faeces and urine – Augustine's phrase – of childbirth, the closeness of woman to all that is vile, lowly, corruptible, and material was epitomized; in the 'curse' of menstruation, she lay closer to the beasts; the lure of her beauty was nothing but an aspect of the death brought about by her seduction of Adam in the garden. St John Chrysostom warned: 'The whole of her bodily beauty is nothing less than phlegm, blood, bile, rheum, and the fluid of digested food.'[88]

Compare Yeats:

> Love is all
> Unsatisfied
> That cannot take the whole
> Body and soul;
> And that is what Jane said.[89]

Warner has outlined the Christian theological argument that 'woman was womb and womb was evil':

> When Augustine, Ambrose and Jerome endorsed virginity for its special holiness, they were the heirs and representatives of much current thought in the Roman empire of their day. And in this battle between the flesh and the spirit, the female sex was firmly placed on the side of the flesh. For as childbirth was woman's special function, and its pangs the special penalty decreed by God after the Fall, and as the child she bore in her womb was stained by sin from the moment of its conception, the evils of sex were particularly identified with the female. Woman was womb and womb was evil: this cluster of ideas endemic to Christianity is but the extension of Augustine's argument about original sin.[90]

Hillman makes the point that as long as the physical body and matter generally represent the feminine principle, then whatever is physical will continue to receive anti-feminine projections, so that matter, evil, darkness and female will continue to be interchangeable concepts. The female body in particular will have 'a *doubly* negative cast':

> The material aspect of the feminine, 'her human body, the thing most prone to gross material corruption' (papal wording of bull declaring the Assumption of the Virgin Mary as dogma, 1950), will have a *doubly* negative cast.

The more female the material, the more will it be evil; the more materialized the female, the more will it be dark. Upon the physical body of the feminine the fantasies of female inferiority become most florid, since just here the 'abysmal side of bodily man with his animal passions and instinctual nature' is constellated.[91]

Another aspect of the rejection of the body was the behaviour of the Christian saints, who inflicted on it every kind of torture and misery, from starvation to flagellation. Asceticism, chastity and celibacy became the hallmark of the virtuous, of men and women dedicated to the holy life. Virginity became the 'gateway' to immortality: 'Let us love chastity above all things,' Augustine wrote, 'for it was to show that this was pleasing to Him that Christ chose the modesty of a virgin womb.' Augustine, as Warner writes, thus bound up three ideas in a causal chain: the sinfulness of sex, the virgin birth, and the good of virginity.[92]

In this way the spiritual life was irrevocably divided from the natural life; so love of God could not be born of love of life. On the contrary, the virgin and the martyr offered their bodies to Christ in the belief that virginity and martyrdom would bring them closer to God. The body was to be sacrificed to the spirit in the belief that in this way evil would be vanquished: 'The root, and the flower, too, of virginity, is a crucified life', wrote John Chrysostom.[93]

On the other hand, the asceticism of certain Christian saints has to be placed in the context of shamanic experience, where the aim in both is to transcend the limitations that keep people bound to earthly needs and concerns, closing them to another kind of perception that has always been called 'visionary'.[94] The withdrawal into the wilderness, a model set by Jesus himself, or the self-imposed fast of the Christian ascetics can be understood as an enactment of the sacrifice or death to the old way that in all mystical traditions marks the entrance to a more profound understanding. Initiation into the deeper mysteries of life requires in all traditions that people perform a ritual that separates them from everyday life 'in the world', so enabling them to experience a 'second birth' into a new kind of seeing and hearing that is the result of what the alchemists called the *Opus Contra Naturam*, the work against nature.

The distinction in kind between the denigration of the body and all physical, instinctive life and the shaping, ordering and relating of the body and physical life to the ends of the individual as a whole is obviously crucial here. It may never have been helpful to distinguish the elements of this question into terms such as 'spirit' and 'matter', but it certainly is not helpful to polarize the two sides of a conflict into different kinds of entities, and then make one superior to the other. Even if, provisionally, we accept a distinction into 'spirit' and 'matter' – at least in our language – the task of bringing 'them' into harmony is made almost impossible if there is an inherent prejudice against one or the other. What may be less obvious is that it is the images of male and female in the psyche that lie, often invisibly, behind more grandiose statements about what is, or is not, a life of value. Hillman's discussion is central:

> The matter–spirit relation and the difficulties of their harmony reflect, from the psychological point of view, prior difficulties in the harmony of those opposites we call mind and body or, even deeper, male and female ... In other words, the uniform world-picture will depend on the male and female images of the psyche, for even world-pictures are also in part psychological phenomena ... The transformation of our world-view necessitates the transformation of the view of the feminine. Man's view of matter moves when his view of the feminine moves ... The uniform world-image in metaphysics requires a uniformity of self-image in psychology, a conjunction of spirit and matter represented by male and female. The idea of female inferiority is therefore paradigmatic for a group of problems that become manifest at the same time in psychological, social, scientific, and metaphysical areas.[95]

ORIGINAL SIN

The idea of female inferiority may also be paradigmatic for the conception of 'original sin'. What does the world picture of Genesis tell us about the relation between the male and female images of the psyche? That the male images are valued and the female images are not. The primary valuing is, of course, the Father God, who makes heaven and earth through his word, as something apart from himself. The created world then takes on the female image of inferiority, for creation is not of the same substance as the creator. Nature and human nature as part of creation are not divine, for the divine transcends them. In relation to the divine, they are flawed. Adam is female in relation to God, shaped out of the clay and given the breath of life, but male in relation to Eve, who is drawn from his body without the breath of life. Eve is then female in relation to Adam, and 'doubly female' in relation to God. The female human is doubly flawed, as Hillman noted, so that through her the inherent flaw in all creation is exposed. The breath of life is male because it comes from God to Adam, but not Eve, and the clay that comes from nature is female.

In Latin 'breath' is 'spirit', *spiritus* (coming from the father); 'nature' comes from 'birth', *natus*; and matter comes from mother, *Matrix*: Mother Nature. Spirit is male and nature or matter is female – inferior, fallen. Human nature, being female in relation to God, is fallen, sinful. Eve, as doubly fallen, doubly sinful, cannot obey God. Adam could but, because of Eve, does not.

We suggest that the fallacious reasoning here stems from the fact that female images are out of balance with the male images in the human psyche. At some points they are even in direct opposition to each other. No conjunction or harmony between them is possible when they are transferred on to a world picture that is then believed as true. The disharmony between transcendence (male) and immanence (female) will not be experienced as an imbalance to be reflected on, but as the necessary order of things. In studying the writings of the people who formulated the doctrine of original sin, the underlying drama of male and female images may be borne in mind.

Doctrinal Christian thought continued the opposition between the human and the divine, and between nature and spirit, by understanding the divinity of Christ in terms of the redemption of humanity. Christ was to be the Second Adam, who removed, through his death and resurrection, the curse placed upon the first. In Paul's words: 'For since by man came death, by man came also the resurrection of the dead. For as in Adam all die, even so in Christ shall all be made alive' (1 Cor. 15:21–2). It is as if it were believed that by denigrating the one, the other was magnified.

The idea of the Fall, with the related idea of original sin, was therefore central for Christianity in a way that it was not for Judaism, for it provided the point for the counterpoint, which is Redemption. The doctrine of original sin is mainly the creation of the Christian Fathers, who either regarded Eve as the original sinner, or as not capable of sin at all since she was not capable of moral choice. They developed this doctrine in the third and fourth centuries AD, constructing their theories on the second and third chapters of Genesis, and expanding the ideas not of Jesus, but of Paul, who wrote of sin in the same vein as death: 'Wherefore, as by one man sin entered into the world, and death by sin, and so death passed upon all men, for that all have sinned' (Rom. 5:12). They came to believe that the 'sin' of Adam in disobeying God's commandment (Eve is here excluded) impaired a world that had been created perfect.

Origen (third century AD), the most learned and prolific writer of all the Fathers, believed, however, that the Fall did not spoil an already existing world but actually brought it into being. So, following Philo, he held that the coats of skin with which God clothed the nakedness of Adam and Eve were the actual bodies that clothed the soul expelled from its supersensible realm. As we can see below, however, this led him to regard the whole material world as inherently contaminated:[96]

> Everyone who enters the world is said to be affected by a kind of contamination. By the very fact that he is placed in his mother's womb, and that the source from which he takes the material of his body is the father's seed, he may be said to be contaminated in respect of father and mother ... Thus every man is polluted in father and mother and only Jesus my Lord came to birth without stain. He was not polluted in respect of his mother, for he entered a body which was not contaminated.[97]

Perhaps the ultimate statement of original sin may be left to Calvin, who, in 1559, some 1,300 years after Origen, said:

> Therefore original sin is seen to be an hereditary depravity and corruption of our nature, diffused into all parts of the soul ... For our nature is not merely bereft of good but is so productive of every kind of evil that it

cannot be inactive. Those who have called it concupiscence have used a word by no means wide of the mark, if it were added (and this is what many do not concede) that whatever is in man, from intellect to will, from the soul to the flesh, is all defiled and crammed with concupiscence; or, to sum it up briefly, that the whole man is in himself nothing but concupiscence . . .[98]

It was Augustine (AD 354–430), however, who was the main formulator of the doctrine of original sin.[99] As Elaine Pagels argues in her book *Adam, Eve and the Serpent*, Augustine effectively transformed much of the teaching of the Christian faith: 'Instead of the freedom of the will and humanity's original royal dignity, Augustine emphasizes humanity's enslavement to sin. Humanity is sick, suffering, and helpless, irreparably damaged by the fall, for that "original sin".'[100]

As a result of his reflections, theologians believed that life on earth was a curse that was passed from Adam to all future generations by the process of heredity. The fateful means was then the involuntary impulse of desire that led to the sexual act of procreation. Augustine's relentless logic even named the *impulse* to sexuality – lust – as evil, not the act itself, which was barely tolerable even within marriage: 'We ought not to condemn marriage because of the evil of lust, nor must we praise lust because of the good of marriage.'[101]

Warner clarifies Augustine's position:

Augustine suggested that either the hereditary taint was transmitted through the male genitals themselves during intercourse, and that the body itself, not the soul, was genetically flawed by the Fall, or that because a child cannot be conceived outside the sexual embrace, which necessarily involves the sin of passion, the child is stained from that moment. The premise for this literal connection of intercourse and original sin was the virgin birth of Christ. The son of God chose to be born from a virgin mother because this was the only way a child could enter the world without sin.[102]

It seems to be a feature of Augustine's thought that he cannot conceive of the divine without conceiving of what he calls 'the devil':

By a kind of divine justice the human race was handed over to the devil's power, since the sin of the first man passed at birth to all who were born by the intercourse of the two sexes, and the debt of the first parents bound all their posterity . . . The method by which man was surrendered to the devil's power ought not to be understood in the sense that it was God's act, or the result of God's command: rather he merely permitted it, but he did so with justice. When God deserted the sinner, the instigator of the sin rushed in.[103]

Still trying to explain how death and evil entered a world created by a good and omnipotent God, Augustine places the blame for sin on humanity. (So also does the Yahwist writer of the Flood story in Genesis, when he has Yahweh remove the curse he had put on the ground, yet still maintain that 'the imagination of man's heart is evil from his youth' (Gen. 8:21).)

The doctrine of original sin deprived humanity of any innate divinity, and instead named woman and man as innately corrupt and condemned to sin eternally. There was no intrinsic good in the natural world and in human nature. But human beings cannot mistrust their own natures and at the same time trust the divine, since the divine, whatever else the word conveys to those for whom it is meaningful, is at least the name for the source of our being, and if our being is tainted, then so must be our divinity. It is, therefore, consistent with Augustine's premiss that having found our nature tainted 'from the mother's womb',[104] he cannot imagine it redeemed by recourse to any indwelling divine presence, since how would we recognize its voice?

We are not, then, to listen to the depths of our own being and begin the challenging task of discriminating the true from the false, but are to displace our devotion on to an external authority, the Church, which will *relate* us to what we *are* not. For this to happen, we are to believe its doctrines and observe its rituals, starting at birth to baptize away sin. Inevitably, from this starting point, humanity requires an intermediary between its innate sinfulness and the goodness of God, so the abstraction of 'the Church' replaced the immanence of the Holy Spirit dwelling immediately (and without need of interpretation) within all life.

If humanity is corrupt, then woman, because of Eve, is more so. Here, Augustine's position is disclosed in what he does not say:

> Eve would not have believed the serpent, nor would Adam have preferred his wife's wish to God's command . . . The transgression happened because they are already evil; that evil fruit could come only from an evil tree, a tree which had become unnaturally evil through unnatural viciousness of the will . . . The grievousness of Adam's fall was in proportion to the loftiness of his position. His nature was such as to be capable of immortality if it had refused to sin; his nature was such as to display no strife of flesh against spirit; his nature was such as to show no struggle against vice, not because it surrendered to vice, but because there was no vice in him . . . The sin with which God charged Adam was a sin from which he could have refrained . . . and a sin which was far worse than the sins of all other men just because he was so much better than all others. Hence the punishment which straight-away followed his sin was so severe as to make it inevitable that he should die, though it had been in his power to be free from death . . . Now when this happened the whole human race was 'in his loins.' Hence in accordance with the mysterious and powerful natural laws of heredity it followed that those who were in his loins and were to come into this world through the concupiscence of the flesh were condemned with him . . . And so the sons of Adam were infected by the contagion of sin and subjected to the law of death. Though they are infants, incapable of voluntary action, good or bad, yet because of their involvement in him who sinned of his own volition, they derive from him the guilt of sin, and the punishment of death: just as those who are involved in Christ, although they have done nothing of their own volition, receive from him a share in righteousness and the reward of everlasting life.[105]

In this passage Eve's part in the engendering of the human race is strikingly absent, since it is in Adam's 'loins' only that the whole human race exists *in potentia*. As the medical historian Edelstein observes: 'The theory of the human body is always a part of philosophy.'[106] Furthermore, Eve is guilty of listening to a 'serpent', whereas Adam 'fell' from the 'loftiness of his position' of being apparently the only one of them capable of immortality. Eve is placed in communion with a reptile of the earth (concretely visualized), while Adam communes with 'his wife' – understandably beguiled (for this one time only) into assuming she is his moral equal – and he communes with God, who made him but not her. Adam names the animals, as he does his wife, but he does not converse with them. Again, the implication is not hard to find: Eve is closer to, that is, 'more like', the animals without souls, and furthest from the specifically human condition of conscience and self-consciousness which Adam embodies. The imagery of Genesis draws her as an instinctive not a moral being. She liked the look of the tree – it was 'good for food' and 'pleasant to the eyes', and 'to be desired' to make one wise, as though (woman that she was) she assumed that wisdom was instantly available simply by virtue of being desired. Yet take the story not literally but symbolically, and the meanings change into their opposite. Symbolically, the feminine principle in human beings of both sexes is more receptive to the instinctive and intuitive wisdom that transcends the limits of any one conscious viewpoint, and is therefore 'closer to God'. Here, the serpent is the image of that divine curiosity which disturbs the established order so that we are drawn deeper into understanding. Then, like the caduceus of intertwining snakes, the magic wand of Hermes, god of imagination, the serpent transforms and heals the limitations of an exclusively conscious viewpoint, dogmatically held. But literally interpreted, as a woman who takes the word of a serpent over God's injunction, she is closer to the devil (doubly female).

The anomalies in Augustine's discussion fall into place when we read elsewhere: 'The image of God is in man and it is one. Women were drawn from man who has God's jurisdiction as if he were God's vicar because he has the image of the one God. Therefore, woman is not made in God's image.'[107]

Philip Sherrard sets the legacy of Augustine in perspective. It is, he writes,

> one of the paradoxes, and also one of the tragedies, of the western Christian tradition that the man who affirmed so strongly the presence of God in the depths of his own self and so the ultimate independence of the human personality from all worldly categories should as a dogmatic theologian have been responsible more perhaps than any other Christian writer for 'consecrating' within the Christian world the idea of man's slavery and impotence due to the radical perversion of human nature through original sin. It has been St Augustine's theology which in the West has veiled down to the present

day the full radiance of the Christian revelation of divine sonship – the full revelation of who man essentially is.[108]

Although the idea of humanity's innate sinfulness has been held in the unconscious psyche for many centuries, it can be re-evaluated in the same way that any idea can once it has become conscious. In any other discipline we might ask 'why do we need this idea?' It purports to explain what Antony on the murder of Julius Caesar calls 'the evil that men do', which 'lives after them'.[109] But in so far as it explains that, it does not explain the good that men do, which also lives after them. On the contrary, like any negative idea, it is more likely to create and sustain the thing it condemns. Blake's words 'Error, or Creation, is Burnt up the Moment men cease to behold it'[110] may be relevant to the suggestion that in perpetuating the belief of primordial sin, we bring about the conditions where 'sin' is engendered, for we deprive ourselves of the habit of trusting ourselves and looking within for moral guidance. However, Blake's fundamental conviction was that 'everything that lives is Holy'. It is sad that the insight Augustine recorded late in his life was not available to him in time to redeem his conviction of his own and humanity's sinfulness: 'Too late came I to thee, O thou Beauty both so ancient and so fresh, Yea, too late came I to love thee. And behold, thou wert within me, and I out of myself, where I made search for thee.'[111]

MARY AS THE SECOND EVE

Central to Christian doctrine from the fourth century AD was the teaching that as Christ was the Second Adam, so Mary was the 'Second Eve', that Mary through her virginity had redeemed the sin of Eve. The paradise that had been lost was now regained, since the transmission of original sin had been finally interrupted by the untainted birth of Christ. As Jerome said, 'Now the chain of the curse is broken. Death came through Eve, but life has come through Mary.'[112] And Irenaeus declared: 'Eve by her disobedience brought death upon herself and on all the human race: Mary, by her obedience, brought salvation.'[113]

It is fundamentally Mary's virginity that is the cornerstone of Christian theology, for without it there could be no 'Son of God' and no suspension of the laws of nature that manifest in the human being as original sin 'from the mother's womb', as Saint Augustine locates it. Jesus would have been a man like other men, and it would have been impossible to render him Christ the Redeemer of Sin. So, in the Christian tradition it was essential to provide a doctrine of the immaculate conception of Jesus, and equally essential, later, to extend the idea of immaculate conception to Mary herself, so that she would also be completely free of any taint of the 'original' sin, now unquestionably human sexuality. Logically, Mary's mother, Anne, should also have had the taint removed from her, and so,

Figure 22. *The Annunciation*, Fra Angelico, *c.* 1432–3. The orange wings of
the angel, whose tips alight in the Garden of Eden at the moment of Adam
and Eve's expulsion, fragment the focus of the picture. The eye cannot rest
with either Mary or Adam and Eve, but, alternating between them, finally
acknowledges their relationship through the angel.

also, the whole line of ancestresses back to and including Eve. Divinity of
parentage and a miraculous birth are common to all mythic traditions as a
way of acknowledging the one who becomes the hero or the saviour of the
community,[114] but this myth bore the unique burden of redeeming the
whole of nature.

Mary's virginity was defined in imagery that banished sexuality and
birth from embodying an aspect of divinity. She becomes the mother of
the Redeemer and the mother of all believers, but she is no longer the
mother of all living, as Eve was. So the natural processes of birth by
which all living creatures come into being are rejected as links in the
corrupting chain of original sin. Mary's womb, unlike Eve's, is uncor-
rupted by human fecundation, or the human processes of birth. In the
imagery of the Song of Songs, it is 'a garden enclosed . . . a spring shut
up, a fountain sealed' (S. of S. 4:12).

Mary served only to make things worse for Eve. As Tertullian himself
explains it: 'Eve becomes more evil because Mary is the perfect woman.'
He explains further:

Eve believed the serpent, Mary believed Gabriel; the one sinned by believing, the other by believing effaced the sin. But did Eve conceive nothing in her womb from the devil's word? She certainly did. For the devil's word was the seed for her, so that thereafter she should give birth as an outcast, and give birth in sorrow. And in fact she bore a devil who murdered his brother; while Mary gave birth to one who should in time bring salvation to Israel.[115]

Mary became virgin before, during and after the birth of her son (*aeiparthenos*). There could be no 'rite of passage' either in or out of her womb, which therefore remained uncontaminated either by the sexual act, or by the blood, 'urine and faeces' of birth. Everything 'natural' had to be removed from association with her, because what was natural was bound to the corruption of sexuality and the decay of death. Woman, through whom birth came, was, by inverse logic, the one through whom death came. Coitus, Phillips writes, became 'the means by which the sins of the fathers and mothers are visited on the sons and daughters. Sin, sexuality and death were thus woven into the tapestry depicting Eve; obedience, virginity, and eternal life became shining attributes of Mary.'[116]

Virginity was identified with freedom from sin, which implicitly turned sexuality into the primary sin. However, the association of virginity with freedom from sin, and so with the promise of eternal life, involved the Christian Fathers in the contradiction that death could be overcome only by denying the natural process of entry into life. Evidently, the way to achieve immortality was not to be born at all! The theoretical assumption that Christianity has not devalued nature and that there is no dualism involved in its teaching is thoroughly undermined by the 'logic' of these images.

What was the effect on women in particular of this absolute polarization of spirit and nature, which identified 'spirit' with the immaculate Mary and 'nature' with the sinful Eve? If they could not emulate Mary's virginity, they were condemned to align themselves with Eve. There was no way in which they could combine within themselves the opposing roles of virgin and mother, for their motherhood could never achieve Mary's perpetual virginity (the inviolate hymen), nor their virginity her fortunate motherhood. They could, therefore, identify themselves only with Eve. In the Judaeo-Christian tradition of mythic images women had none of the variety of models that existed in Greece in the figures of Athena, Artemis and Aphrodite, as well as Demeter, Persephone, Hera and Hestia, goddess of the hearth and home. Instead, as either Mary or Eve, the reality of woman was wholly imagined in sexual or relational terms as mother, wife, virgin or whore. Even Mary Magdalene, who might have escaped conventional definition, was called a 'penitent whore'. Where is the image of woman independent of relationship to man or child unless, to go full circle, it be Lilith?

EVE IN PROTESTANT THEOLOGY

With the Reformation there might have been a hope of a new interpretation of the Genesis myth, and with it a change in attitude towards women
and men. Not only did the old ideas endure, however, but they were
given new confirmation by Luther and his successors. Luther and Calvin
in the sixteenth century both started out following the first chapter of
Genesis, and declaring woman to be equal to man. But then, working out
the reasons for the Fall, they both came to the conclusion that it was
Eve's independence that was the cause of her being able to lead Adam
into sin: and so determined that woman should be the compliant partner
of man, subject to his will in all things. This subjugation is punishment
for her sin and the expression of divine justice, such that any refusal on
the part of woman to accept the social order must be understood as a
further sin: a refusal to accept the judgement of God.[117] Woman's place in
relation to man's was to be based on Eve's to Adam's. She is, Luther
writes, in his act of nailing, like 'a nail driven into the wall':

> Now there is added to these sorrows of gestation and birth that Eve has
> been placed under the power of her husband ... This punishment, too,
> springs from original sin, and the woman bears it just as unwillingly as she
> bears those pains and inconveniences that have been placed upon her flesh.
> The rule remains with the husband, and the wife is compelled to obey him
> by God's command. He rules the home and the state, wages wars, defends
> his possessions, tills the soil, builds, plants, etc. The woman, on the other
> hand, is like a nail driven into the wall. She sits at home and ... does not go
> beyond her most personal duties ... Women are generally disinclined to
> put up with this burden, and they naturally seek to gain what they have lost
> through sin. If they are unable to do more, they at least indicate their
> impatience through grumbling. However, they cannot perform the functions
> of men: teach, rule, etc. In procreation and in feeding and nurturing their
> offspring they are masters. In this way Eve is punished; but, as I said at the
> beginning, it is a gladsome punishment if you consider the hope of eternal
> life and the honour of motherhood which have been left her.[118]

This attitude, which was in essence no different from the early Christian
and medieval ideal, found its way into Lutheran, Calvinist and Puritan
teaching. 'It cannot be denied', wrote Calvin reluctantly, 'but that the
woman was created after the image of God, though in the second
degree.'[119] Luther, commenting on Genesis, drew on the old Iron Age
imagery to make the same point: 'For as the sun is more excellent than
the moon, so the woman, although she was a most beautiful work of God,
was none the less not the equal of the male in glory and prestige.'[120] The
notion of woman is thus rendered equivalent to the notion of fallen
woman, so she becomes in her person a living reproach to the sinfulness
of her nature at having merited the punishment of subjugation.

For Calvin, the subordination of women to men took its justification from the hierarchical order that God intended. It reflected the divinely appointed social order in which man was to rule and woman was to obey. As the Good Book said: 'Thy desire shall be to thy husband, and he shall rule over thee.'

> For this speache, 'Thy lust shall belong to thy husband' is as much in effecte, as if he should denied that shee should be free, on her owne, but subject to the rule of her husband, to depend upon his will and pleasure: As if he should say, Thou shalt desire nothing but what the husband will. Even so the woman, which had perversely exceeded her boundes, is restrained and bridled.[121]

These sentiments informed the work of successive Protestant theologians, until this century, in the writings of Karl Barth, a final 'nail' fixes Eve's descendants in their place: 'Woman does not have a single possibility apart from being man's helpmeet ... Being herself the completion of man's humanity she has no further need of a further completion of her own.'[122] It is his view that the 'command of the Lord' does not dishonour or humiliate anyone. Rather, 'it puts both man and woman in their proper place', which, for woman, is to be woman: 'The essential point is that woman must always and in all circumstances be woman; that she must see and conduct herself as such and not as a man.'[123] There is no mention here of the possibility of man being himself the completion of woman's humanity, and no conception of man and woman each finding the completion of their humanity in their own unique individuality, or in their relation to their own divinity, still less the heretical idea that 'God's humanity' could be explored through human beings. In contrast, the Van Eycks' conception of Adam and Eve (Fig. 23) makes no judgement between them, and draws them as partners in relationship on the soul's journey.

In the continuing story of Eve can be read the result of the imbalance between the masculine and feminine principles that was ratified in the story of the *Enuma Elish*. The myth, with its Jewish, Christian and Islamic interpretations, has persisted, but the original historical situation and human experience that brought it into existence have been forgotten. Furthermore, the symbolic meaning of the myth as the birth of consciousness is completely obscured to those who take it as divine revelation. The innocent phrases that explore humanity's most testing moment have been abstracted from the narrative, generalized out of context, and wrenched into shapes that support the prevailing social order. The 'nervous discord' between the image and the word can be overcome if the myth is read symbolically as a tragic myth that treats of one dimension of human existence, the *kathodos* or going down, but not the *anodos*, the coming up into the mythic vision. But, read concretely, the image is sacrificed to the interpretation of the word, and so the inherent joyousness of the images cannot reach the feelings they exist to move. Any myth

Figure 23. Adam and Eve; detail from *The Mystic Lamb* in the Ghent Altarpiece, Hubert and Jan Van Eyck, 1432. St Bavo, Ghent, Belgium.

taken literally confuses two levels of understanding or two modes of discourse, and so is bound to destroy the life it was conceived to discover. To this, Genesis is no exception.

EVE AND NATURE

There are now more urgent implications of the consistent misreading of this myth throughout the last 2,000 years of our mythological tradition. And these affect, quite crucially, our present attitudes to nature and the 'body' of the Earth. There has never been in Christianity, as there was in the goddess cultures, an understanding of the Earth as a 'living being', still less an awareness that Everything was Holy, since belief in divine immanence was doctrinally dismissed as belief in spirits. The goddesses and gods of pagan cultures were thought of as demons, and the values expressed through them were regarded as demonic. Yet the Oxyrhynchus Manuscript gives the words of Jesus that show that the earlier vision of the sacredness of nature was an integral part of his teaching:

> Who then are they that draw us and when shall come the Kingdom that is in heaven?
> The fowls of the air and of the beasts whatever is beneath the earth or upon the earth, and the fishes of the sea, these they are that draw you. And the Kingdom of heaven is within you and whosoever knoweth himself shall find it. And, having found it, ye shall know yourselves that ye are sons and heirs of the Father, the Almighty, and shall know yourselves that ye are in God and God in you.[124]

If nature is not believed to be intrinsically divine, and instead is only 'made' by the deity as something separate from the whole, and if the physical processes of birth and begetting are experienced as a transmission of sin from generation to generation, then it is hardly surprising if they are eventually regarded as mechanistic. Consequently, nature has been progressively desacralized from Augustine, through Aquinas, to the development of science from the sixteenth century to the present day. It was Francis Bacon who said that nature should be 'hounded in her wandering ... bound into service ... made a slave'. Borrowing the language of the Inquisition, nature was to be 'put in constraint' and the aim of the scientist was to 'torture' her secrets from her.[125] Descartes also wrote that humanity's ultimate purpose was to become the 'Lords and Masters of Nature'.[126] Such language would be inconceivable in a culture that believed in divine immanence.

Until very recently matter was regarded as so emptied of spirit that it was thought to be 'inert', even 'dead'. Jung said:

> Today we talk of 'matter'. We describe its physical properties. We conduct laboratory experiments to demonstrate some of its aspects. But the word

'matter' remains a dry, inhuman, and purely intellectual concept, without any psychic significance for us. How different was the former image of matter – the Great Mother – that could encompass and express the profound emotional meaning of Mother Earth.[127]

Science now suggests that there is no such thing as 'death' in matter, for even the decomposed body, reduced to atoms and molecules, *is* 'alive'. Although Christian doctrine taught that human beings had souls and that they were a composite unity of body and soul, it did not, in the Western tradition, teach that the divine, therefore, dwelt within them. Moreover, the identification of the body with evil, and of the soul with a state of primordial and inherited sinfulness, effectively deprived both human nature and nature of any intrinsic divinity.

Aristotle was a vital factor in this process, for his works, translated into Latin from the beginning of the twelfth century, had a radical effect on doctrinal Christianity through their influence on Thomas Aquinas. It was at this point that the Platonic image of a great chain of being, emanating from the source of life in the highest pleromatic sphere and descending by a succession of hierarchical stages, infusing the lowest emanation of the manifest world with being, was lost. It was replaced by the Aristotelian idea that the universal cannot be present in a particular substance or entity. The same notion is also found in Tertullian's writings: 'Flesh does not become spirit nor spirit flesh.'[128] Through Aristotle's influence on Aquinas the idea is developed that there are two orders, a supernatural and a natural, and that humanity belongs to the natural order rather than to the supernatural. Soul is reduced to the rational principle in human beings, which cannot know God through participation in the life emanating from the source, but can only learn *about* God. Its knowing is not informed by the active intelligence and insight of divine wisdom present within it or co-inherent with it, but is something more like intellect, or the ability to reason, which is created *by* God but not part *of* God.

The soul, and even more the body, is not then an emanation of the creator, who stands apart from both body and soul in the way that the creator stood apart from creation in Genesis. The effect of this doctrine was to split spirit once again from nature, and the unmanifest life from the manifest. Aquinas's thought, steeped in the rigid distinction between universal and particular made by Aristotle, compounded the impact of the doctrine of original sin, for it stated once again that there could be in nature and humanity no indwelling divine spirit. The teaching of Jesus that humanity as the son was part of the Father (just as in the goddess culture humanity had been the child of the Mother) could have bridged this great divide. However, the doctrine of the Incarnation of Christ developed by the Church could not allow this, for the divine event was interpreted as taking place uniquely, in one man only on behalf of humanity, but not within all humanity, nor in the whole of creation. So the insight contained in Jesus' words in the Gnostic Gospel of Thomas was lost, and the wound in the soul was not healed but exacerbated.

Here Jesus creates an image beyond duality, significantly bringing into complete harmony the male and female images of the soul:

> When you make the two one, and when you make the inner as the outer and the outer as the inner and the above as the below, and when you make the male and female into a single one, so that the male will not be male and the female (not) be female . . . then you shall enter (the Kingdom).[129]

And again, he offers an unforgettable image of divine immanence:

> Cleave a (piece of) wood, I am there;
> lift up the stone and you will find Me there.[130]

The way we look upon nature reflects ideas *about* nature, which in turn reflect the way we look upon human nature. We might wonder if the notion of original sin was begotten by those who could not love life in its entirety, for no mystic of any tradition excludes one part of life from the whole. Is 'Yahweh's' curse (literally taken) then not rather the Yahwist's curse, and the curse also of those who followed him, the rage of humanity against what it sees as its own annihilation? By contrast, Blake directs our thought inwards: 'To the Eyes of the Man of Imagination, Nature is Imagination itself. As a man is, so he sees. As the Eye is formed, such are its Powers.'[131] As in every culture, the poet's vision is one of unity:

> Vast chain of being! which from God began,
> Nature's aethereal, human, angel, man,
> Beast, bird, fish, insect, what no eye can see,
> No glass can reach; from Infinite to thee,
> From thee to nothing. – On superior pow'rs
> Were we to press, inferior might on ours;
> Or in the full creation leave a void,
> Where, one step broken, the great scale's destroyed;
> From Nature's chain whatever link you strike,
> Tenth, or ten thousandth, breaks the chain alike.[132]

The image of a path of descent and ascent for angelic beings or souls, which occurs in Jacob's dream of the ladder extending between heaven and earth, and which inspired Blake (Fig. 24), may also convey the idea of a continuous chain of relationship throughout creation.

The myth of the Garden of Eden could also be understood as symbolizing the memory of an original wholeness, which is forgotten in the eating of the fruit of the Tree of Knowledge, drawing us into time and consciousness, and sending us each on a unique journey of exploration. But the fruit of the Garden that has been ingested, continues to live inside us as the impulse to remember the state of union before dismemberment in time, for the memory persists in echoes and glimpses that cannot be

Figure 24. *Jacob's Dream*; William Blake, 1805.

explained and will not go away. Yeats's 'Anima Mundi' and 'Great Memory', Jung's 'Collective Unconscious' and Black Elk's 'Sacred Hoop of the World'[133] may come from this source, as may the often dreamed-of 'Akashic Records' as well as Plato's theory of Knowledge as Recollection, *Anamnesis*. Nearer to our own time, the idea, nourished by the Neo-platonic tradition, that the soul retains the memory of its place of origin but can no longer perceive it, is expressed by Shakespeare through Lorenzo's love for Jessica:

> How sweet the moonlight sleeps upon this bank!
> Here will we sit, and let the sounds of music
> Creep in our ears; soft stillness and the night
> Become the touches of sweet harmony.
> Sit Jessica. Look how the floor of heaven
> Is thick inlayed with patines of bright gold;
> There's not the smallest orb which thou behold'st
> But in his motion like an angel sings,
> Still quiring to the young-ey'd cherubims;
> Such harmony is in immortal souls;
> But whilst this muddy vesture of decay
> Doth grossly clothe it in, we cannot hear it.[134]

14

MARY:
THE RETURN OF THE GODDESS

The threefold terror of love; a fallen flare
Through the hollow of an ear;
Wings beating about the room;
The terror of all terrors that I bore
The Heavens in my womb.

W. B. Yeats

Jesus, the Imagination.

William Blake

When the fifteenth-century French triptych in Figure 1 is open, Mary is the declared Great Mother Goddess in whose body lives God, the Father, as her son, holding the cross of destiny for Christ, his son. In turn, God's son lies back into the lap of God as a child upon his knee, even as God himself is seated, as it were, in the lap of Mary, who becomes thereby his Goddess Mother.

When the triptych is shut (Fig. 2), the symbolic reading of Mary in the mythic tradition is also closed, and Mary is restored to the more familiar posture of the human mother with the divine child who is to redeem the sin of the world-apple of Eve, which Mary, as the Second Eve, holds in her hand. But, once opened, the meaning of the closed and literal picture is never the same, and the eye is drawn irresistibly to the crack down the centre through which the symbolic depths were irrevocably disclosed. The outward figure of human maternity reveals itself to be an illusion of incarnation that the inward timeless drama comprehends.

Doctrinally, this would be heresy, and, predictably, the same disjunction between orthodox word and image that began with Eve is perpetuated in Mary; for, in complete contradiction to the New Testament text and canonical statements, the poetic vision of Mary – in icon, painting or hymn – brings her to life in the old images of the past. Here she is drawn as the Great Mother of Life and Death, Queen of Heaven, Earth and Underworld, Goddess of the Animals and Plants, and Goddess of the Wisdom of the Soul.

Mary is the unrecognized Mother Goddess of the Christian tradition. Apart from the first chapter of Luke, where she holds the centre of the stage in the story of the Annunciation, Mary appears very infrequently in

Figure 1. (*Left*) Vierge Ouvrante, open; carved and painted wood,
fifteenth century AD. France.
Figure 2. (*Right*) Vierge Ouvrante closed; fifteenth century AD. France.

the Gospels, and then she plays a completely subordinate role to her son.
Yet within 500 years of her 'death' a pantheon of images enveloped her
until she assumed the presence and stature of all the goddesses before her
– Cybele, Aphrodite, Demeter, Astarte, Isis, Hathor, Inanna and Ishtar.
Like them, she is both virgin and mother, and, like many of them, she
gives birth to a half-human, half-divine child, who dies and is reborn.
Jesus, like Attis, Adonis, Persephone, Osiris, Tammuz and Dumuzi before
him, descends into the underworld of hell, where regeneration has always
taken place, and his ascent and resurrection, like theirs, is understood to
redeem all incarnate being from the limitation of mortality and time.

Following the symbolic pattern of the earlier deities in whom this
central mystery has been enacted, Jesus, as *bios*, the Son – archetype of
incarnate being – born from *zoe*, the Mother – archetype of the source of
being – suffers dismemberment in time, and is then restored to that
source that is at once the origin and end of incarnation. When, in pictures of *The Coronation of the Virgin,* Jesus offers Mary the crown as they
sit together on the Throne of Heaven, it is difficult not to look through
the Christian tradition to the myth of the 'sacred marriage' of *zoe* and
bios, which, in every tradition, signifies transformation. Campbell's introduction to Mary locates her within the mythic tradition:

It is simply a fact – deal with it how you will – that the mythology of the dead and resurrected god has been known for millenniums to the neolithic and post-neolithic Levant . . . The entire ancient world, from Asia Minor to the Nile and from Greece to the Indus Valley, abounds in figurines of the naked female form, in various attitudes of the all-supporting, all-including goddess . . . And so it came to pass that, in the end and to our day, Mary, Queen of Martyrs, became the sole inheritor of all the names and forms, sorrows, joys, and consolations of the goddess-mother in the Western World: Seat of Wisdom . . . Vessel of Honour . . . Mystical Rose . . . House of Gold . . . Gate of Heaven . . . Morning Star . . . Refuge of Sinners . . . Queen of Angels . . . Queen of Peace.[1]

THE MAKING OF A GODDESS

'The "making of a goddess" ', Harrison writes, 'is always a mystery, the outcome of manifold causes of which we have lost count.'[2] Nearly 2,000 years after the Gospels were written, the 'Virgin Mary', in the dogma of the Catholic Church, is Mother of God, Perpetually Virgin, Immaculately Conceived, and Assumed into Heaven, Body and Soul, where she reigns as Queen. Yet Mary's birth and death are not even mentioned in the Scriptures, so this picture of her cannot offer itself as a factual description of a particular historical person, but must, yet again, be the continuing story of the human imagination.

Reading this liturgy to Mary in relation to the figure in the Gospels, it is astonishing how far she has come from the original story, as most of the images that her name brings to mind have found their way to her afterwards. In the New Testament, Mary is only a human woman, who 'found favour with God' (Luke 1:30). All stories about her agree that she is the mother of Jesus, but only Matthew calls her a virgin unequivocally, saying that before Mary and Joseph 'came together, she was found with child of the Holy Ghost' (Matt.1:18). Luke implies that she is a virgin, though his purpose is less to wonder at the miracle of Mary's physical intactness than to point to the divinity of her child, for if she is virgin, then her child must be the child of God, not of a man: 'For with God nothing shall be impossible.'

> Then said Mary unto the angel, How shall this be, seeing I know not a man?
> And the angel answered and said unto her, The Holy Ghost shall come upon thee, and the power of the Highest shall overshadow thee: therefore also that holy thing which shall be born of thee shall be called the Son of God. (Luke 1:34–5)[3]

In the New Testament Mary's significance is entirely secondary: she is the inviolate vessel for God's holy 'word'; she bears the Christ, but she is not herself a goddess. Her character, in so far as she is given one, is a model of loving obedience to something higher than herself. She also has her own source of strength, for, in Luke at least, she is reflective, and where the signs of her son's divinity break through, she 'keeps' these things in her heart and 'ponders' them. Like any mother, she sees beyond her child and fosters his growing. But in all this she is simply the mother of Jesus.

Even where she is presented as a virgin mother, she is not the only woman for whom the laws of nature are suspended. Before the angel visits Mary, he appears to Zacharias on behalf of his wife, Elizabeth, Mary's cousin, who, in spite of her many years and barren womb, is to give birth to John the Baptist, the one who proclaims and baptizes Jesus as the Christ. For both women, it is their relation to Christ that brings divine intervention and, with Mary, divine impregnation.

None the less, by AD 431, at a council in Ephesus presided over by Cyril of Alexandria, Mary was proclaimed not just 'Christ-bearer' but 'God-bearer', *Theotokos*; so what had happened? By the fourth century the status of Mary was obviously already a matter of concern, for Epiphanius, the Christian Father, made a precise distinction: 'Let Mary be honoured, but let the Father, the Son and the Holy Spirit be adored.' At the First Council of Constantinople in the fourth century Mary's virgin motherhood was proclaimed as a way of securing the divinity of Christ by pointing to the suspension of natural law in the manner of his incarnation. Now, early in the fifth century, the Patriarch of Constantinople, Nestorius, insisted that Christ had two natures, a human one and a divine one, which meant that Mary was the bearer of Christ, but could not be the bearer of God. The Bishops of Syria agreed with him, but Cyril, the Patriarch of Alexandria, did not. A council was then convened to discuss this question at Ephesus, but Cyril declared the council open before the Syrian bishops had arrived, and immediately excommunicated Nestorius, who had no supporters present to argue his case. Such was the rather dubious and very human foundation for the conclusion whose divine sanction was nevermore to be doubted.

Ephesus was, significantly, the very place where the great temple to Artemis, or Diana as she was called in Roman times, had stood for many centuries. The cult of Artemis or Diana had been repressed in AD 380 by the Emperor Theodosius, and the people, deprived of their goddess, readily turned to Mary instead. The first picture of Mary had appeared in the catacombs in the second century AD, but from now on portraits of Mary began to proliferate, one of them said to have been painted by Luke himself. Another was sent from Jerusalem to Constantinople, where, hundreds of years later, it was to be carried into battle on a chariot, so, it may be observed, re-enacting the old role of the Goddess of War. Portraits from the end of the fourth century and beginning of the fifth show Mary seated in the same position as Isis with Horus, wearing the mural crown of Cybele or Diana, and with the gorgon of Athena painted on her breast.

Athena's own temple, the Parthenon, became Mary's church only 100 or so years later, sometime between AD 500 and 600.

It had taken less than a century for Mary to take over the role of Isis, Cybele and Diana, the remaining goddesses, whose cults had dwindled with the decline of the Roman Empire and were, in any case, often suppressed, with their temples closed and their teachers and priests banished. In fact, it looks as if the imagery of the older goddesses had passed directly on to the figure of Mary, inspired by the needs of the people and perhaps also by the understanding of the priests that these long-established customs of devotion had to be understood in terms of the new religion. Sometime between AD 400 and 500 the Temple of Isis at Soissons in France was dedicated to the 'Blessed Virgin Mary'. Isis and Cybele had been 'Mother of the Gods'; Mary was now 'Mother of God'.

The implications of this position were addressed in AD 451, when, at the Council of Chalcedon, the Fourth Ecumenical Council of the Church, Mary was awarded the greatest honour in Christendom: she was given the official title of *Aeiparthenos*, 'Ever-Virgin', so she was now deemed to be virgin before, during and after birth (leaving faithfully to God the question of how the baby was born at all).

After the fifth century Mary's abrupt removal from the human condition slowed down, and her cult grew by concentrating on what was already established: her divine motherhood and her role in the conception of Christ, which was understood as her virginity. As had happened with Isis in Rome, the Christian Fathers were obliged at different stages to redefine her position in response to popular demand. Feasts of the Virgin were now for the first time instituted in Byzantium, commemorating her role in the Incarnation – first the Annunciation, and then her Virginity. By the beginning of the seventh century a further crucial distinction between Mary and ordinary humanity emerged: the conviction that she could not die. Around AD 600 the feast of the Dormition, or Falling Asleep of the Virgin, was celebrated on 15 August, and fifty years later two more days of the year were set aside for her Nativity and Presentation in the Temple, based on the Apocryphal book of James. Later in the seventh century, these feast days were brought to Rome by monks escaping from the Holy Land, which was being invaded by the Muslims, and then the feast of the Presentation became, significantly, the feast of Mary's Purification. It was moved from 21 November to 2 February, the dark time of the old year, offering then, most subtly, a new image of the light conquering the darkness. Purity from the natural process of conception – sex – now symbolically banished what, in the pagan feast of lights of the same date, used to be the spirits of plague, famine and earthquake, but was now implicitly redefined as the dangers of the flesh.

Mary's cult reached its height in the Middle Ages and early Renaissance, from the eleventh to the fifteenth century. Between 1170 and 1270, for instance, in France alone over 100 churches and 80 cathedrals were built in her honour. She was constantly celebrated in the poetry and music of the troubadours, and painted over and over again by artists who saw beyond the religious iconography of the time to what she had been in the past and what she was to become several centuries later; for in 1854 the Catholic Church declared Mary to be 'immaculately conceived' as well as 'immaculately conceiving', thereby reassuming the virgin imagery of the ancient goddesses, though with fatally new, limited and literal meaning. This papal bull, entitled *Ineffabilis Deus*, was given in response to an immense popular demand that had begun in the twelfth century, as though something fundamental was felt to be missing in the existing ways of relating to the sacred dimension. Its importance is clear from the fact that it was followed by another bull sixteen years later, which declared as dogma the infallibility of the pope, effectively making it impossible to challenge the Church on any article of dogma.

The theology in which the image of Mary was enclosed had the same material and literal cast of mind as that which indicted Eve. It is as though it was thought that the divine could be imagined merely by reversing the conditions that obtain for humans. The dogma declared that Mary was preserved from all taint of 'original sin', even from 'concupiscence' or the 'incentive to sin'. Quite what she was thereby preserved from became a matter for unremitting inquiry. The idea of Mary's 'Immaculate Conception' had been initiated by Augustine, convinced that, though Mary was born into the world in the normal way from her mother, Anne, she must somehow be exempt from the sinfulness he had declared implicit in it, by which he meant, presumably, the lust of her parents in the coital act. (*Maculare*, which in Latin means 'to stain' or 'to pollute', is, then, how every human being comes into incarnation.) Augustine did not feel, to be precise, that Mary had actually been conceived 'immaculately', but that she was made immaculate, retrospectively, as it were, by her son through her perfect obedience to divine will.

As the New Testament offered no reference to Mary's 'divine' birth, or even her divine life, the argument was theoretical and counterfactual. Mary must have been immaculate or she could not have been Christ's mother. Quite where her immaculateness was to stop was then a considerable problem. Bernard of Clairvaux, in the twelfth century, for instance, understood the elevation of Mary's conception to be inseparable from undue reverence to the intercourse of her parents. In the thirteenth century Duns Scotus made the issue more palatable by obscuring it, suggesting that 'the Virgin had been *preserved* from sin from the moment of her conception until the Redemption of the Cross, when she, like all the human race, had been saved'.[4] The Protestant Churches never accepted the doctrine of the Assumption, any more than the Immaculate Conception of Mary, and Luther refused to celebrate the feast of 15 August: hence in the sixteenth century came the instruction: 'Ye shall sing no more praises to Our Lady, only to Our Lord.'

But this elevation to the more-than-human condition was obviously still not sufficient to answer what was missing in the hearts and minds of the Catholic people, and the priests as well. A little less than 100 years after the 1854 declaration of Mary's 'Immaculate Conception', in 1950, a petition was signed by 8 million people. As a result, Pope Pius XII declared the Assumption of the Virgin as official doctrine, stating that Mary was 'taken up body and soul into the glory of heaven',[5] an announcement that was greeted with thunderous applause in the square in front of St Peter's Basilica. Only four years later, in 1954, the Catholic Church proclaimed her 'Queen of Heaven', though notably not 'Queen of Earth', while she had effectively been 'Queen of the Underworld' for many centuries in her capacity as merciful intercessor with her son for the souls of the dead.

At this point, in the doctrinal view, she stands between Earth and Heaven as the principal mediator between the human and divine dimensions of life. The special position she holds is reflected in the worship that is deemed appropriate to her. God is owed *latria*, adoration, while the saints may receive *dulia*, veneration, but Mary is entitled to *hyperdulia*, superior veneration; less than fully divine, but more than fully human.

Even in orthodox doctrine, then, it seems as if the 'making of a goddess' is close to completion, or complete in all but name. But if Mary has grown to the stature of a goddess, and yet she is not formally recognized as being wholly divine, we may wonder whether the collective psyche of our time is caught in a fundamental contradiction. In many Catholic countries Mary is worshipped as totally and devoutly as were the goddess figures of old, yet this 'goddess' does not bring forth the world from the inexhaustible source that is herself, the original symbolic meaning of 'virgin'; she is only a maiden pure from the 'sin' of sexual relationship, chosen to bear divinity but not herself divine. She cannot, therefore, inhabit the archetypal reality of the Great Mother, with the result that, when she is worshipped, the whole of life cannot be experienced through her. Only Mary's son is truly divine, and he must return to his Father, who sent him, leaving his mother, as it were, neither here nor There.

'Between' Earth and Heaven, albeit as their mediator, is not the same as beyond yet within both, when their opposition is shown to be illusory. By this time in the history of the images of earth and heaven, 'earth' no longer signifies the divine immanent in nature, but represents fallen nature, or 'this world', and 'heaven' represents transcendent spirit, or 'the next world'. So from within Christian premises it is understandable that in formal Catholic doctrine Mary is Queen of Heaven only. But because she is not also Queen of Earth, as were the goddesses of old, Heaven and Earth as the two terms of the polarity are out of balance from the start. In fact, Mary has what divinity she has not because she offers an image of the whole of nature in all its manifest and unmanifest mystery, but only by virtue of being set apart from the laws of nature within which humanity is held. This means that the Christian figure of Mary cannot serve as an image of *zoe* in all its totality, since nature, or earth, now called by the inanimate name of 'matter', is still under the deathly sentence of Eve, and, as fallen, cannot be the other and complementary term of spirit or heaven. The feminine principle has not been doctrinally acceptable as a sacred entity for at least 2,000 years, and consequently any union of masculine and feminine principles in the language, image and word of orthodox theology is unthinkable.

However, it is difficult to explain the persistent discussion concerning the status of Mary without turning to the deeper levels of the psyche that continue to be moved whatever the doctrine. For many Catholics, perhaps the majority, it simply does not matter whether Mary is called a goddess; she moves the heart by any name, whatever position she is given in working out a scheme of things. *Madonna*, a recent book of pictures and hymns throughout the ages, shows that Mary was variously prayed to as 'Mother of the Word', 'Star of the Sea, Glorious Mother of God', 'Wide-Open Gate of Heaven', 'Our Ambassadress and our Hope', 'Queen of Angels', 'Queen of Apostles', and 'Harrier of Hell'.[6] It is notable that, as many a Protestant theologian has roundly protested, in art, for the most part, Jesus is either a newly born infant or dead!

This raises the fascinating question of the inherent self-regulating balance of the collective psyche as a whole. This is the idea, proposed by Jung, that if the conscious psyche of individuals or of groups (such as nations or even the human race as a species) has become distorted, then the unconscious psyche will, apparently intentionally, compensate for this distortion by insisting on an opposing point of view in order to restore the balance.[7] How else to make sense of the constant debate over Mary lasting hundreds and hundreds of years, gathering to a crescendo in the last 150 years, which is essentially a debate on how human, or divine, she was and is? Why would it matter whether Mary was a goddess or not unless there were an overwhelming need to include an image of the feminine in the conception of the divine?

The last 2,000 and even 4,000 years have seen the demise of the feminine principle just as they have seen the increasing mastery of nature. This process seems both inevitable and, in broad outline, lawful, but from this historical moment, when the earth is progressively being laid waste by those who depend on it for their life, it also seems to have gone too far. It would not be surprising, then, if there were some counterbalancing impulse whose purpose was to reassert, in new form, the carriers of those values that had been too sweepingly rejected. Politically, we can see this expressed in the Feminist Movement, which challenges pervasive cultural assumptions on the inferior status of women as defined by the ruling patriarchy; philosophically, it is expressed in the 'New Age' exploration of intuition as the feminine mode of knowing needed to complement the 'masculine' mode of knowing through the intellect.[8] The Green environmental movement, which calls in many different voices for the earth to be respected and cared for in a new way, and 'Gaia consciousness', which asks that we see our earth as a living being and a sacred entity, would also belong to this process of collective revisioning. These values are all 'feminine' in the archetypal sense that they are the values of immanence, known through feeling, loving, imaginative involvement – gnostic knowledge – which requires a commitment from the whole person, a knowledge that comes from a *relationship* with the thing known.

In orthodox Catholic religion this general theme is focused on the ever-increasing stature of Mary, or, more precisely, the mode of relating to the sacred that the image of Mary makes possible. It may be more than coincidence that she was granted a royal place in 'Heaven' – assumed without question by the earlier goddesses – only in the 1950s, at the very time when, after the devastation of the Second World War, the full implications of the nuclear bomb were being registered.

The wider point being made here is that even when the 'status' of an image is archetypal, that is, belonging to the structure of the human psyche, the image itself still needs to be understood in its local historical context. The two dimensions of such an image, the archetypal and the historical, do *not* exclude each other, but are both required for an estimation of its meaning and implications.

Marina Warner's outstanding book on the myth and cult of the Virgin Mary, *Alone of All Her Sex*, explores the figure of the Virgin in its historical context, insisting on the importance of seeing how the images arose in response to prevailing attitudes and circumstances:

> By emptying history from the figure of Mary, all the various silks interwoven for centuries on the sensitive loom of the mind are deprived of context, of motive, of circumstance, and therefore seem to be the spontaneous expression of enduring archetypal ideas. Once the combination of historical and social circumstances is ignored, the reasons for such a symbol are also obscured, and the distortions and assumptions the symbol perpetuates in our lives become invisible.[9]

The semiologist Roland Barthes, quoted by Warner, reminds us that 'in myth, things lose the memory that they once were made', and that the principle of myth is that it 'transforms history into nature'.[10] But once we have rightly restored to things this memory, and given back to the image its name and local habitation, there is still, it seems, a question left to ask: *why* were they made at all?

In discussions of mythology a distinction is often drawn between 'innate' archetypal ideas and extrinsic cultural and historical products,[11] as though an archetype, being fundamental, were also 'timeless' and a priori, and so unable to enter into history and change. Without engaging in the metaphysical, and specifically Kantian, issues here,[12] it seems simpler to observe that one of the ways we realize an image is archetypal is because

we see it continually turning up in different cultures and different times:
we see a pattern, as well as the particular local instance. Studying a
mythic image over thousands of years, there gradually emerges a pattern
of constancy and variation that allows an evaluation of how these ideas are
expressed, sometimes finely, sometimes crudely, sometimes only partially.
Consequently, studying the history of the goddess image in all its manifestations through the succeeding ages, it seems possible to point to an
evolution in the image such as would confound any absolute distinction
between archetype and history, and indeed would seem to call for a
history of the archetype itself. In this case, we could infer that 'history'
had modified the archetype, even as the 'archetype' had shaped history,
though both terms tend towards vagueness once they have become polarized abstractions.

This reinstatement of the devalued feminine principle through the
image of Mary has long been happening in art, and the rest of this chapter
aims to suggest how the pervasive influence and significance of Mary can
be understood by seeing her in the context of the millennial tradition of
the mother goddess, as its latest embodiment. From the long reach of
mythological and historical perspective, which invites us to stand outside
our own cultural tradition, we may also subject the image itself to some
scrutiny, asking how vital and complete an image is it, and – which is
essentially the same question – can the image of Mary express the essence
of the feminine archetype?

Mary as the Great Mother Goddess

Figure 3 shows the Great Mother gathering humanity within her robe,
protecting it from fear and harm. She gazes impersonally upon eternity,
transcending and transforming the troubles of the little people nestling
for comfort in the wide folds of her embrace. A statue such as this points
to what is most relevant in any discussion of divinities: that all over the
Catholic world statues of Mary are hung with gifts, not just jewellery and
candles fit for a queen, but the personal mementos of gratitude for the
birth of a child and the recovery from a frightening sickness. How many
of us have, perhaps with some surprise, come upon a little shrine to Mary
carved in the hollow of a rock, apparently miles from anywhere? Her
festivals are celebrated with masked processions, dancing and music that
involve the whole community, and are looked forward to all year round.
In the tiny island of Gozo off Malta, to take one example, the statue of
Mary in Figure 4 – constructed, incidentally, 100 years before the Vatican
officially declared her Assumption into Heaven – is carried around the
town every year on 15 August, the day of the Feast of the Assumption; it
is so heavy that six of the strongest men, bearing it on their shoulders, are
unable to lift their feet, but must shuffle them flat upon the ground for
several hours. On the tiny island of Kalymnos near Kos, where a church

Figure 3. (*Left*) *Schutzmantel-Maria aus Ravensburg*, Michael Erhart, *c*. 1480.
Figure 4. (*Right*) *Our Lady of the Assumption*. Gozo Cathedral, Gozo, Malta.

to Mary was built on top of the hill to commemorate miraculous healing cures, three days are set aside for the festival of the Assumption, and people come from all the neighbouring islands, camping on the shores, year after year. A Polish funeral in Brighton ended with a remembrance to 'Our Lady, the Virgin, Mother of Mankind'.

Then there are the visions of Mary: 21,000 in the last 1,000 years, of which 210 were reported between 1928 and 1971. Many of the churches were constructed on the site of a vision, including the sanctuary of Lourdes, a place of annual pilgrimage for many. Pope John Paul II declared 1988 to be 'The Year of Marian Devotion'.

The Virgin's link with the goddess tradition is also reflected etymologically in her name, 'Maria', which comes from the Latin *mare*, meaning 'sea'. All the Great Mothers are born from the primeval ocean or the watery abyss, the primordial womb of life from which all created forms emerge: the ideogram for the Sumerian goddess Nammu was the sea; Isis was 'born from the all-wetness'; Hathor is 'the watery abyss of heaven'; Nut, the sky goddess, lets fall her milk as rain; Aphrodite is born from the foam of the sea. The brightly painted 'mermaids', flinging their arms and hair to the winds of every quarter on the prows of ships, may be a folk remnant of this inheritance.

Mary is sometimes known as the net and her son as the divine fisherman, just as in Sumeria Dumuzi, the son–lover of Inanna, was called 'Lord of the Net'. This theme is echoed in the image of Christ as 'fisher of men'. The sea-shell, sacred to Aphrodite and the image by which the initiates of Eleusis recognized each other, became, in the Middle Ages, the talisman of the pilgrims journeying to the great shrine of Santiago de Compostela in northern Spain. Mary inherited her title *Stella Maris* – 'Star of the Sea' – from Isis, evoking the heavenly sea of the night sky as well as the earthly ocean. Again, like Isis, Mary became the patron of ships and sailors, life-saving in an age of nightly navigation by stars. In Sicily, for instance, where once the eye of Horus, son of Isis, was painted on the prow of the local fishing boats, now the sign of the Virgin takes its place.[13] In Alchemy Mary became the star that guided the pilgrim who set sail on the uncharted waters of the great sea of the soul. Eithne Wilkins, in her book *The Rose Garden Game*, draws these images together:

> The stone boat of Isis that commemorates the ritual boat once carried in procession in antique Rome, when the mystery religions flourished there, is still preserved outside the church called Santa Maria della Navicella, Our Lady of the Boat. Appositely the apse mosaic is a representation (the earliest of its kind) of the Great Mother, a brilliant sixth century Madonna enthroned, herself a throne for the regal Child . . . The same symbols join together continually, whatever the framework of belief may be. A means of transport, whether boat or chariot (such as that of Isis with roses for wheels) or the travelling moon, is a universal symbol of the feminine principle, and the Great Mother, whether as the rose sailing on the waves of the sea or as the rose that is the haven, is also the sea itself, the vast

Figure 5. *The Virgin Mary in a Ship.* Chapelle de la Rotonde, Boulogne-sur-mer.

watery womb, the depth. The Lady is symbolized as the sea, the traveller
on the sea, the haven, and the rose. It was when Aphrodite was born,
foam of the sea, that the roses first bloomed on her island, and doubtless
the sea was then rained on and sprinkled with roses as Botticelli
imagined.[14]

A poem by Petrarch expresses the appeal of such a metaphor:

> Bright Virgin, steadfast in eternity,
> Star of this storm-tossed sea,
> Trusted guide of every trustful pilot,
> Turn your thoughts to the terrifying squall
> In which I find myself, alone and rudderless . . .[15]

In an apocryphal story about her Mary weaves the veil of the temple.[16]
The dynamic of this story is again the image of the Great Mother, who
spins life out of herself, giving form to and clothing incarnation in the
person of her son, yet drawing a veil between the two aspects of herself,
unmanifest and manifest. As eternity spinning time, growth and destiny,
she weaves the great web of life in the image of a mother with a child in
her womb, who weaves life into form out of her body in ways still
unknown to us. The *Moirae*, the three Greek goddesses of fate, born
from the Underworld and Night, from Zeus and Themis; the Cretan
goddess of childbirth, Eileithyia; Athena; and Penelope waiting for Odysseus were all spinners and weavers of the threads of destiny, and Mary
stands as the last link in this chain of transmission. Wilkins continues:

> Whether in Greek, Germanic, Mayan or other myth, the Fates are always
> spinners and weavers, the archaic female triad outside space and time . . .
> The Great Mother herself spins and weaves because she is the primal
> embodiment of the triad of the weavers of all things earthly, of growth, of
> time, of destiny. The primordial lady spins out of her own being the thread
> of time and weaves it to make the tissue of things, just as the woman spins
> in herself the tissue of another being's flesh. . . . Spinning and weaving are
> occupations proper to the Virgin Mary as Great Mother and it is probably
> not accidental that two parts of spinning-wheel machinery are called 'the
> maiden' and 'mother of all', or that the number fifteen plays a significant
> part both in spinsterist lore and in the rosary.[17]

In the fairy-tale of the Sleeping Beauty (originating in the Greek myth
of Hera and Zeus's wedding feast, to which one of the goddesses was not
invited) it is significant that the life of the princess and the whole court is
suspended at the moment when she pricks her finger on the spindle of the
woman spinning in the top of the tower, as foretold in the curse of the
Wicked Fairy, who had been overlooked at the christening of the child
attended by all the other 'god-mothers', a term by now mythologically
resonant. The lunar symbolism of the tale is evocative of older meanings:
the princess is fifteen when she pricks her finger, the first day of the

Figure 6. *The Annunciation*; fresco fragment, twelfth century.
Church of Sorpe, Spain.

waning moon, when the spinning goddess of the moon begins to loosen
the threads of the cloth she has woven. The Wicked Fairy, as the one not
invited, is the rejected goddess of the dark moon, whose lore must be
included in a total image of the web of life.

In the early twelfth-century Catalan Annunciation picture in Figure 6
the artist's intention may have been, as Neumann comments, 'no more
than to represent the Madonna engaged in an everyday womanly activity',
but 'unconscious forces produced a work of archetypal grandeur . . . the
Madonna is still the Great Goddess who spins destiny – though here
destiny is the redemption of the world'.[18] In the south German painting
in Figure 7 the thread from the spindle passes from Mary's hands directly
through the brow of the baby lit up *in potentia* in her womb, and thus,
Neumann concludes, 'the act of spinning regains its true and original
meaning: the mother becomes the spinning goddess of destiny; the child
becomes the fabric of her body.'[19]

Figure 7. *The Virgin Mary Spinning*; Upper Rhenish Master, *c.* 1400.

Mary as the Birth-Giving Goddess

And she brought forth her first born son, and wrapped him in swaddling clothes, and laid him in a manger; because there was no room for them in the inn. (Luke 2:7)

This event is celebrated as Christmas in many countries, and, to speak colloquially, always has been. Let us stand back for a moment and look at the story of Christmas mythologically.[20]

All over the world, for countless millennia, people have participated in a religious ritual at the winter solstice, when the sun's downward course is arrested and it turns back, as it seems, to earth. This change of state in the bleak mid-winter of the year was experienced as the rebirth of the sun and commemorated as the birth day of the sun god, the luminous divine child. Like the heavenly sun arising from the depths of darkness, these divine sons were born at midnight, hidden in the depths of the earth, in a cow-byre, in the reeds, in a cave, out of a rock, in a manger. The cry 'The Virgin has brought forth! The light is waxing' would have echoed in various tongues across the centuries. In Mesopotamia he was called Tammuz and Dumuzi; in Egypt he was called Osiris and Horus, and, later, Aion; in Greece, Dionysos, Helios and Orpheus; in Persia and Rome, Mithras.

Such parallels were not lost on the early founders of the Christian Church. St Jerome, as we have seen, related the tears of the baby Jesus to

562 *The Myth of the Goddess*

those of the women bewailing the death of Adonis, all echoing in the same groves of Bethlehem.[21] Originally, the birth of Christ was celebrated twelve days after the solstice on 6 January, the day of Epiphany (Manifestation) in the Christian calendar, when Jesus was manifested to the wise men from the East. In those days this was also the date of the festival in Egyptian Alexandria of the birth of Aion (a later version of Osiris) from the Greek Kore, 'the Maiden', identified with the Egyptian Isis, whose particular star was Sirius. Every year for hundreds of years Egyptians had watched for Sirius to rise on the horizon, for this announced the rebirth of Osiris as Horus and the rising of the flood waters of the Nile, bringing to the people life and eternal life together.

This ritual was described by an early Christian writer, Epiphanius, who, although writing about heresy in the fourth century AD, saw the relevance of the older ritual to the birth of Jesus:

> After they have kept all-night vigil with songs and music, chanting to their idol, when the vigil is over, at cockcrow, they descend with lights into an underground crypt, and carry up a wooden image lying naked on a litter, with the seal of a cross made in gold on its forehead, and on either hand two similar seals, and on either knee two others, all five seals being similarly made in gold. And they carry round the image itself, circumambulating seven times the innermost temple, to the accompaniment of pipes, tabors and hymns, and with merry-making they carry it down again underground. And if they are asked the meaning of this mystery, they answer: 'Today at this hour the Maiden (Kore) that is, the Virgin gave birth to the Aeon.'[22]

This is a description not of a fourth-century Midnight Mass and Christmas Day, but of the Festival of Kore in her temple at Alexandria.

Now, in the fourth century AD the birth of Jesus Christ was declared by the Western Church to have 'happened' on 25 December, the day of the winter solstice as reckoned by the Julian calendar, the day after the three days (apparent) standing still of the sun (Latin: *sol* = sun; 'stice' comes from *sistere* = to stand still), when the light begins to increase. Christ's birth now coincided exactly with the rebirth of the sun, and the title of *Sol Invictus* (the 'Unvanquished Sun') was accorded to him, as it had been to Mithras, and before him to those other beings whose birth had been regarded in different traditions as divine. Christ's holy day was then moved from Satur(n)day to Sun-day. The meaning for Christians was, of course, unique: 'Day-spring, Brightness of the Light eternal, and Sun of Justice, come and enlighten those who sit in darkness and the shadow of death.'[23]

But the symbolism of the light conquering the darkness is common to all the hero myths from the late Bronze Age onwards, following the myth of the *Enuma Elish*, in which Marduk, the solar hero, vanquishes the Mother Goddess Tiamat, who thereby becomes the darkness. Long before that, however, in the lunar goddess cultures, the sun was born from the moon, his mother, or the heavenly cow, and darkness was not then hostile but the condition of rebirth.

Folk wisdom also recognizes a universal theme, for many of the rituals still surrounding Christmas have meanings that transcend the boundaries of age, culture and belief. The evergreen tree we call the Christmas tree, with candles flickering on its branches and gifts strewn around its roots, was once honoured as the Tree of Life, or the World Tree. Uniting the dimensions of heaven, earth and underworld, it was the cosmic axis at the centre of the world, the *Axis Mundi*, through which the eternal energies of creation poured continuously into time. The greenness of the Tree of Life at this darkest moment was then, and is still under a different name, the sign and the promise of life eternally renewed. So the flames of the tree celebrate the rekindling of that heavenly fire in its winter underworld of death and proclaim the victory of the light over dark. Similarly, the silver star on the top of the Christmas tree, the one the Magi saw, is as a mythic image the pole star of the world axis, and the bright star of Inanna, Isis, Aphrodite and Venus, accompanying all the divine births all over the Near East.

These festivals of delight are far from the doctrinal Christian preoccupation with the intact hymen of Mary, the mother of Jesus. As suggested in Chapter 13, the 'immaculate conception' of Jesus, that is, the literal virginity of his mother, was an idea that arose retrospectively as a way of pointing to the divinity of Christ. In fact, a belief in the divine impregnation by a god of a mortal woman who gives birth to a hero or demi-god belongs to all the traditions of the pre-Christian world *except* the Judaic. The idea of virgin birth applied to the king or high priest named as the goddess's son–lover, as well as to the many gods and heroes of legend. Warner draws attention to the fact that in the 'pre-Christian Roman Empire virgin birth was a shorthand symbol, commonly used to designate a man's divinity' and that it became a title associated with men who were outstanding individuals, whether as spiritual teachers or great military leaders. 'Pythagoras, Plato, Alexander were all believed to be born of woman by the power of a holy spirit. It became the commonplace claim of a spiritual leader.'[24]

The story of the virgin birth of Jesus is told only in Matthew and Luke, and the fact that Joseph plays no apparent part in his conception seems to contradict the idea of the genealogical descent from David, for the Davidic blood would not have been transmitted to Jesus unless Joseph was his father. And if Joseph was his father, what is the relevance of the virgin birth? The two are not compatible with each other. In the apocryphal stories and iconography of the couple, it is significant that Joseph is generally depicted as an older man, who, symbolically, is thereby transformed from her nuptial husband into her father. There is evidence that the earliest surviving manuscript of Matthew (the Mount Sinai manuscript) was altered to make the virgin birth story credible. The passage in Isaiah 7:14, 'Behold a virgin shall conceive and bear a son', is one of the main texts used to affirm the doctrine of the virgin birth, but this interpretation has no foundation in Jewish religion, and owes its existence to the interpretation given to the Greek translation of the Hebrew word *almah*, the one actually used by Isaiah.[25] When the Hebrew texts were translated into Greek for use in the Greek-speaking Jewish communities established outside Palestine during the third century BC, the Hebrew word *almah* was translated by the Greek word *parthenos*, which had the meaning of maiden or unwedded girl. If Isaiah had meant virgin, he would have used the word *bethulah*, but this word was never interpreted as someone who conceived miraculously, only as a girl who had had no sexual experience or had not yet begun menstruation, or as one who couldn't conceive.[26] Elizabeth, Mary's cousin, was virgin in this sense; she had not had a child. Her conception of John the Baptist was, in this sense, not a divine impregnation, but a divine intervention that put an end to her sterility, in the same way that divine intervention had, in the Old Testament, given children to the wives of Abraham, Isaac, Jacob and Samuel.

Paradoxically, it is Mary's very humanity as a mother – our readiness to identify with a woman about to give birth with nowhere to go – that predisposes us to take the symbolism of virginity literally because she does not 'feel symbolic'. Whereas all the goddesses were automatically virgin in the symbolic sense of being sufficient unto themselves for the act of conception and birth, the idea of their literal virginity would have been absurd in the way that any confusion of levels of discourse is absurd. But rendering Mary as human and virgin together is equally perplexing, for it also confuses the archetypal and the human dimensions: symbolically virgin is only for goddesses and literally virgin is not for human mothers. Christianity has taught that the 'miraculous' birth without the 'sin' of sexuality is believed to redeem the Eve of its own invention, but it perpetuates the Judaic tradition of belittling the human order to honour the divine. It exalts a woman to the level of a goddess, creating as a goddess creates – at once mother and virgin – yet denies her either the title of goddess or the complete humanity of a woman. As Warner writes, 'In the very celebration of the perfect human woman, both humanity and women were subtly denigrated.'[27]

THE LUNAR MYTH

Leaving aside the doctrinal intention of the Church and returning to the picture of Mary created in art, we find that the archetypal lunar myth clothes the figures of Mary and Jesus, drawing their story into the ancient and ever-renewing pattern of the cycle of the moon and its phases. Mary here becomes a Goddess of the Moon, whose image, like Inanna and Isis before her, is the crescent moon and the star, and her robe is the blue of the sky and the sea, the same blue as the robe of Isis and Demeter and the lapis lazuli necklace of Ishtar. Like all the lunar goddesses, Mary is virgin and mother, and the drama of her destiny follows the changing cycle of the moon, though with one crucial difference. She gives birth to her son with the crescent, mothers him at the full moon but does not, of course, marry him; she mourns the loss of her son in the three days between his crucifixion and resurrection – those three days of darkness when the moon is gone and Jesus has descended to hell, harrowing or ploughing the underworld dimension to release the life buried there – in lunar symbolism, to awaken the dormant light of the returning crescent. Mary's lament for her sacrificed son echoes the lament of all previous goddesses for their sacrificed son or daughter, and the three Marys who surround the drama of his Passion recall the three visible phases of the moon, the trinity of goddesses of destiny. On his return he is greeted as 'the gardener', the resurrected life, by Mary of Magdala, who anoints him with precious balm before his death, as all the previous son–lovers had been anointed by the high priestess of the goddess. In the Greek Orthodox Church Mary takes the role of her son and also enters the realm of the moon's darkness for three days during what is called her 'dormition' before her ascension, when she is reunited with her son, who now crowns her in a ceremony

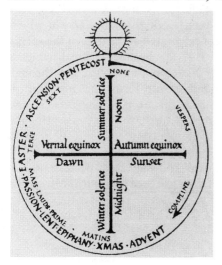

Figure 8. The Christian calendar in relation to the symbolism of the year.

that is like the sacred marriage rite of the full moon, known to Christian doctrine as the 'Coronation of the Virgin'. This full moon rite of 'marriage' is, as it were, displaced, so that the completion of the cycle takes place afterwards, in the symbolic region of eternal life. As though in commemoration of this lunar mystery, the timing of Easter every year is not set for a fixed date, but follows the changing course of the full moon in relation to the spring equinox.

Lunar and solar symbolism are intriguingly reflected in the Christian calendar in a way that exactly corresponds to their mythological history. When the drama being celebrated is one of transformation, the timing of the rituals follows the moon's course; for example, Christ's resurrection is arranged for the Sunday following the first full moon after the spring equinox. But when the 'event' belongs to the solar heroic model of the conquest of darkness by the light principle, the calendar follows the course of the sun; for example, the birth of the child 'happens' at the winter solstice when the sun is reborn out of the dark of the old year. Alan Watts, in his book *Myth and Ritual in Christianity*, which is essential reading for this subject, clarifies this:

> In the cycle of the Christian Year the rites of the Incarnation are governed by the solar calendar, since they are connected with the Birth of the Sun, and so fall upon fixed dates. On the other hand, the rites of the Atonement, of Christ's Death, Resurrection, and Ascension, are governed by the lunar calendar, for there is a figure of Death and Resurrection in the waning and waxing of the moon.[28]

The son born to the mother is, in the perennial mythological pattern, the Sun born to the Moon, the Light risen out of the depths of Darkness and the rebirth of the year. Christ was called the 'Sun of Righteousness', the 'Light of the World'.[29] Easter, which in Latin countries is derived from the Latin word *pascha* (from the Hebrew word *pesach*, the Passover), derives in English from the Anglo-Saxon Goddess of the Dawn, whose name was Eoestre, and whose rites were celebrated at the time of the spring equinox, the dawn of the agricultural year. The number of the disciples is the solar number twelve, representing one revolution of the sun through the twelve months of the year, but together with Jesus, the thirteenth, it becomes the thirteen months of the lunar year. So it reconciles solar and lunar time, and unites the solar principle of rebirth with the lunar principle of transformation. On the lunar model, related to the life of growth, vegetation and the agricultural year, Jesus' life is cut off at the end of the old year, as in the Neolithic era the year god may have been cut down with the sickle like the corn, and in Crete the tree was cut down as the dying god. The tree reappears in the symbolism of Jesus, for the cross he hangs upon as the death of the world is the Tree of Life in its dying phase before rebirth.

Mary as Queen of Heaven

In the painting in Figure 9 the celestial robe of the Queen of Heaven takes the same colour as the heavenly blue of the angels, and Mary stands among a flurry of wings almost as if they all came from her own body. It is as though the sky had dropped its blue momentarily upon the earth.

> *Ave, Regina caelorum,*
> *Ave, Domina Angelorum:*
> *Salve radix, salve porta,*
> *Ex qua mundo lux est orta.*

> Hail, Queen of Heaven,
> Hail, Lady of the Angels:
> Salutation to thee, root and portal,
> Whence the light of the world has arisen.[30]

This gesture of greeting and joy, now sung at the evening service of Compline when the sun has set, finds the same expression of image as was once addressed to Inanna, Ishtar and Isis – 'Hail, Great Lady of Heaven!' as the hymn went – 4,000 years before. Then the goddesses were

Figure 9. *Mary, Queen of Heaven*; The Wilton Diptych, French school, 1395.

personified in the stars of the morning, Sirius and Venus, and Mary also is invoked in the image of the morning star in Monteverdi's Vespers of 1610: 'Tell me, who is She Who rises bright as the dawn and I shall bless Her.' The star that guided the wise men from the East and came and stood over where the young child was had always been a sign of the goddess, hanging above the head of the seated goddess in Sumerian seals. In Egypt the bright star Sirius (Sothis) was identified with Isis, who rose when the rising waters of the Nile were about to give birth, flooding the parched lands with the fertilizing power of Osiris. Mary with the twelve stars circling her head like a halo of light is like Inanna–Ishtar, who, as moon goddess, wore as her crown the twelve constellations through which the sun – her son – moved. Like the moon, Mary became the Mistress of the Waters, guardian of the rhythmic ebb and flow of the womb; and, like Artemis and Aphrodite, and probably like the Palaeolithic Goddess of Laussel, with one hand holding the horn of the crescent moon and the other gesturing to her rounded belly, Mary also became goddess of fertility and childbirth.

In Christianity these 'pagan' connections are disguised and spiritualized, and the images appear to derive from sources entirely within the Christian framework of belief. So the iconography of Mary's relation to the moon, stars, sun and heaven takes its ostensible reference from the passage in Revelation, when what was revealed to John in a cave on the island of Patmos was a vision that could have come straight out of Sumeria,

Figure 10. (*Left*) *Mary, Queen of Heaven*; c. 1500. Netherlands.
Figure 11. (*Right*) *Mary with nimbus and roses*; late fifteenth century.
Northern Netherlands.

but reached him, in the manner of archetypal imagery everywhere, as an epiphany of an order never seen before: 'And there appeared a great wonder in heaven; a woman clothed with the sun, and the moon under her feet, and upon her head a crown of twelve stars' (Rev. 12:1).

This woman is totally different in feeling from the modest, submissive Mary of the Gospels, yet the two figures were often cast as the same one, perhaps as part of the process of magnifying the human woman into the divine queen. Mary is drawn or sculpted standing on the crescent moon in the centre of a round or oval disc with vibrant streams of light emanating from her form to the circumference, often circled with roses. The sculpture in Figure 10 hangs from the ceiling of St Catherine's Convent in Utrecht, Holland, high above every head, while on a nearby wall a more traditional Mary is painted feeding her child against a hedge of climbing roses, framed by a cosmic halo, brilliant like the first rays of the rising sun (Fig. 11).

However, John's text continues in a way that places this lovely vision of the old goddess within the warring perspective of the Iron Age hero myth, and so entirely changes its meaning:

> And she being with child cried, travailing in birth, and pained to be delivered.
>
> And there appeared another wonder in heaven; and behold a great red dragon, having seven heads and ten horns, and seven crowns upon his heads.
>
> And his tail drew the third part of the stars of heaven, and did cast them to the earth: and the dragon stood before the woman which was ready to be delivered, for to devour her child as soon as it was born.
>
> And she brought forth a man child, who was to rule all nations with a rod of iron: and her child was caught up unto God, and to his throne.
>
> . . . . .
>
> And there was war in heaven . . . (Rev. 12:2–5, 7)

It is significant that Astarte stands with the crescent moon upon her head (see Chapter 1, Fig. 42b), while Mary stands upon the crescent moon, epitomizing in one image the radical difference in feeling towards the natural world between pre-Christian and Christian religion. The moon, once the goddess herself, is often drawn, following the rest of the passage, in the shape of a curved and flattened dragon, complete with tail and claws (Fig. 12), the red dragon conquered by Michael and his angels. Later, dragon, serpent, the Devil and Satan are amalgamated into one opposing being, but the further identification of them or it with the crescent moon is one that exactly reflects the orthodox Judaeo-Christian deposition of the lunar world of rhythm and renewal. The inherent contradiction of this image of the woman crying in the travails of childbirth, as though she were the cursed Eve, with the image of Mary bringing forth her child virginally and without suffering appears not to have been noticed.

Figure 12. *The Glorification of the Virgin*; Geertgen tot St Jans, *c.* 1490–5.

This image was none the less taken by the Christian Fathers as the text for the idea of Mary as the Second Eve trampling the serpent of the First Eve underfoot. As hero as well as virgin, she is thereby given the role of the old Virgin Goddess who was co-opted into war, but her enemy, the dragon, is – to read mythologically with Tiamat in mind – the split-off aspect of her former unity, who is now, repressed and devalued, inevitably seen as the embodiment of evil. In this interpretation Mary, as the image of the goddess apparently but not actually restored, is now drawn in wholly male terms, doing battle, like the hero, with the dragon who was once herself and was once the whole of nature as divine.

However, in the official canons of the Church, Mary's Assumption into Heaven and her role as Queen of Heaven are intimately bound up together – as is reflected in the temporal proximity of their official announcements – and this gives a new meaning both to 'heaven' and to 'queen'. What is new in the title of Queen of Heaven is that Mary has had to rise up from the meagre earth to reassume it, and it is here that the doctrine of her 'assumption' into heaven 'body and soul' – or, rather, soul *and* body – reminds us that she has to travel on behalf of humanity the unmeasurable distance no human being can contemplate. The ancient 'heaven', with no such distance between sacred and profane, was an image that invoked the abiding presence of a reality beyond appearances yet everywhere within them, beyond what the eye can see and the ear can hear, yet visible and audible to the inner vision and inner listening in all that can be seen and heard – the sense in which Jesus uses it in the quotation from the Gospel of Thomas on pages 602–3. The new heaven is poised above earth, or even pitched against earth, as a spiritual reality defined as superior to matter, different in kind, so not even potentially inherent in it. This is a heaven that the corruptible and sinfully lusting flesh of the body cannot enter, and so must, excepting Mary, die first. As Warner says, 'The Assumption dogma depended on the Christian equivalence between sex and death, and consequently between the Virgin's purity and her freedom from the dissolution of the grave.'[31] It is notably only after death, which is to say, 'dormition', that Mary reaches heaven as its queen, but the heavenly goddesses of old were always living and did not, once and for all, live and die. In Mary, as in Eve, narrative and symbol compete for meaning.

If it is reasonably enough objected that Mary is not, in dogma, a goddess, and so her elevation has to be envisaged in (all too) human terms, then we are back to the problem of the consequences of imagining divinity from less than the whole of the psyche. That is, if, dogma or not, Mary is *experienced* as divine – which in the olden days was called 'a goddess' – then her ascent from earth to heaven must subtly diminish earth, that is to say, the sacredness of earthly life, which is the possibility of the divine immanent in creation. Jung, talking of the tension between the opposites of spirit and matter, argues that, understood concretely, the

Figure 13. *The Assumption of the Virgin*; Titian, 1518.

Assumption is a 'counterstroke that does nothing to diminish the tension between opposites, but drives it to extremes', while 'understood symbolically, however, the Assumption of the body is a recognition and acknowledgement of matter'.[32] No problem, he writes elsewhere, can be solved at the same level at which it arose,[33] which means here that the attempt, if such it was, to respiritualize the body must fail because it ends up by depriving the body of substance.

But even a symbolic understanding is, in our view, confused in the same way. Matter cannot be recognized or acknowledged from the point of view of its 'opposite' – spirit. Only by collapsing both of the apparent opposites can a new language emerge from a level beyond both extremes. To put it another way, the reinstatement of the feminine principle fails because only part of the feminine principle is acknowledged, and so the split is perpetuated, or perhaps worse, enshrined.

MARY AS THE SECOND EVE

As suggested in Chapter 13, the doctrine of Mary as the redeemer of the sin of Eve underlined still further the dissociation of spirit and body, for to be the redeemer Mary had to be perpetually virgin, untainted by sexual relationship with another human being. During the first centuries of the Christian era another doctrine was formulated that the Church was the Virgin Mother and Bride of Christ and that *it* was the Second Eve, Redeemer of the First Eve. The Church came to be called by Eve's name, the 'Mother of All Living'. In this way, the Church took over the former role of the Mother Goddess, which, of course, it could not possibly fulfil without dismissing those depths of the psyche that experience the replacing of a living image with an abstract idea as a violation. None the less, Mary is often depicted holding a model of a church in her arms, or set inside a church as its personification.

The Christian reading of the virginity of Mary as *literal* contrasts totally with the earlier understanding of the virginity of the mother goddess as symbolic: the wonder of nature perpetually renewing herself from the source that is herself. Mary's virginity in Christianity cannot redeem the fallen Eve, but only compounds the idea that there was a sin in the beginning, and that there is something intrinsically wrong in human nature which has to be atoned for. This is a harsh indictment of the loneliness of separation and the bewildering anticipation of death, and not least the implicit identification of the tragedy of the human condition with sexuality, which brings life. As Warner comments:

> The Immaculate Conception remains the dogma by which the Virgin Mary is set apart from the human race because she is not stained by the Fall . . . As the icon of the ideal, the Virgin affirms the inferiority of the human lot. Soaring above the men and women who pray to her, the Virgin conceived

Figure 14. *Tree of Death and Life*; miniature by Berthold Furtmeyer, 1481.
From Archbishop of Salzburg's missal.

without sin underscores rather than alleviates pain and anxiety and accentuates the feeling of sinfulness. The state her votaries believe to be hers must always elude them, for all creatures except her are, they are told, born in sin. Mary is indeed Eve's other face.[34]

In the miniature in Figure 14 the faces of the two women are identical, and their heads incline away from the central point of the tree in antithetical relationship: Eve, predictably naked, offering to humanity the apple of death, which she is passing on from the serpent; and Mary, predictably clothed, offering the redeeming apple of life. The position of the serpent arising from the not-to-be-seen phallus of Adam is presumably less than coincidental. On Eve's side of the tree lies the grinning skull, while Death waits for her on the right, and on Mary's side of the tree – the Life side – the cross with the crucified Christ poised as on a branch, himself the fruit of her miraculously intact womb.

It is, of course, understandable that having excluded divinity from nature, these same laws of nature would need to be suspended in order to, as it were, let divinity enter 'back into life' to heal this separation. But, again, it is a rectification that perpetuates the original mistake, which was not one of human nature, but of the limitations of human understanding, for if a myth is interpreted literally, it can no longer serve as a vehicle for

Figure 15. Glorified Madonna; Spanish woodcut, fifteenth century.

metaphysical exploration. However, if the myth of Mary's divine impregnation is understood symbolically, what is redeemed through the union of the 'human' and the 'divine' is the partiality of human reflection upon the meaning of life and death. The 'child' born of this 'conception' is a new vision, which redeems the split between nature and spirit because it sees their separation as ultimately illusory, or 'true' only at a lower level.

Alan Watts offers a richer and more comprehensive understanding of the symbolism of Mary in what he calls 'Christian mythology':

> The Virgin Mother is, first of all, *Mater Virgo* – virgin matter or the unploughed soil – that is to say, the Prima Materia prior to its division, or ploughing, into the multiplicity of created things. As Star of the Sea, *Stella Maris* (*mare* = Mary), the Sealed Fountain, 'the immaculate womb of this divine font,' she is likewise the Water over which the Spirit moved in the beginning of time. As the 'Woman clothed with the sun, and the moon under her feet,' she is also everything signified in other mythologies by the goddesses of the moon, which shines by the sun's light, and appears in the night surrounded (crowned) with stars. As the Womb in which the Logos comes to birth she is also Space, signified in the common artistic convention of clothing her in a blue mantle, spangled with stars.[35]

Watts comments: 'The symbolism is of the Virgin as *Rosa Mundi*, Rose of the World – that is, of the created order, *maya*, which flowers from its divine Centre.'[36]

MARY: THE LOST GODDESS OF EARTH

Mary, as the last in the chain of goddesses through whom the beauty of the earth becomes numinous, is scarcely known for her relation to the earth for the reasons given above. Yet already in the fifth-century-Greek 'Akathistos Hymn' to the Virgin images of corn, wheat and vine reappear,

Figure 16. *The Little Paradise Garden*; 'The Master of the Paradise Garden',
c. 1410.

linking Mary with the fertility of the earth and, through Cybele, Demeter,
Aphrodite and Inanna, with the Neolithic Mother Goddess of the life-
giving soil. Mary as the fountain of life, the rose garden, the fragrance of
the lily and the pillar that is the Tree of Life are images that decorate the
golden pages of the Books of Hours, often blending quite naturally with
the astrological symbolism that still, in the fourteenth and fifteenth centuries, registered the character of the months of the year. It is fitting to find
them first in a Greek hymn, since Greece is one of the lands that for at
least six millennia has revered the image of the goddess:

> Hail to you through whom joy will shine out;
> hail, redemption of fallen Adam;
> hail, deliverance of the tears of Eve;
> hail, height unattainable by human thought;
> hail, depth invisible even to the eyes of angels;
> hail to you, the throne of the king;
> hail, star that heralds the sun;
> hail, womb of divine incarnation;
> hail to you through whom creation is reborn;
> hail to you through whom the Creator becomes a child:
> hail, wedded maiden and virgin . . .
> Hail, vine of the unwithered shoot;
> hail, field of the immortal crop;
> hail to you who harvest the harvester, friend of man;
> hail to you who plant the planter of our life;
> hail, field that flourishes with a fertility of compassion;
> hail, table that bears a wealth of mercy;
> hail to you who make a meadow of delight to blossom;

hail to you who make ready a haven for souls . . .
Hail, mother of lamb and shepherd,
hail, flock of the fold endowed with reason . . .
hail, key of the gates of paradise;
hail, for the skies rejoice with the earth;
hail, for the earth chants in chorus with the heavens . . .
hail, rock giving water to those who thirst for life;
hail, pillar of fire, leading those in darkness . . .
Hail, flower of incorruptibility . . .
hail, tree of brilliant fruit, from which the faithful are fed;
hail, branch of fair-shading leaves, under whom many take shelter . . .
hail to you who bring opposites together . . .
hail to you who have filled the nets of the fishermen;
hail to you who draw forth from the depths of ignorance . . .
hail, boat for those who wish to be saved;
hail, harbour for the sailors of life . . .
hail, inexhaustible treasure of life . . .[37]

Here are many of the images already familiar from older cultures: the gate and the door from the Neolithic; and the lapis lazuli gate of Ishtar's temple; tree, rose, lily (the incorruptible flower) and fountain from the garden of Sumeria. The holy city with its tower, or ziggurat, which is also the sacred mountain, ladder, pillar or Tree of Life connecting earth with heaven also come from Sumeria. The 'tree of brilliant fruit from which the faithful are fed' could describe the goddesses Nut, Hathor and Isis giving the food and drink of eternal life to their faithful. She 'who brings the opposites together' in Egypt was Isis, relating obscurely to a line that says 'hail, ocean overwhelming the Pharaoh of the mind'. The lily and the rose belonged to the goddess in Egypt, Sumeria, Crete and Greece, and wherever the association was made between beauty and divinity. Inanna, Ishtar, Nut, Hathor and Isis, as well as Demeter of the Mysteries of Eleusis, live on in this Christian iconography of the Virgin.

In Figure 17 Mary lies upon a bed of corn covered by a quilt embroidered with the heads of sheep as though she were, like Inanna, the 'shepherdess' who had given birth to the Lamb. The whole picture, in bright colours of blue and gold, is a joyous celebration of the harvest. Pamela Berger's book *The Goddess Obscured* describes the continuity of the tradition of the grain goddess from pre-Christian to Christian times, and how fiercely the Christian priesthood in Europe fought to eradicate all traces of it.[38] An inversion of imagery, as had happened in Sumeria during the third millennium BC and in Palestine during the first millennium BC, happened also in Europe under Christianity. The old festivals sacred to Cybele as *Magna Mater* in the days of the Roman Empire were now celebrated on days renamed as sacred to the Son of God or to certain saints, and the old earth spirits were named as demons. Female saints took the place of the grain goddess, so that, except for Brigid, each saint belonged to a legend that brought her to a field at the time of sowing and,

Figure 17. *Mary on a Bed of Corn*; the Rohan master; *c.* 1400.

because of her presence, a miraculous growth of grain occurred. This process began in the Middle Ages, but by the twelfth century Mary had taken over this role, becoming, like her ancient predecessors, ultimately responsible for the sustaining and nourishing of humankind. In the exquisite illustration of the Grain Miracle, Mary appears as Queen of Earth, source of the grain, the harvest and so of humanity.

The medieval legend tells of how, during the Flight into Egypt (a story inspired itself by the goddess Isis, who bequeathed her images to Mary in the first to fourth centuries AD), the Virgin and the infant Jesus come to a field where a farmer is ploughing and sowing his seed. The Virgin or the child warns him that if he should see a band of soldiers in search of the holy family and hear them asking whether they had seen a mother and her child pass by, he should say that he had seen them pass when he had ploughed and sowed the field. The family leaves the field behind and, instantly, the newly sown seed sprouts and then grows to its full height and stands there, gold and ripened, ready for harvest. Herod's pursuing soldiers appear. The farmer tells them that, yes, a mother and her child had passed by 'when I first began to sow the seed'.[39] Berger comments:

> The twelfth and thirteenth century texts and artworks that incorporate the Virgin's Grain Miracle testify to a transformation that had already taken place. The steps of this transformation of the grain protectress into the Virgin are impossible to uncover. When the tale emerges in the twelfth

century, however, it appears in several different places, cropping up in France, Ireland, Wales, and Sweden. The extent of this diffusion suggests that the tale had a long history in the oral tradition before these versions were recorded in art and literature.[40]

Among the phrases associated with the telling or acting out of this Grain Miracle in the Middle Ages was one that referred to the Virgin being led around the field, just as had happened for millennia:

> Our Lady turned around it,
> She who was very frightened,
> And towards Egypt went she,
> And Saint Joseph led her.
> They came toward a husbandman
> Who was sowing wheat in the furrow.[41]

Berger suggests that these words could refer to 'the poet's unwitting preservation of the ancient ceremonial of the female deity going around the field to protect the land and energize the seed', and that the poem 'reflects an earlier ritual drama, an enactment that supplanted the annual early spring procession of the grain goddess around the field at sowing time'.[42]

Following an 'appearance' of Mary as a corn goddess to a merchant in Milan in the fifteenth century, which was then painted and hung in the Duomo of Milan, Mary was widely known in Italy and Germany as the Corn Maiden. The astrological sign of Virgo in the harvesting month of September, in which the maiden characteristically holds up an ear of corn, was undoubtedly allied to this revived image of Mary, as it had been earlier to Kore or Persephone, daughter of the Corn Goddess Demeter.

Figure 18. *The Madonna of the Sheaves*; woodcut, perhaps Bavarian, c. 1450.

Figure 19. 'Madonna from Munster near Dieburg';[43] cast stone sculpture of Mary holding the baby Jesus and the Tree of Life, 1900.

Spring has always had a goddess to call its own. Either Persephone came back to see her mother, Demeter, or Aphrodite returned from the deep waters of her winter bath, or Isis gave birth to Horus. Ishtar greeted the rebirth of Tammuz, and Inanna was released from Ereshkigal's dark embrace to reassume her title 'the Green One'. The month of May, nine days after the spring equinox, became Mary's month officially only in the eighteenth century, but long before that she had been celebrated as the epitome of the delight of spring on May morning, as she is still, with flowers and dancing and processions in which her statue is carried around the town.

But however fruitful in the image of 'Nature's motherhood', as Gerard Manley Hopkins calls her in his poem beginning 'May is Mary's month', Mary is not simply pictured sitting on the earth before the Tree of Life as its epiphany, as in the Minoan seal (see Chapter 3, Fig. 11). Generally, when she takes over the ancient domain of the 'Lady of the Plants', her transcendent qualities are emphasized in the manner of the Christian spiritualization of the natural world. In the cast-stone statue in Figure 19 Mary, wearing a crown of fruits and flowers just like Demeter, holds in one hand the baby and in the other a branch as the Tree of Life with her son crucified upon its central stem. Without interpretation, though, the image on its own could depict the perennial drama of the two phases of birth and death: the child and the dying consort, the bud and the tree that has to be cut down for the renewal of growth.

Mary as Goddess of the Animals

The ox and the ass nuzzling over the crib of the baby Jesus are so central
to depictions of the Christmas scene that it comes as a surprise to remember that they were not part of the original story in the Gospels.
Looking simply at a typical picture of the birth scene, we could be
looking at the old goddess of the animals, where the once stylized abstract
of the goddess between two symmetrically placed beasts on either side of
her has given way to the narrative moment when her fertility is realized.
From this point of view, the entrance of the shepherds with their sheep is
integral to the gathering of all the animals around their mistress in the
cow-byre, as an image of the fertility that she had in her care. A further
meaning to the invariable appearance of ox and ass is offered by Campbell,
who points out that these were also the animals that symbolized the
opposing factions of Osiris and Seth – a fact, he says, that would have
been instantly recognizable at that time – so that in this way the birth
of the Christ child as the union and transcendence of opposites was
registered.[44]

Mary is also often found sitting on a lion throne, placing her in the long
tradition of goddesses whose rulership of the powers of nature is expressed
by standing or sitting upon the lion (see Chapter 6, Fig. 31). Without
having seen similar pictures in earlier cultures, it is easy to overlook the
significance of the statement that is implicitly being made. The Etruscan
mother goddess in Figure 20, for instance, sits massively on her throne,

Figure 20. (*Left*) Etruscan Mother Goddess; stone sculpture, fifth century BC.
Figure 21. (*Right*) *Mary on the Lion Throne*; 1360. Hermsdorf, Germany.

Figure 22. *La Sainte Pureté dans la Fortresse*; studio of Hans Memlinck, active
c. 1465–94. The Virgin Mary(?) standing in an amethyst mountain,
guarded by two lions.

with two human-faced sphinxes to support her, while the joyous and
fruitful Mary in Figure 21 sits on a throne with tamed lions at her feet.
The Etruscan and the Christian figures are very similar in outline yet the
Etruscan goddess has all the solidity of the Neolithic goddesses, while
Mary, by contrast, is light and playful, almost childlike.

The placing of the woman rising out of the body of the mountain in
Figure 22 recalls unmistakably the Minoan Goddess of the Animals standing on top of her mountain flanked by lions from Crete (see Chapter 3,
Fig. 27). Here, too, are two lions at the foot of the amethyst mountain, at
once fierce and heraldic; in fact, the picture is so reminiscent, the question
arises how did the artist 'know'?

Earlier goddesses of the beasts, such as Artemis, also grasped birds as
well as deer, lions and bulls, as descendants of the Neolithic bird goddess.
The only remnant of this in the Christian tradition is the dove, formerly
the bird of the Minoan Goddess, Inanna and Aphrodite, in their capacity
as goddesses of the relationship of all orders of being through love. As the
image of the Holy Spirit descending from the opened heavens and 'lighting on' Jesus as he is baptized, the dove has no explicit connection with

Mary in the Gospels, and in fact the dove that almost invariably accompanies the angel in the Annunciation pictures was not originally 'there'. Similarly, artists have added the dove to pictures of Mary's childhood as a sign of the Holy Spirit already inherent in her. None the less, it remains significant that the dove symbolizes the albeit fleeting immanence of God, the Father – his epiphany made visible – which is obviously why the story of the Annunciation seemed incomplete without it. The question why the Holy Spirit, which is neuter in Greek, *Hagion Pneuma*, and masculine in Latin, *Spiritus Sanctus*, is symbolized in a feminine image belonging to the deposed goddess culture will be considered in the next chapter on Sophia.

MARY AS THE GODDESS OF DEATH AND THE UNDERWORLD

Although as late as the eighteenth century Mary was described in a work of devotion as 'the most blessed Virgin (who) rules over the infernal regions . . . the sovereign mistress of the devils', [45] it still seems strange to describe her, the intercessor and mediator for the souls of the dead and dying, as a 'goddess of death or the underworld', probably because the original unity of the Great Mother who rules over life as well as death has gone, and so the meaning of a goddess of death has changed. Christian mythology has no Mother of Life, so how can it have a Mother of Death, she who takes back the children to whom she had given life?

The Christian name for the underworld is 'hell', a name of a Germanic goddess of the underworld, called Hel. She is the sister of the uroboric Midgard, serpent of the ocean that encloses the earth, and sister, too, to the devouring 'Fenris-wolf'. So the resonances are still there in the image of the underwater abyss that swallows up lives, as well as the serpent who regenerates them. In early pictures, as in the Winchester Psalter, for instance, hell is imagined as a whale with wide-open jaws, ready to swallow sinners into its bottomless belly. Christ, who redeems Adam and Eve, is then cast as the archetypal hero doing battle with the dragon-whale. But more often there is an imaginative gap, since the change from mother to father creator brings with it a corresponding change in the imagery of death, and into this gap, soon to become a yawning cavern, was projected all the torments that fear creates, concretized, as in Babylonian times, into demons with tails and pitchforks, boiling pitch, sulphur and everlasting fire. Creation by the Word means death by the Word, and death was generally envisaged as a punishment for sin and sin was inevitable.

Into this situation the merciful, forgiving, figure of Our Lady enters as the last hope of reprieve from eternal damnation, reassuming the ancient titles of the Sumerian goddess Ninhursag, 'She who Gives Life to the Dead', and of Inanna, who was called the 'Forgiver of Sins'. Theologically, Mary enters as a compassionate mother whose heartfelt plea no son

Figure 23. *Madonna della Misericordia*; Piero della Francesca, *c.* 1445–8.

could refuse. Her intercession with Christ, the Judge, metaphorically tips the scales of justice (sometimes held by St Michael) in favour of the redemption of the accused sinner, even as in Egypt the feather of the goddess Maat is weighed against the heart of the dead person. In Michelangelo's painting of the Last Judgement, Mary's body, with arms protectively crossed and eyes cast down, inclines away from Christ's implacably raised arm, in mute protest against the harshness of his judgement. However, in practice, as in Piero della Francesca's painting in Figure 23,

Mary's awesome reality is all encompassing, and it is to her that the fearful soul looks for mercy. The Apocalyptic stories all testify to the belief that if only she can be reached, then forgiveness is assured, because Mary alone can accept the whole human being. It is curious that although the character of Jesus is known from the Gospels, and it is his drama that is enacted, in this final scene of life Mary becomes almost more accessible than him. She can be swayed by feelings of compassion for the suffering of sinners, whereas he, the righteous judge, only enacts the law whatever the punishment, in spite of the fact that in the Gospels he is the one who refuses to judge. As Christianity continued to grow over the centuries, the figure of Mary the Mother gathered to herself the meaning of the loving teachings of her son, who was sometimes by contrast allotted the surprising role of the dispassionate Father, almost as though an archetypal pattern of feminine and masculine principles were reasserting itself. The most important prayer to Mary, the Hail Mary, said all over the Catholic world, has as its closing plea that she would 'pray for us sinners, now and at the hour of our death'.

Mater Dolorosa

Michelangelo's *Pietà* in St Peter's Basilica is probably the most well-loved of the countless *pietà* shared by the Christian world, for in the mourning of the mother for her son can be felt the universal human loss of all that is finest in life, even finally that life itself.

As the 'Mater Dolorosa', Mary's lament for her crucified son echoes the lament of Inanna for Dumuzi, Ishtar for Tammuz, Isis for Osiris, Aphrodite for Adonis, Demeter for Persephone and Cybele for Attis; and the women weeping at the tomb take up the cry of the women who wept for Tammuz in the temple at Jerusalem. Briffault records that

> as late as the tenth century AD, a traveller in Arab countries observed: 'All the Sabaeans of our time, those of Babylonia as well as those of Harran, lament and weep to this day over Tammuz at a festival which they, more particularly the women, hold in the month of the same name.'[46]

The last temple of Isis at Philae was closed by Justinian in the sixth century AD, and in the same century poetry appeared in Syria of Mary mourning for her dead son:

> I am overwhelmed, O my son
> I am overwhelmed by love
> And I cannot endure
> That I should be in the chamber
> And you on the wood of the cross
> I in the house
> And you in the tomb.[47]

Figure 24. *Pietà*; marble statue by Michelangelo, 1499. St Peter's Basilica, Rome.

The words of Inanna's lament for Dumuzi are not far away:

> Tell me where is my house, my mute, silent house,
> My house in which a spouse no longer lives, in which I no longer greet a son,
> I, the queen of heaven, am one in whose house a spouse no longer lives, in whose house I no longer greet a son.[48]

Ishtar's grief for Tammuz speaks in the same images:

> Him of the plains why have they slain?
> The shepherd, the wise one,
> The man of sorrows why have they slain?[49]

And Isis' lament for Osiris:

> Come to thy house, come to thy house . . .
> O beautiful Boy, come to thy house,
> Immediately, immediately.

I do not see thee,
My heart weepeth for thee,
My two eyes follow thee about.
I am following thee about that I may see thee . . .
Come to thy beloved one,
Come to thy beloved one, Beautiful Being, triumphant![50]

In Christian doctrine Mary knows that her son will rise from the dead, and participates in the eternal necessity of his sacrifice. Yet again, it is only in an image such as Piero della Francesca's that Mary embodies the principle of eternity, for, unlike the Bronze Age goddesses, she did not initiate the ritual sacrifice of her son, so her mourning takes on a more human quality. As Warner says, it is through Mary that the Crucifixion, the Deposition, and the Entombment, as they are called in the Christian tradition, come to life: 'She made the sacrifice on Golgotha seem real, for she focused human feeling in a comprehensible and accessible way.'[51]

None the less, the tears she weeps, like the lunar dew and milk, are given the power to regenerate life, and, like Persephone, the pomegranate she often holds in her hand suggests her role as guardian of the under-world's mysteries of transformation, like the goddess of the waning and dark moon. For millennia death had become comprehensible through the image of the Mother, as though when death struck the mind of humanity, so did an image of consolation and compassion that took the shape of the Mother who gave that humanity birth. Mary's inclusion in the image of life beyond death may belong to this memory.

THE BLACK VIRGIN

Standing in underground crypts of cathedrals and upon the altars of remote and humble churches and chapels, the image of the Black Virgin also relates to the realm of the dark moon, the creative depths from which the old light has gone but from which new light is born. Earlier goddesses were on occasion cast as black, as though to summon the heart to the impenetrable mystery of the creative source. Isis in Apuleius' vision wears a black robe, Cybele was worshipped as a black stone, and Demeter and Athena also had black versions of themselves. Artemis of Ephesus, the place where the powers of the goddess tradition were 'transferred' to Mary, was also strikingly black. We do not know which goddess speaks the words in the Song of Songs 'I am black but comely, O ye daughters of Jerusalem' (S. of S. 1:5), except that she is a Shulamite, which is 'one who has found peace' and may also be the female counterpart of Solomon, whose name contains the word *shalom*, which means 'peace'. None the less, this is the basic text in the Judaeo-Christian tradition for the relation between wisdom and blackness, which was made in earlier times through the symbolism of the moon.

Figure 25. *Notre Dame de Marsat*; wood,
twelfth century. Puy-de-Dôme, France.

The Black Virgin is found mostly in France, Spain, Switzerland and
Poland. Ean Begg's book *The Cult of the Black Virgin* traces the sources
of the Black Virgin chiefly to Isis, Cybele and Artemis of Ephesus, and
follows the resurgence of this image in the twelfth century, when it was
brought back to the West by the Crusaders. He gives an evocative description of the way Christianity absorbed the generalized worship of the
Great Goddess of many names:

> In Christianity the feminine principle was represented by Black Virgins,
> White Virgins and a host of female saints, each having her own symbol and
> specific nature. As Christianity gradually asserted itself, the great bronze
> and marble statues of the pagan deities were destroyed. Smaller, household
> images or votive offerings, hidden in the earth, in cleft rocks or hollow
> trees, survived, especially in remote country places. Some were lost, some,
> perhaps, still visited as fairy trees and stones, long after their true nature
> had been forgotten. The memory of them may have influenced a later
> generation of religious sculptors. In addition, at the time of the Crusades,
> original pagan statues, or images based on them, were brought back from
> the east by returning warriors, as Madonnas.
>
> Apart from the candle-smoke theory, this is the simplest and most widely
> held explanation for the existence of Black Virgins in Europe. They would
> thus be a survival, and a continuation under a new name and a new religion,
> of goddesses from the classical world.[52]

Statues of the Black Virgin are often found on the sites of the ancient
goddesses, or where the Cathars lived, or where there was a cult of Mary

Magdalene, with whom she was significantly associated. Many of the statues have an androgynous look about them, as in Figure 25,[53] offering a very different portrait of the Madonna from the submissive mother of the Gospels. Sometimes the images invoke the grandeur of the Gnostic Sophia, who was with God in the beginning, and whose name in Greek means 'Wisdom'. Certainly, miracles and apparitions surround the Black Virgins, especially those relating to the physical processes of childbirth and sickness, together with an unusual tolerance towards what Hamlet calls 'country matters'.[54] It is as though all the denied feelings of orthodoxy found in their opaque darkness a place to wonder anew at the magical healing powers of nature herself. (See Chapter 15, pp. 643–7.)

MARY MAGDALENE

Mary Magdalene was a figure of such suggestive mystery that legends continually wove themselves around her, pointing to what was missing for the human imagination in the image of Mary the Virgin Mother. There has always existed some confusion as to whether there are three separate women in the Gospels: Mary of Bethany, who was Lazarus's sister; the 'sinner' who anointed Jesus' feet with oils and dried them with her hair; and the woman called Mary Magdalene; or whether the three women are all one – Mary Magdalene – declared by name to be the one who witnessed the Resurrection, and so of paramount importance. Certainly, the profusion of Marys is arresting, together with Mary the Mother, given the

Figure 26. *St Mary Magdalene*; Pietro Perugino, *c.* 1494.

derivation of the name from the sea, and the number three suggesting the symbolism of the lunar trinity. The Gospels do not clarify the identity of Mary Magdalene, so the stories to which the fascination of this ambiguous figure gave rise are primarily stories about the reclamation of sexuality for the Christian imagination. In practice, however, the term 'Magdalene' became the name for a house for the reclamation of prostitutes!

Mark refers to Mary Magdalene by name as one 'out of whom he [Jesus] had cast seven devils' (Mark 16:9), and Luke speaks of a woman following Jesus who 'had been healed of evil spirits and infirmities', who was called Mary and came from the town of Magdala, and out of whom Jesus had exorcised seven devils (Luke 8:2). Just before this, Luke gives an account of the dinner with the Pharisee when an unnamed woman washes Jesus' feet with her tears, dries them with her hair and then anoints them, a juxtaposition that invites a conflation of the two women, especially by those who read Jesus' forgiveness of her sins – 'for she loved much' – as referring to the large number of the woman's erotic amours rather than to the simple much-loving act she had just performed. In Matthew and Mark the same story occurs, but it is given greater significance by being set just before the Last Supper, in Bethany, though the unnamed woman is not called a sinner. She anoints not the feet of Jesus, but his head, more in the ceremonial manner of anointing a king, and evocative of the way that in Sumeria kings were anointed by the priestess in the ceremony of a ritual sacrifice. When the disciples are indignant for the waste of oil on the grounds that it could have been sold and given to the poor, Jesus asks that her action be seen not as a celebration but as an embalmment: 'For ye have the poor always with you; but me ye have not always. For in that she hath poured this ointment on my body, she did it for my burial' (Matt. 26: 11–12; cf. Mark 14: 3–8). It is immediately after this scene in both accounts that Judas goes to the priests to betray him.

In Luke, Mary Magdalene is implicitly present at the burial and deposition, but she sees only the empty sepulchre, not Christ risen (Luke 24:4). In Matthew, Mary Magdalene and 'the other Mary' – probably the Mary referred to as the mother of James and Joseph, Zebedee's children – are present at the crucifixion and then keep watch over the sepulchre. On the third day the two Marys come to see the sepulchre and are greeted by the angel, and on their way back they are met by Jesus, who tells them to tell his brethren that he is risen (Matt. 27:56 – 28:10). But when this same story is told by Mark, it has the crucial addition that the two Marys, Mary Magdalene and Mary the mother of James, with Salome, had brought 'sweet spices, that they might come and anoint him' (Mark 16:1). When Mark then tells the story of Jesus' appearance to 'Mary Magdalene, out of whom he had cast seven devils' (Mark 16:9), the association of devils and the sinner who anointed Jesus for his burial make the identification of the exorcized Mary Magdalene with the unnamed loving sinner whose sins were forgiven her almost irresistible.

However, a further complication is introduced by John, who, describing the raising of Lazarus, explicitly identifies Mary of Bethany with 'that Mary which anointed the Lord with ointment, and wiped his feet with her hair' (John 11:2). John gives the scene in the following chapter in much the same way as the other Gospels, though without referring to Mary as a sinner: 'Then took Mary a pound of ointment of spikenard, very costly, and anointed the feet of Jesus, and wiped his feet with her hair' (John 12:3). But John does not make any connection between Mary of Bethany and Mary Magdalene, which, given his earlier precision, he would have done had he believed them to be the same person. In fact, in his Gospel, Mary Magdalene stands apart from all the others because of the moving depth of her encounter with the angels and then with Jesus himself. As she stands outside the empty sepulchre weeping, the angels 'say unto her, Woman, why weepest thou?' She replies:

> Because they have taken away my Lord, and I know not where they have laid him.
>
> And when she had thus said, she turned herself back, and saw Jesus standing, and knew not that it was Jesus.
>
> Jesus saith unto her, Woman, why weepest thou? whom seekest thou? She, supposing him to be the gardener, saith unto him, Sir, if thou have borne him hence, tell me where thou hast laid him, and I will take him away.
>
> Jesus saith unto her, Mary. She turned herself, and saith unto him, Rabboni; which is to say, Master.
>
> Jesus saith unto her, Touch me not; for I am not yet ascended to my Father. (John 20: 13–17)

The most important thing about the controversy surrounding Mary Magdalene is not whether she was or was not in fact also Mary of Bethany and/or the 'sinner', but why so many people have minded so much about it. In other words, what does the controversy mean? In John, where her personal sorrow finds expression in one of the loveliest passages, she is the first to see the body of Jesus gone and the first to see Christ risen, and the one entrusted by him to tell the disciples of his resurrection from the dead. At the simple level of narrative, her devotion to him is rewarded with the greatest gift anyone could imagine, that the one mourned returns to life. But in a universe where nothing is conceived to be random, she is unaccountably singled out, and it is not surprising that the Gnostic Gospels of Philip and Mary interpreted this unaccountability in terms of a love between Jesus and Mary, and consequently a special initiation, which medieval tradition continued in the image of Mary as 'the Lightbearer'.

Read symbolically, however, the state of mind that the figure of Mary Magdalene embodies – one of loving commitment, active caring and complete trust – is poetically appointed to be that most suited to seeing beyond appearances into their inherent reality, even where that

Figure 27. Mary Magdalene; detail, panel of Calvary
Triptych, Rogier van der Weyden, *c.* 1440.

confounds the apparently absolute logic of common sense. This was the true meaning of Gnosticism, that knowledge is won through the imaginative engagement of the whole being in what is known – *gnosis*.

The picture of a sorrowful woman holding a jar of anointing oil is the one most characteristic of Mary Magdalene in early Renaissance paintings, and this image followed her in legend to Provence, where a shrine was dedicated to her in the cave of Ste Baume hidden in a mountain ridge near St Maximin. Her relics were claimed to exist in many places in the south of France, since the three Marys, together with Martha and Lazarus, were believed to have arrived by boat at the place called after them, Les Saintes Maries de la Mer.[55] The image of weeping was also one of her defining qualities, for the word 'maudlin', which passed into the English language via the French, derived from her name.[56]

One doctrinal advantage of identifying the three Marys as one is that her weeping gains in addition that specifically Pauline Christian emphasis on repentance for sin, the 'sin' for a woman being assumed without question to be sexual, and the woman assumed therefore to be a whore whom Jesus had forgiven and who had herself repented. In fact, the response of Jesus elsewhere to the woman taken in adultery totally contravened and transformed Jewish law laid down in Leviticus, which would have had the woman stoned to death, whereas Jesus asks 'he who is without sin' to cast the first stone at her (John 8: 3–12). The fascination with the penitent whore is still a fascination with sexuality, albeit reformed and redeemed into humble service, a questionable prurience, which finds its apotheosis in Wagner's Kundry, the once wild amoral spirit of nature who ends up drying the feet of Parsival with her tangled hair and receiving for her reformation one chaste kiss upon her tear-stained brow.

In the light of the mythological tradition that preceded her, the significance of Mary Magdalene's 'mistaking' of the risen Christ for the 'gardener' is supremely resonant, because the gardener was the name given to the son–lover of the goddess in Sumeria, where Inanna's tears also flowed for the loss of her lord. Furthermore, the ceremony of the sacrifice of the son–lover included the ritual of anointing by the temple priestess, so it becomes another curious coincidence that the name 'Magdalene' means literally 'She of the temple-tower'. Again, the association of prostitution and anointing is suggestive because the role of the temple priestess of the goddess religion included both these tasks as sacred rituals, though the term 'prostitution' cannot convey the original religious meaning of the practice. The act of anointing recalls Gilgamesh's lament for Enkidu, in which he is interpreted as saying: 'The harlot who anointed you with fragrant ointment laments for you now',[57] but the word 'harlot' was a translation of the word *quadishtu,* which in its original sense meant 'sacred hierodule or priestess'. The number of seven devils cast out of Mary Magdalene is interesting in this connection, for it may have taken its reference from the seven Annunaki, or spirits of the underworld, which were also the seven planetary gods of Babylon, and may have found their way as a sacred number into Canaan. When, therefore, Mary Magdalene of the 'devils' is treated as one with the 'sinner', it is just possible that behind the story of exorcism and forgiveness is a further story of the conversion of a temple priestess from the Canaanite religion to the new teaching of Jesus.

It seems as if the very extremity of virgin motherhood embodied in Mary itself created the need for the other extreme: the woman who was not chaste, but whose original 'sin' had been redeemed. The flaw in the thinking that one extreme will be corrected by another, which characterizes all literal thinking, fails here as elsewhere because both alternatives remain at the same level. Both virgin and whore are cast wholly in sexual terms – in their relations to men – and the difference is ultimately only one of different kinds of service. Yet in the narrative it is Mary Magdalene, not Mary the Mother, who ultimately transcends her doctrinal definition since she performs the human task of mourning and laying out the dead body, and witnesses all the phases of the drama of transformation; she is the one to whom Christ speaks the moving words that mark him as not any longer of this world: 'Touch me not.' It is she who is then the mediator between the mystery of the Resurrection and the ordinary understanding of the disciples, who hear it from her as her story of her Lord.

MARY AS GODDESS OF WAR

It cannot pass without mention that the dark phase of the moon, which is embodied in Mary's underworldly aspect, also parallels the ways in which other goddesses have been conceived. Mary's emblem has been repeatedly pinned to the standards of Christian armies in the role that describing Ishtar, Astarte or Anath would be called 'Goddess of War' – that is, death to others. The alliance of politics with official religion has, presumably, no greater claim to holiness in Christian history than it does in any other 'holy war'. Victories were often attributed to the Virgin's intervention, like the icon of Mary that was thought to have brought victory at Lepanto; and sometimes a representation of Mary was itself fought for, like the Virgin of Vladimir.[58] Feast days to the Virgin were instituted afterwards to commemorate God's will being done on earth as it was envisaged in heaven, even when the opposing army was itself Christian, but 'another kind' of Christian, or 'heretics'.[59] Now, perhaps, this role is more subtly registered; for instance, in a little village in Crete called Kolumbari, the Feast of the Assumption is celebrated as usual with insignia of the Virgin carried in procession around the village, followed by all the villagers, but flanked on either side by the army in full uniform.

MARY AS THE DAUGHTER OF
THE GREAT MOTHER ANNE

In one of Leonardo's great paintings Mary is shown as the daughter of Anne, with the emphasis on Anne as the Great Mother on whose lap Mary sits in a curious sideways posture as though she were part of her mother's body (Fig. 28). The three faces form one line, with the child and his mother holding the dramatic focus of the picture, while Anne comprehends the whole scene in the serenity of her expression, at once beyond the drama yet participating in it as its ultimate author. The positioning of their feet, so that Mary's foot seems to be Anne's and Anne's seems to be Mary's, refers us to a tradition of inheritance from one perennial source. Also the positioning of the leg of the lamb across the knee of Jesus to rest on the ankle of Mary, as though, from another perspective, it completes the leg of Jesus, gives him the impression of a little hoof, like Pan, the spirit of awakened nature.

Many paintings and sculptures throughout the Catholic world portray Anne and Mary as a 'great' and 'little' mother, generally fused together as though they were in essence one being. This conveys the original grandeur of the Great Mother, while keeping strictly to the Mary of the Gospels, who is modest, submissive and concerned, and who is often portrayed as herself a child in relation to her mother. One of the earliest Christian

Figure 28. *Virgin and Child with St Anne*; Leonardo da Vinci, *c.* 1508–10.

images, in the church of St Maria Antiqua in the Roman forum, has St Anne holding Mary in her arms. Generally, the son is also included, and so perpetuates a tradition of mother, daughter and child known from Crete, and possibly even earlier from Anatolia, continued through the myth of Demeter, Kore–Persephone and Triptolemos, the divine son.

In the imagery of mother and daughter, there are echoes from the past of Demeter and Persephone as the source and its manifestation, and, closer to Christianity, echoes also of the Gnostic Great Mother Sophia and her daughter, which may have found their way into the apocryphal literature that grew up around Mary from the second century to the Middle Ages. Sometimes the gaze of eternal foresight found on the face of Anne as she looks beyond the human drama of her daughter and her daughter's son would be disconcerting if we did not recall the Sophia who was 'there' at the beginning of all things.

Figure 29. *Madonna and Child with St Anne*; Masaccio and Masolino,
c. 1427–8.

MARY AND THE HOLY SPIRIT

The dove that – not in the Gospels but in the pictures of Gospel stories –
hangs above the head of Mary, whispers in her ear, or is poised midway
between her and God across a stream of light in the moment of Annunciation, is interpreted as having been 'sent' by God 'to' Mary as the epiphany
of 'His' presence: the image of the 'Holy Spirit'. Yet the conjunction of
dove and female in the earlier traditions would have been understood as
the Mother Goddess with the dove that was her epiphany, and the two
together as the heavenly and the earthly aspects of the goddess, which, in
still earlier traditions, would have been unified in one being called the
Bird Goddess. In the Christian tradition it is assumed without question
that the dove comes *to* Mary, whereas, formerly, it would have been
assumed to have come *from* her. In many pictures of any tradition the
direction of the bird's flight is simply a matter of interpretation.

The dove, once the epiphany of the divine feminine, has now become the epiphany of the divine masculine, so it may be worth reiterating what the bird, and specifically the dove, originally signified. The bird in the Neolithic era was identified with the Great Mother as the moving spirit of 'the great sea' of the heavens, source of the waters that fertilized the earth. In the Bronze Age the bird as the Great Mother lays the universal egg on the primeval waters in both Egypt and Greece. The bird accompanies the goddess in Sumeria, Crete and Egypt, as later in Greece, and a dove hovers above the dead person in Egyptian tomb paintings as an image of the soul. An Akkadian bas-relief shows a large dove carried by two male attendants, image of the goddess Anna, a descendant of Inanna (compare the name of St Anne). The presence of the mother goddess Rhea is signified by doves, and Zeus, her child, was fed by doves when a baby. In the Iron Age the Phoenician moon goddess, Ashtoreth, drives in a chariot pulled by doves, and the dove is the bird of Aphrodite, goddess of love. Demeter holds in one hand a dolphin and in the other a dove, and a dove sits in the lap of her daughter, Persephone, in the underworld. In the Judaic tradition of Noah and his ark, derived from the Sumerian Ziusudra or the Babylonian Utnapishtim and his ark, the dove was the messenger of new life, the news that land had risen above the flood. The dove was not, therefore, an image that came into being uniquely when God saw his son baptized in the River Jordan.

However, the dove still retains its *archetypal* feminine connotations, for, as the Holy Spirit, it signifies the relationship between the divine and the human realms, and it is this that brings the transcendent god into creation as an immanent presence. The divine presence of Yahweh in the Wisdom literature of the Old Testament used to be experienced as feminine, either as the Shekhinah or as Sophia, as the Presence of God or the Wisdom of God. If the feminine principle had not been lost as a sacred entity, there would inevitably have been some relation between 'God' and Shekhinah/Sophia, and 'God' and Mary as a parallel union of masculine and feminine principles in their heavenly and earthly aspects. The language of the Annunciation – 'The Holy Ghost shall come upon thee, and the power of the Highest shall overshadow thee: therefore also that holy thing which shall be born of thee shall be called the Son of God' – unmistakably recalls, in the image of 'overshadowing', the Shekhinah.

In this case the Holy Trinity would have constituted a father, mother and a child, or an unmanifest, a manifest aspect, and an aspect that belongs to both and so relates the two to each other. This would have then been the sacred marriage of transcendence and immanence which brings about the new vision, the child. Of course, this is not the story that is given, but it is fascinating that the story that the images tell, underlying the formal Christian story – and, it may be, thereby contributing to its imaginative power – is one of harmony and archetypal complementarity.

As we have seen, the idea of a trinity as a unity is lunar in origin, going back to the three visible phases of the moon – the waxing, the full and the waning – experienced as the three-fold nature of the one Great Goddess of the eternal cycle. Referring to Egyptian sources in particular, Frazer comments: 'The conception of the triad or trinity is, in Egypt, probably as old as the belief in gods ... If the Christian doctrine of the Trinity took shape under Egyptian influence, the function originally assigned to the Holy Spirit may have been that of the divine mother.'[60]

Probably by the fourth century, when the Apostles' Creed was being formulated, and certainly by the eighth century, when it was finally completed, the Holy Spirit in Latin was irrevocably masculine, *Spiritus Sanctus*, which had considerable implications for the lost feminine dimension of the divine. The imagery of the Creed still suggests in fact that the Holy Spirit was a Mother – 'conceived by the Holy Ghost, born of the Virgin Mary' – so that the conception of Jesus was understood as having taken place at two levels, within a divine and then a human mother, though Mary is only the vessel, not the 'egg'. But the Holy Ghost is of masculine gender. So, as with Adam and Zeus, but more subtly, the conceiving capacities of the female are appropriated by the male, if only in the implicit reference of linguistic gender.

JESUS IN THE TRADITION OF THE SON–LOVER OF THE GODDESS

In the Near East sacred ritual had been for many thousands of years focused on the myth of the Mother Goddess and her son–lover. It would be strange if the ancient goddess tradition converged so completely on Mary but left her son utterly unique, without any mythic structures to support him. Whatever interpretation one might finally like to make of these parallels, it seems to be undeniable, as Frazer proposed, that the perennial mythic images of the dying and resurrected god gathered round the figure of Jesus of Nazareth, so it is very difficult – if indeed it is even possible – to distinguish 'myth' from 'reality'.

With the exception of Dumuzi's lament in Sumeria and the bridegroom's song in the Song of Songs, Jesus is the first of the 'son–lovers' whose voice we hear, or at least whose voice has come down to us. He is the first actually to teach the meaning of his sacrifice, and the first to take that sacrifice upon himself willingly. In the tradition that clothed him, the son–lovers of earlier times were not drawn as consenting to their death or understanding it. If that is a valid comparison, then from any perspective this represents a crucial movement of consciousness to a higher level.

The question that arises from any parallels between Christianity and religious beliefs many thousands of years older than itself is why and how this myth came to surround the life of someone called Jesus, who was at least an extraordinary teacher. Christians say that it is because Jesus was

Figure 30. *The Crucifixion*; Evesham Psalter, *c.* 1250. English.

the Son of God, as doubtless did the Sumerians of Dumuzi, the Babylonians of Tammuz, the Phrygians of Attis, and the Greeks of Dionysos and Adonis. Outside the framework of belief this question is ultimately unanswerable and obviously beyond the scope of this book, so we shall simply point to the resemblances between the different cultural stories and images in order to reveal the one thing that is common to all of them: the human psyche.

The cross upon which Christ hangs in Figure 30 is shown as the two crossed branches of a living tree, with all but the essential branches cut back to the stem, rendering the cross as the ever-living Tree of Life. Let us review the symbolism of the Tree of Life to point to the universality of this image. Once the epiphany of the Mother Goddess, the dramas of the Tree of Life followed the growing of humanity. Trees gave birth to gods and heroic redeemers, and then the gods themselves were seen embodied in the tree's rising sap and the dynamic and ever-renewing phases of its growth. Dumuzi, son–lover of Inanna, was called 'Son of the Abyss: Lord of the Tree of Life'. In Egypt the sun god was born variously from the heavenly cow, Hathor, the female body of Nut, the sky goddess, or from the highest branches of the tree of Isis, or Hathor in another of her manifestations. The brother–husband of Isis, Osiris, who, as the setting sun, became lord of the underworld, was reborn from a tree: his coffin was washed ashore and an erica tree grew up around it, and, after a time of gestation, the tree released him back into life; when, dying again, a pillar of wood (the *Djed* column) was raised upright as the sign of his eternal life.

There was also a tree for Queen Maya to lean against as she gave birth to the Buddha, and it was beneath the boddhi tree that the mature Buddha sat until he reached enlightenment. In Greece the myrtle tree gave birth to Adonis, lover of Aphrodite and god of regeneration, whose death and

Figure 31. *Christ on the Tree of Life*; mosaic ceiling of the Church of San Clemente, Rome, *c.* 1500.

rebirth were mourned and celebrated every year in the springtime season of renewal. Mithras, the Persian and Roman sun god, came forth from a tree (or sometimes a cave) at the time of the winter solstice as the *Sol Invictus*, a title that fell naturally to Jesus, 'born' at the same time. Imaginal trees surround the life of Jesus. His earthly father was a carpenter, fashioner of the cut tree, and in the *Rig Veda* the architect of the universe, Tvastri, is imagined as a carpenter, fashioning the world into being.[61]

Doctrinally, the symbolism of the cross is understood from within the Christian faith with no reference to its universality as a symbol for believers of any creed. Here, the cross as the Tree of Life is placed in symbolic counterpoise to the Tree of Knowledge, and so is an image of the final redemption of the original Fall. In art Christ is also sometimes placed hanging on a tree of grapes, linking his sacrifice with that of the dismembered god of the Greek tradition, Dionysos, and also illuminating his statement: 'I am the vine, ye are the branches' (John 15: 5). Sometimes, as in the Byzantine mosaic on the ceiling of the Church of San Clemente (Fig. 31), the death and resurrection of Christ are portrayed as one image. There the golden and joyously spiralling Tree of Life takes back into itself the body of Jesus, the trunk of the tree serving as the cross upon which Christ hangs surrounded by doves. The Tree of Life here both contains and transforms the cross of its central branches, and the drama depicted is one in which the Lord of the Tree of Life, cut down for the

Figure 32. *Christ of the Apocalypse*; South Porch, Royal Portal, Central Tympanum, Chartres Cathedral, twelfth century.

birth of all, returns home, like many Lords before him, to the place beyond opposites and so to the source of rebirth.

In this connection the symbolism of Palm Sunday and Ash Wednesday in the Christian year is interesting, since the ashes placed on the foreheads of the faithful are the embers of last year's palm leaves, which have been blessed with holy water and the sign of the cross, a ceremony that, symbolically, revives the life-force of the Tree of Life. The mass of Palm Sunday, which begins the Holy Week that ends in the resurrection at Easter, starts with a consecration of branches of palm and olive, not the customary bread and wine. In fact, the whole of Holy Week takes on the character of a Mystery drama, in which the events of the 'passion' of Christ are re-enacted every year, just as they were in the Mysteries of Attis in Rome, or in the Mystery plays of Osiris at Abydos, which culminated in the raising of the *Djed* column, the wooden pillar of the Tree of Life and the sign of resurrection: 'Osiris is risen', the people cried.

If Christ took over the role of the Lord of the Tree of Life, he was also given the role of Lord of the Beasts, guardian and ruler of the animal world of nature, and, as it now became, of animal instinct also. In Figure 32 Christ is carved in the south portal of Chartres Cathedral at the centre of two winged animals, the lion and the bull, one eagle and one winged man or angel. Without a knowledge of the 'text' that gave rise to them, the only difference between this and earlier images is that the Lord is not here grasping his beasts and birds, as once Artemis did, but sits enthroned in an oval as though he were emerging from an opening womb, which, as revelation, of course he is. John's vision in Revelation in the Christian text, however, came to him, fascinatingly enough, in the images of what were then the four 'cardinal' signs of the Chaldean zodiac (which, 2,000 years later, have become the 'fixed' signs of the contemporary zodiac) – Taurus, Leo, Scorpio and Aquarius – an image, therefore, of totality with Christ as the *Axis Mundi*. When adapted to Christian symbolism, these signs of the four world quarters became the four Evangelists: Luke as the

Figure 33. *The Crucifixion*; woodcut, *c.* 1830. Rennes, France.

bull, Mark as the lion, John as the eagle (an earlier image of the sign of Scorpio) and Matthew as a winged angel, once the god who carried two jars of water, like Hapi, the Nile god, pouring the waters of life upon the parched ground.[62]

The nineteenth-century woodcut in Figure 33 also works with the symbolism of the cross as the Tree of Life, but its difference from the older symbolism is instructive. The cross rises out of, and away from, the sphere of the world, represented by the skull with the serpent circling around it, offering the specifically Christian emphasis on transcendence as the way of unifying the opposites, given here in the images of sun and moon. A striking addition are the dismembered heads and limbs hanging from the heart-shaped rose wreath, suggesting a link with earlier traditions of sacrifice, which took the explicit form of dismemberment rather than hanging from a tree. What is common to both forms is that the body of the divine being is offered as sacrifice for the 'body' of life. The mystery, here as in the earlier mysteries, is that eating the bread and drinking the wine of our everyday life can return us, symbolically, to the original substance of the divine being whose life is not time-bound but eternal. Briffault draws the parallels:

> The lamentations of the women of Syria, Egypt, Babylon and Greece over the Divine Son were also lamentations for the Saviour who had paid for them the price of death. For the Divine Son was ever the 'Saviour' whose death is the pledge of the moon's gift of eternal life. Initiation into the mysteries of Dionysus was believed to secure eternal salvation.[63]

The most obvious difference in orthodox Christian thought from the earlier manifestations of this myth is that Christ's sacrifice is deemed to have occurred at a particular time in history, and so, inevitably, to have transformed the very concept of historical time. It is as though the flow of time at that moment is suspended, and history becomes a frieze upon which we must read backwards to a beginning (the Fall) and forward to an ending (the Second Coming, which is to be the Last of Time). The original myth assumed and articulated the notion of cyclical time – the lunar model of birth, death and rebirth as a continuous process – and now superimposed, as it were, upon this model is the Christian concept of linear time in which the god's birth, death and rebirth happen once and for all, even though they are celebrated every year. Linear time predisposes a reading of the myth as historical rather than symbolical, whereas in earlier versions, where the sacrifice 'happened' perennially, the idea of it occurring once and then being over would have seemed impossible, or equivalent to interrupting the perpetual flow of the life-process in and out of all created beings.

The earlier gods were experienced as the *whole* of creation, whose deaths could be mourned and whose rebirths rejoiced in, both as a way of preparing the human mind for its own death and as a way of acknowledging the presence of an underlying ground of being, a reality independent of the forms of its manifestation, which places death in a perspective beyond what can be felt through the senses. That this process can be observed every year in the barren tree and the empty field serves to relate human suffering to the universal experience of nature. When the sowers of the seeds in autumn were instructed by their priests alongside them in the fields not to cry out the name of Dionysos but to mourn instead for Jesus, what would have been the difference? Doctrinally, it would, or should, have been uniquely different because Jesus, unlike Dionysos, died, not *as* creation but *for* our sins, and his sacrifice redeems not the *dying* world but the *fallen* world. Subtly, therefore, the emphasis is shifted from the tragedy of the human condition to the sinfulness of human nature, just as it was with Eve. The natural world in its waxing and waning phases remains, in orthodox pronouncements, implicitly excluded from redemption.

This is rarely the feeling of the Jesus in the Gospels, however, and particularly not in the Gospel of John, which is also the closest in feeling to the recently discovered Gnostic 'Gospel According to Thomas', found in an urn in Nag Hammadi in Egypt in 1945, written in 140, translated into Coptic in 500, and still around, therefore, when the four Gospels were being worked upon, since they were not finally fixed until the beginning of the fourth century. The Gospel of Thomas was made up of 114 sayings of Jesus, *logia*, many of which are similar enough to those in the four Gospels either to have derived from a common source or to be one of the originals from which the four Gospels drew. The crucial distinction between the Gospel of Thomas and the others is the consistent inwardness of the Gnostic text, in which the 'Kingdom' is not 'in heaven', or 'in the sea', but it is 'within you and it is without you' (Logion 3).

His disciples said to Him: 'When will the Kingdom come?' Jesus said: 'It will not come by expectation; they will not say, "See here" or "See there".

But the Kingdom of the Father is spread upon the earth and men do not see it.' (Logion 113)

This, and others like it (which will be explored in Chapter 15), imply, as Campbell says, 'a theology of immanence',[64] which the Pauline Church obscured, if not re-interpreted, into a theology of transcendence, thereby restoring the very idea of the fallen world that Jesus had taught was an illusion. This reinterpretation can be seen at work in the translation, from the Greek in which the New Testament was written, of some of the central concepts. *Hamartia*, for instance, is translated 'sin', but in the Greek actually means the 'missing of the mark', a term without guilt or shame beyond the correcting of the 'aim'. Similarly, the word translated as 'repentance' comes from the Greek *metanoia*, which means literally a 'turning about of the mind' or, as we might say, a change of heart. In the Greek, which is the closest to the language of Aramaic, which Jesus spoke, the notion of guilt and judgement is missing. Watts, himself once a Christian priest, points out the difference:

> While it is all too true that the 'missing of the mark' called egocentricity underlies all the enormities of human behaviour, Christians have seldom recognized that the inculcation of shame, horror, and guilt is in no sense a cure for sin. It is merely the opposite of misconduct ... For sentimental guilt by no means destroys egocentricity, being nothing other than the sensation of its wounded pride – a pride which it then labours to restore by acts of penitence and piety.[65]

By contrast, the distance between the two kinds of vision can be clearly seen in the saying (quoted in Chapter 13 and more fully in Chapter 15) from the Gospel of Thomas:

> Cleave a (piece of) wood, I am there;
> lift up the stone and you will find Me there. (Logion 77)

Here, all the earth is unquestionably sacred, even where one might not have thought to look, and so also become all the natural images that Jesus takes for his miracles and parables in the Synoptic Gospels: the loaves and fishes whose source never runs out, the water transformed into wine, the ear of wheat falling into the ground, the good shepherd and his sheep, the vine and the branches, the true husbandman. In the Last Supper Jesus takes for his commemoration the body and the blood of the earth in the bread and wine, which are to be transformed into his own body and blood in the ritual of re-membering the fragmented body of *bios*, the temporal, manifest life, which needs continually to be reunited in the human heart with its eternal source, *zoe*. In this sense Jesus does not have to be the one and only Son of God who entered the history of humanity one particular day, for he is the symbol of a 'Christ' in any and every human being.

Figure 34. *The Coronation of the Virgin*, detail of the Florentine Diptych, fourteenth century.

THE SACRED MARRIAGE

The image of a sacred marriage between god and goddess was not possible in orthodox Christianity, where Mary was a human woman and the Great Father God ruled supreme in heaven. However, the urge towards a union of masculine and feminine principles was expressed in some of the excluded Gnostic texts in the idea that Jesus loved (and even married) the woman who carried the sacred vessel, Mary Magdalene. From a reading of the included Gospels alone, it seems almost unthinkable that twelve centuries later pictures would appear with Jesus and his mother relating to each other in the nuptial symbolism of a bridal pair. Yet, without a knowledge of the official interpretation, what else would be made of the fourteenth-century diptych from Florence in Figure 34 and probably the painting in Figure 35 as well? In both paintings, and many others like them, Mary sits enthroned beside Jesus not as his mother but as his bride. In the diptych from the Florentine school, the two scenes of birth and death are brought together in harmony at the apex, as though in fulfilment of the meaning of the scenes below.

The Coronation of the Virgin was an image that, once portrayed in Christian iconography in the twelfth century, must have answered some need that was previously missing, for it was soon reflected in the great Gothic cathedrals that rose in the following centuries, where Mary appears crowned as Queen of Heaven in the portals of Chartres and Notre Dame. It was in these centuries also that the great hymns to her – the Regina Caeli, the Regina Caelorum and the Salve Regina – were composed. Generally, there is no difference between Jesus and Mary in age. In the moving rendering of this theme by Agnolo Gaddi the identical robes of the two figures merge into one and, as Christ places the crown reverently upon Mary's head, it is as though once again there is a celebration of the

Figure 35. *The Coronation of the Virgin*, Agnolo Gaddi, tempera on wood,
c. 1370.

Figure 36. *Jesus and the Dormant Mary*, mosaic in the Basilica of St Maria
in Trastevere, Rome, thirteenth century.

Hieros Gamos, or Sacred Marriage, of the sun and moon, which was the
supreme moment of the Mysteries of pre-Christian cultures. However,
there is the crucial difference that it is the son who acknowledges the
mother as bride, rather than the mother who acknowledges her son as the
bridegroom and thereby becomes his bride. Here, he crowns her; she does
not crown him.

In the thirteenth-century mosaic in Figure 36, added a hundred years
later to the mosaic of the sacred marriage in the Basilica of St Maria in
Trastevere, the reversal of roles can be seen in this moment of passing
over from the earthly to the heavenly world. Mary is sleeping the sleep
that to ordinary mortals is death, and Christ holds the baby that is her
soul, as though he were himself the mother out of whose heavenly body
the baby had come. No longer does Mary the mother hold in her arms
Jesus the baby, as an image of *zoe* giving birth to *bios* in the way that
eternity 'gives birth' to time. Now Christ, the spiritual mother, taking
precedence over his earthly mother, brings her eternal soul into being as
she leaves her earthly body. Christ is here the image of *zoe*, and Mary has
become an image of *bios*, the fairest face of humanity, resurrected from
the human condition through her son's willing sacrifice of himself.

One century earlier the theology was more questionable, as the earliest
mosaic of the divine couple (Fig. 37), constructed high up in the apse of this
same church in Rome, suggests. Christ is seated beside a woman of the same
age as himself, or even younger. His arm rests lightly around her shoulder as
he gathers her to himself in the gesture of a bridegroom to his bride. Apart

Figure 37. *Jesus and Mary on the Throne*; mosaic of the Basilica of St Maria in Trastevere, Rome, twelfth century.

from the fact that the hand of the Father is poised above his head, placing him at the centre of the picture, there is no difference of status between them: he is the one who protects her, and she sits easily within his embrace, as many a picture of husband and wife throughout the ages. Yet the movement of the scene comes from the gestures of her hands, as she holds up the scroll upon her knee and points to the face of Jesus haloed in the cross. This, mythologically, is the reunion at the full moon, when the son, born at the crescent, sacrificed at the waning and lost at the dark moon, is reborn as the lover who claims as his bride she who gave him birth. Here, *bios* and *zoe* have again become one, and the duality of male and female, life and death, time and eternity, is transcended.

A new 'incarnation' of the myth of the goddess and her son–lover seems to manifest when human consciousness is ready to deepen its understanding by searching for a new revelation of life's meaning. It is as though the numinosity of the images gives birth to a new moment of consciousness, which helps to bring about a transformation of the image of the deity in a particular culture at a particular time. The new revelation that allows humanity's values to evolve emerges from the depths of the human soul, whose most ancient image of itself is the goddess. The Soul of the World, described here as *zoe*, endlessly renews herself in humanity, her son, in a new manifestation of her being. The image of the son has been understood as the generative principle within the life of vegetation, and as the king whose life embodied the life of the tribe, and as the hero whose conquest of the dragon of darkness released the light of eternal life. Now Jesus, the most recent son–lover of the goddess, becomes the voice of the timeless wisdom of the soul that speaks to humanity – as *bios*.

The numinous power of the perennial myth captured the imagination of the ancient world. New beliefs took form, crystallized and died as the myth was robbed of its numinosity by a literal interpretation of its meaning. The repeated death and rebirth of the son of the goddess, and later the god, represent the many revelations that have taken place in the gradual evolution of human consciousness. Many times, it seems, humanity has had to pass through the cultural disintegration that marks the transitional stage of darkness between the death of the old system of beliefs and the birth of the new. But again, once the moment of inspiration has passed, the myth has been understood literally rather than symbolically, and countless thousands of people have been sacrificed to the 'truth' of a revelation that was believed, this time, to be final and complete.

It seems that whenever the depths of the soul are touched by the need to go beyond the literal interpretation of formal doctrine, the old lunar myth is evoked again and the archaic images re-emerge. At the deepest level of symbolic imagery Mary, as *zoe*, brings the unmanifest divine world into manifestation as *bios*, in the person of her son. He is offered, or offers himself, as sacrifice in order that this translation of life from one dimension to another may flow back and forth. Mary is then the new incarnation of the old poetic vision, which is timeless because it reflects *zoe*; Jesus is the *bios* in historical time who teaches the poetic vision. As both divine and human, he belongs to both realms and so he is the intermediary between the source and its manifestation. It is the poetic vision that gives birth to the new order, for this is the language of the soul.

It may be that a rhythmic interchange between archetypal feminine and masculine images (goddesses and gods) is necessary in order to evolve. To remain fixed in either mode may arrest the process of movement. It is interesting that Ishtar, Isis and Cybele were all at one point demoted by the supremacy of the new gods, yet they returned even stronger some centuries later, as though the inspiration had run out of the prevailing order and a balance were required. The gods articulate aspiration and the heroic quest: they give the 'word' to the whole that is implicit in the poetic vision. But when this 'creation' is complete, when the voice has been given and the urgency and effort of the quest are concluded, there seems to be an inherent danger of falling into literalization and historicization, which kill the life in the old myth. When this happens, the old order has to give way to a new expression of the poetic vision out of which the new order is born. If we can set the Christian myth in this context also, then the poetic vision is here the mother to the new consciousness, the son. In the Christian story, as in all the others, the mythic tradition is still visible in the timeless images with which the story is clothed.

15

SOPHIA:
MOTHER, DAUGHTER AND BRIDE

O no man knows through what wild centuries roves back the rose.

Walter de la Mare

The Holy Spirit of Wisdom as the guiding archetype of human evolution is one of the great images of universality. Transcending the limitations of any one religious belief, it is an image that embraces all human experience, inspiring trust in the capacity of the soul to find its way back to the source. Where are we to look for the finest expressions of the human spirit in every civilization if not to the stories of the quest that inspire and illumine human life? From Gilgamesh's search for the herb of immortality to Odysseus' long sea journey home to Penelope, from the medieval quest of the Grail knights to the modern scientific search for the unified field, the impulse is the same: to discover the living presence that informs the phenomenal world and brings into being the exquisite order of the universe. In this chapter on Sophia, the Holy Spirit of Wisdom, the image of the goddess moves inwards, and becomes the inspiration of the quest for the sacred marriage – the reunion of the two aspects of consciousness so long separated from each other.

The Greek word *Sophia* means 'wisdom'. In the twelfth-century picture in Figure 1 Mary, in her aspect as Sophia, is seated upon the lion throne, as were all the goddesses before her. The divine child is held on her lap and her right hand holds the root of the flower, which blossoms as the lily, disclosing that she is the root of all things. The dove, for so many thousand years the principal emblem of the goddess, rests on the lily, and a stylized meander frames the right-hand side of the scene. All these images relate the medieval figure of Sophia to the older images of the goddess, which reach back into the Neolithic past. But here the goddess is given a specific emphasis, which offers an image of Wisdom as the highest quality of the soul and suggests that, evolving from root to flower, the soul can ultimately blossom as the lily and, understanding all things, soar like the bird between the dimensions of earth and heaven. Nor is this Christian image unrelated to that of the shaman lying in trance in the cave of Lascaux, for there, also, the bird mask he wears and the bird resting on his staff symbolize his flight to another dimension of consciousness.

Figure 1. Mary as Sophia on the lion throne; illuminated manuscript,
c. 1150. Eynsham Abbey, Oxfordshire.

To discover the root of the idea of Wisdom we have to go back once
again to the Neolithic era, when the goddess was the image of the Whole,
when life emerged from and returned to her, and when she was conceived
as the door or gateway to a hidden dimension of being that was her
womb, the eternal source and regenerator of life (see Chapter 2, Fig. 5).
Earlier chapters have shown how the idea of Wisdom was always related
in the pre-Christian world to the image of the goddess; Nammu and

Inanna in Sumeria, Maat and Isis in Egypt, and Athena and Demeter in Greece. Even the passages in the Old Testament that describe Hokhmah, the Holy Spirit of Wisdom, powerfully evoke her lost image, though here the image is dissociated from the word.

But as we move into the Christian era there is a profound shift in archetypal imagery as Wisdom becomes associated with Christ as Logos, the Word of God, and the old relationship between Wisdom and the goddess is lost. Now, the archetypal feminine is finally 'deleted' from the image of the divine, and the Christian image of the deity as a trinity of Father, Son and Holy Spirit becomes wholly identified with the masculine archetype. Because of a sequence of theological formulations – grounded on the assumption that nature was inferior to spirit, and that whatever pertained to the female was inferior to the male – the image of the Holy Spirit lost its former association with the feminine Hokhmah, or Sophia, and was assimilated, first in Judaism, and then in Christianity, to the concept of the masculine Logos, the Divine Word. This theological development effectively erased the ancient relationship between Wisdom and the image of the goddess.

Gnostic Christianity, however, retained the older tradition and the image of Sophia as the embodiment of Wisdom survived. Here she was the Great Mother, the consort and counterpart of the male aspect of the godhead. When the Gnostic sects were repressed by the edicts of the Emperor Constantine in AD 326 and 333, the image of Sophia as the embodiment of Wisdom was again lost. However, after an interlude of several hundred years, it reappeared in the Middle Ages, in the great surge of devotion to the Virgin Mary and the pilgrimages to the shrines of the Black Virgin, as well as in the philosophical impulse of these times, expressed in the writings of great scholars, such as John Scotus Erigena (AD 810–77), who, although he lived at the time of Charlemagne, had a profound influence on the philosophy of the later Middle Ages. Then, in the sudden manifestation of the Order of the Knights Templar, the Grail legends, Alchemy, the troubadours and the Cathar Church of the Holy Spirit, Sophia, or Sapientia, as the image of Wisdom, became the inspiration, guide and goal of a spiritual quest of overwhelming numinosity.

It is a fascinating story, and one that reveals the soul's constant attempt to restore relationship and balance between the feminine and masculine archetypes reflected in the images of goddess and god. Further, it seeks to give emphasis through the feminine archetype to the intuitive, inward-looking tendencies of the soul as well as to the nurturing, compassionate qualities traditionally defined as feminine, which may not be valued in societies where only the masculine archetype is named as divine.

THE LOSS OF THE FEMININE IN THE IMAGE OF THE HOLY SPIRIT

The opening words of the Gospel of St John, 'In the beginning was the Word, and the Word was with God, and the Word was God', need to be read with the passage quoted below from the Book of Ben Sirach (24:3). Here Sophia is 'in the beginning' with the deity; she is the Word emanating as creation:

> I came out of the mouth of the most High,
>   and covered the earth as a cloud [mist].
> I dwelt in high places,
>   and my throne is in a cloudy pillar.
> I alone encompassed the circuit of heaven,
>   and walked in the bottom of the deep.
> I had power over the waves of the sea, and over all the earth,
>   and over every people and nation. (Sir. 24:3–6)

The imagery of both passages has a resonance that relates them to each other, and with the older Sumerian verses spoken by the goddess:

> Begetting Mother am I, within the Spirit I abide and none see me.
>   In the word of An I abide, and none see me
>   In the word of Enlil I abide, and none see me
> In the word of the holy temple I abide, and none see me.[1]

Yet the connection between them may pass unnoticed because the Sumerian verses are not generally known and because the Book of Ben Sirach is part of the Apocrypha, and therefore does not belong to the canonical texts available to most readers of the Bible. And so in St John's Gospel 'the Word' emanating from the ground of being has left behind the feminine image of Sophia, who has vanished from the scene as completely as if she had never existed. How did it come about that the image of Wisdom as the Holy Spirit came to be associated in Christianity with Christ as Logos, the Divine Word, and no longer with Sophia?

A great deal seems to depend on the endings of nouns in different languages. The historical movement was from the feminine image of Hokhmah (Sophia), to a Greek image that was neither feminine nor masculine (*Hagion Pneuma*), to the masculine image of the Greek word *Logos*, and eventually to the Latin *Spiritus Sanctus*. The Greek *Hagion Pneuma* was neuter, with the sense of an abstract idea; however it was personified as the dove, which discloses the former relationship to the goddess. But now the concept of the Trinity, which originally came from the triune lunar goddess, and was later named as the Sumerian trinity of Mother (Ki), Father (An) and Son (Enlil), becomes wholly masculine. The Holy Spirit is now conceived as masculine, although its image remains the dove of the goddess. The former connection of the Holy Spirit with

Sophia (Hokhmah) and the origin of her image in the Great Mother was lost to consciousness. Soon no one except the persecuted Gnostic sects remembered the mythological connection between the goddess, the dove, light, and wisdom.

Engelsman, in her book *The Feminine Dimension of the Divine*, tells the story of how this came about, not so much by any deliberate intention as by a process that seemed natural enough at the time, given the general antipathy towards the imagery of the 'pagan' goddess among theologians who were struggling to formulate the doctrine of Christianity. The Old Testament image of Sophia as the consort of Yahweh and as the crafts-woman of creation, who is also 'active in the world' as a guiding presence and intelligence within all appearances, vanishes in the early centuries of the Christian era, as does the Gnostic image of Sophia as consort of the deity and the 'womb' of creation. In the Gnostic myth, as we shall see, the ancient connection is retained, however obscurely, between the mother goddess, as Sophia, and Christ, her son, who is sent by the Mother–Father Source to rescue their daughter.

But in the tradition of Western Christianity the connection between the son and the mother goddess appears to be lost when the doctrine is formulated that Christ was the son of a divine father and the human Mary. Jesus Christ, as the incarnate 'Word', son of the heavenly father, assumes the qualities that once belonged to Sophia. The feminine image of Wisdom is now lost in the all-encompassing fatherhood of the deity, and Jesus comes to be seen as wisdom incarnate as Logos. One of the reasons for this translation of Wisdom from a feminine to a masculine image must surely lie in the loss of the actual image of the goddess, a process that originated, as we have seen, in the Wisdom Books of the Old Testament. The Greek and Latin words for wisdom, like the Hebrew word, have the feminine gender, but in the English language 'wisdom' carries no associations with either gender and so gives no hint of the imagery that once belonged to it in the goddess cultures. It becomes simply an abstract noun rather than an image of the archetypal feminine.

The theologians and churchmen who formulated the doctrines of the Incarnation and the Trinity at the Councils of Nicaea and Chalcedon in AD 325 and 451 – doctrines that were the foundation of the edifice of Christian theology – inherited the Iron Age attitudes of the patriarchal cultures in which they lived. They assumed, without questioning their premises, that nature was inferior to spirit and the female to the male. They defined their doctrines on the basis of the legacy they received from the Old Testament, which clearly differentiated the beliefs and practices of Judaism from those of the surrounding pagan cultures and rejected the image of the goddess. With no feeling for the older images, it is easy to understand how the intellect, split off from its psychic ground, became entangled in its own formulations and came to believe that these were divine revelation.

The writings of the Jewish philosopher Philo (early first century AD) were crucial to the transfer of the wisdom imagery from Sophia to Christ. He lived in Alexandria at the turn of the millennium, and his writings had a great influence on Christian as well as Jewish theologians. Philo, attempting to bridge the gap between Greek Stoic philosophy and Judaism, was the first theologian to formulate the concept of the Logos as the *intermediary* between the father god and his creation, and to identify the Wisdom imagery of the Old Testament with the Greek concept of Logos. Philo's writings were imbued with a strong antipathy towards the female, as in the passage quoted in Chapter 13, p. 512.

In complete accordance with the general beliefs of the time, whatever was female was inferior and secondary to the male. The contrast between the 'life of the world' and the 'life of the spirit' was made by associating worldly life, the physical senses and the body with natural life, and all of these with the image of the female. Spiritual life, in contrast, was associated with the mind and intellectual activity, and with the image of the male. 'Progress', Philo wrote, 'is indeed nothing else than the giving up of the female gender by changing into the male, since the female gender is material, passive, corporeal and sense-perceptible, while the male is active, rational, incorporeal and more akin to mind and thought.'[2]

This sounds like a restatement of Aristotelian thought. Philo writes of Sophia as the *daughter* rather than the *consort* of the father god and, in a telling passage, evocative of Athena and Zeus, asks how Wisdom, the daughter of the deity,

> can be rightly spoken of as a father? Is it because, while Wisdom's name is feminine, her nature is manly? ... For that which comes after God, even though it were the chiefest of all other things, occupies a second place, and therefore was termed feminine to express its contrast with the Maker of the Universe who is masculine, and its affinity to every thing else. For pre-eminence always pertains to the masculine, and the feminine always comes short of and is lesser than it. Let us, then, pay no heed to the discrepancy in the gender of the words, and say that the daughter of God, even Wisdom, is not only masculine but father, sowing and begetting in souls aptness to learn, discipline, knowledge, sound sense and laudable actions.[3]

Within 100 years, as Engelsman writes, Philo's influence on Christian theologians, compounded with their own doctrines, had broken Sophia's power so that Wisdom was no longer personified as a feminine image:

> She was superseded by a masculine figure who took over her roles ... Ultimately, Sophia's powers were so totally preempted by Christ that she herself completely disappeared from the Christian religion of that time.[4]

The lost myth of the mother goddess and her son gradually makes its return in the doctrines formulated by the early Church during the course of the third to fifth centuries. It reappeared in the doctrine of Mary's perpetual virginity and in the title of God-bearer (*Theotokos*) that was bestowed on her at the Council of Chalcedon in 451. Mary's Immaculate Conception of her son, as Jung among others has pointed out, makes her different from other mortals by removing from her the 'stain of sin', and therefore suggests that she is a goddess and her son a god.[5]

This dogma was the first stage in raising Mary to the status of the ancient goddess, a process that has apparently taken place quite unconsciously in Christianity over the last 2,000 years. Another version of the old myth returned in a strange guise: the Church itself became mother and assumed the former nurturing imagery of the goddess. Clement of Alexandria (AD 150–220) wrote of the Church that 'she alone had no milk because she alone did not become woman, but she is both virgin and mother, being undefiled as a virgin and loving as a mother; and calling her children to her, she nurses them with holy milk.'[6] The Church nourished the faithful, as the goddess had once nourished her sons, the kings of Sumeria and Babylonia, with the milk from her breasts.

More specifically, the Church assimilated the attributes and functions of Sophia. The Church, from the beginning conceived as feminine, was Mother. She was the Bride of Christ, as Israel had been the bride of Yahweh. And she was the embodiment of Wisdom. The text of the Song of Songs was used to support the idea that the Church was the beloved of Christ and the repository of Wisdom. The Church was described by one early Christian writer, Methodius, as 'a power by herself, distinct from her children; whom the prophets . . . have called sometimes Jerusalem, sometimes a bride, sometimes Mount Zion, and sometimes the Temple and Tabernacle of God.'[7]

The Church's task as mother was, like Sophia's, to draw the human soul to her and so to Christ, but this authoritative intermediary deprived her children of trust in their own souls; or of visualizing the Holy Spirit of Wisdom, now personified by Christ, as the ground of their being and the wise presence of a directing consciousness within the soul. Although the rich tradition of contemplatives and mystics belonging to both the Eastern and Western stream of Christianity kept alive this inner approach to the image of Christ, the Western Church became increasingly secular in its aim to increase its terrestrial authority and insisted on absolute obedience to the 'law' of its doctrine.

It was a natural corollary of the Church's identification of itself with the archetype of the Great Mother that it should fall victim to mythic inflation for many centuries, in the same way that the kings of earlier times had fallen victim to mythic inflation in their assumption of the divine role of 'sons' of the goddess. One symptom of this inflation was the unconscious emulation of the goddess in her role (created by humanity) as goddess of war. In the extirpation of heresy, the Western Church assumed the pitiless mantle of the Goddess of Death split off from the Goddess of Life. The persecution of anything or anyone that threatened her doctrine reveals the dangerous, compulsive behaviour of an archetype when it is unconsciously 'appropriated' by an individual or an institution. The institution, identified with the archetype, becomes inflated by the numinosity of the divinely appointed role it accords to itself. In this way, believing that it was executing the divine will by eradicating the evil of heresy, the Church became itself the actual embodiment of the evil it saw in others, and the antithesis of its own teaching. How can the long history of the intolerance and arrogance of Christianity towards other faiths and 'primitive' peoples be explained except as mythic inflation? (Today, any individual or group of people who identifies 'good' exclusively with their own religious or political ideas, and 'evil' with those of other groups, may fall victim to the same psychic disorder. It seems as if this psychic danger can be avoided only if no claim is made to being infallible and if the emphasis is placed always on the quest for greater understanding, which must involve relationship.)

The substitution of Christ as Logos for Sophia as the Holy Spirit is only one strand in the story of how the image of the feminine was excluded from the Christian Trinity. With the formulation of Christian doctrine in the early centuries of this era, the emphasis of Christianity on the masculine archetype was, so to speak, fixed. The image of the goddess and god as together the creative source and ground of life, and of the sacred marriage between them, was implicit in the images of the Christian myth, yet could not be fully honoured because nature and human nature were contaminated by the idea of the Fall, and so the precious legacy inherited from the Mysteries of the pagan world was almost lost. The faint reflection of the image of union lingered in the concept of the marriage between Christ and his Church, or between Christ and the community of the elect, which followed the Judaic precedent of the relationship between Yahweh and the mystical community of Israel. But this 'humanization' of the goddess image could not contain the soul's need for an image of union between goddess and god, which symbolized the unity of life in the union of creator and creation, and anticipated the experience of the reunion of consciousness with its ground. With the evolution of consciousness taking humanity ever further away from nature and the instinctual ground of life, mental and spiritual processes increasingly came to be seen as unrelated to physical ones, and intellect as superior to instinct. The only numinous image that could bring these two aspects of life together again was the sacred marriage between goddess and god. In selecting these images, and continually re-creating the image of the sacred marriage, the soul gave expression to a deep inward need for its regeneration through the union of these two aspects of itself that had grown so far apart.

The Old Testament marriage of the people of Israel to Yahweh and the New Testament marriage of the Church to Christ could not satisfy the soul's need for a *divine* image of wholeness to express the mysterious unity of all life. Jung comments on the soul's need to have the image of the feminine 'metaphysically anchored in the figure of a *divine* woman, the bride of Christ. Just as the person of Christ cannot be replaced by an organization, so the Bride cannot be replaced by the Church. The feminine, like the masculine, demands an equally personal representation.'[8] Only now, perhaps, after nearly 4,000 years of a split between spirit and nature, which has deeply injured the 'natural' aspect of life and all aspects of the feminine, can the growing understanding of the soul help us to heal this wound. Jung drew attention to the great importance of the doctrine of the Assumption of the Virgin; in his view, if its symbolic meaning is understood, it restores to humanity both the divinity of the feminine and the image of the sacred marriage, so preparing the ground for the birth of new understanding: 'Mary as the bride is united with the son in the heavenly bridal-chamber, and, as Sophia, with the Godhead.'[9] But, as has been suggested in the chapter on Mary, the earth aspect of the archetypal feminine is still excluded from divinity; from the standpoint of human consciousness, therefore, nature and the body remain split off from spirit.

GNOSTIC CHRISTIANITY

No study of Christianity is complete without including Gnosticism: for Gnosticism is the source of the underground stream that flowed beneath Christian doctrine into Alchemy and many other spiritual movements in the Middle Ages, and Gnosticism itself grew out of the esoteric or mystical stream of the Egyptian, Hebrew and Greek religions. In Alexandria, the great city founded by Alexander the Great in 328 BC, all three traditions met and mingled in a climate of tolerance that was assured as long as Greek influence prevailed there. In the first century AD Alexandria had a million inhabitants and two of the five divisions of the city were Jewish. More Jews lived here than in Palestine and, mixing freely with Egyptians and Greeks, their attitude to other religious traditions was liberal.[10] The earliest group of Christians was that established in Jerusalem by James, known as the brother of Jesus, after Jesus' death. When James was murdered by the Sanhedrin in AD 62, the persecuted Jewish-Christian community in Jerusalem dispersed, some going to Alexandria, others to Syria, and Edessa in Mesopotamia. In Alexandria the Gospel fell on ground prepared by traditions of metaphysical inquiry which had long been the focus of discussion among the Jewish and Greek communities in this city; these were concerned with the nature of the universe, the origin of evil, the fall and redemption of the soul and the survival of the soul after death. 'Christianity', Jung comments, 'would never have spread through the pagan world with such astonishing rapidity had its ideas not found an analogous psychic readiness to receive them.'[11]

By the second century AD there was still great freedom in the early Christian Church established in Alexandria. But in Rome a different spirit already prevailed, inspired by the authoritarianism of the Roman Empire, and this spirit ultimately brought about the persecution and suppression of the Gnostic Christians. The history of Christianity might have been very different if the Jewish Gnostic teacher Valentinus, who had moved from Alexandria to Rome, had been elected Bishop of Rome in AD 140 instead of Pius I, who later became pope. But Pius was chosen, and the groups that Valentinus represented and the texts they used as the foundation of their teaching were gradually suppressed and lost. Valentinus was expelled from the Christian Church in Rome by AD 150. The recent discovery of the Nag Hammadi scrolls and the work of scholars in this century, in particular Elaine Pagel's book *The Gnostic Gospels*, have greatly expanded our knowledge of the Gnostic Christian groups. (Until now, because they were suppressed and their texts destroyed, the existence of this controversy was known mainly through the polemics of the exasperated early Christian bishops who struggled to eradicate these 'unorthodox' groups.)

The original Gnostic groups took their name from the Greek word *gnostikoi*, an adjective, not a verb. There are two Greek words for knowledge. One means knowledge in the sense of information gathered: *epistemi*. The other, *gnosis*, means knowledge in the sense of insight or understanding, which requires the participation not merely of the intellect but of the whole being. It is knowledge discovered with the intuition – the eye of the heart – which has no need of the intermediary of a priesthood, but is directly perceived. It is in the second sense, drawing on the idea of wisdom as insight, that the Gnostic sects interpreted their 'knowledge'.

From the Gospels that are familiar to us, as well as from these other 'resurrected' ones, it seems that the essence of Jesus' teaching was to transmit this *gnosis*, or knowledge of the heart. He attempted to heal the fragmentation in the soul by returning men and women to its deeper instinctual wisdom, through which they might recover the *Kingdom* – the treasure of relationship with the ground of life. Deeply learned in the rabbinic tradition, he nevertheless stood against it in his emphasis on the universality of his teaching, in his sensitivity and response to suffering, in his repudiation of the cruelty, oppression and literalism of the rabbinic 'Law' as it was then practised. Both sets of Gospels have sayings in common that are attributed to Jesus. It seems most likely that the group of Jewish Christians in Jerusalem, led by James, recorded the Aramaic sayings of Jesus and that these were transmitted to early Christian groups in other cities. We know the story of early Christianity only from the Pauline writings in the New Testament, which do not mention the earliest community in Jerusalem or the importance of the role of James. Some of the Gnostic writings are definitely earlier than the Gospels familiar to us, as early as the second half of the first century AD.[12]

The Gnostic Gospels show that their deepest concern was with how to awaken the soul to awareness of its divine nature and its innate potential for the growth of insight and understanding; how to transform consciousness from a state of 'sleep' to one of 'wakefulness'. Their record of the teaching of Jesus shows him to be concerned not with beliefs and worship but with the act of *metanoia*, or 'turning around' to face the inner world of the soul. The mythological imagery of the Gnostic texts is often overwhelming and baffling, yet they also offer a very human image of the relationship between Jesus and his disciples, who, it is now clear, included women. They show, too, the difficulties the disciples themselves had in understanding, let alone transmitting to others, Jesus' teaching about the need for the transformation of consciousness.

In the early centuries of Christianity there was evidently a great variety of beliefs and many groups had a markedly individual character. The 'orthodox' Christian bishops struggled to establish a strong and unified Church, and at first to curtail, then to suppress this abundance of 'revelation'. One bishop, Irenaeus, bitterly remarked that 'every one of them generates something new every day'.[13] One may feel some sympathy with their efforts, yet Christianity has been greatly impoverished for having repressed a tradition that might have given it a far deeper understanding of the soul, as well as a deeper insight into the philosophical teachings of other religions and the parallels in these with its own tradition.

The astonishing number of Gnostic texts (fifty-two) so amazingly recovered in 1945 from Nag Hammadi in the Egyptian desert have, therefore, restored to us an essential part of our religious heritage. There are Jewish, Greek and Egyptian texts, which show how eclectic is the cultural background of Gnosticism. Pagels, in her book *The Gnostic Gospels*, has explained much that was obscure about the early history of the Christian Church and the various Gnostic sects that flourished during the first three centuries of the Christian era. The texts disclose many images relating to the goddess tradition, which were lost with the suppression of these sects. Indeed, their discovery amplifies the theology of the present forms of Christianity, for they show how much was repressed and destroyed in order for it to impose its doctrines. As Pagels writes:

> Every one of the secret texts which gnostic groups revered was omitted from the canonical collection and branded as heretical by those who called themselves orthodox Christians. By the time the process of sorting the various writings ended – probably as late as the year 200 – virtually all the feminine imagery for God had disappeared from orthodox Christian tradition.[14]

Among the texts that were suppressed were those that told the story of Sophia, the Great Mother, consort of the Great Father; and the story of their daughter, also called Sophia, and their son, Christ, who went to the rescue of his sister. It is a most dramatic myth about the fragmentation and reintegration of the soul. In this Gnostic myth the earlier lunar images of the mother and daughter goddess are reanimated, but the orientation of the mythology is now specifically towards an inner world, an invisible archetypal world, and loses its relation to the cycle of the seasons.

It is as if the Gnostic myth continues the tradition of the Eleusinian Mysteries of Demeter and Kore and those of Attis and Cybele in Rome, with their emphasis on the regeneration of the soul. The Gnostic myth of Sophia personifies the human soul as the *daughter* of the Great Mother.

In this myth, which had many different versions, Sophia appears as the primal Virgin Mother, consort of the Father God, and as the power through whom the creative source of life brings itself into being: the womb that generates all worlds and levels of being as her child. Like the Egyptian Maat and Hokhmah in the Old Testament, she personifies Wisdom. Like Inanna, Hokhmah and the Shekhinah of later Kabbalistic mythology, she personifies Light. The mother Sophia gave birth to a daughter, the image of herself, who lost contact with her heavenly origin, and in her distress and sorrow brought the earth into being, and became entangled and lost in the chaotic realm of darkness that lay beneath the realm of light: a darkness or underworld that was identified with the earth sphere whose gates were guarded by fearsome planetary spirits, the archons. A curtain or barrier came between the worlds of light and darkness, making it impossible for the daughter Sophia to return to her parents. She was condemned to wander in this dark labyrinth, 'endlessly searching, lamenting, suffering, repenting, laboring her passion into matter, her yearning into soul'.[15] This Gnostic myth, appearing 1,000 years after the Hebrew myth of the Fall, describes the same *tragic* human experience of the separation of consciousness from its source.

The individual human soul in this myth is a 'spark' or element of the cosmic or universal soul, the creation of the Mother and Father in the transcendent world of the Pleroma. The soul, 'incarcerated' in the body, has lost all memory of her 'home', and is in great distress: 'Having once strayed into the labyrinth of evils, the wretched soul finds no way out, she seeks to escape from the bitter chaos and knows not how she shall get through':[16]

> Sometimes she mourned and grieved,
>   For she was left alone in darkness and the void;
> Sometimes she reached a thought of the light which had left her,
>   And she was cheered and laughed;
> Sometimes she feared;
>   At other times she was perplexed and astonished.[17]

Like Persephone, the soul cries out in her distress to her Mother and Father in the transcendent world of the Pleroma. As in the earlier Greek myth in which Hermes descends to rescue Persephone, the Virgin Mother Sophia, in response to her daughter's call, sends her son to rescue his sister. Her son is Christ, the embodiment of her Light and Wisdom, who descends into the darkness of his parents' furthest creation to awaken his sister to remembrance of her true nature.

There are echoes in this new lunar myth of the descent of the Sumerian

Inanna into the dark underworld of her sister goddess Ereshkigal, her 'death' or severance from the light, heavenly world of her origin, her three days of 'death' and her rescue by Enki, the god of wisdom. Ereshkigal's underworld kingdom has now become the world, as fearful a place as any Babylonian vision of life after death. In Sophia's exile we can see Eve's expulsion from the Garden of Eden, and suddenly this older myth can be read as a story of consciousness losing the memory of its 'home' as it leaves the paradise of the Garden. Similarly, in the fairy-tales of Sleeping Beauty and Snow White the Gnostic myth gleams through every word, even to the hedge of thorns that stands between the prince and princess, and Snow White lying asleep in her glass coffin.

The radical difference between the Sumerian myth of Inanna and the new myth is that the world itself has now become the underworld, the world of the dead, and human existence is compared to an entombment. Jesus' rigorous saying comes to mind: 'Follow me; and let the dead bury their dead' (Matt. 8:22). The split between light and darkness is apparently absolute and final, yet, as with all lunar myths, this is a temporary illusion. It was possibly even more difficult then than it is now to understand this kind of myth not literally but in a metaphysical sense, that is, in relation to states of consciousness and the fragmented human psyche. Consequently, many Gnostics projected the darkened state of consciousness that they deplored in the human soul on to the world, and the orthodox Christian commentators who recorded their beliefs also interpreted them in this literal sense. So, in this mythological universe, everything that belonged to creation was believed to be contaminated by evil, including religion, which was subject to error because it was the creation not of the Pleroma, but of the darkened consciousness of the soul.

The Gnostic myth is the first to express the fourfold image of Mother, Father, Daughter and Son, which must surely descend from Sumerian and Babylonian mythology, and to offer an image of the totality of human experience in life in these four divine figures. It reflects the plight of human consciousness in that era, through the image of Sophia's total bondage and suffering. But, true to its lunar character, it is also a myth of release, for it offers an image of a return to wholeness, and the possibility of psychic transformation through the rescue and awakening of the daughter Sophia.

Sometimes the 'unconscious' semi-divine being is portrayed as feminine, as the daughter Sophia; at others, it is masculine, as the *Anthropos*, or divine son, who 'fell' into matter and forgot his relationship to the world of his origin. The myth of the *Anthropos* resembles the older myth in which the son–lover is sacrificed and descends into the darkness of the underworld for the sake of the regeneration of life, and is restored to life by his mother, the goddess. The rescue and redemption of the myriad parts of the sacrificed and suffering god who has poured himself into life as the 'sparks' of the soul forms the essence of the Gnostic myth. Both

myths in their feminine and masculine forms tell the story of the awakening of the sleeping consciousness and its return to its 'home' in the Pleroma.

The soul was compelled continually to reincarnate in a new body as
long as she knew nothing of her true nature and so had no longing to
return through these seven dimensions to her 'home'. This idea of the
reincarnating soul reveals a further link with the cyclical traditions of the
goddess culture. In her state of sleep, the soul had no choice to determine
her fate; no free will. In Gnostic texts she is called 'a poor desolate
widow' and a prostitute who is defiled by many robbers. (These terms
once described Ishtar and were later to appear in the imagery of the
Shekhinah.) The soul is asleep, blind or drunk, according to the different
metaphors used in the Gnostic texts. The Holy Spirit, or Light of Wisdom
within her, her true self, shines in this darkness, but the soul, in her
trance-like state, cannot perceive it. The Christian Gospel of John, which
many Gnostic sects used, expresses this in the words: 'And the light
shineth in darkness; and the darkness comprehended it not' (John 1:5). It
was in this way, owing a great deal to Babylonian and Persian mythology,
that certain Gnostic myths explained the creation of the world and of
humanity, as well as the existence of suffering. Humanity is not evil, but
unconscious; ignorant rather than inherently sinful. As Socrates said, no
one sins willingly. Men and women are the victims of a fate they cannot
control, precisely because they do not know that they are controlled by it.

Gnostic myth offers an anguished image of human suffering, loneliness
and terror, but seeks a luminous and courageous solution to it. The
Gnostics, including the Jewish Gnostics, tried to go beyond any image of
divinity hitherto formulated, to one that could be expressed only as Light,
and that could be revealed to people only through an inward experience
of their own soul, not through belief or obedience to any religious authority. 'Knock on yourself as upon a door and walk upon yourselves as on
a straight road.'[18] The first priority of their teaching was to awaken the
soul to knowledge of its predicament. The salvation of both the individual
and the cosmic soul was not dependent upon a saviour's sacrifice to
redeem human beings but upon their 'bringing forth' or 'giving birth' to
the saviour in the depths of their own consciousness, sacrificing their
ignorance and awakening from their sleep. The theme that pervades Gnostic thought is not that of 'original sin', but of the soul's captivity or
entanglement in a *tragic* fate that can be changed only through a creative
act of insight and inner growth. So the Gnostic teacher Valentinus taught:
'What liberates is the knowledge of who we were, what we became; where
we were, whereinto we have been thrown; whereto we speed, wherefore
we are redeemed; what birth is, and what rebirth.'[19] As the soul awakens,
she becomes aware of her indwelling spirit, personified by Christ, who
says to her: 'I am thou and thou art I; and wheresoever thou art I am
there, and I am sown (or scattered in all); from whencesoever thou willest
thou gatherest Me; and gathering Me thou gatherest Thyself.'[20]

The Sacred Marriage of Soul and Spirit

The quest in Gnostic myth takes a dual form: the soul's longing for the light she desires to reach and the longing of the divine parents to rescue their daughter, sending their son, Christ, as Divine Saviour to accomplish this mission. The underlying unity of soul and spirit is expressed in the image of marriage. At the interface between inner and outer worlds, the spirit, as the bridegroom, emissary of the Divine Mother–Father, comes to meet the 'enlightened' soul, his bride, and the two become one. Gnostic ritual celebrated this 'sacred marriage' of soul and spirit. The spirit was visualized as 'the robe of glory', the 'greater self' of the soul, similar to the image of the Egyptian *Ka* that comes to meet the soul after death. There the soul says: 'O great divine beloved Soul (the goddess Nut), come to me'[21] and the *Ka*, or Great Soul, says, 'Behold I am behind thee, I am thy temple, thy mother, forever and forever.'[22] In a Gnostic text the meeting of the two 'parts' of the soul who become one in one likeness is most beautifully described in a poem called 'The Hymn of the Pearl' or 'The Hymn of the Robe of Glory':

> And my bright robe, which I had stripped off,
> And the toga wherein it was wrapped,
> From the heights of Hyrcania
> My parents sent thither,
> By the hand of their treasurers,
> Who in their faithfulness could be trusted therewith.
> And because I remembered not its fashion –
> For in my childhood I had left it in my Father's house –
> On a sudden as I faced it,
> The garment seemed to me like a mirror of myself.
> I saw it all in my whole self,
> Moreover I faced my whole self in (facing) it.
> For we were two in distinction,
> And yet again one in one likeness.[23]

The primary revelation of the Egyptian, Greek and Roman Mysteries was that the eternal body was the 'Ground', 'Mother' or 'Father' of the consciousness temporarily focused in the physical body. The initiate knew that at death he or she would be reunited with this ground, this greater self to which he or she belonged as child to parent. In this century many people are returning to these ideas, which have such an ancient lineage. Jung called this ground the 'Self' – the greater consciousness that underlies and directs the 'lost' part of itself towards reunion.

The 'resurrection' body, so called because it was the 'luminous' ground of the soul, was neither born nor died with the physical body. It was 'eternal'. (The same idea is expressed by Paul in his discussion of terrestrial and celestial, or 'incorruptible', bodies, and earthly and heavenly houses (1 Cor. 15:40 and 2 Cor. 5:1–8), but the division between the earthly and heavenly dimensions seems absolute, with no possibility of experiencing the heavenly body while still in the earthly one.) The Gnostics' vision of this 'light' body beneath the physical form, gave them, like the initiates of the Mysteries before them, the knowledge that there was no death; matter was rendered translucent to them by their insight into its true nature. Today it might be called the 'sub-atomic' body, or, as in David Bohm's image, 'the Implicate Order'.[24] The 'light' body was thought of as male, in contrast to the physical body, which was described as female. In certain Gnostic texts Jesus appears to his disciples after his resurrection in his 'body of light', and it is helpful to consider the passages in I Corinthians 15 together with these Gnostic texts in order to understand the 'resurrection of the body' in a different sense from the literal one usually given in Christian teaching (see Chapter 13, pp. 533, 545).

The great contribution of the Gnostics to the further evolution of consciousness was their emphasis on awakening through understanding or insight rather than belief. Their teaching about the need of individuals to discover the Christ, or divine consciousness within themselves, brought them into conflict with the orthodox Christians, whose teaching was (and still is) that salvation can only come through belief and belonging to the Church. The myth of the unconscious soul and the possibility of her awakening to the guidance of the Holy Spirit of Wisdom appears to be the creation of the Gnostics, yet it was inherited from the esoteric traditions of Sumeria, Egypt and Greece. At the beginning of the Christian era the Gnostic myth expressed something so deeply relevant to human need that it survived 1,400 years of persecution. It offered people a new myth about the soul in the imagery of the old goddess myth.

The Gospel of Thomas[25]

In 1956 Professor Gilles Quispel discovered the Gospel of Thomas in Cairo and realized that it contained material from the Jewish tradition and, most significantly, that it was related to the earliest Jewish-Christian congregation in Jerusalem. Scholars now accept that this Gospel transmits the original Aramaic sayings of Jesus that were preserved by the members of his brother James's group, and that this was one of the earlier sources drawn on for the sayings in the Gospels of Matthew and Luke.[26] One or more members of this group went to Edessa and established a centre of teaching there, and the Gospel of Thomas transmits the essence of this teaching. The Gospel opens with the words: 'These are the secret words which the Living Jesus spoke and Didymos Judas Thomas wrote. And He said: "Whoever finds the explanation of these words will not taste death."' There are many familiar passages in the Gospels of the New Testament in which Jesus speaks as the embodiment of Sophia, the divine light of Wisdom, but there are other passages from the Gospel of Thomas that are not so well known.

... Within a man of light
there is light
and he lights the whole world. When he
does not shine, there is darkness. (Logion 24)

Jesus said: I will give you what
eye has not seen and what ear
has not heard and what hand has not touched
and (what) has not arisen in the heart
of man. (Logion 17)

In another logion, or saying, from this Gospel, Jesus says:

I am the Light that is above them all.
I am the All; the All came forth from Me
and the All attained to Me.
Cleave (a piece of) wood, I am there;
lift up the stone, and you will find Me there. (Logion 77)

The Kingdom, this Gospel suggests, was the revelation of the nature of
reality made accessible by progressive insight into the mysteries of the
soul, by the bringing together of the two 'bodies', the terrestrial and
celestial consciousness. Jesus taught that the Kingdom would not come
by waiting for it nor could one say of it 'Here it is' or 'There it is'. Rather,

... the Kingdom
of the Father is spread upon the earth and
men do not see it. (Logion 113)

So how may it be discovered?

Let him who seeks, not cease seeking until he
finds, and when he finds, he will
be troubled, and when he has been troubled, he will
marvel and he will
reign over the All. (Logion 2)

Jesus told his disciples:

If you bring forth that within yourselves,
that which you have will save you.
If you do not have that within yourselves,
that which you do not have within you will kill you. (Logion 70)

Whoever achieves *Gnosis*, as the Gospel of Philip says, is 'no longer a
Christian but a Christ',[27] an idea that is reflected in the Gospel of John in
the New Testament:

But as many as received him, to them gave he power to become the sons
of God, even to them that believe on his name:
Which were born, not of blood, nor of the will of the flesh, nor of the will
of man, but of God. (John 1:12–13)

By a strange twist of 'fate' the numinous ground within the human being, which was approaching the threshold of consciousness in many individuals and was personified by Jesus as a teacher of Wisdom, was lost as Jesus was transformed into a god to be worshipped. Instead of the ground *within* the soul being recognized as divine, and related to the underlying divinity of the whole of life, the old literal pattern of the worship of a god was emphasized and the separation between consciousness and its ground was perpetuated. Immanence was sacrificed to transcendence. Christians were taught that as long as they believed, belonged to and obeyed the Church, they were redeemed by the sacrifice of Jesus' death on the cross. And so, as Jung has pointed out, the divine image came to stand *outside* man and woman, rather than within:

> The demand made by the *imitatio Christi* – that we should follow the ideal and seek to become like it – ought logically to have the result of developing and exalting the inner man. In actual fact, however, the ideal has been turned by superficial and formalistically-minded believers into an external object of worship, and it is precisely this veneration for the object that prevents it from reaching down into the depths of the soul and transforming it into a wholeness in keeping with the ideal. Accordingly, the divine mediator stands outside as an image, while man remains fragmentary and untouched in the deepest part of him ... An exclusively religious projection may rob the soul of its values so that through sheer inanition it becomes incapable of further development and gets stuck in an unconscious state. At the same time it falls victim to the delusion that the cause of all disaster lies outside, and people no longer stop to ask themselves how far it is their own doing.[28]

The symbolic interpretation of Jesus' teaching about the immanence of the indwelling spirit within all human beings as well as the whole of natural life is often obscured in the Western Christian tradition. With the Council of Chalcedon in 451, Jesus became the exception – the *only* incarnation of this light, the *only* 'son of God' – rather than a man who has realized his true, divine, being and become the voice and mouthpiece of Hokhmah or Sophia: the model, therefore, of what all human beings may become, because this, essentially, is who they are.[29]

The history of the mythic imagery that preceded Christianity in the great civilizations of the Bronze Age is not widely known, and it seems important to relate the Christian myth as it was formulated in the councils of the early Church to the mythology of the goddess and her son–lover. Unless one remembers the tendency of the soul continually to reformulate the old myth, such a restatement of it might seem remarkable. It is most unlikely that the convergence of a timeless myth with the person of Jesus was a deliberate decision taken by the bishops gathered at Chalcedon; on the contrary, they would have been at pains to ensure that such a thing did *not* happen. But the power of the myth to enter the imagination invited its reformulation, and so it came to clothe both the images of the father god and his son, and the figures of Mary and her son Jesus. However, in its reformulation, the element in the teaching of Jesus most vital to the further evolution of consciousness was obscured. For while the doctrine that Jesus Christ, the son of God, was consubstantial with the godhead, yet distinct from it in his humanity – therefore both divine and human – restated the goddess myth imagery of *zoe* and *bios*, the belief that he was the one and only incarnation of the godhead veiled the 'new' insight that all people have within them the potentiality of realizing their divine nature and becoming the 'sons' or 'daughters' of God. Moreover, because the earlier revelation was lost to consciousness, the Incarnation could not be understood in the sense that the divine presence is incarnate in the whole of visible creation as the 'Son'. True to the process whereby what is unconsciously lost is projected on to an image of an adversary, the Christian Church soon lost the image of totality and created another separation between those who 'believed' its teaching and were therefore 'saved', and those who did not and so were not 'saved'. The same separation was projected topographically on to heaven and hell, which were to receive the 'saved' and the 'damned'.

The image of totality was lost twice over as the feminine aspect of the godhead – defined in the Gnostic image of Sophia as the Divine Mother – was rejected when Christ as Logos replaced Sophia as the Holy Spirit. Although Mary's elevation to the status of God-bearer (*Theotokos*) and the doctrine of her perpetual virginity soon allowed her to take the place of the Virgin Mother of previous cultures in the affection of the people, nevertheless, in its rejection of the human process of birth it split nature from spirit and divided life into two 'halves', as Judaism, when it rejected the image of the goddess, had also done.

The identification of Jesus with the image of the son of the deity, who was immaculately conceived and born of a virgin, gave divine authority to the New Testament and to the Church as its interpreter, and may have ensured its survival, but the Wisdom tradition of the Kingdom of God as the divine ground of life and the human soul had to go underground, and Western civilization was deprived for many centuries of an insight that might greatly have enriched it.

The Androgyny of the Divine in Gnostic Christianity

The Gnostic Christian image of the deity was androgynous, both male and female, Mother and Father. How did the orthodox Christian image of the deity come to be conceived as uniquely male? Once again, the explanation may lie in a break in transmission between the gender distinctions intrinsic to the Hebrew and Greek languages and those of Latin and later European languages. The aspect of the godhead as Holy Spirit – as Hokhmah and Sophia – was feminine in Hebrew and Greek until it became assimilated to the masculine concept of Logos, and then to the Latin *Spiritus Sanctus*, which also had a masculine gender. In English there is no gender distinction between nouns, so there is no means of conveying the gender of something by means of the spelling of a word. One can say, 'God is wisdom', 'God is beauty', 'God is truth' and so on, but there is no way of knowing whether these qualities are imagined as masculine or feminine in character, as there is in earlier languages.

The Gnostics, including the Jewish Gnostics, made an important contribution to the restoration of balance in the Judaeo-Christian image of God by describing the deity as both mother and father, and the emanations from the primal source as both female and male in essence; a hierarchy of divine beings or energies mediating between the unmanifest ground of being and the manifest world.

The restoration of the image of the goddess is startling, so much so that one scholar has maintained that there are grounds for concluding that Gnosticism was an expression of the cult of the Mother Goddess.[30] It is true to say that Gnosticism appeared in precisely the areas that had for millennia seen the worship of the goddess – Syria, Egypt, Asia Minor and Mesopotamia. Jewish Gnostics had access both to the tradition of the biblical Wisdom literature and, if they lived in Syria, Mesopotamia or Egypt, to the traditions of the goddess and her son–lover long existing in these regions. The underlying image of the sacred marriage pervades Gnostic texts and, most importantly, was one of their main sacraments. So we find that, as in the earlier myths, the original semi-divine being, or *anthropos*, is sometimes portrayed as daughter, sometimes as son, sometimes as the brother–sister pair. The emphasis is on the quest, as now one, now the other, goes in search of his or her 'lost' counterpart, and their reunion and return to the divine world of their origin is celebrated in the sacred marriage.

Pagels, in her book *The Gnostic Gospels*, writes that Gnostics prayed to the Divine, Feminine, Virgin Sophia as the 'mystical, eternal Silence', as 'Grace, She who is before all things', as the 'Invisible within the All' and as 'incorruptible Wisdom, or Gnosis'.[31] The Sumerian 'tone' of each of these phrases is striking. Again, Pagels refers to a group of Gnostic sources that claimed to have received a secret tradition from Jesus through James, his brother, and through Mary Magdalene – sayings no doubt recorded by the original group in Jerusalem. She writes that members of this group prayed to both the divine Father and Mother: 'From Thee, Father, and through Thee, Mother, the two immortal names, Parents of the divine being, and thou, dweller in heaven, humanity, of the mighty name ...'[32] Pagels quotes a definition of God by the Gnostic teacher Valentinus in which he suggests 'that the divine can be imagined as a dyad; consisting, in one part, of the Ineffable, the Depth, the Primal Father; and, in the other, of Grace, Silence, the Womb and "Mother of All"'.[33] Pagels writes that 'he goes on to describe how Silence receives, as in a womb, the seed of the Ineffable Source; from this she brings forth all the emanations of divine being, ranged in harmonious pairs of masculine and feminine energies.'[34] The creative dyad is given very clear expression in the following passage:

> Before the universe, the First was revealed. In the boundlessness he is a self-grown, self-constructed father who is full of shining, ineffable light. In the beginning he decided to have his form come to be as a great power. Immediately the beginning of that light was revealed as an immortal, androgynous man. His male name is 'the Begetting of the Perfect One'. And his female name is 'All-wise Begettress Sophia'. It is also said that she resembles her brother and her consort.[35]

In another similar text, called 'The Sophia of Jesus Christ', the risen Jesus, teaching his disciples, says:

> I desire that you understand that First Man is called Begetter, Mind who is complete in himself. He reflected with the great Sophia, his consort, and revealed his first-begotten, androgynous son. His male name is called 'First-Begetter Son of God'; his female name is 'First Begettress Sophia, Mother of the Universe'. Some call her Love. Now the First-begotten is called 'Christ'.[36]

The androgyny of the primal source is reflected at every level of the hierarchy of creation until it appears in our own, manifesting as the two 'halves' of the soul, masculine and feminine.

Sometimes one has the impression that certain elements in the Gnostic texts are derived from the apocryphal Wisdom literature of Judaism lost after the Babylonian Exile, because they are so rich in the symbolism of Sophia (Hokmah). The image of light, associated with both goddess and god as far back as Sumeria, recurs again and again in connection with the divine unity. It is quite clear that the trinity of Father, Mother and Son is really based on a dyad that is carried through a chain of numberless creations. Each 'Son' created from above, from a union of the male and female aspects of the divine source, has a consort, each archangel or angel a 'reflection', so that any concept of a duality of Mother and Father, or a trinity of Mother, Father and Son, has to be extended to a quaternity that includes a daughter, who is the bride of the son and the mother of the next level of creation.[37]

In the 'Gospel to the Hebrews' Jesus refers to the Holy Ghost as 'My Mother, the Spirit'. The 'Apocryphon of John' tells how John had a vision of the Trinity:

> While I was contemplating these things, behold the heavens opened and the whole creation which is under heaven shone and the world was shaken. And I was afraid . . . and I saw in the light a youth who stood by me. While I looked at him he became like an old man . . . There was not a plurality before me, but there was a likeness with multiple forms in the light, and the

forms appeared through each other, and the likeness had three forms. He
said to me, John, John, why do you doubt, and why are you afraid . . . be
not timid! I am the one who is with you for ever. I am the Father, I am the
Mother, I am the Son.[38]

The idea that the Holy Spirit was feminine – the Mother – was foreign
only to *Gentile* Christians. Professor Quispel writes that 'Jewish Christians
were entirely convinced that the Holy Spirit was a feminine hypostasis.'[39]
This is a most important consideration in relation to the passages describing the baptism of Jesus, where the Holy Spirit descends on him in the
likeness of a dove (Matt. 3:16). In a fragment from the Jewish Christian
Gospels, the Holy Spirit says to Jesus at his baptism: 'My Son, in all the
prophets I was waiting for Thee.'[40] 'Here', writes Quispel, 'we come to a
very simple realization: just as birth requires a mother, so rebirth requires
a spiritual mother. Originally, the Christian term "rebirth" must therefore
have been associated with the concept of the spirit as a feminine
hypostasis.'[41]

There is one particular Gnostic text that is electrifying in its reflection
of the imagery of the Virgin Mother and must surely contain fragments of
earlier texts now lost, possibly even a Mesopotamian temple incantation,
which may have belonged to the same source as the verses spoken by
Hokhmah in Proverbs and Ben Sirach quoted in Chapter 12. From our
knowledge of Sophia, it is clear that in the few lines given below from a
longer text she herself is speaking as Wisdom, as once Inanna spoke in
Sumeria and Isis in Egypt.

The Thunder, Perfect [Whole] Mind[42]

I was sent forth from (the) power,
   and I have come to those who reflect upon me,
   and I have been found among those who seek after me.
Look upon me, you who reflect upon me,
   and you hearers, hear me.
   You who are waiting for me, take me to yourselves.
And do not banish me from your sight.
   And do not make your voice hate me, nor your hearing.
   Do not be ignorant of me anywhere or any time. Be on your guard!
   Do not be ignorant of me.

For I am the first and the last,
I am the honored one and the scorned one,
I am the whore and the holy one.
I am the wife and the virgin.
I am the [mother] and the daughter.
I am the members of my mother.
I am the barren one
   and many are her sons.
I am she whose wedding is great,

and I have not taken a husband.
I am the midwife and she who does not bear.
I am the solace of my labor pains.
I am the bride and the bridegroom,
    and it is my husband who begot me.
I am the mother of my father
    and the sister of my husband,
    and he is my offspring.

    . . . . .

I am the silence that is incomprehensible
    and the idea whose remembrance is frequent.
I am the voice whose sound is manifold
    and the word whose appearance is multiple.
I am the utterance of my name.

    . . . . .

Why have you hated me in your counsels?
For I shall be silent among those who are silent,
    and I shall appear and speak.
Why then have you hated me, you Greeks?
    Because I am a barbarian among (the) barbarians?
For I am the wisdom (of the) Greeks
    and the knowledge of (the) barbarians.
(I) am the one whose image is great in Egypt
    and the one who has no image among the barbarians.
I am the one who has been hated everywhere
    and who has been loved everywhere.
I am the one whom they call Life,
    and you have called Death.
I am the one whom they call Law,
    and you have called Lawlessness.
I am the one whom you have pursued,
    and I am the one whom you have seized.
I am the one whom you have scattered,
    and you have gathered me together.

Women as Disciples and Teachers of Gnosis

Women in the Gnostic Church could teach, heal, prophesy and hold any rank within it that men did, including that of bishop. This was a source of great irritation to the orthodox Christians. Tertullian exclaimed: 'These heretical women – how audacious they are! They have no modesty; they are bold enough to teach, to engage in argument, to enact exorcisms, to undertake cures, and, it may be, even to baptize.'[43] Defining the way he believed women ought to behave, he wrote, echoing Paul: 'It is not permitted for a woman to speak in the church, nor is it permitted for her to teach, nor to baptize, nor to offer (the eucharist), nor to claim for herself a share in any *masculine* function – not to mention any priestly office.'[44]

Pagels observes that from the year 200 'we have no evidence for women taking prophetic, priestly, and episcopal roles among orthodox churches'.[45]

Apart from the Gnostic Church, the only exception to the exclusion of women from priestly office in the 2,000 years of Christianity is the heretic twelfth-century Cathar Church of the Holy Spirit, in which, as in the Gnostic Church, women held the rank of bishop, administered the sacraments, taught, baptized and healed the sick. With the exception of Judaism and Islam, the Christian refusal to allow women to hold priestly office is in striking contrast to the entire previous history of religion in Egypt, Mesopotamia, Crete, Syria and Greece, where, from the inception of the Bronze Age, women had been priestesses in all the temples of the goddess. (It cannot pass without wondering how deeply this exclusion has wounded woman's soul and curtailed her expansion as a human being.) In none of the three 'patriarchal' religions, Judaism, Christianity and Islam, was there an image of the mother, wife, sister or bride of the father god. These images are to be found only within the mystical or repressed traditions of the three religions. With no metaphysical image of woman, and with no longer any 'sacred' role in society, how could women, and equally men, relate within themselves to all the different aspects of the archetypal feminine?

In the Gnostic Gospels women can discover a long-lost image of themselves. The Gospel of Philip relates that the mother, sister and companion of Jesus are all called Mary. This threefold image suggests the lunar mysteries of the threefold goddess, the original lunar trinity. Mary Magdalene, the closest companion of Jesus, appears in several of the Gnostic Gospels as one of the disciples, and there is no doubt in these texts of the importance of her role in the Jerusalem group in earliest Christianity. The Gospel of Mary says that, as mentioned in the Gospels of Mark and John, she was the first to see the risen Christ. (It is interesting to recall, as noted in Chapter 14, that Mary mistakes Jesus for the gardener as he 'returns from the underworld' and that 'the Gardener' was one of the most ancient titles of the Sumerian son–lover.)

In the 'Dialogue of the Savior' Mary is one of three disciples who receive a particular revelation from Jesus, and is spoken of as 'a woman who knew the All'. A text called *Pistis Sophia*, written at Luxor, in Egypt, during the third century AD, describes the journey of the soul, interpreting the words of the Psalms in terms of Gnosticism.[46] It may have been written by a woman or a group of women and records an important teaching given by Jesus to the disciples after the Resurrection. It says that as well as the disciples mentioned in the Gospels known to us, there were present at that gathering four women disciples of Jesus: Mary Magdalene; Martha; Mary, the mother of Jesus; and Salome. Each one of these, as well as several male disciples, questions Jesus, but Mary Magdalene's questions far outnumber the rest; indeed, the entire text is almost a dialogue between Jesus and Mary Magdalene. Mary, in pursuit of her desire to learn more, repeatedly says, 'My Lord, be not wroth with me if I question thee concerning all with precision and certainty.' Peter, annoyed by her monopoly of Jesus' attention, becomes irritated with her, and Mary, alarmed, says at one point, 'I am afraid of Peter, because he threatened me and hateth our sex.'[47] Jesus always praises Mary's insight, and says that because they have truly understood his teaching, 'Mary Magdalene and John, the virgin, will tower over all my disciples and over all men who shall receive the mysteries in the Ineffable. And they will be on my right and on my left. And I am they, and they are I.'[48] This is a change indeed from the image of women offered by the four Christian Gospels, in which there are no women disciples.

In other texts Peter's envy of Mary explodes. The Gospel of Mary, which may have been written by a woman – even perhaps Mary Magdalene herself originally – tells how Jesus, appearing in his 'body of light' to the disciples, urged them to go forth and preach the gospel of the inner kingdom. 'Beware that no one lead you astray, saying, "Lo here!" or "Lo there!" For the Son of Man is within you. Follow after him! Those who seek him will find him. Go then and preach the gospel of the kingdom.'[49]

But after he had left them, the disciples, overcome with doubt and despair, felt they could not accomplish what he asked.

Then Mary stood up, greeted them all, and said to her brethren, 'Do not weep and do not grieve nor be irresolute, for his grace will be entirely with you and will protect you . . .'

Peter said to Mary, 'Sister, We know that the Savior loved you more than the rest of women. Tell us the words of the Savior which you remember – which you know (but) we do not nor have we heard them.' Mary answered and said, 'What is hidden from you I will proclaim to you.' And she began to speak to them these words: 'I,' she said, 'I saw the Lord in a vision and I said to him, "Lord, I saw you today in a vision." He answered and said to me, "Blessed are you, that you did not waver at the sight of me. For where the mind is, there is the treasure." I said to him, "Lord, now does he who sees the vision see it [through] the soul [or] through the spirit?" The Savior answered and said, "He does not see through the soul nor through the spirit, but the mind which [is] between the two – that is [what] sees the vision . . ."'

When Mary had said this, she fell silent, since it was to this point that the Savior had spoken with her. But Andrew answered and said to the brethren, 'Say what you (wish to) say about what she has said. I at least do not believe that the Savior said this. For certainly these teachings are strange ideas.' Peter answered and spoke concerning these same things. He questioned them about the Savior: 'Did he really speak privately with a woman (and) not openly to us? Are we to turn about and all listen to her? Did he prefer her to us?'

Then Mary wept and said to Peter, 'My brother Peter, what do you think? Do you think that I thought this up myself in my heart, or that I am lying about the Savior?' Levi [Matthew] answered and said to Peter, 'Peter, you have always been hot-tempered. Now I see you contending against the woman like the adversaries. But if the Savior made her worthy, who are you indeed to reject her? Surely the Savior knows her very well. That is why he loved her more than us.'[50]

Pagels notes the political implications of Mary's words: 'As Mary stands up to Peter, so the Gnostics who take her as their prototype challenge the authority of those priests and bishops who claim to be Peter's successors.'[51]

These texts have a ring of authenticity, and are interesting for the very human light they shed on the relationship between the disciples. One point of recording these encounters would seem to be to offer a different and perhaps more complete view of Jesus' relationship with his disciples than that shown in the more familiar Gospels. These few extracts from some of the Gnostic texts give us a very intimate view of the disciples, who evidently included both men and women, and a realistic impression of the various relationships between them. We hear their voices speaking to each other and to Jesus, and sense their uncertainty in the face of the immense responsibility they had assumed.

The figure of Jesus is too numinous for the Gnostic texts to be dismissed as irrelevant or heretical. Everything that can be known about him needs to be considered and evaluated, and these newly discovered voices from an era that is all too remote and obscure provide not only a new approach to an understanding of his teaching but also a fascinating insight into the voice of the soul. The Gnostics never thought of themselves as heretics but as the inheritors of an authentic transmission of teaching from Jesus.

The Gnostic sects were suppressed by two edicts of the Emperor Constantine, the 'Christian' emperor who, it is not generally known, had his wife boiled alive and his son murdered. These two edicts of AD 326 and 333 prohibited the Gnostics' meetings and ordered their Gospels to be burned. It was in this way that the orthodox branch of Christianity prevailed over the Gnostic one, supported by the political structure of the Roman Empire, which empowered it to eliminate 'heretics'.

SOPHIA IN THE DARK AND MIDDLE AGES

In the first quarter of the sixth century, in a prison cell in Pavia, one of the greatest scholars of the age gave way to despair as he confronted his imminent death on the orders of the barbarian emperor Theodoric. His name was Boethius (480–524). As he waited, poised between life and death, he had a vision:[52]

While I was quietly thinking these thoughts over to myself and giving vent to my sorrow with the help of my pen, I became aware of a woman standing

Figure 2. Sophia appearing to Boethius in his cell; frontispiece to an English manuscript of Boethius, *De Consolatione Philosophiae*, 1150–75. Winchester or Hereford.

over me. She was of awe-inspiring appearance, her eyes burning and keen beyond the usual power of men. She was so full of years that I could hardly think of her as of my own generation, and yet she possessed a vivid colour and undiminished vigour. It was difficult to be sure of her height, for sometimes she was of average human size, while at other times she seemed to touch the very sky with the top of her head, and when she lifted herself even higher, she pierced it and was lost to human sight. Her clothes were made of imperishable material, of the finest thread woven with the most delicate skill. (Later she told me she had made them with her own hands.) Their colour, however, was obscured by a kind of film as of long neglect, like statues covered in dust. On the bottom hem could be read the embroidered Greek letter Pi, and on the top hem the Greek letter Theta. Between the two a ladder of steps rose from the lower to the higher letter. Her dress had been torn by the hands of marauders who had each carried off such pieces as he could get. There were some books in her right hand, and in her left hand she held a sceptre. (p. 35)

A long dialogue between Boethius and the woman followed, in which she revealed herself to be Sophia. Speaking to him over several days, she answered his questions, transforming his understanding of life's apparent injustice, and giving him the strength he needed to face his terrible death.

Boethius was able to write down his long dialogue with Sophia before he was tortured to death. Miraculously, it has come down to us as *The Consolation of Philosophy*. It influenced generations of scholars and was reverently read by Charlemagne in the ninth century. Eventually, in twelfth-century Italy, it reached Dante, whose image of Beatrice as the guiding spirit of Wisdom in the human soul was perhaps inspired by the figure of Boethius' Sophia.

Figure 3. *The Black Virgin.*
Montserrat, Spain.

The Resurgence of the Gnostic Sophia

The Gnostic tradition, which had been forced underground in the early centuries of Christianity, reappears in the twelfth century. Four powerful movements concentrated during the Middle Ages mainly in France and northern Spain manifest as the long-lost voice of the hidden tradition. These were the Order of the Knights Templar,[53] the Cathar Church of the Holy Spirit, Jewish Kabbalism and Alchemy. Perhaps a fifth should be added, for the influence of Sufi scholars and poets in Spain and southern France was a powerful catalyst for the resurgence of the Gnostic tradition.[54] The Gnostic ideas were spread by the troubadours and by the immense popularity of the legends of the quest for the Holy Grail. It is in these diverse movements, so strangely allied with each other and with the great popular movement of devotion to the Black Virgin, that the feminine principle once again becomes the focus of consciousness. It may have been only a handful of individuals – even Jews, Christians and Muslims working together – who precipitated this resurgence. The emphasis in all of them was not on the goddess as such, but on Sophia, or Sapientia, as the image of the Wisdom to which the soul aspires on its journey back to its source. The science of the soul's transformation was hidden in an elaborate code of symbols known as Alchemy, or the Hermetic Art. This secret teaching nourished not only the Cathar heretics, but other groups of individuals within the Order of the Knights Templar, as well as Jewish

Kabbalists and Islamic philosophers and mystics. It was woven into the symbolic imagery of the Grail legends, Dante's *Divine Comedy* and the *Romaunt de la Rose*, and carried all over Europe by the troubadours, many of whom were initiates of the teaching they concealed in the allegorical imagery of their love poems. It is carved into the stone structure of the Gothic cathedrals, and the intricate symbolism of their great rose windows.

At the Courts of Love in France, where these ideas were nurtured, woman was celebrated for her beauty, compassion, intelligence and learning. For the first time since the Gnostic groups 1,000 years earlier, she began to be treated as an individual and given a social position and a cultural role apart from that of wife, mother or concubine. She became the inspiration of an astonishing flowering of poetry, philosophy, song and literature, as well as the chivalric ideal, which did much to transform her life. The troubadours made her the personification of Sophia, and addressed her in language that evoked the Song of Songs. Until these Courts of Love appeared, woman had been (and still was) presented by the Church to society as a lewd, wicked, treacherous creature, fatally flawed by the sin of Eve, whose destiny it was to be ruled by her husband, to experience sex only for the purpose of procreation, and to serve her lord in the same way and on the same contractual basis as the medieval vassal served his overlord. The troubadours began to free sexuality and eroticism from guilt. They offered to men a new image of themselves, as gentle, courtly and cultivated instead of dedicated only to conquest and prowess in war. Their songs were a glorification of life, a celebration of being. Tragically, their vision died with the Papal (Albigensian) Crusade of 1209 against the Cathar heresy and the persecution that lasted throughout the thirteenth century. The carnage that ensued eviscerated a people and destroyed a brilliant culture. The Languedoc, as an early focus of the spiritual impulse that laid the foundations of the cultural development of Europe, never recovered. Christian civilization let slip another moment of *kairos* when it could perhaps have altered the fate brought into being by the ever-increasing emphasis given to the masculine archetype.

The Cathar Church was known as the Church of the Holy Spirit and the Church of the Grail. At the heart of its teaching was a Gnostic text called 'The Secret Book of John', possibly the same 'Apocryphon of John' that was found at Nag Hammadi. It claimed that the ancient Church of the Holy Spirit derived from the actual teaching of John, who, as the disciple leaning on Christ's breast at the Last Supper, was the one with his ear closest to Christ's heart. The Church was spoken of as 'the cup that gives out manna' and 'the precious stone' – images that connect it with the symbolism of the Gnostic cup, or *krater*, and with the chalice of the Grail, as well as with the image of the goddess. The Holy Spirit, Sophia, and her messenger, the dove, became the secret inspiration and emblem of a dedicated group of men and women who said of themselves, echoing the experience of persecuted Christians, Gnostics and Jews: 'We lead a life hard and wandering. We fly from town to town like sheep among wolves. We suffer persecution like the Apostles and Martyrs, yet our life is holy and austere. These things are not difficult, for we are no longer of this world.'[55]

Like the Gnostics, the Cathars taught that Christ was the image of the indwelling divine spirit in the human soul, and that human beings could awake from their sleep of ignorance to awareness of this spirit. They could awaken their own soul, as the prince in the fairy-tales awoke the Sleeping Beauty and Snow White. They could devote themselves to this work of self-understanding, as a lover to his beloved. The second birth, or resurrection of the soul, was the process of awakening to awareness of their divine nature and the guiding spirit within it. The Cathars, like the Gnostics, believed the world was in darkness because it was ruled by an evil principle that held everything in its thrall, including the Christian Church. The Church, which was exceedingly corrupt at this time, not surprisingly felt itself threatened by this teaching and did its utmost to eradicate it, finally succeeding when Pope Innocent III instigated the Papal Crusade of 1209. Yet Bernard of Clairvaux, founder of the Cistercian Order, who was sent by the Pope to preach against the heretics, could find no fault with their way of life. With hindsight, it is clear that all three, Gnostics, Cathars and the orthodox Church, were gripped by the Iron Age belief that evil must exist as the counterpart to good, and each projected it upon their spiritual opponents, reserving the quality of 'goodness' to themselves. In this state of mythic inflation there was no room for 'goodness' in the other.

The Knights Templar, whose growth coincided roughly with the growth of the Cathar Church, and whose Order was destroyed with barbaric cruelty in 1309, 100 years after the Albigensian Crusade, may also have been Gnostics. The image they were said to worship – *Baphomet* – was a cryptographic name that concealed its secret meaning – Sophia.[56] The Templars were celibate, and included women as well as men in their Order, even choosing them to be the head of it. Like the troubadours, they took the dove as their emblem.

THE SHEKHINAH

In Kabbalah – the mystical Jewish tradition that appears in the Middle Ages in Spain and southern France – the association of the Holy Spirit with the feminine aspect of the divine is restored in the image of the Shekhinah. The rise of medieval Kabbalism belongs to the same psychic impulse that evoked the resurgence of feminine imagery at this time. To some extent, its different expressions almost restored the feminine archetype to the position it had held in the Bronze Age. Within the framework of Kabbalistic teaching the image of the Shekhinah, like that of Sophia, reaches far back into the foundations of the Bronze Age goddesses of Mesopotamia and Egypt, and also, later, to the images of Asherah and Astarte in Canaan. What is truly extraordinary is that the old imagery of these goddesses survived in Jewish Kabbalism into the European Middle Ages and beyond. How, and by whom, one wonders, was this tradition preserved? Was it the Jews settled in Mesopotamia, perhaps in the area of Babylon or Basra, who passed it from one generation to another, until at last it was carried to the shores of France and Spain? Because so few scholars compare the images of different cultures, vital associations may have been overlooked and the continuity with the past has not been perceived. Wallis Budge was one of the first scholars to notice the relationship between Egyptian and Sumerian mythology and to refer to its influence on Judaic and Gnostic imagery.[57] As shown in Chapter 12, Patai's study of the Hebrew goddess has made a vital contribution to the continuity of goddess imagery over an immense expanse of time. What becomes clear through a study of the tradition is that Jewish Gnosticism was the medium of transmission from the archaic Babylonian imagery to that of Jewish Kabbalism. Although the study of Kabbalism properly might begin in Babylonia in the sixth century BC – from the time of the Exile – or even earlier, it has been placed in this part of the book because it is only in the Middle Ages that it emerges clearly into the religious structure of the age.

The Hebrew noun *Sh'khinah* is derived from the verb *shakhan*, which means literally, 'the act of dwelling'.[58] There is no allusion to the Shekhinah as a feminine being in the Old Testament, but the way for this image to manifest was prepared by the verses in the Pentateuch that referred to the 'presence' or 'glory' of Yahweh as the visible cloud overshadowing or hovering over the Tabernacle (Exod. 40:34–8) and by the later concept of Hokhmah in the Wisdom Books. The first mention of the Shekhinah in Jewish writings appeared during the first century AD,[59] and to begin with had the meaning of the manifestation or aspect of the deity that could be apprehended by the senses.[60] The extensive mythology relating to the image of the Shekhinah and the Shekhinah–Matronit as a feminine deity, however, developed fully only during the Middle Ages.

The definitive text of Kabbalism – the *Zohar* – was written in the thirteenth century, and the popular movement derived from these early beginnings reached its full flowering only in the sixteenth and seventeenth centuries. Certain Kabbalistic images go back to the Jewish philosopher Philo of Alexandria, the same Philo who gave a new definition to the image of Wisdom.[61] They were also influenced by texts written during the seventh and eighth centuries in Babylon and Byzantium[62] and during the ninth century in Basra.[63] These texts found their way to Europe, where, by the beginning of the eleventh century, they became the foundation of the Kabbalism that developed in the Jewish communities in Spain and south-western France. The communities in Babylon and Basra were the descendants of the exiles who had remained behind in Mesopotamia in 538 BC. It is interesting that Kabbalism returned to the Near East as a result of the expulsion of the Jews from Spain in 1492, when a group of Kabbalists settled at Safed, in Galilee; from there Kabbalism spread to Asia and Africa as well as to Jewish communities elsewhere in Europe.

The myth of the Shekhinah in Kabbalistic teaching says that she was the source or foundation of the created world, embodied above all in the image of Light.[64] She is the immanence of the divine in the world, transmitter of the light of the godhead through all the cycles of manifestation until she generates the world we know. This recalls nothing so much as the radiance of Inanna and her descent through the seven planetary spheres or gates to the 'Underworld' of her sister goddess Ereshkigal. And it is almost identical to the Gnostic myth of Sophia explored earlier in this chapter. Like the moon, the Shekhinah reflects the light of the source. She is so tiny that her presence could be accommodated even in the ark of bulrushes that held Moses, yet so great that her body extended for millions of miles. She is the Holy Spirit: Light generating all forms of life. Her 'name' is so holy that, like Yahweh's, it is not spoken of directly, and she is referred to as 'That Woman, That Female', rather than by her ineffable name. Like Mary, she takes the role of intercessor between the human and the divine realms, able to intercede with Yahweh on behalf of humanity.[65] The line between the Shekhinah as the 'presence', manifestation or attribute of Yahweh and as a distinct entity is very finely drawn and not by any means clear, for only the feminine gender of her name distinguishes her from Yahweh. It is the gender ending that gives the texts referring to the Shekhinah their 'feeling' and establishes their feminine quality.

The Shekhinah was identified by the Kabbalists with the radiance of the Holy Spirit, the fiery Pleroma from which all creation, including the human soul, emanates. This Holy Spirit, radiance or 'glory of God', which was compared by the Kabbalists to a great sea, was the first creation, or emanation, from which all other creations or emanations have flowed. The Shekhinah is immanent in the human soul as its divine 'ground' or radiant 'body', and can be revealed personally to men and women. She is their deepest self, the holy presence of 'the glory of God' within them. The sacred marriage in Kabbalism is, as it is in Gnosticism as well as in mystical Christianity and Islam, the union of the soul with this Holy Spirit. Through the radiant light of the Shekhinah everything is linked to everything else, as if connected through a luminous skein of being. *Ainsoph*, the indescribable and ineffable mystery of the ground of life, is both the source of the skein and is immanent, through the Shekhinah, in creation, in every particle and aspect of it. What is called nature is therefore the epiphany of the Divine. The Shekhinah was called Queen, Daughter and Bride of Yahweh, and was, by implication, the mother of all human souls, although in Kabbalism she was specifically the mother of 'the mystic community of Israel' and ultimately of every Jewish individual. These souls are 'sparks' of the fiery Shekhinah, which are 'scattered' in exile and have to be 'gathered together' again to their source. (Compare the similar imagery in the Gnostic Gospel of Eve quoted on p. 622.) The Shekhinah was addressed as the 'Mystical Eden' – an enfolding presence, not a place – as well as the 'holy apple garden', the 'great sea' and the fountain that transmits life from the unmanifest source into manifestation.[66] Life, or creation, is conceived in the divine union between Yahweh and the Shekhinah. Sexual imagery and the image of light are used in text after text to show how 'the ray which emerges from Nothing, is, as it were, sown into the "celestial mother" . . . out of whose womb the Sefiroth (creative energies) spring forth, as King and Queen, son and daughter'.[67] One has to return to the creation myths of Sumeria and Egypt for the clearest source of this imagery. The many pictures of the ray of light impregnating the Christian Mary come to mind as a parallel image. One of the primary texts used in the Middle Ages for the contemplation of the union of the deity with the Shekhinah was the Song of Songs. The blackness of the Shekhinah, her garb of mourning that conceals the glory of her Light, is a theme that is always related to the image of Wisdom.

Like the Gnostics in their myth of Sophia, Kabbalism stressed the myth of the Shekhinah's exile. There seem to be two kinds of exile connected with her image: the first was 'mythological' and arose out of the expulsion of Adam and Eve, when the Shekhinah shared the exile from the Garden with all humanity. The second exile was 'historical' and specific to the history of the people of Israel. In the early history of Israel the Shekhinah, or 'glory of God', dwelt first of all in the Tabernacle, as the presence overshadowing the Ark of the Covenant, going before it as a pillar of cloud by day and a pillar of fire by night (Exod. 40:38). Later, when the Ark was placed in the Temple built by Solomon, the Shekhinah dwelt there. However, she disappeared at the time of the destruction of the first Temple (586 BC), when the Ark was lost and the Jews were taken into captivity in Babylon, and she did not return with them to Israel at the end of their exile in 538 BC. She will not return until the coming of the Messiah, and she cannot return until the broken unity of the godhead is restored through her reunion with her divine bridegroom. The image of exile, therefore, is not only associated with her failure to return to the Holy Land, but with her exile from the godhead, as if her being immanent in creation had cut her off from her 'other half', her transcendent source and spouse. In her exile she is named 'the Widow', and the 'Stone of Exile' (*Lapis Exulis*), the 'Precious Stone' and 'the Pearl'. Some of these images are inherited from the earlier goddesses and are rediscovered in Alchemy and the Grail legends. The Shekhinah weeps, as Rachel wept for her children, as she waits for her exile to end. Rabbinic prayer is directed towards bringing this about and to hasten the time of her return. As long as her exile lasts, creation is cut off from the transcendent deity.

The cause of her cosmic exile was believed to be Adam's sin. Scholem explains what this was:

> The Sefiroth [creative energies of God] were revealed to Adam in the shape of the Tree of Life and the Tree of Knowledge; . . . instead of preserving their original unity and thereby unifying the spheres of 'life' and 'knowledge' and bringing salvation to the world, he separated one from the other and set his mind to worship the Shekhinah only without recognizing its union with the other Sefiroth. Thus he interrupted the stream of life which flows from sphere to sphere and brought separation and isolation into the world. From this time there has been a mysterious fissure, not indeed in the substance of Divinity but in its life and action . . . Only after the restoration of the original harmony in the act of redemption, when everything shall again occupy the place it originally had in the divine scheme of things, will 'God be one and His name one'.[68]

It is this fissure that separates the Shekhinah from Yahweh and maintains her state of exile by 'breaking' the chain of relationship between the source and its manifestation, and therefore rupturing the unity of life.[69] One of its effects was to 'scatter' the light of the Shekhinah into the myriad sparks, or *scintillae*, that are the souls of human beings, an image that Jung refers to in his exploration of the nature of the psyche.[70] Until these are gathered up again, the unity of life cannot be restored, and the exile of the Shekhinah cannot end. It seems as if the scattering of the Shekhinah is a condition of spirit manifesting as the physical world. Here, once again, we encounter the distinction between life as *zoe* and life as *bios*.

The Matronit, or 'matron', was the name given to that aspect of the Shekhinah that remained in exile with her people on earth, which was called 'the Daughter'. The deep devotion of the less sophisticated members of the communities, who found in Kabbalah a compassionate mother figure to whom they could relate in their daily lives and appeal to for help in their suffering, was identical with the devotion expressed by the great body of Catholic Christians to the Virgin Mary. The image of the Shekhinah as the 'Matronit' reinstated the old imagery of the mother goddess. Furthermore, the idea of the 'Holy Family', or four aspects of the godhead, which developed in Kabbalism to include the four distinct deities of Father, Mother, Son and Daughter, gave each individual an archetypal image of his or her own experience of life.[71] Sexuality was included in the relationship of these deities to one another, and so human beings, by imitating the divine union, had restored to them the sense of sacrality that was believed to have been lost with the expulsion of Adam and Eve from the Garden. It is a remarkably balanced vision.

Within the space of a few hundred years Kabbalism had developed an image of a goddess that reinstated in many details the earlier image and provided an essential counter-balance to the rigorous masculinity of the

Judaic deity. Interestingly, Scholem observes that the introduction of the idea of the feminine element in God

> was one of the most important and lasting innovations of Kabbalism. The fact that it obtained recognition in spite of the obvious difficulty of reconciling it with the conception of the absolute unity of God, and that no other element of Kabbalism won such a degree of popular approval, is proof that it responded to a deep-seated religious need.[72]

Yet, he continues, Kabbalism, 'both historically and metaphysically, is a masculine doctrine, made for men and by men. The long history of Jewish mysticism shows no trace of feminine influence. There have been no women Kabbalists.'[73] Nevertheless, no doubt because the soul ultimately insists on the inclusion of the feminine archetype, the image of the Shekhinah became vitally important to this tradition, which kept alive the image of the consort of Yahweh and the sacred marriage between them, whereas orthodox Judaism saw in Wisdom only an attribute of God.

What emerges from this exploration of the important role played by the Shekhinah in Kabbalah is that a large slice of history has been, as it were, excised from the Judaism familiar to most people. The fact that there was a feminine component of the deity both in biblical times and much later, in Kabbalism and Hassidism, is certainly unknown to most Christians, if not to many Jews. The direct line of descent of this imagery from the Bronze Age and beyond, from the Neolithic era, is unknown also. The monotheistic stance of the Judaic and Christian god gives an incomplete reflection of the soul, which has always affirmed the need for a feminine principle in the deity to express the totality of its experience of life and the full reach of its imagination.

THE BLACK VIRGIN

The mythology of the Shekhinah was paralleled in Christian culture by the great upsurge of popular devotion to the Virgin Mary, and in the flowering of feminine imagery in mystical Christianity, Alchemy and the Grail legends. It is hard to be sure what precipitated the dramatic eruption of the feminine archetype in the twelfth and thirteenth centuries. What is certain is the release it gave to the imagination and to a feeling of revelation, which expressed itself in the creation of every kind of beauty, from the Gothic cathedrals to illuminated manuscripts, and in a new mythology that found its voice in poetry and song. It was as if the soul were impregnated once more, as it had been in the greatest moments of earlier cultures, with a vision of the marvellous. This vision drew its inspiration from the Wisdom literature of the Bible, in particular from the Song of Songs, as well as from the Sophia of the secret Gnostic tradition whose imagery has been explored above, and from the image of the goddess, which was now, mysteriously, given new life in the devotion to Mary.

Figure 4. *The Black Virgin.*
Dorres, Pyrenees.

The three traditions – Gnostic, Jewish and Christian – all contain
elements of the imagery and mythology of the Sumerian and Egyptian
Mother Goddess, together with their association with light and wisdom,
but all three have lost the original unity of earth and heaven that the
image once embraced. The curtain or barrier that came between the
Gnostic worlds of light and darkness and separated the daughter Sophia
from her mother in the Pleroma, and the 'fissure' that appeared between
the Shekhinah and Yahweh, can be compared with the angel with the
flaming sword who barred Adam and Eve from the Garden of Eden.
These can all be understood as images that describe humanity's sense of
alienation as consciousness drew ever further away from its instinctual
ground. The different 'revelations', or myths of redemption and return,
and the image of the feminine as the primary agent facilitating this return
– as the compassionate intercessor between the deity and humanity – came
into being as expressions of the urgent need to recover the lost experience
of wholeness and so the oneness and unity of life. The black robe that
hides the Shekhinah, like the robe or veil of Isis, symbolizes the un-
fathomed mystery of the identity of creator and creation and, at the same
time, the darkened or fragmented consciousness of humanity, which
cannot perceive it and so inevitably prolongs both the 'exile' of the Light
and the Holy Spirit of Wisdom, and the exile of humanity from the
eternal ground.

Hieratic, majestic, austere, the Black Virgin gazes out from the windows of Chartres Cathedral, or sits enthroned in the crypt, holding her son in the manner of the goddess holding life, her child. So much interest surrounds her today that she is once again becoming the focus of pilgrimage. Her image is stolen from churches where she has sat for centuries undisturbed, and must now be hidden as a precaution against thieves. In Poland she has been the inspiration of a persecuted people, and a Pope addresses his prayers to her.

In the Middle Ages the shrines of the Black Virgin were the most venerated in Europe. As pointed out in Chapter 14, the cult sites that had once been venerated as sacred to the goddess were rededicated by the Christian Church to the Virgin Mary and the powers that had once belonged to the goddess were 'transferred' to Mary, for the people would not be separated from their millennia-long devotion to this image. These sites were often in the crypt of a church, or in a cave, or were marked by a sacred well, tree or stone, which belonged to the mythology of earlier goddesses – Isis, or Cybele, or Minerva (the Roman Athena), who were worshipped far into the Christian era. The worship of the goddess existed in France, as Chapters 1 and 2 have shown, in the Palaeolithic and Neolithic eras, but in 600 BC Greeks sailing from Phocaea on the coast of Asia Minor founded Marseilles and brought with them new images of a mother goddess similar to those found in their homeland. Later, with the Roman occupation of Gaul, the cults of Isis, Cybele and the Roman goddesses travelled with them throughout the Roman Empire. Then, with the coming of Christianity, the shrines of the goddess were slowly rededicated to the Virgin Mary. Statues of the goddess, their wood blackened by age, or perhaps stained black, were brought back from the Holy Land by Crusaders and placed in the shrines where Mary was now venerated. Others were mysteriously 'revealed' to a community by an ox or a bull, which uncovered a long-lost statue of the goddess as it ploughed the field, and then, naturally, this statue 'became' Mary. The association of the bull with the statue of the dark goddess unmistakably discloses the image of the pre-Christian Great Mother.

From the tenth century onwards there is a veritable explosion of veneration for the Black Virgin, and the places sacred to her began to draw more devotees than the cult of either the father god or his son. Now, suddenly, kings, saints and pilgrims flocked to bow their heads before the Black Virgin at Le Puy, Rocamadour, Mont St Michel and Montserrat in Spain, beseeching her favour and endowing her shrines with immense wealth and treasure. Soon her statues, clothed in magnificent robes and jewels or left unadorned in their stark grandeur, marked the stages on the great pilgrimage route to Santiago de Compostela in northern Spain. Miraculous cures proliferated at her shrines. In particular, women prayed to her for a safe delivery in childbirth; pilgrims for a safe journey; criminals for release from their sins. The people worshipped Mary as they had always

Figure 5. *The Black Virgin.*
Solsona, Spain.

worshipped the goddess, but for some the statues of the Black Virgin
symbolized Sophia–Sapientia, the symbol of the secret Wisdom tradition
studied in many places in Christian Europe, offering a sign to the pilgrim
that said: 'If you are in search of Wisdom, you may pursue your quest
here in safety.' For everywhere at that time the breath of heresy trembled
before the zeal of orthodoxy and whatever could not be taught openly as
part of Church doctrine, had to be taught in the utmost secrecy, under
fear of torture and death by fire.

The symbolism of the Black Virgin returns us once again to the Song of
Songs, to the bride who is 'black but beautiful'. It returns us to Cybele,
whose symbol was a black stone, a meteorite, and to the black images of
Demeter, Artemis and Isis, and to the black-robed, exiled Shekhinah, the
'Precious Stone'. It evokes the blackness of the night sky in which the
moon and the evening star are the brightest luminaries, and the mystery
of space as a mother who gives birth each night to the moon and stars and
each morning to the sun. Above all, the Black Virgin holding her son,
Christ, on her lap, gives us the image of the light shining in darkness, and
the esoteric, hidden teaching of Gnosticism and Alchemy. Countless were
the troubadours who knelt before the image of the Black Virgin that once
stood in the great abbey church of La Daurade in Toulouse, and pledged
their devotion to her with the words: 'Lady, I am yours, as long as my life
endures' (Bernard de Ventadour). Their songs to her recall the words of
Solomon: 'I loved her and sought her out from my youth. I desired to

make her my spouse, and I was a lover of her beauty' (Wisd. 8:2). The Black Virgin is the key, not only to the mystical and alchemical literature of the twelfth and thirteenth centuries but to the tremendous surge of cathedral and abbey building of that period. Bernard of Clairvaux, who spent many years contemplating the images of the Song of Songs, dedicated his first and indeed all subsequent Cistercian abbeys to 'Notre Dame', and cathedral after cathedral followed this dedication. So, for troubadour, monk and mystic, the phrase 'Notre Dame' embraced far more than Mary, the mother of Jesus. For the alchemist also, as he struggled to reach the innermost secrets of nature and to release the hidden spirit buried in the depths of his soul, 'Notre Dame' carried a numinous meaning.

Black is the colour that is associated with Wisdom, as the dark phase of the lunar cycle, where light gestates in the womb, is transformed and brought forth anew – an association that is as old as the Black Stone of the Ka'aba, which was once the epiphany of the Great Goddess, and as the robe or veil of Isis. The image of the Black Virgin embodies the ageless Wisdom of life, the ageless Wisdom of an invisible dimension hidden within the outward form of nature, which brings it into being, informs and guides it, or contains it, as a mother her child. The child she holds is life itself to which eternally she gives birth; she is *zoe* holding *bios*. At the same time the Black Virgin symbolizes the fathomless mystery of the soul, which must follow the star that guided the wise men if it is to understand these mysteries and itself give birth to the divine child.[74]

ALCHEMY

The figure of Alchemy sits enthroned beneath the figure of Christ on the central pillar of the Porch of Judgement, at the threshold of the Cathedral of Notre Dame in Paris, her feet touching the ground, her head in the heavenly 'waters'. In one hand she holds a sceptre and in the other, two books, one closed, one open. Against her body rests a nine-runged ladder. We may recognize in her the figure of Sophia, who presides over the mysteries of her temple, which everywhere manifests the teaching of the hermetic art of Alchemy, concealed in the closed book she holds. In another part of the cathedral a bearded figure leans intently forward. He wears the Phrygian cap of the devotee of Cybele. Was he perhaps the architect or master mason who planned the building of this hieroglyph in stone?

Alchemy is at least 2,500 years old; probably older still, flourishing in Bronze Age Sumeria and Egypt. In the twelfth and thirteenth centuries, as part of the psychic movement described above, there was a resurgence of Alchemy. The science of Alchemy is expressed in images that have baffled generations of contemplatives who have struggled to understand

Figure 6. Alchemy (Philosophy). Central portal of Cathedral of Notre Dame, Paris.

their symbolic language. Many fairy-tales, rich in alchemical and Gnostic symbolism, no doubt came originally from the alchemists themselves. Alchemy is one of the few traditions in which imagery and practice rather than theory are the teacher. The images throughout are taken from nature, and so are known to all and therefore accessible to all, yet their meaning cannot be grasped by the intellect alone, which is often confused and infuriated by them, as it is by the Zen Koan. They have to become the subject of meditation, or the process that Jung called 'active imagination', and their meaning may be suddenly revealed only after years of contemplation. The alchemists were careful to stress that

> all error in the art arises because men do not begin with the proper subst-
> ance, and for this reason you should employ venerable nature, because from
> her and through her and in her is our art born and in naught else: and so
> our magisterium is the work of Nature and not of the worker.[75]

With Nature as guide, the main purpose of Alchemy was to discover the processes whereby spirit becomes matter and, starting with 'base matter', to proceed by successive transformations of it in their 'vessel' to the revelation of the ultimate essence that underlies and gives birth to the outward form.

This was a process both chemical and philosophical, and the two were inextricably involved with each other. The chemical transformations, as with any spiritual transformation, reflected the transformations of under-standing in the soul of the alchemist. Fire, as Bronowski has said, was 'the element by which man is able to cut deeply into the structure of matter'.[76] The passionate longing to penetrate to the mysteries of the incorruptible substance underlying matter was the inner fire that compelled the alchemist to devote his life to this study. In this context one may recall Jesus' saying in the Gospel of Thomas: 'Whoever is near to me is near to the fire, and whoever is far from me is far from the Kingdom' (Logion 82). Gold, the philosopher's stone, was the primary image of this incorruptible 'substance' that could regenerate and transmute life, and gold was the symbol of the transformed consciousness that would ultimately be able to perceive the mystery of the 'fiery light' that created and sustained life. The legacy of Gnostic ideas is clearly apparent in this imagery. The 'Great Work' of Alchemy aimed to discover the nature of 'spirit' and to see face to face the 'body of light' that was the foundation of the human body as well as the 'matter' of the universe. The alchemical marriage between sun and moon, king and queen, spirit and soul (including body), expressed the essential identity of spirit and nature, so healing the split that had developed in human consciousness between these two aspects of life.[77]

Figure 7. *The Sacred Marriage*; from *Splendor Solis*, Trismosin.

Whoever this secret revealed itself to had penetrated to the mystery of creation and knew there was no death, for he or she understood how life continuously regenerated itself; how the manifest emanated from the unmanifest and 'dissolved' again into the unmanifest. The birth of the 'Son', the divine child, born of the union of king and queen, symbolized not only the alchemists' transformation of matter into its incorruptible essence, but the transformation of their understanding into the quintessential gold, symbol of the eternal, radiant light of the spirit. All blackness, in the ordinary (non-lunar) sense of ignorance and the attitudes and forms of behaviour destructive of life, had been washed and burned away by the many repeated transmutations of the 'base matter' of human psychic 'blindness'. The black, chaotic cloud or stone of the *prima materia* or *nigredo*, 'darker than darkness', symbolized this base matter that had to be placed in the alchemical vessel and washed, distilled, cooked and transformed. The alchemists were often called 'washerwomen' and they prayed to be relieved of 'the horrid darkness of our minds'. The Great Work, or Hermetic Art, had a multiple healing effect. Insight cleansed the soul of the fear, anger, hatred and envy that were the root of all the negative projections that originate from human anguish, suffering and ignorance. And understanding released the soul from bondage to the 'planetary powers' of the Gnostics, or the compulsive patterns of behaviour and conditioned attitudes that had fettered it in the course of human evolution. The alchemical process removed from nature the god-image and life, the projections that had been 'fixed' on them by religious belief and social custom.

The four stages of progressive insight into these mysteries were described by four colours: black, white, red and gold. The lightening or whitening of the dark night was followed by the 'reddening' associated with the rosy colour of dawn, and this in turn by the golden radiance of the sun, but the arduous process of transformation had to be repeated many times before the Work was completed.

A passage from the early fourteenth century calls upon the imagery of the Virgin Birth to bring Alchemy to life, showing how its symbolism was understood to refer to the transformation of the soul. It comes from Petrus Bonus of Ferrara, who is quoting from a letter written by Rhazes, an Islamic physician and alchemist who lived in the tenth century:

> The old philosophers have beheld the Last Judgment in this art, namely the germination and birth of this stone, which is miraculous rather than rational; for on that day the soul to be beatified unites with its former body through the mediation of the spirit, to eternal glory . . . So also the old philosophers of this art knew and maintained that a virgin must conceive and bring forth, because in their art the stone conceives of itself, becomes pregnant, and brings itself forth . . . The philosophers also knew that God must become man on the last day of this art, whereon is the fulfilment of the work; begetter and begotten become altogether one; old man and boy, father and

son, become altogether one; thus all things are made new. God himself has entrusted this magistery to his philosophers and prophets, for whose souls he has prepared a dwelling place in his paradise.[78]

The continuity of the goddess myth from the Song of Songs in the Old Testament to the Middle Ages, and its application to the art of psychic transformation or rebirth, are shown by the following passage from the *Aurora Consurgens*, which Marie Louise von Franz suggests may have been written by Thomas Aquinas:

> This is Wisdom, namely the Queen of the south, who is said to have come from the east, like unto the morning rising, to hear, to understand, yea and to see the wisdom of Solomon, and there was given into her hand power, honour, strength, and dominion, bearing upon her head the crown of the kingdom shining with the rays of twelve stars, prepared as a bride adorned for her husband, and having on her garments written in golden letters in Greek, in barbarian script, and in Latin: Reigning I will reign, and my kingdom shall have no end for all them that find me and subtly and ingeniously and constantly seek me out.[79]

In her Foreword to the text and commentary on it von Franz tells how Jung, when he had finished the first draft of his *Mysterium Coniunctionis*, had a serious illness during which he experienced the great visions of the *Coniunctio* that he describes in his memoirs (Chapter X). When he saw her again after his illness, he told her that what he had written in the text was true. 'I don't need to alter the text. But I only know now how real these things are.' And she writes: 'Might it not be that St Thomas Aquinas, too, only experienced on his deathbed, when the Song of Songs flooded back into his memory, how real Wisdom and a union with her can be?'[80]

Jung's extensive studies on Alchemy are the foundation of his understanding of the soul's power to heal itself. He took the actual stages of Alchemy as a model for the transformation of the soul. He extends and explains the metaphor in his discussion of the magnificent images in Goethe's *Faust*, which he calls 'the last and greatest work of Alchemy':

> Goethe is really describing the experience of the alchemist who discovers that what he has projected into the retort is his own darkness, his unredeemed state, his passion, his struggles to reach the goal, i.e., to become what he really is, to fulfil the purpose for which his mother bore him, and, after the peregrinations of a long life full of confusion and error, to become the *filius regius*, son of the supreme mother.[81]

THE GRAIL

With the Grail legends we enter the sphere of the marvellous. The mystery of the Holy Grail infuses the Middle Ages with the image of the age-old quest, which now turns irrevocably inwards, following the yearning of the seeker's heart and the need to follow a path that cannot be taught but only found and is unique to each individual. There is no authorized way or teacher to be followed, for all ways already found, known and proven, are wrong ways, since they are not the person's own. The chalice, vessel, cup, dish and stone that are the primary images of the Grail evoke the archetype of the Feminine, which becomes the inspiration, guide and goal of the knights' inner quest. In the thirteenth-century legend *La Queste del Saint Graal*, when the vision of the veiled Grail appears to the knights in King Arthur's banqueting hall to summon each to their quest of unveiling it, they decide to ride forth singly, for to go in a group would have been shameful. When all the knights had put on their arms, attended mass and expressed their gratitude to their king, they 'entered into the forest, at one point and another, there where they saw it to be thickest, all in those places where they found no way or path'. So they started their spiritual journey as individuals, each trusting to his own authority and to the mysterious power of his calling.

Where did these legends come from to illumine the sky of medieval Europe with a new animation of the ancient vision? The Grail legends familiar to us were written down during the course of only fifty years, in the last quarter of the twelfth and the first quarter of the thirteenth century, an era that coincides with the zenith of both the Cathar Church

Figure 8. *The Apparition of the Grail to the Knights*; from the *Chronique de Hainault, c.* 1450.

and the Templar expansion. No text earlier than this time has so far been found, yet it is clear that, like the Gospels, the stories contain elements of earlier myth and tales. Through the rich fabric of the legends the lineaments of the Bronze Age myth of the Mother Goddess and her son–lover are disclosed.[82]

The Grail images cannot be separated from Gnosticism and Alchemy, nor from the mythology of the goddess and her son–lover, nor even perhaps from Kabbalism. The 'Fisher King', like Osiris, Adonis and Attis, lies wounded in the groin, unable to regenerate the Wasteland earth.[83] Who else should he be but the ever-dying and ever-resurrected son–lover of the goddess? Fish, as well as bread and wine, was the principal food consumed at the ritual meal, both in the Mystery cults and in early Christian ritual. Tammuz, in Babylonia, was called 'Lord of the Net', and Oannes, who appeared from the waters to teach wisdom to the Babylonians, was half fish, half man. Jesus was the 'fisher of men' and one of his greatest miracles was the transformation of seven loaves of bread and a few small fish into food for the multitude of 4,000 people who followed him (Mark 8:5–10).

Parzival's mother in Wolfram von Eschenbach's version of the Grail story is called 'clear as the light of the sun'.[84] Parzival himself is called 'the Green One', who restores the waters of life to the earth, and also the 'son of the Widow', the Widow being one of the titles of the goddess who has lost her consort during his sojourn in the underworld, as well as a title of the Shekhinah in her exile. This title is as old as Sumeria, for the lamentations of Inanna and Ishtar for their consort bewail their widowed state. Who are the knights who tend the Fisher King and act as guardians of the Grail but those who faithfully kept alive the sacred mysteries of the soul's regeneration?[85] The dove was the emblem of the Grail knights and was embroidered on the crimson robes worn by the troubadours at their forest meetings. Dove and fish are so closely related to the Grail that it is impossible not to connect all three images with the rites and mythology of the pre-Christian goddess.

Vessel and stone were the primary images of the goddess, beginning as her epiphanies in the Neolithic era, and ending with the mysterious images in Alchemy and the Grail legends. Cybele's sacred stone was moved from Pergamum to Rome. The Shekhinah was called the 'Precious Stone'. The deeper one penetrates into the imagery of the Grail, the more the influence of pre-Christian and Gnostic ideas can be discerned and the more these can be understood as a reflowering of the earlier mythology. Gnosticism, whose sacred vessel was the *krater*, or chalice, celebrated rituals that included both a sacred marriage and a sacred feast. There is no doubt, writes Jessie Weston, who was the first scholar to point out the relationship between the Grail images and the pre-Christian cult of the goddess and her son–lover, 'that what we now know as Gnosticism enshrines in its few and fragmentary remains the tradition of a great system of early

Christian esoteric teaching and practice'.[86] Around the images of the
Wisdom Mysteries the myth-makers of the Grail from all over Europe
wrought a tapestry of legends that still have the power to entrance.

The goddess appears in different guises. Now she is Cundrie, the spirit
of nature, who is the Grail messenger and wears a black hood embroidered
with 'a flock of turtle doves'.[87] Now she is a hideous old hag with 'two
teeth like boars' tusks', an image that clearly recalls the death of the son–
lover (Tammuz, Osiris, Attis and Adonis) by the boar. In one story she
demands of King Arthur that Gawain should marry her in return for
answering a riddle that saves the King's life. Gawain discovers – as he
reluctantly kisses her on his wedding night and grants her the choice of
whether she shall be transformed into a beautiful woman by night or by
day – that she becomes this woman before his eyes.[88] One can almost hear
the echo of the ancient words, 'How fair is thy love, my sister, my
spouse.' Wisdom sends forth her call to the knights, who become her
lovers. Disguised as a hideous hag, she guides them to embrace their own
darkness and transform it through love. At the quest's end she reveals to
them the secret treasure of the Grail, the chalice that overflows with
nourishment for all and the vision of the soul's reunion with its Divine
Ground; a vision that, like the revelation of Pentecost, bestows the
longed-for experience of unity, and thereby heals all wounds and assuages
all sorrow.

What is the Grail then, but the inexhaustible vessel, the source of life
continuously coming into being, energy pouring into creation, energy as
creation, the unquenchable fountain of eternal being? There had been
other images of the source of creation, but no myth before this had linked
that image to the spontaneous outpouring of an individual heart, rendering
the outward Grail consubstantial with the inward point of becoming life
in the human being. If we relate that image to ourselves, it is the place in
us where life comes into being inside us, in a place before or beyond
desiring and fearing, just pure becoming. It is an image that emerges in
very different cultures separated by time and space, and so must be a
reflection of certain powers or spiritual potentialities in the psyche of
every human being. By contemplating this and other mythic images, we
evoke these powers in our own lives. The Grail, now as then, is a symbol
that can unify different traditions in a new image of the human being
released from bondage to tribal custom or religious belief, serving the
world through individual love, following wherever the heart leads.

How is the Grail attained? Wolfram's answer, conveyed firstly through
Parzival's failure to ask the question that came from his heart, and then
through the terms on which he and Gawain finally succeed, is that it is
won through the act of compassion that comes instinctively out of an
individual who lives his or her own authentic life.

CINDERELLA

The story of Cinderella belongs with the image of Sophia. Fairy-tales speak with the immemorial wisdom of the soul to draw attention to what has been lost or denigrated by the conscious cultural tradition. They tell the story of what has happened to the missing dimension and what still needs to happen for the balance in archetypal imagery to be restored. So many elements from earlier cultures live in this story that it is impossible to say when and where it may have originated. One thing is certain: its importance to the soul is shown by the universality and duration of its appeal. Cinderella tells the story of a single theme that runs from the mythology of the goddess culture to the Mysteries of the pagan world and the Wisdom literature of Judaism. It can be followed through Gnosticism and mystical Christianity to Alchemy, the Grail legends and the most cherished fairy-tales. It was nurtured by the mystics of the Jewish, Christian and Islamic religions. It is the story of the soul's birth into the manifest world, her loss of memory of her divine origin, her quest for understanding of herself and her relationship to the divine source or world from which she has emanated and to which, in full knowledge of who she is, she may return.

Who is the fairy godmother but Sophia herself, Divine Wisdom, the Holy Spirit – mother, source and womb – the light and intelligence that is the very ground of the soul? Who else should preside as godmother over her daughter's quest for insight, illumination and union? Responding to Cinderella's call for help, she initiates the work of transformation, making possible her meeting with the Prince, and bringing her, after the lunar three days' trial or darkness, to the royal marriage. The tale of Cinderella tells the story of the soul's transfiguration as she is changed from weeping, soot-blackened drudge into radiant bride.

The story of Cinderella has many possible interpretations, but Harold Bayley, in the early years of this century, was the first to see it as the story of the soul's awakening and to connect it with the Song of Songs and with Sumerian, Egyptian and Gnostic myths. In his book *The Lost Language of Symbolism* he traced the historical transmission of many different stories and symbols that centred around the image of light hidden in darkness, a light that had to be rescued and restored to its rightful place. Through a profound knowledge of the etymology of words, and an equally profound knowledge of European paper-making and the water marks that were the medium of transmission for alchemical and Gnostic ideas during an era of cruel persecution, he drew an astonishing picture of the relationship between mythology and the fairy-tales that found their way into many different centres of European culture. Some 345 versions of the story of Cinderella had been gathered together and published by the Folklore Society[89] shortly before Bayley started to write his book, and he drew on this wealth of material to show the relationship between the fairy-tale and the older myths.

So much has been lost with the passage of the centuries, and only now, in this century, can the fragments be recovered and pieced together. The familiar Cinderella of the fairy-tale may seem far removed from the Greek myth of Persephone crying out to her mother, Demeter, or the Gnostic myth of the daughter Sophia weeping in her exile from her mother in the heavenly dimension; nor does she immediately suggest the black Shulamite of the Song of Songs or the exiled Shekhinah. Yet a knowledge of mythology suggests that a relationship between them cannot be fortuitous. In this tale and those of 'Sleeping Beauty' and 'Snow White', the earlier myths and the Bronze Age image of the sacred marriage shine through and connect the soul receptive to their numinosity with these mythic roots.

Fire, light and the dazzling luminosity of the starry dimension are all images that were associated through the ages with the radiance of Wisdom, which, as a fusion of love and insight, or *gnosis*, expresses the union of queen and king, the highest feminine and masculine qualities of the soul. In the fairy-tale these are personified by Cinderella and the Prince. Cinderella's particular quality of sustained devotion to whatever she was asked to do is stressed in every version of the story. The Prince's capacity for insight is shown in his recognition of Cinderella and in the tenacity and single-mindedness of his quest for his 'true' love.

Transformation is the theme of the story of Cinderella, and the alchemist presiding over the great work is Wisdom herself, who, with a wave of her wand, transforms mice into snow-white horses, lizards into footmen, a pumpkin into the golden (or crystal) coach, a rat into the coachman and, of course, Cinderella herself into a vision of beauty arrayed in dresses that reflect the radiance of stars, moon and sun.

The arduousness of the work of transformation is stressed in some versions of Cinderella more than others; for example, in the one where her stepmother throws a heap of seeds on to the ground for the girl to sort into piles. This is identical to the scene in the story of Eros and Psyche in which Psyche is given the same task by her mother-in-law, the goddess Venus. Doves and sparrows, which belong with the image of the goddess in Sumeria and Egypt, help Cinderella to sort the seeds and also, in some versions, point out to the Prince that a false bride wears the slipper destined for Cinderella, by drawing attention to the blood flowing from the injured feet of the ugly sisters.

Cinderella's dresses, her 'robe of glory', are described as 'blue like the sky', woven of the stars of heaven, of moonbeams, sunbeams, or made of all the flowers in the world.[90] Sometimes the metaphor of the sea appears and her dress is 'sea-coloured' or 'like the waves of the sea' or 'as the sea with fishes swimming it' and as the 'colour of the sea covered with golden fishes'.[91] Sometimes, like Isis, she is robed in jet black; sometimes her dresses shine like the sun or gold, covered in diamonds and pearls, 'of splendour passing description', and giving forth the tinkling sound of bells. In one story Cinderella's dress 'rings like a bell as she comes downstairs', which recalls the sistrum of the goddess Isis and also the bells that rang out at the approach of the Shekhinah.[92] But it also recalls the description of the robe worn by the initiate in the Gnostic poem 'The Hymn of the Robe of Glory': 'I heard the sound of its music which it whispered as it descended.'[93]

'How beautiful are thy feet with shoes, O prince's daughter!' says the bridegroom in the Song of Songs (S. of S. 7:1). Cinderella's shoes or slippers are described as made of crystal, or gold or blue glass, or embroidered with pearls. Without her glass slipper, Cinderella would not have been recognized, and it could fit only her whose standpoint had become translucent to the light of Wisdom.

Cinderella is instructed by her godmother to leave the palace before midnight or risk being transformed back into her former state. What could be the meaning of this? Could it be that midnight marks the interface between the dimensions of eternity and time? To fail to hold the balance between them is to risk being fixed in one, unable to relate to or remember the other dimension of experience. To stay at the ball beyond midnight is to forget human values and human relationships, losing touch with everyday life. Not to ask to go to the ball is to remain in bondage to the limitation of a 'fallen', fragmented consciousness, without access to another level of perception.

The image of the soul's journey weaves like a golden thread through mythology and literature that spans 5,000 years. It first appears in Sumeria, when Inanna, Queen of Heaven and Earth, surrenders her glorious apparel at each of the seven gates on her way to the underworld kingdom of her sister, Ereshkigal, reassuming them after her three-day 'crucifixion' in darkness as she ascends to the light. The soul, as Eve, is banished from the Garden of Eden and goes into exile, as does the 'widowed' Shekhinah and the Gnostic daughter, Sophia. The Cinderella of the fairy-tale personifies all these earlier mythic figures, who, in turn, personify the human soul and the predicament of the darkened 'light' that has no knowlege of itself. As in the stories of Sleeping Beauty and Snow White, the soul awakens to the kiss of the Prince, who, as the solar bridegroom, consort of the moon goddess, personifies the divine life principle.

What is the relevance of the story of Cinderella in the new age that is dawning? The image of the sacred marriage between nature and spirit, goddess and god, has been notably absent in the orthodox Judaeo-Christian tradition, and this has inflicted a deep wound on the soul, which has yet to be healed. The fairy-tale restores the image of union between the two primary archetypes and has, so to speak, 'carried' it for our culture until such time as the need for it could become conscious. The growing recognition in human consciousness of the plight of the feminine archetype embraces the image of the soul's suffering and ignorance of herself, and of the earth, nature and the physical body, which, split off from spirit, are also suffering and in need of rescue. Cinderella personifies these aspects of the feminine value so long relegated to the role of servant. The 'resurrection' of the feminine archetype has been prepared by those who, in the centuries of persecution, often sacrificed their lives to the transmission of the Wisdom tradition so that it would not vanish into oblivion.[94] It may even have been one of them – whether Jew, Christian or Muslim – who first imagined this fairy-tale, drawing on the repository of myth inherited by the mystical tradition of all three cultures from their Sumerian, Babylonian and Egyptian past. This tradition taught the immanence of the divine in nature and human nature. It declared the need to discover the presence of the radiant spiritual essence hidden within the myriad forms of life and the darkness of unreflecting human consciousness. They would each have recognized, as Harold Bayley did, that Cinderella, 'the bright and shining one, who sits among the cinders and keeps the fire alight', is 'the personification of the Holy Spirit dwelling unhonoured amid the smouldering ashes of the Soul's latent, never totally extinct, Divinity'.[95]

16

THE SACRED MARRIAGE OF GODDESS AND GOD: THE REUNION OF NATURE AND SPIRIT

O sweet spontaneous
earth how often have
the
doting
      fingers of
prurient philosophers pinched
and
poked

thee
, has the naughty thumb
of science prodded
thy
    beauty   . how
often have religions taken
thee upon their scraggy knees
squeezing and

buffeting thee that thou mightest conceive
gods
    (but
true

to the incomparable
couch of death thy
rhythmic
lover

    thou answerest

them only with

      spring)

         e e cummings

I am certain of nothing but of the holiness of the
   Heart's affections and the truth of Imagination –
What the imagination seizes as Beauty must be truth . . .

        John Keats

> The old gods are dead or dying and people everywhere are searching,
> asking: What is the new mythology to be, the mythology of this unified
> earth as of one harmonious being?
>
>   Joseph Campbell

This book has tried to tell the story of the mythic images that themselves
tell the story of the evolution of consciousness. And if it is true that one
way in which humans can apprehend and know their own being is by
making it visible in the image of their goddesses and gods, then it may be
through such images as these that consciousness tells its own story.

The myth of the goddess has moved through several stages of diminishing influence from the Palaeolithic Age to the present, and these have
registered the way humanity looks upon itself and its world. In our
Western culture there is now formally no goddess myth and so no feminine
dimension in the collective image of the divine. This means that contemporary experience of the archetypal feminine as a sacred entity is no
longer available as an immediate reality in the way that it used to be.
Although the myth of the goddess partially survives in the figure of Mary,
the Virgin, as intermediary, it is still ultimately excluded from the prevailing myth of the god. If we review the historical stages of the demise of the
goddess myth, we can gain some perspective on where we stand at this
particular point.

In the beginning the Great Mother Goddess alone gives birth to the
world out of herself, so that all creatures, including the gods, are her
children, part of her divine substance. Everything is living, animated –
with soul – and sacred. Today's distinctions between 'spirit' and 'nature',
'mind' and 'matter' or 'soul' and 'body' have no place, for humanity and
nature share a common identity. This was the myth that prevailed in the
Palaeolithic, Neolithic and Bronze Age Crete. It is still found in what are
called (probably for that reason) 'primitive' societies and, of course, in
poetry.

Thereafter the Mother Goddess unites with the god – once her son,
now her consort – to give birth to the world. Here the distinction is made
between the eternal womb and its temporal phases (whether of the moon
or the seasonal life of vegetation), and the focus of the myth is on the
relationship between the Mother Goddess and the god, her 'son–lover'.
Everything is still alive and sacred, but the duality of that which endures
and that which changes – *zoe*, the eternal and inexhaustible source, and
bios, its expression in time – prepares the way for the distinction between
energy and form, later to become that between 'nature' and 'spirit'. This
was the myth of Inanna and Dumuzi in Bronze Age Sumeria, Ishtar and
Tammuz in Babylonia, Isis and Osiris in Egypt, Aphrodite and Adonis in
Greece and Cybele and Attis in Anatolia.

In the next stage the Mother Goddess is killed by the god, her great-great-great-grandson, who then makes the world from her dead body, and the human race from the blood of her dismembered son–lover. This was the late Bronze and early Iron Age Babylonian myth of Tiamat, the mother goddess whose corpse was split apart into earth and heaven by the superior wind-and-fire-power of the sky-and-sun god Marduk. Creation is now dissociated from the creative source, and the world is no longer a living being and a sacred entity; on the contrary, it is seen from Marduk's perspective as the inert and inanimate substance that we call 'matter', which can be shaped and ordered only by 'spirit'. The considerable implication here – which mythically underlies much destruction of the earth as well as the 'holy' wars against other human beings – is that the conquest of matter releases spirit.

Finally, the god creates the world alone without reference to the Mother Goddess, either through self-copulation (the Egyptian Atum) or through the power of the Word. This was the Bronze Age myth of the Egyptian Ptah, whose tongue translated the thoughts of his heart, and the Iron Age myth of the Hebrew Yahweh–Elohim, who made heaven and earth in the beginning and saw that it was good. In the popular version Adam is made of the clay of the inanimate earth and comes alive only when spirit is breathed into him, and Eve is derived from Adam. Here, the world is set still further apart from its creator and cannot share in the sanctity of the original source. The creator is transcendent to creation, not immanent in creation as was the mother goddess before him. The transcendent god – Pure Spirit – creates nature and then, in addition, transfers some of this spirit (or, breathes His spirit) into the body of the human being(s), but not into the bodies of animals, plants, soil and stones. After the expulsion, when the earth is cursed to dust and thistles, Nature itself (not Herself) becomes a punishment for the inevitably inferior spiritual 'nature' of humanity. In the Hebrew creation myth, inherited by the Islamic and Christian traditions, there is no relation whatever to the Mother Goddess, who is no longer even an enemy and has disappeared from view.

One way of understanding the long historical process of the replacing of the myth of the goddess by the myth of the god is to view it as the gradual withdrawal of humanity's participation with nature. This process brings with it the corresponding emptying of animate life from nature and the transference of that life into humanity, which is then cast in a relation of opposition to nature. If the relation to nature as the Mother is one of *identity*, and the relation to nature from the Father is one of *dissociation*, then the movement from Mother to Father symbolizes an ever-increasing separation from a state of containment in nature, experienced no longer as nurturing to life but as stifling to growth. Historically, this process can be described as one in which humanity has discovered itself to be progressively independent of the natural phenomena among which it lives, increasingly capable of differentiation and selection, and so, in theory, more and more able to shape and order the world to its own ideas. From the perspective of the god myth, then, the perception of differences that leads to the setting apart of pairs of opposites – spirit and nature, mind and matter, transcendence and immanence, reason and instinct, good and evil, life and death, male and female – is an obviously life-enhancing activity, without which (to think again in opposites) life would fall into inchoate chaos.

Since we are the inheritors of the mythic and social system of the god for over 4,000 years, it would be difficult for us to disagree. One of the results of the god myth is that consciousness has already evolved by gathering the numinosity once experienced in (or as) natural phenomena into itself. It is often assumed that the next stage of evolution will take the form of the last one, and achieve an even greater freedom from the given conditions of life in order to transform them still further. Yet it is not hard to see that the conditions of life have changed over the long duration of the god myth, not least in the way that consciousness now looks upon itself. It would be strange indeed if a tribal myth that arose so long ago, in so small a territory, were able to relate to people of the entire planet.

In this last century three major and apparently unrelated discoveries have undermined the value of continuing the direction of the last 4,000 years, and it is significant that they all point to the same conclusion: the need to comprehend the world as one whole. The most obvious is the splitting of the atom, whereby humanity has achieved sufficient distance from the substance and structure of the material world to restructure it so that it – and the human race along with it – no longer exists. Einstein's own conclusion from this was that 'with the splitting of the atom everything has changed save our mode of thinking, and thus we drift towards unparalleled disaster'.[1]

The second discovery, addressed in this book, comes from the studies of archaeology, anthropology, comparative mythology and archetypal psychology, all of which show the people of the earth not only as sharing in the common human condition of how to understand life, but also as attempting to understand it in similar ways. It has not been possible before this century to study the myths and legends of different cultures and to read them together, so we have been ignorant of their extraordinary resemblances to each other. This common bond between widely differing cultures and times cannot but call for a fundamentally new image of the human race as a unity, however much humankind appears to differ in its secular detail.

The third discovery – made, as it were, by consciousness about itself – is that the earlier scientific model of consciousness as entirely independent of what it sees and does cannot stand. Participation (to come full circle) cannot be finally eradicated. In subatomic physics the absolute distinction between mind and matter, made first by Aristotle and more recently by Descartes, which implies the distinction between the observer and the observed, cannot be sustained. This means that, in the end, we can never speak about nature without at the same time speaking about ourselves.[2] The frame of mind of any investigation – which includes the beliefs, values and unconscious assumptions of the investigator – is, then, not just an essential component of what is discovered, but actually creates dynamically 'what happens' in ways yet to be fully understood. Relationship is again the fundamental reality within which the two terms – observer and observed, subject and object – are brought into being together.

The same kind of conclusion also follows from studies of the unconscious mind in Depth Psychology, in which the conscious mind has been found to be not only answerable to other levels in the psyche, but also, to a greater extent than was ever realized, to be actually dependent for its finest expressions upon these deeper levels, or at least upon a harmonious relation with them. Add to this the common knowledge, upon which psychosomatic medicine draws, that unconscious 'thoughts' are registered in the body, that we cannot 'think straight' when we are sick or tired or angry, and Psyche and Soma emerge as ultimately unseparate. How can we then finally distinguish conscious from unconscious, mind from matter and spirit from nature, except as a linguistic definition of a range of experience, whose purpose is to interrupt the continuum at certain points for particular reasons that have nothing to do with the things in themselves? In the language of mythology this is to say that the myth of the goddess is not absent from the collective psyche just because it is disregarded. In fact, it is exactly where we might expect to find it – in the collective unconscious of the race.

These discoveries, separately and together, point to the need for the new mode of thinking for which Einstein calls, where life is experienced as a living whole, in which humanity participates in a relation of mutual dependence along with all the other creatures of the earth. This, ironically, is precisely the genius of the old goddess myth, even though originally that vision was bound into the constraints of worshipping a personalized image: the Goddess. However, no vision depends upon the literal terms of its earlier manifestation, so the question that arises here is how can the 'new' myth of the Earth as one harmonious being be disengaged from the old form of the myth, which was imagined as a recognizably human figure elevated to divine status, but frequently limited by the same recognizably human traits of character as her worshippers?

The issue for our purposes, then, is whether there can be a 'goddess myth' without a Goddess; or, to put it another way, can we have a 'goddess' without having to believe 'she' exists as a literal divine being? Can the vision of nature as a sacred, living unity, in which the human race is experienced as one whole and consciousness belongs to all life whatever form it takes, exist without a belief in 'the Mother' immanent as creation? And could it co-exist with a belief in 'the Father' transcendent from creation? Or do both Mother and Father, Goddess and God, have to be dissolved as *literal personified* realities so that they may reappear as *symbolic* realities of two essential ways of comprehending what Jesus in the Gospel of Thomas calls 'the All'?[3] *Then* both of these kinds of understanding life, or ways of experiencing the numinous, can be seen to be necessary and true, and both, therefore, require each other to become whole. In the literal language of the old myth this union was the Sacred Marriage of Goddess and God; in the symbolic language of the new myth it is the 'sacred marriage' of 'god' and 'goddess', images that can be translated into the more prosaic but more negotiable terms of the reunion of transcendence and immanence, spirit and nature, soul and body, in order to make possible a new mythic vision – the 'child'.

Before these terms can be reunited in a new myth, they have to be brought into balance with each other; from our point in history, this is effectively the question as to how the goddess myth can be brought back into consciousness so that its values may again become available and complement (not replace) the prevailing myth of the god. It may be more difficult than we envisage to regain that mode of being that the long debased goddess myth originally expressed. D. H. Lawrence, writing of the Etruscans (*c.* 1000–300 BC) as he perceived them through their art, offers a poetic image of the participating consciousness that the goddess myth at its best affords:

> The natural flowering of life! It is not so easy for human beings as it sounds. Behind all the Etruscan liveliness was a religion of life … Behind all the dancing was a vision, and even a science of life, a conception of the universe and man's place in the universe which made men live to the best of their capacity. To the Etruscan all was alive; the whole universe lived; and the business of man was himself to live amid it all. He had to draw life into himself, out of the wandering huge vitalities of the world. The cosmos was alive, like a vast creature … The whole thing was alive, and had a great soul, or *anima*: and in spite of one great soul, there were myriad roving, lesser souls; every man, every creature and tree and lake and mountain and stream, was animate, and had its own peculiar consciousness.[4]

Not as easy as it sounds, and especially after centuries of being dismissed as pantheism by orthodox religion, or as childish fantasy by Baconian and Newtonian science and Cartesian philosophy. Yet a myth does not simply vanish from the world of the collective psyche any more than an event of great moment in the past is irrevocably lost to the individual psyche; and especially not a myth that existed for at least 20,000 years before the myth that superseded it. Rather, it changes its aspect, disguises its mode of operation and reappears in another form. But, like any less than fully conscious attitude, it cannot simply be summoned at will; it has to be sought, elicited, tracked in the shadowy underworld of subliminal image and symbolic implication; discerned in innuendo, pause, juxtaposition, contradiction; and persuaded to re-emerge in the gaps between what we call rational thinking. We might expect to find it disguised as the implicit structural image of a scientific hypothesis, or as the hidden impulse within 'alternative' culture; it might be what is intended by 'new' in today's 'New Age'. Yet as long as it is not fully conscious, it may mislead us with over-simplified dogma or confuse us with claims of its innate superiority, or it may merely fail to make its own voice heard because we are listening in the wrong place. For instance, we may talk of the desacralization of nature and the laying waste of the earth; or the need to transcend the opposites of spirit and nature, mind and matter, thinking and feeling; or the importance of dissolving the boundaries of *our* country, race, customs and *theirs* – but we can forget that the very *oppositional* language of our inquiry prevents us from experiencing what we talk about.

Perhaps the first step is to call into question the language and current patterns of thinking that we unreflectively employ as a solution to any problem – those methods that reflect an imbalance since they derive from the prevailing mythic and social system of the god *without* the goddess; in other words, an excessively dissociated point of view. We might expect, then, that our mode of inquiry would be too rational, too conceptual, too ideal; that it would tend to concentrate on differences and exclude similarities, that it might undervalue the intuitive response, the feeling, the image and the symbolic framework that accord meaning to the endeavour and the energy for carrying it through.[5] Above all, we could anticipate that our habit of thinking in opposites might have dulled us into assuming that they are absolutes in themselves and not provisional distinctions of inseparable terms belonging to one underlying unity, distinctions that are justified only by the increase of consciousness and expansion of life that they make available.

When was it in the Western tradition that oppositions became fixed and lost their relation to the whole that renders them aspects of a larger entity? The first occurrence of a mythic image that was drawn in absolutely negative terms was the Babylonian mother goddess Tiamat, who was pictured as a life-threatening dragon *in relation to* the sky god Marduk, where the relation was one of combat, shown, as it were, from Marduk's point of view. There are no pictures of Tiamat on her own (or none that has survived), so the original mother who gave birth to all the gods was no longer a living reality. She had become only the 'Terrible Mother', who kills life – quite literally 'red in tooth and claw'[6] – and who, it followed, must be killed herself for the sake of life. She was called Evil and Marduk was called Good.

However, this was the late Bronze and early Iron Age, a time of continual invasion and conquest, when, apparently coincidentally, predictable planetary cycles observed in the heavens offered an objective image of order that did not have to depend on some mysterious and invisible power. The sky and solar gods that the invaders brought with them were

Figure 1. The Opposition of Tiamat and Marduk; Assyrian relief, *c.* ninth century BC.

set apart from the earth, and their repeated and unchanging cycles suggested planning and intelligence, in the light of which the spontaneous creations of an all-encompassing mother nature appeared dark, chaotic and full of menace. It was also a time of transition, when the god myth of the nomadic conquerers was being imposed upon the goddess myth of the settled agricultural communities, with their seasonal rites and lunar orientation. With historical hindsight, the wholly negative image of the mother goddess can be seen to be also an image in transition and not an absolute statement, valid for any situation.

The relevance of this age to ours might seem questionable, but mythically it was the last occasion (with the exception of aspects of Greek mythology) when the goddess was central to the drama, and when the opposition of the god to the goddess was consciously and publicly registered. Subsequently, through the influence of Babylonian on Hebrew mythology, the conquest of the goddess by the god was an assumption of such proportions that it was no longer formally mentioned, even though it frequently broke through the official myth in poetic asides. The defeat of the goddess (the withdrawal of participation from nature) was, at that time, the condition for the beginning of civilization. That is to say, the ties with blood and soil, where humanity felt itself to be personally involved in the living rhythms of nature, which therefore limited and determined the freedom of human nature, were seen as a threat to the creation of a way of life that depended more on organization and conceptualization.

The image of *opposition* – of the heroic consciousness banishing chaos to create and order the world – became the model for the way of thinking by which civilization was sustained, and so it entered Judaeo-Christian thought as the basic structure through which the world was perceived and the quality of life was ensured. It is the dramatic focus of the story in Genesis: the Tree of the Knowledge of Good and Evil; the Tree of Life in the Garden of Eden, and Death outside it. Somewhat inevitably, this paradigm of thinking in opposites, which was the language of tribal consciousness, has remained unchanged.

If we analyse the image of opposition enshrined in the battle of Tiamat and Marduk, we find that what is imagined is the heroic moment of victory over the old order when the new order is established. As such, the image parallels the initial rites of any new stage of consciousness, where what is to be left behind has to be opposed by what is to come into being in order that the habitual hold of the past be relinquished. But once the new stage of consciousness has been achieved, there is no further need for the challenge of an 'enemy', and both terms – victor and vanquished, order and chaos, god and goddess – may be dissolved and reunited at a higher level. If, however, this transitional stage is not left behind when it has served its purpose, then the growth of consciousness is arrested at this point of its development, with the result that what was originally simply relative is abstracted from the larger framework in which this dynamic process took place. It is subsequently regarded as an absolute – a composite statement, in this case, about the threat of the indigenous goddess culture, the inherent chaos of nature, and the incipient dangers of participation. Here the political needs of the conquering nation – what we might call 'survival' or 'tribal' thinking – have infiltrated the ways of thinking about how to live beyond survival (the debate on the *quality* of life), and then the tribal orientation on its world has become the unconscious exemplar for the 'triumph' of conscious thought.

This is what we are suggesting has happened to all the so-called oppositions we have inherited – goddess and god, nature and spirit, and so on – but extending to the way we think 'tribally': that is, in terms of *my* self or *our* group, community, country (and god), where the customs and values of one specific 'tribe' are held to be of intrinsically greater worth than those of another 'tribe', in disregard or ignorance of their ultimately mutual dependency as members of the human race. These ideas then enter our discussions with fixed definitions and attributes, and the most damaging of these is the supposedly inherent conflict between them. This predisposes us to see them oppositionally and hierarchically and not as complementary terms within one underlying identity, which is what they are seen to be as soon as the phase of conflict is past.

In individual psychology a radical and permanent split in the psyche between 'good things' and 'bad things' is generally interpreted as a sign that the natural growing of the psyche has been arrested by something that could not be accepted as it was nor placed in a wider framework that would render it intelligible and so tolerable. Then a way is sought to heal the split, so that the intolerable feeling that conflicts with the established view of the world is not repressed into unconsciousness and subsequently projected and discovered outside in the figure of a person or a group of people who are seen as an enemy threatening the conscious position. In collective consciousness, also, perhaps we should see the habit of thinking in absolute and fixed oppositions as a symptom, a sign that something is out of balance. There seems to be no reason why we should not talk of a collective complex as well as an individual complex, where a complex is defined as an unconscious and unresolved conflict that cannot move into the next stage of growth. In an individual the complex is the point at which that person cannot relate to others, since he or she is drawn to project the unconscious image outwards upon others, rather than to respond genuinely to who is actually there. Similarly, taking a transitional, and so provisional, division of a unity into two opposing aspects for an absolute definition about the opposing nature of the two aspects – seeing all life finally in dualistic terms – also prevents genuine relationship with what is actually 'there'.

If we apply this analysis to what has been called 'the Problem of Evil', a phrase that implies that Evil 'exists' as an intrinsic force in the universe, or even as a dimension of the deity itself, then 'evil' becomes not a terrifying metaphysical abstraction but a *linguistic* opposite to 'good', *both* terms requiring a context to render them intelligible at all. When the context is supplied – this act was good, this act was evil – we are back to the human realm of specific value judgements, which cannot be abstracted, generalized and subsequently concretized in some supersensible realm without profound distortion.

Ultimately, therefore, we are suggesting that consciousness, as it has evolved through the god myth, has become confused with tribal consciousness, which, at least in its initial formative stage, tends to demand an opposite to secure its own identity and to project the unresolved conflicts of its own tribe on to 'the other'. This other, the alien, then becomes 'the enemy' to be sacrificed – the 'evil' to be cast out for the 'good' of the tribe:

> Be it thy course to busy giddy minds
> With foreign quarrels; that action, hence borne out
> May waste the memory of the former days.[7]

Such is the last pragmatic advice given by Henry IV to his wayward son, Harry, who, on succeeding his father in the following play, declares in full conviction: 'No King of England, if not King of France'.[8]

By contrast, mythic or sacred themes and images, as we have seen, are not confined within tribal and cultural boundaries, but cross all the borders of the ancient and modern world. To reiterate a point made in Chapter 1, 'the sacred' is not a *stage* in the history of consciousness that people grow out of or into, but it is at least an element in the *structure* of consciousness, belonging to all people at all times. (Even if, as many would prefer, this statement is reversed to read that the structure of consciousness is but one form of the sacred, the point is that one way or the other it is always there.) As an essential part of the character of the human race, then, it is unquestionably required for a perspective on that other aspect of being human: that is, born into a specific family within a specific tribal group at a specific time. For in the same way that an individual's 'tribal' nature – where he or she acts not morally but out of self-interest – can be forgiven when it is seen as a reaction to a wound and an attempt to restore wholeness, so, possibly, can the tribal character of the race be analogically placed in the context of the unclosed wound of our specifically human consciousness – that original separation from nature, when good and evil, eternity and time, life and death, fall apart into apparently irreconcilable opposites. Here is Rilke:

> Death is the side of life averted from us, unshone upon by us: we must try to achieve the greatest consciousness of our existence which is at home in both unbounded realms, inexhaustibly nourished from both . . . The true figure of life extends through both: there is neither a here nor a beyond, but the great unity in which the beings that surpass us, the 'angels', are at home . . . We of the here and now are not for a moment hedged in the time-world, nor confined within it . . . we are incessantly flowing over and over to those who preceded us . . . We are the bees of the invisible, *Nous butinons éperdument le miel du visible, pour l'accumuler dans la grande rûche d'or de l'invisible.* [We deliriously gather the honey of the visible, to accumulate it in the great golden hive of the invisible.][9]

It is arguable that mythic images are the fundamental inspiration for the evolution of consciousness. If that is so, then it becomes a matter of supreme importance that mythic images achieve their most complete expression, for they serve as guides for the evolution of the species. Yet what criteria can we bring to bear upon them beyond what they offer us themselves? Looking back over millennia, it seems as if, in the goddess cultures, the image of the god was trying to break free from the totality of the Mother Goddess – in the person of the son who grew to become her consort – just as in the god cultures the image of the goddess was trying to reassert its claim to rule in consort with the Father God. How else to explain the persistence of Sophia in the Old Testament and in the Gnostic heritage, or the hidden goddess worship of the Hebrews that would not answer to the Law of the One God? Or the irresistible rise of Mary so many centuries after the Book was, as it were, closed? It is as though both images are required to do justice to the fullness of life, as though without the archetypal balance of feminine and masculine images the evolution of consciousness would eventually become one-sided and so distorted.

Yet what evidence is sufficient to claim that the sacred images of goddess and god (whether as literal or symbolic realities) reach their finest expression when they are complementary to each other, separate yet united, 'two distincts, division none', as Shakespeare has it in his poem entitled appropriately 'Venus and Adonis'? Is it (when personified) the ritual delight in a celebration of a divine marriage of heaven and earth, with its parallels both to the celestial union of moon and sun and the earthly union of woman and man? Or (when symbolic) is it the intellectually satisfying balance in which hitherto opposing principles are reconciled, or the aesthetic experience of harmony between the feminine and masculine polarities? Or is the reason common to all these that the union of the two *creates* the third, so that the sacred marriage brings forth new life at every level, from the birth of a human child to the birth of a new vision – the divine 'child'?

From a different point of view, the physicist David Bohm offers a critique of what he calls the 'fragmentation of consciousness', discussing how the way we think *about* things, assuming that we are in principle separate *from* them, creates a fragmentary world:

> The widespread and pervasive distinctions between people (race, nation, family, profession, etc.) which are now preventing mankind from working together for the common good, and indeed, even for survival, have one of the key factors of their origin in a kind of thought that treats *things* as inherently divided, disconnected, and 'broken up' into yet smaller constituent parts. Each part is considered to be essentially independent and self-existent. When man thinks of himself in this way, he will inevitably tend to defend the needs of his own 'Ego' against those of the others; or, if he identifies with a group of people of the same kind, he will defend this group in a similar way. He cannot seriously think of mankind as the basic reality, whose claims come first. Even if he does try to consider the needs of mankind he tends to regard humanity as separate from nature, and so on.

Figure 2. The Sacred Marriage; Tell Asmar, Iraq. Sumerian cylinder seal, early third millennium BC.

Figure 3. The Sacred Marriage of
Hera and Zeus, wood carving,
c. late seventh century BC.

What I am proposing is that man's general way of thinking of the totality, i.e. his general world view, is crucial for overall order of the human mind itself. If he thinks of the totality as constituted of independent fragments, then that is how his mind will tend to operate, but if he can include everything coherently and harmoniously in an overall whole that is undivided, unbroken, and without a border (for every border is a division or break) then his mind will tend to move in a similar way, and from this will flow an orderly action within the whole.[10]

And again:

Being guided by a fragmentary self-world view, man then acts in such a way as to try to break himself and the world up, so that all seems to correspond to his way of thinking. Man thus obtains an apparent proof of the correctness of his fragmentary self-world view though, of course, he overlooks the fact that it is he himself who has brought about the fragmentation that now seems to have an autonomous existence, independent of his will and of his desire.[11]

But it is difficult to disengage, even momentarily, from our current world-view when this means standing back from the assumptions of our mythological inheritance, in particular the fundamental distinction between creator and created. As suggested in Chapter 13 in relation to Eve, the advantage of understanding the 'oppositional paradigm' historically is that it frees us from the assumption that it belongs to the nature of things and, more widely, that a fragmentary world-view is all there can be.

Figure 4. Husband and wife on Etruscan sarcophagus; sixth century BC.

However, ironically, much of contemporary psychology – the discipline that might have been expected to contribute most to a new understanding – is itself structured on divisive language, and so falls often imperceptibly into divisive thinking: 'the conscious' and 'the unconscious', when used as nouns implying totally separate realms of being; the 'life-instinct' and the 'death-instinct' (Freud); the 'good breast' and the 'bad breast' (Klein) – where Freud's opposition is theoretically projected back into the mind of the infant; '*the* Shadow' (Jung); and, not least, the one that was first, the relegation of the myriad energies of psychic life into the three distinct categories of 'id, ego and super-ego' (Freud).

Similarly, it needs to be continually restated that 'feminine' and 'masculine' are not things in themselves, not archetypal figures of an absolute differentiation with fixed and predetermined fields of application. They are terms in continual relationship, which take their meaning from each other: for example, containing and emerging, receptive and active, conserving and dynamic; the ground and its differentiation, the whole and the part. But while their apparent opposition exists only at the extremes of their polarity, it is these extremes that are recorded in language as definitions, especially when they are used as nouns and not as verbs or adjectives. The terms may perhaps best be understood as different modes of consciousness, or different ways of experiencing and expressing life at any one moment, available to any human being of whatever gender. The archetypal masculine mode of consciousness has come historically to be associated with linear thinking, intellect, reason, Logos; the archetypal

Figure 5. Etruscan Sun God and Moon Goddess.

feminine mode of consciousness with analogical thinking, intuition, feeling, Eros. Each needs the other to be whole, and when either predominates both are thrown out of balance: 'Thoughts without content are empty; and intuitions without concepts blind', as Kant puts it.[12] It is not helpful to take the further step of applying these modes invariably to specific 'things' (that is, to create things out of the modes), when, for instance, consciousness is identified with the masculine archetype and unconsciousness with the feminine archetype.[13] Consciousness can be receptive and synthetic, as when it allows a new pattern to take form, and unconsciousness can be active and dynamic, as in dreams and visions, or 'slips' of the tongue.

Figure 6. Coronation of the Virgin; Rheims Cathedral.

Perhaps the best model for understanding how feminine and masculine
modes interrelate is offered by the yin–yang symbol in Taoist philosophy.
Here, dark (yin, feminine) and light (yang, masculine) are equally contained within a circle, divided by an S curve, each 'half' containing a spot
of the other's colour and nature. What is immediately apparent is that the
black and the white are not divided down the middle with a straight line,
so creating opposites that are clearly delineated and absolute, but instead
the distinction is provisional, alternating, continually in play. Each contains the other in embryo, and the force of the curve is to send the mind
around the circle, and not to allow it to become fixed in one part or
another, nor to begin at any particular place. Consequently, we are
directed to understanding yin and yang not so much in terms of opposition, but rather in terms of complementarity, where the separation of each
from the other makes possible the perception of both at once. In so far as
there is difference, then, there is mutual dependence: the sense of movement created by the alternations of colour and shape, and, further, the
way that the movement changes the more intensely it is contemplated
suggest that here we are in the presence of principles or realities that
escape precise definition and exact application. In the West this perception
is made easier for us because the words and symbols of yin and yang have
no previous association or public reference, so we cannot resolve the
tension of the paradox by reducing it to something already known and
explaining it away conceptually. What we have to do instead is to experi-

Figure 7. Yin–yang symbol.

ence what we habitually separate too distinctly in a new way: that is, not as opposites that tend to conflict, but as complements that tend to relate. Following this model, we would have to consider any problem that arose not as one of finding a resolution to conflicting opposites, but one of discovering the just or appropriate relation between them, which would inevitably redirect us to their underlying identity.

Dark and light, winter and summer, unconsciousness and consciousness are opposing terms only as a negation of each other – that is, as linguistic definitions rather than as a faithful reflection of the totality of our experience. Dark is not light, but what of twilight or dawn, or the 'wolf-light', as the Homeric 'Hymn to Hermes' has it? The danger is that, distanced from the unruly nature of actual experience, we tend to structure our thoughts in terms of our definitions, and so limit our perceptions to match the limitations of language. Only poetic language with its paradoxical imagery, its resonant symbols, the play of tone, sound, texture and rhythm, can claim to be as flexible and responsive to ambiguity and ambivalence as human experience, but the language of everyday speech is too functional, too fast, too adapted to the needs of action. Then opposites serve to introduce a framework, one that may in origin have been vital for survival: fight or flight, friend or foe, true or false, good or bad. Less survivally, there also evolved differences of conviction as to what was true, good, beautiful, and what was not, and when something was true, good, beautiful, and when it was not. The more complex the experience, the less valuable is the language of a simple opposition, which may indeed create an opposite to simplify life rather than to describe it, and still less to explore it:

> They said to Him: Shall we then, being children,
> enter the Kingdom? Jesus said to them:
> When you make the two one, and
> when you make the inner as the outer
> and the outer as the inner and the above

> as the below, and when
> you make the male and female into a single one,
> so that the male will not be male and
> the female (not) be female . . .
> then shall you enter the Kingdom.[14]

It seems clear that a new *poetic* language has to evolve to allow back into consciousness a sensibility that is holistic, animistic and lunar in origin, one that explores flux, continuity and phases of alternation, offering an image not of exclusive realities, nor of final beginnings and endings, but of infinite cycles of transformation. In other words, it is only through Imagination that the reunion of the goddess myth with the god myth can take place. As Blake says, 'To the Eyes of the man of Imagination, Nature is Imagination itself. As a man is, so he sees.'[15] These eyes see with 'double vision':

> For double the vision my eyes do see
> And a double vision is always with me.
> With my inward eye 'tis an old man grey,
> With my outward, a Thistle across my way.[16]

Owen Barfield, in *Saving the Appearances*, concludes his discussion by making an important distinction between what he calls 'original participation' and 'final participation'.[17] Original participation is, in our terms, the relation to nature of the old goddess myth, in which humanity and the natural world are bound within a common identity. Final participation, on the other hand, which is the only participation possible after the long process of withdrawal from original participation, re-creates through the 'systematic use of imagination' the old participative relation to nature but in an entirely new way.[18] It involves, therefore, a dual relation to nature, in which our contemporary experience of nature as separate from us is honoured but transformed by a *conscious* act of participation in which our identity with nature is experienced at a new level of unity. This, in the language of mythology, is again the sacred marriage of god and goddess.

But what is Imagination? All poets agree that it is a unifying activity in which the mind and the heart perceive as one – the thought of the heart. For Jung it is a 'transcendent function' in which conscious and unconscious aspects of the psyche are united at a new level.[19] Coleridge describes Imagination as synthetic and vital: 'it dissolves, diffuses, dissipates, in order to recreate';[20] like the poet, it 'brings the whole soul of man into activity . . . [it] reveals itself in the balance or reconciliation of opposite or discordant qualities: of sameness, with difference; of the general, with the concrete; the idea, with the image; the individual, with the representative'. Imagination, he concludes, is 'the soul that is everywhere, and in each; and forms all into one graceful and intelligent whole'.[21] This description is embodied in his moving image of Nature as an Eolian wind harp that 'plays' as the wind plays through it:

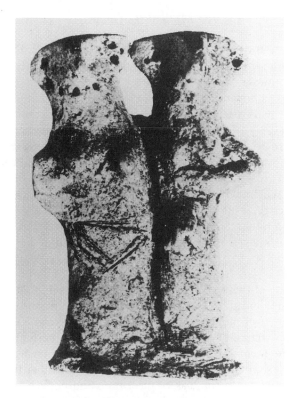

Figure 8. The Sacred Marriage: *The Gumelnitsa Lovers*; Neolithic stone sculpture. East Balkan civilization, *c.* 4500 BC. Cascioarele, Romania.

And what if all of animated nature
Be but organic Harps diversely fram'd,
That tremble into thought, as o'er them sweeps
Plastic and vast, one intellectual breeze,
At once the Soul of each, and God of all?[22]

Without pursuing a study of the Imagination here,[23] we can at least understand by the term a way of relating that tends to perceive in or through images and symbols, that involves and unifies the whole being and brings together as one the inner and the outer worlds. 'I see it feelingly', says the blind Gloucester to King Lear,[24] articulating the play's subsidiary theme: that vision is moral vision.

It is significant that with the formal disappearance of the goddess myth there has also been an undervaluation of the image. No graven images were to be made of the Unknowable and Unpronounceable Yahweh lest Yahweh be reduced to the ontology of the creatures of Yahweh – an obviously impossible demand on the human heart, which was simply solved by the doubly reductive expedient of calling 'Him' 'He'. The eighth-century Nicean Council also drew an unimaginative distinction between 'adoration' and 'veneration' of images, with the similar aim of declaring that the divine was not present in the image.[25] The image was an allegory only; it pointed, but it *was* not; compare Wallace Stevens: 'As in images we awake ... It is, we are.'[26] Of course, this paralleled the instructions as to how to feel about the Virgin Mary – that image that was springing up everywhere – who was also not to be confused with the divine. The eyes – of 'Single Vision and Newton's Sleep', to call upon Blake[27] – were to be directed upwards to the vanishing Heavens, not downwards or around to the appealing body of Earth. 'Mankind has forgotten how to think symbolically', Jung diagnosed, but we cannot remember if the Imagination is not valued as a mode of perception that brings knowledge. This is gnostic knowledge, which is a way of knowing won through a total relationship, not conceptual knowledge 'about' something when the knower is not implicated in the known.

To gather some of these strands together, it would seem that a revaluation of the epistemological importance of image, feeling and intuition – and of the total response of the whole being however it manifests – is a prerequisite for any new mode of thinking to emerge. Then the highly developed skills of the fragmented consciousness may not only be engaged in dissecting ever smaller units of the natural world but also, and at the same time, be directed inwards, to the task of discriminating between those images, feelings and intuitions that arise spontaneously from the twilight depths of the psyche. Like the flail of Osiris, it is needed to sift the original from the tired, the life-enhancing from the self-regarding, and to accept those that weigh no more than the feather of truth.

The fate of 'feeling' has followed the fate of the image during the supremacy of the god myth, excluded from knowledge as image was excluded from divinity. Feeling has been so long falsely opposed to thinking, as intuition has to reason – the former supposedly subjective and so unreliable, the latter objective, beyond personality – that their potentiality for knowledge has not been fully explored. In ancient Egypt the hieroglyph for thought was a heart, proclaiming as ancient truth the timeless poetic insight that, without the barriers of formal language, it is obvious that feelings think and thoughts feel when thinking and feeling are well conducted. When they disagree, this is a sign that something is wrong.

If we try to stand outside our mythological inheritance and consciously compensate for the neglect of archetypal feminine values, we would treat as highly relevant the way we *feel* about 'nature' and our planet Earth, and, more generally, the way we feel about a hypothesis, an argument, an idea, a piece of information, a person – and then we would try to evaluate our feeling as we would an idea. This is conscious participation. We might discover that not everything that is inspiring is a fantasy of wish-fulfilment, a delusion of denial and an invitation to behave irrationally. If, say, the prospect of the rivers and seas full of factory waste, the fish, seals and dolphins dying, the trees withering from acid rain, the air clouded with smog, people across the world from us starving, moves us, then this should not be written off as sentimentality, with the argument that it is too large to do anything about (actually, a familiar strategy for shrugging off inner conflict). On the contrary, the feeling of horror or regret may itself reflect an awareness of belonging to a unity in which what happens in one part of the universe affects in some way what happens everywhere else.

Imagination, as a unifying activity of the whole being, will be totally absent where there is only opposition. It would advise us to distrust a conclusion that sets reason and feeling against each other, where the means and the end can be separated (one used to justify the other, as though both were not one), where quantity vies with quality, where context is abstracted, rule is generalized, and the individual matter is not 'translucent' with the universal. Consequently, the character of the one who knows is entirely relevant to evaluating what that person knows, and, further, how it was known. It would follow from this that certain kinds of 'knowledge' would be ultimately self-contradictory: studying the workings of life in an animal that was dead, for example, caged and killed as a means to an end, as though (to return to Genesis) the naming of animals conferred for ever the right to subdue them.

'What is within surrounds us', writes Rilke.[28] If Imagination sees a unity whose participants are in continual relationship, then it will be concerned with discovering the laws of relationship between particular terms, and with those hypotheses that propose a holistic vision as a way of understanding aspects of life or life itself. Holistic paradigms of the universe, necessarily including humanity as belonging to the whole, cannot deny to nature the consciousness or 'spirit' that humanity claims for itself. These are the conclusions of the 'New Biology' and the 'New Physics', new in the paradoxical sense that the old organic image of nature has replaced the late mechanistic image of the past four centuries, which has radical implications for the way we live; in fact, it completely changes the kind of interpretations we are used to making. For example, adopting a holistic model of the individual psyche, such as Jung's 'homeostatic principle', in which the psyche is understood as a self-regulating system, changes the way a symptom (say, apparently irrational or destructive behaviour) is interpreted: not just as a problem to be explained in terms of a past trauma, but as an attempt on the part of the whole psyche to heal itself.

Similarly, a hypothesis such as James Lovelock's 'Gaia Hypothesis',[29] in which the Earth (as the name of the Greek Mother Goddess Earth would suggest) is seen also as an organic self-regulating whole, involves human beings in a new kind of interpretation of natural phenomena. Rupert Sheldrake's theory of 'Morphic Resonance',[30] which proposes that what is learnt by a particular species in one part of the world facilitates learning in another, changes the interpretation of the world as inhabited by self-contained, isolated units. So does David Bohm's theory of the 'Implicate and Explicate Order', which claims that the manifest diverse three-dimensional world we see is enfolded in an unmanifest implicate order, which is its ground. This ground is also called the holomovement, whose movement is a folding and unfolding, emphasizing 'the unity of unity and diversity', and 'the wholeness of the whole and the part'.[31]

Significantly, like Lovelock, Bohm also falls into the old imagery of the mother goddess to summon an image of the whole, when, for instance, he describes the Implicate Order as an 'ocean of energy'.[32] Fritjof Capra also calls on the image of a cosmic web – 'an interconnected web of relations' –

Figure 9. *Family Group*; Henry Moore, 1944.

to describe the discoveries of subatomic physics,[33] recalling the Neolithic goddess and her spindlewhorls, the Greek spinners of destiny, Artemis, the spinner, and pictures of the Virgin Mary with the thread of human destiny spinning from her womb. Whether or not we understand what is happening in modern science, we can at least say that the imagery in which the discoveries are described is highly evocative.

Once a vision of life as an organic whole is accepted in principle, humanity becomes in one sense a co-creator with nature, in so far as it can foster, ignore or destroy its identity with nature, for nature's continued existence depends ultimately on the kind of consciousness we bring to bear on it. This, at a new level, is a restatement of the old symbolic life of the original participating consciousness in which the rising of the sun and the coming of the rain were believed to require the assistance of human rituals. As Jung writes:

> As a matter of fact we have actually known everything all along; for all these things are always there, only we are not there for them. The possibility of the deepest insight existed at all times, but we were always too far away from it. What we call development or progress is going round and round a central point in order to get gradually closer to it. In reality we always remain on the same spot, just a little nearer or farther from the centre . . . Originally we were all born out of a world of wholeness and in the first years of life are still completely contained in it. There we have all knowledge without knowing it. Later we lose it, and call it progress when we remember it.[34]

Remembering this knowledge, in full and final participation, humanity can assume that original creative delight in nature as the greater form of itself. In the language of mythology this is the sacred marriage of goddess and god.

Chief Seattle's words, quoted in full in Chapter 1 in relation to the Palaeolithic era, may perhaps be understood symbolically in relation to the opportunity of our age:

> Will you teach your children what we have taught our children? That the earth is our mother? What befalls the earth, befalls all the sons of the earth. This we know: the earth does not belong to man, man belongs to the earth. All things are connected like the blood which unites us all. Man did not weave the web of life, he is merely a strand in it. Whatever he does to the web, he does to himself.[35]

APPENDIX 1
PREHISTORIC TIMES

The history of the human species may be most roughly charted as follows:

1 ?
2 *Homo habilis*: 5,000,000(?) to 1,600,000 BC.
3 *Homo erectus*: 1,600,000 to 75,000 BC.
4 Archaic *Homo sapiens: Homo sapiens neanderthalensis*; 500,000 to 40,000 BC.
5 Modern *Homo sapiens: Homo sapiens sapiens* (Cro-Magnon Man); *c.* 40,000 BC.[1]

The earliest species of *Homo sapiens* was Neanderthal Man, who made exquisite tools and also experimented with various symbols. These people used bear skulls ritually, structured their sanctuaries, buried their dead ceremonially, sprinkled red ochre for a symbolic purpose and may have made notational marks of a simple kind.

Neanderthal Man was replaced or absorbed about 40,000 BC by a different type of human being – modern *Homo sapiens* – who was given the name of Cro-Magnon Man, and in whom we can recognize our own kind of consciousness.

The Palaeolithic, or Old Stone, Age period of human evolution lasted for about one million years, ending about 10,000 BC. It has two main divisions, called the Lower (early) Palaeolithic and the Upper (late) Palaeolithic. The early Palaeolithic lasted through successive periods of glaciation, from about one million years ago to 50,000 BC. The later, or Upper, Palaeolithic begins where we can first discern the emergence of *Homo sapiens sapiens*, about 50,000–40,000 years ago, and ends with the beginning of the Neolithic period, *c.* 10,000 BC. The Upper Palaeolithic era is usually divided into five separate periods.

1 The Mousterian: roughly 50,000 to 30,000 BC. During this period stone slabs and bone fragments appear, incised with lines that have been identified with notations of lunar cycles, but there do not seem to be figurative works of art. It was bitterly cold because of widespread glaciation. The principal animals hunted were the woolly mammoth, the woolly rhinoceros, the bear and the reindeer, which were among the few animals able to survive in this climate.

2 The Aurignacian: roughly 30,000 to 25,000 BC. During this period the gradual retreat of the glaciers created a warmer climate, in which the frozen tundra was transformed into steppe, and animals could survive that were not seen before, such as the horse, bison, wild ox and deer. The eastern and western ends of the Pyrenean mountain chain were not covered by glaciers, and a more temperate climate prevailed here than anywhere else in northern Europe. Much as it does today, an alpine zone merged into coniferous forest and this in turn blended into deciduous forest, providing food and shelter for a wide variety of plant and animal life. The climate generally resembled that of modern Siberia. Carvings of the human figure and paintings and engravings of animals begin to appear in the caves.

From the Aurignacian period onwards the great caves of northern Spain and south-western France, together with the figurines found in Germany, Czechoslovakia and Russia, suggest the rituals of an immensely extended culture that reached from Spain to Siberia and formed the foundation of the later Neolithic and Chalcolithic cultures.

3 The Gravettian: roughly 25,000 to 20,000 BC.

4 The Solutrean: *c.* 20,000 to 15,000 BC. A very cold, wet period. The mammoth hunt was at its peak over a vast area stretching from western Europe to Siberia and across to North America. Forests appeared as the climate became warmer.

5 The Magdalenian: *c.* 15,000 to 10,000 BC. The early Magdalenian period was again very cold, but later it grew warmer, and the herds of animals who thrived in a colder climate moved eastwards, followed by the hunters. Those who stayed behind continued to live with the focus of their lives on the great river valleys and on the caves. During the first 4,000 years of the Magdalenian period, Palaeolithic art reached its highest level of expression in the caves.

APPENDIX 2
THE CHRISTIAN GOSPELS

It is surprising to discover that the four Gospels as we know them today were not eyewitness accounts written by the evangelists they have been named after, but are a later compilation of older material – written down at least a generation after the time of Jesus – which has been rearranged and altered to fit in with the criteria of the compilers. These criteria were, it is believed, both theological and practical, in the sense of meeting the beliefs as well as the teaching needs of the early Christian congregations in places very far from Galilee and Jerusalem and the Jewish community where Jesus lived. As John Bowden writes in his book *Jesus: The Unanswered Questions*: 'One evangelist does not hesitate to change the words of another, and all do this for primarily theological reasons . . . or to fit in with their own portrait of Jesus, not to produce a more accurate historical account of him.'[1]

It appears that in the first and second centuries there were four different centres of Christianity: Alexandria, Syria, Greece and Rome, and that there were not four Gospels shared by these early Christian communities but many gospels. A Christian moving from one city to another might hardly recognize the teaching he found in the second city as the same as he had received in the first. The Gospel of Mark is believed to have been written in Rome, while Matthew is thought to have been written in Alexandria, Luke in Antioch and John in Ephesus. None of the three Synoptic Gospels – Matthew, Mark and Luke – is earlier than the third quarter of the first century AD (*c*. 70–90). The Gospel of Mark, compiled in Rome about AD 69–75 and denigrating of the Jews, is believed to be the earliest. The later authors of the Gospels of Matthew and Luke (*c*. AD 80–90) drew on the Gospel of Mark for the narrative material and the basic outline of the life of Jesus; of 661 verses in Mark, more than 600 are reflected in Matthew and about 350 in Luke.

The Gospels of Matthew and Luke also drew from an older written Greek source, colloquially known as Q, from the German word *Quelle*, meaning source. This source, although written in Greek, was translated from, or based on, an earlier Aramaic text or orally transmitted sayings. It is believed the Aramaic material was written down before the middle of the first century and translated into Greek by AD 70. But to make the matter more complicated still, the compilers of the Gospel of Matthew drew on another, older source, whose stories are unique to this Gospel, and the compilers of Luke also drew on an older source (different from Matthew's source) for stories that are specific to this Gospel. The compilers of Luke were careful to weave references from the Old Testament into their stories, so that the events of Jesus' life are presented in such a way that they seem to be the fulfilment of older prophecies. The earlier texts on which all three Gospels drew have so far not been discovered, perhaps because so many of the texts circulating among different Christian groups in the first 300 years of Christianity were destroyed when this abundance of material was 'rationalized' into the four Gospels we know. With the discovery of the Gnostic texts from Nag Hammadi in 1945, the framework has been widened and it seems clear that in some texts, such as the Gospel of Thomas, the compilers of both the Synoptic Gospels and the Gnostic one have drawn on the same source of *logia*, or sayings.

The Gospel of John is thought by most scholars to be later than the other three, although there is the suggestion that parts of it were earlier, even possibly the whole of it, because it refers to the Temple in Jerusalem prior to its destruction in AD 70 (The Pool of Siloam, John 9:7).[2] It is very different in tone from the others and closer to the Aramaic language used by Jesus.

The original Gospel stories and teachings were no doubt at first transmitted orally and then written down by Jews, most probably by the close friends and disciples of Jesus. After the destruction of the Temple, the earliest Christian community in Jerusalem was no longer tolerated, for after this event Judaism narrowed its framework and excluded and destroyed elements that it once might have included within it, much as the Christian Fathers, faced by the proliferation of Gnosticism, excluded the Gnostic sects and destroyed their texts. Jewish Christianity had its beginnings in the countryside of Galilee. Hellenistic Christianity under its leader, Paul, evolved in the highly sophisticated centres of Hellenistic culture, where the earlier stories were arranged and altered to suit Paul's own theological ideas and the needs and expectations of the Christian congregations. The letters of Paul were written roughly half-way between the death of Jesus and the compilation of the Gospels.[3] Yet there is no mention in Paul's writings, or those attributed to him, of the early life of Jesus, his parents or family, his miracles and parables, or even his trial and execution. It is possible that James – believed to be Jesus' brother and the leader of the earliest Christian group in Jerusalem – and Paul did not agree with the content or method of each other's teaching. But by AD 68 both had been murdered. These are some of the reasons why the Christianity presented by Paul is very different from that offered by the Gospels. With the move from Jerusalem to the centres of Hellenistic culture, Bowden writes, 'the message changes. The centre of Jesus' preaching is the kingdom of God; the centre of Paul's preaching is Christ crucified and risen ... In other words, the Jesus who *has* the message changes into the Christ who *is* the message.'[4]

Within 300 years of Paul's death his interpretation of Jesus' life and teaching had prevailed. The suppression of the Gnostic sects by Constantine in AD 326 and 333 removed the last resistance to the survival of a different image of Jesus and his teaching. At the Council of Nicaea in 325, convened by Constantine, Jesus was declared to be 'of one substance with God' from all eternity. It was at this Council that the Creed that is still recited today in the Christian churches was formulated. It was approved by the Council of Chalcedon in 451, so establishing the foundation of the two Christian doctrines of the Incarnation and the Trinity. Even though the compilers of the Gospels do not name Jesus as God, and even Paul did not do so, in these Councils Jesus is declared to be the only Son of God. From this a theology was to grow that had very little in common with the earliest image of the man of Galilee.

THE TITLE OF 'CHRIST'

The name Jesus is the Greek form of the Aramaic name Jeshua (in Hebrew, Joshua). 'Christ' is the Greek equivalent of the Hebrew word 'Messiah', and was used by the Christian communities in Greece. The evidence of the Gospels suggests that Jesus himself never used the title Messiah (Christ) and did not refer to himself as the 'Son of God'. These titles were given to him later by his Gentile followers and were elaborated by them within the context of the Graeco-Roman world, where, as a result of their deliberations, the prophetic elements in the Old Testament were inextricably entwined with Greek Platonist philosophy.[5] The result of this strange fusion of mythologies was the doctrine formulated at Nicaea and Chalcedon. Bowden comments:

> The Chalcedonian Definition came at the end of a long process of theological controversy ... Its formulation was a diplomatic as well as a theological exercise; at various points force had to be used to secure the triumph of what eventually became the 'orthodox' party, and historical accident also played a role. However, once established, the Definition took on the authoritative status it has enjoyed since and, like a satellite going into orbit, jettisoned the forces of thrust which had set it in its place. Now it was in the heavens, and Christians came to believe that God himself had put it there – as part of his revelation, in the same way as the Bible was his revelation.[6]

NOTES AND REFERENCES

PREFACE

1. Joseph Campbell, *The Hero with a Thousand Faces*, p. 13.
2. C. G. Jung, *Collected Works*, Vol. 9:1, *The Archetypes and the Collective Unconscious*, para. 271.

PART I THE MOTHER GODDESS AND HER SON-LOVER

Chapter 1 In the Beginning: the Palaeolithic Mother Goddess

1. Quoted in full in Joseph Campbell, *The Way of the Animal Powers*, p. 269.
2. ibid., p. 68.
3. Alexander Marshack, *The Roots of Civilization*, p. 290.
4. Herbert Kuhn, *On the Track of Prehistoric Man*, p. 64.
5. Joseph Campbell, *Primitive Mythology*, p. 306.
6. Quoted in Campbell, *Primitive Mythology*, pp. 307-8.
7. André Leroi-Gourhan, *Treasures of Prehistoric Art*, p. 144. Quoted by Campbell, *The Way of the Animal Powers*, p. 62.
8. André Leroi-Gourhan, *Préhistoire de l'Art Occidentale*, p. 120.
9. Sir Laurens van der Post, in the course of a story-telling evening, 17 December 1989. See also Robert Briffault, *The Mothers*, pp. 339-45 for the prevalence of this custom in other tribes and countries.
10. Marshack, op. cit., p. 57.
11. Mircea Eliade, *A History of Religious Ideas*, Vol. 1, pp. 9-12.
12. Campbell, *Primitive Mythology*, p. 330.
13. Gertrude Levy, *The Gate of Horn*, p. 48.
14. Campbell, *The Way of the Animal Powers*, p. 73.
15. Interview with Professor Jean-Phillippe Rigaud, director of prehistoric antiquities in Aquitaine, *National Geographic*, October 1988, p. 448.
16. Riane Eisler, *The Chalice and the Blade*, p. 5.
17. Henri Breuil, *Four Hundred Centuries of Cave Art*.
18. Ailton Krenack, from the Krenacki Indian nation, in personal conversation, Altamira, Brazil, February 1989.

19. Mircea Eliade, *Shamanism*, p. 470.
20. ibid., p. 19.
21. See Laurens van der Post, *The Heart of the Hunter*.
22. Campbell, *The Way of the Animal Powers*, p. 25.
23. Based on notes taken during a television programme on the ritual paintings of the Bushman and the Australian Aborigine, 1989.
24. See drawing in Marija Gimbutas, *The Language of the Goddess*, p. 213.
25. Eliade, *Shamanism*, p. 481.
26. ibid., p. 486.
27. T. S. Eliot, 'Dry Salvages', *The Four Quartets*, p. 102.
28. André Leroi-Gourhan, *The Dawn of European Art*, p. 75.
29. C. G. Jung, *Collected Works*, Vol. 5, *Symbols of Transformation*, p. xxiv.
30. Laurens van der Post, *The Lost World of the Kalahari* and *The Heart of the Hunter*.
31. See Don Cupitt, *The Sea of Faith*. This is a book from a six-part television series of the same name. See particularly programme three: 'Darwin, Freud and Jung'.
32. C. G. Jung, *Collected Works*, Vol. 8, *The Structure and Dynamics of the Psyche*, para. 673.
33. This goddess is called a Parthian goddess of the second century AD by Erich Neumann, but is entitled 'Astarte from second-century BC Babylon' by the Louvre.
34. C. G. Jung, *Collected Works*, Vol. 8, *The Structure and Dynamics of the Psyche*. We regret that we are unable to give the exact reference for this quotation.

Chapter 2 The Neolithic Great Goddess of Sky, Earth and Waters

1. Laurens van der Post and Jane Taylor, *Testament to the Bushman*, p. 142.
2. Greek: *neo* = 'new'; *lithos* = 'stone'; *chalcos* = 'copper'.
3. Greek: *meso* = 'middle'.
4. Marija Gimbutas, *The Goddesses and Gods of Old Europe*, p. 205.
5. Joseph Campbell, *Primitive Mythology*, p. 139.
6. Robert Briffault, *The Mothers*, Chapter 8.
7. Mircea Eliade, *A History of Religious Ideas*, Vol. 1, pp. 40–1.
8. Marija Gimbutas, *The Language of the Goddess*, preface, p. xv and p. 1.
9. Gimbutas, *The Goddesses and Gods of Old Europe*, preface.
10. ibid., p. 85.
11. ibid., p. 24.
12. Riane Eisler, *The Chalice and the Blade*, p. 18.
13. ibid., p. 20.
14. Marija Gimbutas, *The Early Civilizations of Europe*, Chapter 2.
15. ibid., Chapter 2.
16. ibid., Chapter 2.
17. Gimbutas, *The Goddesses and Gods of Old Europe*, p. 159.
18. Gimbutas, *The Language of the Goddess*, pp. 3–23.
19. ibid., p. 3.
20. ibid., p. 101.

21. Gimbutas, *The Goddesses and Gods of Old Europe*, p. 205.
22. ibid., pp. 169–95.
23. André Leroi-Gourhan, 'La fonction des signes dans les sanctuaires paléolithiques', *Bulletin de la Société Préhistorique Française*, 55, 1958.
24. The Musée de L'Homme in Paris displays the masked and costumed figures from central and Eastern Europe that originated in Neolithic Old Europe.
25. Gimbutas, *The Goddesses and Gods of Old Europe*, p. 169.
26. ibid., pp. 181–90.
27. ibid., p. 181.
28. Marija Gimbutas, 'The First Wave of Eurasian Steppe Pastoralists into Copper Age Europe'; see also 'The Beginning of the Bronze Age in Europe and the Indo-Europeans: 3500–2500 BC'; 'Three Waves of the Kurgan People into Old Europe, 4500–2500 BC'; and 'Remarks on the Ethnogenesis of the Indo-Europeans in Europe'.
29. Gimbutas, 'The First Wave of Eurasian Steppe Pastoralists into Copper Age Europe'.
30. Gimbutas, *The Goddesses and Gods of Old Europe*, preface.
31. Compare the effect of the Indo-European (Aryan) invasion on the civilization of the Indus Valley and the absorption of the Vedic pantheon of gods by the older Dravidian peoples of India.
32. Gimbutas, *The Goddesses and Gods of Old Europe*, preface.
33. ibid., preface.
34. Quoted by M. J. Vermaseren, *Cybele and Attis*, p. 10.
35. James Mellaart, *Earliest Civilizations of the Near East*, p. 77.
36. James Mellaart, *Çatal Hüyük*, p. 176.
37. James Mellaart, 'Excavations at Çatal Hüyük, 1965; Fourth Preliminary Report', *Anatolian Studies 16*, pp. 180–2.
38. Mellaart, *Çatal Hüyük*, p. 117.
39. In Tibet to this day bodies are laid out on a rock after death. The bones of the dead person are ground to powder and the flesh is offered to the vultures that attend the burial site. In this ritual, perhaps similar to that practised at Çatal Hüyük, the flesh body is offered back to the cycle of life as food for the vultures.
40. Mellaart, *Çatal Hüyük*, pp. 152–3.
41. Buffie Johnson, *Lady of the Beasts*, p. 62. No reference is given for this comment.
42. Mellaart, *Çatal Hüyük*, pp. 180–201.
43. ibid., p. 148.
44. Greek: *mega* = 'great', *lithos* = 'stone'.
45. Mircea Eliade, *The Sacred and the Profane*, p. 13.
46. Michael Dames, *The Silbury Treasure*, pp. 1, 42.
47. See Alexander Thom, *Megalith Sites in Britain*.
48. Glyn Daniel, *The Megalith Builders of Western Europe*, p. 74.
49. Gimbutas, *The Language of the Goddess*, p. 223.
50. Daniel, op. cit., p. 100.
51. Eliade, *A History of Religious Ideas*, Vol. 1, p. 116.
52. Henri Frankfort and H. A. Frankfort, *Before Philosophy*, p. 12, quoted in Dames, op. cit.

53. Euan Mackie, *The Megalith Builders*, p. 113.

54. Dames, op. cit., p. 58.

55. Daniel, op. cit., p. 82.

56. The archaeologists Jacquetta Hawkes and Sir Leonard Woolley write: 'Nothing can shake the evidence of hundreds upon hundreds of little clay, bone and stone effigies of the mother goddess ... Their presence has been repeatedly mentioned in the account of the rise and spread of the primary farming communities.' *Prehistory and the Beginnings of Civilisation*, Part II; quoted in Dames, op. cit.

57. See the recent discoveries of Dr Romana Unger-Hamilton, Institute of Archaeology, University College, London, which have pushed back the origins of agriculture in the Neolithic era by 2,000 years. She has brought evidence to show that people in the Middle East were planting cereals as early as 11,000 BC. (Report in *The Independent*, 21 July 1988.)

58. Eisler, op. cit., p. 9.

59. Gimbutas, *The Language of the Goddess*, p. 321.

60. C. G. Jung, *Collected Works*, Vol. 8, *The Structure and Dynamics of the Psyche*, para. 729.

Chapter 3 Crete: the Goddess of Life, Death and Regeneration

1. Homer, *Odyssey*, 19.

2. Nikolaos Platon, *A Guide to the Archaeological Museum of Herakleon*, p. 27f; quoted in Carl Kerenyi, *Dionysos: Archetypal Image of Indestructible Life*, p. 6.

3. Kerenyi, op. cit., p. 11.

4. H. A. Groenewegen-Frankfort, *Arrest and Movement*, p. 186; quoted in Kerenyi, op. cit., p. 10.

5. Marija Gimbutas, *The Goddesses and Gods of Old Europe*.

6. R. F. Willetts, *Cretan Cults and Festivals*, p. 6; see also Sir Arthur Evans, *The Palace of Minos*, Vol. 1, p. 14.

7. Evans, op. cit., Vol. 2ii, pp. 183–5.

8. Evans, op. cit., Vol. 2ii, p. 277.

9. Martin P. Nilsson, *Geschichte der Grieschen Religion*, Munich, C. H. Beck'sch, 2nd edn, 1955 and 1961, Vol. 1, p. 298; quoted in Joseph Campbell, *Occidental Mythology*, p. 46.

10. Erich Neumann, *The Great Mother*, p. 118.

11. Gertrude Levy, *The Gate of Horn*, p. 230, and Mircea Eliade, *A History of Religious Ideas*, Vol 1, p. 134.

12. Willetts, op. cit., p. 70, and Sir Arthur Evans, *The Mycenaean Tree and Pillar Cult*.

13. Gimbutas, op. cit., p. 186.

14. J. V. Luce, *The End of Atlantis*, London, Thames and Hudson, 1968, p. 158; quoted in Riane Eisler, *The Chalice and the Blade*, pp. 108–9.

15. Campbell, op. cit., p. 72.

16. Quoted in Gimbutas, op. cit., p. 182.

17. Kerenyi, op. cit., p. 41.

18. Virgil, *Georgics*, IV, 63; quoted in Gimbutas, op. cit. p. 183.

19. Trs. Jules Cashford.
20. Levy, op. cit., pp. 231–2.
21. Nikolaos Platon, *Crete*, pp. 161–77.
22. Homer, *Odyssey*, 1.
23. ibid., 22.
24. Kerenyi, op. cit., pp. 23–5.
25. Henri Frankfort, *Kingship and the Gods*, p. 67.
26. Kerenyi, op. cit., p. 16.
27. Evans, op. cit., Vol. 3, pp. 145–6.
28. Gimbutas, op. cit., p. 43.
29. Willetts, op. cit., p. 181.
30. Campbell, op. cit., pp. 47–50.
31. Charles Picard, *Les Religions Préhelleniques: Crète et Mycènes*, Paris, 1948, p. 152, quoted in Eliade, op. cit., Vol. 1, p. 133.
32. Martin P. Nilsson, *The Minoan-Mycenaean Religion and its Survival in Greek Religion*, p. 354.
33. Willetts, op. cit., p. 81.
34. See Maria-Gabriel Wosien, *Sacred Dance: Encounter with the Gods*.
35. Homer, *Iliad*, pp. 352–3.
36. Willetts, op. cit., p. 199.
37. Sir James G. Frazer, *The Golden Bough*, Vol. 4, *The Dying God*, p. 76.
38. This is an abbreviated version of the story which can be found in full in Robert Graves, *Greek Myths*, pp. 292–348.
39. Jane Harrison, *Prolegomena to the Study of Greek Religion*, passim.
40. Frazer, op. cit., p. 74.
41. ibid., p. 69.
42. ibid., p. 71.
43. ibid., p. 72.
44. ibid., p. 31.
45. Campbell, op. cit., p. 60.
46. Carl Kerenyi, *The Gods of the Greeks*, p. 109.
47. Kerenyi, *Dionysos*, pp. 268–72.

Chapter 4 The Bronze Age: The Mother Goddess and Her Son–Lover

1. Carl Kerenyi, *Dionysos: Archetypal Image of Indestructible Life*, p. xxxv.
2. Heinrich Zimmer, *The Art of Indian Asia*.
3. Joseph Campbell, *Occidental Mythology*, p. 64.
4. The word *numen* is Latin, and means a 'nod', derived from the Greek *nouein*, meaning 'to nod', and the Greek *pneuma*, meaning 'breath', 'wind' or 'spirit'. *Hagion Pneuma* is the Christian 'Holy Spirit'. *Numen*, and its adjectival form 'numinous', have been discussed by Rudolf Otto in his book *The Idea of the Holy*, and can be understood colloquially as a 'nod from a god', that is, the coming alive of a divine presence.
5. Joseph Campbell, *Oriental Mythology*, p. 12.
6. Joseph Campbell, *The Mythic Image*, pp. 72–4.
7. Erich Neumann, *The Origins and History of Consciousness*, pp. 5–170.

8. S. N. Kramer, *Sumerian Mythology*, p. 40. Enlil has many attributes in common with the Egyptian god Shu, and with the Aryan god Varuna, who made the three worlds of heaven, earth and the air between them, which was his breath.

9. S. N. Kramer, *From the Poetry of Sumer*, p. 45.

10. R. T. Rundle Clark, *Myth and Symbol in Ancient Egypt*, p. 44.

11. ibid., p. 65.

12. Campbell, *Occidental Mythology*, pp. 117–19.

13. William W. Hallo and J. J. A. Van Dijk, *The Exaltation of Inanna*.

14. S. N. Kramer, *The Sumerians*, pp. 127–8.

15. Neumann, op. cit., p. 131.

16. ibid., p. 131.

17. Campbell, *Occidental Mythology*, p. 7.

18. Mircea Eliade, *A History of Religious Ideas*, Vol. 1, pp. 187–8; see also Riane Eisler, *The Chalice and the Blade*, pp. 42–59.

19. Eliade, op. cit., p. 187.

20. Campbell, *Oriental Mythology*, p. 176.

21. Campbell, *Occidental Mythology*, p. 121.

22. Eliade, op. cit., Vol. 1, p. 191. Compare also the oral tradition of Vedic India. Gurdjieff in the course of his travels noted that the heroic tales that were still recited orally closely resembled the ancient Babylonian epics (Ernest Scott, *The People of the Secret*, Chapter 8).

23. Stuart Piggott, *Prehistoric India*, p. 329.

24. Campbell, *Oriental Mythology*, pp. 126–7.

25. Eliade, op. cit., Vol. 1, p. 187.

26. ibid., Vol. 1, p. 36. 'Among the Assyrians, the Iranians, and the Turko-Mongols, the techniques of hunting and war are so much alike as to be hardly separable.'

27. Campbell, *Occidental Mythology*, pp. 21–2.

28. D. A. Mackenzie, *Myths of Babylonia and Assyria*, p. 16.

29. Kramer, *From the Poetry of Sumer*, p. 27.

30. Sir James G. Frazer, *The Golden Bough*, Vol. 8, *The Spirits of the Corn and the Wild*, pp. 261–2.

31. Mircea Eliade, *The Sacred and the Profane*, p. 138.

32. Neumann, op. cit., p. 279.

33. Joseph Campbell, *Myths to Live By*, p. 137.

34. Hesiod, *Theogony*, quoted in Walter Burkert, *Structure and History in Greek Mythology and Ritual*, p. 57.

35. Campbell, *Oriental Mythology*, p. 72.

36. Edgar Wind, *Pagan Mysteries of the Renaissance*, p. 133.

37. See Campbell, *Primitive Mythology*, pp. 151–69, and Frazer, *The Golden Bough*, Vol. 4, *The Dying God*; also Eliade, *A History of Religious Ideas*, Vol. 1.

38. Frazer, *The Golden Bough*, Vol. 4, *The Dying God*, pp. 211–12.

39. Frazer, *The Golden Bough*, Vol. 9, *The Scapegoat*, p. 227.

40. ibid., p. 227. See his note on the Crucifixion of Christ at the end of the book, pp. 412–23.

41. Sir Leonard Woolley, *Ur of the Chaldees*, pp. 45–6.

42. Erich Neumann, *The Great Mother*, Part II.
43. Marija Gimbutas, *The Goddesses and Gods of Old Europe*, p. 196.
44. Sandars, op. cit., p. 92.
45. Homer, *Odyssey*, Book 24.
46. ibid.
47. Sandars, op. cit., p. 27.
48. ibid., p. 29.
49. ibid., pp. 29–30.
50. ibid., p. 26.
51. ibid.
52. ibid.
53. Trs. by G. A. Reisner, quoted in Jacobsen, *The Treasures of Darkness*, p. 137.
54. ibid., p. 231.
55. Quoted in Neumann, *The Origins and History of Consciousness*, p. 56.
56. Campbell, *Oriental Mythology*, p. 80.
57. John Gray, *Near Eastern Mythology*, p. 56.
58. Campbell, *Oriental Mythology*, p. 139.
59. ibid.
60. Jacobsen, op. cit., p. 77.
61. ibid., pp. 77–8.
62. From 'The Dialogue of a Man with his Soul', a version of the Egyptian poem compiled by the authors from translations of the Berlin Papyrus 3024. See also Campbell, *Oriental Mythology*, p. 138, and Bika Reed, *Rebel in the Soul: A Sacred Text of Ancient Egypt*, New York, Inner Traditions International, 1978.

Chapter 5 Inanna–Ishtar: Mesopotamian Goddess of the Great Above and the Great Below

1. Stephen Langdon writes that the sign employed to write the name of Inanna–Ishtar from first to last probably represented a caduceus, a staff with intertwined serpents coiled around it; *Tammuz and Ishtar*, p. 87.
2. A phrase borrowed from the poetry of Thomas Traherne's *Centuries of Meditations*, 1:29.
3. Langdon, op. cit., p. 153.
4. Raphael Patai, *The Hebrew Goddess*, p. 136.
5. Titles gathered from various source books and poems.
6. From D. Wolkstein and S. N. Kramer, *Inanna, Queen of Heaven and Earth*, p. 93.
7. Langdon, op. cit., Chapter 1.
8. S. N. Kramer, *From the Poetry of Sumer*, pp. 11–12.
9. See S. N. Kramer, preface to *Sumerian Mythology*, and Chapter 8, 'The Legacy of Sumer', in *The Sumerians*.
10. Sir Leonard Woolley, *The Sumerians*, pp. 186–7. The relationship with the Indus Valley civilization is clear from a comparison of the images that are common to both, in particular those of the goddess and the serpent god. See Heinrich Zimmer, *The Art of Indian Asia*.
11. Euan Mackie, *The Megalith Builders*, p. 195.

12. Lord Byron, 'Hebrew Melodies: The Destruction of Sennacherib'.

13. Cylinder seals show many features that are not characteristic either of the rivers and swamps of the Mesopotamian river valleys or of the Arabian or Syrian desert.

14. Zimmer, op. cit. It is only by comparing the imagery and mythology of the goddesses and gods of India and Sumeria that one concludes that the relationship between them must have been much closer than is realized. A thousand years after the Aryan invasions *c.* 1500 BC, the older mythology reasserts itself.

15. Kramer comments further: 'In the centuries that followed, however, the status of woman in Sumerian society deteriorated considerably, although even then she could own property and on occasion buy and sell without consulting her husband.' *From the Poetry of Sumer*, p. 27. See 'The Sumerian Woman: Wife, Mother, Priestess, Goddess' in Denise Schmandt-Beserat (ed.), *The Legacy of Sumer*, 1976.

16. Kramer, *From the Poetry of Sumer*, p. 27.

17. 'For some reason or other, one is forced to conclude, the role of the goddess Ki, Mother Earth, had been usurped by the male deity Enlil.' ibid., pp. 27–8.

18. From 'Inanna and the *Huluppu*-Tree' in Wolkstein and Kramer, op. cit.

19. Ki-Ninhursag, the oldest goddess of Earth, is Belit-ili in Akkadian. An, the god of heaven, is Anu or Anum. Inanna is Ishtar. Nanna, the moon god, is Suen or Sin. Enki, the god of the waters of the abyss, is Ea.

20. Joseph Campbell, *The Inner Reaches of Outer Space*, p. 34. See also his *Oriental Mythology*, pp. 120–1.

21. Quoted by Kramer, *From the Poetry of Sumer*, pp. 29–30. This translation, Kramer says, is based on an unpublished edition of the text prepared by Miguel Civil. Compare the almost identical imagery in a poem to Aphrodite; see Chapter 9, p. 353.

22. Named as Mount Sumeru in Hindu mythology. It is interesting that Sumeru should sound so like Sumer or Sumeria.

23. Gertrude Levy, *The Gate of Horn*, p. 169.

24. Later Classical authors wrote that the ziggurat of Babylon was coloured to represent the seven regions of the heavenly worlds – imagery that descends to Dante's *Divine Comedy* (see Levy, op. cit., p. 170, footnote).

25. Kramer, *From the Poetry of Sumer*, p, 43.

26. The cosmic gods of the Vedic (Aryan) and then the Hindu pantheon bear a strong resemblance to the Sumerian trinity of male gods: An, Enlil and Enki. An may be compared with Brahma, Enlil with Shiva, and Enki with Vishnu. Again, Enki or Ea may be compared to Vishnu, who rests on the coils of the great serpent. In Hinduism it is the cosmic embrace of goddess and god that sustains the universe and is the source of all created forms (see Zimmer, op. cit.).

Professor Wallis Budge thought that both Sumerians and Egyptians derived their gods from a common and exceedingly ancient source; see his *The Gods of the Egyptians*, Vol. I, p. 190. India must not be left out of this equation, for the civilization of the Indus Valley shows many points of contact with that of Sumeria, and was, indeed, flourishing at the same time, in the third to mid-second millennia BC, when it was interrupted and radically altered by the Aryan invasions. The old goddess culture later reasserts itself in the rich pantheon and the mythology of the Hindu goddesses and gods, and in the deities of Mahayana Buddhism. Indian mythology offers many insights into a better understanding of Sumeria.

27. Henri Frankfort, *Kingship and the Gods*, p. 284.
28. Kramer, *From the Poetry of Sumer*, p. 29.
29. Seton Lloyd, *The Archaeology of Mesopotamia*, pp. 117–18.
30. Leonard William King, *Legends of Babylonia and Egypt in Relation to Hebrew Tradition*, p. 111.
31. See Frankfort, op. cit., p. 284. He refers to the verse in the Gospel of Mark (4:28): 'For the earth bringeth forth fruit of herself; first the blade, then the ear, after that the full corn in the ear.'
32. Wolkstein and Kramer, op. cit., p. 146.
33. An Assyrian text reads: 'Weak wast thou, Assurbanipal, when I satiated thee on the lap of the queen of Nineveh.' Langdon, op. cit., p. 56.
34. Compare the Egyptian text images, where Hathor and Isis nourish kings – 'Thy Mother is the great Wild Cow' (Pyramid Text 729, quoted by Frankfort, op. cit., p. 174). Also the Indian mother goddess as a cow; hence the sacredness of cows in India.
35. Stephen Langdon, *Sumerian and Babylonian Psalms*, p. 13.
36. Compare the double-headed axe held by the Cretan goddess and by the Anatolian goddess Cybele, as well as that held by the god Shiva in Hindu mythology.
37. Wolkstein and Kramer, op. cit., p. 169.
38. 'Hymn to Ishtar', quoted in D. A. Mackenzie, *Myths of Babylonia and Assyria*, p. 54.
39. Robert W. Rogers, *Cuneiform Parallels to the Old Testament*, p. 126.
40. Thorkild Jacobsen, *The Treasures of Darkness*, pp. 136–7.
41. Compare this lion imagery with that of the goddess Durga in India.
42. See the passages referring to this transformation in Levy, op. cit.
43. In India the sycamore fig and the pipal tree were sacred to the goddess; see Zimmer, op. cit.
44. Langdon, *Tammuz and Ishtar*, p. 153.
45. Kramer, *From the Poetry of Sumer*, p. 92.
46. Langdon, *Tammuz and Ishtar*, p. 155.
47. These must be the prototypes of the *Asherim* of the Old Testament.
48. Levy, op. cit., p. 95.
49. Quoted by M. Esther Harding in *Woman's Mysteries*, p. 159.
50. Tantricism in India may be descended from the pre-Aryan goddess culture there. Some method of initiation of the same kind may also have existed in Sumeria.
51. See Harding, op. cit., for a discussion of this ritual.
52. Woolley, *The Sumerians*, p. 108.
53. These children were known as 'virgin-born', meaning that they were born of the priestesses of the temple, possibly the high priestess.
54. W. W. Hallo and J. J. A. Van Dijk, *The Exaltation of Inanna*.
55. Wolkstein and Kramer, op. cit., p. 101.
56. Campbell, *Occidental Mythology*, p. 46.
57. Sir James Frazer, *The Golden Bough*, Vol. 4, *The Dying God*, pp. 69–76.
58. The belt or girdle is one of the images that belong to the Virgin Mary.

59. Langdon, *Tammuz and Ishtar*.
60. Kramer, *From the Poetry of Sumer*, p. 86.
61. Compare the role of Zeus, 'the Thunderer', and Indra, who wields the thunderbolt in Vedic mythology.
62. Ishtar was called 'the fearful dragon of the great gods'. The dragon, as flying serpent, brings together the ancient sky and water epiphanies of the Neolithic Great Mother.
63. Thorkild Jacobsen, 'Pictures and Pictorial Language (The Burney Relief)' in *Figurative Language in the Ancient Near East*, Mindlin et al. (eds.), London, School of Oriental and African Studies, 1987, p. 2.
64. Kramer, *From the Poetry of Sumer*, p. 76.
65. ibid., p. 76.
66. Hallo and Van Dijk, op. cit., p. 51.
67. Quoted in Jacobsen, *The Treasures of Darkness*, p. 231.
68. Kramer, *From the Poetry of Sumer*, pp. 45–6, quoting from a study by Gertrude Farber-Flugge.
69. Rogers, op. cit., p. 162.
70. From a hymn to Ishtar, quoted in Rogers, op. cit., p. 162.
71. Wolkstein and Kramer, op. cit., p. 21.
72. Kramer, *The Sumerians*, p. 174–83.
73. Kramer, *From the Poetry of Sumer*, p. 96.
74. Langdon, *Tammuz and Ishtar*, Chapter 1.
75. Jacobsen, *The Treasures of Darkness*, p. 26. Compare the words of Jesus: 'I am the vine and ye are the branches. He that abideth in me and I in him, the same bringeth forth much fruit: for without me ye can do nothing' (John 15:5).
76. ibid.
77. Eugene Goblet d'Alviella, *The Migration of Symbols*, p. 157. See his chapter on the symbolism of the Tree of Life.
78. Compare the image of the ram caught in a thicket in the story of Abraham's intended sacrifice of Isaac (Gen. 22:13). The older ritual of the sacrifice of a 'king's son' is here transformed as the animal sacrifice is substituted for the human one.
79. Kramer, *From the Poetry of Sumer*, p. 37.
80. Langdon, *Tammuz and Ishtar*, from an unpublished manuscript in Berlin.
81. Jacobsen, op. cit., p. 33.
82. Wolkstein and Kramer, op. cit., p. 36.
83. ibid., p. 107.
84. Langdon, *Journal of the Royal Asiatic Society*.
85. Wolkstein and Kramer, op. cit., p. 40. Compare the Song of Songs, 'I am come into my garden, my sister, my spouse . . .' (S. of S. 5:1).
86. ibid., pp. 37, 39.
87. Kramer, *History Begins at Sumer*, p. 286.
88. Wolkstein and Kramer, op. cit., p. 38.
89. ibid., p. 44.
90. H. Frankfort, 'The Burney Relief' in Ernst F. Weidner (ed.), *Archiv für Orientforschung*, Berlin, Zwölfter Band, 1937–9, pp. 128–35. See also note 91.
91. Jacobsen, 'Pictures and Pictorial Language (The Burney Relief)' in *Figurative*

Language in the Ancient Near East, Mindlin *et al.* (eds.), London, School of Oriental and African Studies, 1987, pp. 4–5.

92. Wolkstein and Kramer, 'The Descent of Inanna', op. cit., p. 71.
93. ibid., p. 83.
94. ibid., p. 84.
95. ibid., p. 87.
96. ibid., p. 89.
97. See Sir Leonard Woolley, *Excavations at Ur.* Sumerian scholars have searched for evidence of the ritual of the sacrifice of kings and the immolation of the court, but there are no texts that relate to this practice.
98. Compare the negative confession in the Egyptian ritual of the dead.
99. Compare the flagellation of Jesus.
100. Kramer, *The Sumerians,* p. 151.
101. Campbell, *Oriental Mythology,* p. 44.
102. Langdon, *Tammuz and Ishtar,* pp. 166–70. The month of ritual mourning is still observed in the Christian calendar as Lent, and in the Islamic calendar as Ramadan.
103. Wolkstein and Kramer, op. cit., p. 86.
104. Kramer, *From the Poetry of Sumer,* p. 93.
105. It was this ritual mourning that Ezekiel was referring to when he wrote: 'Then he brought me to the door of the gate of the Lord's house which was toward the north: and behold, there sat women weeping for Tammuz' (8:14). Ezekiel lived near Nippur during the exile of the Hebrews in Babylon, and would have been familiar with Babylonian temple rituals. It was here that he had his great vision of the temple in Jerusalem.
106. Langdon, *Tammuz and Ishtar,* p. 14.
107. Adonis was buried in a tree trunk, like Osiris, and cast into the sea at Byblos.
108. Frazer, *The Golden Bough,* Vol. 4, *The Dying God* and Vol. 5, *Adonis, Attis and Osiris.*
109. Langdon, *Tammuz and Ishtar,* p. 14.
110. Compare also the Buddhist imagery of 'awakening' human beings from their sleep of ignorance – *avidya.* A Buddhist saying is: 'Incomparable are the Wake!'
111. Levy, op. cit., pp. 101–2.
112. In Akkadian, Ereshkigal is called Irkalla, the underworld is Arallu. In Hebrew culture, the underworld is Sheol, in Christian, Hell, a word that comes from the name of the Norse goddess of the underworld, Hel.
113. James Pritchard, *The Ancient Near East,* Vol. 1, p. 59; see also Sandars, op. cit., p. 92.

Chapter 6 Isis of Egypt: Queen of Heaven, Earth and Underworld

1. See Chapter 4, pp. 153–4; see also R. T. Rundle Clarke, *Myth and Symbol in Ancient Egypt,* p. 18.
2. New Kingdom hymn, quoted in Rundle Clark, op. cit., p. 103.
3. The parallels between this part of Isis's story and Demeter's in the Homeric 'Hymn to Demeter' are testament to a direct continuity of tradition.

4. The Paris Stele, the Louvre, C. 286; quoted in Georges Nagel, 'The Mysteries of Osiris in Ancient Egypt', *The Mysteries*, Eranos Yearbooks, 2, p. 122.
5. The sources of this myth are Plutarch, 'Isis and Osiris' in *Moralia*, Book 5, pp. 31–49; and Joseph Campbell (after Frazer), *Primitive Mythology*, pp. 424–7.
6. Pyramid Text; quoted in Rundle Clark, op. cit., p. 113.
7. Pyramid Text, ibid., p. 111.
8. Pausanias, *De Phocis*, x, p. 323; quoted in Henri Frankfort, *Kingship and the Gods*, p. 192.
9. Rundle Clark, op. cit., p. 157.
10. Pyramid Text 1636 b; ibid., p. 188.
11. Quoted in Frankfort, op. cit., p. 190.
12. Plutarch, op. cit., 366–7, p. 97.
13. Quoted in Rundle Clark, pp. 125–8.
14. Plutarch, op. cit., p. 93.
15. Quoted in Frankfort, op. cit., p. 195.
16. Quoted in Rundle Clark, op. cit., p. 119.
17. Quoted in Frankfort, op. cit., pp. 186–7.
18. Plutarch, op. cit., 367–8, p. 103.
19. Quoted in Frankfort, op. cit., pp. 195–6.
20. Plutarch, op. cit., 368, p. 105.
21. ibid., p. 121.
22. Quoted in Rundle Clark, op. cit., p. 115.
23. Joseph Campbell, *Oriental Mythology*, p. 81.
24. Extracts from 'The Lamentations of Isis and Nephthys' (Berlin Papyrus 1425), after the translation by James Teackle Dennis, *The Burden of Isis*, London, John Murray, 1910, pp. 21–7. Compare the translation by E. A. Wallis Budge, *Osiris and the Egyptian Resurrection*, Vol. 2, pp. 222–40 (quoted in Chapter 14, pp. 585–6). See also Harold Bayley, *The Lost Language of Symbolism*, who points out the similarities between this and the Song of Songs.
25. Pyramid Text, 834; quoted in Erich Neumann, *The Origins and History of Consciousness*, p. 222.
26. Quoted in Manfred Lurker, *The Gods and Symbols of Ancient Egypt*, p. 47.
27. From Dennis, op. cit., p. 25.
28. E. A. Wallis Budge, *The Book of the Dead*, London, Routledge & Kegan Paul, 1974, p. xvii.
29. From E. A. Wallis Budge, *The Papyrus of Ani*, New York, Metropolitan Museum of Art and Alfred A. Knopf Inc., 1976, p. 94.
30. See I. E. S. Edwards, *Tutankhamun: His Tomb and Its Treasures*. New York, Metropolitan Museum of Art, 1976.
31. Pyramid Text 207–12, quoted in Frankfort, op. cit., p. 121.
32. E. A. Wallis Budge, *The Gods of the Egyptians*, Vol. 1, p. 205.
33. Plutarch, p. 131.
34. Budge, *The Gods of the Egyptians*, Vol. 1, p. 204.
35. Pyramid Text 1652; quoted in Frankfort, op. cit., p. 66.
36. Quoted in Frankfort, op. cit., p. 67.
37. Henri Frankfort, *Ancient Egyptian Religion*, pp. 12–13.
38. ibid., p. 13.
39. See Mircea Eliade, *The Myth of the Eternal Return or, Cosmos and History*, pp. 1–48.

40. R. A. Schwaller de Lubicz, *Symbol and the Symbolic*, p. 14.

41. George Hart, *A Dictionary of Egyptian Gods and Goddesses*, London, Routledge & Kegan Paul, 1986, p. 189.

42. Frankfort, *Ancient Egyptian Religion*, p. 7.

43. ibid., pp. 6–7.

44. See Campbell's detailed discussion of the Narmer Palette in *Oriental Mythology*, pp. 51–8.

45. See the picture in Veronica Ions, *Egyptian Mythology*, p. 79.

46. The analogous idea of humanity contributing to divinity, or, as Jung puts it, 'God coming to know himself in man' is explored later in Gnostic thought.

47. Budge, *The Gods of the Egyptians*, Vol. 1, pp. 429–35.

48. John Romer, *People of the Nile*, p. 167.

49. Frankfort, *Ancient Egyptian Religion*, p. 4.

50. Rundle Clark, op. cit., p. 88.

51. Quoted in Lucie Lamy, *Egyptian Mysteries: New Light on Ancient Knowledge*, p. 82.

52. Frankfort, *Ancient Egyptian Religion*, p. 17.

53. Erich Neumann, *The Great Mother*, p. 223.

54. Rundle Clark, op. cit., pp. 28, 87.

55. Mummy of Soutywes, no. 2611m. *c.* 1100 BC. The Louvre.

56. Lamy, op. cit., p. 17.

57. ibid., p. 17.

58. ibid.

59. Schwaller de Lubicz, *Le Roi de la Théocratie Pharaonique*; quoted in Lamy, op. cit., p. 17.

60. Frankfort, *Ancient Egyptian Religion*, p. 64.

61. Eliade, op. cit., p. 92.

62. Lamy, op. cit., p. 51.

63. Arthur Versluis, *The Egyptian Mysteries*, London, Arkana, p. 15.

64. Eliade, op. cit., p. 92.

65. Lamy, op. cit., p. 84.

66. Abbreviated from Budge, *The Gods of the Egyptians*, Vol. 1, pp. 372–87.

67. Quoted in Rundle Clark, op. cit., p. 189.

68. ibid., p. 192.

69. ibid., pp. 194–5.

70. ibid., p. 195.

71. ibid.

72. See Martin Bernal, *Black Athena*.

73. Quoted in Joan C. Engelsman, *The Feminine Dimension of the Divine*, pp. 64–6.

74. Pausanias; quoted in Budge, *The Gods of the Egyptians*, p. 219.

75. Apuleius, *The Golden Ass*, p. 228.

76. Quoted in Rundle Clark, op. cit., p. 88.

77. Apuleius, op. cit., pp. 227–8.

Chapter 7 *Tiamat of Babylon: The Defeat of the Goddess*

1. Quotations from the *Enuma Elish* are from L. W. King, *The Seven Tablets of Creation*, unless otherwise stated. The epic was copied by the scribes of

Assurbanipal for his library at Nineveh from older Babylonian texts, the
originals of which were kept in Babylon itself.

2. Sir James G. Frazer, *The Golden Bough*, Vol. 4, *The Dying God*, p. 108.

   See the myth in the Indian *Rig Veda* in which the god Indra defeats the great
   serpent dragons Danu and her son Vritra, and releases the imprisoned waters
   so that the land is once again rendered fertile after the terrible drought of
   summer. See also John Michel, *City of Revelation*, for the annual celebration
   in Britain of the myth of St George and the Dragon.

3. Also called Bel, which, like Baal, means 'Lord'.

4. Quoted in Joseph Campbell, *Occidental Mythology*, pp. 78–9. This description
   of Marduk closely resembles the Indian god Shiva in Hindu mythology.

5. Trs. Thorkild Jacobsen, *The Treasures of Darkness*, p. 179.

6. In some versions Marduk's head is cut off and humanity is made from his
   blood. See the Vedic myth in which a god (*purusha*) sacrifices his body to
   bring the world into being.

7. Jacobsen, op. cit., pp. 190–1.

8. N. K. Sandars, *The Epic of Gilgamesh*, pp. 62–3.

9. King, op. cit., pp. 131–7.

10. Campbell, op. cit., pp. 80–1.

11. Quoted in Campbell, op. cit., p. 75.

12. C. G. Jung. We regret we are unable to find this reference. See Chapter 1,
    note 35.

13. Laurens van der Post, *Jung and the Story of our Time*, pp. 23–4.

14. Joseph Campbell, *Myths to Live By*, p. 140. Compare the *Mahabharata* in
    India.

15. Homer, *Iliad*, trs. E. V. Rieu, Harmondsworth, Penguin Books, Penguin
    Classics, 1950, pp. 128–9.

16. Assyria intervened in Israel and Syria when Ahaz, King of Judah, bought its
    help against the allied armies of those countries. The people of Israel were
    deported and Judah became a tributary of Assyria.

17. Jane Harrison, *Prolegomena to the Study of the Greek Religion*, introduction, p. x.

18. Lord Byron, 'Hebrew Melodies: The Destruction of Sennacherib'.

19. Quoted by Jacobsen, op. cit., p. 231.

20. ibid., p. 232.

21. ibid., p. 228, from the Erra Epic Tablet IV, lines 27–9.

22. ibid., p. 232, from Assurbanipal, *Annals*, IV.

23. Quoted by Campbell, *Occidental Mythology*, p. 214, from Eduard Meyer,
    Geschichte des Altertums, Stuttgart and Berlin, J. G. Cotta'sche Buchhandlung
    Naschfolger 2–5, Aufln. 1925–37, Vol. III, p. 161.

24. Mircea Eliade, *The Sacred and the Profane*, pp. 157–8.

25. C. G. Jung, *Collected Works*, Vol. 8, *The Structure and Dynamics of the Psyche*,
    para. 326.

26. See Joseph Campbell, *The Hero with a Thousand Faces*.

27. See Indra's slaying of the serpent dragon Vritra in the Vedic Hymn:

    > Like a vehement bull, he took to himself the soma,
    > Drank the pressed drink from three mighty bowls,
    > Picked up his weapon, the fiery bolt,
    > And slew the first-born dragon. (*Rig Veda* 1. 32A, verse 3)

28. John Gray, *Near Eastern Mythology*, p. 85.
29. ibid.
30. Homeric 'Hymn to Apollo', trs. Jules Cashford.
31. Apollonius of Rhodes, *The Voyage of the Argo*, pp. 150–1.
32. C. G. Jung, *Collected Works*, Vol. 14, *Mysterium Coniunctionis*, para. 756.
33. See the Vedic hymns for the similar epiphanies of the sky gods in Aryan India.
34. John A. Phillips, *Eve: The History of an Idea*, p. 7.

Chapter 8 Goddesses of Greece: Gaia, Hera, Artemis and Athena

1. Walter Burkert, *Greek Religion*, p. 48.
2. Jane Harrison, *Prolegomena to the Study of Greek Religion*.
3. Trs. Jules Cashford, in *Harvest*, 1988.
4. Hesiod, quoted in Riane Eisler, *The Chalice and the Blade*, p. 108.
5. Aeschylus, *The Libation Bearers*, p. 127. All quotations from the plays of Aeschylus, Sophocles and Euripides are from David Grene and Richmond Lattimore (eds.), *Greek Tragedies*.
6. Aeschylus, *The Eumenides*, pp. 1–2.
7. Joseph Campbell, *The Hero with a Thousand Faces*, p. 13.
8. Robert Graves, *Greek Myths*, pp. 27–8.
9. Pausanias, viii, 2, 4; quoted in Harrison, op. cit., p. 263.
10. Graves, op. cit., pp. 30–1.
11. ibid., pp. 30–1.
12. Hesiod, *Theogony*, 116–41. All quotations of Hesiod are from Dorothea Wender (trs.), *Hesiod and Theognis*, unless otherwise stated.
13. ibid., pp. 176–218.
14. Pausanias, x, 12, 10; quoted in Harrison, op. cit., p. 263.
15. Hesiod, *Works and Days*, 225. See F. M. Cornford, *From Religion to Philosophy*.
16. Sophocles, *Oedipus Rex*, 24–8.
17. ibid., 97–100.
18. ibid., 313.
19. Carl Kerenyi, *Zeus and Hera: Archetypal Image of Father, Husband and Wife*, p. 135.
20. Marija Gimbutas, *The Goddesses and Gods of Old Europe*, p. 149.
21. ibid., pp. 149–50.
22. For a fuller discussion of this ceremony, see Kerenyi, op. cit., pp. 141–7.
23. Homer, *Iliad*, 14, 346–53.
24. ibid., 14, 213.
25. Harrison, op. cit., p. 316.
26. Kerenyi, op. cit., p. 123.
27. Homer, op. cit., 8, 476–83.
28. Virgil, *Aeneid*, 7, 312.
29. Kerenyi, op. cit., p. 125.
30. E. Gerhard, *Etruskisches Spiegel*, Vol. V, p. 60.
31. Burkert, op. cit., p. 131.

32. Homer, op. cit., 8, 18–28.
33. Kerenyi, op. cit., pp. 3–20.
34. James Hillman, 'And Huge is Ugly', in John Button (ed.), *The Green Fuse*, p. 192.
35. Hesiod, *Theogony*, 209.
36. Homer, *Odyssey*, 9.
37. Trs. Jules Cashford, in *Harvest*, 1987.
38. Aeschylus, *Agamemnon*, 133.
39. Aeschylus, fragment, 342.
40. Homer, *Odyssey*, 6, 102–8.
41. Harrison, *Themis*, p. 114.
42. Homer, *Iliad*, 5, 51–2.
43. ibid., 21, 483–4.
44. Euripides, *Hippolytus*, 165–8.
45. Ginette Paris, *Pagan Meditations*, p. 119. See her discussion of abortion as a sacrifice to Artemis, pp. 139–48.
46. Gimbutas, in *The Goddesses and Gods of Old Europe*, observes that 'in the cave of Acrotiri near ancient Kydonia, a festival in honour of Panagia (Mary) Arkoudiotissa ("she of the bear") is celebrated on the second day in February' (p. 200).
47. Burkert, op. cit., p. 151.
48. D. H. Lawrence, *Women in Love*, Harmondsworth, Penguin Classics, 1950.
49. Euripides, op. cit., 71–8.
50. ibid., 94–5.
51. ibid., 102–3.
52. Burkert, op. cit., pp. 151–2.
53. Aeschylus, fragment, 170.
54. Sophocles, *Trachinian Women*, 214.
55. Harrison, *Themis*, p. 502.
56. Carl Kerenyi, *The Heroes of the Greeks*, p. 146.
57. Tacitus, quoted in Barbara Walker, *The Woman's Encyclopaedia of Myths and Secrets*, p. 59.
58. ibid., p. 59.
59. E. Cassirer, *The Philosophy of Symbolic Forms*, Vol. II, p. 218. See also Neumann, *The Origins and History of Consciousness*, p. 369.
60. Homeric 'Hymn to Athena', trs. Jules Cashford.
61. See Carl Kerenyi, *Athene: Virgin and Mother in Greek Religion*, pp. 17–18. As Plutarch puts it: 'The Greeks are correct in saying and believing that the dove is the sacred bird of Aphrodite, that the serpent is sacred to Athena, the raven to Apollo, and the dog to Artemis.' 'Isis and Osiris', p. 165.
62. Hesiod, *Theogony*, 52–3.
63. J. J. Bachofen, *Myth, Religion and Mother Right*.
64. Harrison, *Prolegomena*, p. 303.
65. Aeschylus, *The Eumenides*, 658–66. See Riane Eisler's discussion in *The Chalice and the Blade*, pp. 78–89.
66. Aeschylus, *The Eumenides*, 736–8.
67. Harrison, *Prolegomena*, p. 304.
68. Gimbutas, op. cit., p. 148.

69. Hillman, op. cit., p. 190.
70. Kerenyi, *Athene*, p. 7.
71. Walter F. Otto, *The Homeric Gods*, p. 54.
72. Homer, *Iliad*, I, 193–200.
73. Sophocles, *Ajax*, 832.
74. Joseph Campbell, *Occidental Mythology*, p. 154.
75. ibid., p. 154.
76. Harrison, *Prolegomena*, p. 187.
77. Graves, op. cit., I, pp. 17, 244.
78. Homeric 'Hymn to Athena', trs. Jules Cashford.
79. Burkert, op. cit., p. 142.

PART II: THE SACRED MARRIAGE

Chapter 9 Goddesses of Greece: Aphrodite, Demeter and Persephone

1. First Homeric 'Hymn to Aphrodite', trs. Jules Cashford, in *Harvest*, 1987.
2. Second Homeric 'Hymn to Aphrodite', trs. Jules Cashford.
3. Homer, *Iliad*, 14, 294–6.
4. Euripides, *Medea*, 844.
5. Erich Neumann, *The Great Mother*, p. 145: 'With the development of the patriarchate the Great Goddess has become the Goddess of Love, and the power of the Feminine has been reduced to the power of sexuality.'
6. Hesiod, *Theogony*, 189–99. All quotations of Hesiod are from Dorothea Wender (trs.) *Hesiod and Theogonis* unless otherwise stated.
7. Aeschylus, *Danaides*.
8. Jane Harrison, *Prolegomena to the Study of Greek Religion*, p. 312.
9. Homer, *Odyssey*, 8, 270.
10. Edgar Wind, *Pagan Mysteries in the Renaissance*, p. 125.
11. Ginette Paris, *Pagan Meditations*, p. 18.
12. ibid.
13. Euripides, *Hippolytus*, 555.
14. Harrison, op. cit., p. 308.
15. Sir James G. Frazer, *The Golden Bough*, Vol. 5, *Adonis, Attis, Osiris*, p. 32. See also Martin Bernal, *Black Athena*, p. 127.
16. Harrison, op. cit., p. 565.
17. ibid., pp. 292–300.
18. Euripides, *Hippolytus*, 528–32.
19. Plato, *Symposium*, trs. W. R. M. Lamb, Cambridge, Mass., Harvard University Press, and London, Heinemann, Loeb Classical Library, 1935, Vol. 3, pp. 74–245, 189d–93d.
20. Euripides, *Hippolytus*, 1268–79.
21. Frazer, op. cit., p. 257.
22. Homer, *Iliad*, 5, 500–1, trs. Jules Cashford.

23. G. E. Mylonas, *Eleusis*: 'We may assume that tradition, in general, places the introduction of the cult of Demeter in the second half of the fifteenth century BC', p. 14. See Eugene Goblet d'Alviella, *The Mysteries of Eleusis*, p. 7, and Mircea Eliade, *A History of Religious Ideas*, Vol. 1, p. 294: 'The Mysteries were celebrated at Eleusis for nearly two thousand years.'
24. Hesiod, *Theogony*, 969–71.
25. Harrison, op. cit., p. 564, note 3.
26. Homer, *Odyssey*, 5, 125.
27. 'All commentators agree that the Hymn relates events which occurred long before its composition. The first sanctuary was built in the fifteenth century BC.' Mylonas, op. cit., p. 41.

    Kerenyi finds the earliest reference to Persephone in the Middle Minoan period in Crete, shortly before 2000 BC (Carl Kerenyi, *Eleusis*, p. xix). This picture of Persephone is shown in Fig. 11.
28. Walter F. Otto, *The Homeric Gods*, p. 36.
29. Harrison, op. cit., p. 158.
30. Trs. Jules Cashford.
31. Bernal, op. cit., pp. 118–19.
32. Harrison, op. cit., p. 567.
33. ibid., p. 121.
34. Walter Burkert, *Greek Religion*, p. 245.
35. Walter F. Otto, 'The Meaning of the Eleusinian Mysteries', in *The Mysteries: Papers from the Eranos Yearbooks*, 2, p. 19.
36. Harrison, op. cit., p. 122.
37. ibid., p. 124.
38. Plutarch, 'Isis and Osiris', p. 161.
39. Burkert, op. cit., p. 286.
40. ibid., p. 286.
41. Harrison, op. cit., p. 543.
42. Mylonas, op. cit., p. 264.
43. P. Foucart, *Les Mystères d'Eleusis*, Paris, 1914, p. 392ff.
44. Kerenyi, *Eleusis*, p. 80.
45. Sophocles, Fragment from 'Triptolemos'; quoted in Burkert, op. cit., p. 289.
46. Pindar, Fragment 137a; quoted in Burkert, op. cit., p. 289.
47. Harrison, op. cit., p. 563.
48. Goblet d'Alviella, op. cit., p. 26.
49. Kerenyi, *Eleusis*, p. 27.
50. Harrison, op. cit., pp. 563–4.
51. Kerenyi, *Eleusis*, p. 92.
52. Kerenyi, *Eleusis*, p. 27.
53. Harrison, op. cit., p. 555.
54. Kerenyi, *Eleusis*, p. 128.
55. ibid., p. 128.
56. Euripides, *Hypsipyle*, fragment 757.
57. Quoted by Harrison, op. cit., p. 549.
58. Goblet d'Alviella, op. cit., p. 65.
59. ibid., p. 65.

Chapter 10 Cybele: Great Goddess of Anatolia and Rome

1. *Orphei Hymni*, G. Quandt (ed.), Berlin, 1941; quoted in M. J. Vermaseren, *Cybele and Attis*, p. 10.
2. Trs. Jules Cashford, *Harvest*, Vol. 35, 1989–90, p. 209.
3. Sophocles, *Philotectes*, 391, quoted in Vermaseren, op. cit., p. 81.
4. Vermaseren, op. cit., p. 36.
5. ibid., p. 49.
6. G. B. Pighi, *La Poesia Religiosa Romana*, Bologna, 1958, quoted in Vermaseren, op. cit., p. 87.
7. Julian, *Orat.*, G. Rochefort (ed.), V, 159a, Paris, 1963, quoted in Vermaseren, p. 32.
8. Walter Burkert, *Structure and History in Greek Mythology and Ritual*, p. 103.
9. Vermaseren, op. cit., p. 22.
10. ibid., p. 24.
11. ibid.
12. Sir Leonard Woolley, *Ur of the Chaldees*, p. 57, and Sir Arthur Evans, *The Palace of Minos*, Vol. 4i, p. 348.
13. E. O. James, *The Cult of the Mother Goddess*, p. 87.
14. Vermaseren, op. cit., p. 24.
15. ibid., p. 39.
16. Lucretius, *De Rerum Naturae*, C. Bailey (ed.), ii, 600–609, Oxford, 1947, quoted in James, op. cit., p. 170.
17. Vermaseren, op. cit., p. 27.
18. Virgil, *Aeneid*, X, 252–5, quoted in Vermaseren, op. cit., p. 86.
19. Julian, Chapter VI, 112, quoted in Vermaseren, op. cit., pp. 86–7.
20. Pighi, op. cit., quoted in Vermaseren, op. cit., p. 87.
21. Vermaseren, op. cit., pp. 72–3.
22. Pamela Berger, *The Goddess Obscured*, pp. 33–4.
23. ibid., p. 38.
24. Burkert, op. cit., pp. 104–5.
25. Vermaseren, op. cit., p. 109.
26. ibid., p. 110.
27. Osiris's member had a similar function.
28. Jane Harrison, *Themis*, p. 26.
29. Burkert, op. cit., p. 103.
30. James, op. cit., p. 166.
31. Burkert, op. cit., p. 104.
32. Franz Cumont, *The Mysteries of Mithra*, p. 179.
33. The image of Lazarus comes to mind.
34. Firmacus Maternus (*de errore profanarum religionum*), writing in AD 350 about the false doctrines of the pagan religions; quoted in Vermaseren, op. cit., p. 116.
35. William Anderson, *The Rise of the Gothic*, p. 108.
36. ibid., p. 109. See also his *Green Man*.
37. Henry Corbin, *Creative Imagination in the Sufism of Ibn Arabi*, pp. 55–67. Ibn Arabi was the disciple of *Khidr*, who is also called 'The Hidden Imam'. He may be understood as the inner, invisible guide of the seer and mystic, personifying the very essence of his being. Corbin writes that *Khidr* 'is

indeed associated with every aspect of Nature's greenness' and that this in turn is connected with a 'special mode of perception implied by the presence of *Khadir*, a mode of perception that is bound up with the extraordinary pre-eminence accorded to the color green in Islam'. The colour of the supreme centre of man's being, the 'mystery of mysteries', is green. It is interesting to bear this in mind when considering Jung's vision of the green Christ.

38. C. G. Jung, in his *Collected Works*, Vol. 13, *Alchemical Studies*, para. 267, quotes the following passage from an alchemical treatise describing Mercurius:

'I contain the light of nature; I am dark and light; I come forth from heaven and earth; I am known and yet do not exist at all; by virtue of the sun's rays all colours shine in me, and all metals. I am the carbuncle of the sun, the most noble purified earth, through which you may change copper, iron, tin, and lead into gold.'

39. C. G. Jung, *Memories, Dreams and Reflections*, p. 201.
40. Jane Harrison, *Prolegomena to the Study of Greek Religion*.
41. ibid., p. 489.
42. Vermaseren, op. cit., pp. 121–3.
43. Julian, III, 106, quoted in Vermaseren, op. cit., p. 87.
44. Harrison, *Prolegomena*, p. 573.
45. ibid., p. 534:

By a most unhappy chance our main evidence as to the Sacred Marriage of the mysteries comes to us from the Christian Fathers; their prejudiced imaginations see in its beautiful symbolism only the record of unbridled license. We may and must discredit their unclean interpretations, but we have no ground for doubting the substantial accuracy of their statements as to ritual procedure. They were preaching to men who had been initiated in the very mysteries they describe, and any mis-statement as to ritual would have discredited their teaching.

46. ibid., pp. 535–6.
47. ibid., p. 535.
48. Harrison, *Themis*, pp. 54–5.
49. Gertrude Levy, *The Gate of Horn*, p. 293.

Chapter 11 The Iron Age: the Great Father God Yahweh– Elohim

1. Compare the imagery of creation in the *Rig Veda X*:

The non-existent was not, the existent was not; then the world was not, nor the firmament, nor that which is above the firmament . . . How could there be the deep unfathomable water? . . . There was no indication of day or night; That One unbreathed upon breathed of his own strength, other than That there was nothing else whatever. There was darkness covered by darkness in the beginning, all this world was indistinguishable water.

Raymond Van Over (ed.), *Eastern Mysticism*, New York, New American Library, 1977, Vol. 1, p. 65.

2. Joseph Campbell, *The Hero with a Thousand Faces*, p. 249.

3. Joseph Campbell, *Occidental Mythology*, p. 95.

4. The *Enuma Elish*; see Chapter 7, note 1.

5. Frazer writes: 'The account of creation given in the first chapter of Genesis, which has been so much praised for its simple grandeur and sublimity, is merely a rationalised version of the old myth of the fight with the dragon.' *The Golden Bough*, Vol. 4, *The Dying God*, p. 106.

6. Robert Graves and Raphael Patai, *Hebrew Myths*, p. 27; see also p. 33.

7. ibid., p. 31.

8. ibid.

9. ibid., p. 26.

10. Graves and Patai say of this passage that the phrase *nahash bariah*, describing Leviathan, could also mean 'bolted in serpent', which refers back once again to Marduk's struggle to contain Tiamat. ibid., p. 33.

11. John A. Phillips, *Eve: The History of an Idea*, p. 12.

12. S. N. Kramer, *From the Poetry of Sumer*, p. 45.

13. Breasted writes in his *Memphite Theology*, 1901, p. 54: 'The above conception of the world forms quite a sufficient basis for suggesting that the earlier notions of *nous* and *logos*, hitherto supposed to have been introduced into Egypt from abroad at a much later date, were present at this early period.'

14. Phillips, op. cit., p. 13.

15. Graves and Patai, op. cit., p. 25.

16. Campbell, *Occidental Mythology*, p. 105.

17. S. H. Hooke, *Middle Eastern Mythology*, p. 119.

18. Graves and Patai, op. cit., p. 25.

19. A similar connection exists between the Latin *homo* (man) and *humus* (earth), both of which can be traced to an ancient Indo-European root that in Greek produced *chthon* (earth), *chamai* (on the earth) and *epichthonios* (human). Graves and Patai, op. cit., p. 63, note 1.

20. Genesis 2, 3 originally dated to before the Exile of 586 BC, but was altered after the Exile, or possibly earlier, after the dispersal by Assyria in 721 BC of the ten tribes of the northern state of Israel.

21. Northrop Frye, *The Great Code: The Bible and Literature*, p. 54.

22. ibid., p. 41.

23. ibid.

24. S. N. Kramer, *History Begins at Sumer*, p. 196.

25. Frye, op. cit., p. 142.

26. N. K. Sandars, *The Epic of Gilgamesh*, p. 110.

27. ibid., pp. 111–12.

28. From *Assyrian and Babylonian Literature*, New York, D. Appleton & Co., 1901, quoted in B. Walker, *The Woman's Encyclopedia of Myths and Secrets*.

29. Sandars, op. cit., p. 112.

30. See Frye's discussion in *The Great Code*, p. 143.

31. Kramer, op. cit., p. 189.

32. Sandars, op. cit., p. 63.

33. Hooke, op. cit., p. 126.

34. ibid., pp. 125–6.

35. James B. Pritchard, *The Ancient Near East*, Vol. 1, p. 234.

36. See extracts from *The Burden of Isis* in Chapter 6, pp. 240–1, and Chapter 6, note 24.

37. The Masoretic text for verse 3 of the same text reads: 'A man of pains and acquainted with disease'. Verses 10–12, which follow in the Masoretic text, evoke the image of Job, the 'suffering servant'.
38. Mircea Eliade, *A History of Religious Ideas*, p. 172.
39. Owen Barfield, *Saving the Appearances*, p. 111.
40. ibid., p. 110.
41. William Shakespeare, *The Tempest*, III, ii.
42. Barfield, op. cit., p. 109.
43. ibid., p. 113.
44. Gerhard von Rad, *Old Testament Theology*, p. 11.
45. Merlin Stone, *The Paradise Papers*, pp. 119, 128–30.
46. Barfield, op. cit., p. 109.
47. Raphael Patai, *The Hebrew Goddess*, p. 28.
48. ibid., pp. 28–9.
49. ibid., p. 30.
50. Elaine Pagels, 'The Suppressed Gnostic Feminism', *The New York Review*, 26, no. 18, November 22, 1979, 42.
51. Graves and Patai, op. cit., p. 28.
52. ibid., p. 28.
53. C. G. Jung, *Letters*, Vol. 2, p. 434.
54. Jane Harrison, *Themis*, p. 28.
55. Patai, op. cit., p. 86.
56. Ilan Halevi, *A History of the Jews*, p. 37.

Chapter 12 The Hidden Goddess in the Old Testament

1. Ilan Halevi, *A History of the Jews*, p. 45.
2. Gerhard von Rad, *Old Testament Theology*, Vol. 1 and Mircea Eliade, *A History of Religious Ideas*, Vol. 1, p. 186.
3. Raphael Patai, *The Hebrew Goddess*, p. 29.
4. ibid., pp. 25–6.
5. ibid., p. 69.
6. ibid., p. 94. His conclusion is based on the studies of the Ark made by Gressman and Morgenstern. See bibliography in *The Hebrew Goddess*.
7. ibid., pp. 94–5.
8. ibid., p. 69.
9. ibid., p. 70.
10. ibid., p. 71.
11. It is most interesting that, in his discussion of the Kabbalistic Tetrad, Patai notes that the four principal Canaanite deities of this era – El, Asherah, Anath and Baal, the Father, Mother, Daughter and Son – re-emerge in the medieval Kabbalistic literature as the four divine elements of the Tetragrammaton, Yahweh (YHWH), the name of God. The four elements are Wisdom (*Hokhmah*), Understanding (*Bina*), Beauty (*Tif'eret*) and Kingship (*Malkhut*). Wisdom is identified with the Father, Understanding with the Mother, Beauty with the Son, and Kingship with the Daughter. See the 'Kabbalistic Tetrad' in Patai, op. cit., p. 116.
12. Eliade, op. cit., p. 185.
13. Patai, op. cit., p. 61.

14. ibid., p. 61.
15. John Gray, *Near Eastern Mythology*, p. 87.
16. Patai, op. cit., p. 54.
17. Lawrence Burdin-Robertson, *The Goddesses of Chaldea, Syria and Egypt*, p. 125.
18. ibid., p. 126.
19. Patai, op. cit., p. 57.
20. Owen Barfield, *Saving the Appearances*, p. 111.
21. Patai, op. cit., p. 85.
22. ibid., p. 41.
23. ibid., p. 51.
24. Barfield, op. cit., p. 149.
25. Northrop Frye, *The Great Code*, p. 152.
26. Joseph Campbell, *Occidental Mythology*, p. 127.
27. Edmund Leech and D. Alan Aycock, 'Why did Moses have a Sister?' in *Structuralist Interpretations of Biblical Myth*, pp. 33–66.
28. Patai, op. cit., pp. 98, 287.
29. ibid., p. 287.
30. ibid., p. 288.
31. Campbell, op. cit., p. 138. He comments further that 'whereas elsewhere the principle of divine life is symbolized as a divine individual (Dumuzi–Adonis–Attis–Dionysos–Christ), in Judaism it is the People of Israel whose mythic history thus serves the function that in other cults belongs to an incarnation or manifestation of God' (p. 139).
32. Frye, op. cit., p. 107.
33. Rad, introduction to *Wisdom in Israel*, p. 9.
34. Gudea cylinder A, trs. Scharff and Moortgat, abridged; quoted by Campbell, op. cit., p. 118.
35. Quoted in Joan C. Engelsman, *The Feminine Dimension of the Divine*, pp. 64–6.
36. ibid., p. 75.
37. See *The Burden of Isis*, trs. James Teackle Dennis, London, John Murray, 1910; see also Chapter 6, pp. 240–1, and Chapter 6, note 24.
38. Henry Vaughan, 'The Night'.
39. G. R. S. Mead, *The Wedding Song of Wisdom*.
40. C. G. Jung, *Collected Works*, Vol. 9ii, *Aion*, paras. 303, 308.
41. Samuel Taylor Coleridge, *Biographia Literaria*, p. 139.

> They and only they can acquire the philosophic imagination, the sacred power of self-intuition, who *within themselves* can interpret and understand the symbol, that the wings of the air sylph are forming within the skin of the caterpillar, those only who feel in their own spirits the same instinct which impels the chrysalis of the horned fly to leave room in the involucrum for antennae yet to come. They know and feel that the potential works in them, even as the actual works on them!

Chapter 13 Eve: the Mother of All Living

1. W. B. Yeats, 'The Philosophy of Shelley's Poetry', in Alexander Norman Jeffares (ed.), *Yeats: Selected Criticism and Prose*, London, Macmillan and Pan Books, 1980, p. 65.

2. C. G. Jung, *Collected Works*, Vol. 8, *The Structure and Dynamics of the Psyche*, para. 805.
3. Joseph Campbell, *Occidental Mythology*, p. 17.
4. S. H. Hooke, *Middle Eastern Mythology*, p. 115.
5. See Robert Graves and Raphael Patai, *Hebrew Myths*, p. 69. They point out that Eve's name is the Hebrew form of the goddess Heba, Khebet or Khiba, who was the Hittite equivalent of Anath, who, in Babylonia, was Ishtar.
6. Campbell, op. cit., p. 31.
7. John A. Phillips, *Eve: The History of an Idea*, p. 15.
8. ibid., p. 15.
9. Eugene Goblet d'Alviella, *The Migration of Symbols*, p. 157.
10. ibid., pp. 153, 173. See his discussion of the 'Symbolism and Mythology of the Tree', pp. 118–76.
11. See Gurdjieff's exposition of understanding as the result of the union of Knowledge and Being. P. D. Ouspensky, *In Search of the Miraculous*, pp. 64–8.
12. Campbell, op. cit., p. 106.
13. Erich Neumann, *The Origins and History of Consciousness*, p. 49.
14. See the symbolism of the shaman's rod in Mircea Eliade, *Shamanism*.
15. Joseph Campbell, *The Mythic Image*, p. 294.
16. Northrop Frye, *The Great Code*, p. xviii. Quoted in Chapter 10.
17. See Aldous Huxley, *The Doors of Perception*, pp. 23–4.
18. The Ophite sect took Yahweh as evil and the serpent as good, but the level of fairy-tale interpretation remains the same.
19. N. K. Sandars, *The Epic of Gilgamesh*, p. 106.
20. Yeats, 'Sailing to Byzantium', in *Collected Poems*, p. 218.
21. Goethe, *Faust*, trs. P. Wayne, Harmondsworth, Penguin, 1969, p. 67.

> Two souls, alas, are housed within my breast,
> And each will wrestle for the mastery there.
> The one has passion's craving crude for love,
> And hugs a world where sweet the senses rage;
> The other longs for pastures fair above,
> Leaving the murk for lofty heritage.

22. Erich Fromm, D. T. Suzuki and Richard de Martino, *Zen Buddhism and Psychoanalysis*, p. 87.
23. Erich Fromm, *You Shall Be As Gods*, pp. 70–1.
24. T. S. Eliot, 'Burnt Norton', *Four Quartets*, p. 16.
25. This text, probably dating to before AD 400, was translated from an original Hebrew text in the centuries between 100 BC and AD 200. See the Introduction by M. D. Johnson to 'The Life of Adam and Eve', in James H. Charlesworth (ed.), *The Old Testament Pseudepigrapha*, Vol. 2, pp. 249–52.
26. Charlesworth, 'The Life of Adam and Eve', p. 287.
27. ibid., p. 295.
28. Louis H. Ginzberg, *Legends of the Jews*, Book 1, p. 66.
29. ibid., p. 67.
30. *The Zohar*, Harry Sperling and Maurice Simon (trs.), London, Soncino Press, 1984, 5 vols., I, 20a.
31. Edward Whitmont, *The Return of the Goddess*, p. 125.

32. 'Inanna and the *Huluppu*-Tree', in D. Wolkstein and S. N. Kramer, *Inanna*, p. 9.
33. ibid., p. 9.
34. In the Masoretic text the translation reads 'night-monster'.
35. Raphael Patai, *The Hebrew Goddess*, p. 230.
36. ibid., p. 224.
37. *Zohar*, I, 19b, quoted in Patai, op. cit., p. 237.
38. Phillips, op. cit., p. 104.
39. Philo Judaeus, *Hypothetica*, Chapter 11, verses 14–17, in F. H. Colson and G. H. Whitaker (trs.), *Philo*, Vol. 10; quoted by Phillips, op. cit., p. 51.
40. *Zohar*, III, 19a.
41. The Testament of Reuben from H. F. D. Sparks (ed.), *The Apocryphal New Testament*, p. 519.
42. The lion and the dragon are both images of the Mother Goddess.
43. Ginzberg, op. cit., p. 67.
44. Phillips, op. cit., p. 57.
45. Luther, *Lectures on Genesis*, Chapters 1–5, p. 151, quoted in Phillips, op. cit., p. 58.
46. Whitmont, op. cit., p. 124.
47. See Peter Brown, *The Body and Society*, for the position of women in early Christian society.
48. Hesiod, *Works and Days*, trs. after H. G. Evelyn-White, pp. 55–77. Harrison comments on Hesiod's poem:

    Through all the magic of a poet, caught and enchanted himself by the vision of a lovely woman, there gleams the ugly malice of theological animus. Zeus the Father will have no great Earth-goddess, Mother and Maid in one . . . but her figure *is* from the beginning, so he remakes it.

    (Jane Harrison, *Prolegomena to the Study of Greek Religion*, p. 285.)
49. Hesiod, *Works and Days*, 94–100.
50. Hesiod, *Theogony*, trs. H. G. Evelyn-White, 590.
51. Jane Harrison, 'Pandora's Box', *Journal of Hellenistic Studies*, 20: 108–9.
52. Hesiod, *Theogony*, 573–90.
53. ibid., 585–90.
54. Tertullian, *De Corona Militis*, quoted in Phillips, op. cit., p. 21.
55. John Chrysostom (*c.* 347–407), *In Mattheum Homili*, xxxii, *Ex Capitae*, xix (a), Migne, *Patrologiae Graecae*, Vol. 56, p. 803; quoted in Phillips, op. cit., p. 22.
56. Phillips, op. cit., p. 20.
57. A similar synthesis, or abstraction, can be seen in the astrological symbolism of Aquarius, the Water Bearer, who in the oldest zodiac pictures (e.g., the second-century-AD zodiac in the Temple of Denderah, and the eleventh-century York zodiac in England) carries the two vessels of life and death. In the later zodiacs the Water Bearer carries only one vessel, and the richness of the original symbolism is lost.
58. Dora and Erwin Panofsky, *Pandora's Box*, p. 12.
59. Compare the vase imagery of the Virgin Mary, the sealed vessel, and the vase or jar of oil that Mary Magdalene holds; also the alchemical vessel in Alchemy; all of which carry the same image of containment as Pandora's urn.

60. Apuleius, *The Golden Ass*, pp. 14–26. Panofsky, op. cit., pp. 17–19.
61. Thomas Aquinas, *Summa Theologiae*, 1, 93, 4 ad.1; quoted in Marina Warner, *Alone of All Her Sex*, p. 179.
62. Aquinas, op. cit., 1a., 92, i; quoted in Phillips, op. cit., p. 35.
63. John Milton, *Paradise Lost*, Bk. 4, 299.
64. James Hillman, *The Myth of Analysis*, pp. 217–18. Simone de Beauvoir comments on the same subject:

> Humanity is male and man defines woman not in herself, but as relative to him; she is not regarded as an autonomous being ... She is defined and differentiated with reference to man and not he with reference to her; she is the incidental, he is the Absolute – she is the Other.

(The Second Sex, p. 16)
65. Claus Westermann, *Genesis*, 1–12, p. 357; quoted in Phillips, op. cit., p. 115.
66. Aristotle, *On the Generation of Animals*, 729a, 22, quoted in Hillman, op. cit., p. 228.
67. Aquinas, op. cit., 1a, 92, quoted in Phillips, op. cit., p. 35.
68. *The Image of Man*, London, Arts Council Publication, 1982, p. 180.
69. Plato, *The Timaeus*, in R. D. Archer-Hind (ed.), *The Philosophy of Plato and Aristotle*, New York, Arno Press, 1973, 42, D.
70. Freud, *An Outline of Psychoanalysis*, SE, XXIII, pp. 193–4; quoted in Hillman, op. cit., p. 241.
71. Hillman, op. cit., p. 243.
72. C. G. Jung, *Collected Works*, Vol. 6, *Psychological Types*, para. 9.
73. Quoted in Phillips, op. cit., frontispiece.
74. ibid., p. 41.
75. C. G. Jung. We regret we are unable to find this reference.
76. John Milton, *Paradise Lost*, Book 10, 867–95.
77. Phillips, op. cit., pp. 44–5.
78. H. Kramer and J. Sprenger, *Malleus Maleficarum*, p. 47.
79. Tertullian, *On the Apparel of Women*, quoted in Phillips, op. cit., p. 76.
80. Tertullian, *Adversus Hermogenem*, pp. 2–3, quoted in H. Bettenson (ed.), *The Early Christian Fathers*, p. 108.
81. Tertullian, *De Carne Christi*, pp. 4–5, quoted in Bettenson, op. cit., p. 125.
82. Quoted by Phillips, op. cit., p. 77.
83. Marina Warner, *Alone of All Her Sex*, p. 306.
84. Kramer and Sprenger, op. cit., p. 43.
85. Gregory Zilboorg, *A History of Medical Psychology*, New York, Norton, 1941, pp. 161–2.
86. Montaigne, *Essais*, Vol. IX, p. 22, quoted in Zilboorg, op. cit.
87. Donnah Zohar, *Quantum Self*.
88. Warner, op. cit., p. 58.
89. W. B. Yeats, 'Crazy Jane on the Day of Judgement', *Collected Poems*, pp. 291–2.
90. Warner, op. cit., p. 57.
91. Hillman, op. cit., p. 219.
92. Warner, op. cit., p. 54.
93. John Chrysostom, from *De Virginitate*, quoted in an encyclical letter of Pope Pius XII, 25 March 1954.

94. See Mircea Eliade, *Rites and Symbols of Initiation*, p. 102.

95. Hillman, op. cit., pp. 216–17.

96. J. W. Trigg, *Origen*, p. 109.

97. Origen, 'Hom. in Leviticum', xii, 4, in Bettenson, op. cit., p. 220.

98. Henry Bettenson (ed.), *Documents of the Christian Church*, p. 213.

99. Augustine conceived the doctrine of original sin in response to the heresy of the British monk Pelagius. See Elaine Pagels, *Adam, Eve and the Serpent*, pp. 124–6. See also the important book by Uta Ranke-Heinemann, *Eunuchs for Heaven: The Catholic Church and Sexuality*, which was published too late to be included in this discussion.

100. Pagels, op. cit., p. 99.

101. Augustine, *De Nuptiis et Concupiscentia*, 1, 8 (7), quoted in Warner, op. cit., p. 54.

102. Warner, op. cit., p. 54.

103. Augustine, *De Trin*, 13, quoted in H. Bettenson (ed.), *The Later Christian Fathers*, p. 220.

104. Augustine, quoted in Pagels, op. cit., p. 131.

105. Augustine, *de Civ. Dei*, 14. 13, and *Op. imp. c. Jul.* 6. 22, quoted in Bettenson (ed.), op. cit., pp. 196–7.

106. Hillman, op. cit., p. 219.

107. *Corpus Iuris Canonici*, quoted in E. and G. Strachan, *Freeing the Feminine*, p. 122.

108. Philip Sherrard, *The Rape of Man and Nature*, p. 21.

109. William Shakespeare, *Julius Caesar*, III, ii.

110. William Blake, 'A Descriptive Catalogue: Vision of the Last Judgement', in *Poetry and Prose of William Blake*, ed. Geoffrey Keynes, p. 651.

111. Augustine, *Confessions*, Book X, Chapter 27.

112. Letter 22, Philip Schaff and Henry Wave (trs.), *The Nicene and Post Nicene Fathers of the Christian Church*, 6:30, quoted in Warner, op. cit., p. 54.

113. Irenaeus, *Adversus Haereses*, III, xxii, 4, in Bettenson (ed.), *The Early Christian Fathers*, p. 74.

114. See Otto Rank, *The Myth of the Birth of the Hero*, New York, 1941, and Joseph Campbell, *The Hero with a Thousand Faces*.

115. Tertullian, *De Carne Christi*, p. 17 in Bettenson (ed.), *The Early Christian Fathers*, p. 126.

116. Phillips, op. cit., p. 135.

117. See Rosemary Radford Ruether's discussion in *Sexism and God-talk: Towards a Feminist Theology*, Boston, Mass., Beacon Press, 1983, pp. 97–9.

118. Luther, op. cit., 69, 115, quoted in Phillips, op. cit., p. 105.

119. John Calvin, *Commentary on Genesis*, Book ii. 9, quoted in Phillips, op. cit., p. 99.

120. Luther, op. cit., 69, 115, quoted in Phillips, op. cit., p. 104.

121. Calvin, op. cit., Chapter 2, verse 18, quoted in Phillips, op. cit., pp. 105–6.

122. Karl Barth, *Church Dogmatics*, 3:2, p. 287.

123. ibid., 3:4, p. 170.

124. Quoted from the Oxyrhynchus Manuscript in Frank C. Happold, *Mysticism*, pp. 174–5.

125. Francis Bacon, quoted by Carolyn Merchant in *The Death of Nature*, p. 169.

126. Descartes, quoted in Maurice Ashe, *New Renaissance*, p. 59.

127. C. G. Jung, *Man and His Symbols*, p. 85.
128. Tertullian, *Adversus Praxean*, 16, in Bettenson (ed.), *The Early Christian Fathers*, p. 122.
129. The Gospel of Thomas, Logion 22.
130. ibid., Logion 77.
131. William Blake, Letter to the Revd Dr Trusler, 23.8.1799, in Geoffrey Keynes (ed.), *Poetry and Prose of William Blake*, p. 835.
132. Alexander Pope, *An Essay on Man*, lines 237–46.
133. John G. Neihardt, *Black Elk Speaks*, p. 43.
134. William Shakespeare, *The Merchant of Venice*, V, i.

Chapter 14 Mary: the Return of the Goddess

1. Joseph Campbell, *Occidental Mythology*, p. 45. The attributions to Mary are from *Aspirations from the Litany of Loreto*, fifteenth century; sanctioned 1587.
2. Jane Harrison, *Prolegomena to the Study of Greek Religion*, p. 270.
3. Marina Warner, *Alone of All Her Sex: The Myth and Cult of the Virgin Mary*, p. 11. The parallel between the image of 'overshadowing' and the shekhinah is significant.
4. Quoted in ibid., p. 242.
5. *Munificentissimus Deus*. The Papal Bull of 1954 was called *Ad Caeli Reginam*.
6. *Madonna*, London, Orbis Publishing, 1984. See also Bruce Bernard, *Mary Queen of Heaven*.
7. 'Moral, philosophical, and religious problems are, on account of their universal validity, the most likely to call for mythological compensation.' C. G. Jung, *Collected Works*, Vol. 7, *Two Essays on Analytical Psychology*, para. 284.
8. See Robert Ornstein, *The Psychology of Consciousness*, Chapter 7: 'The Education of the Intuitive Mode', pp. 143–79.
9. Warner, op. cit., p. 335.
10. ibid.
11. ibid., p. xxiv.
12. The question, for example, as to whether there can be a priori empirical statements (Emmanuel Kant, *Critique of Pure Reason*) is not relevant when 'archetypal' is used as an adjective conferring value rather than 'archetype' used as a noun. See James Hillman, *Archetypal Psychology: A Brief Account*, p. 11.
13. Warner, op. cit., p. 263.
14. Eithne Wilkins, *The Rose Garden Game*, p. 147.
15. Petrarch, 'Hymn to the Virgin', quoted in Warner, op. cit., p. 263.
16. The Protoevangelium, also known as the Book of James, second century. See Wilkins, op. cit., p. 94.
17. Wilkins, op. cit., pp. 96–7.
18. Erich Neumann, *The Great Mother*, p. 233.
19. ibid., p. 233.
20. The following section was adapted in Jules Cashford, 'Universal Christmas', *Financial Times: Weekend Edition*, 24 December 1989.
21. St Jerome, in Sir James G. Frazer, *The Golden Bough*, Vol. 5, *Adonis, Attis, Osiris*, p. 257.

22. Quoted in G. R. S. Mead, *Thrice Greatest Hermes*, Vol. III, pp. 160–1.
23. 'O Oriens', sung during Advent at Vespers on 21 December, from the Breviary.
24. Warner, op. cit., p. 35.
25. Geza Vermes, *Jesus the Jew*, pp. 215–18.
26. ibid., p. 222.
27. Warner, op. cit., Prologue, p. xxi.
28. Alan Watts, *Myth and Ritual in Christianity*, p. 126.
29. See Watts's chapter 'Christmas and Epiphany', ibid., pp. 115–37.
30. Quoted in ibid., p. 102.
31. Warner, op. cit., p. 92.
32. C. G. Jung, *Collected Works*, Vol. 9, *Psychology and Alchemy*, para. 197.
33. Compare C. G. Jung, *Collected Works*, Vol. 13, *Alchemical Studies*, para. 18. 'All the greatest and most important problems of life are fundamentally in- soluble . . . They can never be solved, but only outgrown.'
34. Warner, op. cit., p. 254.
35. Watts, op. cit., pp. 107–8.
36. ibid., p. 101.
37. Extracts from the 'Akathistos Hymn', in Constantine A. Trypanis (ed.), *The Penguin Book of Greek Verse*, Harmondsworth, Penguin, pp. 374–89.
38. Pamela Berger, *The Goddess Obscured*, pp. 49–76.
39. ibid., p. 90.
40. ibid.
41. ibid., p. 92.
42. ibid. pp. 93, 94.
43. The description of this statue in German is '*Mutter Gottes*'. Dr Theo Julich from the Hessisches Landesmuseum, Darmstadt, writes in a letter: 'The term "Mother Goddess" related to the Madonna from Munster is definitely wrong. This error derives from a misunderstood translation of "Mutter Gottes", which is the German genitive and means "Mother of God". Our type of sculpture is described by the English terms "Virgin and Child" or "Madonna".'
44. Joseph Campbell, *The Mythic Image*, p. 32.
45. Quoted in Warner, op. cit., p. 329.
46. Robert Briffault, *The Mothers*, p. 397.
47. Quoted in Warner, op. cit., p. 209.
48. S. N. Kramer, *From the Poetry of Sumer*, p. 93.
49. Stephen Langdon, *Tammuz and Ishtar*, p. 14.
50. 'The Lamentations of Isis and Nephthys', in E. A. Wallis Budge, *Osiris and the Egyptian Resurrection*, Vol. 2, pp. 222–40. See Harold Bayley, *The Lost Language of Symbolism*, where he compares this to the poetry of the Song of Songs, pp. 170–2.
51. Warner, op. cit., p. 211.
52. Ean Begg, *The Cult of the Black Virgin*, p. 49.
53. See the commentary on this and other statues in Begg, op. cit., p. 197.
54. Hamlet: 'Lady, shall I lie in your lap?'
    Ophelia: 'No, my lord.'
    Hamlet: 'I mean my head upon your lap.'
    Ophelia: 'Ay, my lord.'
    Hamlet: 'Do you think I meant country matters?'

(William Shakespeare, *Hamlet*, III, ii.)

55. Jacopus de Vaoragine, in *The Golden Legend*, published in 1275, and translated by Caxton in the fifteenth century.
56. This is still reflected in the pronunciation of Magdalen College, Oxford.
57. N. K. Sandars, *The Epic of Gilgamesh*, p. 95.
58. Bernard, op. cit., p. 14.
59. See Warner, op. cit., Chapter 20.
60. Sir James G. Frazer, *The Golden Bough*, Vol. 4, *The Dying God*, pp. 5–6, footnote.
61. Betty Radice and Wendy Doniger O'Flaherty (eds.), *Hindu Myths*, Harmondsworth, Penguin Books, Penguin Classics, 1975, pp. 56–71.
62. Lucie Lamy, *Egyptian Mysteries: New Light on Ancient Knowledge*, p. 5.
63. Briffault, op. cit., pp. 376–7.
64. Campbell, *Occidental Mythology*, p. 369.
65. Watts, op. cit., p. 141.

Chapter 15 Sophia: Mother, Daughter and Bride

1. Stephen Langdon, *Sumerian and Babylonian Psalms*, p. 13.
2. Quoted by Joan C. Engelsman in *The Feminine Dimension of the Divine*, p. 102.
3. ibid., p. 103.
4. ibid., pp. 119–20.
5. C. G. Jung, *Collected Works*, Vol. 11, *Psychology and Religion: West and East*, para. 690 and footnote.
6. Clement of Alexandria, quoted in E. O. James, *The Cult of the Mother Goddess*, p. 197.
7. Quoted by Engelsman, op. cit., p. 135.
8. Jung, op. cit., para. 753.
9. ibid., para. 743.
10. At this time there were some 6 million Jews spread throughout the Roman Empire, whose population was about 60 million. Of these only about 500,000 lived in Palestine. Those Jews who adhered to the orthodox rabbinic tradition in Palestine numbered about 6,000. The Jews who lived in the Diaspora outside Palestine were liberal in their outlook and did not follow a single system of beliefs. Hence their ability to exchange ideas with Greeks and Egyptians in Alexandria.
11. Jung, op. cit., para. 713.
12. Helmut Koester, 'Introduction to the Gospel of Thomas', in James M. Robinson (ed.), *The Nag Hammadi Library in English*, p. 117.
13. Irenaeus, quoted by Elaine Pagels, *The Gnostic Gospels*, p. 19.
14. Pagels, op. cit., p. 57.
15. Hans Jonas, *The Gnostic Religion*, Preface.
16. ibid., p. 52.
17. Robert M. Grant, *Gnosticism*, p. 171.
18. 'The Teaching of Sylvanus', in Robinson, op. cit., p. 356. Compare Jesus' sayings in the Gospels of Matthew (7:7) and Luke (11:9).
19. Quoted in Jonas, op. cit., p. 45.
20. Epiphanius, 'The Gospel of Eve', trs. G. R. S. Mead in *Fragments of a Faith Forgotten*, p. 439.

21. Quoted in Henri Frankfort, *Kingship and the Gods*, p. 67.
22. From an inscription on a sarcophagus in the Louvre.
23. Mead, op. cit., pp. 406–14. See also the translation by Jonas, op. cit., pp. 113–15.
24. David Bohm, *Wholeness and the Implicate Order*. See also Philip Sherrard, *The Rape of Man and Nature*, p. 37.
25. The Logia from the Gospel of Thomas are from the translations by A. Guillaumont *et al.*
26. AD 140 is the date given by Professor Quispel for the Gospel of Thomas, although he believes the sayings in it came from the earliest group of Jewish Christians in Jerusalem.
27. Robinson, op. cit., p. 140.
28. C. G. Jung, *Collected Works*, Vol. 9, *Psychology and Alchemy*, para. 7.
29. Dr Geza Vermes has pointed out in his book *Jesus the Jew* that the Christian Church teaches that the Jesus of history and the Christ of the faith are identical. His book, as he says in the introduction, is written to show that Jesus, 'so distorted by Christian and Jewish myth alike, was *in fact*, neither the Christ of the Church, nor the apostate and bogey-man of Jewish popular tradition'. In particular, he comments, it may be helpful to understand the original significance of the four titles associated with Jesus: Prophet, Messiah, 'son of Man' and 'son of God', for, in the context of the time in which Jesus lived, and the Jewish community in which he taught, they had a very different meaning from what they came to mean in later Christian belief. Writing of the title 'son of God' as it was defined at the Council of Chalcedon, he says:

> Whether Jesus would have reacted with stupefaction, anger or grief, can never be known. One thing, however, is sure. When Christianity later set out to define the meaning of *son of God* in its Creed, the paraphrase it produced – 'God of God, Light of Light, true God of true God, consubstantial with the Father' – drew its inspiration, not from the pure language and teaching of the Galilean Jesus, nor even from Paul the Diaspora Jew, but from the Gentile-Christian interpretation of the Gospel adapted to the mind of the totally alien world of pagan Hellenism. (p. 213).

30. Bousset, *Hautprobleme der Gnosis*, Gottingen, Reitzenstein, 1907, quoted in E. O. James, *The Cult of the Mother Goddess*, p. 192.
31. Pagels, op. cit., p. 54.
32. ibid., p. 49.
33. ibid., p. 50.
34. ibid.
35. 'Eugnostos the Blessed', in Robinson, op. cit., p. 214.
36. ibid., p. 217.
37. ibid., p. 206.
38. ibid., p. 99.
39. Quispel, *The Birth of the Child*, p. 23.
40. ibid.
41. Rebirth through the Mother as the *Ka*, or the greater self as the divine embrace, was originally an Egyptian concept, and in the Mysteries of Eleusis, Cybele and Isis the initiate became at once the 'child' of the goddess as Mother, and the bridegroom of the goddess as Wisdom – experiences later embodied in Gnostic and Alchemical symbolism.

42. Robinson, op. cit., p. 271. Professor Quispel translates the title of this areta-
logy (hymn of praise) as 'Thunder, the Whole Mind'. Wholeness, in Jung's
definition, is an image that belongs to the feminine archetype, whereas perfection belongs to the masculine archetype.

43. Tertullian, quoted in Pagels, op. cit., p. 60.

44. Tertullian, quoted ibid., p. 60.

45. ibid., p. 61.

46. Professor Quispel dates the fourth book of the *Pistis Sophia* to the first half of
the third century – about 225 – and the first, second and third books to the
second half of the third century and comments that it shows the office of
prophetess existed at this time in Jewish communities in Egypt. (Open Gate
Seminar, Bristol 1988)

47. Mead, *Pistis Sophia*, p. 135.

48. ibid., p. 193.

49. Robinson, op. cit., p. 472.

50. ibid., pp. 472–3.

51. Pagels, op. cit., p. 14.

52. All quotations are from V. E. Watts, *Boethius, The Consolation of Philosophy*.

53. The Templars, whose extraordinary rise to power coincided approximately
with the growth of the Cathar Church and Kabbalism, had access to both
Islamic and Jewish mystical teaching.

54. Ernest Scott, *The People of the Secret*.

55. From an Albigensian text. It has been suggested by Frances Yates that one
of the 'treasures' taken with them by the four escaping Cathars on the night
before the rest of the defendants of the citadel of Monségur were burned
was John Scotus Erigena's (810–77) *De Divisione Naturae*. It is thought this
was condemned by the papacy in 1225 because of its connection with the
Cathars (Yates, *Lull and Bruno*, London, Routledge & Kegan Paul, 1982,
p. 114f).

56. See Hugh Schonfield, *The Essene Odyssey*, p. 164. He mentions that the
records of the Inquisition describe a casket that was found in Templar hands,
surmounted by 'a great head of gilded silver, most beautiful, and constituting
the image of a woman'.

57. E. A. Wallis Budge, *The Gods of the Egyptians*, Vol. 1, p. 281; see also Gershom Scholem, *The Origins of the Kabbalah*.

58. Raphael Patai, *The Hebrew Goddess*, p. 99.

59. ibid., p. 98.

60. ibid., p. 99.

61. ibid., p. 111.

62. ibid., p. 113.

63. A group of Sufi scholars in Basra completed an encyclopedia of knowledge in
980, which was transmitted to Spain by Muslim scholars. From the tenth to
the fifteenth century, Arabs, Jews and Christian scholars and mystics worked
together, and the Kabbalah may have developed partly from their cooperation,
as well as from texts being brought into Spain from the Near East. (See Scott,
The People of the Secret.)

64. See Gershom Scholem, *Major Trends in Jewish Mysticism* and *Kabbalah*.
Kabbalah meant literally 'reception', in the sense of something received from
ancient masters. Scholem writes that:

The encounter between the Gnostic tradition . . . and neoplatonic ideas concerning God, His emanation, and man's place in the world, was extremely fruitful, leading to the deep penetration of these ideas into earlier mystical theories. The Kabbalah, in its historical significance, can be defined as the product of the interpenetration of Jewish Gnosticism and Neoplatonism.

(*Kabbalah*, p. 45.) See also Patai's chapter on the Shekhinah, op. cit.

65. Patai, op. cit., pp. 139, 151–2.
66. Images drawn from the books of Scholem and Patai.
67. Scholem, *Major Trends in Jewish Mysticism*, p. 227.
68. ibid., p. 232.
69. Scholem, *Kabbalah*, p. 164.
70. See C. G. Jung, 'The Nature of the Psyche' in *Collected Works*, Vol. 8, *The Structure and Dynamics of the Psyche*.
71. See Patai, op. cit., for the chapter on the Kabbalistic Tetrad.
72. Scholem, *Major Trends in Jewish Mysticism*, p. 229.
73. ibid., p. 37.
74. Meister Eckhart, the great mystic who so narrowly escaped being condemned as a heretic, expressed this understanding with the words: 'It is of more worth to God, his being brought forth spiritually in the individual virgin or good soul, than that he was born of Mary bodily.'
75. *Artis Auriferae*, 2 vols., Basle, 1593; quoted in Jung, *Collected Works*, Vol. 16, *The Practice of Psychotherapy*, para. 411.
76. J. Bronowski, *The Ascent of Man*.
77. Compare the imagery of the marriage of the King and the Matronit in Kabbalism and the sacred marriage of Gnostic ritual.
78. Quoted in Jung, *Collected Works*, Vol. 13, *Alchemical Studies*, para. 392.
79. Marie-Louise von Franz (ed.), *Aurora Consurgens*, London, Routledge & Kegan Paul, 1966, p. 210.
80. ibid., from the Foreword, p. xiii.
81. Jung, *Collected Works*, Vol. 16, *The Practice of Psychotherapy*, para. 407.
82. Jessie Weston, *The Quest of the Holy Grail*.
83. The fish swallowed the phallus of Osiris, the missing 'piece' of re-memberment.
84. Wolfram von Eschenbach, *Parzival*, p. 330.
85. The Order of the Knights Templar has sometimes been identified with the Grail knights.
86. Weston, op. cit., pp. 105–6.
87. Eschenbach, op. cit., p. 386. It is strange to find that the feminine element is absent from Wagner's opera *Parsifal* (*Parzival*). Indeed, with the exception of Kundry (Cundrie), the whole opera is entirely a male affair. There is no bringing together of the two great images of the feminine and masculine archetypes – the vessel and the lance – nor is there any reference to the theme of the sacred marriage. In Wolfram von Eschenbach's story, on which Wagner based his study of Parzival, Parzival marries a queen called Condwiramurs, and Fierefiz, his half-brother, marries Repanse de Schoie, the Grail-bearer.
88. This story is beautifully told by Heinrich Zimmer in *The King and the Corpse*.
89. Marian Roalfe Cox, *Cinderella*, London, The Folklore Society, 1893.
90. ibid. and Harold Bayley, *The Lost Language of Symbolism*, Vol. 1, Chapters VIII and IX.

91. Roalfe Cox, op. cit., and Bayley, op. cit.
92. Patai, op. cit., pp. 102–3: 'The Shekhinah rang before him like a bell.'
93. Bayley's rendering of the lines in Mead, *Fragments of a Faith Forgotten*, p. 413.
94. These were not only the Cathars and Templars, but also those who were in later centuries tortured and sentenced to death by the Inquisition for having affirmed the theology of Divine Immanence, among them Giordano Bruno.
95. Bayley, op. cit., pp. 194–5.

Chapter 16 The Sacred Marriage of Goddess and God: the Reunion of Nature and Spirit

1. Albert Einstein. We regret we have been unable to find the source of this quotation.
2. See Fritjof Capra, *The Turning Point*.
3. Gospel of Thomas, Logion 77.
4. D. H. Lawrence, 'Last Poems', in *The Complete Poems of D. H. Lawrence*, Vol. 1, p. 17.
5. See Jung's essay 'Two Kinds of Thinking', in *Collected Works*, Vol. 5, *Symbols of Transformation*, paras. 4–46.
6. 'In Memoriam', lvi. Tennyson's description of the unadorned state of Nature, following Darwin's description in the *Origin of Species*.
7. William Shakespeare, *Henry IV, Pt. 2*, IV, iv.
8. William Shakespeare, *Henry V*, II, ii.
9. *Letters of Rainer Maria Rilke, 1910–1924*, trs. Jane Bannard Green and M. M. Herter, New York, Norton, 1947, pp. 373–4.
10. David Bohm, *Wholeness and the Implicate Order*, Introduction, p. xi.
11. ibid., pp. 2–3.
12. Immanuel Kant, *Critique of Pure Reason*.
13. Erich Neumann, *The Great Mother*, p. 148.
14. Gospel of Thomas, Logion 22.
15. William Blake, *Complete Poetry and Prose*, Geoffrey Keynes (ed.), p. 835.
16. ibid., p. 860.
17. Owen Barfield, *Saving the Appearances*, throughout the book, but especially: 'The essence of *original* participation is that there stands behind the phenomena, *and on the other side of them from me*, a represented which is of the same nature as me.' (p. 42)
18. ibid., p. 146.
19. C. G. Jung, *Collected Works*, Vol. 8, *The Structure and Dynamics of the Psyche*, paras. 131–93.
20. Coleridge is speaking here of what he calls the 'secondary Imagination', which he distinguishes from the 'primary Imagination':

The primary Imagination I hold to be the living Power and prime Agent of all human Perception, and as a repetition in the finite mind of the eternal act of creation in the infinite I AM. The secondary Imagination I consider as an echo of the former, coexisting with the conscious will, yet still as identical with the primary in the *kind* of its agency, and differing only in *degree*, and in the *mode* of its operation. It dissolves, diffuses, dissipates in order to re-create; or where this process is rendered impossible, yet still at all events it struggles to idealize and to unify. It is essentially *vital*, even as all objects (*as* objects) are essentially fixed and dead.

(*Biographia Literaria*, XIII, p. 167)

21. ibid., XIV, pp. 173–4.
22. Samuel Taylor Coleridge, 'The Eolian Harp', *The Portable Coleridge*, p. 66.
23. For further reading, see Henry Corbin, *Mundis Imaginalis*; Raymond Avens, *Imagination is Reality*; and works by James Hillman and Gaston Bachelard; and Blake, Keats, Coleridge and Yeats.
24. William Shakespeare, *King Lear*, IV, vi.
25. James Hillman, 'The Pandaemonium of Images: Jung's contribution to Know Thyself', *Healing Fiction*, pp. 70–5. The whole of this book is essential reading.
26. 'The Study of Images I', *Collected Poems of Wallace Stevens*, p. 463, quoted in Hillman, op. cit., p. 74.
27. Blake, op. cit., p. 862.
28. Rainer Maria Rilke, *The Duino Elegies*.
29. J. E. Lovelock, *Gaia: A New Look at Life on Earth*.
30. Rupert Sheldrake, *A New Science of Life*; see also his *The Presence of the Past*.
31. Bohm, op. cit., p. 192.
32. ibid.
33. Capra, op. cit.
34. C. G. Jung, Letter to M. R. Braband-Isaac, 22.7.39, in *C. G. Jung: Letters*, Gerhard Adler and Aniela Jaffé (eds.), Vol. I, pp. 274–5.
35. Quoted in Joseph Campbell, *The Way of the Animal Powers*, p. 251.

Appendix 1 *Prehistoric Times*

1. These dates are based on the table given in Joseph Campbell, *The Way of the Animal Powers*, p. 22.

Appendix 2 *The Christian Gospels*

1. John Bowden, *Jesus: The Unanswered Questions*, p. 38.
2. Wilson, op. cit., p. 40.
3. Bowden, op. cit., p. 47.
4. ibid., p. 7.
5. ibid., p. 7 and pp. 82–3. See in particular, Chapters 1, 2, 3, 5. See also Dr Geza Vermes' analysis of the titles of Jesus within the context of the Jewish community in which he lived, in his book *Jesus the Jew*. For a bibliography on this immensely complicated subject, see John Bowden.
6. Bowden, op. cit., p. 74.

SELECT BIBLIOGRAPHY

Adler, Gerhard, *Dynamics of the Self*, London, Coventure Ltd, 1979.

Aeschylus, *The Oresteian Trilogy*, trs. Philip Vellacott, rev. edn, Harmondsworth, Penguin Books, 1959.

Anderson, William, *The Holy Places of Britain*, London, Ebury Press, 1983.

The Rise of the Gothic, London, Hutchinson, 1985.

Green Man: The Archetype of Our Oneness with the Earth, London, Harper Collins, 1990.

Apollonius of Rhodes, *The Voyage of the Argo*, Harmondsworth, Penguin Books, 1959.

Apuleius, Lucius, *The Golden Ass*, trs. Robert Graves, Harmondsworth, Penguin Books, 1950.

Ashe, Maurice, *New Renaissance*, Bideford, Devon, Green Books, 1987.

Atkinson, R. J. C., *Silbury Hill*, London, 1967.

Stonehenge, rev. edn, Harmondsworth, Penguin Books, 1979.

Avens, Robert, *Imagination is Reality: Western Nirvana in Jung, Hillman, Barfield & Cassirer*, Dallas, Spring Publications Inc., 1980.

Bachofen, Johann Jakob, *Myth, Religion and Mother Right*, trs. Ralph Mannheim, Bollingen Series LXXXIV, Princeton, N.J., Princeton University Press, 1967.

Barfield, Owen, *Saving the Appearances: A Study in Idolatry*, rev. edn, Hanover, New Hampshire, Wesleyan University Press, 1989.

Baring, A., 'Cinderella: An Interpretation', in Nathan Schwartz-Salant and Murray Stein (eds.), *Psyche's Stories*, Wilmette, Illinois, Chiron Publications, 1991.

Barth, Karl, *Church Dogmatics*, Edinburgh, T. & T. Clark, 1961.

Bayley, Harold, *The Lost Language of Symbolism: An Inquiry into the Origin of Certain Letters, Words, Names, Fairy Tales, Folklore and Mythologies*, London, Williams and Norgate Ltd, 1912.

Beauvoir, Simone de, *The Second Sex*, New York, Knopf, 1974.

Begg, Ean, *The Cult of the Black Virgin*, London, Arkana, Routledge & Kegan Paul, 1985.

Begouën, H. and Breuil, H., *Les Cavernes du Volp*, Paris, Arts et Métiers Graphiques, 1958.

Berger, Pamela, *The Goddess Obscured: Transformation of the Grain Protectress from Goddess to Saint*, Boston, Mass., Beacon Press, 1985.

Bernal, Martin, *Black Athena: The Afroasiatic Roots of Classical Civilization*, London, Free Association Books, 1987.

Bernard, Bruce, *Mary Queen of Heaven*, London, Macdonald Orbis, 1987.

Bettenson, Henry (ed.), *The Early Christian Fathers*, Oxford, OUP, 1956.
Documents of the Christian Church, Oxford, OUP, 1963.
The Later Christian Fathers, Oxford, OUP, 1963.

Blake, William, *Complete Poetry and Prose*, ed. Geoffrey Keynes, London, Nonesuch Press, 1961.

Bly, Robert (ed.), *News of the Universe: Poems of Twofold Consciousness*, San Francisco, Sierra Club Books, 1980.

Boardman, John, *Athenian Black Figure Vases*, London, Thames and Hudson, 1974.
Athenian Red Figure Vases: The Archaic Period, London, Thames and Hudson, 1975.

Bohm, David, *Wholeness and the Implicate Order*, London, Routledge & Kegan Paul, 1980.

Bowden, John, *Jesus: The Unanswered Questions*, London, SCM Press Ltd, 1988.

Breasted, James H., *Development of Religion and Thought in Ancient Egypt*, Chicago, Scribner, 1912.

Breuil, Abbé Henri, *Four Hundred Centuries of Cave Art*, trs. Mary E. Boyle, Montignac, Centre d'Études et de Documentation Préhistoriques, 1954.

Briffault, Robert, *The Mothers: A Study of the Origins of Sentiments and Institutions*, abr. Gordon Rattray Taylor, London, Allen & Unwin, 1959.

Brown, Peter, *The Body and Society*, London, Faber & Faber, 1989.

Budge, E. A. Wallis, *The Gods of the Egyptians: Studies in Egyptian Mythology*, 2 vols., New York, Dover Publications, 1969.
Osiris and the Egyptian Resurrection, 2 vols., New York, Dover Publications, 1973.

Burdin-Robertson, Lawrence, *The Goddesses of Chaldea, Syria and Egypt*, Enniscorthy, Eire, Cesara Publications, 1975.

Burkert, Walter, *Structure and History in Greek Mythology and Ritual*, Berkeley, Los Angeles and London, University of California Press, 1979.
Greek Religion: Archaic and Classical, trs. John Raffan, Oxford, Basil Blackwell, 1985.

Burl, A., *The Stone Circles of the British Isles*, New Haven, Conn., Yale University Press, 1976.
Prehistoric Avebury, New Haven, Conn., Yale University Press, 1979.

Button, John (ed.), *The Green Fuse: The Schumacher Lectures 1983–8*, London, Quartet Books, 1990.

Cade, C. Maxwell, and Coxhead, Nona, *The Awakened Mind: Biofeedback and the Development of Higher States of Awareness*, Shaftesbury, Dorset, Element Books, 1989.

Cameron, D. O., *Symbols of Birth and of Death in the Neolithic Era*, London, Kenyon Deane, 1981.

Campbell, Joseph, *The Hero with a Thousand Faces*, Bollingen Series XVII, 2nd edn, Princeton, N.J., Princeton University Press, 1968.
Myths to Live By, London, Souvenir Books, 1973.
The Masks of God: Oriental Mythology, Harmondsworth, Penguin Books, 1970.
The Mythic Image, Bollingen Series C, Princeton, N.J., Princeton University Press, 1974.

The Masks of God: Creative Mythology, Harmondsworth, Penguin Books, 1976.
The Masks of God: Primitive Mythology, Harmondsworth, Penguin Books, 1976.
The Masks of God: Occidental Mythology, Harmondsworth, Penguin Books, 1976.
Historical Atlas of World Mythology: Vol. 1: The Way of the Animal Powers, London, Times Books, 1984.
The Inner Reaches of Outer Space. Metaphor as Myth and as Religion, New York, Alfred van der Marck Editions, and Toronto, St James Press Ltd, 1986.
Campbell, Joseph, with Moyers, Bill, *The Power of Myth*, New York, Doubleday, 1988.
Capra, Fritjof, *The Turning Point*, London, Wildwood House, 1982.
Carson, Rachel, *The Silent Spring*, London, Hamish Hamilton, 1963.
Cashford, Jules, 'Homeric Hymn to Artemis', *Harvest: Journal for Jungian Studies*, Vol. 33, 1987–8, pp. 204–7.
'Homeric Hymn to Aphrodite', *Harvest: Journal for Jungian Studies*, Vol. 33, 1987–8, pp. 204–7.
'Homeric Hymn to Gaia', *Harvest: Journal for Jungian Studies*, Vol. 34, 1988–9, pp. 155–60.
'Homeric Hymn to the Mother of the Gods', *Harvest: Journal for Jungian Studies*, Vol. 35, 1989–90, pp. 207–10.
'Joseph Campbell and the Grail Myth', in John Matthews (ed.), *The Household of the Grail*, Wellingborough, Northants., Aquarian Press, 1990.
Cassirer, Ernst, *An Essay on Man*, New Haven, Conn., Yale University Press, 1945.
The Philosophy of Symbolic Forms, 3 vols., trs. Ralph Mannheim, New Haven, Conn., Yale University Press, 1955–65.
Charlesworth, James H. (ed.), *Old Testament Pseudepigrapha*, Vol. 2, London, Darton, Longman and Todd, 1985.
Charon, Jean E., *The Unknown Spirit*, London, Coventure Ltd, 1983.
Coleridge, Samuel Taylor, *Biographia Literaria*, Oxford, OUP, 1907.
The Portable Coleridge, Harmondsworth, Penguin Books, 1977.
Cook, Roger, *The Tree of Life: Symbol of the Centre*, London, Thames and Hudson, 1974.
Corbin, Henry, *Creative Imagination in the Sufism of Ibn Arabi*, trs. Ralph Mannheim, Princeton, N.J., Bollingen Series XCI, Princeton University Press, 1969.
Cornford, F. M., *From Religion to Philosophy: A Study in the Origin of Western Speculation*, Brighton, Harvester Press, 1980.
Cumont, Franz, *The Mysteries of Mithra*, Chicago, The Open Court Publishing Company, 1910.
Cupitt, Don, *The Sea of Faith*, London, BBC Publications, 1984.
Dames, Michael, *The Silbury Treasure: The Great Goddess Rediscovered*, London, Thames and Hudson, 1976.
The Avebury Cycle, London, Thames and Hudson, 1977.
Daniel, Prof. Glyn E., *The Megalith Builders of Western Europe*, London, Hutchinson, 1958.
The First Civilizations, New York, Crowell, and London, Thames and Hudson, 1968.
Demargne, Pierre, *Aegean Art*, London, Thames and Hudson, 1964.
Doresse, Jean, *The Secret Books of the Egyptian Gnostics*, London, Hollis & Carter, 1962.

Downing, Christine, *The Goddess: Mythological Images of the Feminine*, New York, Crossroad Publishing Co., 1984.

Driver, G. R., *Canaanite Myths and Legends*, Edinburgh, T. & T. Clark, 1956.

Eisler, Riane, *The Chalice and the Blade: Our History, Our Future*, San Francisco, Harper & Row, 1987.

Eliade, Mircea, *The Sacred and the Profane*, trs. Willard R. Trask, New York and London, Harcourt, Brace Jovanovich, 1959.

The Myth of the Eternal Return or, Cosmos and History, Bollingen Series XLVI, trs. Willard R. Trask, Princeton, N.J., Princeton University Press (pb), 1971.

Shamanism: Archaic Techniques of Ecstasy, Bollingen Series LXXVI, trs. Willard R. Trask, Princeton, N.J., Princeton University Press (pb), 1972.

Rites and Symbols of Initiation, trs. Willard R. Trask, New York, Harper & Row, Torch Books, 1975.

Myths, Dreams and Mysteries: The Encounter Between Contemporary Faiths and Archaic Reality, trs. Philip Mairet, New York, Harper & Row, Torch Books, 1975.

A History of Religious Ideas, 3 vols., trs. Willard R. Trask, Chicago, University of Chicago Press, 1978–85.

Eliot, T. S., *Four Quartets*, London, Faber & Faber, 1979.

Ellenberger, Henri F., *The Discovery of the Unconscious: The History and Evolution of Dynamic Psychiatry*, New York, Basic Books Inc., 1970.

Engelsman, Joan C., *The Feminine Dimension of the Divine*, Philadelphia, Westminster Press, 1979.

Eschenbach, Wolfram von, *Parzival*, trs. A. T. Hatto, Harmondsworth, Penguin Books, 1980.

Evans, Sir Arthur, *The Mycenaean Tree and Pillar Cult*, London, Macmillan, 1901.

The Palace of Minos, 6 vols., London, Macmillan, 1930.

Fox, Robin Lane, *Pagans and Christians*, London, Viking, 1986.

Frankfort, Henri, *Kingship and the Gods*, Chicago, University of Chicago Press, 1948.

Ancient Egyptian Religion: An Interpretation, New York, Harper & Row, Torch Books, 1961.

The Intellectual Adventure of Ancient Man, Chicago, University of Chicago Press, 1977.

Franz, Marie-Louise von, *Aurora Consurgens*, London, Routledge & Kegan Paul, 1966.

Frazer, Sir James George, *The Golden Bough*, 13 vols., London, Macmillan, 1911–15.

Fromm, Erich, *The Art of Loving*, London, George Allen & Unwin, 1957.

You Shall Be As Gods, New York, Holt, Rinehart & Winston, 1966.

Fromm, Erich, Suzuki, D. T. and De Martino, R., *Zen Buddhism and Psychoanalysis*, London, Souvenir Press, 1974.

Frye, Northrop, *The Great Code: the Bible and Literature*, New York and London, Harcourt, Brace Jovanovich, 1982.

Gadon, Elinor W., *The Once and Future Goddess: A Symbol for our Time*, Wellingborough, Northants., Aquarian Press, 1990.

Gage, Anne [Anne Baring], *The One Work: A Journey Toward the Self*, London, Vincent Stuart Ltd, 1961.

Galland, China, *Longing for Darkness: Tara and the Black Madonna*, New York, Viking Penguin, 1990.

Gimbutas, Marija, 'The Beginning of the Bronze Age in Europe and the Indo-Europeans: 3500–2500 B.C.', *Journal of Indo-European Studies*, 1, 1973.

'The First Wave of Eurasian Steppe Pastoralists into Copper Age Europe', *Journal of Indo-European Studies*, 5, Winter 1977.

'Three Waves of the Kurgan People into Old Europe, 4500–2500 B.C.', *Archives Suisses d'Anthropologie Générale*, 43, 2, 1979.

The Early Civilizations of Europe, Monograph for Indo-European Studies 131, Los Angeles, University of California Press, 1980.

The Goddesses and Gods of Old Europe, 6500–3500 B.C.: Myths and Cult Images, London, Thames and Hudson, 1982.

'Remarks on the Ethnogenesis of the Indo-Europeans in Europe', *Ethnogenese Europaischer Volker*, Stuttgart–New York, Gustav Fischer Verlag, 1986.

The Language of the Goddess, San Francisco, Harper & Row, 1989.

Ginzberg, Louis H., *Legends of the Jews*, Vol. I, Philadelphia, The Jewish Publication Society of America, n.d.

Goblet d'Alviella, Eugene, *The Migration of Symbols*, Wellingborough, Northants., Aquarian Press, 1979.

The Mysteries of Eleusis: The Secret Rites and Rituals of the Classical Greek Mystery Tradition, Wellingborough, Northants., Aquarian Press, 1981.

The Gospel According to Thomas, Coptic text established and translated by A. Guillaumont *et al.*, Leiden, E. J. Brill, 1976.

Gottlieb, Freema, *The Lamp of God: Shekhinah as Light*, London, Aaronson, 1989.

Graillot, H., *Le cult de Cybèle, Mère des Dieux à Rome et dans l'Empire Romain*, Paris, 1912.

Grant, Robert M., *Gnosticism, an Anthology*, London, Collins, 1961.

Graves, Robert, *Greek Myths*, London, Cassell, 1955.

The White Goddess: A Historical Grammar of Poetic Myth, New York, Farrar, Strauss & Giroux, 1972.

Graves, Robert and Patai, Raphael, *Hebrew Myths: The Book of Genesis*, New York, Greenwich House, 1983.

Gray, John, *Near Eastern Mythology*, London, Hamlyn, 1982.

Grene, David and Lattimore, Richmond (eds.), *Greek Tragedies*, 3 vols., Chicago, University of Chicago Press, 1963.

Grigson, Geoffrey, *The Goddess of Love: The Birth, Triumph, Death and Return of Aphrodite*, London, Quartet Books, 1978.

Hadingham, E., *Early Man and the Cosmos*, London, Heinemann, 1983.

Halevi, Ilan, *A History of the Jews: Ancient and Modern*, London, Zed Books, 1987.

Hallo, William W. and Van Dijk, J. J. A., *The Exaltation of Inanna*, New Haven, Conn. and London, Yale University Press, 1968.

Happold, Frank C., *Mysticism – A Study and an Anthology*, Harmondsworth, Penguin Books, Pelican, 1963.

Harding, M. Esther, *Woman's Mysteries, Ancient and Modern*, New York, Harper & Row, 1971.

Harrison, Jane Ellen, *Mythology*, New York and London, Harcourt, Brace Jovanovich, 1963.

Themis: A Study of the Social Origins of Greek Religion, London, Merlin Press, 1963.

Myths of Greece and Rome, Falcroft, 1976.

Prolegomena to the Study of Greek Religion, London, Merlin Press, 1980.

Hawkes, J., *Dawn of the Gods: Minoan and Mycenaean Origins of Greece*, London, Chatto & Windus, 1968.

The First Great Civilizations: Life in Mesopotamia, the Indus Valley and Egypt, New York, Knopf, 1973.

Hawkins, G. S., *Stonehenge Decoded*, London, Souvenir Press, 1966.

Herodotus, *The Histories*, trs. Aubrey de Selincourt, Harmondsworth, Penguin Books, Penguin Classics, 1954.

Hesiod, *Theogony and Works and Days*, trs. Dorothea Wender, Harmondsworth, Penguin Books, Penguin Classics, 1973.

Theogony and Works and Days, trs. H. G. Evelyn-White, Cambridge, Loeb Classical Library, 1950.

Hillman, James, *The Myth of Analysis*, New York, Harper & Row, Harper Colophon Books, 1978.

Re-Visioning Psychology, New York, Harper & Row, Harper Colophon Books, 1977.

The Thought of the Heart, Eranos Lectures 2, Dallas, Spring Publications Inc., 1981.

Archetypal Psychology: A Brief Account, Dallas, Spring Publications Inc., 1983.

Healing Fiction, Barrytown, N.Y., Station Hill Press, 1983.

Hirsch, Udo; Mellaart, James; Balpinar, Belkis, *The Goddess of Anatolia*, Milan, Eskenazi, 1989.

The Holy Scriptures According to the Masoretic Text, Philadelphia, The Jewish Publication Society of America, 1955.

Homer, *Odyssey*, trs. E. V. Rieu, Harmondsworth, Penguin Books, Penguin Classics, 1946.

Iliad, trs. Richmond Lattimore, Chicago, Phoenix Books, 1961.

Hooke, S. H., *Middle Eastern Mythology*, Harmondsworth, Penguin Books, Pelican, 1963.

Huxley, Aldous, *The Doors of Perception*, London, Chatto & Windus, 1954.

Ions, Veronica, *Egyptian Mythology*, London, Newnes Books, 1982.

Jacobsen, Thorkild, *The Treasures of Darkness: A History of Mesopotamian Religion*, New Haven, Conn., Yale University Press, 1976.

James, E. O., *Myth and Ritual in the Ancient Near East*, London, Thames and Hudson, 1958.

The Cult of the Mother Goddess, London, Thames and Hudson, 1959.

Jelinek, Jan, *Encyclopédie Illustrée de l'Homme Préhistorique*, Paris, Grund, 1975.

The Jerusalem Bible, London, Darton, Longman and Todd, and New York, Doubleday, 1968.

Johnson, Buffie, *Lady of the Beasts: Ancient Images of the Goddess and Her Sacred Animals*, San Francisco, Harper & Row, 1988.

Jonas, Hans, *The Gnostic Religion*, Boston, Mass., Beacon Press, 1958.

Jung, C. G., *Collected Works*, 20 vols., eds. Sir Herbert Read *et al.*, trs. R. F. C. Hull, London, Routledge & Kegan Paul, 1957–79.

Memories, Dreams and Reflections, London, Collins and Routledge & Kegan Paul, 1963.

Letters, selected and edited by Gerhard Adler in collaboration with Aniela Jaffé, trs. R. F. C. Hull, London, Routledge & Kegan Paul, 2 vols., 1973–6.

Man and His Symbols, London, Pan Books, 1978.

Jung, C. G., and Kerenyi, Carl, *Introduction to a Science of Mythology: The Myth of the Divine Child and the Mysteries of Eleusis*, trs. R. F. C. Hull, London, Routledge & Kegan Paul, 1951.

Jung, Emma and Franz, Marie-Louise von, *The Grail Legend*, trs. C. G. Jung Foundation, London, Hodder & Stoughton, 1971.

Kerenyi, Carl, *Eleusis: Archetypal Image of Mother and Daughter*, New York, Schocken Books, 1967.

The Heroes of the Greeks, trs. Prof. H. J. Rose, London, Thames and Hudson (pb), 1974.

Zeus and Hera: Archetypal Image of Father, Husband and Wife, Bollingen Series LXV, trs. Christopher Holme, Princeton, N.J., Princeton University Press, 1975.

Dionysos: Archetypal Image of Indestructible Life, Bollingen Series LXV:2, trs. Ralph Mannheim, Princeton, N.J., Princeton University Press, 1976.

Athene: Virgin and Mother in Greek Religion, trs. Murray Stein, Zurich, Spring Publications, 1978.

The Gods of the Greeks, trs. Norman Cameron, London, Thames and Hudson (pb), 1979.

King, Leonard William, *Babylonian Religion and Mythology*, London, 1897.

The Seven Tablets of Creation, London, 1902.

Legends of Babylonia and Egypt in Relation to the Hebrew Tradition, London, OUP, 1918.

Koltuv, Barbara Black, *The Book of Lilith*, York Beach, Maine, Nicolas-Hays Inc. (pb), 1986.

Kramer, H. and Sprenger, J., *Malleus Maleficarum*, trs. Montague Summers, London, Pushkin Press, 1951.

Kramer, Samuel Noah, *History Begins at Sumer*, London, Thames and Hudson, 1958.

The Sumerians, Their History, Culture and Character, Chicago, Chicago University Press, 1963.

The Sacred Marriage Rite: Aspects of Faith, Myth and Ritual in Ancient Sumer, Bloomington, Ind., Indiana University Press, 1969.

Sumerian Mythology, Philadelphia, University of Pennsylvania Press, 1972.

From the Poetry of Sumer: Creation, Glorification, Adoration, Berkeley and Los Angeles, University of California Press, 1979.

Kuhn, Herbert, *On the Track of Prehistoric Man*, trs. A. H. Brodrick, London, Hutchinson, 1955.

Laming-Empéraire, Annette, *Lascaux, Paintings and Engravings*, trs. E. F. Armstrong, Harmondsworth, Penguin Books, 1959.

La Signification de l'Art Rupestre Paléolithique, Paris, Picard, 1962.

Lamy, Lucie, *Egyptian Mysteries: New Light on Ancient Knowledge*, London, Thames and Hudson, 1981.

Langdon, Stephen, *Sumerian and Babylonian Psalms*, Paris, Librairie Paul Geuthner, 1909.

Tammuz and Ishtar, Oxford, OUP, Clarendon Press, 1914.

Sumerian Liturgies and Psalms, London, 1919.

Lawrence, D. H., *The Complete Poems of D. H. Lawrence*, Vivian De Sola Pinto and Warren Roberts (eds.), London, Heinemann, 1972.

Leech, Edmund and Aycock, D. Alan, *Structuralist Interpretations of Biblical Myth*, Cambridge, CUP, 1983.

Leroi-Gourhan, André, 'La fonction des signes dans les sanctuaires paléolithiques', *Bulletin de la Société Préhistorique Française*, tome LV, 1958.

    Les Religions de la Préhistoire, Paris, Presses Universitaires de France, 1964.

    Treasures of Prehistoric Art, trs. Norbert Guterman, New York, Harry N. Abrams, 1967.

    Préhistoire de l'Art Occidentale, Paris, Editions d'Art Lucien Mazenod, 1971.

    The Dawn of European Art, trs. S. Champion, Cambridge, CUP, 1982.

Levy, Gertrude Rachel, *The Gate of Horn: A Study of the religious conceptions of the Stone Age, and their influence upon European thought*, London, Faber & Faber, 1948.

Lloyd, Seton, *The Archeology of Mesopotamia*, London, Thames and Hudson, 1978.

Lossky, Vladimir, *The Mystical Theology of the Eastern Church*, trs. by members of the Fellowship of St Alban and St Sergius, London, J. Clarke, 1957.

Lovelock, James E., *Gaia: A New Look at Life on Earth*, Oxford, OUP, 1979.

Luke, Helen M., *Woman, Earth and Spirit: The Feminine in Symbol and Myth*, New York, Crossroad Publishing Co., 1981.

Lurker, Manfred, *The Gods and Symbols of Ancient Egypt: An Illustrated Dictionary*, London, Thames and Hudson, 1980.

Mackenzie, Donald A., *Myths of Babylonia and Assyria*, London, Gresham Publishing Co., 1915.

Mackie, Euan Wallace, *The Megalith Builders*, London, Book Club Associates, 1977.

Marinatos, Dr Nanno, *Art and Religion in Thera: Reconstructing a Bronze Age Society*, Athens, 1985.

Marinatos, S., *Crete and Mycenae*, London, Thames and Hudson, 1960.

Marshack, Alexander, *The Roots of Civilization*, London, Weidenfeld & Nicolson, 1972.

Mead, G. R. S., *Fragments of a Faith Forgotten*, London, John M. Watkins, 1931.

    Hymn of the Robe of Glory, also called the Hymn of the Pearl, London and Benares, Theosophical Publishing Society, 1908.

    The Wedding Song of Wisdom, London and Benares, Theosophical Publishing Society, 1908.

    Pistis Sophia, A Gnostic Miscellany, London, John M. Watkins, 1947.

    Thrice Greatest Hermes, 3 vols., London, John M. Watkins, 1949.

Mellaart, James, *Earliest Civilizations of the Near East*, London, Thames and Hudson, 1965.

    Çatal Hüyük, A Neolithic Town in Anatolia, London, Thames and Hudson, 1967.

    The Neolithic of the Near East, New York, Scribner, 1975.

Merchant, Carolyn, *The Death of Nature*, New York, Harper & Row, 1980.

Michel, John, *City of Revelation*, London, Garstone Press, 1972.

    The View over Atlantis, London, Abacus, 1973.

Milton, John, *Paradise Lost*, London, Longman, 1971.

Mylonas, G. E., *Eleusis and the Eleusinian Mysteries*, Princeton, N.J., Princeton University Press, 1961.

Neihardt, John G., *Black Elk Speaks*, Lincoln, Nebraska and London, University of Nebraska Press, 1979.

Neumann, Erich, *The Great Mother*, Bollingen Series XLVII, trs. Ralph Mannheim, Princeton, N.J., Princeton University Press, 1955.
The Origins and History of Consciousness, Bollingen Series XLII, trs. R. F. C. Hull, Princeton, N.J., Princeton University Press (pb), 1970.

New Bible Commentary, Leicester, Inter-Varsity Press, 1970.

Olson, Carl (ed.), *The Book of the Goddess Past and Present: An Introduction to Her Religion*, New York, Crossroad Publishing Co., 1983.

Ornstein, Robert E., *The Nature of Human Consciousness*, San Francisco, W. H. Freeman & Co., 1973.
The Psychology of Consciousness, Harmondsworth, Penguin Books, 1986.

Otto, Rudolf, *The Idea of the Holy: An Inquiry into the non-rational factor in the idea of the divine and its relation to the rational*, trs. John W. Harvey, Oxford, OUP, 1958.

Otto, Walter F., *The Homeric Gods: The Spiritual Significance of Greek Religion*, trs. Moses Hadas, London, Thames and Hudson, 1979.

Ouspensky, P. D., *In Search of the Miraculous: Fragments of an Unknown Teaching*, London, Routledge & Kegan Paul, 1975.

Pagels, Elaine, *The Gnostic Gospels*, London, Weidenfeld & Nicolson, 1980.
Adam, Eve and the Serpent, London, Weidenfeld & Nicolson, 1988.

Panofsky, Dora and Erwin, *Pandora's Box*, Bollingen Series LII, Princeton, N.J., Princeton University Press, 1962.

Paris, Ginette, *Pagan Meditations: The Worlds of Aphrodite, Artemis and Hestia*, trs. Gwendolyn Moore, Dallas, Spring Publications Inc., 1986.

Patai, Raphael, *The Hebrew Goddess*, 3rd edn, Detroit, Wayne State University Press, 1990.

Perera, Sylvia Brinton, *Descent to the Goddess: A Way of Initiation for Women*, Toronto, Inner City Books, 1981.

Phillips, John A., *Eve: The History of an Idea*, San Francisco, Harper & Row, 1984.

Piggott, Stuart, *Prehistoric India*, Harmondsworth, Penguin Books, 1950.

Platon, N., *Crete*, Geneva, Nagel, 1966.

Plutarch, 'Isis and Osiris' in *Moralia*, Book 5, trs. Frank Cole Babbitt, London, William Heinemann, Loeb Classical Library, 1969.

Pope, Maruin H., *Commentary on the Song of Songs*, New York, Doubleday, 1977.

Pritchard, James B. (ed.), *The Ancient Near East: An Anthology of Texts and Pictures*, 2 vols., Princeton, N.J., Princeton University Press, 1958.

Quispel, Prof. Gilles, *The Birth of the Child*, Eranos Lectures, Dallas, Spring Publications Inc., 1973.

Rad, Gerhard von, *Old Testament Theology*, trs. D. M. G. Stalker, London, SCM Press, Vol. I, 1962; Vol. II, 1965.
Wisdom in Israel, trs. James D. Martin, London, SCM Press, 1972.

Ranke-Heinemann, Uta, *Eunuchs for Heaven: The Catholic Church and Sexuality*, trs. John Brownjohn, London, Deutsch, 1990.

Ransome, H. M., *The Sacred Bee in Ancient Times and Folklore*, London, Allen & Unwin, 1937.

Rawlinson, H. C., *The Cuneiform Inscriptions of Western Asia*, London, 1861.

Rilke, Rainer Maria, *Selected Poetry*, ed. and trs. Stephen Marshall, London, Picador, 1982.

Robinson, James M. (ed.), *The Nag Hammadi Library in English*, 2nd edn, trs. Members of the Coptic Gnostic Library Project of the Institute for Antiquity and Christianity, Leiden, E. J. Brill, 1984.

Rogers, Robert W., *Cuneiform Parallels to the Old Testament*, London, Gordon Press, 1977.

Romer, John, *People of the Nile: New Light on the Civilization of Ancient Egypt*, London, Michael Joseph (pb), 1989.

Rundle Clark, R. T., *Myth and Symbol in Ancient Egypt*, London, Thames and Hudson, 1978.

Ruspoli, Mario, *The Cave of Lascaux: The Final Photographic Record*, London, Thames and Hudson, 1987.

Sandars, N. K. (ed.), *The Epic of Gilgamesh*, Harmondsworth, Penguin Books, Penguin Classics, 1960.
Poems of Heaven and Hell from Ancient Mesopotamia, Harmondsworth, Penguin Books, 1972.

Sayce, Archibald Henry, *Hibbert Lectures*, 1887.

Scholem, Gershom, *Major Trends in Jewish Mysticism*, New York, Schocken Books Inc., 1961.
The Origins of the Kabbalah, Princeton, N.J., Princeton University Press, 1967.
Kabbalah, New York and Ontario, Meridian Books, 1978.

Schonfield, Hugh, *The Essene Odyssey*, Shaftesbury, Dorset, Element Books, 1984.

Schürer, Emil, *The History of the Jewish People in the Age of Jesus Christ*, 3 vols., rev. Geza Vermes *et al.*, Edinburgh, T. & T. Clark, 1973–86.

Schwaller de Lubicz, R. A., *Symbol and the Symbolic: Ancient Egypt, Science, and the Evolution of Consciousness*, trs. Robert and Deborah Lawlor, New York, Autumn Press, 1978.

Scott, Ernest, *The People of the Secret*, London, Octagon Press, 1983.

Shakespeare, William, *The Complete Works*, Oxford, OUP, 1986.

Sheldrake, Rupert, *A New Science of Life*, London, Blond & Briggs, 1981.
The Presence of the Past, London, Blond & Briggs, 1988.

Sherrard, Philip, *The Rape of Man and Nature*, Ipswich, Golgonooza Press, 1987.

Smith, Morton, *Jesus the Magician*, Wellingborough, Northants., Aquarian Press, 1985.
The Secret Gospel, Wellingborough, Northants., Aquarian Press, 1985.

Sparks, H. F. D. (ed.), *The Apocryphal New Testament*, Oxford, Clarendon Press, 1984.

Speiser, E. A., *Akkadian Myths and Epics*, Princeton, N.J., Princeton University Press, 1957.

Spretnak, Charlene, *Lost Goddesses of Early Greece: A Collection of Pre-Hellenic Myths*, Boston, Mass., Beacon Press, 1984.

Stone, Merlin, *The Paradise Papers*, London, Virago, 1976.

Strachan, Elspeth and Gordon, *Freeing the Feminine*, Dunbar, Labarum Publications Ltd, 1985.

Thom, Prof. Alexander, *Megalithic Sites in Britain*, Oxford, OUP, 1967.
Megalithic Lunar Observatories, Oxford, OUP, 1971.
Megalith Remains in Britain and Brittany, Oxford, OUP, 1979.

Traherne, Thomas, *Centuries of Meditation*, London, Bertram Dobell, 1908.

Trigg, Joseph W., *Origen: The Bible and Philosophy in the Third Century Church*, London, SCM Press, 1985.

Trump, D. H., *Malta, an Archaeological Guide*, London, Faber & Faber, 1972.
  The Prehistory of the Mediterranean, Harmondsworth, Penguin Books, Pelican, 1981.
Urbach, E., *The Sages: The World and Wisdom of the Rabbis of the Talmud*, Jerusalem, Harvard University Press, 1979.
van der Post, Laurens, *The Lost World of the Kalahari*, Harmondsworth, Penguin Books, 1962.
  The Seed and the Sower, Harmondsworth, Penguin Books, 1963.
  The Heart of the Hunter, Harmondsworth, Penguin Books, 1965.
  Jung and the Story of Our Time, Harmondsworth, Penguin Books, 1978.
van der Post, Laurens, and Taylor, Jane, *Testament to the Bushman*, Harmondsworth, Penguin Books, 1985.
Van Over, Raymond (ed.), *Eastern Mysticism, Near East and India*, Vol. I, New York, New American Library, 1977.
Vermaseren, Maarten J., *Cybele and Attis*, trs. A. M. H. Lemmers, London, Thames and Hudson, 1977.
Vermes, Geza, *Jesus the Jew*, London, Collins, 1973.
Virgil, *The Aeneid*, trs. W. F. Jackson Knight, rev. edn, Harmondsworth, Penguin Books, 1958.
Vries, Ad de, *Dictionary of Symbols and Imagery*, Amsterdam, Elsevier Science Publishers, 1984.
Walker, Barbara G., *The Woman's Encyclopedia of Myths and Secrets*, San Francisco, Harper & Row, 1983.
Ward, William Hayes, *Seal Cylinders of Western Asia*, New York, J. P. Morgan Library/AMS Press, 1910.
Warner, Marina, *Alone of All Her Sex: The Myth and Cult of the Virgin Mary*, London, Pan Books (Picador), 1985.
Watts, Alan, *Myth and Ritual in Christianity*, London, Thames and Hudson, 1954.
Watts, V. E. (trs.), *Boethius, The Consolation of Philosophy*, Harmondsworth, Penguin Books, 1969.
Weber, Renée, *Dialogues with Scientists and Sages: The Search for Unity*, London, Routledge & Kegan Paul, 1986.
Wender, Dorothea (trs.), *Hesiod and Theognis*, Harmondsworth, Penguin Books, 1973.
Weston, Jessie, *The Quest of the Holy Grail*, London, Frank Cass & Co., 1964.
Whitmont, Edward C., *The Return of the Goddess*, New York, Crossroad Publishing Co., 1982.
Wilber, Ken (ed.), *The Holographic Paradigm and Other Paradoxes: Exploring the Leading Edge of Science*, Boulder, Colo. and London, Shambhala, 1982.
  Up from Eden: A Transpersonal View of Human Evolution, London, Routledge & Kegan Paul, 1983.
  No Boundary: Eastern and Western Approaches to Personal Growth, Boston, Mass. and London, New Science Library, 1985.
Wilkins, Eithne, *The Rose Garden Game: The Symbolic Background to the European Prayer-Beads*, London, Victor Gollancz, 1969.
Willetts, R. F., *Cretan Cults and Festivals*, London, Routledge & Kegan Paul, 1962.
Wilson, Ian, *Jesus: the Evidence*, London, Weidenfeld & Nicolson, 1984.

Wind, Edgar, *Pagan Mysteries in the Renaissance*, Harmondsworth, Penguin Books, Peregrine, 1967.

Wolkstein, Diane and Kramer, Samuel Noah, *Inanna, Queen of Heaven and Earth: Her Stories and Hymns from Sumer*, London, Rider and Co., 1983.

Woolley, Sir Charles Leonard, *The Sumerians*, Oxford, OUP, 1928.

The Excavations at Ur, London, Ernest Benn, 1954.

Ur of the Chaldees, London, The Herbert Press, rev. edn, rev. P. R. S. Hoovey, 1982.

Wosien, Maria-Gabriel, *Sacred Dance: Encounter with the Gods*, London, Thames and Hudson, 1974.

Yeats, W. B., *Collected Poems*, London, Macmillan, 1952.

Zimmer, Heinrich, *Myths and Symbols in Indian Art and Civilization*, ed. Joseph Campbell, Bollingen Series VI, Princeton, N.J., Princeton University Press, 1946.

The King and the Corpse: Tales of the Soul's Conquest of Evil, ed. Joseph Campbell, Bollingen Series XI, Princeton, N.J., Princeton University Press, 1948.

Philosophies of India, ed. Joseph Campbell, Bollingen Series XXVI, Princeton, N.J., Princeton University Press, 1951.

The Art of Indian Asia: Its Mythology and Transformations, ed. Joseph Campbell, Bollingen Series XXXIX, Princeton, N.J., Princeton University Press, 1955.

Zohar, Donah, *Quantum Self*, London, Bloomsbury Publishing Co., 1989.

ESSENTIAL READING

Barfield, Owen, *Saving the Appearances: A Study in Idolatry.*

Campbell, Joseph, *The Hero with a Thousand Faces*; *The Masks of God: Primitive Mythology*; *The Masks of God: Occidental Mythology*; *The Masks of God: Oriental Mythology.*

Eliade, Mircea, *A History of Religious Ideas*, Vols. 1 and 2.

Gimbutas, Marija, *The Goddesses and Gods of Old Europe*, *The Language of the Goddess.*

Harrison, Jane, *Prolegomena to a Study of Greek Religion.*

Hillman, James, *The Myth of Analysis.*

Johnson, Buffie, *Lady of the Beasts.*

Jung, Carl Gustav, *Collected Works*: Vol. 5, *Symbols of Transformation*; Vol. 8, *The Structure and Dynamics of the Psyche.*

Neumann, Erich, *The Great Mother.*

Patai, Raphael, *The Hebrew Goddess.*

Phillips, John A., *Eve: The History of an Idea.*

Warner, Marina, *Alone of All Her Sex.*

ACKNOWLEDGEMENTS

The authors and publisher gratefully acknowledge the following sources for permission to use copyright material.

Abingdon Press: excerpts from *Wisdom in Israel*, Gerhard von Rad.

Bantam Books: *Myths to Live By*, Joseph Campbell.

Beacon Press: *The Gnostic Religion*, Hans Jonas, 1958; *The Goddess Obscured: Transformation of the Grain Protectress from Goddess to Saint*, Pamela Berger, 1985.

Peter Bedtick Books Inc.: excerpts from *Near Eastern Mythology*, John Gray.

Basil Blackwell: *Greek Religion*, Walter Burkert.

E. J. Brill: *The Nag Hammadi Library in English*, edited by James M. Robinson.

British Broadcasting Corporation: paraphrase from BBC programme *Chronicle: Images of Another World*, transmitted on 19 April 1989.

Cambridge University Press: *The Dawn of European Art*, André Leroi-Gourhan.

Jonathan Cape Ltd: *The Second Sex*, Simone de Beauvoir.

Frank Cass & Co. Ltd: *The Quest of the Holy Grail*, Jessie Weston.

Chiron Publications: excerpts from *The Feminine Dimension of the Divine*, Joan Chamberlain Engelsman (Chiron Publications, 1987), reprinted by permission of the publisher.

William Collins Sons & Co. Ltd: *Jesus the Jew*, Geza Vermes.

Constable & Co. Ltd: *Handbook of Egyptian Religion*, Adolf Erman.

Curtis Brown Ltd: excerpts from *The Megalith Builders of Western Europe*, Prof. Glyn E. Daniel.

Darton, Longman and Todd Ltd: excerpts taken from *Old Testament Pseudepigrapha*, Vol. 2, James H. Charlesworth, published and copyright © 1985 by Darton, Longman and Todd Ltd, and used by permission of the publishers.

Darton, Longman and Todd Ltd and Doubleday & Co. Inc.: excerpts taken from *The Jerusalem Bible*, published and copyright © 1966, 1967, 1968 by Darton, Longman and Todd Ltd and Doubleday & Co. Inc., and used by permission of the publishers.

Element Books: *The Essene Odyssey*, Hugh Schonfield.

Eranos Foundation, Ascona: 'The Birth of the Child', Gilles Quispel. Article based on a lecture given at the Eranos conference in Ascona (Switzerland) in 1971 and originally published in *Eranos 40–1971*, Eranos Foundation, Ascona; with grateful acknowledgement to Professor Gilles Quispel.

Faber & Faber Ltd: *Four Quartets*, T. S. Eliot; *The Gate of Horn*, Gertrude Levy.

J. G. Ferguson Publishing Company: *Man and his Symbols*, C. G. Jung (ed.), Aldus Books, 1964; permission granted by the J. G. Ferguson Publishing Company.

Golgonooza Press: *The Rape of Man and Nature*, Philip Sherrard. Golgonooza Press, 1987, and with kind permission of Philip Sherrard.

Victor Gollancz Ltd: *The Rose Garden Game*, Eithne Wilkins.

Granada Publishing Ltd: *Myths to Live By*, Joseph Campbell.

Paul Hamlyn Publishing: excerpts from *Near Eastern Mythology*, John Gray.

Harcourt, Brace Jovanovich Inc.: excerpts from *The Great Code: The Bible and Literature*, Northrop Frye, copyright © by Northrop Frye, reprinted by permission of Harcourt, Brace Jovanovich, Inc.; excerpt from *The Sacred and the Profane*, Mircea Eliade, copyright © 1957 by Rowohlt Taschenbuch Verlag GmbH, English translation copyright © 1959 and renewed 1987 by Harcourt Brace Jovanovich, Inc., reprinted by permission of Harcourt Brace Jovanovich, Inc.; excerpts from 'Burnt Norton' and 'Dry Salvages' in *Four Quartets*, copyright © 1943 by T. S. Eliot and renewed 1971 by Esme Valerie Eliot, reprinted by permission of Harcourt, Brace Jovanovich, Inc.

Harper & Row, Publishers, Inc.: excerpts from *Eve: The History of an Idea*, John A. Phillips, copyright © 1984 by John A. Phillips; excerpts from *The Language of the Goddess*, Marija Gimbutas, copyright © 1989 by Marija Gimbutas; *The Chalice and the Blade: Our History, Our Future*, Riane Eisler; *The Nag Hammadi Library in English*, James M. Robinson (ed.), copyright © 1978 by E. J. Brill; excerpts from *The Women's Encyclopedia of Myths and Secrets*, Barbara Walker, copyright © 1983 by Barbara Walker; excerpts from *Ancient Egyptian Religion, An Interpretation*, Henri Frankfort, copyright 1948 by Columbia University Press; *The Death of Nature*, Carolyn Merchant; all the foregoing reprinted by permission of Harper & Row, Publishers, Inc.

Harvard University Press: *Hesiod: The Homeric Hymns; Fragments of the Epic Cycle, Homerica*, trs. Hugh G. Evelyn-White, Cambridge, Mass., Harvard University Press, 1914; *Herodotus*, Vols. I–IV, translated by A. D. Godley, Cambridge, Mass., Harvard University Press, 1920, 1921, 1922, 1924, reprinted by permission of the publishers and the Loeb Classical Library.

Harvill Press: excerpts from *Myths, Dreams and Mysteries*, Mircea Eliade, copyright © 1960 by Harvill Press, renewed © 1988 by Harvill Press, reprinted by permission of Harper & Row Publishers Inc.

William Heinemann Ltd: *The Complete Poems of D. H. Lawrence*, coll. and ed. with Introduction by Vivian De Sola Pinto and Warren Roberts, Vol. I, reprinted by permission of Laurence Pollinger Ltd (Literary Agents) and the Estate of Frieda Lawrence Ravagli.

Herbert Press: excerpt from *Ur of the Chaldees*, Sir Leonard Woolley.

Hutchinson Publishing Group: *Inanna, Queen of Heaven and Earth: Her Stories and Hymns from Sumer*, copyright © 1983 by Diane Wolkstein and Samuel Noah Kramer, reprinted by kind permission of the authors. *The Rise of the Gothic*, copyright © 1985 by William Anderson, reprinted by kind permission of the author.

Jewish Publication Society of America: *Legends of the Jews*, Vol. I, Louis H. Ginzberg.

Liberal Arts Press: excerpts from *Hellenistic Religions: The Age of Syncretism*, Frederick L. Gaunt.

Macmillan Publishers Ltd: *Collected Poems*, W. B. Yeats; *The Palace of Minos*, Sir Arthur Evans, Vols. II and III; *The Golden Bough*, Sir James George Frazer, by permission of A. P. Watt Ltd on behalf of Trinity College Cambridge.

Meridian Books: *Kabbalah*, Gershom Scholem, copyright © Keter Publishing House Jerusalem Ltd.

Merlin Press Ltd: *Themis: A Study of the Social Origins of Greek Religion*; and *Prolegomena to the Study of Greek Religion*, Jane Ellen Harrison.

New American Library: *Eastern Mysticism*, Vol. I, *Near East and India*, Raymond Van Over (ed.).

Northwestern University Press: *The Myth of Analysis*, James Hillman.

W. W. Norton & Company, Inc.: *A History of Medical Psychology*, Gregory Zilboorg; *Letters of Rilke, 1910–1924*, Rainer Maria Rilke, trs. Jane Bannard Green and M. M. Herter.

Oriental Institute of the University of Chicago: excerpts from Oriental Institute Publications.

Oxford University Press: *The Complete Works of Shakespeare*, 1986; *Megalithic Lunar Observatories*, Professor Alexander Thom, 1971; *The Land of Ur*, Hans Baumann, 1969; *The Apocryphal New Testament: The Testament of Reuben*, H. F. D. Sparks (ed.), 1984; *Tammuz and Ishtar*, Stephen Langdon, Clarendon Press, 1914; *The Concise Oxford Dictionary of Quotations*: quotation from Henry Vaughan; *Biographia Literaria*, Samuel Taylor Coleridge; *Documents of the Christian Church*, Henry Bettenson, 1963; *The Early Christian Fathers*, Henry Bettenson, 1956; *The Later Christian Fathers*, Henry Bettenson, 1963.

Zdenek Pavlik, Director of Artia Foreign Trade Corporation, Czechoslovakia, for permission to use photographs from *Encyclopédie Illustrée de l'Homme Préhistorique*.

Penguin Books Ltd: *The Voyage of Argo*, Apollonius of Rhodes, trs. E. V. Rieu, copyright © E. V. Rieu, 1959, 1971; *The Golden Ass*, Apuleius, trs. Robert Graves; *Hesiod and Theogonis*, trs. Dorothea Wender; translation copyright © A. T. Hatto, 1980; *Parzival*, Wolfram von Eschenbach, trs. A. T. Hatto; translation copyright © A. T. Hatto, 1980; *Prehistoric India*, Stuart Piggott, copyright © Stuart Piggott, 1950; *The Oresteian Trilogy*, Aeschylus, trs. Philip Vellacott, copyright © Philip Vellacott, 1956, 1959; *The Consolation of Philosophy*, Boethius, trs. V. E. Watts, copyright © V. E. Watts, 1969; *Odyssey*, Homer, trs. E. V. Rieu, copyright © the Estate of E. V. Rieu, 1946; *Testament to the Bushman*, Laurens van der Post and Jane Taylor, copyright © Jane Taylor and Magasoma Holding B.V., 1984; *Mysticism: A Study and an Anthology*, F. C. Happold, copyright © F. C. Happold, 1963, 1964, 1970; *Iliad*, Homer, trs. E. V. Rieu, copyright © the Estate of E. V. Rieu, 1950; *The Aeneid*, Virgil, trs. W. F. Jackson Knight, copyright © G. R. Wilson Knight, 1956, 1958; *The Epic of Gilgamesh*, trs. N. K. Sandars, copyright © N. K. Sandars, 1960, 1964; *Electra and Other Plays*, Sophocles, trs. E. F. Watling, copyright © E. F. Watling, 1953; all the foregoing reproduced by permission of Penguin Books Ltd.

Princeton University Press: *The Ancient Near East: An Anthology of Text and*

Pictures, Vol. 1, James B. Pritchard (ed.), copyright © 1958 © renewed 1986 by Princeton University Press; *The Hero with a Thousand Faces*, Joseph Campbell, Bollingen Series XVII, copyright 1949 Princeton University Press, © 1976 renewed by Princeton University Press, excerpt p. 249 reprinted by permission of Princeton University Press; *Zeus and Hera: Archetypal Image of Father, Husband and Wife*, Carl Kerenyi, trs. Christopher Holme, Bollingen Series LXV, Princeton University Press, 1975; *The Mythic Image*, Joseph Campbell, Bollingen Series C, copyright © 1974 Princeton University Press, excerpts pp. 87, 72–4, 294 reprinted with permission of Princeton University Press; *Shamanism: Archaic Techniques of Ecstasy*, Mircea Eliade, trs. Willard Trask, Bollingen Series LXXVI, copyright © 1964 Princeton University Press, excerpts pp. 19, 478, 481, 486 reprinted by permission of Princeton University Press and Penguin Books Ltd; *Creative Imagination in the Sufism of Ibn Arabi*, Henry Corbin, trs. Ralph Mannheim, Bollingen Series XCI, copyright © 1969 Princeton University Press; *The Origins and History of Consciousness*, Erich Neumann, trs. R. F. C. Hull, Bollingen Series XLII, copyright © 1954, © renewed by Princeton University Press; *The Great Mother: An Analysis of the Archetype*, Erich Neumann, trs. Ralph Mannheim, Bollingen Series XLVII, copyright 1955 Princeton University Press, © 1983 renewed by Princeton University Press, excerpts, pp. 233, 191, 330, 326, 147, 148 reprinted with permission of Princeton University Press; *Aurora Consurgens*, Marie-Louise von Franz (ed.), trs R. F. C. Hull and A. S. B. Glover, copyright © 1966, Bollingen.

Quartet Books Ltd: *The Goddess of Love: The Birth, Triumph, Death and Return of Aphrodite*, Geoffrey Grigson.

Random Century: excerpts from *Women's Mysteries Ancient and Modern*, Esther Harding.

Routledge & Kegan Paul: *Dialogues with Scientists and Sages*, Renée Weber (ed.); *Cretan Cults and Festivals*, R. H. Willetts; *The Cult of the Black Virgin*, Ean Begg; *Dionysos: Archetypal Image of Indestructible Life* and *Dionysus*, Carl Kerenyi; *Arrest and Movement*, H. A. Groenewegen-Frankfort; *Collected Works*, Vols. 1–20, C. G. Jung; *Wholeness and the Implicate Order*, David Bohm.

Schocken Books: *Eleusis: Archetypal Image of Mother and Daughter*, Carl Kerenyi; *Major Trends in Jewish Mysticism*, Gershom Scholem.

School of Oriental and African Studies, London: excerpts from 'Pictures and Pictorial Language: The Burney Relief', Thorkild Jacobsen, in *Figurative Language in the Ancient Near East*, 1987.

SCM Press: *Jesus, The Unanswered Questions*, John Bowden; *Old Testament Theology* and *Wisdom in Israel*, Gerhard von Rad.

Shambala Publications Inc.: *No Boundary*, Ken Wilbur, 1979.

Soncino Press: *The Zohar*, Harry Sperling and Maurice Simon (trs.).

Souvenir Press Ltd: *Oriental Mythology*; *Occidental Mythology* and *Primitive Mythology*, Joseph Campbell.

Sphere Books Ltd: *Faust*, Johan Wolfgang von Goethe.

Spring Publications Inc.: *Pagan Meditations: The Worlds of Aphrodite, Artemis and Hestia*, Ginette Paris; *Athene: Virgin and Mother in Greek Religion*, Carl Kerenyi, trs. Murray Stein.

Thames and Hudson Ltd: *Earliest Civilizations of the Near East*, and *Çatal Hüyük: A Neolithic Town in Anatolia*, James Mellaart; *Cybele and Attis*, M. J. Vermaseren; *Myth and Ritual in Christianity*, Alan Watts; *Egyptian Mysteries:*

New Light on Ancient Knowledge, Lucie Lamy; *The Cult of the Mother Goddess*, Edwin Oliver James; *The Goddesses and Gods of Old Europe*, Marija Gimbutas; *The Heroes of the Greeks*, Carl Kerenyi; *Myth and Symbol in Ancient Egypt*, R. T. Rundle Clark; *History Begins at Sumer*, Samuel Noah Kramer; *Aegean Art*, Pierre DeMargne.

Theosophical Publishing House Ltd: *The Wedding Song of Wisdom*, G. R. S. Mead.

Times Books London: *The Way of the Animal Powers: Historical Atlas of World Mythology*, Vol. 1, Joseph Campbell.

University of California Press: *From the Poetry of Sumer: Creation, Glorification, Adoration*, Samuel Kramer, material from pp. 24, 27, 28, 29, 30, 37, 45–6, 71–2, 86, 87, 88, 93 and 96, copyright © 1979 The Regents of the University of California.

University of California at L.A.: 'The Early Civilizations of Europe', Monograph for Indo-European Studies 131.

University of Chicago Press: *A History of Religious Ideas*, Vols. 1–2, Mircea Eliade; *Greek Tragedies*, David Grene and Richmond Lattimore (eds.).

University of Pennsylvania Press: *Sumerian Mythology*, Samuel Noah Kramer.

Unwin Hyman Ltd: extract from *The Mothers*, Robert Briffault, reproduced by kind permission of Unwin Hyman Ltd.

A. P. Watt Ltd: *Hebrew Myths*, Robert Graves and Raphael Patai. By permission of A. P. Watt Ltd, on behalf of The Trustees of the Robert Graves Copyright Trust and Raphael Patai. A. P. Watt on behalf of Trinity College, Cambridge: *The Golden Bough*, Sir James George Frazer.

Wayne State University Press and Raphael Patai for permission to quote from *The Hebrew Goddess* © Wayne State University Press.

Weidenfeld & Nicolson Ltd: *Alone of All Her Sex: The Myth and Cult of the Virgin Mary*, Marina Warner; and for permission to quote and reproduce illustrations from *The Roots of Civilization*, Alexander Marshack; *The Gnostic Gospels* and *Adam, Eve and the Serpent*, Elaine Pagels.

Wesleyan University Press: excerpt from *Saving the Appearances: A Study in Idolatry*, Owen Barfield, courtesy of Owen Barfield and Wesleyan University Press 1989, copyright © Owen Barfield 1985 and 1988.

Yale University Press: *The Philosophy of Symbolic Forms*, Vol. 2, Ernst Cassirer, trs. Ralph Mannheim; *The Exaltation of Inanna*, William W. Hallo and J. J. A. van Dijk; *The Treasures of Darkness*, Thorkild Jacobsen.

Zed Books: *A History of the Jews: Ancient and Modern*, Ilan Halevi.

Every effort has been made to trace the copyright holders. The authors and publishers would be pleased to hear from any copyright holders not acknowledged.

PICTURE SOURCES

All photographs are by Simon Constable-Maxwell unless otherwise specified. All drawings from the books by Marija Gimbutas are by the kind permission of the author and all photographs from her books are by Simon Constable-Maxwell with the kind permission of Marija Gimbutas and Thames and Hudson as, owing to the recent events in eastern Europe, we were unable to obtain photographs from the museums. Photographs from *Çatal Hüyük, A Neolithic Town in Anatolia* by kind permission of Professor James Mellaart and Thames and Hudson. Photographs from *The Palace of Minos* by kind permission of Macmillan & Co. Photographs from *The Roots of Civilization*, Alexander Marshack, by kind permission of Weidenfeld & Nicolson Ltd.

Chapter 1

All drawings by Robin Baring unless otherwise stated.

Fig. 1. Courtesy of Musée d'Aquitaine, Bordeaux, France. All rights reserved. Fig. 2. Courtesy of Musée de l'Homme, Paris. Fig. 3. Courtesy of Musées Réunis du Louvre, Paris. Fig. 4. Courtesy of Naturhistorisches Museum, Vienna. Fig. 5. Courtesy of Naturhistorisches Museum, Vienna. Fig. 6. Anthropos Institut, Moravske Museum, Brno. Photographs from J. Jelínek, *Encyclopédie Illustrée de l'Homme Préhistorique*. By permission of Artia, Prague. Fig. 7. Anthropos Institut, Moravske Museum, Brno. Photograph from Jelínek. By permission of Artia, Prague. Fig. 8. Drawing after A. Salmony, 'Some Paleolithic ivory carving from Mezine', *Artibus Asiae*, 12, No. 1/2 (1949): 107, Figs. 1 and 2. Fig. 9. Anthropos Institut, Moravske Museum, Brno. Photograph from Jelínek. By permission of Artia, Prague. Fig. 10. Drawing after Alexander Marshack, *The Roots of Civilization*, p. 315. Fig. 11. Drawing after illustration in Joseph Campbell, *The Way of the Animal Powers*, p. 72. Fig. 12. Anthropos Institut, Moravske Museum, Brno. Photograph from Jelínek. By permission of Artia, Prague. Fig. 13. Courtesy of Archaeological Museum, Volos, Greece. Photograph: Tap Service, Athens. Fig. 14. Drawing by Anne Baring after Marshack, p. 284. Fig. 15. Drawing by Anne Baring after Marshack, p. 309. Fig. 16. Photograph: Editions Larrey, Toulouse. Fig. 17. From Marshack, pp. 144–5, courtesy of Weidenfeld & Nicolson. Fig. 18. From Marshack, p. 48, courtesy of Weidenfeld & Nicolson. Fig. 19. Anthropos

Institut, Moravske Museum, Brno. Drawing after Marshack, p. 295. Fig. 20. Institute of Archaeology of the Academy of Sciences, USSR. Drawing from illustration in *Encyclopédie Illustrée de l'Homme Préhistorique*, p. 452. Fig. 21. Drawing from illustration in *Encyclopédie Illustrée de l'Homme Préhistorique*. Fig. 22. Institute of Archaeology of the Academy of Sciences, USSR. Drawing after Joseph Campbell, *The Way of the Animal Powers*, p. 72. Fig. 23. Drawing after Chovkoplias in *Encyclopédie Illustrée de l'Homme Préhistorique*, p. 446. Fig. 24. Drawing after Marshack, p. 174. Fig. 25. Drawing after Henri Begouën and Abbé H. Breuil, *Les Cavernes du Volp*, Paris, Arts et Métiers Graphiques, 1958, p. 48. Fig. 26. Drawing after Begouën and Breuil, p. 11. Fig. 27. Photograph: Jean Vertut. Fig. 28. Photograph: Jean Vertut. Fig. 29. Drawing after Begouën and Breuil. Fig. 30. Drawing after Begouën and Breuil, p. 51. Fig. 31. Photograph: Jean Vertut. Fig. 32. Photograph: Jean Vertut. Fig. 33. Courtesy of Musées Réunis du Louvre. Figs. 34–36. Robin Baring. Fig. 37. Drawing after detail of *The Mystic Lamb* in the Ghent Altarpiece, Hubert and Jan Van Eyck. Fig. 38. Robin Baring. Fig. 39. Courtesy of the Trustees of the British Museum. Fig. 40. Codex Vigilianus y Albedense. Biblioteca del Monasterio de San Lorenzo de El Escorial. Courtesy Patrimonio Nacional, Spain. Fig. 41. Drawing after illustration in Roger Cook, *The Tree of Life*, p. 112. Fig. 42. (a) Courtesy Musée d'Aquitaine. All rights reserved. (b) Courtesy of the Louvre, Paris. Fig. 43. Courtesy of Museum Boymans-van-Beuningen, Rotterdam.

Chapter 2

All drawings by Lyn Constable-Maxwell unless otherwise stated.

Fig. 1. Drawing after Marija Gimbutas, *The Goddesses and Gods of Old Europe*, p. 132. Fig. 2. Courtesy of Naturhistorisches Museum, Vienna. Fig. 3. Drawing after Gimbutas, p. 90. Fig. 4. Koszta Jozsef Museum, Szentes, Hungary. Photograph from Gimbutas, p. 128. Fig. 5. Photograph: Lauros-Giraudon. Fig. 6. Drawing after Gimbutas, p. 87. Fig. 7. (a) Photograph courtesy of National Archaeological Museum, Bucharest. (b) Photograph from Gimbutas, p. 202. Fig. 8. National Archaeological Museum, Bucharest. Photograph from Gimbutas, p. 121. Fig. 9. Photograph from Gimbutas, p. 121. Fig. 10. Photograph from Gimbutas, frontispiece. Fig. 11. Volos Archaeological Museum. Photograph: Tap Service, Athens. Fig. 12. Drawing after Gimbutas, p. 101. Fig. 13. Drawing after Gimbutas, p. 136. Fig. 14. Drawing after Gimbutas, p. 103. Fig. 15. (a, b) Drawing after Gimbutas, p. 107. (c) Drawing after Marshack, p. 284. (d) Drawing after Gimbutas, p. 36. (e, f) Drawings after Gimbutas, pp. 166–7. (g) Drawing after Sir Arthur Evans, *The Palace of Minos*, Vol. 1, fig. 405d. Fig. 16. Drawing after Gimbutas, p. 103. Fig. 17. Courtesy of the National Museum, Belgrade. Fig. 18. National Museum, Athens. Photograph: Tap Service, Athens. Fig. 19. Philipi Museum, Macedonia. Photograph from Gimbutas, p. 203. Fig. 20. Philipi Museum, Macedonia. Photograph from Gimbutas, p. 203. Fig. 21. Drawing after Gimbutas, p. 101. Fig. 22. Courtesy of Musée des Augustins, Toulouse. Fig. 23. Courtesy of the Museum of Fine Arts, Boston, Mass. H. L. Pierce Fund. Fig. 24. Courtesy of the Louvre, Paris. Fig. 25. National Museum, Athens. Photograph: Hirmer. Fig. 26. Plovdiv Archaeological Museum. Photograph from Gimbutas, p. 104. Fig. 27. National Archaeological Museum, Bucharest. Photograph from

Gimbutas, p. 206. Fig. 28. National Archaeological Museum, Bucharest. Photograph from Gimbutas, p. 212. Fig. 29. Courtesy of Aegyptisches Museum, Staatliche Museen, Berlin. Fig. 30. Courtesy of the National Museum, Belgrade. Fig. 31. Drawings after Gimbutas, pp. 172, 174. Fig. 32. Drawings after Gimbutas, pp. 169, 171, 100. Fig. 33. Drawings after Gimbutas, p. 187. Fig. 34. Drawing by Robin Baring after Gimbutas, p. 184. Fig. 35. Courtesy of Archaeological Museum, Cracow, Poland. Fig. 36. Photograph from Gimbutas, p. 218. Fig. 37. National Museum, Athens. Photograph: Tap Service, Athens. Fig. 38. Volos Archaeological Museum. Photograph: Tap Service, Athens. Fig. 39. (a) Tornai Janos Museum, Hodmezovasarhely. (b) Koszta Jozsef Museum, Szentes, Hungary. Photographs from Gimbutas, pp. 210, 84. Fig. 40. Goddess. National Archaeological Museum, Bucharest. Photograph: Lauros Giraudon. Fig. 41. God. National Archaeological Museum, Bucharest. Photograph: Lauros Giraudon. Fig. 42. Oltenita Archaeological Museum, Romania. Photograph from Gimbutas, p. 229. Fig. 43. Courtesy of private collection, New York. Fig. 44. Courtesy of the Trustees of the British Museum. Fig. 45. Courtesy of Museum of Anatolian Civilization, Ankara. Fig. 46. Drawing by Robin Baring after Professor James Mellaart, *Çatal Hüyük*, p. 120. Fig. 47. Minoan shrine with doves. Drawing by Robin Baring after Evans, Vol. 1, p. 220. Fig. 48. Courtesy of Museum of Anatolian Civilization, Ankara. Fig. 49. Drawing by Robin Baring after Mellaart, p. 113. Fig. 50. Drawing by Robin Baring after Mellaart, p. 127. Fig. 51. Drawing by Robin Baring after Mellaart, p. 116. Fig. 52. Drawing by Robin Baring after Mellaart, p. 169. Fig. 53. Drawing by Robin Baring after Mellaart, p. 119. Fig. 54. Photograph from Mellaart, p. 157, courtesy of Professor James Mellaart. Fig. 55. National Archaeological Museum, Athens. Photograph: Hirmer. Fig. 56. Drawing by Robin Baring after Mellaart, p. 163. Fig. 57. Drawing by Robin Baring after Mellaart, plate 40, p. 90. Fig. 58. Drawing by Robin Baring after Mellaart, p. 111. Fig. 59. Photograph from Mellaart, p. 185, courtesy of Professor James Mellaart. Fig. 60. Photograph from Mellaart, p. 185, courtesy of Professor James Mellaart. Fig. 61. Photograph from Mellaart, fig. 83, p. 149, by kind permission of Professor James Mellaart and Thames and Hudson. Fig. 62. Photograph: Clive Hicks. Fig. 63. Drawing by Robin Baring. Fig. 64. Photograph from *La Préhistoire du Morbihan*, p. 54. Courtesy of La Société Polymathique du Morbihan. Fig. 65. Courtesy of La Société des Lettres de Rodez. Photograph: Balsan. Fig. 66. Drawing by Robin Baring after Marija Gimbutas, *The Language of the Goddess*, p. 289. Fig. 67. Photograph: Photograph: Clive Hicks. Fig. 69. Photograph: from H. Bayley, *The Lost Language of Symbolism*. Fig. 70. Drawing by Robin Baring after Michael Dames, *Silbury Hill*, p. 161. Fig. 71. Photograph: Mario Mintoff, courtesy of M.J. Publications, Malta. Fig. 72. Photograph from James Mellaart, *Çatal Hüyük*, p. 145, by permission of Thames and Hudson. Fig. 74. Photograph: Mario Mintoff, courtesy of M.J. Publications, Malta. Fig. 75. Photograph: Mario Mintoff, courtesy of M.J. Publications, Malta.

Chapter 3

All drawings by Lyn Constable-Maxwell unless otherwise stated.

Fig. 1. Photograph from Sir Arthur Evans, *The Palace of Minos*, Vol. 2ii, Supp. pl. XXVI. Fig. 2. Collection Dr Giamalakis, Herakleion. Photograph: Tap Service,

Athens. Fig. 3. Courtesy of Museum of Fine Arts, Boston, Mass.; gift of Mrs W. Scott Fitz. Fig. 4. Photograph: Tap Service, Athens. Fig. 5. Drawings after Marija Gimbutas, *The Goddesses and Gods of Old Europe*, p. 93, and James Mellaart, *Çatal Hüyük*, p. 124. Fig. 6. Photograph: Hirmer. Fig. 7. Photograph: Tap Service, Athens. Fig. 8. Drawing after Evans, Vol. 4i, p. 163. Fig. 9. Photograph: Tap Service, Athens. Fig. 10. Drawings after Gimbutas, pp. 186–7. Fig. 11. Photograph from Evans, Vol. 2i, p. 341. Fig. 12. Ashmolean Museum, Oxford. Photograph from Evans, Vol. 3, p. 458. Fig. 13. Courtesy of Staatliche Antikensammlungen und Glyptothek, Munich. Fig. 14. Museum Nauplion. Fig. 15. Museo Nazionale delle Terme, Rome. Photograph: Alinari. Fig. 16. Archaeological Museum, Herakleion. Drawing by Robin Baring. Fig. 17. Archaeological Museum, Herakleion. Drawing by Robin Baring. Fig. 18. Archaeological Museum, Herakleion. Photograph: Hirmer. Fig. 19. Photograph from Evans, Vol. 4i, p. 169. Fig. 20. Drawing after Gimbutas, p. 182. Fig. 21. Drawing after Sir Arthur Evans, 'Ring of Nestor', *Journal of the Hellenic Society*, XLV. Fig. 22. Museum of Fine Arts, Boston, Mass. Drawing by Robin Baring after Jane Harrison, *Prolegomena to the Study of Greek Religion*, p. 443. Fig. 23. Photograph from Evans, Vol. 1, p. 430. Fig. 24. Drawing after Gertrude Levy, *The Gate of Horn*, plate 9. Fig. 25. Archaeological Museum, Herakleion. Photograph: Tap Service, Athens. Fig. 26. (a, b) Archaeological Museum, Herakleion. Drawing after and photograph from Evans, Vol. 2ii, p. 437. (c) Egyptian Museum, Berlin. (d, e) Photograph from Evans. (f) Drawing after Evans, p. 432. Drawings by Robin Baring. Fig. 27. Archaeological Museum, Herakleion. Photograph: Tap Service, Athens. Fig. 28. Photograph: Tap Service, Athens. Fig. 29. Courtesy of the Louvre, Paris. Fig. 30. Archaeological Museum, Herakleion. Photograph: Hirmer. Fig. 31. Archaeological Museum, Herakleion. Photograph: Tap Service, Athens. Fig. 32 (a) Drawing after Neumann, *The Great Mother*, p. 114. (b) Courtesy of Trustees of the British Museum. (c) Drawing after Neumann. (d) National Museum, Copenhagen. Photograph from Levy, p. 220. (e) Photograph: Hirmer. Fig. 33. Drawing by Robin Baring from a vase in the National Museum, Athens. Fig. 34. Museum Aghios Nicholaos, Crete. Photograph: Tap Service, Athens. Fig. 35. Ashmolean Museum, Oxford. Photograph from Evans, Vol. 3, p. 153. Fig. 36. Archaeological Museum, Herakleion. Photograph: Tap Service, Athens. Fig. 37. Drawing by Robin Baring after Levy, p. 224. Fig. 38. National Museum, Athens. Photograph: Hirmer. Fig. 39. Archaeological Museum, Herakleion. Photograph: Tap Service, Athens. Fig. 40. Archaeological Museum, Herakleion. Photograph: Hirmer. Fig. 41. Photograph from Evans, Vol. 1, p. 160. Fig. 42. Photograph: Hirmer. Fig. 43. Photograph from Evans, *The Palace of Minos*, Vol. 1, p. 161. Fig. 44. Photograph: Hirmer. Fig. 45. Courtesy of Staatliches Antikensammlungen und Glyptothek, Munich. Fig. 46. Photograph: Tap Service, Athens. Fig. 47. Museo Nazionale, Palermo. Photograph: Hirmer. Fig. 48. Courtesy of the Ashmolean Museum, Oxford. Fig. 49. Photograph from Evans, Vol. 3, p. 226. Fig. 50. Photograph: Tap Service, Athens. Fig. 51. Courtesy of the Royal Ontario Museum, Canada. Fig. 52. Archaeological Museum, Herakleion. Photograph from Pierre Demargne, *Aegean Art*, plate 443, courtesy of Editions Gallimard, Paris.

Chapter 4

Fig. 1. Photograph courtesy of Christie's, London. Fig. 2. Courtesy of Griffith Institute, Ashmolean Museum, Oxford. Fig. 3. Courtesy of the Trustees of the British Museum. Fig. 4. Courtesy of Mme Catherine Garrige, Musée Guimet, Paris. Photograph: Georg Helmes. Fig. 5. Museum Aleppo. Photograph: Hirmer. Fig. 6. Courtesy of the Louvre, Paris. Fig. 7. Courtesy of the Trustees of the British Museum. Fig. 8. Courtesy of the Trustees of the British Museum. Fig. 9. Courtesy of the Louvre, Paris. Fig. 10. Photograph from drawing in W. H. Ward, *The Seal Cylinders of Western Asia*, p. 58. Fig. 11. National Museum, Baghdad. Photograph: Hirmer.

Chapter 5

Fig. 1. Courtesy of the Oriental Institute of the University of Chicago. Fig. 2. The Pierpont Morgan Library. Photograph of line drawing of cylinder seal in W. H. Ward, *The Seal Cylinders of Western Asia*, p. 153. Fig. 3. Courtesy of the Trustees of the British Museum. Fig. 4. Courtesy of the Trustees of the British Museum. Fig. 5. National Museum, Baghdad. Photograph: Hirmer. Fig. 6. National Museum, Baghdad. Photograph: Hirmer. Fig. 7. Photograph courtesy of the National Museum, Bangkok. Fig. 8. Drawing by Robin Baring after cylinder seal impression in J. Hawkes, *The First Great Civilizations: Life in Mesopotamia, the Indus Valley and Egypt*, p. 36. Fig. 9. Courtesy of the Trustees of the British Museum. Fig. 10. Photograph: Hirmer. Fig. 11. Courtesy of the Trustees of the British Museum. Fig. 12. Photographs from line drawings in Ward, p. 152. Fig. 13. Courtesy of the Lands of the Bible Foundation, Jerusalem. Photograph: Zev Radovan. Fig. 14. Photograph courtesy of the National Museum, Baghdad. Fig. 15. (a) Courtesy of the National Museum, Baghdad. (b) Photograph: Hirmer. Fig. 16. Courtesy of the Louvre, Paris. Fig. 17. Photographs from line drawings in Ward, p. 384. Fig. 18. Photograph from line drawing in Ward, p. 372. Fig. 19. Courtesy of the Trustees of the British Museum. Fig. 20. Drawing by Robin Baring after a photograph in *Iranische Denkmaler*, Deutsches Archaeologisches Institut, Teheran, 1976. Fig. 21. Courtesy of the Louvre, Paris. Fig. 22. Drawing by Robin Baring after photograph in Joseph Campbell, *The Mythic Image*, p. 283. Fig. 23. Courtesy of the Louvre, Paris. Fig. 24. Photograph from Ward, p. 134. Fig. 25. Courtesy of Staatliche Museen, Berlin. Fig. 26. Courtesy of the Trustees of the British Museum. Fig. 27. Courtesy of the Oriental Institute of the University of Chicago. Fig. 28. British Museum. Photograph from Ward, p. 138. Fig. 29. Courtesy of the Louvre, Paris. Fig. 30. Private collection on loan to the British Museum. Photograph courtesy of Christie's, London. Fig. 31. Photograph after line drawing in Ward, p. 56. Fig. 32. Photograph of line drawing in Ward, p. 40.

Chapter 6

Fig. 1. Photograph: Hirmer. Fig. 2. Drawing by Robin Baring after E. A. Wallis Budge, *Osiris and the Egyptian Resurrection*, Vol. 1, p. 5. Fig. 3. Photograph: Peter Clayton. Fig. 4. Courtesy of the Trustees of the British Museum. Fig. 5. Photograph: William MacQuitty. Fig. 6. Photograph from R. T. Rundle Clark, *Myth and Symbol in Ancient Egypt*, p. 101. Fig. 7. The Louvre, Paris. Courtesy of

RMN. Fig. 8. The Louvre, Paris. Courtesy of RMN. Fig. 9. Photograph from Budge, Vol. 1, p. 58. Fig. 10. Photograph: Peter Clayton. Fig. 11. Courtesy of the Trustees of the British Museum. Fig. 12. Courtesy of the Griffith Institute, the Ashmolean Museum, Oxford. Fig. 13. Courtesy of Museum of Fine Arts, Boston, Mass. Harvard University, MFA Expedition. Fig. 14. Photograph: Peter Clayton. Fig. 15. Photograph from Neumann, *The Great Mother*, p. 140. Fig. 16. Courtesy of the Trustees of the British Museum. Fig. 17. Photograph: Hirmer. Fig. 18. Photograph from Henri Frankfort, *Ancient Egyptian Religion*, frontispiece. Fig. 19. Photograph: Peter Clayton. Fig. 20. Courtesy of the Trustees of the British Musuem. Fig. 21. Photograph: Hirmer. Fig. 22. Deutsches Archaeologisches Institut, Cairo. Photograph from C. G. Jung, *Collected Works*, Vol. 5, *Symbols of Transformation*, p. 241. Fig. 23. Photograph: Peter Clayton. Fig. 24. Cairo Museum. Photograph from Hannelore Kischkewitz, *Egyptian Art: Drawings and Paintings*, London, Hamlyn, 1989, plate 50. Fig. 25. Courtesy of Leiden Museum, Netherlands. Fig. 26. Photograph: William MacQuitty. Fig. 27. Photograph from Egypt Exploration Society. Fig. 28. Courtesy of the Trustees of the British Museum. Fig. 29. Photograph: Peter Clayton. Fig. 30. Drawing after Rundle Clark, p. 107. Fig. 31. Courtesy of Leiden Museum, Netherlands. Fig. 32. Photograph: Peter Clayton. Fig. 33. Drawing after Neumann, p. 144. Fig. 34. Courtesy of Egyptian Museum, Staatliche Museum, Berlin.

Chapter 7

Fig. 1. Courtesy of the Trustees of the British Museum. Fig. 2. Drawing by Robin Baring after Ward, p. 201. Fig. 3. British Museum. Photograph from Lenormant. Fig. 4. Courtesy of the University Museum, University of Pennsylvania. Fig. 5. Courtesy of the Oriental Institute of the University of Chicago. Fig. 6. Courtesy of Staatliche Museen, Berlin. Fig. 7. Courtesy of Staatliche Antikensammlungen und Glyptothek, Munich. Fig. 8. Courtesy of Caisse des Monuments Historiques, Paris. Fig. 9. Courtesy of The Metropolitan Museum of Art, New York; Harris Brisbane Dick Fund, 1934.

Chapter 8

Fig. 1. Courtesy of the Louvre, Paris. Fig. 2. Photograph courtesy of Deutsches Archaeologisches Institut, Istanbul. Fig. 3. Museo Nazionale, Palermo. Photograph: Hirmer. Fig. 4. National Museum, Athens. Photograph: Hirmer. Fig. 5. Photograph: Deutsches Archaeologisches Institut, Athens. Fig. 6. Photograph from Sir Arthur Evans, *The Earlier Religions of Greece*, p. 34, fig. 15. Fig. 7. Courtesy of Antikensammlung, Staatliche Museen, Berlin. Fig. 8. Courtesy of Antikenmuseum, Staatliche Museen, Berlin. Fig. 9. National Museum, Athens. Photograph: Tap Service, Athens. Fig. 10. Museo Archeologico, Florence. Photograph: Alinari. Fig. 11. Drawing by Robin Baring, after Carl Kerenyi, *The Gods of the Greeks*, plate Va. Fig. 12. Courtesy of the Trustees of the British Museum. Fig. 13. Drawing by Anne Baring after illustration in Erich Neumann, *The Great Mother*, p. 169. Fig. 14. Muzeo Nationale, Naples. Photograph: Mansell Collection. Fig. 15. Photograph from Kerenyi, p. 129. Fig. 16. Courtesy of Museum of Fine Arts, Boston, Mass.; James Fund and by special contribution. Fig. 17. Photograph: Tap Service, Athens. Fig. 18. Drawings by Robin Baring after

Kerenyi, p. 121, and Jane Harrison, *Prolegomena to the Study of Greek Religion*, p. 307. Fig. 19. Courtesy of Antikenmuseum, Staatliche Museen, Berlin. Fig. 20. Staatliche Antikensammlungen und Glyptothek, Munich. Photograph: Hirmer. Fig. 21. Acropolis Museum. Photograph: Hirmer. Fig. 22. Photograph: Tap Service, Athens. Fig. 23. Courtesy of the Louvre, Paris. Fig. 24. Courtesy of the Trustees of the British Museum. Fig. 25. Courtesy of the Trustees of the British Museum.

Chapter 9

Fig. 1. Vatican Museum, Rome. Photograph: Hirmer. Fig. 2. *The Birth of Aphrodite*. Museo Nazionale, Rome. Photograph: Hirmer. Fig. 3. Uffizi Museum, Florence. Photograph: Alinari. Fig. 4. Courtesy of the Louvre, Paris. Fig. 5. Courtesy of the Louvre, Paris. Fig. 6. Courtesy of the Ashmolean Museum, Oxford. Fig. 7. Courtesy of the Trustees of the British Museum. Fig. 8. Courtesy of the Trustees of the British Museum. Fig. 9. Uffizi Gallery, Florence. Photograph from Joseph Campbell, *Occidental Mythology*, p. 15. Fig. 10. National Museum, Athens. Drawing by Robin Baring after Jane Harrison, *Prolegomena to the Study of Greek Religion*, p. 275. Fig. 11. Herakleion Museum. Drawing after Carl Kerenyi, *Eleusis*, p. xix. Fig. 12. Museo Nazionale, Reggio Calabria. Photograph: Hirmer. Fig. 13. National Museum, Athens. Photograph: Tap Service, Athens. Fig. 14. Photograph: Hirmer. Fig. 15. Drawing by Robin Baring from Peter Levi, *Atlas of the Greek World*, Oxford, Phaidon, 1980, p. 65. Fig. 16. Photograph: Hirmer. Fig. 17. Photograph: Hirmer. Fig. 18. National Museum, Athens. Photograph: Tap Service, Athens. Fig. 19. Photograph from Campbell, p. 49. Fig. 20. Courtesy of The Metropolitan Museum of Art, New York; Fletcher Fund, 1956. All rights reserved.

Chapter 10

Fig. 1. Courtesy of the Louvre, Paris. Fig. 2. Courtesy of the Louvre, Paris. Fig. 3. Photograph courtesy of Museum of Anatolian Civilization, Ankara, and Deutsches Archaeologisches Institut, Istanbul. Fig. 4. Drawing by Robin Baring after M. J. Vermaseren, *Cybele and Attis*, p. 22. Fig. 5. Photograph from Sir Arthur Evans, *The Palace of Minos*, Vol. 4i, p. 348. Fig. 6. Photograph courtesy of the Museum of Anatolian Civilization, Ankara, and Deutsches Archaeologisches Institut, Istanbul. Fig. 7. Photograph from Evans, Vol. 1, p. 505. Fig. 8. Courtesy of The Metropolitan Museum of Art, New York; gift of Henry G. Marquand, 1897. All rights reserved. Fig. 9. Museo Nazionale, Naples. Photograph: Mansell Collection. Fig. 10. Courtesy of Soprintendenza Archeologica della Lombardia, Milan. Fig. 11. Courtesy of Soprintendenza Archeologica per Il Veneto. Fig. 12. Museum of St Rémy de Provence, France; Collection Hotel de Sade, Rodez. Photograph: Folliot-Reveilhac. Fig. 13. Courtesy of the Trustees of the British Museum. Fig. 14. Photograph: Clive Hicks.

Chapter 11

Fig. 1. Photograph: Peter Clayton. Fig. 2. Drawing by Lyn Constable-Maxwell after E. A. Wallis Budge, *The Gods of the Egyptians*, Vol. 1, p. 498. Fig. 3. Courtesy of the Louvre, Paris. Fig. 4. Photograph: Editions Houvet-la-Crypte, Chartres.

Chapter 12

Fig. 1. Courtesy of the Louvre, Paris. Fig. 2. Courtesy of the Lands of the Bible Archaeology Foundation, Jerusalem. Photograph: Zev Radovan. Fig. 3. Courtesy of the Trustees of the British Museum. Fig. 4. Courtesy of the Griffith Institute, Ashmolean Museum, Oxford. Fig. 5. Courtesy of Israel Antiquities Authority, Jerusalem. Fig. 6. Courtesy of the Louvre, Paris. Fig. 7. Courtesy of the Louvre, Paris. Fig. 8. Courtesy of The Metropolitan Museum of Art, New York; gift of Harris D. Colt and H. Dunscombe Colt, 1934. All rights reserved. Fig. 9. Drawing by Anne Baring after E. A. Wallis Budge, *The Gods of the Egyptians*, Vol. 2, p. 279. Fig. 10. Courtesy of the Trustees of the British Museum. Fig. 11. Courtesy of the Louvre, Paris. Fig. 12. Courtesy of Staatliche Museen, Berlin. Fig. 13. Herbert Gute, copy of the wall painting from the Synagogue at Dura Europos, showing the *Finding of Moses*, courtesy of Yale University Art Gallery.

Chapter 13

Fig. 1. Courtesy of the Trustees of the British Museum. Fig. 2. Biblioteca del Monasterio de San Lorenzo de El Escorial. Courtesy Patrimonio Nacional, Spain. Fig. 3. Courtesy of Courtauld Institute, London; Lee Collection. Fig. 4. Photograph: Alinari. Fig. 5. Cathedral of Notre Dame. Photograph: Clive Hicks. Fig. 6. Photograph: Peter Clayton. Fig. 7. Kunsthistorisches Museum, Vienna. Fig. 8. Photograph from Jane Harrison, *Themis*, p. 431. Fig. 9. (a) Drawing after Joseph Campbell, *The Mythic Image*, p. 294. (b) Drawing after Ward, p. 127. Fig. 10. Courtesy of the Rodin Museum, Paris. Photograph: Bruno Jarret. Fig. 11. Courtesy of the Condé Museum, Chantilly. Photograph: Lauros-Giraudon. Fig. 12. Photograph: Alinari. Fig. 13. Photograph from line drawing in Ward, p. 139. Fig. 14. Drawing from Barbara Black Koltuv, *The Book of Lilith*, p. 64. Fig. 15. Courtesy of the Louvre, Paris. Fig. 16. Photograph: Bibliothèque Nationale, Paris. Fig. 17. Courtesy of Kunsthistorisches Museum, Vienna. Fig. 18. Courtesy of the Museum of Fine Arts, Boston, Mass.; gift by subscription, 1890. Fig. 19. Copyright Rubenshuis, Antwerp. Courtesy of the Board of Burgomaster and Eldermen, Antwerp, Belgium. Fig. 20. Galleria Antica e Moderna, Florence. Photograph: Alinari. Fig. 21. Galleria Antica e Moderna, Florence. Photograph: Alinari. Fig. 22. Courtesy of the Prado. Fig. 23. Photograph and permission by the Institut Royal du Patrimoine Artistique. Copyright A.C.L. Bruxelles, Belgium. Fig. 24. Courtesy of the Trustees of the British Museum.

Chapter 14

Fig. 1. Musée de Cluny, Paris. Courtesy of Musées Réunis du Louvre. Fig. 2. Musée de Cluny, Paris. Courtesy of Musées Réunis du Louvre. Fig. 3. Courtesy of Staatliche Museen Preussischer Kultur Besitz, Berlin. Fig. 4. Gozo Cathedral, Malta. Fig. 5. Photograph from Sylvie Girard, *Flandre-Picardie*, Paris, Larousse, 1988, p. 37. Fig. 6. Courtesy of Museo de Arte de Cataluña, Barcelona. Fig. 7. Courtesy of Staatliche Museum, Berlin. Fig. 8. From Alan Watts, *Myth and Ritual in Christianity*, p. 85. Fig. 9. Courtesy of the Trustees, the National Gallery, London. Fig. 10. Courtesy of St Catherine's Convent, Utrecht. Fig. 11. Courtesy of St Catherine's Convent, Utrecht. Fig. 12. Courtesy of Museum Boymans-van-

Beuningen, Rotterdam. Fig. 13. Santa Maria Gloriosa dei Frari, Venice. Photograph: Alinari. Fig. 14. Courtesy of Bayerische Staatsbibliothek, Munich. Fig. 15. Courtesy of Biblioteca Universitaria, Valencia. Fig. 16. Courtesy of Stadel Institute, Frankfurt-am-Main. Fig. 17. Courtesy of Museum Mayer van den Bergh, Antwerp, Belgium. Fig. 18. Photograph from Glaser, Gotische Holzschnitte, plate LIII, in Erich Neumann, *The Great Mother*, p. 264. Fig. 19. Courtesy of Darmstadt, Hessisches Landesmuseum, Germany. Fig. 20. Museo Archeologico, Florence. Photograph: Alinari. Fig. 21. Courtesy of Wroclaw, Muzeum Narodowe we Wroclawiu, Poland. Fig. 22. Courtesy of Musée Jacquemart André, Paris. Photograph: J. Bulloz. Fig. 23. Museo del Sepolcro, Borgo Sansepolcro, Italy. Photograph: Alinari. Fig. 24. Courtesy of S. Pietro in Vaticano. Fig. 25. Photograph: Loic-Jahan, Grasse. Fig. 26. Borghese Gallery, Rome. Photograph: Alinari. Fig. 27. Courtesy of Kunsthistorisches Museum, Vienna. Fig. 28. Courtesy of the Louvre, Paris. Fig. 29. Uffizi Gallery, Florence. Photograph: Alinari. Fig. 30. Courtesy of the British Library. Fig. 31. Photograph: Alinari. Fig. 32. Photograph: Clive Hicks. Fig. 33. Photograph of drawing in Watts, *Myth and Ritual in Christianity*, p. 155. Fig. 34. Courtesy of The Museum of Fine Arts, Boston, Mass. Fig. 35. National Gallery of Art, Washington, DC. Samuel H. Kress Collection. Fig. 36. Photograph: Alinari. Fig. 37. Photograph: Alinari.

Chapter 15

Fig. 1. Courtesy of Bodleian Library, Oxford. Ms. Bodl. 269, fol. iii recto. Fig. 2. Courtesy of Bodleian Library, Oxford, Ms. Auct. F. 6. 5, fol. 1 verso. Fig. 3. Photograph: Jean Dieuzaide (Yan), Toulouse. Fig. 4. Photograph: Jean Dieuzaide (Yan), Toulouse. Fig. 5. Photograph: Jean Dieuzaide (Yan), Toulouse. Fig. 6. Cathedral of Notre Dame, Paris. Fig. 7. Courtesy of the British Library. Fig. 8. Courtesy of the Bibliothèque Nationale, Paris.

Chapter 16

Fig. 1. British Museum. Photograph from Lenormant. Fig. 2. Courtesy of the Oriental Institute of the University of Chicago. Fig. 3. Photograph: Deutsches Archaeologisches Institut, Athens. Fig. 4. National Museum of Villa Giulia. Photograph: Alinari. Fig. 5. Courtesy of the Fitzwilliam Museum, Cambridge. (The Fitzwilliam Museum questions the authenticity of these statues.) Fig. 6. Photograph: Clive Hicks. Fig. 7. Drawing by Lyn Constable-Maxwell. Fig. 8. Oltenita Archaeological Museum, Romania. Photograph by Simon Constable-Maxwell from *The Goddesses and Gods of Old Europe*, courtesy of Marija Gimbutas and Thames and Hudson. Fig. 9. Courtesy of the Henry Moore Foundation.

The front cover shows *The Glorification of the Virgin* by Geertgen tot St Jans (Courtesy of the Museum Boymans-van-Beuningen, Rotterdam); Gaia, Goddess of Earth (Courtesy of Deutsches Archaeologisches Institut, Istanbul); the Goddess of Laussel (Courtesy of Musée d'Aquitaine, Bordeaux); Minoan snake goddess (Photograph: Tap Service, Athens); the Black Virgin, Montserrat, Spain

(Photograph: Jean Dieuzaide (Yan), Toulouse); the Goddess Inanna–Ishtar (Photograph courtesy of Christie's, London).

MAPS

Map 1. Adapted from Joseph Campbell, *The Way of the Animal Powers*, p. 71. Map 2. Adapted from Marija Gimbutas, *The Goddesses and Gods of Old Europe*, p. 16. Map 3. After Marija Gimbutas in Riane Eisler, *The Chalice and the Blade*, p. 249. Map 4. After Marija Gimbutas in Riane Eisler, *The Chalice and the Blade*, p. 249.

INDEX

Numerals in **bold** type represent sections or chapters devoted to the entry. Numerals in *italics* refer to illustrations.

187, 216, 272, 391, 582, 608, 626;
persecuted 638; Philo's influence on
614; priesthood 297, 513–14; psyche,
effect of vengeful father-god on 465;
repentance 591; ritual 164, 460; saints
405, 531; sexuality 352, 523–4, 526;
symbols 412, 440, 491; theology,
cornerstone of 537; theology,
Catholic 521; thought 503, 667;
tradition(s) 359, 364, 390, 644, 661;
wife, role of 515, 519; writers 523;
writings 525, *see also* Bible, New
Testament, Old Testament; *see
also* Christianity, Gnostic(s), Judaeo-
Christian
Christianity 274, 283, 435, 447, 611,
615; early centuries of 270, 283, 404,
572, 626; intolerance of 616; mystical
478–9, 643, 655; original sin in 514,
532–7; pagan connections in 568;
resurrection of the body in 624;
Western 536, 613, 626; women and
283, 503, 513–14, 517, 520, 521,
524–6, 528–31, 539, 631; *see also*
Catholicism, Christian, Gnostic(s)
Christmas 561–3, 580
Chronos 307–9, 313, 315, 317, 353, 360,
367, 370, 372, 383
Chrysostom, St John 517, 530–1
Chrysaor 342
Cicero 389
Cinderella **655–8**
Circe 294, 295
circumcision 407
Cistercian Order 638
Clement of Alexandria 380–2, 415, 615
Coffin Texts 234, 237
Coleridge, Samuel Taylor 485, 676
Collective Unconscious 40, 41–2, 45,
105, 283–4, 447, 484, 490, 504, 546,
554, 663, 679, 681
Combe Capelle Man 20
communion 460
communities, beginning of established
47, 55
Conneda 31
consciousness 664; archetypal
masculine and feminine modes of
672–3; birth of 154, 488, 506;
collective 668; differentiation of in

the Neolithic 427; evolution of 41,
47, 82, 104–5, 144, 154–5, 157–8,
174, 183, 273–4, 281–5, 297, 417,
444, 461, 608, 616, 660, 662, 667,
669–70; the Fall as the myth of the
birth of 504–8; fragmentation of
670–1, 678; and gods in the Bronze
Age 152; Jesus' teaching about 619;
lunar and solar modes of 319;
separation from source 620;
separation into male and female
elements 75; Theseus as questing
143; tribal 668; *see also* participation
Constantine, Emperor 611, 634
Corn 375, 377, 381, **389–90**; *see also*
wheat
Corinthians 623–4
cosmic conflict, Babylonian image of,
419
Council of Constantinople, First, 550
Cranach the Elder, Luca, 491
creation: of Adam 423, 425–6, 527; of
Eve **425–6**, *492, 493*, 520; Eve as
secondary **519–20**, 525; father god
role of 494; interrelatedness of 274,
353; myths 418–19, 422–6, 488, 510–
11, 521, 540, *see also* Adam, *Enuma
Elish*, Eve, Isis, Osiris; unity of 245
Crete 52, 54, 59, 103, 112, 131, 165,
250, 270, 299, 359, 374, 454, 456,
660; and Anatolia 88; art of 106–7,
127, 300; Bronze Age 58, 148, 299,
660; bull in 134–5, 140, 141, 309;
culture of 54, 107; Demeter and 366–
7; goddesses of **106–44**, 323, 337, 445
labyrinth dance of 34, 45; New Year
in 119; religious life of 106; sacred
knot in 194; sacrifice in 309; status of
women in 159; Zeus's childhood in
316
cross: as *Axis Mundi* 488, 563, 600; as
Tree of Life 579, 598–602; *see also*
Christianity
crusades 443
Cucuteni vase(s) 46, 68, 72
Cummings, e.e. 659
Cumont, Franz 409
Cundrie 654
Cybele 82, 146, 176, 191, 198, 281, 359,
369, **391–415**, 460, 480, 548, 550–1,

N

Nabu 421

Nag Hammadi 618–19, 637

Nammu xiv, 64, 152, 185–8, 194, 200, 207, 219, 223, 279, 420, 454, 473, 557, 610

Nanna 166, 200, 216

Nanshe 205

Naram Sin, the stele of *167*

Narmer Palette 252

Nature 107, 335, 356, 469, 503, 554, 666, 669; desacralization of xi, 435–6, 543–6, 665; divine as immanent in 144, 284, 364, 438, 663; and Eve 543–6; as fallen in Judaeo–Christian tradition 417, 426, 487, 495, *see also* original sin; humanity as child of 3, 71, 680; as the 'Kingdom' 602–3; polarization of humanity and xii; polarization of spirit and xii, 274, 539, 543, 572, 574, 617, 627, 660, 673; reunion of spirit and xv, 659–81; separation of humanity from 151–2; as teacher 602; as Thou 99; *see also* divinity, Great Mother Goddess, Mother Goddess, immanence, *zoe*

Nausicaa 322

Neanderthal Man 16, 71, 299

Near East 54, 129, 140–1, 145, 155, 299, 424, 144, 158, 121, 180, 209, 285

Nebo, Mount 465

Nehemiah 422

Nekhbet 246, 256

Neolithic 9, 13–14, 40–1, **46–105**, 144, 135, 147, 161, 168, 245, 252, 284, 325, 374, 387, 421, 438, 473, 477, 499, 609–10; Great Goddess of the **46–105**, 109, 111, 148, 184, 188–9, 299–300, 304, 311, *323*, 391, 407; Old Europe **52–82**, 84, 94, 101, 103–4, 109–10, 113, 128–30, 144, 149, 155, 181, 280, 301, 323, 364, 396, 399

Neoplatonic tradition 356, 546

Nephthys 58, 60, 228, 230, 234–7, 240–1, 243–4, 260, 266, 271, 451, 480; *see also* Isis

Nergal 421

Nestor, Ring of 127, 323, 339, 560

Nestorius 550

net 65, 112, 126, 130, 209, 557–8, 653

Neumann, Erich 152, 155, 161, 168, 257, 352, 560

New Age 554, 665

New Biology 679

New Grange 94, 97–8

New Kingdom 238, 264, 271

New Physics 609, 679

New Testament 155, 177, 178, 415, 427, 547, 549, 552, 600–1, 603, 616, 624–5, 627; Colossians 515; Corinthians 515, 533, 624; Ephesians 514; John 390, 590–1, 602, 612, 625, 632; Luke 547, 549–50, 561, 563, 589, 624; Mark 589, 632, 653; Matthew 522, 549, 563–4, 589, 621, 624, 630, 634, 600–1; Paul 401, 591, 618; Revelations 568–9, 600; Romans 533; Timothy 514

Niaux 15, 37, 112

Nicaea and Chalcedon, Councils of 613, 677

Nidaba 195

Nin-dub 471

Nineveh 179, 180, 289

Ningal 200

Ningizzida 43, 208, 497; *see also* Tree of Life

Ningursu 471

Ninhursag 168, 311, 420, 425, 430, 454, 457, 582; and Euki 493; *see also* Inanna, Ki-Ninhursag

Ninlil 200; *see also* Enlil

Nin-ninna 216–17, 510

Ninshubur 206, 216

Ninsun 220

Nin-ti 493; *see also* Eve

Nintu 430; *see also* Inanna

Ninurta 201

Nippur 178–9, 180, 184

Nisaba 471; *see also* Gilgamesh

Noah 61, 426, 430–1, 449; and the ark 596; the dove of 43

Notre Dame 604, 647

numinous 8–9, 149–50; *see also* sacred

Nun 225, 257, 260, 262–3

Nut 58, 153, 225, 227–8, 242, 252, **256–60**, 264, 266, 496, 557, 576, 623; *see also* Geb, Shu

O

Oannes 63, 208, 473, 653; *see also* fish